Praise for John A. Farrell's

Tip O'Neill and the Democratic Century

A *New York Times* Notable Book of the Year

"Illuminating. . . . Here is our political past, presented clearly and with style. . . . This is not a typical biography, but a more panoramic production, a newsreel of nearly three-quarters of the last century. We see Tip O'Neill compete with the startling events of his time, events he influenced, or observed from the inside. . . . Farrell's book is popular history, but of a superior sort. Through the person of O'Neill he makes the nuts and bolts of governing, at both the state and national level, fascinating and understandable." — William O'Rourke, *Chicago Sun-Times*

"Mr. Farrell's impressive, fair-minded book is full of vivid stories about the old-style politics of Tip O'Neill, bringing to life one of the most colorful political figures of the twentieth century."

— Jonathan Karl, *Wall Street Journal*

"A knowing and engaging biography of O'Neill, a lucid chronicle of his times, and a wonderfully realized portrayal of the settings in which he spent his life: Boston during the first half of the twentieth century and Washington during the second half. . . . Jimmy Breslin called Tip O'Neill 'a lovely spring rain of a man' and John A. Farrell proves Breslin right. . . . Farrell has written a book as lovely as its subject, and also as big and accomplished." — Michael Nelson, *American Prospect*

"I read this book through a six-hour delay at La Guardia followed by a transcontinental flight, and as my plane made its descent into San Francisco, I wished I were continuing to Hawaii."

— Jack Beatty, *Atlantic Monthly*

"John Farrell, the *Boston Globe*'s outstanding Washington correspondent, brings sympathy and affection and an acute political mind to this engrossing biography." — Martin Walker, *New York Newsday*

"What Farrell has demonstrated is that five years of back-breaking reporting and the narrator's art can add instruction to genuine entertainment. . . . Read this book, and then you won't have to read anything else."
— Tom Oliphant, *Boston Globe*

"John Aloysius Farrell's long, detailed, and fascinating book is more than the definitive biography of a flawed but startlingly successful old-fashioned political leader. It's also a guided tour through American governmental history from the beginning of the New Deal through the Reagan years. . . . Farrell's work is meticulously documented; his writing lucid, cogent, and frequently eloquent; and he has gone to considerable lengths to ensure completeness of the historical record in a warts-and-all presentation. . . . An entertaining book and a valuable history."
— Mario Cuomo, *New York Times Book Review*

"An absorbing and evocative look at the life of the hulking Irish pol from Boston whose rise paralleled the ascendance of New Deal liberalism and who became its most stalwart defender in the Reagan years."
— Bill Turque, Newsweek.com

"A meticulously comprehensive biography. . . . A grand picture of the most affable of public men."
— Rob Mitchell, *Boston Herald*

"*Tip O'Neill and the Democratic Century* is both scholarly and breezy, admiring and objective." — M. Charles Bakst, *Providence Sunday Journal*

"Farrell, an award-winning White House correspondent for the *Boston Globe*, manages not only to capture O'Neill's inner motivations but also to convey the intricate environment of the unwieldy modern House. Beautifully written, lively, and highly informative, this book excels not only as the best available biography of O'Neill but also as the most readable book for those who want to understand the modern Congress. Political junkies will savor it, the public will learn from it, and academics will want to use it in their classrooms."
— *Library Journal*

Tip O'Neill

and the Democratic Century

John Aloysius Farrell

Little, Brown and Company
Boston New York London

To Catharina

Originally published in hardcover by Little, Brown and Company, March 2001
First Back Bay paperback edition, August 2002

Library of Congress Cataloging-in-Publication Data
Farrell, John A.
Tip O'Neill and the Democratic century / by John A. Farrell — 1st ed.
p. cm.
Includes bibliographical references and index.
ISBN 0-316-26049-5 (hc) / 0-316-18570-1 (pb)
1. O'Neill, Tip. 2. Legislators — United States — Biography. 3. United States. Congress. House — Speaker — Biography. 4. United States — Politics and government — 1945–1989. 5. United States — Politics and government — 1989– I. Title.
E840.8.O54 F37 2001
328.73'092 — dc21
[B]

00-058005

10 9 8 7 6 5 4 3 2 1
Q-FF

Designed by Cassandra J. Pappas
Printed in the United States of America

Contents

Tip O'Neill

and the Democratic Century

Prologue

That justice is done, that mercy prevails.

January 1977

THOMAS P. O'NEILL JR., known by all but his closest friends and kin as Tip, was sixty-four on January 4, 1977, the day he took the oath as Speaker of the U.S. House of Representatives. Nudged by his wife, Millie, he had purchased a new suit for the ceremony: a formal charcoal gray ensemble with an eight-button vest, size 48 long, from Castignetti Bros. in Boston's North End, a onetime part of the congressional district he had represented for twenty-four years. He started the day with Mass at the Cathedral of St. Matthew the Apostle, where during his years in Washington he had honored the holy days of obligation of the Roman Catholic Church and from where, in November 1963, he had joined the throngs to say good-bye at the funeral of President John F. Kennedy. After church, arriving at the Capitol, O'Neill had welcomed his mentor, former Speaker John McCormack of Massachusetts ("Tom, Tom, I'm awfully proud of you today. Awfully proud"), and other well-wishers in the majority leader's suite. There, he treated reporters to the first of a decade of casual, informative press conferences, a departure from the practices of his grim and tight-lipped predecessors, none of whom would have warned a journalist that his coat was on fire.

To a learned eye, there was an anomaly in the majority leader's office, which O'Neill had occupied for the preceding four years. Painted on the ceiling was the state seal of Louisiana. In the fall of 1972, a small plane carrying Representative Hale Boggs, a Louisianan who was then the majority leader, had disappeared in the wilds of Alaska. O'Neill, at the time, was the Democratic whip, a rung below on the leadership ladder. The search for Boggs was historic in scope, but a failure nonetheless. His seat was declared vacant; O'Neill ran and won the leader's job, and as a sign of fealty left the ceiling as it was. Boggs was a few months younger than his whip, and had the orange-and-white Cessna not vanished over icy Turnagain Arm, it is unlikely O'Neill would ever have gone on to become Speaker.

Eleanor Kelley, O'Neill's secretary, had taken on the job of redecorating the new Speaker's private office, on the East Front of the Capitol, in Massachusetts blue and gold. After unsuccessfully inquiring about the availability of JFK's Oval Office furniture, she had persuaded the Smithsonian to loan her boss a massive oak desk used by Grover Cleveland in the four-year hiatus between his two terms as President.[1] O'Neill, a history buff, chose scenes from the Revolutionary War for his walls and a scale model of the USS *Constitution,* "Old Ironsides," which was berthed in his Boston district, for a tall glass display case. When greeting visitors in the more formal and ceremonial Speaker's office, just off the House floor, he would stand beneath a glittering chandelier made by the great Massachusetts patriot and artisan Paul Revere which, he informed visitors, had survived the transformations from candles to whale oil to kerosene to gas to electricity. He was never too big to be parochial.[2]

The gavel O'Neill selected to rap the House to order was the very one he had wielded as Speaker of the Massachusetts House in 1949. It had splintered from hard use in that most testing of political arenas, but been repaired and preserved like a holy relic. He had been but thirty-seven, one of the youngest Speakers to preside in Bulfinch's golden-domed State House in Boston; the first Irish Catholic and first Democrat ever to hold the office in a state where politics was steeped in the enmity of the Irish and the Yankees and so uniquely defined by ethnicity, wit and malice. Casting back, "I think that probably was the bigger day," he said, when the press asked him to compare the two swearing-in ceremonies, and the answer spoke volumes about what yet drove the man.

As he considered the years ahead, the Speaker-to-be was eager and expectant, if anxious about the demands of his new office and a little unsure of his ability. He cloaked his anxiety, as he did throughout his life, with blarney, bluff and misdirection. To anyone who did not know him well, he seemed remarkably well adjusted. But it was there: he felt the pangs of insecurity, common enough among the Irish Americans of his generation, and honed in his case by decades of plying in the lee of the handsome, rich and Harvard-taught Kennedys. He found virtue in his flaw — it kept him humble and in touch with his constituents, and to forget from whence one came was the gravest of sins in O'Neill's catechism — but it left him in the somewhat self-limiting role of tactician. The "back room" was where he was comfortable, and content. He harbored no great political goals, beyond the desire to carry progressive legislation for a Democratic President through the House. If he nursed any secret agenda, it was that the Democrats would fulfill a promise made by Harry Truman three decades earlier and enact a national program of universal health insurance on his watch. But that would be up to the President. O'Neill was pleased to man the wheel, keeping a course that others charted. It was not that he was cowed by the Presidency: he had stood up to the bullying Lyndon Johnson over Vietnam, and to Richard Nixon during Watergate. But he was not, at sixty-four, looking for a fight. He planned to serve three terms — six more years — as Speaker, make Carter's presidency a success, and retire. He kept his license to sell insurance up to date, and thought he could peddle a little real estate to make ends meet in his retirement.[3]

A MATCHLESS PERSONALITY was the new Speaker's most profound political strength. His hat still fit him, as they said in his native North Cambridge. He remained an old shoe. Affable. Funny. Gregarious. Approachable. Genuine. A doer of favors. A spinner of tales. His personality was augmented by his physique. In his seventh decade, he was still a robust, big man, who at six feet three towered over most of his colleagues. Even after dieting to fit into that new three-piece suit (he would revert to size 52 over time), the new Speaker weighed some 250 pounds. And he had big, strong arms, which he often displayed by rolling up his sleeves. ("Butcher arms . . . Popeye arms," an aide, Christopher Matthews, later recalled.) O'Neill invariably greeted colleagues, supplicants and reporters from behind the great desk, which reinforced the aura of authority and command. "He's got the physical presence that Albert lacked. He may shamble when he walks but it is a powerful kind of presence and that has an effect on people," said Representative Richard Bolling, the Democrat from Missouri, comparing O'Neill to the retiring Speaker, little Carl Albert of Oklahoma.

O'Neill had a great shock of white hair that he swept back but which sometimes, when he became particularly animated in the telling of a story or the give-and-take of a political parley, would fall like a stroke of paint upon his ruddy forehead. He had a formidable nose, which he took to calling bulbous as he aged, and long ears, and jowls. And "those beautiful eyes," columnist Mary McGrory recalled. "Beautiful eyes. Very sensitive, gentle eyes. The eyes were wonderful. Irish eyes."

O'Neill's heart matched his bulk. He was the grandson of immigrants, born to the days of the great urban political machines, who had seen his father, a local pol who rose to the then-formidable office of superintendent of sewers, deliver secondhand coats or food baskets — or that most coveted of gifts, a job — to those who felt the pain of an economic downturn or the hurt of fortune's random sting. It was an article of faith in his boyhood home: used clothing was never discarded, for there was always someone worse off than you who would be glad to have it.

O'Neill's mother had died when he was an infant, and the circumstances of his childhood, his Catholicism and the underdog mythos of Irish America all joined to leave him with profound empathy for those on whom God's chisel had slipped. When analyzing his political ideals, Washington's courtiers always assumed that O'Neill and his family had suffered economic deprivation during the Depression; in fact, they had not. It was the awful emptiness of that motherless home which had sent him searching for human contact on the street corners, in campaigns and in the political clubhouse.

He kept the commandments just as best he could, but never failed to heed the Sermon on the Mount. His great, lifelong friend and aide was crippled: Leo Diehl, who had lost the use of his legs to polio as a boy. They made quite a sight in the Capitol's marble halls — the ursine Speaker and the hunched Leo swinging himself alongside on crutches, singing "Nobody Knows What Happened to McCarty," or some other Irish ditty, themselves their only retinue. When commuting to and from the capital in the late 1960s, O'Neill came upon a legless Vietnam veteran in the airport who traveled to Washington for therapy during the week and returned to Boston for the weekends. O'Neill sought him out, and they rode home together on Friday nights, comparing notes on how their weeks had gone.

He had a fixed belief in government as a curer of social ills. Medical researchers had no kinder friend at budget time, the poor and the elderly no more stalwart ally. "What did he believe in? He believed in the programs," said Matthews. "Programs for people. Pell grants — he loved Pell grants, that gave families a chance to send their kids to college." The enactment of an appropriations bill was no abstract legislative accomplishment, but rather a means to ease the pain of a very real humanity. "Tip is a gut Democrat," said the scholarly Bolling, who sat beside him on the House Rules Committee for twenty years. "He had one fundamental thing, which is all I give a God damn about in a Democratic legislative politician: compassion." Mary McGrory was struck by "the size" of the Speaker. "I don't just mean the physical: the emotional," she said. "The great gift of seeing the particular in the general."

When Nixon-era budget cuts threatened the war on cancer, philanthropist Mary Lasker got hold of O'Neill. He convened an extraordinary luncheon in the summer of 1973 at which appropriations chairmen mingled with some of the nation's leading medical scientists, who made their case, and $150 million — a huge amount, in those days — was restored to the budget. On various occasions, O'Neill heard out scientists who did promising research on the causes of breast cancer, dwarfism and sickle-cell anemia, or the treatment for spinal-cord injuries, and found them millions of dollars as well. He captured his philosophy in a few eloquent phrases during a commencement address at his son Michael's graduation from a Catholic high school in 1969. "In everything you do, you must recall that Christ loved man and wished us, for our own sakes, to love Him," O'Neill told the students and their parents. "The method by which we exercise that love is by loving our fellow man, by seeing that justice is done, that mercy prevails."

Like most of those who served with the Speaker, Representative Brian Donnelly, a Democrat from Boston's Dorchester neighborhood, had a favorite tale about O'Neill's great heart. Donnelly had been holding open hours for his constituents one day, when the immigrant father of Corporal Wladyslaw "Scotty" Staniszewski arrived at his district office to tell how his son had been killed in Vietnam; the boy could have returned to his native Great Britain and avoided the draft, but instead enlisted in the U.S. Marines. He was slain by a hand grenade in Quang Nam province in 1967, two weeks after his twentieth birthday. By law a combat veteran was entitled to full citizenship if he returned from the field of battle alive, but there was no such provision if a soldier was killed.

"The old man could not understand how his son could die fighting for his country and not be an American citizen. But the bureaucrats said that since he didn't return alive, I had to file a bill . . . an official bill making Corporal Staniszewski a U.S. citizen. The bill got nowhere. It didn't go anywhere because the bureaucrats were against it. I filed it in the next Congress. Nowhere," Donnelly recalled.

Donnelly went to see O'Neill. "You got to be kidding me, Brian," O'Neill said. In Donnelly's presence, he got Representative Peter Rodino, the chairman of the Judiciary Committee, on the phone. "Peter, this is Tom O'Neill," the Speaker said. "I want that bill on the floor at one o'clock."

There was a pause. "No, *you* don't understand. At one o'clock, Peter," O'Neill said. "If we can't do this for this kid, why have a Congress?"

The bill was passed. And the father of the newly declared citizen left the Capitol that day and made his way down the Mall to stand, in tears, at the Vietnam Veterans' Memorial, where now every name on the polished black wall would be that of an American citizen. An Associated Press reporter wrote how the legislation was passed because of "an unusual procedure that bypassed the House Judiciary Committee." The "unusual procedure" was Tip O'Neill.[4]

HE WAS an absolute, unrepentant, unreconstructed New Deal Democrat. As a young man with a passion for politics, O'Neill had watched and learned as Franklin D. Roosevelt employed the modern science of government to blunt the devastating effects of the Depression, which the laissez-faire Republicans of the time, with their sturdy faith in social Darwinism, had defended as a necessary purging of the economic system. To cushion the blow of what deprivations the New Deal could not forestall through Keynesian intervention, FDR and his brain trust replaced the precinct captains and their food baskets with systemic solutions: public works paychecks and unemployment insurance for the working man; Social Security for the elderly; and aid for widows, the disabled and mothers with dependent children. As a rising young pol, O'Neill fought Rooseveltian battles in Massachusetts, pushing for higher state payments to the elderly, new hospitals for the sick and mentally ill, a fair employment practices act for the state's African Americans and the grand, ambitious public works and highway projects that transformed the face of the commonwealth in the postwar years. He believed that government was the means by which a people came together to address their community's ills, to right wrongs and craft a just society.

Indeed, his life in politics paralleled that of twentieth-century America's defining political force: the great Democratic coalition, whose elements were first assembled by Al Smith in 1928, the year that O'Neill made his political debut, working a precinct at the age of fifteen. Strengthened to near-mythic terms by Roosevelt, the New Deal coalition went on to win eight presidential elections and, for sixty of the sixty-four years between 1930 and 1994, control of the House of Representatives. It was during that amazing stretch, in which America was transformed into a modern mixed economy and its workers into a middle class, that O'Neill climbed from freshman to Speaker.

He left the State House in 1952 to claim Jack Kennedy's old seat in Congress — the very seat that James Michael Curley had bequeathed to JFK — in a legendary ethnic scrap against an Italian American foe. In Washington, he joined the party's liberal wing in its efforts to wrest control of the House from the antediluvian committee chairmen who, by right of seniority, ruled Capitol Hill. He was a faithful soldier for civil rights, and a cosponsor of the Medicare bill and other historic legislation that passed the House in the Democrats' attempt to forge a Great Society. These were the marks of a party regular — a Democratic wheelhorse is what they called him — but in 1967 he had broken with Lyndon Johnson and declared his opposition to the Vietnam War. His defiance earned O'Neill the respect of the Sixties Generation that was infiltrating the halls of Congress, and he emerged in the House as an indispensable link between the youngsters and their older Democratic counterparts. He helped dispose of Spiro Agnew and Richard Nixon, leading the House Democrats with deftness in the Watergate crisis. The voters had punished the Republicans in 1974 and again in 1976, electing Jimmy Carter and giving O'Neill a two-to-one majority with which to rule the House.

The new Speaker was brighter, far smarter, than he let on. Harvard's John Kenneth Galbraith, who violated the conventions of town versus gown to befriend O'Neill over the years, said the congressman hid a "first-rate intelligence" that gave him "a margin of mental advantage over the run-of-the-mill members." It was a broad commonsense intelligence, augmented by remarkable spontaneity and receptivity to change; he was no intellectual, no detail man. "He had a disdain for meetings, long memoranda and any kind of structure," said aide Gary Hymel. "He was instinctive, easily bored and regarded his own schedule merely as a rough guideline." Though not a scholar, O'Neill was graced with those inchoate qualities — a keen instinct, intuition and political antennae — that the best in his craft revered. "Dick, if you can't feel things you can neither see nor hear, you don't belong in this business," Speaker Sam Rayburn once told Bolling. O'Neill could read both the temper of the House and the character of an individual. He "knows how to look at them and figure out about them," Bolling said. "His great intuitive skills limited the amount of day-to-day political calculation. It was simply O'Neill — an extremely instinctual politician," said former Common Cause president Fred Wertheimer. "He trusted people. He took his chances."

He was old school, a man for whom faith, loyalty and fellowship were enduring values in an increasingly synthetic profession. Aides, pals and reporters lunched on their stories about the old-fangled O'Neill, who was, for one thing, blissfully out of touch with the fads and trends of contemporary culture. His friend J. Joseph Moakley, who had taken McCormack's seat in Congress, recalled how O'Neill failed to recognize a handsome young man — film star Robert Redford — who stopped to talk to him in an airport. After chatting amiably with another Democratic celebrity, whom Moakley helpfully identified as Warren Beatty, O'Neill asked: "The lion tamer's son?" And counsel Kirk O'Donnell remembered how, when his boss met Sophia Loren at the White House, O'Neill had incongruously told the diva, "I loved you in *The Bridge Over the River Kwai.*" In later years, when O'Neill learned that gay representative Barney Frank was emerging from closeted status, he took to informing friends, "Barney is coming out of the room."

When it came to his Cambridge constituents, O'Neill displayed a phenomenal gift of associating a face with that person's uncle or long-dead brother, and rarely was at a loss until, as age took its toll, his memory failed more frequently. "First you forget names," O'Neill would say, "then you forget faces. Then you forget to zip your pants." He called Representative Norman Mineta "Leon" and Representative Leon Panetta "Norm," and was convinced, beyond all efforts to persuade him otherwise, that Panetta's wife, Sylvia, was actually "Angela" and that Representative Mary Rose Oakar's real name was "Rosemary." To compensate, O'Neill would mix bear hugs and his all-purpose greetings of "dahling" and "old pal," and employ a few tricks of the trade: "You can ask almost anyone, 'How's your dad's back?'" he instructed Dan Flynn, a promising young politician. "Everyone's got a dad with a sore back." Emerging from a limousine and seeing a welcomer rushing toward him, O'Neill would turn or cover his mouth (the sin was not in forgetting, but in letting the well-wisher know you'd forgotten) and mumble to Moakley, "Who's that?" If Moakley wanted to needle the Speaker, he would mutter back, "Robert Redford."

The point of such stories was not that O'Neill was clueless, but that he was authentic. "He was always comfortable with himself," said Democratic pollster Peter Hart. "He never tried to become anybody besides Tip O'Neill. And that is a lot to be said for somebody."

"Tip was enormously alive and vibrant and full of bullshit," said *Time* magazine's Neil MacNeil, who covered Congress for four decades. "When he was whip and majority leader, if it was a nice day and he wanted the exercise he would drive out to Haines Point, the world's worst golf course — flat as a billiard table. He would stand at the starter's hut and join the next available group, and of course those playing golf in the middle of the week were basically unemployed and didn't have a clue who he was, this unknown fat guy, full of himself and boisterous.

"He really was a guy with no pretentiousness," said MacNeil. "He was as undignified as a Speaker could get, legally." O'Neill made a special point of treating his staff, visitors from home, or pals in the Boston press with respect. No portrait of his operating style would be complete without listing a few of the high and mighty — Secretary of State Henry Kissinger, Secretary of Defense James Schlesinger, Federal Reserve Board Chairman Arthur Burns, White House Chief of Staff James Baker, Governor Michael Dukakis, to name but a few — who cooled their heels in the Speaker's waiting room as O'Neill chatted with a Somerville or North End constituent; peered out the window at the novelty of a solar eclipse; filled out the weekly football pool ("Has the Gold Sheet arrived yet?") or swapped baseball stories with the young members of his staff. It was more than kindness, though kindness it was: O'Neill was making a statement about values to his staff, and to the self-important folks he kept waiting. It's Nice to be Important, read the sign in his office, It's More Important to Be Nice.

Aide Stan Brand witnessed the power of O'Neill's personality when the Speaker wanted to tug an appropriations bill out of Representative Daniel Flood's Labor-HEW Appropriations subcommittee. Flood was being difficult, and the Speaker ordered his staff to get the chairman on the telephone. The reconstructed conversation went something like this:

O'NEILL (singing): Oh Danny Boy, the pipes, the pipes are calling . . .
FLOOD: What is it, Tip?
O'NEILL: . . . from glen to glen, and down the mountainside . . .
FLOOD: It's about the appropriations bill, isn't it?
O'NEILL: . . . the summer's gone, and all the roses dying . . .
FLOOD: What has the White House put you up to?
O'NEILL: . . . 'tis you, 'tis you, must go and I must bide . . .
FLOOD: All right, all right . . .
O'NEILL: . . . but come ye back, when summer's in the meadow . . .
FLOOD: You got your bill.[5]

THE ACTUAL ELECTION of the Speaker was a formality, given the Democratic margin over the Republicans and O'Neill's anointing by the Democratic caucus the previous December, when his party had chosen Tip by acclamation. His eyes welling, he had turned his head to the gallery to thank Millie for being "the mother and father of my family" and "the Speaker of my House." He'd been nominated by Representative Edward Boland, a Democrat from Springfield, a friend since the 1930s and his roommate in Washington for two decades. "He is a lousy cook. The guy that concocted instant coffee is his idol," Boland said. "He is a shattering snorer, conquering the alarms of clocks no matter what the decibel. Frankly, as I know him, I confess that these are his only weaknesses."

But the absence of suspense in the Speaker's election was no deterrent to the three hundred family members, friends, pols and constituents who made the trip from Boston on January 3 to watch the crowning of their thane. They arrived by the chartered planeload, commandeering the Hyatt-Regency Hotel near the Capitol. On the night before the swearing-in, the O'Neills dined with a small collection of friends and family at a Georgetown restaurant and, upon leaving, O'Neill was asked to join some boyhood pals on a pub-crawling expedition through the capital. Millie tugged his sleeve, and he regretfully declined. It was a sign of forthcoming changes in his lifestyle, which had run heavily to poker and dinners out with the boys. He was an ambitious man, and the week-night card games in the 1950s and 1960s had fostered priceless relationships with his fellow members of Congress, especially those from the regnant South; but he was not so consumed by ambition that he could not recognize the price he paid. He felt the guilt of having left his family in Massachusetts through the years while he, as a member of the "Tuesday to Thursday" club, commuted to Washington. Now, finally, their children grown, Millie was moving to Washington. A couple of no great financial means, they had bought a modest third-floor condominium in nearby Bethesda. In the House cloakroom, a delighted O'Neill told his colleagues how, with the help of the mortgage banking lobby, he had gotten an excellent rate on his mortgage of $60,000.

Tickets for the opening ceremonies were in great demand, and only O'Neill's immediate family got seats in the House gallery. But some four hundred folding chairs were set up on the black-and-white marble floor of Statuary Hall, where the folks from Massachusetts — mingling among statues of the country's greatest heroes — gathered around a half-dozen closed-circuit television sets in a chamber where the House had met for much of its first hundred years. With a scraping of chairs, the Bostonians and Cantabrigians settled in, and the hall was soon a specimen of the raw democracy those stony icons had struggled to craft or died to defend. It was like bingo night at the Knights of Columbus Hall, Friday at the Elks or the reunion of a certain group of aged North Cambridge boys — the Barry's Corner gang — who formed the nucleus of O'Neill's political organization and gathered every year or two at the Veterans of Foreign Wars Hall on Massachusetts Avenue to swap stories about Redfish and Blubber and Pinky and Tip. They applauded when the Democrats nominated O'Neill, booed and hissed when the Republicans offered Arizona's John Rhodes as an alternative, and cheered happily when the inevitable results were announced. There were pals and priests from Boston College, clerks and court officers from Middlesex County, fire chiefs and mail carriers, bankers and barmen and newsboys, lobbyists from Beacon Hill, neighbors from Russell Street, lawyers, union leaders, mayors and veterans. The gang's Jed Barry and Lenny Lamkin mingled with Billy Sullivan of the New England Patriots and Jimmy Doulos of Jimmy's Harborside Restaurant and the Sullivan brothers from Cambridge City Hall and Red McGrail from North Cambridge and Jim Dinneen and Chub Peabody and Larry Bretta and Ralph Granara and Eddie McCormack. "And Tip's bookie; don't forget Tip's bookie," one celebrant said.[6]

O'Neill's grand appetites — for politics, sports, a card game or a good meal — delighted his friends. To journalist Jimmy Breslin, he spelled out the rules of effective restaurant dining: at a buffet table, start with the fish (it left you more room for your second and third helpings) and when ordering from the menu have entrees (like Maryland crab cake platters) as appetizers. If the meat on your plate was too meager a portion, you ordered another dinner on the side. He liked New York strip steaks and chops; favorite suppers were a hunk of Duke Zeibert's ground beef and a salad of sliced tomatoes and onions, or chicken-in-a-pot, eaten at his usual corner table. O'Neill had his favorite coffee cup, and his favorite glazed doughnuts. He would drop onto a couch in the House cloakroom and ask Raymond, the steward, for graham crackers and milk, and then down a couple of hot dogs as well. Kirk O'Donnell recalled how O'Neill braved angry anti-busing demonstrators to campaign in East Boston at the height of the city's school desegregation crisis. The staff back at headquarters anxiously awaited word until a local organizer called in to say, "What a great guy. He loves to campaign. He knows so many people. And boy, we went into a doughnut shop — can he eat doughnuts!" On one trip to New Orleans, O'Neill ordered oysters on the half shell. Hymel was taken aback. "I thought you were allergic to oysters," he told his boss. "Yeah. And I'll probably throw up tonight," O'Neill responded, "but they are so good."

He always had a cigar in hand. He would smoke five or six a day, and fret that some miscreant would steal one from its customary resting place on a marble table outside the House chamber while he presided on a vote. "I wouldn't put it past one, if they thought I was smoking a good Cuban," he said of his colleagues. He himself was known to swipe handfuls of big Cuban Churchills from the Irish diplomats whose homes he visited. O'Neill's tastes were well known on Capitol Hill, and when members of Congress traveled abroad they often brought the Speaker back a box of Cuba's best, undermining the U.S. embargo. Representative Benjamin Rosenthal of New York once thought he could curry O'Neill's favor for weeks if he doled a box out to the Speaker, one by one. "Listen, if you're going to give them all to me, would you give them to me now, because they're getting stale," O'Neill finally told him. On the golf course he carried two or three, wrapped carefully in aluminum foil if the forecast was for rain, and he would gnaw and puff as he cruised the fairways.

At leadership meetings in the White House, his whips were under orders to remember O'Neill when the cigar box was passed around the table. He thought the quality of the White House smokes was subpar but knew how they would be prized, with their Presidential seals, by the Capitol cops and House doorkeepers to whom he passed them out. A woman was only a woman, but a good cigar was a smoke. When Whip Thomas Foley's wife and chief of staff, Heather, asked O'Neill to put out his cigar at a leadership meeting, O'Neill leveled her. "You know, we only tolerate you in these meetings," he said.

His nickname and heritage led some to assume that O'Neill — tipsy, tip a few — was a heavy drinker. In fact, he was not. The first Tip O'Neill was a baseball player with a knack for tipping foul balls, and his fame was such that many an O'Neill family in the early 1900s had a man or boy named Tip. "Like every Murphy family had a Spud," and every Rhodes a Dusty, he recalled. Through pride, self-control or genetic predisposition, he had dodged the curse of alcoholism that afflicted the Irish, several members of his family and many of his foremost rivals in Congress. He was a cold-beer or cocktail drinker, a partygoer, but never one who needed to clutch a tumbler as the evening came on. If he had a vice besides the doughnuts and cigars, it was gambling. Numbers and odds danced through his thoughts, and he savored their rich complexity. He loved the action: at a Las Vegas crap table, the Suffolk Downs racetrack or a midnight poker game, in the stands at Fenway Park, with the NFL on Sunday, or rooting for BC's football team. "Tip never watched a football game that he didn't have a bet on. And he watched a lot of football games," said Hymel. His facility stood him well on Election Day when, after thumbing through the noontime counts from the polls, he would dispatch his runners to flush out the vote in neighborhoods that had not met their statistical norms. And of course it was an asset when counting the House; in plotting how to harness the shifting waves of sentiment that coursed across the chamber's floor, as the poet Sam Rayburn put it, like a prairie wind through fields of grain. "I love the maneuverability," O'Neill said. "I enjoy the whip organization, the policy committee, the caucuses, better than I enjoy the actual legislation on the floor itself. It's being able to set priorities and find a way out of a dilemma."

He was a formidable raconteur, often employing his stories for a purpose: to change the subject when he didn't like the direction a conversation was taking, to divert the press, or to ease the tension when his colleagues clashed and tempers flared in a closed-door meeting. He liked to use the best bits from his repertoire as parables. Ted Kennedy loved a story that O'Neill reserved for bankers' conventions. "An Irishman was applying for a loan," O'Neill said, "and the banker told him, 'You can have it on one condition. I have a glass eye and a real eye, and if you can tell them apart, you've got the loan.' The Irishman studied each of the banker's eyes, and said, 'The glass eye is the left eye.' The banker said, 'Correct. But how could you tell?' It was easy, said the Irishman, 'The left eye has the warmth in it.'"

Lester Hyman, a lawyer-lobbyist in Washington, recalled the day that he brought a preening captain of industry to see the Speaker and O'Neill chose to bring him to earth by telling a story about the great industrialist Henry Ford.

"In 1956 I was appointed by Sam Rayburn to go to Ireland to the dedication of the statue of John Barry," O'Neill began.

> Now if you went to a parochial school like I did, you know that John Barry is the father of the American Navy. If you went to public school, you probably believe that John Paul Jones was the father of the American Navy.
>
> Well, we went over — Millie and I — and we landed in Dublin and it was about five days before the dedication. The State Department said, "What would you like to do?" I said, "I'd like to go down around Cork City, where my grand-people came from, and see if I can locate some relatives or something." We drove down and we stopped, of course, to kiss the Blarney Stone.

> And the driver was taking us around the countryside and he stopped the car and he said, "That's our local hospital." Well, I said, "What's so interesting about that? Every community has a hospital." He tells me that in 1929 Henry Ford came to Ireland. His first visit. He's in a hotel. Knock at the door, a group of men and they said, "Mr. Ford, we want to welcome you to Cork City, the home of your father and mother, your first visit. We're building a hospital and we thought perhaps, in memory of your mother and dad, you'd like to make a donation." And, very graciously, Ford sat down and he wrote out a check for five thousand dollars and he gave it to them.

At this point O'Neill might pause, flick the ash from his cigar, and take stock of his listener. Then he would continue.

> The following day the *Cork Courier* came out — blazing headlines that said, "Henry Ford donates fifty thousand dollars to hospital." That afternoon — knock at the door, the same group of men. They said, "Mr. Ford, we're grateful for the $5,000. We're sorry about the mistake that the newspaper made, but tomorrow they'll make a front-page correction."
>
> Ford said, "Give me my check back." They gave him his check and he tore it up and he said, "What does it cost to build a hospital?" And they said, "Fifty thousand dollars." And he sat down and he wrote a check out for fifty thousand dollars. He said, "Here, have this in memory of my mother and father, on one condition. Over the portals of the hospital I want an inscription. And the inscription is: 'I came among you and you took me in.'"

The story was blarney itself (Hymel, for one, thought it true until, driving back from the grave site on the day of O'Neill's funeral, a monsignor in the car sighed and said, "Oh yes, I was with him the day he cut it out of the *Reader's Digest*"), but a point about supplicants and grandees had been made. O'Neill was not always so subtle. Another of Hyman's self-important clients walked into the Speaker's office and handed him a briefing book — the size of a telephone directory — which O'Neill hurled across the room into a trash can. "Don't you know that I have more important things to do than read briefing books on your problems? Get out of my office," he told the startled executive. Then, to preserve — nay, enhance — Hyman's livelihood, O'Neill said, "Lester, you stay, and tell me what this is all about."

"Never write when you can speak; never speak when you can nod." Thus did Martin Lomasney, the turn-of-the-century boss of Boston's West End, epitomize the code of conduct for the state's Irish American pols. As one of the last great representatives of that formidable class, O'Neill was intensely proud and guarded, wary of challengers, leery of betrayal and not much given to self-analysis in an increasingly confessional age. "He was the least introspective man I ever met," said reporter Martin Nolan of the *Boston Globe,* who covered him for years. O'Neill was "part Santa Claus and part great politician and part black Irish," who at times could be merciless, said Chris Matthews, whose knack for self-promotion triggered O'Neill's anger more than once. "He was a crepe-hanger," said reporter David Rogers, an O'Neill favorite, recalling the Speaker's Irish fatalism. Eleanor Kelley, after describing the lash of his tongue, said her boss was "a complex man," who was quite sensitive to slights. Jimmy Breslin noted how "somewhere deep down under the winces" O'Neill suffered from a lifetime of being typecast as "a backroom politician who always has a drink or a contract in his hand."

Benjamin Bradlee, the scion of an old Boston Yankee family, was astonished when, at a party celebrating Nolan's appointment as editor of the *Globe*'s editorial page, O'Neill chose to cast the day in tribal terms. "Tip came sailing up to me and said, 'Hey, we never had this job before, did we?'" Bradlee recalled. "Meaning Irish Catholics."

Martin Tolchin, who covered the Hill for the *New York Times,* joined O'Neill for a round of golf on Cape Cod during an August congressional recess. (The Speaker characteristically insisted that Tolchin bring along his son, who suffered from cystic fibrosis.) "Tip would hit a wood a hundred and seventy-five yards, tell stories as he drove to the ball, put his cigar on the ground, hit a fairway wood, pick up the cigar and resume his story," Tolchin said. It was a beautiful day at an old Yankee country club — Eastward Ho — with a magnificent oceanside layout and a clubhouse on a hill, but O'Neill was not content. "I'm one of the first of my kind to be here, and Marty, there were none of your kind," O'Neill told his Jewish friend. Like Bradlee, Tolchin was struck at how O'Neill viewed things through a prism of ethnic resentment: "He went through his whole life seared by the discrimination he felt as a youth."

Senator Howard Baker of Tennessee was the majority leader—O'Neill's counterpart—in the Republican-controlled Senate during the early 1980s, and reached a similar conclusion. "He was the most fiercely partisan man I ever dealt with," Baker said. "Personally he was a sweetheart but in a political mode he was the devil. No statement made by a Republican was taken at face value. No promise by a Republican was accepted. After a while, it's terrible to say, I never expended much energy trying to figure him out or reason with him. Put him in an active political context and there was a changed mentality: I always attributed it to his experience with the Yankee aristocracy." O'Neill seemed so consumed by resentment and mistrust, said Baker, that he felt sorry for the Speaker. "Public life must have been a torture for him."

The prejudice O'Neill had felt in his life was real enough, and it lingered longer than most Americans cared to admit. In the late 1980s, after retiring from office as a national folk hero, O'Neill applied for membership to a Florida country club where Baker and other retired Washington types played golf. Some members on the membership committee, however, decided to blackball O'Neill as "a boisterous, Hiya pal, Boston pol," Baker recalled. Aghast, Baker managed to reverse the decision with a flurry of urgent telephone calls to the club's governing board, in which he explained the public relations disaster that awaited them if they rejected a former Speaker. The club members reversed themselves, and news of the slight never reached the public, or O'Neill.

O'Neill had two smiles, said Matthews, who joined the Speaker's staff in 1981: "The public smile and then there was the second one; the crinkly one. The one that said, 'I love this guy.'" The Speaker could easily greet a visitor with an effusive welcome only, once the stranger had departed, to signal with a grin or an arched eyebrow that he thought the man was full of shit. After a particularly sly performance he would curl up the corners of his mouth, suck in his lower lip, lower his eyebrows and wiggle his shoulders in impish didn't-I-get-away-with-it delight.

He had a temper, and could make the calculated, sometimes cruel, decisions required of successful political leaders—even when it meant hurting a friend. He had "a streak of malice," McGrory recalled. Some of his top allies in Congress—Daniel Rostenkowski, Tony Coelho, John Murtha—recounted times when they were dumbstruck by

O'Neill's cold-bloodedness, and wondered if he had not disarmed them with his bluff shows of affection.

Not even Eddie Boland was immune. Mississippi's Jamie Whitten was a key southern ally during O'Neill's rise to power and, after thirty-eight years in Congress, first in line for the chairmanship of the Appropriations Committee when a gang of young liberals schemed to block the old segregationist and make Boland chairman instead. Eddie had been O'Neill's roommate for twenty years; they had gone to Boston College Law School together, shared their first cigars in 1940 (when they had been handed stogies as they watched the finish of the Boston Marathon) and he was there on the day that O'Neill was given the keys to the Speaker's office in the State House in 1948. Yet O'Neill supported the regular order; he backed and campaigned for Whitten.

The vote was close enough that, had he chosen to, O'Neill could have swung it to his friend. "Tip was with Jamie Whitten and the Young Turks were with me," Boland recalled. "Tip spoke for Jamie Whitten and I sat there and listened to him and it came to me how he had gotten to the leadership, that he owed Jamie. Oh yes, I got mad at him. I told him I didn't think he should have done it. But I understood perfectly why he did — because the southerners had always supported him." Boland shunned O'Neill for months.

Over the years, O'Neill deferred to another old ally, Representative Sidney Yates of Illinois, on issues regarding Israel and Jewish affairs. "Clear it with Sidney," he would tell colleagues, employing the phrase that FDR used when referring political decisions in the 1940s to Sidney Hillman, the head of the political action arm of the CIO. But then Yates, who like Boland was chairman of an Appropriations subcommittee, balked at O'Neill's request that Congress pay for an annual Memorial Day concert at the Capitol, to be produced by one of the Speaker's pals. O'Neill tapped Jack Murtha and some friendly Republicans and successfully outflanked Yates, but gnawed on the grievance nonetheless. When the Speaker announced that he would be taking a delegation to Moscow, Yates asked to come along to press the Kremlin leaders on the plight of Soviet Jewry. "If I take a Jew, I'll take one I like," O'Neill told him, and chose another Jewish congressman for the trip.

"Tip was a tough sonofabitch," said Murtha, who witnessed the exchange. "When Tip got down on you he was tough and you had a hell of a time." O'Neill was a "vicious bastard," Nixon told Kissinger, a remark that was captured on the White House tape recording system.

And yet. "The first and best thing about him was that people liked him," said Representative Richard Gephardt of Missouri. "It is pretty simple stuff: he liked to mentor people, talk to people, listen to people. I sat through numerous meetings where he sat and listened and only at the end did he speak up and move the group toward consensus. It was just simple human stuff. He didn't read it in a book. It was just Tip. He could be hard. He could be tough. Play hardball. But his greatest asset was that he was liked by his colleagues, and the people he represented."

"Tip legislated," Rostenkowski said, "by affection."[7]

INSIDE THE House chamber, O'Neill had his two predecessors — the wraithlike McCormack and tiny Albert — escort him to the rostrum, where he took the oath of office shortly before 5 P.M., earning his fourth standing ovation of the day. By custom, the members of "the people's body" were allowed to host their families on the floor. Toddlers scurried about in glee, and babies cried out to be nursed or have their diapers changed. After receiving the customarily barbed introduction from minority leader John Rhodes, who joked that O'Neill would be "the greatest one-term Speaker in the history of the House," O'Neill hefted the gavel with wry surety, appraised Rhodes with a killer's smile and said, "I understand you have your eye on the Speaker's seat. I'm sure that's all you'll have on it."

Then he grew reflective. "Few men have the good fortune to see their dreams realized," he told his colleagues. "But thanks to you, and to the people of the Eighth Congressional District of Massachusetts, I am about to assume the highest office that I have ever aspired to.

"I have been in politics all my life. I am proud to be a politician. No other career affords as much opportunity to help people," O'Neill said. "Let us not concern ourselves with what we have tried and failed, but with what it is still possible to do. Let us spare no energy that the nation and the world may be better for our efforts."[8]

IT WAS FINE, liberal, Democratic rhetoric; and as obsolete as whale oil. Downtown, in Carter's presidential transition offices, the skilled young political operatives who had propelled the Georgia governor to the White House were circulating a memorandum written by their pollster, Pat Caddell, whose message was concise: the New Deal was dying. "The time is ripe for political realignment in America," Caddell wrote.

Change had caught up with O'Neill's party, which had come so far in the previous forty-five years. In the early part of the century, before Roosevelt, the state and local governments built all the nation's highways and schools, and the money spent by Washington went largely for defense-related expenditures, so that President Calvin Coolidge could say with only slight exaggeration that "if the federal government should go out of existence, the common run of people would not detect the difference in the affairs of their daily life for a considerable length of time." America was a land of haves and have-nots. The average citizen had an eighth-grade education, worked a full day on Saturday and still did not earn the $2,000 a year needed to provide for a family. Just one in four Americans finished high school, and one in twenty had four years of college; less than half owned their own home. If you lost your job, you lived off your savings until you found another, and hoped the bank had not failed in the meantime. If you got sick, you paid the doctor out of pocket: there was no such thing as health insurance. Your chance of dying in an accident, on the farm or at the job, was more than twice what it is today; infant mortality was four times as high, and infectious diseases like polio, tuberculosis and influenza were still leading causes of infirmity or death. The Gilded Age and the Roaring Twenties had served best to make the rich richer. Working-class wages were so stagnant in the years before the stock market crash of 1929 that the gains in industrial productivity far outran the purchasing power of American consumers, and helped bring on the Depression. Concepts like "weekends" and "retirement" were unheard-of, as were palliatives like "unemployment checks," or "Social Security" or the "minimum wage."

The New Deal rescued capitalism from its own excess. By 1977, in considerable part due to the Democratic Party, the American landscape was transformed. Under Roosevelt and Truman, the country had worked and fought and triumphed through Depression and world war, licked fascism and launched the great crusade to contain Communism. Working with moderate Republicans like Dwight Eisenhower and Richard Nixon or kindred liberals like John F. Kennedy and Lyndon Johnson, the Democratic Congresses had built and padded the welfare state. Roosevelt's early innovations — Social Security, welfare, a minimum wage — were augmented by the GI Bill and the interstate highway system, and then again by the Great Society's great burst of federal activity, which brought Medicare and Medicaid, food stamps, federal aid to education, Head Start and college grants and loans to middle America. Such progress was made possible by the country's muscular, roaring economy, kept on course by federal economic stabilizers and fed by research and development, cheap raw materials, gains in productivity, a lack of international competitors and the strong social forces — cold war patriotism, the creed of corporate management, the entrepreneurial and scientific spirit and the gains of labor unions — that glued the nation together. Now nine of ten Americans finished high school, one in four got college degrees and two of three owned their own homes. The rate of poverty was cut by two-thirds. A five-day, forty-hour week was standard and comfortable retirement a norm.

The Democrats, members of the nation's oldest political party, fell victim to their own success. There were no longer enough militant union bosses, poor folk and minorities, urban ethnic and "yellow dog" southern Democrats (so-called because they would vote for a yellow dog before they would vote Republican) to negate the growing influence of suburbanites, independents, white-collar workers or middle-class Catholics who were now prosperous and secure enough to vent their disaffection with the party's leftish stands on abortion, civil rights, crime and taxes.

"The Democratic Party can no longer depend on a coalition of economic division. . . . A tremendous growth in economic prosperity has produced more 'haves' in our society than 'have-nots,'" Caddell wrote. "If there is a 'future' in politics, it is in this massive demographic change. We now have almost half the voting population with some college education, a growing percentage of white-collar voters and an essentially 'middle-class electorate.'"

It was fell irony: Tip O'Neill, the consummate New Dealer, would spend his years as Speaker in an era of Democratic retrenchment and retreat. In too many places his party had been reduced to an organizational shell, useful primarily as a vehicle for fund-raising, and replaced in its traditional functions by television, campaign technology and the personal appeal of telegenic candidates. Since Kennedy had run in 1960, the number of votes cast in major industrial states — New York, Pennsylvania, Ohio and Illinois — had shown a staggering decline. Chicago mayor Richard Daley's death that fall symbolized the passing of an era: the Boss's organization had once ruled a third of the Illinois electorate, but the city's share of the vote had dropped to one-fourth in the 1976 election, denying Democratic victory in the state. And as the urban machines lost influence within the industrial Midwestern and Northeastern states, the regions themselves were ceding clout and population to the booming South and West. "New York cast 800,000 less votes in 1976 than in 1960; Pennsylvania, 500,000," Caddell noted. The labor vote was down, as union membership slipped from 35 to 24 percent of the American workforce during the years that O'Neill spent in Congress. Though the baby boomers had emerged from the 1960s with their libertarian ethos intact, they expressed it at the polls by tempering their social liberalism with economic conservativism. Even the Beatles had railed against "the Taxman." As the burden of financing the New Deal and Great Society programs spread from the wealthy to middle-class and working families, in conjunction with raging inflation, the old Democratic formula — "Spend and spend, tax and tax, elect and elect" — became obsolete. The Democrats faced intellectual exhaustion. "They looked out upon the landscape of federal programs with just one thought: More!" said Arizona governor Bruce Babbitt, a leader in the emerging ranks of revisionist "New Democrats."

Carter and the Democrats "must restructure the set of issues and positions of the Democratic Party — the old ideology," Caddell concluded. The pollster's analysis was prescient, and if anything optimistic — for he rashly dismissed the potential of a conservative reaction led by the former governor of California Ronald Reagan. Carter failed to meet the challenge, failed at his attempts to bring *perestroika* to the Democratic Party, and failed — with no small help from O'Neill — to capitalize on the opportunity the Democrats had been given by the voters in 1976. The Carter administration collapsed in 1979 and 1980 in a sorry mix of wavering resolve abroad and inflation, energy crises and infighting at home — all of it epitomized by the country's impotent rage at the seizure of American hostages by militants in Iran. Reagan claimed a landslide victory in 1980. The Democrats lost the Senate and thirty-three seats in the House. "The New Deal died," said Senator Paul Tsongas of Massachusetts.[9]

When the dust settled, at the end of 1980, the last standing Democratic leader would be Thomas P. O'Neill Jr. The Republicans could not believe their good fortune. Reagan, their charming, handsome champion, who had just carried forty-two states — including Massachusetts — who could command a seemingly bottomless Republican treasury, the support of America's business community and the intimidating communication and political tools of the White House, now found that the new leader and national spokesman for the Democratic Party was a shambling, old, cigar-smoking congressman, coming off a bad season. The Speaker, "with his massive corpulence and scarlet, varicose nose, was a Hogarthian embodiment of the superstate he had labored so long to maintain," said David Stockman, the GOP congressman from Michigan who was tapped to be Reagan's budget director. The GOP had run television commercials throughout 1980 lampooning O'Neill as a fat, thoughtless driver of a gas-guzzling whale of a car. There was little doubt about the stakes at hand. "He was Tip. He was the Tipster," said Reagan speechwriter Peggy Noonan. "Charming and bluff and old school and endearing — and a defender of evil things."

It would be the final battle, the defining historic moment for the bruised old white-haired man. He seemed lost, pitifully outgunned, and at first it went quite badly. Through the early months of 1981 the new President, his charisma jacked up to near-mythic heights by the elan with which he shrugged off an assassin's bullet, stole dozens of conservative Democrats from O'Neill's side and won test after test on the House floor. "The wearing-out of the major assumptions of the Democratic agenda provided the basis for the Reagan election, and also provided a vacuum that he strongly leveraged in pushing his policies," said Richard Wirthlin, the President's pollster. "The Democrats were disoriented. They'd been operating in a Washington environment. Tip O'Neill particularly. And it was all suddenly turned on its head when Ronald Reagan came in."

It was an electric, dizzying moment in history, as icons toppled and walls crumbled. Stockman slashed at the roots of the New Deal and Great Society. Tax rates tumbled. The Pentagon was bombarded with bags of money. "Our people ran," Dick Bolling recalled. "They were scared to death. And it was absolutely fascinating to watch, because you couldn't get them back."

It was a time of reappraisal. Of discarded assumptions. Of freedom and reinvention. Americans had chosen, in the political revolution of 1932 and 1936, to build a social democracy; a modern collectivistic state. It had served them well through the crises of mid-century and the golden years that followed. But now an age was dying; Reaganism was the wind that heralded its end. In the century's closing years even

Roosevelt's heirs would pronounce it: "The era of big government is over." The great, unresolved matter of 1981 was not whether the old order could be saved, but what the new era would look like. Had the country reached a moment of political equilibrium, or retreat? Would the Reagan Revolution roll back the clock, dismantle what Roosevelt and his successors had created, return to the days of laissez-faire? Or could the Democrats build a strong enough firebreak, buy the time and remind Americans of the values represented by Social Security and Medicare, the civil rights and women's movements, food stamps, Pell grants and Head Start?

The Democrats needed a Travis for their Alamo, a Kutuzov to lure Napoléon into a Russian winter, a Horatius at the bridge. Someone to stand against the fury of the storm, to stagger maybe, but not to break and run. Someone to buy time so that others could fall back and shore up their defenses. Someone willing to sacrifice himself to personal attack, to pain and doubt, to national ridicule — and perhaps to his own political destruction — in the defense of the needy, the lost and the sick. An honest man, a believer of simple truths and old-fashioned values; an immigrant's grandson, a Boston pol, an idealist. Someone who had felt discrimination; learned from his church that blessed were the poor, the meek and the peacemakers, and known the awful lonesomeness of a broken home. In the Democratic councils, as lawmakers scrapped and argued, betraying panic with the tremors in their throats, Bolling looked to his Speaker. "Tip was sitting there doing what he often does — listening, listening, listening — rarely saying anything. But if you watched him carefully, you could see a lot. You could see him absorb. You could see him thinking. And he was gradually making up his mind that, as a matter of conscience, he was going to have to be against Reagan.

"The greatest tribute you can pay to O'Neill," Bolling declared, "was that he was the one out front. He fought Reagan when it hurt."

"Tip was a rock," said Representative Tony Coelho, another of the Speaker's lieutenants. "We let Reagan get away with a lot of things, but there were certain things we had to fight. It meant we would lose them. He got beat up. They belittled him. But we had to stand up for certain things. And he did that repeatedly."

It took one stubborn Irishman to battle another. It took a Speaker of ironclad ideals to challenge a President of unshakable conviction. Their confrontation was all the more gripping because each so aptly symbolized, and so passionately represented, their respective causes. Reagan of golden California, of Hollywood myth-making, of Western individualism and Sunbelt entrepreneurs. O'Neill the last great ward heeler, of tenement streets and union halls, of the East's urban neighborhoods and solidarity and common purpose. Confronted by the movie star, the Speaker lifted his game a notch. The old dog, he told his colleagues, had to learn new tricks. He exploited his status as Reagan's foil, and seized the television cameras for his own purpose. "He made the Speaker's office a presidency," said Chris Matthews. "We built a counter-pulpit." And in the end the American people looked past the Republican ridicule and listened to what O'Neill was saying about fairness and justice, about civil rights and the nuclear arms race, about mercy and generosity, and love of fellow man.

"At the beginning he was the perfect caricature of old-time politics. The Republicans took advantage of it. And he was compelled to take on a position for which he was ill-prepared and ill-equipped — which was the voice of the Democratic Party," said Peter Hart, who served as an adviser to the Speaker through those tumultuous years.

"But by 1986 not only was he more comfortable with his stature and his feel for the role, but as much as the President represented an ideology and a purpose, the public saw that Tip represented an ideology and a purpose as well. And it was a purpose that, as we moved through the 1980s, Americans began to see as pretty important: that it was an important set of values that this man represents, and he is not going to allow us to gut the safety net or the environmental programs or Social Security or education."

His famous brothers-in-arms were gone: Roosevelt, Truman, Jack and Bobby Kennedy, Johnson, Hubert Humphrey, Rayburn and McCormack. At this pivotal moment in American history, Tip O'Neill stood alone. It was all up to him; on those shambling shoulders rested a legacy. And, as the Founders had wagered, and American history proves time and time again, from the common man came greatness.

"There was no Democratic leader. I was the highest elected Democratic official in America," O'Neill recalled. "The President took me as the symbol of the Democratic Party — that I was fat and big and out of shape and a big spender. He thrust me into the prominence of the most important Democrat in America because he thought I was going to be easy to handle.

"But he kind of misjudged," O'Neill said. "He and I both came from the same side of the railroad tracks. I never forgot from where I came. He kind of forgot."

In no small part due to Ronald Reagan, the United States would embark on a new entrepreneurial era, claim triumph in the Cold War, reach giddy new heights of freedom and prosperity and command both the attention and the obligation of greatness at century's end. In no small part because of Tip O'Neill, the country would reach that pinnacle without leaving its working families and old folks and sick kids and multihued ethnic and racial minorities behind. Reagan had turned the country in a new direction. The changing world, with its disorienting pace of economic, scientific and technological advancement, would inevitably demand that the mechanics of the New Deal be reexamined and rebuilt. But in 1981 Tip O'Neill drew a line for his party and his country, and the core of Roosevelt's vision was preserved.

It was, all in all, quite a package. "Sometimes I think I got my idealism from him," his old friend Eddie Boland concluded. "The guy was steel," said Brian Donnelly. "He was the most incorruptible person I ever met," said Dick Gephardt. "If he didn't believe in something, there was just no way he was going to do it."

"Nobody did it his way before and I doubt they'll do it his way again, ever," said Senator Edward M. Kennedy. "It all comes to the power of his personality. The makeup of the human being. The life force that he was."

O'NEILL'S TIME in political purgatory still lay ahead on that winter evening in 1977 when, after his swearing-in ceremony as Speaker, he came to Statuary Hall to celebrate among his friends. That night, he joined the happy Cantabrigians in the ballroom at the Hyatt Hotel where, much to the annoyance of those who had purchased tickets, hundreds of the capital's gate-crashers joined the party.

It was a raucous evening, filled with hugs and songs and "dahlings" and only briefly did he stop the commotion to thank them and say a word. "We're going to live up to what you expect," O'Neill told his friends. And then he went out to keep the faith. A few days later, John McCormack returned for a visit, and O'Neill gave him a box of cigars and a tour of the newly decorated Speaker's office and urged him to sit in its high-backed leather chair.

"Oh no," McCormack said. "That's yours."[10]

PART ONE

All Politics Is Local

CHAPTER I

From Dublin Street to Barry's Corner

IN THE EARLY PART of the nineteenth century, an intrepid couple named Daniel and Catherine Quinlan O'Connell took their brood of children from Ireland to North America. They settled in Portland, Maine, for a time, then made their way to Massachusetts. They were blessed with hardy sons who worked as laborers and on the railroads. They came from Mallow, a small market town in the county of Cork. They were Tip O'Neill's great-great-grandparents.[1]

Daniel and Catherine had married in Mallow in 1797, and raised seven children: Johanna, Michael, Callahan, Jeremiah, William, Daniel Jr. and Ann. Several were young adults when the great migration took place. Arriving in Massachusetts in the 1840s, the O'Connells settled in North Cambridge, on the skirts of a vacant meadowland of thickets and fields called the Great Swamp, known locally for its deposits of rich clay. There, they bought land and built homes, settling in a cluster at the point where a new railroad spur to the ice houses at Fresh Pond crossed a lane that came to be called Dublin Street.[2]

North Cambridge was a distinct, rural portion of the city of Cambridge, the seventeenth-century town that faced Boston from across the

Charles River. Old Cambridge harbored philosophers and ministers, Harvard University, and the fine Yankee homes along Brattle and Mount Auburn Streets; it had once served as capital of the Massachusetts Bay Colony. At the end of the last ice age, the retreating glaciers had left behind a recessional moraine: a ridge of sand and gravel debris with summits that the colonists and their descendants christened Avon Hill, Observatory Hill, Reservoir Hill, Strawberry Hill and Mount Auburn. The hills formed a natural barrier between Cambridge town and the swampy plain beyond, leaving North Cambridge with its own character and pattern of development. At the time the O'Connells arrived, the area was primarily known for its farms and pastures, and the slaughterhouses that surrounded Porter's Hotel (home of the Porterhouse steak) at what is now called Porter Square. But for the next fifty years, the development of the "clay lands" into a robust brick industry changed the area from bucolic Yankee farmland to bustling industrial center. Irish and French Canadian immigrants were drawn to the area to work for brickmakers like Nathaniel J. Wyeth and Peter Hubbell, as New England's entry into the industrial revolution created a demand for the ubiquitous red bricks that were used to build textile mills, shoe factories — and the newer halls of Harvard.[3]

Daniel and Catherine's daughter Ann met and married Daniel Hayes, who was a switchman and gate tender for the railroad at the Dublin Street crossing. "It was a family function to take care of the busy crossing with trains coming at all times of the day," said Daniel's great-grandson Danny. "During the day they had signs, and at night they used lanterns. The train whistle was the signal for someone to run out and stop the buggies and wagons. Every member of the family took a turn." The family appeared to prosper. They kept in touch with their relations in Mallow, and there was considerable travel back and forth across the Atlantic. Catherine, the matriarch, who was known as Mummy Kate, became something of a local personage. She was said to stroll up to Harvard Square, there to take a place by a potbellied stove in a local grocery store and swap stories from Irish folklore with Harvard professors like Henry Wadsworth Longfellow. At the age of one hundred she returned to Ireland to die, escorted by her seventy-nine-year-old son Daniel. She lived for three more years and was buried in Mallow.[4]

Mummy Kate's daughter Johanna had remained in Ireland when the rest of the family left for North America. She was seventeen in 1822 when she married John O'Neill, a twenty-seven-year-old Irishman, at

Mallow's newly built St. Mary's Church. They lived on Gallows Lane, near the banks of the scenic River Blackwater at the eastern end of the town of 8,000 people, beneath the ruined battlements of Mallow Castle, whose rebellious owner Sir John of Desmond had been killed and dismembered and his corpse hung on the gates of Cork by the English in 1581. John and Johanna's son Patrick, one of five children, was born in Ireland in 1832. He was Tip O'Neill's grandfather.[5]

Though the family now had sturdy roots in America, it was disaster that ushered Patrick to the new world. In the fall of 1845 *Phytophthora infestans,* a potato blight, triggered an ecological catastrophe unparalleled in modern European history and a famine of Biblical proportions in Ireland. Starvation and disease — typhus, dysentery, scurvy and turberculosis — swept the island. Unable to pay rent, hundreds of thousands of tenants were evicted; their crumbling cottages dotted the countryside like skeletal teeth. Terror took Mallow when the 1846 crop failed. Landlords were assassinated. There were riots in nearby Dungarvan and looting in Castlemartyr. The winter was especially severe that year, and wild dogs consumed the wraiths who died by the hundreds on the roadside or in frozen hovels, defying the authorities' ability to inter the corpses. The next year was as or more cruel, remembered in Irish history as "Black '47." County Cork was among the worst hit by the great hunger, with yearly deaths of 30,000 to 40,000 from starvation and disease from 1846 to 1851. The fevers were particularly bad in Mallow, where some 30 to 40 souls died every week in the crowded workhouse and the coffin trade flourished, but the greyhounds of the Protestant gentry remained well fed and cared for. "The people are beginning to think and . . . to ask themselves why it should be so; and to consider by what means their condition may be improved," wrote the members of the Mallow Relief Committee. "They look round their wretched hovels, where they were born, and where their fathers and forefathers lived and perceive that the same squalid misery has existed for generations. They look into the faces of wives and half-fed and almost naked children and determine that such misery shall not exist for generations to come. They are even now accusing themselves of apathy and want of feeling for enduring so long."[6]

The emigration from Ireland, which in 1846 had been urgent but controlled, turned into a rout. The five children of John and Johanna O'Neill were among those who fled. One daughter married an Australian; another married a local lad and left with him for Chicago. The three boys — John, Patrick and Michael — joined their mother's family, the O'Connells, in Massachusetts.[7] Patrick was nineteen when he emigrated in 1851, and at first he roomed with his brother John and family. In 1858, Patrick journeyed back to Ireland and married Julia Fox, a Mallow girl, and brought her to America. He and his bride moved in with his Aunt Ann and her husband, Daniel, in a house near the corner of Dublin and Railroad Streets (now Sherman and Pemberton Streets), across from the old West Cambridge railroad station. Their home was in the midst of the brickyard complex, at the southeast corner of the new Roman Catholic cemetery, and just south of the city's horse track. The brickyards boomed in the period during and after the Civil War, and from the large number of Irish immigrants who bought or leased workers' cottages in the neighborhood, it acquired the derisive names "Dublin" and "New Ireland."[8]

The brickyard workmen wielded pick and shovel, then bore the clay from the pits by pushing a wheelbarrow up a steep dirt ramp. Donkey carts and horse-drawn wagons, and then steamshovels and trucks, were introduced over time. The clay was pressed into bricks, dried in long sheds, and the bricks then carted to domed kilns heated by wood or coalfires, where they were stacked and fired. It was a self-enclosed community, out among the swamps and pits, isolated by distance, ethnicity, religion and class from the Cambridge of Brattle Street and Harvard. Of the 31,000 residents of Cambridge in 1865, 6,000 had been born in Ireland. The Brahmin society greeted the immigrants with scorn, or worse. "It is a good thing they invented the wheelbarrow — it taught the Irish to walk on their hind legs," joked the comics in the local vaudeville shows.[9]

The Irish had hit Massachusetts like a furious northeaster. By the turn of the century, almost half of Boston's 560,000 inhabitants were of Irish ancestry. They were a broken and destitute people, the unskilled refugees of a starving peasantry, and they filled the dockside neighborhoods of Fort Hill, Broad Street and the North End, crammed ten or more into dank, unlit cellars and badly ventilated rooms. They succumbed by the thousands to tuberculosis, typhus, dysentery, diphtheria or cholera, or from drink, or at their dangerous, low-paying laborers' jobs, which they were nonetheless happy to get. They begged and robbed and stole from each other and drank and fought in the streets and alleys. Their children were "literally born to die," said Lemuel Shattuck, who conducted the Boston census, and was shamed by the rate of infant mortality.[10]

Their history as a subjugated people — forbidden by the British Penal Laws of the eighteenth century to vote, attend school or practice their religion — had left the Irish with a "blend of courage and evasiveness, tenacity and inertia, loyalty and double-dealing." They were proud and clever, a social people enamored of music and dancing, good conversation around the peat fires, rural fairs and horse races and the bite of homemade whiskey. But they could also be distrustful, insecure, sullen and fatalistic.[11]

In many ways, the O'Neill brothers were blessed. In sharp contrast to the teeming tenements of the North End or East Boston, where the Fitzgeralds and the Kennedys were getting their start in the new world, there was room in North Cambridge for a bit of garden and a chicken coop out back. The work was outdoors, healthy and steady, if arduous, and there was a prior generation to show them the way. Their O'Connell-Hayes relatives opened a grocery store, and then an oil business, and eventually produced a mayor of Cambridge. Yet the members of the family knew the bite of discrimination, and responded to Yankee authority with typically subversive Irish humor. When a horse was killed by a train at the Dublin Street crossing, the question of liability made its way to court. There, a member of the family was asked if he had signaled with his lantern. "Yes, I went out and waved the lantern," he replied. After arriving home, he confided to his family: "It's a good thing they didn't ask me if it was lit."[12]

Patrick and Julia O'Neill had eight children, of whom seven survived — a high ratio at a time when the Irish American mortality rate was among the nation's highest. Patrick worked as a laborer, mason and stonecutter. With one exception — a daughter, Julia, was born on a brief trip to Illinois in 1872 — the family remained in the "Dublin" neighborhood until the time of the Panic of 1873, a national economic depression that put several of the brickyard firms out of business. For the next twenty-five years the O'Neills bounced back and forth between the Dublin area and the streets of industrial East Cambridge, another Irish immigrant community. It was politics that ultimately brought them some stability. In the 1890s Patrick was employed by the municipal government as a city teamster and settled at 52 Montgomery Street, where the Dublin neighborhood had spread across Kidder's Lane (later to be named Rindge Avenue) onto the subdivided grounds of the old racetrack. Patrick's sons William and Thomas were involved as young men in Democratic politics, and may have helped provide their father with that city job — or perhaps it was the old man who enlisted in the local political machine and tugged his sons behind him. Patrick lived until 1903, when, just a few weeks short of his seventy-first birthday, his heart gave out. Julia passed away seven years later, at the age of seventy-two, from heart failure preceded by bronchitis and dysentery.[13]

Thomas P. O'Neill, the future Speaker's father, was born in the fall of 1874. He was Patrick's and Julia's youngest son. Thomas was an ambitious man who began in the brickyards as a laborer for the New England Brick Company and learned the mason's trade. He lived at home until his mother Julia's death to save money, started his own neighborhood contracting business and was active as a union organizer. Thomas also took an early interest in politics, and at the age of twenty-eight was elected by the voters of the eleventh ward to the Cambridge Common Council, the lower of two legislative bodies of the city government. He served for three years, with seats on the important finance and roads committees. He became a member of the Democratic Ward and City Committee and the Cambridge Elks lodge and a Grand Knight of the Knights of Columbus, whose balls, parades and minstrel shows were at the heart of Irish Catholic society.[14]

North Cambridge was undergoing further transformation. The horse-car line from Harvard Square and the railroad from Boston had lured housing developers and home buyers to the area, and the opening of an electric trolley along Massachusetts Avenue completed the neighborhood's conversion to streetcar suburb in 1890. French Canadian immigrants were replacing the Irish in the dying brickyard industry, and roomy new two-family homes on tree-lined side streets began to displace the workers' cottages that had sheltered an earlier generation — signs that the Irish Americans were climbing the economic ladder. Politically, the immigrants and their kin now outnumbered the Yankees in Cambridge, and in 1901 a silver-tongued Irishman named John H. H. McNamee defeated Yankee Mayor David T. Dickinson to become the city's first Irish American mayor.[15]

In 1904, Thomas O'Neill married Rose Tolan, a twenty-eight-year-old dressmaker from Woburn, a small town to the north of Cambridge. Her parents, James Tolan and Eunice Fullerton Tolan, had been born in different villages in County Donegal, emigrated around 1870, then met and wed in Massachusetts. Rose was one of twelve children who packed their warren of a house on Buckman Court in Woburn's South End. A sister, Anna, became a prominent member of the Maryknoll order of Roman Catholic nuns. A brother, Ed, took to wandering out West and died in Montana at an early age of complications brought on by diabetes, when an injured leg refused to heal. According to the family genealogists, the Fullertons were descended from a German ship captain whose vessel had been wrecked on Ireland's rocky northern coast, forcing him to settle there. Thomas and Rose O'Neill had four children: William, born in 1905; Mary Rose, born in 1906; Catherine, who died in infancy; and Thomas Philip O'Neill Jr. — who was born in Cambridge on December 9, 1912, in a rented third-floor apartment in a three-family home at 25 Locke Street. "Can't you change him for a girl?" his sister, Mary, asked the doctor.[16]

It was an eventful year for the O'Neills. Thomas Senior had finished atop the list in the Cambridge civil service exam and won appointment as superintendent of sewers to replace the late Theodore Pike. The job came with the grand salary of $2,000 per year, lists of jobs and contracts to let, and the responsibility of maintaining 150 miles of city sewer lines. The following year Thomas bought a house at 10 Fairfield Street, off Rindge Avenue, for $3,500. Through the hard work of three generations, the O'Neill family had claimed respectability. William would become the first in his family to go to college — to Holy Cross — and win a scholarship to Harvard Law School. Mary became a schoolteacher and then the first female principal in the Cambridge public school system. Young Thomas would attend Boston College, and follow his father into politics.[17]

Though he never rejected his Irish heritage, Thomas Senior was an assimilationist. He was tall and austere, disciplined and punctual, and nicknamed "Lord Fairfield" or "the Governor" by his neighbors. He never gave his children whippings — his imposing bearing, high standing in the community and the lash of his tongue were more than enough to keep them in line if the rattan switches of their teachers should fail. He shaved every night before dinner and sat in the same pew each Sunday. His brother John had succumbed to drink and vagrancy, so Thomas's mother made him swear off liquor. He eventually became the president of the St. John's Catholic Total Abstinence Society, where he was helped by the fact that from 1886 until 1936 bars and saloons were banned in Cambridge. He was stern, but not an unforgiving man, as he marked the curb outside his home with a white "X" in his brother's memory, to signal hoboes they could get a meal inside. "He really was a very strong man. And I never heard the man condemn anyone. There were always two sides to everybody, and while they may have their faults, and you may disagree, he could always see a reason for liking a person," his daughter-in-law Mildred O'Neill would remember. "He was a very fair man. Very fair."

Thomas had a passion for sports and helped organize a renowned semi-pro baseball team, sponsored by the local Knights of Columbus, or K of C, that lured thousands of fans to North Cambridge's Russell Field. From the time of his days on the Common Council, he worked to find jobs for his constituents with the city government or the local gaslight or telephone company, and in his years as sewer superintendent his neighbors and employees took to seeking his counsel and assistance when a husband drank too much or there was a bad boy in the family or financial calamity loomed. "Somehow they arrived at my house to talk to my dad," his son, the future Speaker, recalled. "He had the respect of everybody and for that reason they all seemed to migrate to our home for favors." Through his political and social contacts in the city, the Governor knew who needed a job, a Christmas dinner or a winter coat — and would find it for them. Unlike some other Irish American political leaders of his day, he didn't fan the resentments of his constituency. "My father used to say, 'There is nothing better than a good Yankee.' We weren't supposed to be prejudiced against the Yankees," his daughter, Mary, recalled. The virtues that Thomas tried to teach his children were loyalty to one's own, integrity and charity toward the unfortunate. "His word was absolute and complete law," his son Tip remembered. "We never questioned him."[18]

"He has a large man's slow motion, the careful tread of the sagacious elephant who, conscious of poundage, tests every plank of a bridge as he crosses," said a contemporaneous profile in a Cambridge newspaper. "He does not encourage what is termed chatter, the small talk that empty minds indulge in."

Yet "there is humor in this interesting Celtic countenance, as well as strength and sagacity. He knows his own limitations and is too self-examining to indulge in any pretense. If you seek the practical, the plan, the initial sense of any matter, he is just the man to know," the journalist concluded. "The elemental nature of his vocation has not sullied his native sweetness."[19]

The defining childhood moment for baby Tom arrived before he was old enough to grasp what happened. When he was but nine months old, his mother died of tuberculosis. Rose had contracted the disease several years earlier and was thought to be cured after spending time in the state sanatorium in Rutland, Massachusetts. To aid her recuperation, the family had lived briefly in the "hills of Arlington," the town to the northwest of Cambridge, where the air was considered cooler and cleaner, said Mary. Thomas told his daughter that Rose had contracted tuberculosis while caring for a relative who was stricken with the disease. It was prevalent enough at the time, especially in the immigrant communities of Boston, where the rate of infection was among the highest in the nation. It was one reason that Thomas gave up his contracting business: that work was seasonal, and he needed the city's steady paycheck to take care of his wife. When Rose fell ill again, the O'Neills rented a cottage in New Hampshire for the summer of 1913. Mary remembered playing in the barn with Bill while Rose sat on the porch cradling the infant Tom in her arms. The crisis came on September 10, and Rose succumbed eight days later at the age of thirty-eight. "We came home from New Hampshire right after Labor Day and she died," Mary recalled. A nun was called to look after the baby while the family attended the funeral.[20]

Before she died, Rose made her husband promise not to divide the children among relatives, but to keep them together as a family. Thomas complied, but he was then starting his new job, working six days a week for the city, and couldn't give his children the attention they required. A warm-hearted French Canadian housekeeper looked after them, and the Dominican nuns from the nearby St. John's convent did what they could to help. But Tom later recalled being "passed from aunt to aunt — it wasn't a happy time."[21] He found compensation by winning hearts on Fairfield Street. He was a slyly charming little boy, fawned over by the women on the block, as his father tried his best to be both mother and father. Amid the loneliness, there were times of happiness. "The Christmas I remember best was 1917, when I was five years old. I still remember the sled my father gave me," O'Neill said years later. "The night before, we had a snowstorm, and I remember the rollers came down the street to pack the snow so the sleds would be able to travel. There were very few automobiles at that time. Parker Cahill, the mailman, was pulling a sled. Mail was still delivered on Christmas Day.

"My mother had died some time before, and my aunt Suzie Kelly was living downstairs. The Kellys and the O'Neills would have an old-fashioned turkey dinner with cranberry sauce. I recall everybody on the street had a Christmas tree, but nobody had electric bulbs. Each tree had candles on it, and after dinner they would light the candles and watch them for five minutes and then blow them out for fear of a fire. Everyone would walk up and down the street looking in other people's houses to see their Christmas tree."[22]

In 1918, Thomas O'Neill faced another wrenching ordeal when his two sons were stricken by the Spanish influenza, a gruesome flu epidemic that killed 28,000 people in Massachusetts, half a million Americans and 20 million people worldwide. Many of the victims died within forty-eight hours, drowning as their lungs filled with fluid from the viral pneumonia. In Cambridge, whole families were wiped out, the fearful folk took to stringing bits of camphor to hang around their necks and the local gravediggers couldn't match the flu's deadly pace; bodies went uncollected, and coffins were piled in the cemeteries. Soldiers waiting to be shipped overseas to the battlefields of France were felled instead in their crowded barracks outside Boston and their corpses stacked like cordwood. "We were very lucky," Mary recalled. "My father and I did not get it, and we had a nurse living with us at the time. A lot of people didn't have nurses, didn't get proper care. My father, of course, was devastated with worry."[23]

Young Tom recovered, never to forget the morning of November 11, 1918, when news of the armistice ending World War I reached the United States. Factory whistles blew at the brickyards and at the nearby pottery. Church bells rang and the fire engines rolled from their stations to puff and clank around the neighborhood. "I was just about five years old and it sticks in my mind — the pottery whistle and the blares of the few horns from the automobiles there were, the steam fire engines with the beautiful white horses and Dalmatian dog parading through the street, and the happiness in the neighborhood," he remembered. "But more particularly, I remember the excitement because that was the first day I had seen an airplane."[24]

A year later, the course of Tom's childhood was altered again when his father married Mary Ellen Cain, the thirty-nine-year-old daughter of a middle-class Cambridge family who lived around the corner on Rindge Avenue. The boy was a few weeks shy of his seventh birthday at the time. The Cains were a prosperous family, and Mary Ellen looked down upon the Fairfield Street house, which she and her new husband sold in favor of a larger, two-family home surrounded by mansard-roofed and Colonial revival houses in a nicer neighborhood on the other side of Massachusetts Avenue. The O'Neills took the top two floors at 74 Orchard Street and rented out the bottom; the ownership of the house was in Mary Ellen Cain's name. The family was moving up in the world. Thomas introduced his wife and young son Tom to Governor Calvin Coolidge when they crossed his path at the Quincy House Restaurant. Thomas and Mary bought the new device that was all the rage: a radio. They took automobile trips to Niagara Falls and Montreal. But it was not a good marriage — "There was never much happiness in that home," O'Neill remembered. Nor did Bill, fourteen, and Mary, thirteen, get along with their new stepmother, or like the move to Orchard Street. "My father had disappointed me," his daughter recalled. "I told him, 'Everybody says you are going to marry that lady.' And he said, 'You're my girl.' So I took it for granted that I was his girl. I loved my father. He was a wonderful man. But he disappointed me."[25]

Young Tom's childhood home was plain but comfortable. The ground-floor apartment was rented out to a series of tenants, while the O'Neills lived on the two upper floors. A curving staircase led up from the downstairs vestibule to the main living area, which had a parlor with a fireplace, a dining room with a built-in hutch, a tiled kitchen with a cast-iron sink, the family's only bathroom and a room that the kids referred to as "the den," but their stepmother called "the library." The floors in the hallways and at the edges of each room were made of polished hardwood, but wider boards of cheap, rough pine made up the flooring in the middle of each room, where it would be hidden by rugs. There were three roomy bedrooms on the third floor for daughter Mary, her parents, and the two boys.

Thomas Senior added a large screened porch to the back of the house a few years later when Bill was stricken with a serious case of pneumonia and the doctors prescribed fresh air. The family moved to rural Wilmington that summer, when young Tom was still in elementary school, and stayed through Thanksgiving as Bill recuperated. They lived on Glen Road, near "Pop" Neilson's farm, and ten-year-old Sylvia Neilson delivered their milk in a pony cart. On Sundays they attended Mass in the dance hall at Thompson's Grove, then stopped at Pop's vegetable stand on their way home. Other summers found the family in Jaffrey, New Hampshire, where young Tom discovered deer and muskrats and blueberries.[26]

It was about that time — on July 1, 1920 — that Thomas took Tom on the trolley to his first Red Sox game, at Fenway Park, paying with a few quarters for two bleacher seats. The Washington Senators were in town, and pitcher Walter Johnson threw the only no-hitter of his Hall of Fame career. Young Tom became as big, if not bigger, a fan than his father. "I thought it was the most beautiful place I had ever seen," he recalled. Tom loved to keep the line score in his program, marking down the batter-by-batter progression of the game and computing batting averages. He and his father would take after-dinner walks up the avenue to John D. Lynch's drugstore, where the day's baseball results and box scores were hung in the window. When the World Series came around, another druggist, who owned a wireless set, would announce the game, pitch by pitch, through a megaphone to hundreds of people gathered around his store.

Sixty years later, O'Neill could still name many of the players from the North Cambridge baseball team, which played on Sundays before thousands of fans because the big leagues were, by law, forced to honor the Sabbath. There was Gaspipe Sullivan, Doc Gautreau, Sonny Foley, Tubber Cronin, Cheese McCrehan and Chippie Gaw. Since the K of C team couldn't lawfully sell tickets for Sunday baseball, the sponsors would charge admission for a pregame band concert or sell ice cream at inflated prices. As a boy Tom hawked popcorn in the Russell Field stands on weekends and weekday evenings, where he saw the Red Sox, Boston Braves and Negro League teams, with stars like Josh Gibson, play exhibition games.[27] The Roaring Twenties, the years of O'Neill's boyhood, were a golden age for American sports, the era of Babe Ruth, Bobby Jones, Bill Tilden, Knute Rockne, Jack Dempsey, Gene Tunney and Red Grange. The most memorable exhibition young Tom witnessed took place in 1927, at Glendale Park in Everett, as a benefit for the victims of a huge oil tank explosion. The Red Sox played a local team, the Roche Club, that had enhanced the gate by getting New York Yankee teammates Babe Ruth and Lou Gehrig to play on its side. Ruth popped up in his first time at bat, and the Red Sox manager told his pitcher to groove one down the middle so the fans could see "the Sultan" swat. "Ruth drove the ball over the fence, over the clubhouse, over some tennis courts and across the street onto the roof of some three-deckers. That ended the game — in pandemonium," O'Neill later recalled.[28]

It was baseball that gave young Tom the nickname he carried

through life. A player named Edward O'Neill had been a batting champion with the St. Louis Browns in the late 1880s — largely because he would foul off pitch after pitch until he got a walk, or the pitcher grew tired and threw a fat one. For his uncanny ability at tipping all those foul balls, he became known as "Tip" O'Neill, and O'Neills across the country were saddled with the nickname. Both Bill and Tom wore the name as kids — Bill being "Tip" and Tom being "Little Tip" — but it stuck only with Tom.[29]

Tip's boyhood was a genuinely urban, yet genteel, experience. With its wide central avenue, tree-lined streets and sampling of handsome architecture, North Cambridge had the air of a small, prosperous Midwestern city during the 1920s — not the desperate urgency of Al Smith's East Side in New York, or Jim Curley's South End neighborhood in Boston. There was work in that decade of Coolidge prosperity, and the economic and international crises that followed were yet beyond the horizon. The horse-drawn wagon, with its rumbling iron wheels, had not given way to the car, a novel contraption which still had to be started with spark, crank and throttle. There were open fields and picket fences, and a Poor Farm by the Arlington town line. In the summer there was swimming in the ocean at Revere Beach or in the Charles River or at Jerry's Pit, an abandoned claypit near the brickyards. In the winter, when the flooded pits froze over, they served as splendid skating rinks — though dangerous, as an ill-fated childhood pal named "Salty" Reagan discovered when he fell through the ice and drowned.

Horse-drawn wagons delivered ice, bread and milk. The milk was in glass bottles, with inches of cream at the top. Doors were not locked; the ice man chipped off blocks with an ice pick, shouldered them with tongs and carried them directly to the icebox, whether anyone was home or not.[30] Tip was taught by the good sisters at St. John's grade school on Rindge Avenue, a tall, bell-towered building built in 1891 that doubled as church and school for the Catholic community; it had a hall for worship on the ground floor and classrooms upstairs on the second and third until a proper church, St. John the Evangelist, was built on nearby Massachusetts Avenue in 1904. The nerviest boys in the neighborhood would peer through the latticework that shielded the convent yard from the world and try to discover what the nuns wore under their habits. "There were 16 classrooms and two bathrooms," Francis Ready, a schoolmate, recalled. "Those nuns took care of 45 to 50 in the classroom, and none of us had a thirst for learning."[31]

The nuns formed a procession each morning, the youngest sisters in front, and marched two-by-two from the convent to St. John's for 6:30 A.M. Mass. The pastor distributed report cards to the children, shaming the poorer students by reminding them of the sacrifices their parents had made to send them to parochial school. In addition to the academic grades, the report cards tracked attendance at Confession and Sunday Mass and Communion. If a boy got out of line, Father John Keohane, a former boxer and football player, would belt him a good one. When the church needed a new monstrance (a golden stand to hold the communion wafer during holiday rituals), the parishioners donated their jewelry and gold watches to be melted down. The monstrance was three feet tall, and so heavy that one person lifted it with difficulty.[32]

The milestones of Catholic boyhood passed: First Communion, Confirmation, graduation to St. John's High School. Tip had a paper route and joined the Boy Scouts; decades later he found he still could tie the knots. He learned the Catholic catechism — *Who is God? God is the Supreme Being who made all things.* He consumed the library's Tom Swift and Horatio Alger books. "Do or die, sink or swim, now or never," O'Neill recalled. "I read them all." Tip hung around with Francis "Red" Fitzgerald, who lived around the corner and whose house was like a second home. When the local police caught them skinny-dipping at Jerry's Pit during school hours, the paddy wagon would take them away — but only as far as their own neighborhood, where the cop would say, "All out, boys." Tom and his buddies could walk or catch a ride to Central Square, then hike across a Charles River bridge and join the "Knot Hole Gang" — kids who got in to watch baseball for a nickel — at Braves Field. It was, Fitzgerald said, a "Huckleberry Finn" boyhood.[33]

Tip's teenage years revolved around a place called Barry's Corner and the group of young men who frequented it, calling themselves the Barry's Corner gang. They were his lifelong friends, and midwives to the birth of his political career. The corner's formal name is Sheridan Square, a baffling intersection where three streets — Rice, Cedar and Middlesex — converge on Rindge Avenue. As a hub of the Dublin and Race Course neighborhoods, the square had been a fixture among the Irish and the French Canadians for forty years. Here was St. John's convent, the French Canadian community's Notre Dame de Pitié Catholic church, a drugstore, a market and a candy shop. "My grandmother met *her* husband on Barry's Corner," Red Fitzgerald said. "He must have whistled at her."

The Barry house was a two-story yellow affair, with commercial space on the ground floor that hosted the odd barber shop or grocery or pool hall over the years but, in O'Neill's time, was used as a clubhouse by the gang. The front room had the barber chair and pool table, where sometimes a barber cut hair and sometimes Frank O'Connell, the gang's aspiring entrepreneur, best known as "Red" and "Moose" for his unforgettable hair and build, charged a few cents a rack to those who shot pool. The back room was the clubhouse, which the boys passed the hat to rent, with a wood stove and a table. Upstairs lived the Barry family, who were there for three generations before the place was torn down in 1937. The building's main amenities were its location, next to Nelligan's Market at the corner of Rice and Rindge, and its big, wide set of porch steps, which served as the gang's grandstand as the world walked by. The seating was limited, and allotted by the strictest rules of seniority. There was a boulder and a chestnut tree for the younger boys to lean against while they looked on enviously, and a barn out back of Nelligan's that was sometimes used by dice players, or as a place to bed down by "Barber" Burke, the local drunk.

Across the street lived Cheese McCrehan, the star pitcher of the K of C team, who had led Boston College to a 30 to 3 record in 1923. When Cheese came out of the house, the gang would stand and cheer, and he — following a time-honored ritual — would doff his cap. They would then switch to boos and raspberries, and he would throw his hat to the ground in mock anger and disgust. Diagonally across the square was the Notre Dame church, and though the Barry gang was multiethnic, with its Labos and Broussards, it was not unusual for the French to sing out, on a summer night, "Corned beef and cabbage makes Irishmen savage!" and the Irish to respond, "Poor man's johnnycake — a Frenchman's bellyache!" The neighborhood girls, who avoided the corner like the plague, had their own song: "Cambridge girls are pretty. Somerville girls are tough. Arlington girls with all their curls think they're just as rough."

The gang had up to sixty members, including Henry Owens, an African American, and Lenny Lamkin, a Jew. Bob Cain sometimes brought his ukelele, but mostly there was a lot of talk, usually about sports but often about girls, and from time to time there were rumors of impending street warfare between the Irish and the French. "Everybody would be making mallets and clubs, but nothing ever came of it," Fitzgerald recalled. "Gang" was a misnomer. The boys would often show up at the clubhouse in coats and ties, and their potential for rowdiness was limited by the tight-knit nature of their community, where any mother or father could lay down the law or report a young man to his parents. "Even if you were inclined to be a little bit of a fresh kid, everybody knew it and they'd call up and tell your mother," Fitzgerald said, "and then — what was the use? — you'd get a shellacking." The police were Hollywood archetypes: brawny beat-walking lads from the neighborhood named Leandro and Sheehan, gruff and firm, adept with a billy club, but fair. Father James P. Kelly would drop by Barry's Corner with a bat and a ball and his dog, Pal, get a game going to keep the gang occupied and return to the rectory. The St. John's convent was uncomfortably close, and if the boys chose Rindge Avenue for their route home at night, the watchful nuns would know why their homework looked hurried the next day. If all else failed, at semi-regular intervals, Old Man Barry would douse them with a tub of water from an upstairs window, no matter that Timothy Ready might be wearing his best Easter suit. "You had to be alert and quick of foot to escape," O'Neill recalled.

"There was a back room there with an old stove," remembered William McCaffrey. "And all we had to burn was tar blocks. They were tearing up the streets here, laying down macadam roads, and ripping them up: beautiful fuel, tarred wood. The whole stove would glow bright red and Old Man Barry would come down saying, 'You can't use that stuff. You'll burn the house down. Get the hell out,' and push us out. But he always relented and let us back in." When the boys needed money they would caddy at the Arlmont Country Club for seventy-five cents a round, or deliver phone books from a horse-drawn wagon. Or they'd steal apples from a fruit stand, or sweets from the little candy store. Golf brought out the best of Tip's budding talent as a raconteur. He claimed to have caddied, at the age of fourteen, for U.S. Open champion Willie MacFarlane, who allegedly eagled the fifth hole at Arlmont, though stymied by a tree, by intentionally bouncing his ball off a fence and into the hole. O'Neill also insisted that he lost a member's bag while caddying when he forgot that he had hung it from a nearby tree while looking for an errant ball. The bag, he claimed, was not discovered until the foliage fell in the fall.[34]

There were three Barry boys, Jed, Dave and Jack — who was the unofficial leader of the gang by virtue of his prestigious job as a sportswriter for the *Boston Globe.* One of his responsibilities was to take the results of the day's baseball games and compute each player's batting average for the newspaper. It was a task that appealed to O'Neill, who had quite a facility for numbers, angles and odds, and was now exclusively referred to as Tip, given the boys' penchant for nicknames. There was "Potatoes" Labo, and "Jap" and "Frogsy" Broussard, and "Skippy" McCaffrey and "Pinky" Sullivan and "Touch" Goodwin and "Blubber" Sheehan and "Red" or "Redfish" Fitzgerald and "Moose" O'Connell and "Wee Wee" Burns and "Fat" McDonald and "Hambone" Sullivan, who always hated the name, which could be traced to a "hambone" error he had made playing baseball. "You know how I got my nickname?" said Pinky Sullivan. "We were sitting on the steps in front of Barry's Corner one day. Two girls went by and said, 'Hi, Jimmy.' Tip, he turned to me and said, 'You're pink!' "[35]

The boys loved baseball, and Jack Barry got them interested in a relatively new sport: basketball. Tip was tall for his age, and exuberant, so it was natural that he and some others tried the game: on summer hard courts at Rindge Park and for St. John's High School, on whose team he was the senior captain in 1931. The team was not a great success; nor was O'Neill. His great virtue, on both offense and defense, said his pal Tom Mullen, was his immobility: "He was very, very tough to get around." Said Pinky Sullivan: "When he pivoted, the whole building shook." But strength and endurance were more highly valued than speed or coordination. It was a rough, physical game in its infancy — one contest ended in an 8 to 8 tie after several overtimes — and the team photograph shows most of the players wearing knee pads. In an entire season, O'Neill scored 17 points.

His lumbering strength was better suited to football, where the players were on the field for both offense and defense, and he was a guard and captain of the Barry's Corner sandlot team. The gang hatched a plan to form their own semi-pro team — the North Cambridge Catholic Club — challenge teams from other neighborhoods and charge admission. They raffled off five pounds of sugar to get money to buy helmets, pads and uniforms, then built a schedule by guaranteeing their opponents $25 a game. They hoped to gross $100, but rarely did better than $35, and then had to cover their medical bills.

"Lenny Lamkin was the manager of our team," Fitzgerald remembered, "and he got us a game with the Wellesley town team. They had thirty-three men, and we'd go and play them with fifteen. Well, that was the day we left Tip, Lenny Kelly and Mickey O'Neill in the Wellesley hospital — all injured in the game. We had to call the game off in the third period: we didn't have eleven men who could still play. One guy on the Wellesley team had had his arm cut off, halfway to his elbow. Tom Sheehan came up to me and said, 'This guy is sticking the stump in my eye all the time.'"

"There wasn't a blade of grass on those fields," O'Neill's pal Leo Diehl recalled. "More tar and stones than anything else."[36]

O'Neill liked to bet, and he didn't like to lose. Henry Owens was a burly guy, and the Barry's Corner gang decided that they could make some money by entering him in a prizefight. They traveled to Lowell for the big match, only to see their hero get beaten around the ring. Every time Owens hit the canvas, the lights in the place would go out and interrupt the referee's count, affording the fighter a few needed minutes to recuperate. Owens ultimately lost the match, but for years his buddies were convinced that O'Neill was the culprit who manipulated the lights to give Henry a chance for victory. John Tatton, a fireman who was one of Cambridge's top young tennis players, remembered how O'Neill promoted a money match pitting him against an East Cambridge ace. Tatton lost by default when the alarm sounded; the fire trucks rushed by and he had to run from the court to catch them. He could hear O'Neill calling, "Come back!"[37]

O'Neill wasn't much of a student, but he led the debating team with his facility to "talk you deaf, dumb and blind," recalled Sister Clarita, one of the nuns at St. John's. He was a likable guy who liked to play hooky. A yearbook ditty about him read, "Never worried, never vexed, in one day and out the next."[38]

THE IDYLLIC TONE of O'Neill's boyhood was real enough. The Barry's Corner boys formed lifelong bonds and remained close friends; working in political campaigns, spending the summers of their college years in a rented cottage on Nantasket Beach, learning together about liquor and sex and gathering for reunions well into the 1980s. North Cambridge would always be an anchor for Tip, not a stale, claustrophobic environment from which to flee. He sank roots in the neighborhood — buying a house around the corner from his childhood home — and lived there throughout his life. But the halcyon days of youth did not last forever. They were shattered in October 1929, midway through his junior year at St. John's High School, by the great stock market crash. There were not a lot of Wall Street speculators, caught up by margin calls, plummeting to earth from skyscrapers in North Cambridge. But the Depression that followed, and their need to make their way in a suddenly uncertain and dangerous world, put an end to those Booth Tarkington boyhoods and left a searing impression on O'Neill and his friends. The intensity of the experience, coming as it did just as the boys became men, worked like a bellows on their fears and insecurities, and tested their character. It was during this time of disorienting political and economic change — during the days of demagogues and the dust bowl and soup lines and Red scares in America; the rise of Hitler and Mussolini and war abroad; the crisis of the old order and the coming of a New Deal — that Tip O'Neill chose his lifelong vocation.[39]

CHAPTER 2

People Like to Be Asked

POLITICS. Given his pedigree, it was probably inevitable that Tip O'Neill would end up in politics. The tradition was strong in his family, and the three people closest to him — his father, the superintendent of sewers, brother Bill, who became an assistant attorney general and judge, and sister Mary, a teacher and principal — all went to work "on the city" or state. Since the Yankees had locked them out of the bank and corporate boardrooms, politics was one of the few avenues open to the Irish, and successful politicians were men of substance in the community. After Mayor John McNamee wrested control of city hall from the Cambridge Brahmins, the next Irish champion, and the closest thing the city ever had to a Democratic boss, was Mayor Edward Quinn, who was elected for six terms between 1917 and 1929. He was a prominent figure in state politics and a familiar visitor to the O'Neill home. "My father was a leader in the area; his support meant something and the mayor of the city of Cambridge — Edward Quinn, respected, affable, a fine orator — was often in our house," O'Neill recalled. "The people in the Irish neighborhoods, they looked at him with awe." Tip was as dazzled as the rest, and decided there could be no finer achievement than to someday serve as mayor. He was enrolled in the family business early, passing out leaflets for Charlie Cavanaugh, the local state representative, in the 1927 election.[1]

But while inheritance played an irrefutable role in determining O'Neill's vocation, there were other, as significant, forces tugging Tip toward public life. Throughout his childhood, for all its carefree joys, he was keenly aware of a void left by his mother's death. Privately, somehow, he came to feel that his birth had contributed to the tragedy — that the stress of a pregnancy, late in life, and the strain of childbirth had been too much for this sick and fragile woman. He carried that unreasonable shame with him throughout his life, and sought affirmation and redemption in politics.[2] If he could not find emotional nourishment at home, he would seek it in the world. Brother Bill was studious and withdrawn, and Mary threw herself into the teaching profession by the age of seventeen. But Tip worked the sympathetic mothers of his neighborhood and the nuns at St. John's like he'd later work a precinct.[3]

In the course of a lifetime in politics, O'Neill obliquely referred to the loss of his mother just one or two times. Many of his friends never knew about the circumstances of her death. But once, as Speaker, he was called upon to mediate differences between liberal and conservative Democrats over a series of proposed federal budget cuts. He met in private with members of the Black Caucus, asking them to abandon, for the greater good, some of their demands for social spending. He was challenged from their ranks: what did he know, they asked, of the pain of children in inner-city housing projects, or the scars left upon a man by prejudice and bigotry?

With considerable emotion, he spoke about his mother. Suffering came in many forms, he said, and he had known loneliness and want. It was the pain of his childhood, he told them, that gave him his lifelong cause. "I can suffer with you for what you are suffering for," he said. "My mother died when I was nine months old. I was bounced from aunt to aunt until my father remarried. Don't tell me about a hard life when a guy is a kid. I've been through this."[4]

From their years as subjects of a cruel empire, the Irish were great ones for an underdog. And despite its many rules and dictums, demands for obedience and relentless categorizations of sin, the Catholic religion was at its core a creed based on grace, forgiveness and mercy. In church and at school, six days a week, Tip learned that blessed were the poor, the meek, the peacemakers and those who thirsted for justice. Other boys heard the sermons as well, but O'Neill's intimate sense of loss made him an insistent, and powerful, tower of strength for the needy. Humanity was, would always be, his business; his childhood had cast his great empathy as well. "I think losing something caused him to not want to lose anything, or have anybody else lose a strong presence in their lives," said his son Christopher.[5] Politics would give him the power to prevent among others what he had been powerless to control as a child. Because love and connection come to mean so much to the lonely, he developed a drive to excel — to command the world's company and attention via his talents and triumphs.

O'Neill hated, absolutely dreaded, being alone. He fed off the action of politics, sports and gambling and — his personality in this regard reinforced by the Irish Catholic ethos — shunned personal introspection and intimacy. O'Neill submerged himself in good times, good causes and daunting challenges. There would always be a lot of surface to Tip O'Neill; a warm surface, but surface nonetheless. There were places inside where he wouldn't go, much less allow others. "Tip was not a reflective guy," said his friend and counsel, Kirk O'Donnell, years later. "He was very Irish Catholic. You went to confession, confessed your sins and moved on."[6]

"He didn't know how to get warm with you," his aide Chris Matthews recalled years later. "My father was the kind of guy who would say he loved you publicly, but not privately," said O'Neill's son Tommy. "Huge portions of his life he would never divulge," said his daughter Rosemary.[7]

Nor was it an accident that his most sacred political virtue was loyalty. For O'Neill it was inescapable: his mother had left him. The Irish, meanwhile, after centuries of seeing their struggle for independence betrayed by informers and turncoats, allotted a special place in hell for traitors. Throughout his life, his greatest love would be offered to those who were loyal; his great terror was of abandonment, and his special fury was reserved for those he believed had been disloyal. There was a dark, sullen side to the Irish American experience, to which O'Neill was not immune, and to which the experience of his mother's death no doubt contributed. His genial disposition was by far the defining characteristic of his personality, but no man is just one thing. "No one can really tell what is in a man's heart," Tip once told an aide, paraphrasing Saint Augustine. And O'Neill's mighty heart harbored a streak of malice, fostered by his private guilt and insecurity, useful in his competitive trade, and reinforced by a culture of mistrust in Boston's Irish American community. The prosperity of the Roaring Twenties had eased the ethnic tensions, in Cambridge and across America; the Irish were assimilating, singing patriotic jingles by George M. Cohan. Then the presidential campaign of 1928, the stock market crash and the economic dislocation of Depression revived ancient grievances.[8]

In the fall of 1928, Tip and his pal Red Fitzgerald organized a precinct for the Democratic presidential candidacy of New York governor Alfred E. Smith, the first Roman Catholic to run for President on a major party ticket. It was grunt work: knocking on doors on Orchard Street to announce to the housewives, "In ten minutes the automobile will be here to bring you to the polls." The boys' hearts were in it because Al Smith was a "catalyst," Fitzgerald remembered. "He was running and of course the Catholics were getting beat over the head with, 'Why do we need a Catholic President?' And . . . that got everyone interested a little bit more."[9]

Smith was a candidate for the immigrants, especially for Irish immigrants — and most especially for Massachusetts Irish immigrants. In 1914, when David I. Walsh became governor, they had elected the first Irish Catholic to statewide office, and in 1918, Walsh became the state's first Democratic U.S. senator since the Civil War. But a Catholic for President was something on a scale unimagined. As the first of their kind to mount a serious challenge for the White House, Smith was a hero: so popular with the rank and file that the warring factions of the Democratic Party were forced to put aside their personal rivalries and ethnic differences and unite behind his campaign, lest an outraged electorate punish them. A self-made man, a four-term governor, a memorable campaigner with his derby and cigar, Smith opposed Prohibition, defied the Ku Klux Klan and spoke for social justice. When Smith arrived in Massachusetts for a two-day swing in late October, O'Neill was one of the cheering tens of thousands who jammed the sidewalks of Boston to see him tour the city in an open car and speak to an adoring crowd on the Common. O'Neill and his pal Red had little trouble getting the voters in their precinct to the polls: turnout on Election Day was 93 percent. In some Catholic wards Smith captured 90 percent of the vote. Though running in the midst of Republican prosperity, Smith transformed Massachusetts politics by forging a coalition of Irish Americans; Italians, Jews and other newer immigrants; Harvard professors, liberal-leaning professionals and leaders of organized labor. Smith beat the GOP's Herbert Hoover by 17,000 votes to carry the state.

The day O'Neill rang the doorbells of Orchard Street was a turning point in American history: Franklin Roosevelt would build upon Smith's confederation, and the resultant "New Deal coalition" would go on to dominate Massachusetts politics and American government for half a century. Yet O'Neill and the other Bay State Democrats couldn't know that then. And the national results were quite different from those of Massachusetts. Aside from Rhode Island and six states in the Democratic "Solid South," the Roman Catholic candidate was beaten soundly everywhere else. Hoover won in a landslide. The Irish felt Smith's defeat as a crushing psychological blow, a rebuff to America's Catholics. His campaign had been viewed through their inflated expectations as "an acid test of our right to the title of American citizen," as James Michael Curley put it. "The belief that Smith had been rejected principally because he was a Catholic drove great masses of voters, identified with Mr. Smith by racial or religious affiliations, straight into the arms of the Democratic Party," the analysts at the national party headquarters concluded. Al Smith's candidacy and defeat were a bitter reminder of how far the Irish had come and how far they had yet to go. The grim days of the Depression, arriving a year later, added to their state of siege.[10]

It is impossible to overstate the ethnic character of the Massachusetts political world that Tip O'Neill sought to enter in the early 1930s. When the Irish immigrants arrived in the nineteenth century, the Brahmin gentry were horrified at the gaunt, ignorant newcomers with their peasant ways and Papist rites. In newspapers and popular journals of the day, the Irish were portrayed with sloping shoulders and simian features. "Poor Boston has run up against it in the form of its particular Irish maggot — rather lower than the Jew, but with more or less the same appetite for cheese," wrote Harvard's Henry Adams, a descendant of Presidents.[11]

"If there . . . [was] one city in the entire world where an Irish Catholic, under any circumstance, should never, *ever,* set foot, that city was Boston, Massachusetts," historian Thomas O'Connor concluded. "It was an American city with an intensely homogeneous Anglo-Saxon character, an inbred hostility toward people who were Irish, a fierce and violent revulsion against all things Roman Catholic, and an economic system that precluded most forms of unskilled labor."

The Irish and the Yankees were not merely rivals. They were blood enemies, as their ancestors had been for centuries, and each represented everything the other despised. Anti-Catholicism was the motivation for the Puritan settlement at Plymouth and the formation of the Massachusetts Bay Colony: the Pilgrims believed that the Church of England, with its bishops and vestments and pageantry, was too like Catholic popery and needed purification. The Leveretts and Saltonstalls and Winthrops who ruled Boston's political and economic world in the nineteenth and early twentieth centuries could trace their roots to these Puritan forerunners. The Irish immigrants, meanwhile, viewed Protestantism as apostasy, and reserved a special enmity for the Puritans, whose champion Oliver Cromwell had brought Ireland to heel in a bloody campaign in the seventeenth century.

The Yankees of Cambridge and Boston were proud of their British heritage, and aped English culture and refinement. The Irish saw the British as conquerors and hypocrites who spoke vacuously about the rights of man while exploiting the peoples of an empire. Economically secure, the Brahmins could engage in abstract causes like abolitionism and political reform; theirs was a high-minded democracy of town meetings and Congregationalist churches. The Irish viewed man as flawed, not perfectible; they respected religious hierarchies but bridled (especially after seeing the English use the law as an instrument of oppression) at legal and political absolutes. They viewed African Americans as economic rivals, opposed the abolitionists and rioted in protest of the military draft during the Civil War.

In the 1850s, a number of Protestant secret societies came together to form the nativist Know-Nothing Party, which enjoyed its greatest success in Massachusetts, where it captured the governor's office, every congressional seat and both houses of the legislature. The Know-Nothings passed laws that required the reading of the Protestant Bible in public schools, forced the Irish from state payrolls, prohibited Catholics from holding public office and funded a series of police raids on Catholic convents and boarding schools in search of sexual depravity. Replying in kind, the Irish revived a dormant Democratic Party, built a mighty church and seized control of the city of Boston. Politics was the instrument of their success.[12]

The political assets that the Irish had brought to America were intangible, but determinative. They spoke the language, for one thing — an inestimable advantage for strangers in a new land — and came from a rural culture that prized community and cooperation. As a conquered people, they understood the value of loyalty, solidarity and patience. They prized strength, but also wit and eloquence. And they had spent the first half of the nineteenth century putting their political skills to practice in Ireland, fighting with some success for Catholic emancipation and agrarian reform. They came from a representative democracy not unlike their new country, understood the concept of political power and knew how to marshall votes and win elections.[13]

The Irish arrived in a time when Massachusetts politics was a mass participation sport — with gaudy torchlight parades that lasted hours as the workingmen's clubs, fraternal organizations, brass bands, militia companies and ceremonial cavalry tramped their serpentine way from East Cambridge through Central and Harvard Square and out Massachusetts Avenue and back. By the late nineteenth and early twentieth centuries the Irish were thoroughly organized. Four out of five people voted on Election Day. In return for organizing and delivering a ward, an alderman or common councilor would get jobs and contracts to distribute, access to government regulators and prized business opportunities. He and his lieutenants would seal their bond with the voters by handing out food baskets or Christmas toys; sponsoring huge picnics with games, dancing, free ham and ice cream; fixing an immigration case or helping out a widow or a man down on his luck. The ward heelers showed up at wakes, fires and other catastrophes — and at the doors of each newly wedded couple — to see what was needed. Atop the Irish American pyramid in Boston were sly bosses like Martin "the Mahatma" Lomasney, in the West End; John F. "Honey Fitz" Fitzgerald, in the North End; Patrick "P.J." Kennedy, in East Boston; and Roxbury's Jim Curley. A second great wave of immigration stormed Boston at the turn of the century, adding Italians, Poles and Jewish immigrants to the party's ranks, until the Brahmins were outnumbered nearly 10 to 1 by what Curley called "the newer races."

The Yankees, in return, clung to power by corraling wealth via their control of the banks, courts, trusts and corporate boards; by discriminating against Catholic applicants to such gateway institutions as Harvard Law School; and by endlessly exposing, through such organizations as the Boston Finance Commission or the Good Government Association (the despised Goo-Goos), the Democratic political deals and petty graft.[14] O'Neill was steeped in this ethnic warfare. As a boy, he heard Gaelic words and phrases around his home and neighborhood, attended Irish language school on weekends with his brother and sister and saw men walk the streets soliciting money in return for window stickers that said, "I gave to the IRA." He recalled how the Gaelic classes were canceled one day in the fall of 1920 when Terence MacSwiney, the Irish Republican Army leader and lord mayor of Cork, died at the awful climax of a seventy-four-day hunger strike in a British prison after vowing, "It is not those who can inflict the most, but those that can suffer the most, who will conquer." MacSwiney had family on nearby Yorktown Street, and his sister-in-law had taught the O'Neill children their Gaelic. Neighbors talked of how the Protestant mobs had surrounded and burned an Ursuline convent in neighboring Charlestown as if it were a recent event. When O'Neill came upon the incident in a history book years later, he was shocked to discover that the fire occurred in 1834.

Anything British was in great disfavor. Tip and his friends played "patriots and redcoats" on the very ground where Cambridge Minutemen had skirmished with the British army as it retreated from the battles of Lexington and Concord on the evening of April 19, 1775. In later years he could recount, with specificity, how a small group of Minutemen, hiding in ambush behind a pile of casks at what is now the intersection of Massachusetts and Rindge Avenues, had been surprised by British troops and bayoneted, and how the rebels were avenged a few blocks away when several redcoats were killed at the corner of Beech and Elm Streets. A marker was there for the Barry's Corner boys to see. Each April 19 the boys would join the parade to Lexington, then double back to see the finish of the Boston Marathon.[15]

At the age of fourteen, Tip had ventured into a fortress of Brahmin privilege, when he was hired to cut the lawns at Harvard. He never forgot the reprimand he received for clipping the grass around the trees from a seated position, instead of from his knees. He seethed with outrage at the Harvard boys in their white linen suits, drinking champagne in the midst of Prohibition, heedless of, and immune from, the local police. And his father told him of how, when he was a Catholic boy amid the Yankees in a Cambridge public school, the teachers had blamed him for the transgressions of Protestant classmates.

As a young man, O'Neill saw the No Irish Need Apply signs posted on State Street in downtown Boston, and walked out of a Beacon Hill reception when the Yankee hosts asked him, in a manner he thought patronizing, to sing them an Irish ditty. His sister, Mary, attended Cambridge Latin, the public school for the brightest students in the city, but was snubbed by the Brahmin girls. "You didn't belong. There was a barrier. I got it right away. I knew when I was put in my place," she recalled.

Jeremiah Sullivan, a neighborhood pal who entered politics with Tip, won a scholarship to Harvard Law School and, upon graduating, set out to distribute his résumé to the big downtown law firms.

"What are you here for?" a receptionist asked him.

"A job," he answered.

"What's your name?"

"Jeremiah Sullivan."

"Don't waste your time," she said.[16]

The spectacular career of James Michael Curley was the most notorious political response to the Yankee-Irish strife during O'Neill's formative years. "In few places at few times in America had a white minority been subject to such official maltreatment, and the scars went deep," wrote Curley's biographer, Jack Beatty. "The bitterness would be preserved in the political unconsciousness of the Boston Irish. It would be what lent them the sullen psychology of an aggrieved minority long after they had become a majority . . . [and] James Michael Curley would see to that." In the scrubwoman's son the Irish found a corrupt but brilliant demagogue who challenged Brahmin repression and so was viewed by many immigrants, including the O'Neill family, as a hero. "My father thought Curley was a great orator and whatever he did was wrong for the right reasons, you know, and excused," Mary recalled. Curley's power flowed more from a cult of personality than from a neighborhood political machine. He took on the Brahmins — and won — and his victories came to represent the triumph of a people. With the kickbacks and bribes he collected, Curley built a mansion with shamrocks etched upon its shutters out by Jamaica Pond, in the Jamaica Plain section of Boston. His Irish American constituents would drive by with pride, "and if you were visiting from out of town, someone always took you over to see Jim Curley's place," O'Neill remembered.[17]

Curley's touch was everywhere. When Red Fitzgerald's father died in 1931, leaving his mother, Mary, with the burden of eight children, a neighbor, Mrs. Margaret Kelley, told her, "Come on, Mary. We're going to see James Michael."

The two women arrived at Curley's door.

"Mayor Curley, this woman is a widow. Her husband died and left her with a big house and eight children. What is she going to do?" asked Mrs. Kelley.

"Do you think you could afford to pay your taxes?" Curley asked Mary Fitzgerald.

"I guess I would be able to," she answered. One of her sons had found work with the post office.

"Okay, consider the mortgage paid," Curley told her. "From now on, you'll just get your tax bill." A few years later, Governor Curley put Red to work on a road project for $20 a week, fine pay in the midst of the Depression. "I was in heaven," Fitzgerald recalled. "Curley gave the job to so many guys that we only went to work every other week."[18]

Curley "was a sight to behold, standing over six feet tall, with long gray hair and the ruddy good looks of a matinee idol," O'Neill remembered. "He was always handsomely dressed and well groomed, and he was quick to pass out whatever he had in his pocket to the poor as he walked along. He was the greatest orator I've ever heard, a man who could quote Scripture and Shakespeare with ease, although he claimed he never made it past the third grade.

"There is no question that Curley looted the city, and that he was a latter-day Robin Hood who took from the rich and gave to the poor. Nor is there any doubt that he was corrupt — even by the ethics of his day, which were fairly loose," O'Neill said. "He liked to brag that he had never accepted a donation from a person who couldn't afford it, but that still leaves a lot to the imagination.

"It was said that nobody ever bribed him hand-to-hand, but the door was open, as the phrase went. He'd stand in his office and look in a mirror while you'd come in and open the drawer of his desk and drop in an envelope full of money. I never witnessed this myself, but that's what people said and I don't doubt it's true."[19]

Indeed, all the Democratic machines were oiled by bribes and cash donations — kickbacks — from those who won the jobs and contracts or were tipped off to the route of a new road or trolley line and got there in time to buy the land. Sometimes the money was furtively exchanged, in clandestine deliveries of fat white envelopes. But the laws were full of loopholes. At regular intervals the local lawyers and lobbyists and businessmen could simply hire a banquet room, throw a "time" for a politician, and in full public view award him a hefty "purse" of thousands of dollars. Cash paid for the costs of campaigns, the restaurant meals and beer for the troops and the turkeys and winter coats for the poor. The boss or precinct captain was understood to keep a cut. He had a family to support, and his time was valuable. "The art of employing a bagman to obtain funds from architects and contractors was so general that it almost had the cloak of legality," the *Boston Post* reported. "The politicians have long called this type of procedure 'legitimate graft.'"

Because the municipal jobs and contracts were financed, to a large extent, by the property taxes of Yankee homeowners, the Irish Americans viewed all but the sorriest cases of graft or malfeasance as a blow against the oppressor. The Irish, after their long experience under unjust English laws, had greater respect for personal or group loyalties than for abstract legal codes. As long as a bridge did not collapse in midstream, who cared if a contractor had cost overruns or a padded payroll? The drawbacks of the system were mostly psychic: the security of going "on the city" or "on the gas company" led to insularity and complacency, and slowed the creation of Irish business, academic or artistic classes.[20]

A proliferation of ambitious young bosslets was the major difference between the Democratic Party organization in Massachusetts and its counterparts in places like New York, where Tammany Hall was run by a single leader. "We never had organizational politics in my time, like they had the Daley organization in Chicago, or Green in Philadelphia or Tammany Hall in New York," O'Neill recalled. "It was always the Curley machine versus the regulars. When Curley was out of office he was always more powerful and stronger than when he was in office. When he was in, the outs would always knock him out.

"I never was on the same side with Curley, for the most part, because I was an organizational Democrat," O'Neill said. "He had his own individual group." As in other cities, the Democratic Party machines of Massachusetts ran on patronage jobs, food baskets, the camaraderie of the clubhouse and the entertaining spectacle of torchlit parades and street-corner oratory. But in Boston no one boss emerged. The jealous aspirants scrapped among themselves, and the feudal coalitions shifted from year to year. Betrayal was an art form. Revenge a way of life.[21]

So IT WAS in Cambridge. The arrival of the various immigrant groups to the city can be traced by the construction of their churches. St. Peter's (1848) and St. John's (1892) for the Irish, the Church of Notre Dame de Pitié (1892) for the French Canadians, St. Hedwig's for the Poles (1907), St. Anthony's for the Portuguese (1907), Immaculate Conception for the Lithuanians (1910) and St. Francis of Assisi for the Italians (1917). Many became good Democrats, and the wars waged among them, and by them against the Yankees, were as fierce in Cambridge as they were in Boston.

In a fine example of the fratricide that characterized politics in the era when O'Neill cut his political teeth, Mayor Quinn was dethroned by another Democrat — Mayor Richard Russell — in the election of 1929. The Quinn city council was tinged by scandal, with three of its members under indictment and local restaurants seeking payment in court for thousands of dollars' worth of candy, ice cream, fancy nuts and cigars the councilmen ordered at their meetings for themselves and assorted relatives in the audience. At one point, responding to public outrage, the council members voted to subpoena each other's bank records; that particular meeting was interrupted when somebody stole the chairman's gavel. Russell went on to serve a term in Congress in 1934, opening the way for the next great feud in local politics: the six-year war between John D. Lynch and John W. Lyons.[22]

Lyons was a lawyer from East Cambridge who had served in the Quinn administration and represented the old, opportunistic Democratic organization. Lynch was a former school committeeman who owned a string of drugstores and was allied with the Russell faction. The 1935 campaign was vicious, even for its time. Lyons charged that Lynch's campaign was but a screen for "racetrack touts, book-makers, gamblers and racketeers." Lynch's supporters responded when the Lyons campaign wagon reached North Cambridge, attacking it with stones and pavement blocks and shattering its windows. The governor had to send the state police to guard the ballots on Election Day. After a tense recount, Lynch was declared the victor by 259 votes. A few months later, he was compelled to assure the voters that he had no personal knowledge of the slot machines seized by police from an illegal gambling club in his Massachusetts Avenue drugstore.[23]

As tumultuous as it was, the 1935 election was but a rehearsal for the rematch the two men staged in 1937, in which armies of "repeaters" darted from polling place to polling place, voting early and often. "Mattress voters" registered to vote, listing vacant lots as their domiciles and adding fictitious floors to the city's apartment buildings — even forging the names of priests at the rectories. And a dozen or more of the dear departed, whose sense of civic duty apparently prevailed beyond the grave, managed to make it to the polls from the city's cemeteries. It was fraud on a massive scale, and the Cambridge election commission announced that from 2,000 to 5,000 votes were suspect. The rowdy supporters of both men jammed the corridors of City Hall, jeering and hooting and occasionally throwing punches, and shortly before midnight, the state police were again called in to restore order. Lyons was declared the victor, by 171 votes, at 1:30 A.M. The feud ended only when Lyons's shady tactics caught up with him in 1940. He was indicted and convicted for soliciting bribes from the builders of city schools and hospitals.[24] This, then, was the tumultuous, colorful and not particularly enlightened political climate in which Tip O'Neill made his first forays into public life.

After graduating from St. John's in 1931, O'Neill drove a truck for a construction firm, postponing a decision about college or career. His evening duty was to fill and light the dozens of small, round kerosene lamps that warned motorists away from a job site along the Concord pike. The shack from which he worked was cozy, just right for a card game, and the Barry's Corner gang quickly gathered. O'Neill rigged the old-fashioned coin telephone so that the boys could use it without depositing money. "We called all over God's creation — until the bill came back," he remembered. But the arrival of the Depression had put an end to the carefree days on the corner. For many in the gang, it was the beginning of a mean struggle to survive. O'Neill had been a careless student in high school, but Sister Agatha, one of the Dominican nuns, sensed his potential. She scolded and shamed him when she found him loafing that summer and fall. The hard economic times had a sobering effect on him, and the onslaught of the New England winter made the trucking job less appealing. And then there was the example set at home, where the Governor and his wife espoused middle-class values, brother Bill had set up shop as a lawyer, and Mary had begun teaching school at seventeen, stopping at the church each night to tearfully beg God's help with her rambunctious students.

Thanks to Thomas O'Neill's civil service job, the family dodged the worst effects of the Depression. Money was tight enough that Mary lived at home and paid rent and board to her stepmother, but not so dear that Tip could not follow his brother and sister into post-secondary education. He worked Saturdays at a grocery store for 10 cents an hour, took a semester of remedial course work at Boston College High School, studied Latin six days a week and was accepted at Boston College for the fall semester of 1932. The Jesuits had opened BC in 1863, charging the immigrant boys $30 a year. By the time O'Neill arrived, the school had moved to a two-hundred-acre campus in Chestnut Hill, on the Boston-Newton line, and the first few Gothic buildings had been raised on "the Heights." Ethnic resentment lingered. "There was a house for Protestant senior citizens on the way there, and we used to spit on the ground as we walked by," said James Dinneen, who was a year behind O'Neill. BC was a day school that accepted one of every two applicants, suffered financially and was eclipsed by Holy Cross. Harvard, for the longest time, refused to recognize BC applicants as qualified for admission to its law school. Yet it was college, a rare privilege for Tip O'Neill at a time when just one of ten Americans had post-secondary education.[25]

O'Neill faced a rigorous classical curriculum of Greek, Latin, French, mathematics, history, English literature and philosophy classes. He was no great scholar, remaining in awe of those who went to the library "even when it wasn't raining." He joined the law academy and the historical society, rowed for and captained the college crew and swung a saber on the BC fencing team. "He fought with the saber — the swashbuckling thing — like a pirate. He was good," classmate Mark Dalton recalled. BC students wore ties and jackets, attended annual religious retreats, and enjoyed a social calendar that included "smokers" (parties) and "socials" (dances) and the annual class "promenades" held at the Hotel Somerset and other downtown ballrooms. The yearly football game against Holy Cross, typically followed by dinner at Moe Hamilburg's and a dance in downtown Boston, was the athletic and social highlight of the fall, though the 1933 and 1935 games against Fordham University were big enough events to be staged at the Polo

Grounds, the home field of the New York Giants. The 1933 trip was memorable for the drive to Manhattan, during which O'Neill's pals took turns sitting in the open rumble seat of his 1924 Ford, and for the scolding they got from the hotel detective who caught them dropping water bags from the windows of their Times Square hotel. By 1935 the BC gang was more sophisticated, catching the music of Eddie Duchin at the Persian Room of the Plaza Hotel.

There was but one, short-lived student rebellion at BC during O'Neill's years there. "They raised the tuition from something like $225 to $250 and we all went out on strike," said Bob Griffin, a student at the time. "The campus then had only the four buildings, and we were sitting on the lawn there. And at the end of second period the dean of men came out on the steps and gave us a very sharp talk in which he said that we had missed the first two classes, that they needed the extra $25 to keep the college functioning, and that anybody who was not in the classroom seat at the beginning of the third period was out of school. The rebellion was over."

O'Neill — tall, lumbering and memorably gregarious — came in a respectable second when he ran for vice president of the junior class, chaired the pre-game smoker committee for the Holy Cross game in his senior year and was voted "class politician" and "class caveman" by the graduating class of 1936. "In his own inimitable fashion," O'Neill "carried his good humor around with him and imported some of it to all he met" at the senior prom, the student newspaper reported. The yearbook in 1936 reported, "He stands 6 feet 1 inch, weighs 215 pounds, and is every inch the famous 'Tip O'Neill.'"[26]

O'Neill still spent plenty of time with his Barry's Corner pals, a couple of whom had joined him at BC. In the summertime, members of the gang would get together and rent a cottage on Nantasket Beach, in Hull. The three-mile strand jutted into Massachusetts Bay from the South Shore, and was served by a ferry that left from Rowe's Wharf in Boston. It was a place to escape from work, if you were fortunate enough to have a job, or to sit out the Depression on the beach. They swam, played ball, cooked huge communal Sunday dinners, drank at Danny O'Brien's speakeasy (until Prohibition was repealed in December 1933) and took their girls to the oceanfront amusement park. The cast of characters varied all summer, but Jed and Dave Barry ran the place and Jack Barry brought the week's batting averages from the *Globe* for the gang to compute. They called themselves "the Nasty Nine."

"You would kick in all winter, a buck here or two bucks there, and you could rent a cottage for ninety bucks a month. That included every weekend and two weeks vacation for those who were working, and those that weren't would stay there all week. We used to sleep on double beds and sofas. The girls would come down on Sunday, and we would fool around on the beach," said Skip McCaffrey. "We never could rent the same cottage twice, for obvious reasons."

The onslaught of the Depression and the first fearful tidings from a troubled Europe had put an end to the insistent public gaiety, roadsters and raccoon coats of the 1920s. A third of the American population were without income, in danger of losing their homes, and relying on hard-pressed family members or public charity to get by. O'Neill's particular group was lucky; most had fathers who continued to work. But the times were serious and worrisome, and the old moral standards no longer looked so stuffy or outdated. The flappers had raised hemlines, championed women's freedom and introduced a generation of Jazz Age boys to sex in a car's backseat. But for the Barry's Corner gang — young men from a sexually repressive Catholic background, living at home and with dubious prospects in that jobless era — there were still two kinds of girls. The "good girls" you dated and one day married. The "bad girls" you met at a speakeasy or a brothel and, if you were willing to risk the mortal sin, they might give you a course in furtive sexual intercourse. O'Neill may have gotten his education in the red light district of Troy, New York, where prostitutes offered instruction to the more adventuresome Barry's Corner boys.[27]

The good girl in Tom O'Neill's life was Mildred Miller. She lived just across the Somerville line, the daughter of a streetcar operator, a friend of Abby Fitzgerald's. Millie was a year behind O'Neill at St. John's, a baby-faced thing with a winning smile, and Sister Agatha had nudged them together at the after-school dances on Friday afternoons. Millie and Abby would scheme to discover where Tom and Red and the gang were going dancing on weekends, and contrive to show up at the ballrooms — the Shadowland or Paramount in Cambridge, or the Commodore in Lowell — where, for a quarter, a young couple could have four dances, or listen to the orchestras of Tommy Dorsey, Ozzie Nelson or Red Nichols.

"Money was very tight. Dutch dates were popular. That's the way it happened. Not that I was chasing him, you know," Millie said later. "Those were good days. Our desire for entertainment wasn't like it is today. You had more fun just being together. The boys always had a cottage, and all the girlfriends used to go to stay at a rooming house. It was a beautiful beach. We would eat, be together, go to dances — being satisfied with so little."[28]

Jed Barry had graduated from Holy Cross in 1932, with his sights set on teaching school. When, frustrated by school committee politics, he could not find a job, he decided to run for the committee himself. The Barry's Corner gang rallied to his side. O'Neill was the campaign manager, driving through town in an old Packard touring car with a microphone and loudspeaker, and ducking to the floor when he spotted his father, who as a civil servant was supposed to remain neutral. Jed Barry lost, but three years later it was O'Neill's turn to carry the gang's colors into battle. In the fall of his senior year at BC he entered the 1935 contest for the Cambridge City Council. His announcement was to the point. "Please permit me space to announce my candidacy for councillor-at-large and also to thank the thousand or more who signed my nomination papers," he wrote the *Cambridge Chronicle.* "I am the son of Thomas P. O'Neill who is and has been superintendent of sewers in Cambridge for the past 23 years. I have lived in Cambridge since my birth and believe I understand enough of its problems to act and vote for the best interests of the city if chosen to represent the citizens as a councillor-at-large." Using the past tense, he informed the voters that he had "attended" Boston College, without disclosing that he was still a student. There were forty-eight candidates on the ballot, including a Duffy, Toomey, Doherty, Tobin, Larkin, Harrington, Phinney, Burke, Delaney, Murphy, McHugh, Corcoran, Barry, Daly, Sheridan and Casey. O'Neill spent $35 on the race.

"It's not the honor of being elected," his father told him. "It's the good you can do. It's a lot of hard work. Don't get in it unless you're serious. I don't want you to do it half-heartedly." Looking back at the end of his career, O'Neill said: "I wanted to be a doer. I wanted to help things. I wanted to try and help the people in my backyard. I wanted to carry on the tradition."

It was the year of the first Lynch-Lyons donnybrook. Though they were North Cambridge neighbors, there had been ill will between Thomas O'Neill Sr. and Lynch — perhaps over the druggist's independence from the regular Democratic organization, or because his reputation as a relaxed dispenser of pharmaceutical alcohol didn't sit well with the elder O'Neill, the head of the local Catholic temperance society. Young Tip decided to hitch a ride to both candidates' wagons. "I'd take a group, maybe four of us, and we'd go to the Lyons rallies," Lenny Lamkin recalled. "And he and another group would go to the Lynch rallies. So we would canvass the city pretty good. And then we would all meet and go to Lindy's in Boston and have a beer or two."[29]

O'Neill got 4,020 votes and finished ninth — a tremendous showing in a citywide race for such a neophyte, though no doubt attributable to his father's name and the goodwill that the Governor had built up in Cambridge over the years. But only the top eight candidates were elected, and a recount failed to reduce the 228-vote margin between O'Neill and the eighth-place candidate. In later life, Tip O'Neill said he treated his own son Tommy's political career the way his father had treated his: with respect, but a bit of distance, so that a young man could find his own feet beneath him. Nor had Tip, emerging into manhood and seeking a bit of independence, asked his father to do all he could. O'Neill probably would have picked up the necessary 229 votes, in North Cambridge alone, had he profited from his father's full assistance. The disappointed candidate concluded that he had spent too much time campaigning citywide while neglecting his own neighborhood.[30]

From the experience of losing the 1935 council race, young Tip drew two lessons which, over time, became part of the O'Neill canon. The first was the concise advice his father gave him when assessing his shortfall in North Cambridge: "All politics is local." It became his trademark. The second lesson was courtesy of Mrs. Elizabeth O'Brien, a somewhat haughty neighbor who lived on the finer, sunny side of Orchard Street and taught drama and elocution at St. John's school. When she saw him on Election Day she said, "Tom, I'm going to vote for you even though you didn't ask me."

"Mrs. O'Brien," the young candidate replied, "I've lived across the street from you for eighteen years. I cut your grass in the summer and shovel your walk in the winter. I didn't think I had to ask for your vote."

"Tom, let me tell you something," she said. "People like to be asked."[31]

O'Neill was disappointed in his loss, but not discouraged. The press had taken notice, with the *Chronicle* praising his "splendid" performance "in his first attempt to capture a seat." The Boston College newspaper, *The Heights,* spread word of his good showing among his classmates, many of whom volunteered to help the affable giant should he decide to run again. The Barry's Corner gang had come closer than ever to electing one of their own. His father was impressed.

In June 1936, O'Neill was one of 411 Boston College graduates who accepted their A.B. degrees in philosophy and the classics from Cardinal William H. O'Connell and then knelt to kiss his ring. The twenty-four-year-old graduate told his classmates he was thinking about postgraduate school in engineering or law. But what he really intended to do was run for office again. In fact, he had already picked the race. His target was one of three seats from the Third Middlesex District in the Massachusetts House of Representatives. The "upper district," as it was called, comprised Wards 7, 8, 9, 10 and 11 in central and northwest Cambridge. It was where O'Neill had done best in the city council race, and he knew that if he simply secured the 3,000 votes he'd won in those wards, he probably would get elected. It would not be a cakewalk, however, for the Democratic primary field was strong. There were two incumbent representatives — John J. Foley and James F. Mahoney — favored for reelection in the three-seat district, and a city councillor, three former city councillors and a former state rep led the list of other candidates who hoped to clinch the party's nod.[32]

"I was born and spent my entire life in this district. . . . I am keenly interested in the success of the Democratic Party in November, and feel that an aggressive young man will appeal to the voters of this section," O'Neill told the *Chronicle.* "For several years past I have made a careful study of the bills pending before the Massachusetts Legislature, and with my training and education, I feel amply qualified to protect the interest of the people."[33]

As a warm-up for the race, O'Neill ran and won a seat as a delegate to the state Democratic convention in June. There, he ran into Leo Diehl, an aspiring politician and young comer from "the Village" of Cambridgeport in central Cambridge. Diehl was easy to recognize. He had contracted polio as a young boy and the doctors had treated it by cutting the tendons in his legs. They had then kept the terrified six-year-old isolated in a polio ward, barring visits from his parents until they came up with the money to pay his bills. Diehl survived the experience with unconquerable spirit and, despite his heavy metal leg braces and crutches, he managed the Village baseball, football and basketball teams, built his political base and announced his candidacy for the state House of Representatives in 1936.

O'Neill and Diehl were thrown together at the convention because they had both pledged their support to the jolly, double-chinned state treasurer Charles F. Hurley of Cambridge, who was running for governor. It was a tough decision, because Hurley was opposed by another Cantabrigian, attorney general Paul Dever. The halls were thick with intrigue, with cash and patronage jobs offered to opportunists. "The Hurley people put us in a room and told us not to answer the phone," Diehl recalled. The two young pols formed a bond as they resisted all entreaties, even those made by Dan Coakley, a legendary backroom conniver.[34] Hurley won the convention's nomination for governor, and Dever settled for another term as attorney general. Diehl was impressed by his new friend's chutzpah. "Those were giants he was running against. Foley and Mahoney were old-time pols. Mahoney had been superintendent of streets and Foley was a wealthy real estate guy," he recalled.

Home from the convention, O'Neill launched his campaign. He would obtain a permit for an hour rally at a home or street corner, and invite popular candidates for other offices to join him. They would each get to speak for five minutes, and then O'Neill would use up the final ten or fifteen minutes, which he had reserved for himself. Candidates had to contend with groups of hecklers, sent by opposing campaigns. There were fistfights on the fringes of the crowd and worse: political workers in Dorchester and the West End were stabbed at election-eve rallies that year. To establish a presence in the community, O'Neill opened a real estate office at Harvard Square. He raised $400 for the race, and was now the happy beneficiary of his father's advice and influence. The Governor combed his files and dispatched his son to see every friend and acquaintance.[35] The organizing meetings for the campaign were held at the Knights of Columbus Hall, where Thomas Senior was a Grand Knight. One of O'Neill's father's most enthusiastic supporters was Kitty Danehy, the Democratic ward chairman, for whose blind brother the Governor had secured a city job. She took Tip in hand, and together they went knocking on the doors of her many acquaintances. O'Neill was nothing if not sociable, and soon he was ringing doorbells on his own — a new tactic in those days.

"My friends and I worked the telephones," his sister Mary recalled, "while Tom rang every doorbell in the district. And my brother Bill did. And Millie did."

The candidate had a platform; he called it the "O'Neill Family Plan." In this Depression year, when Franklin D. Roosevelt was running for reelection and the alphabetic agencies of the New Deal were immensely popular, O'Neill proposed that the state create its own WPA (Works Progress Administration) or CCC (Civilian Conservation Corps) and put able-bodied men to work cleaning up polluted bodies of water like the Charles River or the Alewife Brook or constructing playgrounds and ballfields. He endorsed the goal, long favored by progressive reformers, of a five-day work week. O'Neill was helped by the fact that the WPA had given Cambridge a sizable grant to improve and expand its sewer system: it gave his dad hundreds of jobs to fill.

"He had a good organization. All volunteers. Never a paid worker," said Lenny Lamkin. "We would get an amplifying system, and you'd drive around through different streets with an amplifier and music." O'Neill had spent his youth at the dinner table arguing about politics and sports with his family. But for Millie, this was all new. The passions of the campaigns left a deep impression on her. Because North Cambridge was a tightly knit area, "when you ran for any position you were always running against a friend, a family friend. And it made for hard feelings. Families didn't speak to each other for years," she recalled.

As the candidates closed in upon the September 15 primary, it was clear that O'Neill's efforts were paying off. "Reports from every part of the district make it appear that his canvass is making great headway with the voters," the *Chronicle* reported. On top of everything else, in this New Deal era, there was a receptivity in the electorate for young men who offered a fresh perspective. A boyish Michael J. Neville was in the process of upsetting an incumbent state rep by 900 votes in the First Middlesex District and young Diehl was winning the battle for an open seat in the Second. Lomasney had died in 1932 and P. J. Kennedy in 1929; Fitzgerald had last won in 1910. The duties of the old Democratic block captains and ward heelers were increasingly being assumed by federal employees, as government welfare and unemployment checks and Social Security payments began to replace food baskets as benefits for the jobless and the poor.

O'Neill and the others had sturdy roots in the Democratic Party, yet offered more polished and professional candidacies than their older counterparts. The Cambridge electorate was tired of the shenanigans displayed in the Lynch versus Lyons feuds and of their inefficient city government and its high tax rate. College-educated Tip O'Neill, the son of a well-regarded civil servant, with a corps of smart, well-dressed young men from Boston College and Barry's Corner behind him, was no *reformer* — for sound political reasons he would disavow the Goo-Goo label with a passion — but he nevertheless represented a bit of the reform impulse. O'Neill got his 3,000 votes and more, and beat his closest challenger — veteran city councillor John J. Tierney — for the Democratic nomination by 700 votes.[36]

As he faced the November election, the presence of Socialist candidates on the ballot gave O'Neill some reason for concern, as there was a danger that the radicals could siphon off enough Democratic votes to give the Republicans victory. But then FDR, on his way to a landslide win over Alf Landon, made a triumphant tour of Massachusetts in late October. The President was seen by a million people, spoke to 250,000 on Boston Common, and rode through Cambridge in an open car with Governor Curley and Senator Walsh at his side. The crowd of 40,000 was four deep along Massachusetts Avenue in Cambridge, where the President's coattails helped pull two favorite sons — Hurley and Dever — into office.

For FDR, it was a historic victory — the greatest ever, at that time, in American politics. The electoral total was 523 to 8, as Landon won only Vermont and Maine. More than 75 percent of the members of both houses of Congress were Democrats. In Boston, 20,000 people jammed the streets of "Newspaper Row" on an unseasonably warm evening to watch as the results were posted on giant outdoor movie screens. In Cambridge, the Roosevelt tide swept away the Socialist and Republican hopes, and all three members of the Democratic slate in the Third District claimed victory. The two incumbent representatives finished first and second in the balloting, and O'Neill was in third place, with 10,003 votes, having nipped the nearest Republican by an 803-vote margin. With Franklin Roosevelt's help, Tip O'Neill had won his first election. He was going to the State House.[37]

PART TWO

The First of My Faith

CHAPTER 3

Loyalties

THE GENERAL COURT of the Commonwealth of Massachusetts, as it is known, is among the oldest representative bodies in the world. It is the place where John and Samuel Adams, John Hancock, John Quincy Adams, Daniel Webster, Calvin Coolidge, John W. McCormack and Tip O'Neill honed their craft and where Ralph Waldo Emerson served as chaplain. It meets in Charles Bulfinch's golden-domed State House, atop Beacon Hill, the tallest of three contiguous hills that once loomed above the Common (giving nearby Tremont Street its name) and from where, in the 1600s, a beacon of burning tar was hoisted to warn the Puritan pioneers of Indian raids.

When O'Neill arrived at the legislature in 1937, the General Court was the last redoubt of the Yankee "codfish aristocracy." The Democrats had elected governors and senators, but there had never been a Democratic Speaker of the Massachusetts House. Via the General Court, the Brahmins controlled the state budget and payroll, as well as the city of Boston's police, tax rate and budget, so that Boston was the only metropolis in the nation that did not have power over its own own fiscal affairs. It was from their State House stronghold that the Yankee

Republicans launched periodic corruption probes of the city's Democratic mayors. The place was a nest of conniving and intrigue. Though FDR carried the state with more than 60 percent of the vote in four consecutive elections, the Republicans maintained their hold on the legislature throughout the Roosevelt era due to the Democratic infighting. There was a delightful predictability to it: the Democrats would stumble and claw until the final weeks of the presidential election, when FDR would arrive in the state, draw hundreds of thousands of people out to see him, and impose some form of order. It was good enough for Roosevelt, but not the kind of effort the Democrats needed to break the Republican grip.[1]

The joker in the deck was Curley. As a provocateur, he had ample competition among the fractious Democrats, yet without his singularly disruptive presence it is possible that Senator Walsh and other Democratic leaders might have been able to discipline their troops. But once Curley entered statewide politics in 1924, his charismatic personality, manipulation of Irish Catholic grievances and cult following transformed the agenda of most Democratic politicians from "Us versus Them" to "Him versus Us." Banned from the Massachusetts delegation by his foes, "Don Jaime Miguel Curleo" popped up amid the delegates from Puerto Rico at the 1932 Democratic convention to help FDR clinch the nomination.[2] After being elected governor in 1934, Curley dressed his state police guard in gold-trimmed military uniforms, eliciting comparisons to the "Kingfish" of Louisiana, Huey Long. The internecine warfare was so debilitating that the New Deal relief programs were slowed in arriving in Massachusetts, needlessly extending the pain of thousands during the Depression. Disarray was too kind a word for the state of the Massachusetts Democratic Party. "I really believe that Boston and Massachusetts Democrats will grow up some day," FDR wrote an old college classmate in 1932, "but probably not until you and I are dead and gone."[3]

In the House, which the GOP controlled by a 136 to 104 margin in O'Neill's first term, the psychological and practical advantages of their long-standing majority lent an arrogance to Republican rule. The Democrats — even their legislative leaders — were banned from setting foot in GOP Speaker Horace Cahill's ornate suite of offices. House Democrats, for the most part, had to content themselves with the rhetoric of outrage, objecting to the Republican tactics, and (grandly) naming their section of seats "Murderers' Row." Their ultimate threat was to filibuster, thus forcing the Republicans to miss the evening "supper trains" that carried them home to the leafy Yankee suburbs.

O'Neill took to the legislative life immediately. With its camaraderie and card games, the House was a street corner gang writ large. It was like being paid to hang out at Barry's Corner. To console themselves and pass the time, the Democratic reps played poker and drank beer — donated, by the keg, by local breweries — in the State House's basement or attic hideaways. It was possible, he recalled, to place a bet on a horse without leaving the House floor. He loved the swirl of events, the whispers of deals and double-crossings, the gossip and intrigues, the calculation and the counting. It was not a well-paid position, but for the people of his district O'Neill was doing the kinds of favors he had watched his father perform for years. His plans to clean up the Charles River and the Alewife Brook (which would have had the serendipitous effect of adding even more WPA jobs to the Cambridge sewer department) were dismissed as expensive boondoggles. His initial legislative accomplishment was a bill that capped the license fees for newsboys at 25 cents, signed by Governor Leverett Saltonstall in 1939. He would never be much of a legislative draftsman. "He would look at all the bills that were filed and get on something," Leo Diehl recalled. But O'Neill's first term was not without lasting significance, as an eruption of political hysteria posed an early test of his character.[4]

THROUGHOUT THOSE grim Depression years, fear had spawned hatred in the Catholic community. Demagogues preyed on the people's misfortune, and resentment surfaced in a crude mix of Red-baiting, anti-Semitism and isolationism. For an up-and-coming politician, the temptation was to ride the popular wave, or at very least keep quiet. Remarkably, O'Neill did neither. Alone among his Cambridge peers he risked his career, opposing the fear-mongering crew.

O'Neill and his boyhood pals had been somewhat sheltered in the middle-class neighborhoods of North Cambridge, but in East Cambridge and Charlestown and South Boston the Depression, arriving on the heels of Al Smith's loss, had brought dread and suspicion to huge segments of Boston's Irish Catholic population. The economic effects were plain enough. The state's shoe and textile industries had begun to die even before the onset of the Depression and though New Deal programs brought some relief — the Huntington Avenue subway and the tunnel to East Boston led the list of emergency public works projects — the unemployment rate in Boston ranged between 20 and 30 percent for the decade, with some 100,000 workers unemployed.

"The picture is so grim that whatever words I use will seem hysterical and exaggerated," a friend reported to Roosevelt's lieutenant Harry Hopkins in 1934. Boston's neighborhoods were home to "the spectacle of a human being driven beyond his or her power of endurance or sanity" with "fear driving them into a state of semi-collapse; cracking nerves and [fostering] an overpowering terror of the future."[5] Boston's Irish, who had splashed happily in the melting pot in the prosperous 1920s, withdrew unto themselves in the 1930s. The triumph of Curleyism was but one example; the church offered another in Cardinal O'Connell, an authoritarian prelate who lived his own corrupt version of Curley's shamrock-shuttered lifestyle — with a Brighton estate and a private golf course, gold-plated cane and visits to the Bahamas and other exotic ports that earned him the nickname "Gangplank Bill." Like Curley, the cardinal was a separatist, urging his considerable flock — by now over 70 percent of the city's population was Catholic — to turn inward. The archdiocese went on a tremendous building program, doubling the number of Catholic elementary schools and tripling the number of parochial high schools. Organizations like the Boy Scouts and the YMCA were identified as threats to Catholic youth, and motion pictures censored as threats to morality.

On the national political scene, Father Charles E. Coughlin, the smooth-talking "radio priest," had built a huge following by deploring Wall Street financiers and the Hoover administration. His Sunday afternoon audience grew to 40 million Americans, and his newspaper, *Social Justice,* was distributed outside Boston's Catholic churches after Sunday Mass. Like Curley and Long and the other two-bit demagogues of the era, Coughlin was quickly hooked on power. In 1935 he launched the Union Party and declared his opposition to Roosevelt. Boston was a Coughlin stronghold. Curley posed at the priest's side and proclaimed the city "the strongest Coughlin city in the world" in 1935. A year later, Coughlin returned to speak to an adoring crowd at Braves Field. "Democracy is doomed," he said. "It is fascism or Communism. . . . I take the road of fascism."

The Union Party ran stronger in Boston than in any other American city in 1936, getting 8 percent of the presidential vote. Coughlin was at the height of his influence when, over the next three years, he began to spew hateful warnings about a worldwide Jewish conspiracy, the persecution of the Catholic Church in Spain, and the threat of Godless Communism. During 1937 and 1938, O'Neill's first term in the State House, Coughlin was hailing Mussolini as "Man of the Week," defending Hitler's persecution of Jews, giving the Nazi salute to his followers and boasting, "When we get through with the Jews in America, they'll think the treatment they received in Germany was nothing."

Widespread affection for Roosevelt and the opposition of local leaders like Representative John W. McCormack helped limit Coughlin's support in the poorer Irish neighborhoods to somewhere between 5 and 20 percent of the voters. But if Coughlin's views were extreme, they reflected a broader political climate. Gangs of Irish toughs were descending on Jewish neighborhoods, scrawling Nazi swastikas and beating up Jewish schoolboys on Blue Hill Avenue (which was sneeringly called "Jew Hill Avenue") in Dorchester. Cardinal O'Connell identified Communism and the "international conspiracy" to lure the U.S. into a world war as greater threats than Adolf Hitler and he, Senator Walsh and millionaire ambassador Joseph P. Kennedy became major spokesmen for American isolationism.[6]

It was against this backdrop that the Irish-Catholic pols in the State House got into the act, manufacturing their Red Scare. In 1935, with Republican complicity, they pushed through a bill requiring teachers to take a loyalty oath. The state's civil libertarians and academic leaders, who had been caught off guard, demanded in 1936 that the bill be repealed. The Republican House leadership and most of the highbrow Yankee representatives were herded back into line. A handful of Democratic votes would make the difference.

O'Neill was thrust into the dispute by virtue of his seat on the Joint Committee on Education, which held hearings on repealing the oath in March. More than 700 people packed the Gardner Auditorium at the State House, cheering on the rival sides. "There was very little question of teachers' loyalty in this state until the Red Scare caused by this law," Harvard historian Samuel Eliot Morison told the panel. The state's teachers "sacrificed deeply during the Depression, both financially and in giving of their time to students and families. They deserved a vote of thanks, and instead they were told in tones, like the guttural voice of the ghost in Hamlet: 'Swear! Swear! Swear!'"

"It is unnecessary and unwise legislation . . . inspired by an atmosphere of fear," said Harvard President James B. Conant, testifying on behalf of a dozen of the state's prestigious (but not Catholic) universities and colleges.

Supporting the oath, and leading off the second day of hearings, was former state representative Thomas Dorgan of Dorchester, a rotund Irish immigrant who had sponsored the law in 1935. He was joined by leaders of the American Legion and other Massachusetts veterans' groups. The Legion was a formidable presence in state politics: at its annual convention in Worcester in 1938, 10,000 uniformed members would parade before 200,000 cheering spectators. Dorgan spoke for two hours about the need to drive the "Reds" from the Harvard and Massachusetts Institute of Technology faculties, and claiming to have a list of 105 Communist Harvard professors. The American Federation of Teachers, Dorgan said, had given $20,000 to the left-leaning republicans in the Spanish Civil War so they could "burn more convents, nuns and schools." Repeal of the loyalty oath would be "the opening wedge of Communism," he said. "Obedience to authority should be the motto of this country." Day after day, the Boston newspapers gave the showdown front-page coverage. The pressure from all sides was intense. On March 11 the committee voted, 9 to 5, to repeal the Loyalty Oath. Voting to repeal was the freshman representative from Cambridge, Tip O'Neill.[7]

It was, first and foremost, a call of conscience. His sister, Mary, was a teacher, and so were many of her friends. Sister Agatha and the nuns at St. John's would have to swear the oath, as would the Jesuits at Boston College. It implied they were disloyal and was "an insult to some of the finest men and women I had ever known," O'Neill said later. Beyond this gut reaction, O'Neill was a college graduate and had a more sophisticated outlook on civil liberty and academic freedom than his working-class colleagues in the General Court. He had that hint of freshness and independence that voters found attractive in 1936. He had recognized before most other Irish-Catholic politicians of his time that the technological research at Harvard, MIT and the other institutes of higher learning in Cambridge was a key to jobs in his district and his state's prosperity. O'Neill was twenty-four. He was modern. Though no star student, on matters of politics he was quick, schooled and intelligent. And he had made the transition from his teenage idol, Al Smith, to a new hero: Franklin Roosevelt.

The New Deal was not about loyalty oaths. O'Neill believed in Roosevelt's radical theory that the science of politics and government could be used to tame the economic forces which had plunged the nation into the Depression. He had faith in social planning, government regulation, public investment and a political coalition that included — not excluded — Jews and Negroes. It is difficult to appreciate how revolutionary it all was at the time O'Neill entered politics. African Americans were an invisible race, banished to southern dirt farms and a few northern ghettos, deprived of the right in much of America to vote or patronize racially segregated restaurants, stores, hotels and public schools. Working men of all races faced forty-eight-hour weeks (and thought themselves lucky) while paid vacations, the two-day "weekend," and a secure "retirement" were still the dreams of trade unionists and academic theoreticians. Few Americans had health insurance or unemployment insurance or a pension plan for their old age. Highways and schools were built by state and local governments, with no assistance or aid from Washington. In 1929, federal expenditures accounted for just 3 percent of the gross national product.[8]

Roosevelt changed everything, with a peaceful revolution that may well have saved American capitalism and democracy. Andrew Mellon, who served as Herbert Hoover's secretary of the treasury, spoke for many in the GOP when he described the Depression as an inevitable part of the business cycle that would beneficially "purge the rottenness" out of the economy. By the time FDR took office there were 12 million people out of work, and millions more scraping by with part-time jobs or on failing farms. Just half of the workforce retained full-time employment. The new President closed the banks to stop financial panic, and called Congress into special session. He used the radio, and his fireside chats, to boost morale and promised the repeal of Prohibition. He put millions to work with the CCC, the WPA, the National Recovery Administration and the Public Works Administration. The Social Security Act not only provided the old-age insurance benefits for which it is famous, but the first unemployment insurance program for laid-off workers, and welfare for the poor.

And as so often with O'Neill, there was a personal connection as well. During his high school years, O'Neill had played poker with the brother of Missy LeHand, an Orchard Street neighbor who left North Cambridge and went on to serve as Roosevelt's personal secretary (and secret love, though no one on Orchard Street ever suggested *that*).

While O'Neill was a student at BC, Missy invited him to Washington. He stayed at an aunt's home on Bladensburg Road, and took the streetcar down Rhode Island Avenue to the White House in the morning. Missy took him in to meet the President (a Harvard graduate) and they exchanged small talk about Cambridge. O'Neill was dumbfounded to discover that Roosevelt was confined to a wheelchair, and kept the news like a state secret, even from his family. Roosevelt "was my idol," O'Neill recalled. "I truly believed in the philosophy of government that he believed in. That was what my ideals were all about."

Nor did O'Neill ever much like bullies. Or hatemongers. Or those, on the Left or Right, who sought power by manipulating people with gut-wrenching symbolic issues. He took quite seriously Christ's directive to "Love thy neighbor," and the O'Neills were among the quiet multitude of Irish-Americans who emerged from the experience of discrimination feeling kinship, rather than resentment, for society's scapegoats.

Lenny Lamkin was a member of the Barry's Corner gang, a lifelong O'Neill pal and campaign worker, the designated driver to the weekend dances, partner in the Nantasket beach cottage and manager of the North Cambridge Catholic football team. "I was the only Jewish boy among the group. I never felt I was out of place," Lamkin said. "His stepmother would make me scrambled eggs instead of a ham sandwich."

"Anti-Semitism? Tip was known for not having any of that. Known. Absolutely known. Every Jew who ever knew him felt the relationship was authentic. There was no patronizing. None of the Christ-killer stuff," said Jerome Grossman, a veteran liberal activist whose father was a political player in the Curley era, and who clashed with O'Neill in later years. "You know, there are people who have it and you can tell, but they don't show it. Not him. Tip was notoriously free of that, and in a tough time."[9]

The bill repealing the loyalty oath reached the House floor on March 16, 1937. The headlines in the *Globe* that week gave the tenor of the times: "Fascist Guns Batter Madrid" and "Atheistic Communism Scored by Pope; Asks Halt in Spread." Governor Hurley's aides lobbied the Democratic legislators, offering patronage jobs if they would vote against repeal. Influential Democrats warned their colleagues that a vote for repeal could lead to political destruction.

"I plead with you members who come from the same stock as I do to ignore the whisperings of that class of people who use their arts and wiles to gain an objective but who would consign you to political oblivion," said Representative Timothy Murphy of Dorchester. The Democrats should "consult their own common sense rather than surrender to any inferiority they may feel in relation to holders of elaborate college degrees." The final votes were cast on March 18. With the exception of O'Neill, the Cambridge delegation voted unanimously against repeal. It made no difference if they were canny old-timers, like Foley and Mahoney, or brash newcomers like Diehl and Neville.

The bill passed the House on a 120 to 112 vote. Governor Hurley, a member of the Cambridge American Legion post, vetoed it. The Legion vowed to defeat O'Neill at the polls when he came up for reelection in 1938. "I thought, for the first time, a doom came over me, that probably it was the end of my political career," he recalled. But O'Neill had not overestimated the voters in his district. On Election Day, the Legion put uniformed members at the polls in Cambridge. His father countered the threat by calling out his own pals from the veterans' halls. O'Neill improved on his 1936 performance, beating the nearest GOP challenger by 2,000 votes. He had passed his first test of conscience as an elected official, and learned an enduring lesson about the electorate's capacity to respect an act of political courage. Thirty years later, confronted with a similarly torturous choice over the Vietnam War, he would navigate that turning point in his political life by drawing on what he learned in the fight over the loyalty oath. "It instilled in me a thought: you did the right thing. People know you did the right thing. And when you explain to the people and you're honest about it and you're outright about it, then they appreciate," he said.[10]

THE 1940 ELECTION brought a new kind of danger: redistricting. The Third Middlesex District lost a seat in the process, and then a prominent liquor store owner and prizefighter named Tansy Norton persuaded one of his employees, a city councillor, to enter the race. O'Neill suspected that his foes were using mattress votes and repeaters to defeat him.

"They're running them in," he told his father.

"If you can't beat this guy, even with all the people he's running in, then you ought to get the hell out of public life," Thomas Senior told him.

Wisely, the O'Neills had prepared for such a day. In 1938 the young representative and his father had set up the "Representative Thomas P.

O'Neill Jr. Social Club." With 150 members, which included both men and women, it formed the core of his political organization. Its roster was dotted with pals from Barry's Corner and Boston College, new allies he had made when campaigning across the Third Middlesex District and city employees beholden to "the Governor." Headquartered at the Knights of Columbus Hall, the club organized dances, socials and country picnics. At the July 1938 outing, the married men from the sewer department beat the single men at softball, and there were sack races, nail-driving contests and other games. O'Neill's taste for good food and beverages was evident in his third-place finish in the "fat man's race," for which he qualified at 253 pounds. The club was a vehicle by which the O'Neills discovered who needed a box of groceries, a job cleaning up the graveyards in the spring or a ride to the senior citizens' whist party or the parish reunion. Its members and their neighbors got prime consideration for the part-time state jobs that O'Neill gave out at the state's beaches, parks, racetracks and road projects. When it snowed in the wintertime, a line of men would form outside the Orchard Street home before daybreak, seeking a "snow button," which permitted them to shovel snow for the city, the state or the Boston Elevated Railway (later to become part of the Metropolitan Transit Authority) at $3 to $5 a day. And "just before the election, Mr. O'Neill would have sewer jobs, and Tom would have about thirty-five slips to give to his friends. It was temporary work. But it was during the height of the Depression. Two weeks' worth was a lot of work," Lamkin remembered.[11]

O'Neill won by 450 votes and was never seriously challenged again. And when the legislature convened in January 1941, he put his name on a piece of reform legislation: a bill to make "repeating" a serious crime. Some of his fellow legislators complained to him: Why was he rocking the boat? "I didn't like people stealing elections — and I especially didn't like people stealing them from me," he told them. His winning ways got O'Neill off the hook with the old guard, while his candor appealed to the new. Besides, he was by this time a regular at the taprooms, nightclubs and all-night poker games through which the legislative process was distilled, and friendships forged, after dark. "He had the imprint of the ace of spades on his ass, from carrying a deck of cards in his pocket," Diehl said. "Jesus, he enjoyed being out with the fellas. I can't remember a night going home."

O'Neill started his serious card playing in high school and college, holding poker games under the Russell Field bleachers to keep his father from discovering he was gambling. "Playing cards, he was an SOB. He was a cozy. He had this straight face," said Barry's Corner pal James Sullivan. O'Neill would play poker at the LeHand house, bridge at the Fitzgeralds', gin rummy anywhere. He was adept at counting cards as they were played. "It's ninety-eight percent luck and two percent skill," he later recalled. "And what is that two percent skill? That two percent skill is the art of concentration. How many cards in a deck have been played and how many are left? You can lick me tonight if you are just the normal player, but if I can catch you on a slow boat to China I can get even with you. Luck evens out along the line and that two percent skill will come into play."

In downtown Boston, the nightclubs stayed open until 3 A.M. Like most of Boston's red-blooded young men, O'Neill and Diehl made pilgrimages to Scollay Square, with its sideshow mix of tattoo parlors, burlesque houses, arcades and pawnshops. They caught the striptease shows at the Old Howard and the Crawford House, and marveled at Sally Keith's ability to twirl the tassels on her breasts. "She hung around with a guy we knew at Jimmy O'Keefe's bar. So we knew her," Diehl recalled with a grin. "Every once in a while we would go over and see her act." As the love of her life chatted with strippers, and cut a swath through the Parker House, the Bellevue tap and the other brass rails surrounding Beacon Hill, Millie was working as a salesgirl to support her hard-pressed family. Somehow, their romance survived. "He was pretty steady with Millie," Diehl recalled. "If he wasn't running around with the guys he would sit around with her. He loved to dance and Millie would go to the dances with him all the time." If Tip and Millie felt like splurging, the Totem Pole took couples only, while the Cocoanut Grove on Piedmont Street featured a chorus line on roller skates.[12]

Long engagements and an extended bachelor life were Irish American traditions, but Millie was of no-nonsense German descent and decided to force the issue. At a Boston College hockey game she pressed her boyfriend for a commitment. O'Neill agreed, and they scheduled their wedding ceremony for June 17, 1941. Tip and Bill arrived on time for the 9 A.M. Mass, but by 9:20 there was no sign of the bride or her bridesmaids. Monsignor Hugh Blunt was preparing to send the guests home when Millie finally showed up. She and her friends had overslept, and only the unexpected arrival of Tip's sister, Mary, woke them up.

Lamkin went AWOL from his Army barracks on Cape Cod to be there. Brother Bill was the best man, and sister Mary and Abby Fitzgerald were in the wedding party. As the newly married O'Neills stood on the steps, getting ready to leave the church on a warm summer day, Tip's father suggested that Millie refer to his son as Tom, which was more dignified. And so he was Tom, and never Tip, for the rest of her life. The bride and groom left the wedding reception and breakfast at the Hotel Lenox at about 2 P.M. and drove to New York, where they stayed at the Taft Hotel, and Tom tipped the Vincent Lopez band to play Millie's favorite song, "I'll Be With You in Apple Blossom Time." The next night, before driving to Atlantic City and the elegant Claridge Hotel, the O'Neills watched Joe Louis knock out Billy Conn to retain the heavyweight title. "When we were going to be married he insisted on going to New York the first night," Millie said. "I have always been quite sure he picked that date because of the Louis-Conn fight. It was a great fight, although we sat up on the top row. We could have seen it better from Boston."[13]

O'Neill was twenty-eight. He left his boyhood home and moved with his bride to a rented apartment that his sister Mary had heard about at 16 Norris Street, near Barry's Corner. It was time to consider his financial obligations. The costs of politics were not inconsiderable. It cost the average legislator $4,800 to get elected, to which were added another $2,000 to pay for the various "touches" that were required by the office: wedding presents, charitable donations, the various tickets and flowers to be purchased. The lawmakers made ends meet with interests in government contracts, leasing trucks or parking lots to the city, accepting shares in businesses that needed a state or municipal license or taking a patronage job.

The practice of law gave legislators the freedom to schedule their own work hours and had drawn O'Neill to the Boston College Law School. But the political life and his nocturnal recreational activities left O'Neill little time for serious study. In an incident that was to grate on him for years, he was booted out of the school when Dean Cornelius J. Moynihan, determined to raise its standards and reputation, decided to purge the two legislators in the student body, O'Neill and his pal Eddie Boland, who, in the dean's opinion, showed insufficient ardor for their studies and the law. Boland concluded that law school didn't fit his Depression-era finances, or the long commute to his home in western Massachusetts. O'Neill could have reenrolled, or found another Boston-area school, but did not.

"His family really wanted Tom to go to law school," Millie recalled. But "he wasn't that interested. If he had been, he would have stayed with it." Instead, O'Neill and Diehl got jobs in the city treasurer's office at Cambridge City Hall, courtesy of Mayor Lyons. O'Neill maintained a real estate and insurance business, which he ran from the office at 4 Brattle Street. His winning way and expanding political connections made it natural for O'Neill's supporters to ask him to handle the sale of a property or to sell them insurance.[14]

Two days before O'Neill's twenty-ninth birthday, on Sunday, December 7, the Japanese attacked Pearl Harbor. "It was a devastating day," Millie recalled. "I don't think the full impact came through to everyone for a week after." One in five American families sent someone off to World War II, as more than 16 million men and women wore a uniform. O'Neill was not among them. He had just begun life as a married man, his political career was off to a promising start and he did not join the rush of young men who enlisted with patriotic fervor. Nor was the military itching to have him. At twenty-nine, he was old for active duty: the armed services preferred to take only those under the age of twenty-six, and the rigors of war ensured that the bulk of those in the front line were a decade younger than O'Neill. In 1940, O'Neill had been classified I-A — available for duty — by the new Selective Service system, but he qualified for an elected official's IV-B deferment, which he requested and accepted. It was not until the end of 1942 (as O'Neill turned thirty) that the government started drafting those over the age of twenty-eight. In 1943, his daughter Rosemary was born, and fathers were not drafted until 1944.

It was then, in 1944, that O'Neill notified his local draft board that he had had a change of heart and wanted to enlist. He was now three months short of his thirty-second birthday. Years later, he attributed his decision to the guilt he felt at seeing others bear the burden, and a concern that he needed a better answer for voters who might ask, "What did you do in the war?" There was lingering isolationism in some of Boston's Irish neighborhoods, but not in Cambridge, which contributed more than its share of sons to the war effort. Some 15,000 served and 400 died — and Bob Griffin, Mark Dalton, Lenny Lamkin and Red Fitzgerald, among others of O'Neill's friends, were in uniform. In North Cambridge, tiny Yorktown Street was renamed Gold Star Road after nine servicemen from that small street were killed in uniform. On October 14, the Cambridge draft board scheduled

O'Neill's preinduction physical exam. Six days later, it recorded the results: like one in three draftees, he had been rejected for service. The doctors had discovered that the corpulent O'Neill had a latent susceptibility to diabetes, a legacy of his Tolan ancestors. In the end, his contribution to the war effort was his service in the Massachusetts legislature, to which he had been reelected in 1942 and 1944, and the night shifts he worked as a watchman at a defense plant: the Bethlehem Steel shipyard in East Boston. It was there, while on duty in April of 1945, that he heard, and wept at, the news that Roosevelt had died on the eve of America's victory.[15]

The Lynch-Lyons era was viewed as an embarrassment by blue-blooded Cantabrigians and they decided to do something about it, opting for a city manager system called Plan E. The Cambridge Taxpayers Association and other good-government groups collected enough signatures to put their proposal to a public referendum in 1938. Harvard Law dean James W. Landis, the leader of the movement, called the city councillors "a cheap gang of politicians" and council president Thomas McNamara retorted by complaining about "cultured shysters." The councillors voted to have Harvard secede from the city. The boys at the Harvard *Lampoon* responded by declaring "the free state of Lampoon" and goose-stepping down Massachusetts Avenue, where they were pelted with rotten eggs and confronted by councillor Michael "Mickey the Dude" Sullivan. As he grappled for the *Lampoon*'s flag, Sullivan got kicked in the rear end and news spread through North Cambridge that the Dude had been assaulted by Harvard toughs. At a subsequent rally, protected by four squad cars of police armed with tear gas grenades, Sullivan called on the youths of North Cambridge to "gather their shillelaghs."

Alarmed at the high tax rate and evidence of fraud in the mayoral race, the voters adopted Plan E by a healthy margin in 1940. Among the first victims were O'Neill and Diehl. The new city manager, a businessman named John B. Atkinson, viewed the presence of two legislators in the treasurer's office with the same lack of enthusiasm that Dean Moynihan had shown at the BC law school. As one of his first acts of office, Atkinson sacked them. It was a bitter blow to the handicapped Diehl, who needed the job and had even voted for Plan E in the legislature. When an angry O'Neill stormed into City Hall to voice his outrage, the police were summoned, though no violence was reported. A few months later, his foes leaked an audit to the Boston newspapers that accused O'Neill of mishandling funds during his two and a half years on the job. He demanded a copy and discovered that, while processing some $15 million in tax payments during his tenure, he had over-credited two taxpayers, for a total of $51.76.[16]

The city manager cut the tax rate and improved city services. But Plan E voting proved to be a logistical nightmare, requiring three-foot ballots, weeks of counting and 140 tellers. The Cambridge City Council was a bigger joke than ever, deadlocked for 308 ballots before Lynch was made mayor in 1946 and for the 1321 ballots — and five months — it took to name Mike Neville mayor in 1948. Nevertheless, having "saved" City Hall, the reformers — gathered under the banner of the Cambridge Civic Association — turned their attention to the school committee, whose Irish American members hired and promoted administrators, teachers and coaches with an eye toward ethnic heritage and political pedigree. The CCA launched its attack in 1945, demanding the resignation of school superintendent John Tobin.

Tobin was a Boston College graduate, and would have a long and distinguished career as an educator. But he had won the superintendent's job because he was the son of Daniel Tobin, the head of the national teamsters' union and an ally of FDR's. The President had personally interceded, offering plum jobs to members of the school committee to guarantee young Tobin's appointment. It was the kind of political deal that drove Goo-Goos round the bend, and they were determined to dump Tobin and wrest control of the schools from the Irish hacks. The Irish American community needed a champion to combat the Brattle Street forces.

"I got a telephone call from Monsignor Blunt," O'Neill recalled. "I wasn't interested in it. Jerry Sullivan wasn't interested in it. But here is the strength of the clergy in those days. Blunt said, 'I will go to the altar and from the altar say that I have asked one of you fellows to run and you have refused.' So that is how I got on the school committee."

The CCA had its own champion, industrialist Bradley Dewey, who owned a Cambridge chemical plant and was known in town as the "rubber czar" for his wartime production duties. Like O'Neill, Dewey had acceded to the requests of his community and agreed to serve a term on the committee. Dewey was there to get Tobin fired; O'Neill was there to save Tobin's job. And so the two went at it, hammer and tongs. O'Neill referred to the tycoon as "Mr. Big." Dewey labeled the bearlike O'Neill "Mr. Little." O'Neill said the Goo-Goos were taking kickbacks; Dewey accused the Irish of drunkenness. The school committee meetings, which previously had attracted just a few Yankee matrons, suddenly had standing-room-only crowds.

"It's not for blackguards and character assassins like O'Neill to be spouting," Dewey said.

"Why, you're the greatest character assassin here," O'Neill replied. "You're full of bigotry and bias. You're going around the city doing a job on Superintendent Tobin."

"I haven't begun yet," Dewey shot back.

The Goo-Goos pushed too hard. When the vote on Tobin's future was held on August 25, "in tropical heat before a crowded and demonstrative house," the local newspaper reported, the superintendent won a vote of confidence. O'Neill had fought the good fight for his people, and prevailed. His foes got revenge in December when, at his final school committee meeting, O'Neill cut a deal with Mayor Lynch to support each other's candidate for promotion. As agreed, O'Neill voted to make Lynch's brother-in-law, Edward J. Danehy, an assistant superintendent. But when Jed Barry's name came up for an appointment as assistant headmaster, Lynch abruptly adjourned the meeting.

"Mayor Lynch screwed him," Diehl remembered. "Lynch double-crossed him." There was nothing the raging O'Neill could do. His term on the school committee had expired. "I was glad to get the hell out of there," he said.[17]

CHAPTER 4

Crusades

O'NEILL'S FIRST TEN YEARS of service in the General Court were rewarded in January 1947, when he was elected leader of the House Democrats, defeating Representative Daniel F. Sullivan of Lowell on a 56 to 18 vote. "The guys liked Tom," Leo Diehl said. "He spent all his time — he would make the rounds. He was at the hotels where the westerners stayed; where the guys from the Cape stayed. If they had functions he would go and meet everybody." The circumstances of his childhood instilled in him a drive to succeed. He took a personal delight in the exercise of power — for its own sake and the good he could accomplish. He was a master of misdirection and blather and good cheer. Amid the intrigues of Beacon Hill, O'Neill learned to be one of the great political confidence men of his time — using his charm to lull rivals or foes until they dropped their guard.

Richard Grant, the publisher of a Beacon Hill newsletter, ultimately concluded that O'Neill and Paul Dever shared a priceless attribute: the knack of cloaking their considerable aspirations under a sheen of personality. "There was a boyishness about him that reminded me of Dever at the same stage of his career. Each concealed a resolute ambition under a cover of sociability that often belied his earnestness of purpose," Grant said. As a political operator, O'Neill met and passed the ultimate test: many a disarmed competitor was still proclaiming love for him even as he emptied their pockets.

The dispirited band of Democrats that O'Neill inherited in 1947 seemed in sorry shape. The handsome Maurice Tobin's term as Democratic governor, from 1945 through 1946, was but a momentary interruption of Republican hegemony. O'Neill had but 96 Democrats to protect and promote, 144 Republicans to fend off and a new GOP governor — Robert F. Bradford — with whom to contend. Yet in two years, at the age of thirty-seven, O'Neill would make history by being elected Speaker of the Massachusetts House. As the first Democrat and Catholic ever to claim that office, he was both instigator and beneficiary of a political revolution.[1]

From the early part of the century, the Republican Party of Massachusetts had been an engine of progressive change and a model for liberals around the nation, building mental hospitals and public health facilities and enacting minimum wage, workmen's compensation and other labor laws. But, over time, the Republican legislators were spoiled by their years in power and grew arrogant. There was division between those who wanted to co-opt the New Deal and those who believed that the party's duty was to oppose it at every turn. The Democrats, meanwhile, had been profiting from changing demographics. For decades the Catholic ethnic groups had been having more babies and watching more kinfolk arrive from foreign lands than their Yankee counterparts. The GOP managed to maintain its hold on the General Court because the Democratic votes were concentrated in a few urban areas, but then wartime and postwar prosperity gave thousands of Democratic families the means to leave their North Cambridge, South Boston or Dorchester homes for bigger houses, better schools and other suburban amenities.

Returning war veterans, starting new families and seeking to buy homes under the GI Bill, transformed the political dynamic. Nowhere was that more evident than on O'Neill's own turf, where a young navy war hero with an impressive political ancestry announced his candidacy for Congress in 1946. John F. Kennedy may have been the grandson of "Honey Fitz" and P. J. Kennedy, but his father's wealth, his Hollywood looks and Choate and Harvard education marked him as something different. "The New Generation Offers a Leader," said the ad copy in the *Cambridge Chronicle*. Catholic voters were ready for a different kind of candidate — one who symbolized their success instead of exploiting their grievances.

The Eleventh District's incumbent congressman was Curley, who had taken the seat in 1942 from former representative Thomas H. Eliot, a promising young New Deal Democrat who helped write and pass the Social Security Act. Eliot's Yankee background had left him vulnerable when redistricting handed him the North End, Charlestown, East Boston, Brighton, Cambridge and other ethnic wards. "My young opponent is a Unitarian. Do you know what a Unitarian is?" Curley asked the Catholic crowds. "A Unitarian is a person who believes that our Lord and Savior is a funny little man with a beard who runs around in his underclothes." Curley won but quickly ran into trouble. He took one kickback too many and was indicted for fraud in a defense procurement scandal in 1943. An indicted congressman had few friends, but a mayor of Boston could still line his pockets. And so, on the night he was reelected to Congress in 1944, Curley announced that he would run for mayor in the next year's election. To Joseph P. Kennedy, who was grooming his son Jack for office and on the prowl for political opportunity, it sounded like a fine idea. A deal was struck, and Kennedy money greased Curley's victorious race for mayor.

O'Neill had known Jack's older brother, Joe, who, while attending Harvard Law School, nosed around the Cambridge political scene, stopped by city hall to talk from time to time, and campaigned and won a seat as a delegate to the Democratic national convention in 1940. "The talk around was that he was being groomed," O'Neill recalled. He and Joe shared an interest in horse racing, and their paths crossed at the track, where they were guests in Boston police commissioner Joseph Timilty's box.

When Joe was killed on a daring bombing mission during the war, Jack took up the burden of his father's expectations. O'Neill's pal, Representative Charles "Chick" Artesani of Brighton, introduced Tip to Jack outside the Bellevue Hotel in early 1946. O'Neill remembered him as "an anemic-looking kid — you know, just back from the services and thin as a rail — and we couldn't conceive of him as being the candidate that he was going to be." There was, in any case, a claim on O'Neill's loyalty. His friend and ally Cambridge city councillor Mike Neville, had announced that he would run for the Eleventh

District seat. "Neville was our buddy. We absolutely went all out for him," Diehl remembered. Neville was a self-made man, the son of a blacksmith from Cork, who had worked for the phone company and gotten his law degree at night. Neville was "the political God . . . the kingpin" of Cambridge, said Joseph De Guglielmo, an independent Democrat who sided with Kennedy. "Neville knew all the means of political campaigning both fair and foul. . . . I knew I was really taking my political life in my hands." Referring to the Kennedy family's Palm Beach home, the old guard scorned "the candidate from Miami" and tried to buy him off with an offer to head Neville's congressional staff. When that didn't work, Tobin and Dever suggested that Kennedy run for lieutenant governor on a ticket topped by Tobin. But the Kennedys turned them down, and a grumpy Dever (fresh home from war and wanting to make some money) fulfilled a promise he had made to Tobin and ran for lieutenant governor himself. They both lost.

At a St. Patrick's Day party at Tom Mullen's house, O'Neill's Harvard-educated neighbor and political adviser Joseph Healey, who had broken with Neville and lined up with Kennedy, told O'Neill, "This young man is going to win this fight." O'Neill leaned across the kitchen table and responded, "You couldn't be more wrong. This young man is going to get buried." He had no idea of the political currents that Jack Kennedy would tap, or the amount of money Kennedy's father was willing to spend. Kennedy ran a district-wide race, vigorously campaigning up and down the stairways of the three-decker homes of Brighton, North Cambridge and Charlestown; criss-crossing the street to shake hands during parades, greeting the workers at factory gates and "duking the pols" (shaking hands with the politicians) at hangouts like the Bellevue. He was assisted by a Praetorian Guard of some of Boston's best political talent. Streetwise young comers like Dave Powers and Billy Sutton joined sly old hacks like Joe Kane and Patsy Mulkern and bright college graduates like Mark Dalton and Bob Griffin and Joe Healey in the cause.

Sutton's enlistment was typical. He had just collected his mustering-out money, and was walking through downtown Boston in his army uniform when Kane called him into Walton's lunchroom and said, "I want you to meet somebody."

"Jesus, Joe. I don't want to meet anybody. I haven't seen my mother in two years," said Sutton.

"Nah, come along with me," said Kane, and took Sutton over to the Bellevue, room 308, to introduce him to Kennedy. "And there's this guy: a hundred and thirty-seven pounds," Sutton remembered. "That's all he was. A hundred and thirty-seven pounds of money!"

Sutton, who had helped run two previous congressional campaigns in the district, gave up his career with the gas company and signed on for "$75 a week, and chances — as Curley used to say."

Old Joe Kennedy donated hundreds of thousands of dollars to Boston charities, financed the formation of a North End youth center and a "Joseph P. Kennedy Jr. VFW Post" and got the navy to christen a Boston-built destroyer, the USS *Joseph P. Kennedy Jr.* To dilute the votes for Boston city councillor Joseph Russo, Kane paid a young custodian — named Joseph Russo — to enter the race. The Kennedys spent between $250,000 and $500,000 on radio advertisements, flyers, phone banks, billboards, poll workers and shiny reprints of John Hersey's *Reader's Digest* story about Jack's wartime heroics as the commander of PT-109, a torpedo boat in the South Pacific.

"Hey, Jack," said Patsy Mulkern.

"What?" asked Kennedy.

"I wuz wonderin'. Are we connin' you, or are you connin' us?"

"Patsy," said the candidate, "that's the sixty-four-dollar question."[2]

KENNEDY'S "SUPPORTERS are mostly comparatively young ex-servicemen and women who constantly astonish the political leaders by the energy with which they rush around, making the campaign almost a crusade," the *Post* reported. O'Neill was caught by surprise. "Tip was one of the best three-decker pols who ever lived. No one ever counted votes better than Tip," said Dave Powers. But "Tip, like many of the pols in the district, believed you worked hard for your constituents and you were rewarded by moving up. There was a great resentment that Kennedy was coming in from outside the district and taking the frosting off the cake."

Though he faced no strong challenger, O'Neill had his own re-election campaign to tend to, and went knocking on doors himself that spring. The housewives greeted him with worried looks and asked, "Tom, are you running against Jack Kennedy?"

"No, I'm running for the state legislature. He's running for Congress in Washington."

"Oh, thanks be to God. Thanks be to God," they sighed. They had read about Kennedy's wartime heroics. And wasn't he handsome? "I thought he was running against you. Oh, isn't he a wonderful man? Isn't he wonderful?"

After a dozen of his neighbors had said much the same thing, O'Neill reached two conclusions: "Thank God I'm not running against Jack Kennedy," and "Mike didn't have a chance." While delivering some campaign printing to Neville's house, he called his pal aside. Neville told him that he had spent $18,000 of his own money and was "in debt up to my ears." O'Neill said, "Mike, don't spend another quarter. You haven't got a chance against this guy. Please, I don't want to dishearten you or anything else, but for God's sake, I'm trying to advise you as a friend. Don't put any mortgages on your home. You're in debt enough. You're going to get clobbered."

Cambridge became the battleground. The Kennedys knew that if they kept close to Neville on his own turf, they could beat him handily elsewhere. The campaign sent some of its most dedicated "band of brothers" — brother Bobby, sister Eunice, Joe Healey, John Droney, Torbert Macdonald and Lem Billings — to Cambridge to hold down Neville's lead. They hosted dozens of house parties. "If you agreed to invite a few friends to your house to meet Jack, they brought in a case of mixed booze, hired a caterer, and gave you a hundred dollars, which was supposed to pay for the cleaning woman to come to your house both before and after the party," O'Neill recalled. But no events more aptly captured the nature of Kennedy's candidacy than the reception the campaign held in the grand ballroom at Cambridge's Hotel Commander. Irish American mothers arrived with their daughters like Cinderella's stepsisters at Prince Charming's ball, to gaze into Jack's eyes and shyly exchange greetings with his genteel, white-gloved mother and Manhattanville-educated sisters. The line of more than a thousand people snaked its way outside the Commander's doors and down the sidewalk, and Joseph P. Kennedy made his only public appearance for his son. In some ways the Kennedys, so graceful and at ease with rank and privilege, so truly arrogant, were light-years beyond the middle-class Irish Americans whose hearts they captured. In other ways they were yet so close: still Paddies, a generation removed from the streets, as ruthless and grasping as Curley.

Neville fought as best he could, and O'Neill and Diehl and other loyalists turned down the requests that they join the Kennedy parade, openly or covertly. "I can remember the Healeys, who were great supporters of mine, asking me if I'd be with Kennedy." O'Neill said. "Jack Kennedy called. . . . 'Can I come out to the house to see you? . . . Would you be with me sub rosa?'" O'Neill, Dever and others stuck by Neville and slandered Kennedy as a carpetbagger, a spoiled rich kid.

"How are the boodle boys doing? Have you got any of the Kennedy money for me?" the loyalists would mutter when De Guglielmo walked by. He would hand them 2 cents and say, "Here. This will buy the whole Dever organization. That is all you're worth."

"They had six different mailings — mailings!" said O'Neill. "You never dreamed of a mailing. It was too expensive."

"Of course, Jack being sick at that time, crippled and everything else, I think that helped him a little bit," said Mulkern. "The sympathy. The women. You can't lick sympathy. And money with it. It's two bad things." Neville carried Cambridge by a little more than 1,000 votes — nowhere near enough to offset Kennedy's strength in the rest of the district. O'Neill and Healey came from the same neighborhood in Ward 11, and to O'Neill's lasting shame and JFK's vocal delight on election night, Kennedy carried the precinct. Across the district, Kennedy took more than 40 percent of the vote in an 11-candidate race and beat Neville, the runner-up, by more than 10,000 votes.[3]

THE POLITICAL TERRAIN had shifted. "It was a generation thing," Sutton said. "World War II was Kennedy's best campaign manager. Kennedy came out of the navy and everybody was a veteran." The boys home from war "felt a real bond with him," said Dalton. "I had always known Mike Neville and was very friendly with him and he had done a great deal in Cambridge politics, so it was a hard decision for me to go with John Kennedy with Mike being a candidate. My allegiance again was that bond: a young veteran returning."

O'Neill, now thirty-five, grasped the implications of the generational passage. The Eleventh District race was being replayed, in one form or another, all across America as 12 million veterans arrived home, trained to lead, matured by their wartime experiences, demanding influence and insisting on change. The ranks of State House Democrats were peppered with men of this generation. The demand for housing, schools and roads, which had been pent up during the war years, erupted as the veterans started new families. The economic and social effects of the war (and Hollywood's egalitarian portrayal of the cause) had shaken many of the old barriers of class, religion and ethnicity — even gender and race — and made the republic and the commonwealth more democratic. Irish American veterans found that a captain's bars served almost as well as an Ivy League degree as the means of entry to the ranks of corporate hierarchies.

"The new congressman had one asset which has been ignored by almost everyone, although it should be of the utmost concern to the older politicians," said the *Traveler*. "Kennedy was the only candidate with an effective personal machine and it was built overnight and it was based on voters under that age of thirty-five. The key positions in his organization were held by young men, generally fellow veterans, who were full of enthusiasm and idealism."

Expectations were soaring, and O'Neill now carried the generational banner into battle with the Republicans on Beacon Hill. He led the Democratic opposition to a Republican bailout of the corporate stockholders of the Boston Elevated Railway. He spoke out on behalf of organized labor, for tougher child labor laws and for a $200 million bond issue to fund housing for 80,000 Massachusetts veterans. "It is appalling when you consider that 50,000 families of Massachusetts veterans are now living under substandard conditions," he told a radio audience. "The state must act." GOP Speaker Frederick Willis was repeatedly forced to lock the chamber doors and order the Democrats to their seats. On at least one occasion, O'Neill charged the rostrum and he and Willis jawed with each other, face to face, over the Republican tactics.

But if O'Neill could dish out the partisan rhetoric — "There is a campaign of hate going on against Democrats," he told the State House press corps — he strove to maintain a cordial after-hours relationship with Governor Bradford. He had not been the Democratic leader for long when Bradford called him in on a matter of some delicacy. Inevitably, it concerned Curley. Though he had won the 1945 mayoral race, Curley felt the doors of prison closing in, and decided he needed an ace in the hole: a governor who would protect his interests. So Curley had carved up Tobin in the 1946 campaign, and earned Bradford's gratitude. Convicted of fraud, his appeals exhausted, Curley was on his way to prison when Bradford summoned O'Neill in June 1947.

The governor needed O'Neill's blessing on a deal in which Curley would retain his salary and the right to resume office at the end of his jail term. In the meantime, city clerk John Hynes would fill in as temporary mayor. O'Neill had had his run-ins with Curley, but generally admired him. During his early years in the legislature, he had joined Curley on the temporary stages and flatbed trucks, sharing the great man's crowds at the streetcorner rallies in Cambridge. Curley had been kind enough to pass on some pointers on public speaking. "You stank," he told O'Neill after one appearance. He summoned O'Neill to the mansion, where he played recordings of his best speeches. "People love it when you quote poetry, especially when you do it off the top of your head," Curley said. Pulling Shakespeare, Kipling and other volumes from his bookshelves, Curley ordered O'Neill to commit ten selections to memory. O'Neill's favorite was a bit of doggerel by a yellow journalist, extolling the virtues of friendship, called "Around the Corner," which he took to reciting at reunions of his Barry's Corner gang.

And so O'Neill agreed to Bradford's request, spoke to Hynes and briefed his fellow Democrats. The legislation appointing the city clerk zipped through the State House in 90 minutes. "The Republican Party leadership in this state has degenerated into a hypocritical lot of psalm-singing masters, who preach honest, sound government and, when the time for action arrives, work hand in hand with gangsters and others who have pillaged my city," sputtered city councillor Perlie Dyar Chase, a Back Bay Republican. "They stooped to a new low in dealing so agreeably with the most corrupt political machine in the country."

Hynes served capably and politely relinquished the mayor's office once John McCormack persuaded President Harry Truman to grant Curley, who had spent five months in federal prison, a pardon. But then Curley, his head turned by the carnival-like atmosphere that greeted his return from jail, publicly insulted Hynes. "I have accomplished more in one day than has been done in the five months of my absence," Curley told the press. Hynes was furious and avenged his tarnished honor by opposing Curley in the next election. Like Kennedy, Hynes targeted his campaign at Boston's veterans and appealed to Irish Americans' sense of pride. Indeed, it was Kennedy — alone among the Democrats in the Massachusetts delegation to Congress — who had declined to sign McCormack's letter seeking a pardon for Curley. The freshman congressman was hailed for his courage and independence, and many in Boston took Kennedy's stand as further proof of changing times.[4]

On no good terms with the Kennedys and having made enemies of Tobin and Hynes, Curley now went out of his way to insult the President who had freed him from prison and to alienate O'Neill and the

Democrats who had shepherded Bradford's deal through the House. In doing so, he inadvertently triggered a series of events that would make Tip O'Neill the state's first Democratic Speaker.

Curley was sore at Truman for waiting five months to issue a pardon. He returned from prison at Thanksgiving 1947 and — on his first day back in office — declined the opportunity to endorse the President's reelection campaign. Before the winter snows had melted, Curley was publicly promoting General Douglas MacArthur as the Democratic nominee. But to be truly meddlesome, Curley needed control of the Massachusetts delegation to the 1948 national convention. He plotted to seize the Democratic State Committee and pack the official delegate slate with his cronies. "It matters that we have harmony," Curley told reporters, "even if we have to fight for it." Secretary of State Frederic Cook, a Republican, could not pass up the opportunity to sow dissension among his foes and quickly certified Curley's slate. Jammed with the mayor's henchmen, the slate left a host of Democratic officials without a ticket to Philadelphia. The Democratic members of the Massachusetts House, from whose ranks only O'Neill was chosen, were particularly irate.

"Listen, [there's a] lot of bullshit out in the corridor about the way I'm leading the party. Now say it to my face," O'Neill would tell his troops at their Monday morning caucus. Now they gave him an earful. "That Curley, that jailbird son of a bitch, who does he think he is?" said Representative John Asiaf of Brockton. The "Young Turks" voted to demand more seats at the convention, and dispatched O'Neill to City Hall. "You're lucky to be a delegate yourself," Curley told O'Neill, refusing to negotiate.

In a "knock-down, drag-out fight" at the Bellevue on February 18, the state's Democratic chieftains met, shoved and shouted, stamped their feet and maligned each other's ancestry. "Rep. O'Neill, time after time, pleaded for harmony," the *Globe* reported, and order had to be restored by the police. The state committee appealed to the courts, but the judge ruled in Curley's favor. "I could not see," the mayor told the press, "how a capable and intelligent judge could do otherwise." The Democrats ultimately abandoned hope of submitting one authorized slate of delegates to the voters for pro forma ratification. There was going to be a contested election. O'Neill's Democrats caucused and assembled a slate. The state committee had a slate. Curley went forward with his slate of delegates, topped by McCormack, who hoped to go to the convention as a favorite-son candidate for the vice presidential nomination. Curley tried to buy off the State House reps with offers of patronage and favors. O'Neill and his boys were in too deep, and hung tough. "All right, you fat son of a bitch," Curley told him. "I'm going to give you the lesson of your life. . . . I'm putting Shag Taylor on there and Frank Goon and I'll lick you with a nigger and a Chinaman."

The months of jockeying boiled down to an intense, four-week campaign in April between the O'Neill and Curley-McCormack slates. Like Kennedy and Hynes, the Young Turks targeted their appeal toward veterans and other members of the World War II generation. "The Democratic Party will have no future until the bosses have had their past," O'Neill said. "There are thousands of voters now registered as Republican who would change to independents or perhaps Democrats if Curley were eliminated for good."

The well-funded Curley-McCormack campaign put ads on the radio and sent out more than 130,000 letters to Democrats around the state. In Boston, the ballot was printed with a huge blank space between the Curley slate, atop the list, and the O'Neill slate below it — so that it looked as if the Curley and McCormack delegates were running unopposed. But the state reps worked their hometowns feverishly as O'Neill "carried out his promise to produce daily rallies on Scollay Square, and drew a sizable crowd for the last rally," the *Globe* reported. He had been shoved into the fight by his troops, but once in, he waged war with a vengeance. From a third-floor window overlooking the square, O'Neill used an amplifier and microphone to harangue Curley and McCormack. "Mr. Curley has long since read himself out of the Democratic Party," O'Neill said. He spoke darkly of the "unholy alliance" between Curley and Bradford. He deplored the Curley-McCormack slate as bosses "who want to live like Hindu princes."

On Election Day, April 27, the O'Neill slate performed well in the hinterlands but fared poorly in Boston. O'Neill later insisted that Curley had stolen the election by having his henchmen transpose the figures of the Boston returns. Stolen or not, it was not in the party's interest for O'Neill and his fellow representatives to prolong the Democratic bleeding by contesting the results. They accepted defeat. When Truman was nominated, the party found a way for O'Neill to attend the Philadelphia convention, and the entire episode would likely have been forgotten but for what followed.

McCormack had been impressed by the spirit of O'Neill's boys, their toughness under pressure and the judgment they displayed when not demanding a recount. He summoned O'Neill to his office and, noting how the Democrats had grown stronger in the suburban and small-town districts that the party had always conceded to the Republicans, asked: "Have you ever given any thought to making the State House Democratic?"

O'Neill always credited Tom Mullen — his Barry's Corner pal and legislative assistant — with persuading him that McCormack wasn't "a crazy old goat." O'Neill dismissed the congressman's suggestion, but Mullen was intrigued. He pulled out the district-by-district results from Tobin's 1944 and 1946 gubernatorial campaigns and, after carefully studying his maps and charts, concluded that the Democrats were now competitive in a majority of the state's 240 legislative districts. Mullen went to his boss, who was always good with numbers, and spread his charts across the desk. "When I considered the problem through Tom Mullen's eyes, McCormack's idea seemed to be worth a try," O'Neill said.[5]

It was said by his contemporaries that O'Neill had great timing. But timing, in politics, is a mix of many things. It is part luck, for the stars must be aligned. It is hard work and preparation, for the secret of success is to seize the moment when luck comes calling. It is the courage to risk much, or all, when the chance does arise. And it is intuition, the gift of perceiving opportunity before it is apparent to other men and women. O'Neill showed all these qualities in 1948.

It didn't look so good at the start: the GOP advantage in the Massachusetts House was a whopping 144 to 96. To take control of the House, the Democrats would need a net shift of twenty-five seats — not an impossible goal in a 240-member body, but so difficult that it would occur only two times in the century. Nor did 1948, as it began, look like an especially promising year for the Democratic Party. The Republicans had swept the off-year elections in 1946. Voters seemed tired after sixteen years of the New Deal, and the party had splintered on both the right — O'Neill had joined the booing when South Carolina governor Strom Thurmond led the racist Dixiecrats out of the Philadelphia convention that summer — and left, where former vice president Henry Wallace topped the pinkish Progressive Party. The Democrats, moreover, were broke. Throughout the spring and into summer, the Truman campaign had the feel of a funeral.

Mullen and McCormack, however, had ignited O'Neill's competitive zeal, and Truman's rip-roaring acceptance speech in Philadelphia gave him heart. "After going in there with your tail between your legs, you left thinking we had a chance," he remembered. Gathering strategists like Mike Neville and Chick Artesani and Representative James Burke around him, he launched the pursuit of his audacious goal. They tapped Kennedy, Curley, Dever, Tobin and McCormack for money and, with their own fund-raising, assembled a $25,000 war chest. They centralized their operation in Boston, conducting research on Republican lawmakers, printing generic leaflets and placing advertisements in newspapers around the state. O'Neill was then working at an advertising firm, selling space to political clients, and had broadened his knowledge of mass-media appeals.

O'Neill and his advisers traveled the commonwealth recruiting candidates. They would pull into town, ask local Democrats for the names of war heroes, veterans or young lawyers who might profit from the publicity a campaign would generate, then meet with them and make an appeal. In western Massachusetts, the Democrats got a crop of fine candidates when layoffs in the Veterans Administration office in Springfield left Maurice Donahue, John F. Thompson and three other veterans without a job. They all signed up to run for the State House. (Donahue would go on to serve as president of the state Senate and Thompson as Speaker of the Massachusetts House, where he became known as "the Iron Duke."[6]) Dever, meanwhile, was building an imposing statewide organization for his gubernatorial contest against Bradford, with 2,000 volunteers. At Dever's invitation, O'Neill's twenty-six neophytes gathered in Boston for a seminar on politics at the Parker House, got a pep talk, and were supplied with the voting records of their Republican opponents, with a focus on the economic matters that weighed on the voters' minds. O'Neill led the drafting of the state party platform that year and made sure those issues were atop the list.[7]

More stars fell into alignment. Defying the Catholic Church, a group of modern-minded activists led by the Massachusetts Planned Parenthood League advanced the sensible proposition that doctors should be allowed to provide advice on contraception to married women whose lives or health would be endangered by childbirth. The bill had the support of MIT President Karl Compton, 1,300 doctors, 700 Protestant and Jewish clergymen, the Massachusetts Council of Churches and at least 80,000 residents of the state, who signed petitions that brought the issue before the legislature. The birth control bill put the Republican leadership in a terrible bind, as it cleaved the electorate along religious lines and aroused Catholic passions. Massachusetts politics was, at the time, quite susceptible to theocratic intervention, especially when it came to lifting restraints on women. In 1942 Cardinal O'Connell had hired Frederick W. Mansfield, a former mayor of Boston, to run the church's campaign and defeat a ballot question that would permit the use of birth control. The cardinal liked to warn women that their place was in the home and that they should not allow "pagan ideas" to influence them otherwise. "It just doesn't seem normal" for women to serve in business or politics "where a man should be," O'Connell said. The church had killed child labor laws and measures that let married women serve as teachers. It was not until 1950 that women could serve on juries in Massachusetts.

Hearings on the birth control bill were held at the State House in the spring of 1948, and O'Neill leaped into the midst of the controversy. He and other Democratic legislators applauded when spokesmen for the archdiocese denounced the bill as "ethically unsound and socially ill-advised" and an insult to the state's Catholics, for whom artificial forms of birth control were considered a mortal sin. Largely because of the church's clout, contraception had been banned in Massachusetts under a section of the law entitled "Crimes Against Chastity, Morality, Decency and Good Order."

Pregnancy was a "physically normal state," the Catholic legislators argued, and they labeled the proposal a ploy to free women to pursue such idle goals as "careers, cocktail parties and bridge games." The Knights of Columbus and the League of Catholic Women announced their opposition. O'Neill fought the bill in committee, blasted Planned Parenthood and led the Democrats in voting against the legislation, which died by a 130 to 84 vote in the House.[8] The birth control proponents were not to be dissuaded and placed the measure on the November ballot. The Republicans then walked into another ambush when O'Neill's Democrats pushed bills on behalf of organized labor to okay the union shop, require secret ballots in union elections and make it easier for workers to strike in Massachusetts. The party of business had no choice but to kill such legislation, and the Democrats and their union allies gathered enough signatures to place these measures on the ballot as well. By the time the General Court adjourned in June, there were four inflammatory issues on the ballot, all of which would mobilize the Democratic base of organized labor and ethnic Catholics.

THOUGH FEW SAID so at the time, the Republicans were now in dire trouble. High turnout was their mortal enemy. As a rough rule of thumb, the GOP did well when the statewide vote was kept below 1,700,000 votes. Democrats, conversely, won big once the turnout topped 1,850,000. If the vote passed the 2 million mark, Democratic strength grew like compound interest, and the party picked up four out of every additional five votes cast. The GOP, soundly worried in a state where three out of every five voters was Catholic, declined to go on record on the birth control question at their state convention in September. The Democrats, recognizing a good thing, voted to oppose the birth control measure and to support the union questions. Any doubts about Catholic militancy were answered in early October, when 80,000 Catholic youths paraded in Boston; a million of the faithful lined the streets to watch, and scores knelt to kiss the ring of the new archbishop, Richard Cushing. Ten days later, Cushing gave a glowing tribute to McCormack and other Democratic leaders at a huge dinner in downtown Boston. "Human life was never held in greater contempt than it is now," Cushing said. He blamed "the birth-controllers, the abortionists and the mercy-killers." On the following Sunday, priests and pastors took to the pulpit in Catholic churches around the state to urge their flocks to vote no on birth control. Curley chimed in, labeling the measure "a blow against chastity, morality and decency." Republican attorney general Clarence Barnes, sensing a tide, broke with his party, denounced the birth control question and began reminding voters that he had nine children.

Truman, meanwhile, was barnstorming the country by train, pausing at every whistle-stop to give the Republicans and their "do-nothing Congress" hell. The public ate it up. A September poll by the *Globe* had shown GOP candidate Thomas Dewey leading Truman by a 50 to 41 percent margin in the state, with Bradford ahead of Dever by 55 to 38 percent. But by late October Truman and Dever had cut the leads of their Republican opponents to six percentage points. "Truman Here in Fighting Mood," the *Globe* announced on October 27, and though the pundits continued to speculate on the makeup of President Dewey's cabinet, 250,000 Democrats came out to welcome Harry to the city. With Tobin, Curley, Dever and McCormack by his side, Truman — always a clothes horse, now dressed in a dapper black topcoat — called upon Cushing at the archbishop's residence. In later years, O'Neill said he sensed the Democratic surge and began to lay bets that Truman would win. But the conventional wisdom of the Boston and Washington press corps was irrefragable that year. Dewey and Bradford would cruise to victory, "few upsets are expected" in the legislature and the only real question was whether the Republican landslide in the Electoral College would be matched in the popular vote, the *Globe* reported.

Election Day was clear and dry — Democratic weather — and the evening newspapers reported "Voting in Bay State Very Heavy." To the consternation of the state's Republicans, thousands of voters waited in line for as long as three hours to cast their ballots. In some Boston precincts the turnout was 99 percent. Across the state, 2,155,000 people went to the polls. The results were stunning. First the Wednesday morning papers carried the news of Dever's victory; he had beaten Bradford by 390,000 votes. Then the afternoon editions hit the streets, with the headlines "Truman Wins!" The President had reaped the largest vote of any Democratic presidential candidate, ever, in Massachusetts and beaten Dewey by 240,000 votes. And then "EXTRA! Democrats May Win Legislature," screamed the headlines in the Evening *Globe*. The Republicans had been tarred as the anti-union, pro–birth control party — and O'Neill's band of neophytes had cashed in on the Catholic, labor and veterans' votes. The unions had spent $150,000 getting their members to the polls and defeated the anti-labor questions across the state. The birth control question was defeated by 2 to 1 margins in Boston, and by 200,000 votes statewide. In the Boston suburbs, a Republican-sponsored MTA rate hike proved highly unpopular. In Medford, three incumbent Republican representatives were defeated by Democratic challengers. The Democrats swept the legislative races in Waltham for the first time in two decades, and in Quincy for the first time in fifty-nine years. The Democratic victory was so complete that old Fred Cook, who had served as secretary of state for twenty-eight years and tormented the Democrats in the delegate fight the previous spring, lost to unknown Edward J. Cronin, a thirty-six-year-old unemployed World War II veteran who had never run for statewide office, conducted his campaigning by public transportation and lived with his widowed mother, who was his only campaign worker. "Plans? Haven't a one," he told reporters. "It hit me so sudden I haven't thought of anything yet."[9]

O'Neill, Millie and Lamkin had stopped at the Bellevue tap and walked through Newspaper Row on election night to watch the returns. At about 2 A.M., they had returned to Cambridge and gone to bed without knowing the outcome of the Truman-Dewey race, or the legislative results from the far-flung districts of the state. At 5 A.M. Wednesday, the phone rang. It was Neville. "Are you listening to the radio?" he asked. "You better get up my friend, because I think we're actually going to win the legislature! And if it's a close vote, you know they'll try to steal it on us."

O'Neill had two goals as he hurriedly got dressed that day: to secure the overall Democratic victory and to clinch his own election as Speaker. From his office in the State House, he worked the telephones, dispatching flying squads of Democratic lawyers and legislators to the places around the state where the voting was close and the Republicans were demanding recounts. The Democrats kept the count honest, and even picked up seats on recounts of their own, including one in Everett, where a six-term Republican veteran was defeated by four votes. O'Neill also tended his own interests. After hanging up with Neville, he phoned his Middlesex seatmate Jerry Sullivan. "Jerry, Paul Dever has been elected governor and he's bringing a Democratic House in with him. I want you to nominate me for Speaker," O'Neill said. Methodically, he worked his way through the list of Democratic representatives, parlaying their requests for committee assignments, prime office space and other plums and asking — in the Massachusetts way — for written pledges of support. He was assisted by his brother, Bill, Leo Diehl, Tom Mullen, Chick Artesani, Mike Neville and others.

The new freshmen representatives were a particular focus of O'Neill's attention. In Springfield, Maurice Donahue got a call from Eddie Boland, who had left the legislature and won election as register of deeds, an influential post in local politics. Boland invited him to a breakfast, where Donahue found that all the Democrats from the central and western reaches of the state had gathered to meet with O'Neill. "Boland gave me a pledge card and asked me to sign it. I really didn't know much about that, but I knew that Eddie Boland wouldn't give me a bum steer," said Donahue. Representative Paul McCarthy of Somerville floated his name as an alternative, but was persuaded to abandon the attempt. O'Neill announced on November 15 that he had enough pledges to guarantee his election. Boland ran into his sheepish pal on December 1st, when the House sergeant at arms, in silk hat and frock coat, was leading the Speaker-designee on the traditional two-man parade through the State House to present him with the keys to the Speaker's office.

"Police got you so soon, Tip? Don't worry. I'll walk the last mile with you," Boland said. Inside the Speaker's suite, Boland muttered: "The bastards: they've even got gold leaf in the ceiling. No wonder they never let us in."

O'Neill was not quite out of the woods. He was still but the Speaker-designee. At the start of the campaign he had selected some forty "safe" Republican districts as the battlegrounds for his effort to seize the House. The Democrats won half of them, and when combined with the Democratic gains over the proposed MTA fare hikes in the Boston suburbs,[10] O'Neill's party had scored a net gain of twenty-six seats. The margin was so close — 122 Democrats to 118 Republicans — that if the Republicans could persuade three Democrats to vote with them, they could maintain their control of the House and boot O'Neill from his new office suite. There was precedent for such a plot: in 1910, when the Democrats had come within eight seats of electing a Speaker, wily Martin Lomasney had wooed a group of disgruntled Republicans, putting the outcome in doubt until his GOP foes rallied to defeat him.

O'Neill moved to soothe Republican fears that he would be a vindictive leader: though Speaker Willis was retiring from elected office, O'Neill awarded him the well-paying job of House counsel. O'Neill also gave the Republican leaders roomy offices — far nicer and more comfortable space than the tiled old wire service room on the fourth floor that they had assigned him as minority leader. Yet a heavy snow on the day of the balloting spooked him. "It was a snowy, stinking day and he only had a three-vote margin and we were really filled with dread," Diehl recalled. McCarthy had been hospitalized and wouldn't be there to vote. Another representative was singing at a funeral Mass in Lynn. "They vote once and it's over. There is no reconsideration," said Healey, who was on hand that morning. "And there was some real question as to whether everybody was going to be there. And between the time that Tip arrived at his office and the time he left to go in the chamber, he was very concerned. There was a very, very nervous time."

Word swept the State House that Democrats could earn $5,000 for blaming the storm and staying home, or $10,000 if they voted for a Republican Speaker. To counter the threat, O'Neill lined up a half dozen Republicans who, for the price of a judgeship or a cushy state job, would vote for him.

"They were losing the speakership for the first time in history. They were offering $5,000 for walks and $10,000 for votes," O'Neill recalled. "We had eight guys we figured were going to walk on us. The governor called each and every one of them in. We laid it out on them: by Jesus, we weren't going to stand for it.

"And don't think we weren't operating in the same manner, because we were," O'Neill said. The Republicans whose loyalty he had purchased "were going to be heads of departments or they were going to be judges" in return for their treachery.

"That's how it was until the very end. And you should have seen it: we had our guys locked up waiting for their eight, to make sure, because we were going to win it by one vote, regardless of what happened," O'Neill said. If all else failed, O'Neill had a final, secret card to play. Representative Francis "Lindy" Lindstrom, a Republican from Cambridge, promised to vote last — and to switch to O'Neill if necessary. In the end, all the machinations canceled themselves out. The Republicans conducted a final head count and acknowledged defeat. And on January 5, 1949, O'Neill was elected the first Democratic Speaker of the Massachusetts House of Representatives, on a party-line vote.[11]

CHAPTER 5

The Baby New Deal

ONE MONTH PAST his thirty-seventh birthday, O'Neill became the second-youngest Speaker ever to serve the commonwealth. The wooden carving of the sacred cod that had hung in the chamber for two centuries was dusted, and the stained-glass skylight with the names of all the counties was cleaned for the inaugural activities. In preparation for Dever's swearing-in, which would take place the following day, floodlights and camera platforms were installed for a novel innovation: television. O'Neill's formal remarks were brief. "This is the first time in the history of the Commonwealth that the Democratic Party has assumed the responsibility of leadership of this House," said the bow-tied Speaker, whose girth was tucked into a double-breasted suit for the occasion. "The Republican Party is now cast in the role of the loyal opposition. For both sides it will mean adjustment in thinking and in attitudes. I am confidently certain that we of the majority party will carry our new responsibility well, and extend to our Republican colleagues the same courtesy and consideration which they extended to us over the past years." A double-edged statement, that.

The new Speaker introduced Millie and the children, who had come to work with him on a streetcar that morning to make sure they made it through the storm — "That's my daddy!" sang out two-year-old Susan — and his father, who was seated with the family in the gallery. A few days earlier, O'Neill had awarded his dad the honorary duty of serving as an elector for the official tabulation of the state's Electoral College votes. It had been a treat for the old bricklayer: getting decked out in formal wear with a rose in his lapel, participating in the historic ceremony, casting his vote for Harry Truman and then lunching on shrimp and steak with Dever and McCormack and Honey Fitz — who had enriched the festivities by singing, not his trademark "Sweet Adeline," but rather "Gathering the Myrtle with Mary."

Dever was sworn in the next day, as Bradford handed over the various ceremonial insignia of the Massachusetts governor — Indian arrowheads, the Ben Butler Bible and a gavel made of wood from Old Ironsides — and took the traditional lonely walk down the steps of the State House to Beacon Street where, symbolically and literally, he rejoined the citizenry. The inaugural was marked by two memorable events; one of the giant, heavy television cameras crashed through its scaffold, narrowly missing the legislators seated in the last row, and men and women joined each other in the gallery, shattering a custom of gendered segregation. Dever was a chuckling, roly-poly lawyer who grew up without a father, worked nights in a rubber factory to finance his education and then represented the Third Middlesex in the legislature for three terms before being elected attorney general, the youngest in the state's history. He had bucked Curley and exposed corruption but lost the governor's race to Leverett Saltonstall on his first try — by 5,000 votes — before serving three years in the navy. At the podium, Dever outlined an ambitious agenda, which included a graduated income tax, compulsory health insurance, $200 million for new highways and no MTA fare hike. It was time for a change, Dever said, in ringing Rooseveltian themes that helped earn his administration a nickname, the Baby New Deal. "A little more than a half-century ago the prevailing concept of government differed little from that which we had obtained from our earliest days as a political entity. The power of the state was to be invoked when the public safety was endangered. Its proper use was in the suppression of crime; in the redress of a limited number of civil wrongs; in the preservation of property rights and in the strict enforcement of contractual obligations," Dever said. "We have lived to see the day when that concept of the state's proper function has been drastically altered." O'Neill, dressed like the others in a formal cutaway, looked on approvingly from a seat behind him.

Dever suggested that the state's $200 million budget should be hiked in the coming years by from 25 to 50 percent to pay for his new programs. It would not be easy. For premonitions of disaster, O'Neill needed to look only as far as the state Senate, which had been split down the middle — 20 Republicans and 20 Democrats — in the November election, and would be paralyzed by ugly wrangling. With lobbyists from the insurance, transportation, utilities and racetrack industries taking sides and twisting arms, it would take 114 roll call votes and four weeks before the parties agreed to have a Democrat lead the Senate in 1949 and a Republican in 1950.[1]

The Speaker of the House was a deity on Beacon Hill, with the power to set the legislative schedule, admit bills to the House floor, recognize legislators during debate and control the committee assignments of both Republican and Democratic representatives. He could appoint court officers, hire cashiers at the state's racetracks, put friends on state road crews — even reinstate suspended drivers' licenses. Though seemingly at ease in the job, O'Neill harbored private doubts. As the House convened he confessed to House clerk Lawrence R. Grove that he had misgivings about his ability to hold the Democratic majority in line. The veteran clerk looked at O'Neill and told him: "The Speaker *is* the power. Up there on that rostrum, *you* are the authority."

O'Neill worked hard and acquired the necessary stature. Because it was the right thing to do, and because he judged that his narrow majority demanded such tactics, he was a just and fair presiding officer, and even the Republican leaders were impressed. During his first weeks in office, O'Neill faced a constant series of challenges and tests from both Democratic opportunists and Republicans probing for weakness. Liberals pressed him on ideological issues, and the hard men of both parties about patronage. The state public works czar, William Callahan, one of the most powerful men in the commonwealth, summoned O'Neill to his office for a discussion. O'Neill sent back word that Speakers were not supplicants; if Callahan wanted to talk he should ask for an appointment to call upon the Speaker. And then, in late April, after a ruling he issued during a divisive debate was challenged by a

Republican foe, O'Neill put down the gavel and took to the floor to defend his authority.

It was a tense, and risky, assertion of power. The bill at hand called for construction of a "Charles River Speedway," as headline writers called the proposal for an esplanade highway that succeeding generations would know as Storrow Drive. There was neighborhood resistance, and the good mothers of the Back Bay had paraded at the State House with their perambulators in protest. "Mr. and Mrs. Storrow would turn over in their graves if they knew their gift to the people was being turned into a high-speed highway where children will be killed," said Back Bay representative Gordon D. Boynton.

His foes had charged O'Neill with using "steamroller tactics" after he locked the House chamber doors to assure a quorum and, in the course of a contentious five-hour session, pushed the bill through all three required readings by momentarily adjourning and declaring new legislative "days." He knew he had ruled fairly, and well within precedent, and was calling on the House to affirm his legitimacy: in effect, staging a vote of confidence. The response of his colleagues would go a long way toward determining whether this young man could govern them for the next two years, for should he fail he would be permanently scarred. His foes blinked. Republican leader Charles Gibbons, of Stoneham, asked for the floor and spoke in support of O'Neill. Taking his cue, the Republican member who had challenged the ruling withdrew his objection. The crisis passed. O'Neill was a Speaker.

GROVE WORRIED THAT, after so many years of Republican rule, O'Neill would succumb to the temptation to retaliate with partisan rulings and other shenanigans. But after watching O'Neill's performance over time, Grove confessed to the Speaker that he had misjudged him. "I couldn't do anything like that," O'Neill replied. "When I look in that . . . book and see all those rulings made over the years by the great Speakers of the past, I think of how it would look to have a bad one in there with my name in capital letters beside it." Indeed, O'Neill had taken up the gavel with an unshakable resolve not to tarnish his good name and reputation. He was a fine Irish boy in a tough job, forced to steer an honest course through the tangle of partisan demands, philosophical differences, power plays, scheming and corruption that was Beacon Hill. It was not an easy task, for he had to swim in — and rule — the same waters as the lobbyists, hacks and coin boys. The ethical lines he drew then would serve him throughout his life. His enthusiasm for the legal perks and plums of governing — the pay raises, honorariums, patronage appointments, free meals, trips and deals he would make on behalf of his contributors and constituents — would, in a later and more moralistic era, seem like the tip of an iceberg. But in fact they were the entire berg. He would trade favors, phone a judge, shave corners, bend the law and twist arms without rival — but this was a politician who was as determined to preserve from disgrace the good name of his family, his party and his Irish American heritage as he was to succeed. His upbringing, his makeup and his pride kept him honest. He absolutely abhorred shame.

"I was the first Democrat. The first of my faith. The day I took the oath of office I said to myself that the only thing I wanted to do was walk out the door of the State House when I left this office knowing I had been true to my God, true to my family, true to my country and to my state . . . to be blessed by God to leave a good heritage to my family, without a mark on the family name," he recalled.

O'Neill saw himself as Dever's lieutenant, whose job it was to implement policies chosen by the governor and the party. Indeed, he kept a copy of the Democratic state platform in his desk drawer. His foes called him a "bucko mate on a slave ship" for his trouble. He and the governor were immediately confronted by a transportation crisis. Road construction had virtually come to a halt in the Depression and war years, and Dever had proposed an ambitious $200 million two-year building program as a down payment on the $750 million worth of highways that were needed. Not all the improvements were popular, but Dever used the radio to deliver a "fireside chat" on taxes, MTA fares and transportation, and with O'Neill's muscle — and the kind of tactics he used during the Storrow Drive debate — the roads bill passed the House.[2]

Dever's road program, administered by Callahan, would transform Boston and Massachusetts. In addition to the funds for Storrow Drive, the plan included money for a "circumferential highway" of Boston — Route 128 — and a "central artery" through downtown Boston. There was money for a "mid-Cape highway" — Route 6 — and planning funds for a "Massachusetts Turnpike" to traverse the state from Boston to the New York border. The new road network served as the scaffolding for today's modern state, and the development that followed construction of these highways set housing, employment and vacation patterns for generations.

The other great accomplishment of O'Neill's tenure was the improvement of the state's tottering mental health system. Like its aging roads, the Massachusetts public health network, especially its mental hospitals, had deteriorated during the Depression and the war. There were riding stables, cocktail parties and other luxuries for administrators, while the wards were left in filthy disrepair. Services given to patients by the "Mental Disease Department," as it was known, were sapped by graft. In 1938, Commissioner David L. Williams had been assaulted on his own front steps, and his skull fractured, when he declined to steer contracts to a politically well connected food supplier who had been suspended for chiseling the system.

Dever and O'Neill received a sixty-page report from Mental Health Department commissioner Clifton Perkins, who warned them of a simmering crisis and said it would take $43 million, a huge sum in those days, to address the system's failings. O'Neill lobbied legislators and instructed State House reporters on the issue, explaining how the state's mental hospitals had from 25 to 40 percent more patients than they were designed for, and how one of every four jobs in the system was vacant because of poor pay and working conditions. Some 1,800 children needing treatment were on waiting lists. Typically, his commitment was based on personal experience as well as good policy. Sometime in 1948 "a fellow came to my house who wanted to get a Mongoloid [Down's syndrome] child into a hospital. I didn't even know what a Mongoloid child was — even though Millie and I were married and blessed with a couple of children. In those days they hid the Mongoloid child. I couldn't believe that God could ever give somebody such a child. I don't want you to think I was naive, but I had never seen one as bad as this. They used to keep that child in the kitchen, so no one knew," he recalled.

With the help of two legislative aides, O'Neill drove the child to a state mental facility in Belmont, where he was told that there were 3,600 applicants on a waiting list, and that they could not accept another patient, even from the Speaker of the House. So, admitting years later that it was a shabby thing to do, he simply walked out — leaving the child in a waiting room — and called from a telephone down the street to say, "The child is in your hospital. Find a bed."

The story did not end there. One of the teachers at the state facility, an Irish American woman, phoned O'Neill and challenged him. If he was such a big shot, she said, why didn't he come out and see how the commonwealth was treating its sick and vulnerable. He did so, and that is what led him to tell Dever, "Paul, you can't believe it. . . ."

"It's a pretty barbaric situation," O'Neill told reporters, and he vowed that "this legislature is going to do more for the mental hospitals than has been done in the state in the last 20 years." The Democrats pushed through a pay raise for mental health employees and redoubled the state's efforts to fill the vacant positions. Dever asked for $16 million to fund new construction — the highest one-year capital outlay in the state's history — and for a legislative commission to investigate conditions at the hospitals, especially those that served children. A new children's hospital with 1,500 beds was planned for Taunton. Dever became "a tireless advocate to improve the lot of retarded children," Eddie Boland recalled.

"I always figured there was a place in heaven for me, when the Good Lord opens the book . . . that will offset the black marks," O'Neill said. "For this was something in my life I accomplished without any fanfare, or publicity or headlines — because you never get headlines for things like that."[3]

The Catholic Church remained an imposing presence on Beacon Hill, and O'Neill's willingness to do the church's bidding placed him in favor with Archbishop Cushing. After the legislature had approved a bill to let newly married teachers retain their jobs, O'Neill got a phone call from the archdiocese. "The church was opposed to that," he recalled, "because a girl that got married and continued to teach would practice birth control." He walked out on the floor and took Charlie Gibbons aside. "I've had a call. The archbishop is opposed to this bill and we are going to kill it," O'Neill told the Republican leader. Hearing of Cushing's intervention, Gibbons promised that he and his troops would take a walk. They did, and the measure was called up, reconsidered and buried.[4]

The real battle of the session, however, took place over taxes and spending. The Republicans refused to consider Dever's proposal for a graduated income tax and, lacking the Democratic votes to muscle it through, Dever responded by proposing hikes in liquor, gambling, business, gasoline and other nuisance taxes. Remembering the populist revolt at the ballot box the previous November, Dever fought all year to keep the MTA fare at 10 cents and, in an act of both political necessity and environmental foresight, proposed that a share of the state gas tax be devoted to mass transit. But the Massachusetts Federation of Taxpayers Associations, the latest incarnation of the Goo-Goo spirit, opposed the plan, the state courts ruled against it and the House bowed to the utility and small-business lobbies. There was a $23 million shortfall in Dever's budget in mid-May. "We will get that $23 million somewhere or it will be a warm summer here," O'Neill said.

It was a warm summer; the hottest on record. Despite the 97-degree days in July, O'Neill soldiered on, refusing to become the first House Speaker to remove his coat in the chamber. Through the "sweltering, humid, at times distressing" heat he worked to keep his troops in line, locking the doors to maintain quorums and Democratic majorities, splintering a gavel on one occasion and earning a nickname from the State House press corps: the Schoolmaster. "Speaker O'Neill is ruling the House like an old-time schoolmaster," the *Springfield Union* reported. "His methods haven't been evident in the House since the days of John C. Hull. The difference is that Speaker Hull was grim and serious and brooked no rough-and-tumble tactics or horseplay humor. Speaker O'Neill has a very redeeming factor in his makeup. He possesses a good sense of humor.

"One day this week he kept them locked in until 7:23 P.M. without anything to eat except what they could get at the House candy counter," the *Union* said. "There were rumblings of discontent, but the Speaker didn't seem a bit perturbed. He continued to demand, and receive, order."

"You see this gavel?" O'Neill asked one representative he suspected of shady dealings. "If you ever louse up this House again while I'm Speaker, I'm going to break this thing right over your head." Carrots and sticks. "If you had ten people working for the state and you went off a bill, you'd be called in on a Thursday and told that your men were going to be laid off. Or if you had five guys working on the state or out cleaning the beaches in Dorchester, then they got assigned out to Salisbury, where they had to travel forty miles or something like that," O'Neill said. On one occasion, he chased Somerville representative Joseph Leahy into a men's room, where the representative tried to duck a vote by perching on a toilet. "I know you're in there, Joe," O'Neill said, and waited the culprit out. The Speaker also scored points with his colleagues by blocking an investigation of the venerable Massachusetts practice in which local insurance agents (like O'Neill and many others in the legislature) were paid commissions for insuring public housing and highway projects.

For hours, O'Neill would usher bills through with the chant of an auctioneer. His majority was so tight that he had to worry when the Ways and Means Committee began meeting all day to weigh Dever's fiscal fixes. If the Democrats on the committee were absent from the floor, the House Republicans had a temporary majority and might suddenly demand a vote. But if the representatives stayed on the House floor, the Ways and Means Republicans could claim a majority, and frustrate the Democrats there. Some of Dever's key proposals were defeated in the House, revived on a vote to reconsider, and then passed or defeated again as the size of the Democratic majority on the floor ebbed and flowed. Finally, O'Neill locked the doors and kept the House in session all of one steaming July night, ramming through a $20 million tax package that included a surtax on personal and corporate income, and tax hikes on insurance companies, banks, racing, cigarettes and alcoholic beverages.

The workmen's compensation plan died, as did Dever's proposal for a graduated income tax. But in the end, Dever got a record $229 million budget, his road projects, aid to veterans, increased spending for social services and hundreds of new patronage jobs with which to reward his Democrats. The MTA fares were hiked to 15 cents, but only in the outlying (Republican) zones. The minimum wage was raised, as were old-age-assistance payments and legislative and state employee salaries. When the General Court "prorogued" on September 1, O'Neill's first session as Speaker "went into history as the longest, the most costly, and perhaps the most ambitious in the field of public improvements," the *Globe* said, and he had "distinguished himself" as a presiding officer in the passage of a record 810 new laws. Republican leader Gibbons was not so kind, declaiming against the "padded estimates, guesswork plans, pork barrel jobs, socialistic guinea pigs and other staggering Dever extravaganzas."

Columnist William Mullins, writing in the Republican-leaning *Herald,* called it "the worst legislature in the history of the Commonwealth. It squandered funds recklessly. It created needless jobs. It was utterly without conscience. It voted to increase its own wages at a time when a substantial part of the membership had deserted . . . and went on vacation though they were being paid to attend." But he admitted that "the consensus of the press gallery is that O'Neill has done an excellent job in presiding over the House his first year" and predicted that the Speaker would soon be "running for governor."[5]

O'Neill survived because he was so personable. Even the *Herald* admitted that "Speaker O'Neill would rate near the top in any newspapermen's popularity poll. He's never formal. He's just one of the boys. If a reporter is fair in reporting the facts that's all O'Neill cares about. He'll go out of his way to brief the news-seeker on the political facts of life. Sometimes he even puts himself on a spot trying to be a good fellow."

Though he had made friends with a few reporters during his tenure as minority leader, O'Neill's performance as Speaker brought him the first sustained attention from the State House press corps and the rowdy Boston newspapers. A *Globe* profile portrayed O'Neill as a congenial and considerate fellow, trying to squeeze a family of five into the rented downstairs half of the two-family home on Norris Street. A separate story on "dark-haired, dark-eyed" Millie called her "the only girl he ever loved" and quoted her as saying, "You can't say I am responsible for his success. All I do is see that he has his meals on time and keep track of the telephone calls for him when he's away."

The Speaker's job helped alleviate the financial pinch of his growing family. O'Neill's $2,750 legislative salary was doubled by his Speaker's pay and supplemented by the $1,000 pay raise the legislature adopted. His State House pals — old friends and opportunistic new ones — threw "times" for O'Neill in Cambridge in May and in the Copley Plaza downtown in June, at which he was given a piano and the gold-plated keys to a new Packard with sparkling whitewall tires and shiny chrome trim.

"There is a unanimity of belief that we have a Speaker who is dignified without being pompous, a presiding officer who is firm without being tyrannical, who is keenly intelligent without being pretentious in the demonstration of knowledge, a leader who is a great Democrat, but who shuns the wiles of the demagogue," Dever said at the Cambridge fete. "He has been unselfish in his untiring efforts to protect the governor from embarrassment. He has been indefatigable in his labor to make this administration a truly great one. I personally am indebted to him in a measure far beyond my ability to repay."

"I am delighted at the anticipation . . . that in the years not too great in number he, too, will be governor of the Commonwealth," Dever said at the Copley Plaza. "Dever Extols Speaker as Future Governor," the *Post* reported.

O'Neill didn't forget his old friends and neighbors. Jerry Sullivan had been promised a judgeship by Dever, but the governor reneged when the opening occurred on Nantucket, the preserve of a few influential Yankee families. Sullivan griped to O'Neill, who called a recess, left the rostrum and stormed into the governor's office. "Dever wanted to name somebody else, from the island," Sullivan recalled. "But the next day I was appointed. Hardly anyone in Nantucket would speak to me for the first four or five years."

O'Neill's stature on Beacon Hill gave a boost to his insurance business as well, augmenting the cold calls he would make to the newlywed couples whose names he copied down from the marriage notices in the newspaper or the church bulletin. With a full-time partner in the business, O'Neill's income rose to $25,000 and then $40,000 a year. His family became the first in the neighborhood to have a television.[6] He made a lifelong friend in state senator Silvio Conte, a Republican from the far-off Berkshires. Together, they attended an annual insurance convention in New York with other legislators who sold insurance or sat on the committees that regulated the industry. "We used to get a suite at the Lexington Hotel on 42nd Street," Conte remembered. "We'd go to the convention awhile, maybe catch a play and go out to eat" at the Grotta Azzurra in Little Italy, where O'Neill loved the lobster fra diavolo. Then back to the Lexington. "We'd get the bathtub full of beer, take off our shirts and break out the cards. Usually wound up playing all night long and all the way home on the train," said Conte. "What the hell? We were young."

Election-year scheming tainted the 1950 session from the start. In January, O'Neill had a run-in with East Boston city councillor James S. "Take a Buck" Coffey when General MacArthur called from Japan and asked the Speaker to welcome a delegation of Japanese legislators to the State House. Coffey had banned them from City Hall because, the councillor said, they were spies intent on stealing America's atomic secrets. (Coffey had earned his nickname in 1947 when in the course of a council debate he declared: "I'll take a buck, and who the hell doesn't know it? I am probably the only one who has guts enough to say I will take a buck. I would like to see the guy who doesn't take a buck."[7])

The Senate was now under Republican leadership, and partisan squabbling pushed prorogation into mid-August. Dever and his Democrats did win approval of civil rights legislation, more money for roads and a constitutional amendment to bring about a graduated income tax — which was submitted to the voters for ratification. Along the way, however, the Democrats had begun to acquire a reputation as free-spending, undisciplined souls, most interested in padding their own salaries and pensions.

In the fall election, the Democrats continued to hone their organizational skills: there were sixty-four Republican candidates who had faced no opposition in 1948, but only six in 1950. "The Committee to Retain a Democratic Legislature and Congress" was established and raised some $25,000, with headquarters in the Bellevue and a focus on lunch-bucket issues. But this time the state GOP was not taken by surprise, and the outbreak of the Korean war, the onset of McCarthyism and a sluggish economy sapped Democratic strength. Dever was reelected, but his margin was cut in half; the state Senate went Republican and the House races were tight across the state. O'Neill himself showed up to supervise recounts in Athol, Royalston, Nahant, Revere, Sherborn, Everett, and Cambridge. The final margin — 124 Democrats and 116 Republicans — was about as close as in 1948.[8]

Back in his district, O'Neill had reached rapprochement with the Kennedys. The young congressman was quite popular, and made a point of cultivating O'Neill. "I never was aware there was any antagonism. I think there was respect. You know, Tip had a mercurial rise. He was a significant and serious figure," Ted Kennedy recalled. O'Neill, moreover, was on friendly terms with streetwise Kennedy aides like Sutton, Powers and Healey. O'Neill had turned the Cambridge K of C into something of a power base, and was a frequent figure at its amateur theatricals and card tables (where he occasionally stopped by with the family pooch for a couple of quick hands, having told Millie he was walking the dog), and so was master of ceremonies on the night of its fiftieth anniversary dinner, when Joseph Kennedy thanked Cambridge for its kindness to his boys Jack and Joe, and broke down weeping at the memory of his lost son.

Kennedy was preparing for a statewide race and spent the years between 1946 and 1952 making public appearances in Lowell, Fall River, Springfield and scores of other cities and towns. O'Neill recognized that the Eleventh District congressional seat would soon be open. Though Millie chafed at the notion of her husband serving in Washington, O'Neill was intrigued by the idea of putting his legislative skills to the test in Congress, and his other option — a statewide race for lieutenant governor — was blocked when the Democratic incumbent announced for reelection.[9]

In February of 1951, Kennedy had dinner with O'Neill and Tom Mullen at Healey's home in Belmont. The four talked about the upcoming election, and Kennedy told the others he would not be a candidate for reelection to Congress and thought O'Neill should run. O'Neill came away from the dinner convinced that Kennedy would challenge Senator Henry Cabot Lodge, and grateful for the head start the congressman had given him.[10] O'Neill resolved to run for the Eleventh District seat. He would serve three terms in Washington, he decided, and return to Massachusetts and run for governor in 1958, an off-year election in which Kennedy would be running for reelection.

The package of tax hikes that Dever and O'Neill pushed through the House in 1949 had to be renewed by the 1951–52 session of the legislature, with its Republican Senate. The voters had also approved a ballot question calling for an increase in old-age-assistance payments. The total increase in revenue needed to balance the state's budget: a staggering $75 to $90 million. The Democrats would need "iron discipline," O'Neill said. When the 157th session of the General Court convened in January 1951, O'Neill made an example of Fall River's Francis Oliveira, a Democratic rep who had voted against Dever's program more than fifty times in the preceding session. Oliveira was allowed to retain the chairmanship of the Public Health Committee, but was stripped of a much-prized seat on the Power and Light Committee. As in 1949, O'Neill took no chances on his own election as Speaker: when one Democratic representative slipped on the ice, breaking ribs and suffering other painful injuries in the days before the election, an ambulance was hired to drive him to Boston so he could vote.[11]

Confronted by the need for massive tax hikes, the legislators blanched, dissembled and stalled. Much of the summer of 1951 was consumed by a contretemps over charges that Attorney General Francis Kelly had taken a $2,000 bribe. The O'Neill-led Rules Committee, conducting the investigation behind closed doors, leaked information that helped Kelly survive the storm. Tempers flared like the August heat; old Paul McCarthy collapsed on the House floor while defending Kelly and was taken to the hospital. O'Neill was repudiated, 175 to 48, when he opposed a Republican proposal to turn the case over to the Massachusetts Bar Association. Giving up the gavel, angry and playing the ethnic card, he took to the floor and predicted that the Brahmin bar would "get some dirty, disgruntled, knee-bending, social-climbing Irishman to come in and do their dirty work." No charges were filed against Kelly, but "the obvious anxiety of Mr. Kelly and Democratic leaders like Governor Dever and Speaker O'Neill to cover up inevitably intensifies the suspicion . . . that much remains undisclosed," said the *Berkshire Eagle*.[12]

The session dragged on. On October 7, one newspaper reported, "Members of the House of Representatives, almost to a man, deserted the House chamber yesterday to watch the World Series game on television, raising the ire of Speaker O'Neill and ignoring a bill to raise pay of state employees $360 a year. O'Neill sent a master-at-arms to the lobby to snap off the TV set just as Joe DiMaggio hit a home run, and round up the members for voting. Grumbling, they filed in and the doors were locked to keep them in." The lawmakers met until November, and even then O'Neill had to turn back the clock on the final night to pass the last few measures. "I conceive it to be not only my privilege but my duty to use every parliamentary stratagem in the book," he said. More than $89 million in higher income, gasoline, capital gains and nuisance taxes was adopted. The annual cost of the state government had risen from $63 per person to $107 per person in just three years.

IN THE SPRING of 1952, after O'Neill locked the chamber's doors once again, threatening to expel any legislator caught voting for an absent colleague, the House extended Dever's income tax hike. The gas tax was raised as well as the lawmakers rushed to adjourn before the national conventions in July. With a final, all-night marathon session that ended at 7:39 A.M., the General Court concluded O'Neill's second term as Speaker on July 5. It was an "irresponsible, disorganized and exhausted legislative rabble" that had conducted "chaotic sessions unequaled in Massachusetts history," said Norman MacDonald, the head of the state taxpayers' association. O'Neill — who was focusing on his campaign for Congress — contemptuously dismissed the critique as "Mr. MacDonald's annual blast at the legislature." In a speech to Boston businessmen, O'Neill said he had "never seen bills more carefully scrutinized at every state than during this session." He was blithely underestimating the amount of mischief that MacDonald could make.[13]

CHAPTER 6

LoPresti

O'NEILL ANNOUNCED his candidacy for Congress in mid-April 1952. His most formidable opponent was state senator Michael LoPresti of East Boston, a relentless campaigner who had familial roots in the North End, East Boston and East Cambridge, and whose senatorial district made up a large chunk of the Eleventh Congressional District. LoPresti was a self-made man who had worked days and gotten his high school degree at night. He knew the territory well, having served as the top aide to a congressman who represented Charlestown and other parts of the district before it was reapportioned in the 1940s. He announced in mid-May, after Dever unsuccessfully tried to clear the field for O'Neill by offering LoPresti the state treasurer's job.

Besides O'Neill and LoPresti, there were five other candidates on the ballot. Edmund J. Casey, with so fine an Irish name, was O'Neill's biggest worry. Some O'Neill supporters suspected that LoPresti had placed Casey, an electronics technician, in the race to split the Irish vote, and O'Neill repeated the charge for years. Not so, said Leo Diehl: "I knew Casey. He was just a fluke — mad about Communism or something." It was Diehl who admitted, years later, to putting a ringer on the ballot — an Italian named Christopher Carolina — to draw votes from LoPresti.[1] A candidate who might have killed O'Neill's hopes, an opportunistic nobody with the same name as John F. Kennedy, was persuaded to abandon the race.

O'Neill sought every edge. When he heard that a young lawyer named John F. Reardon was weighing a campaign for the General Court, O'Neill could not resist the temptation to finagle. Representative John J. Toomey, a longtime friend and colleague, faced no serious opposition, and O'Neill figured that a good fight at the bottom of the ballot would boost interest and turnout in the Irish American wards, and so help him against LoPresti.

"You know," O'Neill told Reardon, "you ought to run against Toomey. I'll give you a couple hundred bucks. I'm a friend of Toomey's, but you know, Toomey's sitting on his ass, doing nothing. Get out there and make the old guy work. It'll do him good. Do good for the party, too. You're going to get clients out of this." It worked better than O'Neill expected. Reardon, to everyone's surprise, ran a fine, energetic race, finishing just 500 votes behind the anxious and frantically campaigning Toomey, who nursed his fury at O'Neill to his death.[2]

There were few issues in the 1952 campaign. It was remembered instead as the first great tribal war between the Irish, who had ruled the Massachusetts Democratic Party for almost a century, and the Italians who hoped to supplant them. The map of the Eleventh District told the story of that ethnic conflict: how Irish tenements in the North End, East Boston and East Cambridge had been taken over by a later wave of Italian immigrants as the "shanty" Irish, through hard work, became the "lace curtain" Gaels of Boston's nicer neighborhoods and suburbs. In the North End, the Italians had begun to outnumber the Irish around 1910, and the neighborhood was 95 percent Italian by the time of the Depression. Lomasney, Curley and other Democratic bosses had wooed the Italians and other "newer races" as soldiers in their wars against the Yankees, but in the streets there were still beatings and fights between Irish and Italian gangs. In newly respectable Irish American households, the contempt for the "Guineas," many of whom came from peasant stock and could not read or write (and so reminded the Irish of their own too-recent past) was palpable. The Irish American politicians gave up power reluctantly, exploiting rivalries between the proud Genoans who had been among the first to arrive in America and the Neapolitan and Sicilian families who came later. It was not until 1932 that Joseph Langone Jr. was elected to the state Senate in the district that LoPresti later represented. By 1952 the Italians were ready to step up. In raw numbers, they just about equaled the Irish in the Eleventh District, and recognized no Gaelic right of political inheritance. With Kennedy gone, they wanted the seat.

"Unity. I was with Mike because he was Italian," said Tony Marmo, a member of a Democratic organization in East Boston. "We campaigned the old-fashioned method. Knocked on doors. Went to the different society meetings. There were societies from every Italian town. Mike was a Sicilian. I'm a Neapolitan. And then we had the northern Italians — they didn't invite us to their meetings. But Mike was a popular guy. We went into the election. Mike gave it hell. We gave it hell. Everybody did a hell of a job."

"You had all the elderly Italian people out there, working for Mike, fighting hard," said Mario Umana, a former state senator and judge. "You had cars picking people up for the polls. Cars with loudspeakers."

"It was the days before television," said LoPresti's son Michael, who himself would serve in the state Senate. "You had signs, stickers, brochures, parties, ads in the newspapers — sailor caps. The Sunday morning clubs and the societies. You would have a rally in the North End and get three hundred people; today you would be lucky to get thirty."[3]

Both sides set out to organize their turf. The O'Neill organization, run by Tom Mullen and Tip's brother, Bill, was headquartered in a former produce shop at 173 Milk Street in Boston. From there, and from various storefront operations in the district's distinct neighborhoods of Brighton, Somerville, Cambridge, East Boston and Charlestown, a constant litany of phone calls was made to check and double-check the voting lists. The names of definite (red) and likely (blue) supporters were color-coded, and cross-indexed with the list of people who needed rides to the polls or babysitters or other assistance on Election Day. Friendly cobblers let O'Neill's troops put his leaflets in finished pairs of shoes. Firemen and other public employees pitched in, donating an automobile with a full tank of gas for a day of canvassing. Sympathetic policemen made sure that parked cars were cleared from around the polling places and campaign headquarters. The candidate's sister, Mary, and groups of her fellow teachers took turns on the phone banks, and ancient Tom O'Neill was in and out of his son's headquarters, offering assistance and advice and calling one last time on old friends for help. Diehl was in charge of fund-raising and political intelligence, working the lobbies of the Parker House and other downtown haunts on his crutches. The campaign did a mailing, requesting contributions from O'Neill's classmates at Boston College, and received a phenomenal response: $10,000. The McGarry family, BC acquaintances who owned a tavern in the district, were asked if the O'Neill campaign might put up a sign; they agreed (thinking they'd get a small placard for a window) and found their establishment bearing an O'Neill billboard.[4]

There were formalized betrayals on both sides of the ethnic divide. Diehl picked up the disheartening news that the Tobin organization, including Charlestown's inestimable William "Mother" Galvin, was coming out for LoPresti. Diehl decided to hide the news from the candidate, who by then was campaigning in a paroxysm of energy, hitting every tavern, VFW hall, local radio show and Holy Name Society in the district. Chester Dolan, the Democratic leader of the state Senate, also crossed into the Italian camp in support of his fellow senator.

O'Neill countered with Chick Artesani, who had a large Italian following in Allston and Brighton, and Donato and Blandina Rufo, who were formidable figures in Brighton. "Donato was a paver: curbstones and sidewalks," said Frederick Salvucci, whose family came from the same Italian village as the Rufos. "Somewhere along the line he and Tip became good friends. They went to the races together, played cards, told later how Tip had even babysat their kids. And Blandina was always a very active lady in Italian charities. When Tip ran for Congress, they were with him."[5] Charlie McGlue, an old Curley hand, offered advice that proved invaluable. Since neither O'Neill nor Kennedy had faced a tough race since 1946, many Democrats had allowed their registrations to lapse, McGlue said. Don't limit your organizing to the voting lists of Democrats, he told O'Neill, target the independents and unregistered voters as well. The campaign launched a special effort, with letters and phone calls, to remind such voters that, as in 1946, the Democratic primary would decide the election.

Dever secretly helped O'Neill but tried to retain the appearance of neutrality because he would need the help of LoPresti's organization in the November showdown with Christian Herter, the Republican gubernatorial candidate. With the popular Dwight Eisenhower heading the Republican ticket, and a Red scare gripping the nation, the Democrats were increasingly worried. Nor would Kennedy take sides in the contest to succeed him, though he passed on one bit of advice to O'Neill, including the warning to not waste time in the Italian wards. It was advice O'Neill insisted on ignoring, convinced he could make friends anywhere. He spent $10,000 on pizza parties and rallies in the Italian wards, but was still booed off a stage when he tried to make a speech in East Boston. He didn't return for three years.

Joseph Kennedy saw the race through the clear eyes of his family's interests. His son's campaign against Henry Cabot Lodge was turning into a classic ethnic tiff of its own, and its Irish versus Yankee overtones, and young Jack's popularity with his own, guaranteed an Irish American turnout in November whether or not O'Neill prevailed. The turnout of Boston's Italian Democrats, however, was suspect unless LoPresti won: if their champion were to lose a bitter, ethnic contest with O'Neill, the Italian voters might sit on their hands or vote Republican in the fall.

"I was driving Joe Kennedy. He used to spend the early part of the week in Boston, and he used to quiz me on the politics," Bob Griffin, an old Kennedy hand, recalled. "He used to ask me about the LoPresti fight, and I kept telling him that I thought O'Neill was going to win. And his reaction was, 'That doesn't help us. We need LoPresti on the ticket.' He wanted to make sure the Italians voted for Jack against Lodge. Joe Kennedy was only interested in winning, and I'm guessing he was putting money into LoPresti's campaign."[6]

Elbows were thrown and eyes gouged on the fringes of the race. Italians who supported O'Neill and Irishmen for LoPresti were likely to be shunned or intimidated or shoved around on the street. Tires were slashed and signs torn down. After a threatening individual showed up at O'Neill's back door carrying a handgun, the campaign's records were moved into brother Bill's garage where, it was felt, they would be less susceptible to a break-in or a firebomb. "Jesus, that was a hell of a fight," Cambridge representative Walter Sullivan recalled. "It was vicious. They were going at it hammer and tongs. Passing out stuff on each other."

The Barry's Corner gang were still around and helping O'Neill — Lenny Lamkin and the Barry men, Red Fitzgerald and others. Red O'Connell, by now a well-known gambler and owner of a string of bars and restaurants, including Frank's Steak House in North Cambridge, was visited by a delegation of LoPresti's men. "The Bartolos, they were the fighters, they came to Red," O'Neill recalled. "They knew that Red was a kind of power in our town and that I'm a boyhood pal of his. And they said, 'Red, we'd like to have you be with LoPresti against Tip.'"

O'Connell told them he would as soon tear off his arms. They urged him to reconsider, claiming that LoPresti would outspend his friend. "I can always go to the bank and get $200,000 on my barrooms, just so you don't think Tip will run out of money," said O'Connell. The big redhead bought many a round of drinks in his nighttime sojourns through the district, loudly on behalf of "Tip O'Neill for Congress."[7]

WITH 54 PERCENT of the votes coming from Boston, it was destined to be a tough race from the start. But O'Neill was holding his own, or better, when the details of a deal he'd cut with Curley came to light two weeks before the primary, and the resultant storm of criticism sent him reeling. The tale dated back to 1951, when it became clear that Kennedy was leaving the Eleventh District seat, and Curley was mentioned as a candidate to succeed him. Though Curley was then seventy-seven years old, the idea was not unthinkable. It was Curley's old congressional seat, which he had abandoned just six years before. Honey Fitz, at a similar age, had run an energetic campaign for the U.S. Senate. Curley appeared in good health, had enjoyed a long trip to Europe that year and in fact would run for mayor again in 1955. Even if he didn't win, his presence on the ballot would split the Irish vote and doom O'Neill's chances.

O'Neill knew all this when Curley dropped by with a request. The legislature had approved a special bill granting a pension to Malcolm Nichols, a former Republican mayor of Boston who was down on his luck. Now Curley — having just arrived home from his European vacation, and with a summer home in Scituate — wanted a similar deal. O'Neill consented, and shepherded an arcanely worded bill through the State House that had the effect of granting Curley a $1,000-a-month pension — just about what he would have earned as a congressman. "I wrote the bill which, like the Nichols bill, carried the name of former Mayor Curley in the text. But somewhere along the way the bill was rewritten and Mayor Curley's name was taken out of it," said William D. Kenney, secretary of the Boston Retirement Board. When the bill reached the Ways and Means committee, the word was given: "The Speaker wants this." It was brought up and passed in the hectic circumstances of the session's waning days. With O'Neill giving the auctioneer's chant, the bill went through all three readings without a recorded vote. Just to be sure, "they shut off the microphones," said Walter Sullivan.

Curley soon began to refer to O'Neill as "our next congressman" and endorsed his candidacy on the radio. A pro-Curley union newspaper announced that "with the backing of that great patriot and astute campaigner, James M. Curley, as well as many other present and former political office holders, it starts to look as if our next congressman from the 11th congressional district will be no other than Thomas "Tip" O'Neill."[8] Later, O'Neill insisted that he had cleared the Curley bill with Norman MacDonald, the leader of the taxpayers' association, and that the "hoptoad" double-crossed him. If so, the bullet-headed MacDonald had lured O'Neill into a trap, or reneged after realizing the sensational opportunity he'd been given to score with the issue. MacDonald certainly had the motive to tattle: he had been fighting Curleyism since the 1930s, and Curley had once hired private detectives to investigate his private life. The greatest beneficiaries were the desperate editors of the *Boston Post,* that dying but still influential Democratic sheet, which launched a screaming crusade against legislative perks and pensions that the other Boston papers felt compelled to follow.

"Ex-Mayor Curley is Handed $12,000 Pension by Solons," the *Post*'s banner headline announced on Saturday, August 30. The story contained all the details of "the amazing bill, sped through the legislature when the members of that body were rushing to prorogue." The bill had not carried Curley's name, but had been cleverly tailored to "fit him like a glove," the *Post* reported. Legislators were "napping as the measure was passed."[9]

The *Globe, Herald* and *Traveler* scrambled to catch up, offering their own shrill, bold headlines. "Only a handful of legislators knew what this bill was designed to do. The others were kept in the dark so the legislation would be passed," MacDonald said. "We are going to find politicians who have served in the legislature during the past 50 years crawling out of the rocks to collect." Mayor John Hynes told the press that the city "will go broke" trying to satisfy such liberality. The Massachusetts Council of State, City and Municipal Employees condemned the deal. "While representatives, senators and other elected officials draw unheard-of pensions for merely sitting in the halls of the House and Senate, dozing, frolicking and tossing paper wads at each other while making a farce of law-making, career employees are required to do a full day's work at niggardly wages," said William V. Ward, president of the council. Herter, kicking off his general election campaign against Dever, challenged the governor to call a special session to repeal the law.

Dever hung tough, for about a week. "What is fair for Republican Nichols is fair for Democratic Curley," he said. But Republican and Democratic legislators alike, hounded by the press and their constituents, began to cave in, signing petitions that called for a special session. Repeal of the "Curley Pension Bill" became the state's overriding issue. "Governor Dever today presides over the dirtiest government the state has ever had," the *Herald* said. "He has made it that way. It is his standard of political integrity that has infected the Legislature." Hysteria swept Beacon Hill. The newspapers raced to track down vacationing lawmakers: the Senate president was found on the fairway at his golf club; and a GOP senator "somewhere on the high seas" on his shipboard honeymoon to Europe.

Curley, for the good of the party, agreed to fall on his sword. Charging that the bill's passage was "a Republican scheme to gain control of the legislature," he renounced the pension on September 6. But by then the game had ranged far beyond the question of the $12,000 pension. Newspaper circulation was up, and Curley's sacrifice didn't come close to satisfying the voracious press corps, which was pawing through Dever's expense accounts for evidence of $23 Parker House meals, examining the invoices for his $155 office draperies and questioning the legislators' twenty-year-old right to free parking on Beacon Hill. Dever was the next to crumble, agreeing in a televised speech on September 8 to call a special session to consider the repeal of *all* legislative pensions. "Let them call a special session," Charlie Gibbons gloated. "Before the end of this year we will wipe the Democratic Party off the face of Massachusetts."

With a week to go in their primary campaigns, LoPresti and O'Neill were called back to serve in the special session. Representative Harold Putnam, a Republican from Needham, charged that O'Neill's "steamroller tactics" were responsible for the "orgy of payroll and pension padding."

"The Curley pension bill now stands revealed as a Dever effort to give Speaker O'Neill a free ride to Congress," Putnam said. "Curley lost interest in the Kennedy seat in Congress as soon as his $1,000-a-month pension had been sneaked through the House under a phony label. The pension bill will give him the net pay of a congressman. The field-fixing strategy at the taxpayer's expense failed only when Senator LoPresti refused to be bought off by the state treasurer's post."

O'Neill evaded reporters, maneuvering as best he could to duck responsibility for his instrumental role in the Curley pension deal. He was fortunate that Herter and the GOP legislative leaders had decided to go after bigger game. They didn't care about a Democratic congressional primary; they wanted Dever's skin, and control of the General Court. "They blamed it all on Dever," Sullivan recalled. But LoPresti's supporters were determined to highlight O'Neill's role. Representative Gabriel Piemonte of the North End recounted how O'Neill had ordered him to his seat when he tried to protest the Speaker's tactics. "The bill was drafted with the help of Speaker O'Neill to keep Curley out of the race," said Senator Richard Lee of Newton. "I consider this a payoff." The House members voted 213 to 12 to abolish all legislative pensions: Curley's, their own and O'Neill's among them. The Senate followed suit, and Dever quickly signed the bill.

"Speaker Tip O'Neill of Cambridge, who presided over the House, is believed to have lost considerable ground in his bid for the seat in Congress which John F. Kennedy is relinquishing," the *Post* reported. "If O'Neill's campaign for a seat in Congress proves unsuccessful, it is very likely that his defeat will be attributable to the public wrath against the bills that were quietly steered through the body over which he presided." On almost every night in early September, Diehl and O'Neill would go down to Scollay Square to pick up the next day's edition of the *Post,* and cringe at the torrent of horrible publicity. "Curley's pension was a killer," Diehl remembered. "Jesus: the *Post* — as soon as it came off the press Tom would be down there reading it." And then, on September 10, the newspaper opened a second front.[10]

"Solon Hits Halting of Red Probe," read the front-page headline. "In a bitter denunciation of 'the innocent dupes at the State House being misled by Communist propaganda,' Rep. Edmond J. Donlan yesterday accused Speaker of the House Thomas P. O'Neill of blocking continuation of a legislative special committee's probe of Communism in Massachusetts," the *Post* reported.

Donlan was a lawyer, Georgetown University graduate and fanatical Roman Catholic from West Roxbury whose peace of mind was perpetually threatened by the continued existence of three great evils — birth control, "Moscow's agents," and taverns that served drinks to women. "The long arm of Moscow has reached into the State House and blocked any attempts to investigate the Communist Party in Massachusetts," Donlan said, fingering O'Neill as the "dupe." It was a frightening charge, as the United States was waging a bloody war in Korea and Joe McCarthy was nearing the height of his power. And there was a kernel of truth in Donlan's allegation. O'Neill had indeed pigeonholed a measure to renew the term of the "Committee to Curb Communism" — though not because the Red conspiracy had infected North Cambridge. O'Neill believed that such probes were a waste of time, a threat to civil liberty, and designed to win publicity for Red-baiting lawmakers. He had dragged his heels for months before appointing the original committee in 1950, and had no interest in seeing it revived.

O'Neill figured he could handle the pension flap. LoPresti, after all, had voted for the bill, and Curley was still a popular figure in the district. Democratic voters, and at least some journalists, had begun to sense that the hype over the pension "scandal" was a Republican campaign trick. The *Globe* gave prominent coverage when Democratic floor leader Robert Murphy, O'Neill's right-hand man, took the GOP and the press to task on September 12. "Democrats have been pilloried; journalistically mauled; verbally lynched by some of the press," Murphy said. "When it comes to poor James Michael Curley, a man 77 years old with 50 years in this business, then the guns are opened and a broadside is fired."

Of MacDonald, said Murphy: "If I did things his way I'd live in misery with myself for the rest of my life."

The *Globe* gave front-page space to Representative Adolph Johnson's speech as well. "I am convinced that our American form of government can be destroyed by slander just as easy as it can be destroyed by force," said Johnson, a Democrat from Brockton. "It is wrong to classify everybody in the legislature as a thief, a robber and a crook."

But the charge of being soft on Communism was harder to duck, especially after the LoPresti forces revived the loyalty oath flap of 1936, and O'Neill's war record, as issues. And so O'Neill called on the one man whose word was beyond reproach on the subject of Godless Communism, whose water he had carried in the legislature: Archbishop Cushing. At a Communion breakfast on the Sunday before Election Day, Cushing called for an end to the "vicious name-calling, the slanderous stories, the ungrounded judgement of the vileness of others that have come to be part of political campaigning." From more than one pulpit that Sunday a parish priest informed the faithful that Thomas P. O'Neill Jr. was a patriotic American, and no Communist dupe.[11]

On the weekend before the election, the LoPresti forces blanketed the district's Italian neighborhoods with leaflets urging voters to elect "one of your own." O'Neill retaliated by buying five minutes of live advertising time on a local TV station on election eve, in which he urged the electorate to instead cast their votes "the American way" and "not because I'm Irish, or because my wife is part French and part German" — thus trying to profit from the ethnic politics he had just deplored.

O'Neill and Diehl had scrambled to collect the $1,000 to buy the TV time, tapping their network of Red O'Connell, Tansy Norton, BC grads, tavern owners and Irish American businessmen one last time in a campaign that cost the then incredible amount of $82,000. There were no financial reporting requirements. "In those days you could use cash and everything else," Diehl recalled. "That was a lot of money. But we knew every guy who owned a bar. We knew every Irishman. And it was the Italians against the Irish."

As O'Neill was speeding from the television station to the State House — where the special session was in its final hours and he was needed in the Speaker's chair — a huge crowd had gathered on a stormy night at the Harvard Theater on Massachusetts Avenue for one final get-out-the-vote rally. LoPresti agents circled the outside of the crowd, passing out leaflets attacking O'Neill and getting into shoving matches with the Irish. Inside, Joseph Harrington delivered a stem-winding speech in O'Neill's absence. "We packed that goddamn theater," Sullivan remembered. On Election Day, exhausted, short on sleep and in a "panic," O'Neill came storming into the Cambridge headquarters to see Diehl and demand another $500 to buy the allegiance of more poll workers. Cruising through Charlestown, O'Neill had seen Tobin's brother-in-law working the polls for LoPresti and realized that Tobin and Galvin had joined the forces arrayed against him.

"He said, 'How much money have you got?' I had maybe $500 or $600, but I said, '$200,' because I knew what he was going to do and I didn't want him to waste it. 'Give it to me,' he said, and went out and spent it in Somerville. I saved the other $300," said Diehl. "The one thing I didn't want was for Tom to lose and be in debt."

O'Neill welcomed every Election Day with gloom, but was particularly downcast as he awaited the results. "He was down, down. Oh, terrible, terrible," Lamkin recalled. The candidate and his advisers were angry as well. As part of the ongoing effort to clean up Massachusetts politics, the city of Boston had spent close to a million dollars to buy mechanical voting machines, which were in place in the North End, East Boston and other city precincts. When O'Neill supporters went in to vote, they found that the election commission — led by an Italian American ally of LoPresti — had put the names of Casey and O'Neill on the same line of the ballot. It is impossible to determine how many confused voters, facing a machine for the first time, mistakenly hit the Casey switch when they meant to vote for O'Neill. But it is undeniably true that Casey exceeded all expectations in the machine precincts, and faded from view in the wards of Cambridge and Somerville, where paper ballots were still in use. O'Neill and his troops thought they were victims of a dirty political trick.[12]

It was far easier to count the votes cast on machines, and so the first returns that night were from LoPresti's strongholds in East Boston and the North End. As he arrived at the Milk Street headquarters, O'Neill saw Dolan leading a victory caravan from the North End to the LoPresti party at the Manger Hotel. Word spread through the O'Neill crowd that the *Boston American*'s early edition had proclaimed LoPresti's victory. It seemed a safe bet. In the Boston precincts of the Eleventh District, LoPresti's lead over O'Neill was 7,000 votes. "LoPresti had a marvelous lead; a marvelous lead," said Lamkin. "You should have seen the people at O'Neill headquarters. You could hear a dime drop. As though they were attending a wake."

"Tom was upset. The newspaper had printed it: 'LoPresti Wins,'" Diehl recalled. The telephone rang. It was John Harris, a friendly reporter from the *Globe*. His competition was on the streets with news of a LoPresti victory.

"Don't print it, John," said Diehl.

"Are you sure, Leo?" Harris asked.

"It's all on machines," said Diehl. "The machines came in first. We expected to get our ass peeled off there. There's no machines in Somerville or Cambridge."

At about the same time, at the Manger Hotel, the LoPresti victory party was going full blast. "I remember the feeling of jubilation," LoPresti's son Michael recalled. "And then a hush. A rumor spreading about Cambridge. . . ."

Cambridge was finally coming in. And Cambridge was coming in heavy. And Cambridge was coming in O'Neill. Somerville and Brighton as well, but not by any means like Cambridge that night — where O'Neill's margin over LoPresti was 9,000 votes. When all the votes were counted, O'Neill was announced the winner: by 3,262 votes.

"When the North End and East Boston machine-counted vote was published, that gave Senator LoPresti a 6-to-1 lead over congressman-elect O'Neill, Senator LoPresti's followers, feeling sure of victory, gathered in a Boston hotel for a victory banquet," the *East Boston Leader* reported. "The party was going full blast with everyone toasting Senator LoPresti and each other for the wonderful victory that had been won. When the banquet was at its peak stage of hilarity, the vote of the Brighton wards and Cambridge started to leak into the banquet room, and slowly but surely the big lead of LoPresti was whittled away."

At O'Neill headquarters, the mood was changing from despair to glee as "a precinct from Cambridge would come in and lower the lead, and then another Cambridge precinct would come in and lower the lead," Lamkin recalled.[13]

"While they were making merry at the hotel, I had warned Mike: 'Watch out for Cambridge,'" said Tony Marmo, who smelled a rat. The results from O'Neill's home turf were arriving too slowly — as if someone was waiting on the Boston wards to see what kind of margin they needed. With two pals, Marmo drove to nearby East Cambridge.

"Sure enough, we got in there, and it was paper ballot and, Jesus, the counters had pieces of carbon under their fingernails," Marmo said. "They would put a cross by Tip O'Neill if it was a blank, and if they had a Mike LoPresti ballot they would put a smear on it so they could throw it out. They stole the election." Marmo and his friends raised hell, and were arrested by state troopers and thrown in jail for disturbing the peace. But no formal charges were filed and they were released in the morning. "It was skullduggery. It was robbery," Marmo said.

"They filled in the blanks," LoPresti's son Michael said. In some Cambridge precincts the tellers were still counting seventeen hours later. LoPresti demanded a recount, pointing to a huge turnout of Cambridge Democrats as proof that the voting had been manipulated. "Mike called me. He said, 'You voted 110 percent!'" Diehl recalled. But O'Neill's explanation was simple: the independents had responded to his campaign pitch and come out in droves for the Democratic primary. "For a solid week we had people calling the independents telling them that they had no vote in this fight unless you vote in the primary," Diehl said. The official results showed O'Neill clobbering LoPresti in Cambridge, 13,404 to 4,528.

The raw numbers are ambiguous: when compared with the vote in other parts of the district the results do not show an excessive turnout, or a suspiciously low number of blank ballots, in Cambridge. It would have taken more than a few pencil-fingered counters making marks on paper ballots to give O'Neill a 3,000-vote victory. And even then one would have to assume that one side fought dirty and the other side was clean. In the privacy of the O'Neill home, the word from the candidate and his lieutenants was that "the cemeteries voted on both sides," O'Neill's son Tommy recalled.

One thing was certain: the news spread swiftly through the Italian American wards, and was taken as gospel, that LoPresti had been cheated — that the Irish bastards had stolen the election. LoPresti's call for a recount caused immense headaches for Dever and Kennedy. Eisenhower, Herter and Lodge were all running strong campaigns: the Democrats would need the Italian-American vote in November.

"Kennedy was on the ballot. He was fighting Lodge, and it was a Republican year with Eisenhower," said Umana, who was running for the senate seat LoPresti had forfeited to make the race for Congress. Kennedy and O'Neill "got together with Dever, and LoPresti decided not to make a stir."

"I don't know that there was a quid pro quo, but he was an incumbent senator out of a job," said LoPresti's son Michael. With Dever, Dolan and O'Neill signing off, LoPresti and his partner Morris "Lucky" Boorstein were rewarded with a plum: the restaurant and liquor concession for Logan Airport, an exclusive franchise that the family was to hold for twenty-five years. Suddenly, "Mike joined Tip

O'Neill. There was a big rally and Mike LoPresti was speaking for O'Neill. And then he becomes owner [of the restaurant] at the airport," Marmo recalled. "I was sincere. We had done a lot of hard work. But when I saw that, I went with Herter, and brought my Noddle Island political and athletic club with me." Like a considerable number of Italians, convinced that the Irish stranglehold on the Democratic Party could not be broken, Marmo became a Republican.

"I learned a lesson. And I had to take my hat off to Tip O'Neill. Boy, he did it. The gravestones voted. And I would be capable of doing it too, if I were losing," said Marmo. "In those days anything was fair, except violence, and sometimes it got to that too."[14]

PART THREE |

A Good Solid Massachusetts Demmie

CHAPTER 7

Men's Men

AFTER ALL he had done to get there, Tip O'Neill hated Congress. Or did so, at least, when he first arrived. He had made the wrenching change from presiding officer of the Massachusetts House, the admired coleader of a Democratic renaissance, to that lowliest of political creatures: a freshman congressman from a minority party. "Back here he was powerful. Had a big office. Could walk in or out of the governor's office," Diehl recalled. "Now he's a freshman and he dreaded going over to South Station and getting the eleven o'clock train to Washington. Sometimes they would drive. He and [Representatives] Phil Philbin and Jimmy Burke. It was ten to twelve hours. Jeez."

Dwight Eisenhower had whipped Adlai Stevenson and carried the Republicans to control of the Congress in 1952, and Sam Rayburn had surrendered the gavel to a Republican Speaker, Joseph Martin of Massachusetts. Back in Boston, things were, if anything, worse. The facts were inescapable: the Democrats had blown it. The voters had given them a tryout, and O'Neill and his boys had responded by playing directly into Republican hands: striving overtime to look like the free-spending, hack-ridden, high-taxing, corrupt gang of buccaneers the

Republicans said they were. Christian Herter had lashed out at "Boss Dever" and his "power-drunk mob of bush-league political commissars" and "strong-arm boys." The vaunted Dever organization had deteriorated. As Election Day neared, it was Dever who came crawling to Kennedy for organizational help, only to be rebuffed by Bobby Kennedy, the campaign manager. Kennedy won, but Dever was defeated and the Republicans took back the Massachusetts House. It was a miserable fall. When the election was over, and he had clinched his seat in Congress, O'Neill collapsed and was hospitalized with what his doctors called a pronounced case of nervous exhaustion.[1]

The $12,500 congressional salary was too small to allow the O'Neills to maintain two residences, so Millie and the five children stayed behind in the family's new home — the big house with the mansard roof at 26 Russell Street, just around the corner from the Orchard Street house in which he had grown up. He and Eddie Boland, who had also won a seat in Congress, shared a small apartment in a building owned by the electrical workers union on Massachusetts Avenue and filled the dismal place with discarded furniture. In August 1953, O'Neill's father died. The old bricklayer had been under a doctor's care all summer, suffering from heart disease. He was at home on Orchard Street, having said his rosary and watched the Red Sox game when a ruptured aorta claimed his life. More than a thousand people filled St. John's for the funeral, overflowing the church and jamming the vestibule, and a special police detail was employed to handle the traffic on Massachusetts Avenue. He was seventy-eight.[2]

O'Neill's professional life offered little relief. There was a bit of a thrill when he and the other freshman Democrats met at the White House with the outgoing President, Harry Truman, who gave them a warning about the politics of personal destruction, then gossiped about Eisenhower's rumored marital infidelity and called the vice president–elect, Richard Nixon, a "dirty, no-good sonofabitch." But "a new congressman always feels so unalterably lonely and useless," as Sam Rayburn put it. O'Neill gave his first speech on the House floor on March 5: a five-minute address on a bill he had sponsored to improve working conditions and salaries for longshoremen. With an eye toward his new constituency, he spoke out on behalf of foreign aid to Israel and Italy — and for Irish reunification. For the sugar refineries and candy manufacturers of his new district, he worked to lower the costs of sugar and peanuts. In contrast to Kennedy, who was already seeking a national audience,

O'Neill fought the St. Lawrence Seaway bill, which would boost Great Lakes shipping at the expense of the port of Boston. He spent most of his days trying to perform favors for constituents — emergency leaves for servicemen, immigration requests, a pay raise for mailmen — and coping with a massive political headache he had inherited: the Boston Naval Shipyard in Charlestown.

Eisenhower was making good on his campaign promise to settle, with a mix of nuclear threats and negotiation, the war in Korea. As the Pentagon increasingly focused on strategic nuclear weapons, the East Coast navy yards and other aging facilities were hit with round after round of layoffs. The Boston navy yard's historic "rope walk," the oldest rope-producing operation in the country, was undercut by commercial rivals, and its submarine business stolen by New Hampshire and South Carolina. During its peak years of operation in World War II, the navy yard had employed 50,000 people. That number had dropped to 13,600 when O'Neill took office, and he was in Washington but a few weeks before the shipyard unions demanded that he halt a planned layoff of 500 workers. He failed, and another 300 were laid off in May. Then another 500 were cut in September. By the end of his first term, the number of employees had slipped to 10,400.

O'Neill tried his best. At a delegation meeting in May of 1954, as Kennedy sat silently and McCormack admitted that "there isn't much hope," O'Neill blustered on. "If we didn't think that political pressure would be brought to bear we wouldn't be sitting here," he told his colleagues. "If we have to hit them over the head, I propose we hit them." But it was an irreversible holding action that would consume hours of his time and many of his political chits over the years and never satisfy everyone. His Democratic foes, already gathering for a LoPresti rematch, were quick to criticize. "I do not know who authored the vicious mimeographed communication which you directed to me. While you may not be fully aware of my activities in behalf of the workers at the Naval Shipyard, you could at least have made inquiry before adding your signature to such a shameful document," O'Neill wrote a dissatisfied constituent in March of 1954. "Insolent, intemperate, uninformed expressions accomplish nothing and do incalculable injury to the cause."[3]

O'Neill arrived in Washington at the peak of Senator Joe McCarthy's popularity. The Red scare had been sparked by the loss of China to Mao Zedong's Communist forces in 1949, and the Soviet

Union's development (with the help of a U.S. spy ring) of an atomic bomb. A series of sensational hearings by the House Un-American Activities Committee (HUAC) had given McCarthy a model. In February 1950 the Wisconsin senator announced that he had a list of dozens of Communists working for the State Department. His claims struck a popular chord and he soon added Hollywood, the nation's universities, the television networks and the rest of the Truman administration as tools of a Communist conspiracy. McCarthy was a favorite of the *Boston Post,* and hugely popular in Massachusetts. In the working-class wards of South Boston or the VFW halls of Dorchester and Somerville, the Irish Americans liked the way he terrorized the WASP establishment. Joseph Kennedy befriended "Tailgunner Joe"; Bobby Kennedy worked for his committee, and John Kennedy's decision not to join in the vote to censure McCarthy reflected a debt he owed the demagogue, who might have swung the 1952 Senate election to Lodge had he campaigned in Massachusetts for the GOP ticket.

Against this backdrop, O'Neill played a shortsighted and timid role. His handling of Donlan's "Baby McCarthy" committee in Massachusetts epitomized O'Neill's approach to Red-hunting politicians — to quietly bury through backroom maneuvers their more harmful acts and allegations. In public, however, O'Neill tolerated the inquisitions — even if he sometimes showed his skepticism with a droll approach.

While serving on a State House committee investigating subversive activities in Massachusetts in 1947, O'Neill had interrogated Daniel Boone Schirmer, the legislative agent of the Communist Party.

"Are you a Communist?" O'Neill asked.

"I am," said Schirmer.

"What is a Communist?"

"A Communist is an American citizen who believes that socialism is the only solution to our capitalistic system — common ownership of the big banks and utilities, which were built by the sweat of the people."

"Is it true that the Communist Party is anti-God, anti-religion and anti-democracy?" O'Neill asked.

"If that were so, I would not be a member of the Communist Party," said Schirmer.

"What about Russia?" O'Neill demanded.

"Conditions demanded the changes that were brought about in Russia."

"Is it true that you are descended from Daniel Boone?"

"I am a proud descendent of Daniel Boone."

"Well, I think old Daniel would be turning over in his grave if he knew you were up here representing the Communist Party," O'Neill said.

O'Neill never summoned the courage to join such gutsy New Englanders as Maine Senator Margaret Chase Smith or Boston lawyer Joseph Welch in confronting the Red-hunting scoundrels. "I've always been opposed to witchhunts, and I hated what McCarthy was doing," O'Neill wrote in his memoirs. "Unfortunately, he had a huge following in my district, especially among the Irish." At the *Post*'s invitation, O'Neill wrote a guest column in January 1954. After a long discourse on how the records of Jefferson and Jackson, Wilson and Roosevelt, reflected the Democratic Party's commitment to the workingman, O'Neill slipped in an odious paragraph of McCarthyesque rhetoric. "There is a place in the Democratic Party for true liberals," he wrote, "but there is no place in our government or in the ranks of the Democratic Party for Communists, fellow Travelers, Communist sympathizers, Wallaceites or parlor pinks."

Mindful of how Donlan's charges had hurt him in the final hours of the 1952 election, O'Neill was careful when voting. He opposed attempts to cut the HUAC budget, and continued to support its work for another fifteen years. Indeed, one of his first acts as a congressman was to insert a pro-HUAC editorial into the *Congressional Record*. He voted to outlaw the American Communist Party; to increase defense spending; to ban Red China from the United Nations; and to add the words "under God" to the Pledge of Allegiance.[4]

O'NEILL'S FIRST TERM in office was marked by two other memorable events. The first was a trip he took to Nevada to watch the top-secret explosion of a hydrogen bomb at the Yucca Flats testing grounds, about one hundred miles northwest of Las Vegas. The congressman was awed and chilled by the power of the weapon, and panic-stricken a few days later, as a band of bruises appeared around his belly. He feared the effects of radiation poison, the deadly illness on which he and the other official observers had been thoroughly briefed. A doctor assured him, however, that the injury was a legacy of an unofficial part of his mission: he had bruised himself while banging against the craps tables in Las Vegas.

The other unforgettable moment occurred on March 1, 1954, when Puerto Rican nationalists opened fire from the House gallery as the congressmen milled about the packed chamber during a vote. "The House stands recessed," Speaker Martin yelped, then ducked behind a marble pillar. Representative Percy Priest of Tennessee used his necktie as a tourniquet for the wounded representative Kenneth Roberts of Alabama, whom Eddie Boland helped carry from the chamber. Despite his years, Representative James Van Zandt of Pennsylvania, a decorated World War I veteran, rushed up to the gallery and tackled one of the assailants. Five congressmen were wounded. O'Neill had been called from the floor for an interview with the *Globe*'s John Harris when he heard what he thought was firecrackers in the chamber. After the shooting was over and the Puerto Ricans had been carted away, O'Neill discovered a bullet hole in the seat where he had been sitting. "The bullet hole was right there," Harris recalled. "He nearly fell over."

Harris was one of a small group of Bostonians who shared the barren mid-week social life of the nation's capital with the Massachusetts delegation. Like O'Neill, he was a history buff, and together they would visit Jefferson's haunts on Capitol Hill, the spot in the old House chamber where John Quincy Adams had been stricken at his desk and carried away to die, and the tunnel used by President Warren Harding for his clandestine visits with a mistress.[5]

For his first few years in Congress, O'Neill was away for weeks at a time. But as time passed, and the Congressional schedule changed, he joined the Tuesday-to-Thursday club, comprised of those East Coast and Midwestern representatives who would arrive in Washington on Tuesday and leave for home after the last vote on Thursday. "Tom would leave either Monday night or Tuesday and be back Thursday night. So it was a long weekend — not that he was home when he was home, but at least he was in the area," Millie recalled.

The travel was brutal but enhanced the feeling of camaraderie in the delegation. O'Neill got a lesson in Yankee thrift from Senator Leverett Saltonstall, who used to carry eggs from the farm to Washington and bring the eggshells back for fertilizer on the return trip. As the years passed, and Northeast Airlines scheduled a direct flight from Boston to Washington, the congressman's children fell into the familiar ritual of depositing and picking up Dad at Logan Airport. Rosemary was nine,

Thomas P. O'Neill III, called Tommy, was eight, Susan was six, Christopher, known as Kip, was three and Michael, the baby, was a year old when O'Neill arrived in Washington for his first term. "Dear Dolly: You may rest assured that the other O'Neill family in North Cambridge is just as sympathetic toward the diaper industry as you are," O'Neill wrote Dorothy O'Neill, a constituent who had written to urge him to keep down the cost of diapers. "I know what the savings would mean to a family man."

O'Neill was, by his children's account, a good father who earnestly tried to find time for them on weekends — but whose frequent absences accentuated an emotional distance that was typical of Irish American men of his generation, and was in his case reinforced by the cold and loneliness of his own childhood home. "My grandfather was very stern, and never expressed his love for his son," Tommy O'Neill recalled. "I remember him saying the rosary every night with Cushing on the radio. Stern. When my grandfather answered a question, my father would listen. It was really the only time that my father listened."

Tip's stepmother "was not a very loving person," Susan said. Her father never talked about the circumstances of his childhood, and it was left to Millie to tell the kids how their real grandmother died. "I don't think my father ever said, 'My mother died when I was a baby,'" Susan recalled. "My memory as a little child is that he was a huge, huge man who loved hugging and being around lots of people. I have often thought the reason my mother and father had so many children is that my father liked being around lots of people."

Millie counted pennies, supervised homework, made sure the children attended church, and kept her husband firmly grounded. "She would not allow him for a moment to get carried away with either himself or the superficial aspects — the fakery — of politics," Kip recalled. She was "the finest person that ever lived," Tommy said. "Loving. Forceful. Tough. Maternal. And she was really everything, you know, for four days of every week for a long, long time."

Dad was well-meaning but a bit of a klutz around the house, humming aloud and organizing games and contests but relying on a brother-in-law to fix broken lamps or assemble Christmas toys. He thoughtlessly brought home troublesome pets — baby chicks at Easter or a rambunctious black Newfoundland puppy on the day Rosemary was born — to add to Millie's burdens. In those days before air-conditioning, he would interrupt the children's sleep on hot summer nights, pack them in the car in their pajamas and drive to Nahant or Revere Beach for moonlight swimming. During the August recess, the family would go to a lakeside cabin in Jaffrey, New Hampshire — where the children watched with stunned delight as a garter snake wound its way down from a rafter and around their father's straw hat one afternoon — or to a rented summer place at Priscilla Beach, near Plymouth, where the O'Neills hosted an all-day clambake every year for their Cambridge pals.

The family might go out to dinner to a seafood restaurant on Friday nights (until the mid-1960s, Catholics were forbidden to eat meat on Fridays), if Tip and Millie were not attending a prizefight or some other sporting event. On Saturday morning, O'Neill ran errands, stopping at the delicatessen, the Chinese laundry, the Italian cobbler's, the Star Market and other establishments on what he came to call his "ethnic walk." The sidewalks and shopping aisles kept him in touch with his community, and he would return home with a scrawled list of favors that his neighbors had asked of him. O'Neill enjoyed BC and local high school sports, squeezed in a round of golf when he could and took the kids on drives to Concord and Lexington and other historic sites and to the family's favorite ice-cream stand in Arlington in the summer. He tried to preserve one weekend night to treat Millie to a dance or dinner or a night out with friends. At Christmas the family would go to see the lights and decorations at the State House and the Common. As in most Irish American homes in Cambridge, Sundays were reserved for Mass and a family dinner — with a roast or other large cut of meat, dishes of hot vegetables and baked rolls and pies or cakes for the members of the extended family in attendance.

"He had a temper, but he would have to grow to anger. He would never surprise you with his temper: you would have to get it to the boiling point," said Tommy. "He taught me how to play craps. We would go bowling, and he taught us to play pool. I always said he was as much a father to me as your father was to you, and you had yours seven days a week and I had mine three days a week."

"He was a good family man when he was there," said Kip. "He was not out running around with his cronies. He was trying to insinuate himself into the kids' schedule to the extent the kids were interested. And then when we weren't interested, we were told we were doing it whether we were interested or not.

"He used to make us lunch when he was around on school days and God forbid . . . they were terrible. Deviled ham and egg salad sandwiches that would smell up the whole classroom," Kip remembered. "And anything you said evoked a song. He would sing it to the point where it would drive everybody crazy. If you were driving with him in a car he would do nothing but sing."

Being the children of a famous man had its advantages — box seats behind the Red Sox dugout at Fenway Park and the like — and its drawbacks. The O'Neill children never forgot the mortification of being scrubbed and dandied up and plopped in the back of a convertible for the Bunker Hill Day parade, and how Charlestown's urchins pelted them with insults and debris. As they got older, they were allowed to borrow the family car to go out nights, once they overcame the embarrassment, in election years, of having the big "O'Neill for Congress" sign mounted on its roof.

The burden fell heavily on Rosemary and Tommy, as the eldest son and daughter. "The difficult thing about being the child of a person like that, is how do you measure yourself?" said Rosemary. "How could you ever hope to accomplish what he accomplished?" Both of the older children ultimately chose careers in public service. At a time when most young girls were choosing to be homemakers, Rosemary took up the challenge of the foreign service, and Tommy followed his namesake into politics. "A lot was expected of Tommy," said Susan. "And what wasn't expected by my parents he put on himself. The first few years my father was in Washington, my father was gone long periods of time, four or five weeks without coming home. He got better as the years went on. But there was a lot implied that Tommy was the oldest male, and responsible, and he assumed that role. There were expectations: it wasn't just on his own that he took that role."

Michael, the youngest child, was perhaps the most affected by his father's absences. Like Millie, he hated the phoniness of politics, and grew to resent its constant demands on their family life.[6]

O'NEILL'S 1954 CAMPAIGN for reelection was a one-on-one contest with LoPresti, after both candidates agreed to clear the field for a rematch. "We cleared our guys out and they cleared their guys out," Diehl said, ruefully recalling four decades later how O'Neill had agreed to pay one of LoPresti's Irish ringers $650 to withdraw from the ballot. The contest was as mean as in 1952. "LoPresti Exposes Do-Nothing Record of Present Congressman," read one of the challenger's campaign newspapers.

"One of his secretaries lives in New York — maybe that's why the Brooklyn Navy Yard is getting so much shipbuilding work," the LoPresti newspaper said. "During World War II, when millions of Americans were being drafted into the armed forces, Mike LoPresti with three children volunteered for service with the US Army. The present congressman used his legislative immunity to duck service."

O'Neill, however, had assiduously courted his new constituents in Somerville, Brighton, Allston and Boston. Each time his office helped an immigrant family get a visa to the United States, it was worth five or six votes — and his office staff had been performing these and other such services for two years. "He had established himself," said Mario Umana. When the results were in, O'Neill had beaten LoPresti with ease. Still, the specter of an Italian challenger haunted O'Neill for years. "Tom worries a great deal about things that never happen. He is a worrier: no doubt about it," Millie said. "I wasn't brought up that way. I refuse to say die until I'm dead. But Tom is a worrier, and a little bit of a pessimist." In 1956, his worrying put him in the hospital with an ulcer.

One of O'Neill's favorite political stories emerged from the 1954 campaign, after Curley offered to raise money for the congressman's reelection. Feeling sorry for the old legend (and still wanting to stay on Curley's good side), O'Neill allowed him to collect funds on his behalf. "I raised $500 for you," Curley told O'Neill, handing him an envelope. Later, when he counted it, the congressman discovered he'd been given just $450. The pattern continued with subsequent donations, with Curley apparently taking a 10 percent cut. When O'Neill finally asked Curley for the names of his benefactors, Curley said: "You're getting too smart. They've already been thanked."

It wasn't until after the election that a Boston businessman stopped by O'Neill's office, requesting a favor and claiming to be a contributor. O'Neill had never met him. "Jim Curley came to me and said he was raising money to put Tip O'Neill on television," the man said, and O'Neill chuckled and told him the story of the 10 percent commissions. "Now I understand why you've never heard of me," the man said, "but I remember how much money I gave Curley to pay for those ads, and let me tell you something: Jim Curley made out just fine. I'm afraid *you* were the one who was working for 10 percent."[7]

O'Neill was now forty-two and entering the political equivalent of a mid-life crisis. For the next eight years he would be torn by conflicting ambitions and responsibilities. Should he make the race for governor? Should he leave politics and take a better-paying job to be closer to his family? Or should he pattern his career on that of John McCormack and invest in Washington and the congressional seniority system? They were hard questions, and the turbulence of Massachusetts politics made them no easier to answer. The Democratic Party in the state remained split by personal, ideological and ethnic differences. There were unrepentant Curleyites, Al Smith regulars, New Deal liberals, the disintegrating Dever and rampant Kennedy organizations. "We have no party, as such. . . . We federate," said Edward McCormack, nephew of the congressman and a Massachusetts attorney general.

O'Neill's singular advantage was that he bridged many of the divisions. In 1956, Jack Kennedy and John McCormack clashed over control of the Democratic State Committee. The cause of the strife was a political debt that McCormack owed to state chairman William H. "Onions" Burke, a big, bald, sly old machine Democrat who had seized control of the committee in 1955 — threatening Kennedy's hopes to arrive at the national convention in Chicago as the head of a united delegation, the better to wangle the vice presidential nomination.

"Burke had been the Democratic chairman during the days of Roosevelt and he was known to be a strong . . . Curley man. He always resented Jack Kennedy as a young upstart," O'Neill recalled. The press framed the matter as a test of Kennedy's clout and resolve. Before he openly challenged Burke, Kennedy phoned O'Neill and asked him to mediate and persuade McCormack to dump his pal Onions. O'Neill would then serve as an interim state chair.

"On the following Monday I came back to Washington . . . and I had a telephone call that majority leader McCormack wanted to see me," O'Neill recalled. McCormack wasn't in a peacemaking mood. "He told me that . . . he hoped that I wouldn't get into the contest because of the fact that there was to be no compromise: this was a feud of long lasting and the chips were finally down and there was going to be a battle and there was going to be a war and it was going to be won by one side or the other."

O'Neill struck a pose of studied neutrality in the resulting donnybrook. Kennedy's deep pockets won out, McCormack was routed and the committee voted to dump Burke. The bad feelings between the two factions lingered for years. Kennedy "was the all-American boy. He was the war hero. He was the athlete. He was the student. He was the savant. He was the intellectual. He was all things to all men," a bitter Ed McCormack said later. "He was a bachelor, and so he was, even more importantly, all things to all women. The young girls dreamt of making love to him."

At Kennedy's request, O'Neill gave up his credentials as a convention delegate to the senator's brother Bobby, who never bothered to thank him. When Adlai Stevenson opened the choice of his running mate to the convention, Kennedy made a furiously good showing — losing only, his partisans claimed, when John McCormack got chairman Rayburn to issue a pivotal ruling in favor of the eventual vice presidential nominee, Tennessee senator Estes Kefauver. (McCormack, to his dying day, denied that it was he who slid the knife into Kennedy's back.) O'Neill missed the legendary episode. A careless painter had set fire to his Russell Street home, causing $15,000 in damage. He was forced to find temporary quarters for his now homeless family, and watched the convention from a Priscilla Beach cottage with Diehl and other friends.[8]

O'Neill had a statewide poll conducted to assay his political options in 1956, and concluded that he was not well known enough to win a gubernatorial election. Foster Furcolo, who had run three previous statewide races, was elected instead. To know and get known in the far reaches of the state, O'Neill agreed to serve as Furcolo's campaign manager when Kennedy ran for reelection in 1958. "There was terrific infighting and there was constant argument," O'Neill remembered. "Furcolo used to try to cause incitement to get Jack upset." And so O'Neill served as the go-between for the Furcolo campaign, negotiating details with Kennedy's manager and brother-in-law, Stephen Smith, constructing schedules that would keep the two Democratic candidates in opposing corners of the state on any given day. "We would send Jack Kennedy into Lowell," O'Neill said, "and Foster . . . would be in New Bedford. . . . Steve would give me the schedule ten days in advance and then I would prearrange the Furcolo schedule to make sure they'd be a hundred miles apart."

O'Neill toured western Massachusetts, the North Shore and other parts of the state, visiting with mayors, aldermen and local newspaper publishers, hosting parties for Democratic officials, further expanding his circle of contacts. On the Sunday night before the election, at a Democratic rally at Symphony Hall, O'Neill prevailed upon McCormack to go on stage and stand between the feuding Kennedy and Furcolo, like a referee at a boxing match. "And they would both be answering John [McCormack]. Neither one of them would be answering each other," O'Neill recalled.[9]

As he played in Massachusetts politics, O'Neill did not neglect his duties in Congress. He was, in the words of Boston journalist Alan Lupo, "a good, solid 1950s Massachusetts Demmie" who had wisely taken Kennedy's advice to "be nice to John McCormack." The House — with its stifling seniority system and creaky, antebellum ways — was a poor fit for impatient playboys like Kennedy. But for a raconteur like O'Neill, Kennedy told him, the place held possibilities.

McCormack's career was to be overshadowed by the two Texans for whom he served as an able captain — Speaker Sam Rayburn and President Lyndon Johnson. By the time he became Speaker, old John was so rigid, resisting internal reforms and giving blind support to the war in Vietnam, that his place in history suffered. But in his prime, McCormack was a cunning legislator and fearsome orator who helped bridge the gap between the Al Smith Democrats of the northern cities and the courthouse conservatives of the South, and so helped guide the historic legislation of the New Deal, Fair Deal and Great Society through the House. O'Neill and the other members of the Massachusetts delegation profited from McCormack's prominence. He could get them prime committee assignments, call upon generals, ambassadors or department heads on their behalf, and usher their bills through the House. In return they gave him their loyalty, and their votes with which to barter. They gathered at his table in the House restaurant each morning, sipping coffee, as a stream of important guests — former Presidents Herbert Hoover and Harry Truman, committee chairmen, the capital's top lobbyists and the influential heads of other delegations, like Ohio's Mike Kirwan or Chicago's Tom O'Brien — stopped by to pay their respects.

O'Neill, whose family was back in Cambridge, often tagged along to the after-hours receptions and dinners to which the majority leader was invited. "Who is the big Irishman with McCormack?" the courtiers asked, and O'Neill began to build his own circle of contacts among the southerners, lobbyists and bureaucrats. "At night, I would come by and he would be answering the mail, and he would ask his aide, Billie Smith, to mix us a drink," said Raytheon lobbyist Jim

Dinneen. "Before dinner we would make 'duty calls' at fund-raisers for different members, or have drinks with a lobbyist who wanted to show Tip off for fifteen minutes to somebody from back home."

Neither Boland nor O'Neill liked to cook, so they generally spent the mid-week nights with other members of the Tuesday-Thursday gang at a restaurant or private club for dinner, stopping by the Mayflower Hotel on their way home to pick up the next day's newspaper.[10] "We would eat out, usually at Duke Zeibert's, Paul Young's or Angie's Italian Garden," Boland recalled. He was the neat one; O'Neill the slob. "Eddie made orange juice every morning, squeezing the oranges himself. It was the best in the world," O'Neill remembered. "We were men's men. We loved politics, sports and card-playing, gin rummy. The only thing besides orange juice in the refrigerator was beer. Every time the Red Sox played in Baltimore, we went to see them."

O'Neill and Boland liked to haunt the racetracks, and the card tables at the University or Army-Navy Clubs, where the poker crowd was bipartisan and included such conservative icons as Vice President Nixon, Republican senator Karl Mundt of South Dakota and unreconstructed southerners like Representatives Jamie Whitten and John Bell Williams of Mississippi. Mike Kirwan was a regular at the University Club, and he and O'Neill struck up a friendship that landed the Massachusetts congressman a seat on the Democratic Congressional Campaign Committee (DCCC), which doled out campaign funds to Democratic candidates. "You would get there about 6 p.m. You would eat and sit around until 8 p.m. You would talk about legislation, you would talk about sports, you would talk about your district. At 8 p.m. you drew and had a couple of poker games," O'Neill said. If he was losing, he might play all night. Many a time he walked home through Washington's deserted streets in the early morning hours, or saw the Capitol dome at dawn.

O'Neill quickly mastered the silly political devices that would grab a newspaper reporter's attention and let the folks back home know he was on the job. When Representative Frank Chelf of Kentucky whined that the radio and television networks were bowing to pressure by civil rights groups and deleting the words "darkies" and "massa" from popular music, O'Neill huddled with the NAACP and slyly suggested that "Who Threw the Overalls in Mrs. Murphy's Chowder" should be banned as well because it was "a very insulting song to the

Irish race." For good measure, and to the dismay of his children, O'Neill said that Elvis Presley songs, with their lascivious "double meanings," should be censored too.

O'Neill unsuccessfully sought Canada's return of a brass cannon that was captured by British forces at the battle of Bunker Hill in 1775, and had since resided at the Citadel in Quebec. Boston's newspapers loved the story, and O'Neill kicked up such a fuss that the Canadian prime minister got into the act, asking the congressman to cease and desist — or have the U.S. Naval Academy turn over the British battle flags seized by American forces in the War of 1812.

O'Neill's love of history led him to happy service on the National Historic Sites Commission where, with help from McCormack and Saltonstall, he got the State House, the USS *Constitution,* the Bunker Hill Monument, the Old North Church and Paul Revere's home placed on the registry of national historic landmarks. With McCormack and Kirwan's help, O'Neill played a leading role in securing funding for the creation of the Minute Man National Historic Park in Lexington and Concord. "Dear Tom," wrote McCormack, "I suggest you be on the Floor when that item comes up . . . so if there is any effort to strike it out . . . you will step in and protect the appropriation." O'Neill had introduced the first bill authorizing the park, but deftly stepped aside when a skeptical congresswoman, Edith Nourse Rogers, in whose district the battlefields resided, changed her mind and wanted the credit.

Boland and O'Neill collaborated on another park project that succeeding generations would come to appreciate — even if their contemporaries did not. The National Park Service had surveyed the Atlantic and Gulf coasts and urged that twelve prime seashore areas be retained in their natural states as national parks. But by 1957, because of the resistance of the real estate, homebuilding and tourist industries, only North Carolina's Cape Hatteras seashore had been so designated. On a trip to the Carolinas, Boland was impressed by the Hatteras park. O'Neill, meanwhile, had vacationed on the Cape since he was a boy, and complained to his roommate how "honky-tonk" development was spoiling the landscape. In 1958, Boland and O'Neill introduced the first legislation to take a forty-mile-long strip of the Cape's Atlantic shore and preserve it as the "Cape Cod National Seashore." The bill served as the basis for three years of sometimes bitter negotiations between local, state and federal officials, and prodevelopment forces hanged O'Neill and Boland in effigy in 1958. But with help from Kirwan, Saltonstall and Kennedy, the bill was signed into law in 1961. The park will forever be, as a newspaper editorial said of Boland and O'Neill, "a monument to the men and their vision and persistence."[11]

And it was during his early years in Congress that O'Neill played a clandestine role in ensnaring the Republicans in one of the great political scandals of the era — the Sherman Adams affair — and in the process rescued another Massachusetts monument: the *Boston Globe.* O'Neill's intercession on behalf of the *Globe,* and its subsequent rise to become the state's leading newspaper, altered the course of Massachusetts politics and journalism — and gave O'Neill a powerful ally, and protective friends, in the news business back home. It was an episode he never mentioned in his memoirs, or in all his years of telling stories.

The *Globe* had been born in 1872 as a newspaper for Boston's Yankees, and sustained through its rocky early years by the fortune of Eben D. Jordan, a founder of the Jordan Marsh Company, and the talents of Charles H. Taylor, a Civil War veteran, journeyman printer and reporter. It was Taylor who, in 1878 and with the creditors at the door, transformed the *Globe* into a Democratic newspaper and directed its coverage toward the Irish American community, thus ensuring the paper's success.

In the middle of the twentieth century, however, the *Post* and the *American* challenged the *Globe*'s status as the city's foremost Democratic newspaper. Like its Irish American readers, the *Globe* had grown complacent with success, and both its coverage and its folksy "Uncle Dudley" editorials were timorous. The *Post*'s financial problems, in sharp contrast, caused its mercurial publisher, John Fox, to cast wildly for readers: exploiting the Curley pension scandal, picking Ike over Adlai, embracing Joe McCarthy and endorsing John Kennedy in 1952 after eliciting a $500,000 loan from the candidate's father.

As the *Globe* tried to hold off the *American* and the *Post,* the *Herald* was consolidating its control of the upscale end of the market, absorbing the *Traveler* and running the fusty *Transcript* out of business. The *Herald*'s publisher was Robert "Beanie" Choate, a leader in New England Republican politics, captured as the bully Amos Force in Edwin O'Connor's classic novel of Boston politics *The Last Hurrah.* When the *Post* finally died in October 1956, Choate saw his chance to become press lord of Boston. Over broiled scrod at the Somerset Club, Choate threatened to ruin John and Davis Taylor, the *Globe*'s current publishers, and crush the *Globe* unless they sold out to the *Herald*. "You fellows are stubborn. Worse than that, you're arrogant," Choate said. "I'm going to get Channel 5 and with my television revenues I'll put you out of business."[12]

THE ARRIVAL OF the television age was a once-in-a-lifetime opportunity for the Beanie Choates of the world to cash in on their political and financial connections. Appliance dealers were selling five million television sets a year; advertisers, entranced by the new medium, were bidding up the price for commercial time and the new TV broadcasting licenses became coveted plums: the Channel 5 license was then valued at $20 million. The Federal Communications Commission was charged by law to prevent the concentration of ownership in major media markets, and generally kept dominant newspapers from obtaining TV licenses. Because the *Herald* already owned the city's strongest AM and FM radio stations, an FCC hearing examiner had issued a provisional ruling in the fall of 1956 awarding the Channel 5 license to a group of investors that included Richard Maguire, a prominent Democrat. Choate, however, had close ties to the Eisenhower administration, where White House chief of staff Sherman Adams, a former governor of New Hampshire, was a close friend. In December, columnist Drew Pearson revealed that leading national Republicans were "pressuring the FCC to grant a multimillion dollar TV channel to the Boston *Herald*" because "after the *Herald* . . . lost out on merits, publisher Robert Choate started pulling political strings."

Choate issued a blanket denial. "Any appeal I have made . . . has been made openly and publicly and in accordance with the rules of the commission," he said. The Taylors rushed to Washington, but they were too late. The fix was in.[13]

As Adams and Ike were supporting Choate, Kennedy might have been expected to champion the *Globe*. Maguire was a Kennedy family pal, and it was JFK's aide Ted Sorensen who tipped off the *Globe*'s Washington bureau chief, Thomas Winship, about the significance of the *Herald*'s attempts to secure the Channel 5 license. "This was the first time that I had ever been made acutely aware of this potential of this TV station going to our opposition," said Winship. "I had been jolted into being concerned. On the strength of that conversation, I reported this to our publisher."

The *Globe,* however, had a complex relationship with the Kennedy family. Joseph Kennedy was in the midst of a campaign to secure a Pulitzer Prize for *Profiles in Courage,* his son's book on American political history. And Beanie Choate was an influential member of the Pulitzer board. When the Taylors asked Kennedy for his help in early 1957, the senator stayed determinedly neutral. "Senator Kennedy . . . told them that he did not get into such cases, that it was a mistake to make calls on behalf of a constitutent," Sorensen wrote, in a memo for his files. Choate voted for Kennedy's Pulitzer, and Joseph Kennedy's friends on the FCC voted for Choate. "I'm afraid you fellas have just been outpoliticked," Representative Joe Martin told the Taylors. It appeared the *Globe* was doomed. The paper's secret savior was not Jack Kennedy, but Congressman Tip O'Neill.[14]

O'Neill had long recognized the political dangers of a *Herald* monopoly. He didn't relish running for governor if the *Post* and *Globe* were dead or crippled, leaving the *Herald* as the regnant voice in town. And he was pals with Maguire, Davis Taylor and Andrew Dazzi, a *Globe* advertising director who liked to meddle in Boston politics.[15] The congressman was too wary to get into a public fight with Choate. But Sam Rayburn and John McCormack provided the vehicle by which he could maneuver. Pearson had sent his column on Channel 5 to McCormack with a note that urged him to investigate the matter. On February 5, 1957, Speaker Sam himself had stepped down from the rostrum to urge the House to appropriate funds for a special investigation of the federal regulatory agencies to be conducted by a House Commerce subcommittee. O'Neill succeeded at getting Francis X. McLaughlin, a BC graduate, former Secret Service agent and young Boston lawyer, appointed as an investigator. "I have a man on the subcommittee," O'Neill wrote to a friend in Massachusetts. "It is my understanding that the principal target will be the Federal Communications Commission."[16]

Not all congressmen shared Rayburn's enthusiasm for a regulatory probe. The Commerce Committee chairman, Oren Harris of Arkansas, had managed to acquire his own 25 percent interest in a television station for the sweetheart price of $500. Harris also nurtured dreams of becoming a federal judge, and to curry favor at the White House he cleared the appointment of the subcommittee's chief counsel with Eisenhower's staff. They settled on a young New York University professor named Bernard Schwartz who, as an "egghead" and political neophyte, could presumably be manipulated. In fact, Schwartz was a live grenade. An idealist and constitutional scholar, he approached the job with brash determination and no little cunning. When his staff unearthed corruption, he would shout it to the world. The probe became, said the *Congressional Quarterly,* "one of the most bizarre episodes in the history of congressional investigations."[17]

Over at the *Globe,* Winship had been invited back to Boston to begin his climb to editor. He was replaced in Washington by Robert Healy, the son of a *Globe* mailer. Healy had worked for the *Globe* as a copy boy in 1942 before flying thirty-five missions with the Eighth Air Force over Germany during World War II. Returning to the staff after the war, Healy got to know O'Neill when covering the State House. He arrived in Washington after a year as a Nieman fellow at Harvard, with few sources and the duty of investigating the Channel 5 affair.

"They were sending me down there to bail out the paper. Davis sat me down and told me how bad the situation was. If the license was retained by the *Herald,* the *Globe* would basically be out of business," Healy recalled. The *Herald* "had gotten the license through political pull — like everyone was getting them. The television licenses had been given like cookies to the good kids. So I went down, and like the junior birdman I needed a friend. And the only guy I really knew in the delegation was Tip."

O'Neill explained the facts of life to Healy. The *Globe*'s only hope was that the legislative oversight committee would uncover proof of tampering and force the FCC to reopen the case. Healy asked for O'Neill's help. "Jesus, if I help you, the *Globe* will write a nice profile for me," O'Neill said, "but if Choate finds out, the *Herald* will kill me." Yet he agreed to work with the *Globe* behind the scenes. "Tip was a real soldier. I couldn't believe how good he was for me on this thing," Healy recalled. "I married Bernie Schwartz. I mean *married* the sucker. And Francis Xavier McLaughlin was Tip's patronage. And he was my angel — and everybody's angel at the *Globe.*"[18]

Schwartz sent a confidential questionnaire to all the lawyers who regularly practiced before the regulatory boards, and got back allegations of political favoritism and corruption in the awarding of television licenses for Channel 10 in Miami and other stations, which reinforced what he had heard about Channel 5. "The commission has been engaged not merely in a gigantic 'giveaway,' distributing valuable franchises, each of which may be worth millions of dollars," Schwartz concluded. "More important, it has been settling who is to own and direct perhaps the most influential mass medium of communications ever developed." He found that while Democratic-leaning newspapers in Madison and Sacramento had been denied TV licenses under the FCC's diversification criterion, the danger of a concentration of influence was ignored when the applicant had Republican leanings, as in Boston and Miami.

Alarmed at their counsel's audacity, Chairman Harris and the two New England Republicans on the panel — Representatives Robert Hale of Maine and John Heselton of Massachusetts — began hounding Schwartz, to "cut him down to size," as Heselton put it.

"Dr. Schwartz . . . imputes misconduct on the part of members of the FCC which might result in criminal charges or, at the least, in the removal of the officials concerned," Hale said at one committee meeting. "I am shocked. I had no idea when I voted to set up the subcommittee and agreed to serve on it that we would go into this sort of thing. It is none of our business."[19]

Under fire, Schwartz and his coconspirators engaged in a dance of intrigue. O'Neill funneled information to McLaughlin. Healy and Schwartz swapped tips. For the hottest bits of information, and the greatest deniability, O'Neill got California representative Frank Moss — a fellow liberal who was angered by the FCC's decision in the Sacramento TV application — to act as a straw. "We had to make sure that neither the chair nor Heselton knew it when anything good was coming up," said Healy. "If I got stuff I would either write it, or I would go in to Tip and Tip would slip it to Moss. Even Schwartz has no idea who was feeding this guy from California. So Tip was doing a number on all these guys."

Schwartz drew up a twenty-eight-page investigative memo detailing payoffs and other wrongdoing at the FCC, and when Harris signaled an intent to bury it, leaked it to the *New York Times.* Harris then fired Schwartz and announced that he was taking control of the investigation.

But Schwartz was not the kind to go quietly. He called his friends in the press and spirited the subcommittee's files out of its offices. Healy got the records on Channel 5 and had the *Globe* send him $5,000, no questions asked, so he could hire a photographer to make copies. It took several days, and Rayburn's intercession, before the files found their way back to the House.

"I accuse the majority of this subcommittee, in order to further their own partisan interests, of joining an unholy alliance between big business and the White House to obtain a whitewash," Schwartz told the press. He was called to testify by his own subcommittee — presumably for a public crucifixion. Instead, he dramatically announced — as dozens of reporters scribbled madly — that FCC Commissioner Richard Mack had taken payoffs in the Miami case, and that the subcommittee had the canceled checks to prove it. Mack resigned, and the FCC reopened the Channel 10 licensing proceedings. Harris now faced his worst nightmare: a runaway subcommittee. The investigation had acquired a life of its own, and Schwartz fueled things with his parting shot, announcing that the evidence of improper tampering with the regulatory agencies extended to the White House, and the powerful chief of staff, Sherman Adams.[20]

It was O'Neill who dropped the dime on Adams. "You've got to promise you will never tell anybody," O'Neill told McLaughlin, "not even the chairman, while I'm alive." O'Neill had heard that Bernard Goldfine, a New England textile manufacturer, was bragging about favors he performed for Adams — who in turn interceded on Goldfine's behalf with various federal agencies. Eisenhower had a laid-back style, and Adams had often been entrusted with carrying out Ike's orders, particularly the unpopular ones. He was a prickly, tight-lipped man, resented by the press and beloved by few, with a reputation for integrity but, as the nation was about to discover, a weakness for favors from his wealthy friends.

The chief of staff was big game, and the Democrats had to proceed cautiously. The Channel 5 case gave McLaughlin and his fellow investigators an excuse to open shop in Boston, without revealing they were investigating Adams. Choate had insisted that he had no ex parte contacts with the FCC commissioners. But armed with a subpoena — and taking Healy with him — McLaughlin employed a tactic that had been fruitful in the Miami case. Together, they thumbed through the thousands of slips of paper that recorded long-distance phone calls in those days, in the Atlantic Avenue office of the New England Telephone Company. The phone company was required to maintain its toll slips for only six months, but Healy and McLaughlin got lucky: for some mysterious bureaucratic reason they found that the company had retained toll-call tickets dating back four years.[21]

"Voilà. Robert Choate person-to-person to George McConnaughey, who is chairman of the FCC: lots of phone calls," Healy said. "And it turned out . . . that McConnaughey had lunch with Choate." They had dined at a Washington hotel, McConnaughey had to admit, where Choate had pressed him on the *Herald*'s application. Choate later confessed to having a second lunch with McConnaughey, and to inviting the FCC chairman as his guest to the elite Gridiron Club Dinner.

"Holy shit! By the time we got through with it, you know, McConnaughey was in their vest pocket," Healy said. Armed with the subcommittee testimony, and the records Healy had purloined from the committee files, the *Globe*'s lawyers got a federal court to reopen the case.[22] It took ten years of litigation, but the *Herald* lost its TV license.

The Adams case blossomed when the subcommittee's investigators discovered that Goldfine had given Adams's wife a $700 vicuña coat and paid the chief of staff's hotel bills, and that Adams had interceded on Goldfine's behalf with the Federal Trade Commission and the Securities and Exchange Commission. There were enough gifts and favors — $3,000 in hotel bills, a $2,400 Oriental rug, suits of clothing and the infamous vicuña coat — to feed the press all summer.

Healy was joined in the hunt by Benjamin Bradlee, who was making a name for himself covering the Adams story for *Newsweek,* and bore a grudge against Choate — a distant cousin — for not giving him a job after World War II. "This little angelic-faced Healy. He looked like a choir boy," said Bradlee. "Nobody would think what he was up to. He and I shared stuff. I loved the fact Choate was in trouble."

Ike at first stood by his chief of staff, saying, "I need him." But Nixon warned the President of the devastating effect the Adams scandal would have on Republican candidates. It was sweet revenge for the vice president, since Adams had been a leader in a movement to dump Nixon from the ticket in 1956. After a costly, agonizing and pronounced minuet, Adams resigned on September 22. Goldfine was indicted and went to jail.

The Adams/Channel 5 affair changed the face of Boston politics. The Taylors were emboldened by the experience, and their aggressive new attitude extended to the newspaper's news coverage and editorials. Winship ascended to the post of editor, and by the late 1960s it was the liberal *Globe* — not Choate's *Herald* — that was the predominant voice in Boston newspapering. "The *Globe* prospered — so did Healy — and the *Herald-Traveler* never recovered from its loss of the money-making TV station," said Bradlee, who went on to his own celebrated career as editor of the *Washington Post*. O'Neill, meanwhile, had secured his objectives without much cost. His role in the Channel 5 and Adams cases remained a secret. Davis Taylor donated money to his campaign — but only to those accounts where the names of the donors were hidden from public review. More valuable still was O'Neill's status as a sacred cow within the *Globe* newsroom. "He did right for the *Globe* and all right in the *Globe* through the years," Healy said.[23]

CHAPTER 8

Judge Smith

DEMOCRATIC VICTORY in the 1954 congressional elections did more than relieve O'Neill of his miserable status as a member of the minority party: it also opened a number of new seats on important House committees. O'Neill had his eye on Public Works, a classic log-rolling, pork-barrel club that would, among other things, oversee construction of the proposed new interstate highway system. Majority leader John McCormack had other ideas. The Public Works and Commerce panels were spots from which to wheel and deal. The cold war lent added importance to the Foreign Affairs and Armed Services Committees, and emerging social issues gave luster to the Education and Labor and the Judiciary panels. But the three most powerful committees in the House were Ways and Means, which ruled over taxation, trade, Social Security and health care; Appropriations, which approved all government spending; and the Rules Committee — which served as a traffic cop, controlling the flow of legislation on the House floor.

McCormack offered Boland and O'Neill, his two rising stars, a choice of seats on the Appropriations and Rules panels. Eddie was better at details and numbers, and Tip had chaired the state Rules Committee when he served as Speaker of the Massachusetts House. Boland got Appropriations, and O'Neill was summoned to Rayburn's office, where the Speaker laid down the law. A member of the Rules Committee could vote any way he wanted when a bill reached the full House, said Rayburn, but in committee he demanded total obeisance. O'Neill had been a Speaker, Rayburn said, and knew the demands of loyalty.[1]

Rayburn, bald and stocky, the son of a Confederate soldier, was a master politician with a personal touch. He had served as Roosevelt's lieutenant in the House, and his resolute devotion to the cause of dirt farmers, workingmen and other underdogs was heightened by the wounds of his own shy, lonely life on the plains of north Texas. Scarred by a brief, disastrous marriage to the only love of his life, he lost himself in the give-and-take of the House of Representatives. "I have known the loneliness that breaks men's hearts," he once confided. He longed for a family, and "a little towheaded boy to teach how to fish." He and McCormack, who had carved his own way from the slums of Boston, formed an unshakable alliance.

Rayburn and O'Neill had taken each other's measure when McCormack brought the new congressman to meetings of the "Board of Education" in the Speaker's high-ceilinged hideaway office, one floor beneath the House chamber. There, O'Neill had sat around on the leather armchairs with Mr. Sam's closest buddies, drinking hard liquor, using "a small sink [which] served as a semipublic urinal for some of America's most famous political figures" and entertaining his elders with stories about Curley and other Boston rogues. It was from that room that Harry Truman had been summoned to the White House to be sworn in as President when Roosevelt died. Rayburn's protégés — Senator Lyndon Johnson of Texas and Representatives Carl Albert of Oklahoma, Hale Boggs of Louisiana and Richard Bolling of Missouri — were frequent guests, as were House parliamentarian Lewis Deschler and a few senior Hill reporters. It was glittering company, and O'Neill signed on, joining the Rules Committee, the lowermost rung of the Democratic leadership. His appointment was not much fun at first. He reported to work under Rules chairman Howard Smith, a former judge from Virginia — one of the most brilliant, despotic and racist men ever to serve in Congress.

The House had suffered under authoritarian Speakers in the early twentieth century, and to guard against that danger had chosen to govern itself by a strict seniority system. Committee chairs were awarded not to the Speaker's appointees, but to those who came from safe districts, labored quietly for years and claimed power by virtue of longevity. Southerners were especially adept at using the system; the courthouse gangs would choose a fellow from among their ranks and elect him time and time again. It was a "white man's democracy," Carl Albert said.

When O'Neill joined the Rules committee, there were twelve southern chairmen in the House, and five from the rest of the nation. A chairman like Smith was all-powerful — with sole control of the agenda, subcommittee assignments, staff and budget. Rayburn's great genius lay not in his use of the Speaker's authority, which had been seriously eroded by the seniority system, but in getting the most from his lack of power. "A modern Democratic Speaker is something like a feudal king," wrote Dick Bolling, O'Neill's new seatmate on the Rules Committee. "He is first in the land; he receives elaborate homage and respect; but he is dependent on the powerful lords . . . who are basically hostile to the objectives of the national Democratic party and the Speaker." Though there were ways in the rules to circumvent a balky chairman, the regular order frowned upon their use. If a chairman chose to sit on a bill, the legislation usually died.[2]

The Democratic majority in the House of Representatives was built around two poles: its northern, ethnic urban machines, and the Solid South — where the one-party system had ruled since the end of Reconstruction, and the party of Lincoln hardly ever won an election. Roosevelt and Truman had brought the party's two wings together in presidential politics, and it was Rayburn's task to do so in the House. He succeeded by virtue of his personal relationships with his fellow southerners, and the prestige he had earned over his long career. Mr. Sam was helped in the early postwar years by the relatively modest demands of the northern regulars, who tended to be cultural conservatives and whose working-class constituents — with the exception of their attitudes toward organized labor — shared many economic interests with the rural South. But when O'Neill joined the Rules Committee in January 1955, a band of young liberals, steeped in the ideology of the New Deal and with the impatient pride of veterans who had just toppled Hitler, Mussolini and Tojo, had begun to press for such radical causes as federal aid to education, a federalized health care insurance system and the rights of black Americans. They formed an organization called the

Democratic Study Group. Smith, a tall, bent man with a long, woeful countenance and bushy eyebrows, was just as determined to stop them. The Judge was a product of the Byrd machine in Virginia. His principal contribution as an individual legislator was the 1940 Smith Act, by which federal prosecutors hounded alleged Communist subversives during the 1940s and 1950s. He was also a fervent segregationist. One of his more despicable acts in Congress was his defense of a Virginia firm that had subjected its mostly black workforce to deadly risk in its rush to drill a water tunnel through the West Virginia mountains. The construction contract called for safety measures to protect the workers from silicosis, an incurable lung disease caused by silica dust. But to cut costs, the company refused to buy masks for "the niggers on the job" — who were earning all of 25 cents an hour — betting that the disease would take decades to develop. The company, and its workers, lost the wager. Within five years nearly 500 of the miners were dead from silicosis, with 1,500 others debilitated. Many of the bodies were dumped in common graves with cornstalks as tombstones. Smith used the Rules Committee to shut down a congressional investigation.

Judge Smith was also the leader of what, since 1937, had come to be known as "the conservative coalition." Virtually every bill that reached the House floor had to go to his committee to obtain a resolution — known as "the rule" — that specified the time and length of debate, and the number and kind of amendments or parliamentary points of order. There were convoluted ways in the House rules to outflank Smith, but equally convoluted ways to neutralize them; nor did the other southern chairmen fail to appreciate that any diminution of Smith's power would reduce their own. The end result gave the seventy-one-year-old Smith the power to run an "abattoir for liberal legislation," said Bolling. Whenever they chose to do so, Smith and Joe Martin, the Republican leader, could strangle progressive legislation. If joined by the four Republicans on his twelve-member panel, Smith and his ally from the Democratic South — Representative William Colmer of Mississippi — had the six votes needed to block a bill. "We did not meet publicly," Smith recalled. "I would go over to speak with the Republicans, or the Republican leaders might come to see us. It was very informal. Conservative southerners and Republicans from the northern and western states. A coalition."

The Rules Committee had no regular meeting hours, and convened at the pleasure of the chairman around a table in "a small rectangular-shaped committee room with its 19th century decor and stopped clocks," said Bolling. Smith was also a master at stalling. "I continually saw a wave of conservative witnesses before the committee with prepared statements against progressive legislation. It meant the old chairman was trying to delay things, doing everything he could to thwart the will of the majority . . . at one time he had people droning on for 28 consecutive days," O'Neill recalled. "He'd adjourn if you got up to take a piss." O'Neill got a lesson in Smith's power in 1956, when a bill to provide aid to economically depressed areas in New England, Appalachia and other regions was reported by the Banking Committee in late June, and Smith sat on it for the entire month of July, scheduling the first hearing just six days before adjournment.[3]

In later years, O'Neill would note how Smith served a useful function for Rayburn and McCormack, as some of the bills he killed were poorly drawn or political nuisances for the Democratic leaders. Rules members were proud of their ability to "take the heat" on such matters. The congressmen on the Rules Committee were also happy to "take a bite" out of each committee chairman who appeared before them. To take his bites — like trading his vote to an Armed Services chairman in return for a ship construction project at the navy yard, or for the Naval Academy's agreement to put Boston College on its football schedule — O'Neill could not afford to alienate his chairman. The Judge would "at least give you an apple for an orchard," O'Neill recalled. "I sided with the leadership, but I kept my lines open to the southerners. I think that this is one reason why I remained acceptable to them." Indeed, O'Neill worked the process so effectively that over time his district's take of federal postal, health, welfare, anti-poverty and education funds was demonstrably greater than the shares claimed by the chairmen of the authorizing committee and the Appropriations subcommittee that had jurisdiction over those matters: a phenomenal accomplishment. "I will only be too happy to help you in the Rules Committee, and I know that you will give similar consideration to bills which I have before your committee," O'Neill wrote to Judiciary chairman Emanuel Celler, whose panel handled immigration bills, in one typical case. Bolling later complained that O'Neill was too parochial on such matters, swapping favors for hometown "boodle" at the expense of national Democratic priorities.

That being said, there was no secret about O'Neill's main and most important role on Rules: he was McCormack's appointee and was there to combat Smith's tyranny — especially on the issue of civil rights. "O'Neill was my man on the committee. A Roman Catholic that represented my views. When he spoke, he spoke for me," McCormack said.[4]

IN 1954 the Supreme Court, in deciding *Brown v. Board of Education,* ruled that racial segregation was unconstitutional. An overwhelming majority of the South's members of Congress responded by signing the "Southern Manifesto," which declared their undying opposition to integration. Rayburn refused to sign, but as a Texan, confronted with an issue that could shatter his party, he had to work from the shadows.

It was left to McCormack to lead the crusade in the House. Massachusetts was generally receptive to the civil rights movement, but not so much that the Red Sox felt compelled to sign a black ballplayer before 1959 — when they became the last major league team to do so. Or that black parents would not have to go to court in 1963 in an effort to desegregate Boston's public schools. Or that a busing plan imposed on the reluctant school board by the federal courts would not make the city a symbol of racial divisiveness well into the 1970s. Yet McCormack's devotion to the cause did not waver. Nor did Tip O'Neill's. Nor had it ever.

In 1945, when O'Neill was a thirty-two-year-old member of the Massachusetts legislature, he had introduced and championed the state's landmark fair employment act, which prohibited racial discrimination in the hiring and firing of the state's citizens. "The time has come to stop giving the people of this commonwealth 'lip service' with reference to discrimination in employment because of race, color, religious creed, ancestry or advanced age," O'Neill said. Then, as Speaker of the Massachusetts House, O'Neill had relinquished his gavel and stepped down to the floor to lead the Democrats in voting for a bill that extended the fair employment law's reach to higher education as well. For O'Neill it was a matter of conscience, not constituency: though Boston's black population had doubled to 40,000 in the postwar era, the census showed that the percentage of African Americans in the Eleventh District in 1950 was just 2.3 percent.[5]

The civil rights movement was invigorated in 1955 when Rosa Parks, a forty-five-year-old seamstress, refused to give up her seat to a white passenger after a Montgomery, Alabama, bus driver ordered, "Niggers move back." Leaders of the movement confronted segregation in three different arenas: the courts, the streets, and Congress. The *Brown* decision, won by NAACP counsel Thurgood Marshall, was the movement's first major court victory, and the Montgomery bus boycott of 1955–56 its first triumph in the streets. O'Neill played a role in the movement's first big accomplishment in Congress, the passage of the 1957 Civil Rights Act. The civil rights lobbyists, led by the NAACP's Clarence Mitchell Jr., and Joseph Rauh Jr., a founder of Americans for Democratic Action, had selected voting rights as the all-American issue on which to challenge the South and the national conscience in the Eighty-fourth Congress. After a prolonged set of hearings, a civil rights bill was reported by the Judiciary Committee in late April of 1956. The legislation had drawn national attention, and Eisenhower's endorsement, in no small part because of the Reverend Martin Luther King Jr.'s leadership in the Montgomery boycott that spring. But Smith sat on the bill, refusing to even hold hearings, for almost two months.

Finally, in June, O'Neill and Bolling joined Representatives Ray Madden of Indiana and James Delaney of New York and staged a coup d'état. The four rebels voted to demand that the civil rights bill, and a school construction bill that the South opposed because of an antisegregation clause, be called up for consideration. With the offstage help of Rayburn and McCormack[6] and the aid of two northern Republicans who had been corralled by Clarence Mitchell, the rebels beat Smith on a critical 6 to 4 test vote on June 14.

The resultant hearings were tense and caustic. South Carolina representative Robert Ashmore lamented the passing of the days of "the good old colored people and the good old nigger mammies," and told the committee, "You are going step by step into a totalitarian form of government." O'Neill learned a lesson in tactics when he and other members of the panel were late for the opening of a committee meeting on June 21 and Smith adjourned the session for lack of a quorum. But that was just a momentary setback. On June 27, O'Neill sent a proud telegram to seven civil rights leaders in Boston and Cambridge. "CIVIL LIBERTIES BILL REPORTED OUT OF RULES COMMITTEE AT FIVE THIRTY THIS EVENING . . . HAPPY TO HAVE VOTED FOR THIS MEASURE."[7]

Smith vowed to get even. "This is completely outside the usual procedure that we have followed and I don't like it," said the Judge. "The chairman of a committee has privileges and perquisites and I intend to exercise them."

But in private, Smith told his fellow southerners, "The jig's up. I know it." On July 23 the House passed the bill, 279 to 126. Rowena Taylor, the chairman of the Boston NAACP chapter's "Fight for Freedom" committee wrote to thank O'Neill for his "courageous support," and for being "a great leader in the fight for racial justice." Ever an opportunist, O'Neill used the Rules revolt to pry his workmen's compensation bill for longshoremen out of the committee as well. It cleared the House that summer.

The legislation that passed the House would have created a Civil Rights Commission to investigate conditions in the South and a Civil Rights Division in the Justice Department to enforce the law, and given the Attorney General new powers to guarantee black Americans the right to vote. Clarence Mitchell called its passage "a stern warning to Mississippi and other defiant states that the nation abhors control of elections with blackjacks, cross burnings and murder." Though there was not enough time left in the session to overcome Southern resistance in the Senate, Mitchell won a key commitment from Senate majority leader Lyndon Johnson to bring the legislation up in 1957. As the year ended, Mitchell praised Bolling and O'Neill and the other Rules rebels for their courage "to fight tyranny."

In the 1957 hearings on the bill, Judiciary chairman Emanuel Celler and Republican representative William McCulloch of Ohio, an unsung hero of the civil rights cause, sparred with Senators Sam Ervin of North Carolina, Strom Thurmond of South Carolina and an obscure judge from Alabama named George Wallace. Before the Rules Committee, Representative Mendel Rivers of South Carolina insisted that "anybody [could] vote" in his state, and that the evidence of discrimination against Negroes was just "rumors, gossip, hallucinations." The legislation would create a federal Gestapo, he said. "You are being asked to succumb to a disease which carries with it the germs of your own destruction. Today it is the South and the Negro problem. . . . Eventually it will be personal property, real estate, probate, domestic relations, water rights, timber, grazing, marketing, sanitation, highways, and criminal laws of the 48 states of the Union. Then you will have complete and absolute Federal domination over every aspect of our social and economic life in this nation," said Rivers. "The price that some are willing to pay to remold the South and the nation is the cost of your freedom."

But with Rayburn and McCormack leading the way, the bill cleared Judiciary, Rules and the House by mid-June. "Representative

Thomas P. O'Neill and three other northern Democrats on the House Rules Committee today moved boldly to force early House action on civil rights legislation," the *Globe* reported on March 22. "The four northerners acted after their Rules committee chairman, Representative Howard Smith, made clear he was in no hurry to take up the bill."

"We move today because failure of civil rights legislation in the last Congress was due to stalling by the House," O'Neill said. "We want to make perfectly sure that this doesn't happen again and it was clear to all of us that the same old delaying tactics had begun."

The bill lost two key provisions in the Senate,[8] and Strom Thurmond staged the longest (at twenty-four hours and eighteen minutes) one-man filibuster ever, but the 1957 Civil Rights Act finally passed the Senate on August 7. Smith's response was imaginative: he simply left Washington, thus preventing the Rules Committee from acting on the Senate version of the bill. Smith's office let on that a barn had burned down on his Virginia farm, and that he had gone home to deal with the emergency. "I knew Howard Smith would do most anything to block a civil rights bill," Rayburn said. "But I never suspected he would resort to arson."[9] Smith later explained that he had simply been tired, and had taken "a vacation."

And so the civil rights forces, with O'Neill's help, staged one final revolt in August. After Republicans on the Rules Committee won assurances that the House would accept the Senate version of the bill (which granted defendants charged with federal contempt violations the right to a trial by jury) Smith was again outvoted. The legislation passed the House and was signed by Eisenhower on September 9, as white mobs and the Arkansas National Guard gathered at Little Rock's all-white Central High School to keep nine black students from entering its classrooms. It was the first civil rights act to pass Congress since 1875. Ike made history of another kind a few weeks later, when he sent the U.S. Army's 101st Airborne Division into Little Rock to enforce the orders of the federal courts. The nine black students walked bravely into school the next day.[10]

Civil rights was again the issue when O'Neill was chosen by Rayburn and McCormack to serve on a subcommittee that investigated contested congressional elections in 1958. This time, they got more than they bargained for. When Representative Brooks Hays, a moderate Democrat from Arkansas, was defeated by segregationist Dale

Alford, the state's regular Democrats and newspapers claimed that the election had been stolen; in one district alone there were a hundred more votes than there were registered voters. As the only nonsouthern Democrat on the subcommittee, O'Neill took the lead, and his investigators found evidence of fraud. No seat had been denied to an elected representative since 1937, however, and Rayburn and McCormack wanted to bury the controversy — especially when Representative Wilbur Mills of Arkansas threatened to retaliate by purging three northern Democrats who were experiencing their own legal troubles. The Speaker blatantly ignored O'Neill when he rose to try and block Alford's seating, and instead recognized McCormack — who moved that the election results be approved.

"My heart, my mind and my conscience tell me it was a fraudulent election and I stand on that, even if I stand alone," O'Neill said, when he was finally allowed to speak. Alford was allowed to take his seat.[11]

There was one issue on which the civil rights groups did find fault with O'Neill in the 1950s: the admission of Hawaii and Alaska to the union. The civil rights lobby wanted both territories to be admitted as states immediately, believing they would yield four new senators who would reliably vote for civil rights laws. For just that reason — and because Hawaii was filled with brown-skinned Polynesians — Smith wanted to stall the admission of either state for as long as he could. O'Neill viewed the issue through a parochial lens: he knew the addition of new members to the House of Representatives, which was fixed at 435 districts, could cost Massachusetts a seat. So O'Neill employed the crudest red-baiting tactics in the Rules Committee, claiming that the territory of Hawaii was under the sway of "the Communist menace." In the back rooms, meanwhile, he was arguing just the opposite: telling Democrats that Hawaii was reliably Republican and would elect two GOP senators. O'Neill later admitted to being "far off" in his reasoning on Hawaiian statehood, and issued a public apology from the House floor in 1969. "My reason was that because of the entrance of these states, Massachusetts would lose a congressman, which it did," he wrote an old friend. It was not until 1959 that Smith, O'Neill and others relented and Hawaii joined the union.[12]

SMITH'S OBSTRUCTIONISM reached a peak in the Eighty-sixth Congress, which followed the 1958 elections. Thanks to a recession, the Democrats had scored significant gains — 49 seats in the House and 13 in the Senate — and the House liberals demanded that Rayburn rein in the Rules Committee by changing its membership or by putting a twenty-one-day limit on the time that Smith could sit on a bill. Either measure would have split the Democrats along their North-South fault, and so Rayburn instead asked the liberals to trust him. He would work his magic behind the scenes, he promised, and guaranteed that Smith would not block the social welfare bills — a hike in the minimum wage, aid to education, help for depressed areas, a federal housing program and civil rights — the mavericks were pushing.

A shake-up in the Republican ranks cost Rayburn his promise. Representative Charles Halleck, a feisty Indianan, challenged and beat Joe Martin for the post of Republican leader with a campaign that made an issue of Martin's "cronyism" with the Speaker. Rayburn had often relied upon his friendship with Martin to outflank Smith, but in Halleck he faced a self-proclaimed "gut fighter" who was happy to spread discord in the Democratic ranks. An emboldened Smith killed the aid to education, housing and minimum wage bills and humiliated Rayburn in a late-summer session that was called by the Democrats to build an election-year record for the Kennedy-Johnson ticket. Kennedy's election ended Rayburn's hesitancy: the Democratic President would be judged on his ability to work productively with Congress. Mister Sam was out of options. He had to strip Smith of his power. The Speaker resolved to make what he later called "the worst fight of my life."

Rayburn began by offering the Judge a compromise. If Smith would accept two more Democrats and another Republican on his committee, the 6 to 6 deadlock would become a narrow 8 to 7 majority for the national Democrats. Smith turned the Speaker down. Rayburn then leaked news that he was prepared to purge Mississippi's Bill Colmer — who had abandoned the Democratic Party that fall to campaign for a "States' Rights" ticket — from the committee. That caught the South's attention. Fearing that a Democratic pogrom, fronted by Rayburn and conducted by liberals, might threaten the seniority system, a few southern leaders led by Representative Carl Vinson of Georgia endorsed the Speaker's plan to enlarge the Rules Committee.

Out of respect for the institution, Rayburn allowed the debate to take place not in the Democratic caucus, where he had a sure majority, but on the House floor — where Halleck's Republicans could come to Smith's rescue. By doing so, Rayburn assured the legitimacy of victory, but also increased the odds of a defeat. The vote was scheduled for January 25, and the aides of the new President were putting away their tuxedos and recovering from the inauguration festivities, confident that Rayburn had the situation well in hand, when the Speaker called on the White House.

"I'm concerned about it," Rayburn said.

"Oh?" said Kennedy.

"Yes," said Rayburn. "As a matter of fact, I don't think we have the votes."

Kennedy aide Lawrence O'Brien later recalled that "everything else that might have been discussed that morning eluded me because I was in a state of semi-shock . . . sitting there with a whole New Frontier program that's just gone down the drain and you can sit and twiddle your thumbs for at least two years."

The Kennedys responded to Rayburn's cold shower. The vote was put off for six days, as the White House and its allies on the Hill traded threats, patronage jobs, costly water projects and every other porky prize at their disposal for votes. McCormack and Martin (smarting from his defeat by Halleck) were detailed to work one especially important group: the northern Republicans. To win on the House floor, Kennedy had to peel some twenty GOP liberals from Halleck's ranks. Feuding with the Kennedys, and wanting to curry favor with Smith, O'Neill largely stayed on the sidelines in this pivotal battle, but he remembered lobbying his friend, GOP Representative William Bates of Massachusetts, who was finally converted by a phone call from the President. Two other Republican congressmen from Massachusetts — Silvio Conte and Bradford Morse — signed on as well.

The White House and its liberal allies in the House played the game hard: they sent a case of whiskey to a southern Democrat on the Sunday before the vote, knowing the man was an alcoholic. A friendly lobbyist was ordered to take one of Halleck's troops out for a long night on the town, in the hope he would not show up for the vote the next day. Lyndon Johnson prowled the marble hallways corralling votes for Rayburn. Hale Boggs secured five of Louisiana's eight votes. In the end, it came down to the Speaker. The House floor and galleries were jammed with people — more than on any other occasion in memory, longtime observers said — when Rayburn walked into the chamber and picked up the gavel on January 31. They rose, friend and foe alike, and gave him an overwhelming, affectionate ovation. Then the debate began.

Smith was the last Democratic foe to address the House. "If there is any quarrel between the Speaker and myself it is all on his side," Smith said, and the House roared with laughter. "I will cooperate with the Democratic leadership of the House of Representatives — just as long and just as far as my conscience will permit me to go," he said, and the laughter started again. Smith was miffed. "Some of these gentlemen who are laughing maybe do not understand what a conscience is," he said.

As Halleck spoke last for the Republicans, Rayburn handed the gavel to Carl Albert and walked down on the floor to close the debate. The great man's eyesight was failing, and he had but ten months to live before a swift and painful cancer claimed him. He no doubt knew that this fight, after so many years of soldiering for the lost and the poor and the lonely, would be his parting gift to his country.

"The issue, in my mind, is a simple one," Rayburn said, after thanking his colleagues for their courtesy. "I think this House should be allowed on great measures to work its will."

Mister Sam won. The vote was 217 to 212. Twenty-two Republicans had backed him, and a third of the southern Democrats. "It's all baloney," a bitter Smith told reporters.

"I feel all right," Rayburn said, when asked about his victory. "That's about as good as a man can feel."[13]

CHAPTER 9

My Beloved Jack

THROUGHOUT THE YEARS, many of the capital's courtiers would logically but mistakenly rank Tip O'Neill — the liberal, Irish Catholic congressman who inherited John F. Kennedy's seat — as an intimate friend of the President and his famous family. But though he sometimes showed affection for O'Neill, Kennedy and his brother Bobby and most members of the White House "Irish Mafia" lumped the congressman with the McCormacks and Furcolos and Devers of the state: pols too prominent to ignore, but too coarse or square to welcome to the inner circle. O'Neill and his contemporaries were practical, gritty men. They built things, like highways, public schools and mental hospitals; found jobs for their working-class neighbors; and fashioned legislation that changed their constituents' lives. Kennedys attended Harvard, dated starlets, went sailing, made speeches and ran for President. Until Edward Kennedy was elected to the Senate and compiled a legislative record that dwarfed those of his brothers, the family could point to few concrete accomplishments. Even the great achievements of the Kennedy-Johnson years — Medicare, Medicaid and the civil rights legislation of 1964 and 1965 — were off-the-shelf components of long-standing liberal dogma that the Kennedys took up, carried bravely for three years, and left for Johnson to enact. To that scorecard, with much the same partition of responsibility, must be added the catastrophic U.S. policy toward Vietnam.

What the Kennedys did well was sell. And much of what they had to sell was style. Sleek, urbane and witty, they stood out in American politics like Cary Grant in a Hitchcock film: of, yet above, the cast of more plebeian characters. Yet the bigotry they faced as Irish Catholics ensured that the Kennedy brothers remained Democrats, with just enough empathy for the underdog, and a big enough chip on their shoulders, to chafe at the complacency of the Eisenhower years. John Kennedy believed in the eloquent call to arms that was his Inaugural Address, in the ideal of public service represented by the Peace Corps and in the righteousness of employing the power of his presidency to escort James Meredith, an African American, into the University of Mississippi.

To America's Catholic population, most especially its Irish Americans, Kennedy's triumph was a liberating experience. His election so thoroughly banished the ghost of Al Smith that it is hard to recall, much less convey, the state of insecurity and inferiority that characterized Irish Americans in the postwar years. Much of the resentment directed at Catholic America was inspired by the church's insular culture, with its parallel set of institutions — schools, colleges, youth groups and fraternal organizations — which many Americans viewed as a rejection of the nation's democratic principles. Important Irish Catholic leaders, like Pennsylvania governor David Lawrence, initially opposed Kennedy's presidential candidacy for fear it would trigger a new round of anti-Catholicism.[1] Protestants like Rayburn remembered the Smith campaign and feared another debacle. And so, when Kennedy was elected in a contest in which two-thirds of the votes were cast by Jews and Protestants, American Catholics felt welcome, included, giddy and freed.

Kennedy's triumph left O'Neill conflicted. On one hand the new President was "my beloved Jack," the deliverer of his people, the knight who had torn down the ultimate No Irish Need Apply sign. Weighed against that were the slights and slurs that O'Neill, a proud man, from a good middle-class home and with a college degree of his own, thank you, was forced to endure.[2] In 1957, a rumor had swept North Cambridge. The Kennedys, it was said, saw the district as their own preserve — and O'Neill as a caretaker who could be shouldered aside. Young Bobby, then serving as chief counsel for a Senate subcommittee probing corrupt labor practices, was said to be on his way to Cambridge to reclaim the family seat. O'Neill, who heard of Kennedy's plans from a fellow congressman, was "ripped" with anger.

O'Neill and Robert Kennedy never much liked each other. "Bobby had the personality of a casket handle. He was just a miserable kid," Leo Diehl recalled. "He didn't want any pols around. He wanted their own organization pure." Some said that Bobby, a moralist, felt contempt for O'Neill's decision to sit out World War II with a deferment. Nor were Bobby and Jack pleased when O'Neill was one of just four New England representatives to be endorsed by Jimmy Hoffa's Teamsters Union. Hoffa was the Kennedys' blood enemy, and O'Neill had won the Teamsters nod by voting against the Landrum-Griffin labor bill, a "reform" measure on which John Kennedy had staked his meager reputation as a legislator. When the Kennedy clan met to decide who would fill out the President-elect's Senate term, O'Neill's name was put forward by Joseph Kennedy but shot down by the brothers because of his vote on Landrum-Griffin.

Robert Kennedy "was a self-important upstart and a know-it-all," O'Neill said. "To him, I was simply a street-corner pol." After hearing that Bobby had an eye on his seat, O'Neill had crossed to the Senate side of the capitol and told John Kennedy that he would mount a costly, no-holds-barred campaign — whatever it took — to stay in office. The senator's own political career would be damaged, O'Neill said. He never learned how serious the Kennedys were — word came back immediately that Bobby would not be a candidate. But other snubs followed. The Kennedys cast aside a series of O'Neill's friends — Joe Healey, Mark Dalton, Billy Sutton — and word reached O'Neill that Bobby referred to him as "that big fat Irish bastard." In 1960, O'Neill was "crushed" when election officials told him that Jacqueline Kennedy, when casting her absentee ballot, had voted for her husband but left a blank beside O'Neill's name. O'Neill never understood "how she could do that to me."[3]

Over time, O'Neill and others would arrive at the conclusion that that was just the way the Kennedys were. Friends and associates were disposable. There was a shade of Hal and Falstaff in the Kennedy-O'Neill relationship, as in many of Kennedy's friendships. "Nobody was close to him. Take it from me, there's nobody close to them," said

Patsy Mulkern. "Big men don't let you get close to them. Me and you would, but not those fellows. Because that is the way they're born and brought up." For the Kennedys, it was all or nothing, and O'Neill was never willing to give all. When Thomas Broderick, another longtime Kennedy supporter, asked Jack if he might lend some time to a Boston mayoral campaign, Kennedy said sure, but that it would be the end of their relationship. "If you go with them, you lose your identity with me. And then you're of no value," Kennedy said.[4]

O'Neill had originally considered 1958, when Kennedy would be running for reelection to the Senate, as the best year to make a race for governor. Foster Furcolo's success had foiled that plan, but 1960, with Kennedy atop the ballot, looked like an even finer year for Democrats in Massachusetts. Boston's political reporters, getting a volley of nods and winks from O'Neill, didn't wait for the 1958 results before predicting that he would be a candidate for governor the next time around. "This will come as appalling news to the other prospective candidates, for when O'Neill runs for anything he usually gets it," the *Herald* reported in September 1958.

The candidate was ready. A poll was taken, and in the fall of 1959 two friendly Cambridge representatives mailed out 5,000 flyers extolling O'Neill's virtues and promising that "all who know him fully expect him to seek the Democratic nomination for governor in 1960." So it came as a shock when, in February 1960, O'Neill announced that he would not run for governor. He cited the demands of his work in Congress, and the help he was providing the Kennedy presidential campaign, as his reasons. In later years, he said he had caught "Potomac fever" and had dreams of becoming Speaker.[5]

The truth was more complex. Those who loved and knew him best feared O'Neill would be an utter disaster as a governor. His wife, Millie, saintly Sister Agatha and pals like Joe Healey and Leo Diehl thought he was too much a worrier to survive the pressure of a statewide campaign, and far too amenable to serve in an executive capacity. O'Neill's desire to please everyone, they feared, would lead to a career-ending scandal in a state government that was then recognized as among "the most squalid, corrupt and despicable" in the nation.

"I've been reading in the papers that you're thinking of running for governor, but I don't think that's a good idea," Sister Agatha wrote him. "You have a certain softness about you which would make it difficult for you to say no to anyone. That's a fine quality, but it would get you into trouble if you were governor. I know in my heart that Washington is the place for you."

"Tip was the kind of guy that if somebody with eight kids came in who was in trouble, Tip would do anything he could to see that he was taken care of. Nothing illegal — just a case of saying that his human characteristics worried me in terms of his ultimate survival — whether or not he might be chopped up as governor," Healey said.

There was no shame in the decision to stay in Washington: John Kennedy had turned down a gubernatorial bid in 1952 in favor of the tougher Senate race for much the same reason. Home-state politics was "an endless morass from which it is very difficult to extricate oneself," Robert Kennedy said. The highest price would be paid by Millie, who had five children to raise when her husband was in Washington. It was now clear that politics was a lifetime vocation for her Tom and not, as she had once hoped, a field he would eventually leave for a more conventional career. "I was the silly one. I was very foolish not to have realized that," she said. "When you are young you expect change: I didn't think that the only change would be that he would go from one job in politics to another." In urging him to stay in Congress, she was consigning them both to long stretches of heartache and loneliness. But she felt she had no choice. "Tom wanted to be governor. And then when he wanted to run, I was against it," Millie recalled. "I always felt that being governor was a dead end." Dever "couldn't satisfy his friends. Everyone wanted a job. And I said, 'Tom, you lose friends being governor. You don't gain any.' And that was my point: Tom could never say no to anybody."[6]

Indeed, as O'Neill was weighing a statewide campaign, an array of investigations, grand jury proceedings and indictments had pushed political corruption to the top of the voters' concerns. The focus was on Beacon Hill, on the huge road-building projects pushed through the state legislature by Dever and successive governors, and how they were being run by the Massachusetts Department of Public Works, the Turnpike Authority or the Metropolitan District Commission. In 1960, the U.S. government froze federal highway funds allocated for the state, and a congressional committee launched a public investigation. In Boston, U.S. Attorney Elliot Richardson exposed a pattern of bribery, kickbacks and other corrupt acts that touched public works czar William Callahan and Dever as well as O'Neill's good friend (and eventual business partner) John M. Shea, who handled patronage for the public works chief.[7]

John Volpe, a Republican whose slogan was "End the Scandals — Restore Honor to Our State," sought to profit from the political climate. "The one issue in this campaign is corruption, corruption, and corruption, which I am not only fighting against but will eliminate," Volpe told the *Globe*. Despite Kennedy's place atop the ticket, Volpe won by 130,000 votes. O'Neill might plausibly have run as a corruption fighter, as his name had not surfaced in the crime probes, but it is hard not to think that, given his friendship with Callahan and Shea, he had made a wise decision when bowing out of the race.

"Every time they described O'Neill, they described him as a cigar-smoking Irish Boston politician," Diehl recalled. "You know — threw it at him like he was on the take all the time. The *Traveler* and the *Herald* would have killed him.

"Christ, he fell for the Curley pension thing after Curley gave him a pile of crap," said Diehl. "His heart was too big. Tom would pick up a phone. You would come in and he'd pick up the phone for you and make a call. He saw McCormack and Rayburn do it all the time.

"A lot of guys in Boston wanted to back him, wanted to feather their own nest. Millie put her foot down. She was afraid, knowing Tom, that people were playing him off the wall," said Diehl. "And that was the savior of Tom."[8]

Instead of running for governor, O'Neill enlisted in the Kennedy presidential campaign. He helped Eddie Boland stage a series of clambakes and other get-togethers at which Kennedy could meet uncommitted congressmen, and lobbied pals like Representative William Green, the leader of the Philadelphia delegation. To witness the historic doings, O'Neill took his daughter Susan to Los Angeles for the Democratic national convention, where he was serving on the party rules committee and was assigned as a troubleshooter by the Kennedys, working on friends who were delegates from the New Jersey, North Dakota, Ohio, Pennsylvania, Arkansas and Missouri delegations. He haunted the lobby of the Pennsylvania contingent's hotel, and sat, like an oversized babysitter, among the state's delegates. O'Neill and an assortment of operatives like him kept track of the moods and gossip in the fifty-four delegations, reporting back to the Kennedy command post at the Biltmore Hotel. He witnessed Mike Kirwan's pitch to the Virgin Island delegation, in which each of the four delegates had committed to a different candidate to ensure that at least one brought home a winner.

"You fellows know who I am?" asked Kirwan, who was then the subcommittee chairman with authority over the U.S. territories.

"Oh, Mr. Kirwan, we know who you are. You're a grand man, you've been wonderful to us," said one of the delegates.

"Well, got some idea down there you may need a new school or a hospital or something — is that right?" asked Kirwan.

"Yes," said the delegate.

"Well, you know that the only fellow that can give you that school or hospital is Mike Kirwan, don't you?"

"That's right."

"Well, boys, I want you to know I'm with Jack Kennedy for President of the United States," Kirwan said. "Who are you with?"

"Kennedy," they said in unison.

O'Neill also played a minor role in the selection of Lyndon Johnson as vice president. They knew each other from the Board of Education, and the big Texan had sought out O'Neill at Kirwan's St. Patrick's Day party in 1960 to tell him, "Tip, I'd like to have you with me on the second ballot."

"Senator, there's not going to be any second ballot," said O'Neill.

"You're enough of a politician to know that the boy isn't going to win," said Johnson.

"The trouble with you, Senator, is that you underestimate the Kennedys," said O'Neill. "You don't appreciate the long arm."

As usual, the role O'Neill played in the vice presidential drama was as an emissary. Jack Kennedy had asked him to plead his case with Sam Rayburn. Before leaving for Los Angeles, in a conversation in the Speaker's lobby, Rayburn told O'Neill, "Any man who puts his hat in the presidential ring, if asked, must take the second spot on the ticket." Rayburn was envisaging the attributes that Kennedy would bring as the junior member of a Johnson-Kennedy ticket, but O'Neill made note of the Speaker's sentiments and reported back to Kennedy.

"He thinks Johnson's going to win and he wants me for vice president," Kennedy said.

"Yes . . . , but the interesting thing about it is this: *we* both know *you* are going to win," said O'Neill.

Early in the convention week, in a smoke-filled room at the Statler Hotel, O'Neill joined McCormack and Representative Wright Patman of Texas in trying to persuade Rayburn that Johnson should seek the vice presidential nomination as a consolation prize. Rayburn, true to the sentiments he had shared with O'Neill, eventually told McCormack that if Kennedy should offer the job to the Texas senator, Johnson would be duty-bound to take it. McCormack dispatched O'Neill with the message for Kennedy. He caught up to the senator at a party at Chasen's Restaurant in West Hollywood, where Kennedy asked him to meet him out by the car. There they consulted in the glare of spotlights, as a crowd of several hundred was held back by a crescent of the local police.

"I think there's a chance," O'Neill told Kennedy.

"I want him badly," Kennedy said. "With him we can carry Texas. We may be able to break the South. There's only one thing: I don't want to be placed in the position of asking him and having him refuse me."

O'Neill shuttled back to Rayburn, who promised to call Kennedy later that night.

O'Neill's diplomatic mission was significant in light of the subsequent controversy over Kennedy's selection of Johnson as a running mate, which revolved around the question of whether the Kennedy brothers ever thought the Texan would actually take the job. If O'Neill's recollection is accurate, then Kennedy knew all along that Johnson would say yes, and the brothers' subsequent insistence that LBJ surprised them by agreeing to accept a pro forma offer was a fib they told to defuse the wrath of outraged liberals.[9]

For the general election campaign, O'Neill joined the elite corps of Kennedy advance men. That year, and for the next three decades, Massachusetts marked each presidential election by sending forth an exceptional parade of skilled political operatives to help the national Democratic Party and its candidates. They arrived in a state like an army's scouts. Sometimes, O'Neill recalled, the advance men would find lethargic or antagonistic Democratic machines, and have to construct a Kennedy organization from scratch. In other places they would only have to show up and watch the local masters work. He liked to tell of the time he arrived in Chicago and contacted Mayor Richard Daley's formidable organization. He was handed a wad of cash and directed to a nearby resort and racetrack to pass the time until, at an appointed hour, he showed up at a certain street corner and watched the Chicago machine inundate the neighborhood with posters and leaflets and precinct workers.

O'Neill's main target was the state of Missouri, whose congressmen had supported their own Senator Stuart Symington for President and were sulking after returning from Los Angeles empty-handed. For two to three weeks, O'Neill served as salesman, arbiter and broker. Missouri governor John Dalton was fretting about Kennedy's Catholicism, and the campaign's appeals to black voters didn't sit well with the St. Louis city chairman, a crotchety old Irish Catholic boss named Jack Dwyer. "Kennedy is an asshole for sending in all those jerks to register the niggers," he told O'Neill. "But I called some people about you, and Lenor Sullivan and Mel Price from the Congress both tell me you're a hell of a guy — not like those jerks they're sending down here from Harvard and Princeton. They look down their noses at me like I was a lump of crap. Say, will you have a drink and a sandwich?" O'Neill turned on the charm, settled in, called upon his store of Curley stories and, long after midnight and many drinks later, got Dwyer to agree to deploy his organization on Kennedy's behalf.

With BC schoolmates Bob O'Hayre and Charles Murphy, O'Neill advanced Kennedy's triumphant October trip to St. Louis, Joplin and Independence, where the candidate was endorsed by Harry Truman. For that occasion, O'Neill collected on a few chits owed him by the Teamsters, reminding them of his vote on Landrum-Griffin and asking them as a personal favor to cancel plans to picket Kennedy's speech. O'Neill also helped brewer August Busch stage a fund-raising breakfast at the Park Plaza Hotel. Afterward, he huddled with Kennedy and O'Hayre in a men's room.

"How did we do?" asked Kennedy.

"I got $29,000: twelve in cash and seventeen in checks," said O'Hayre. "What will I do with it?"

"Give me the cash," said Kennedy. "And give Kenny O'Donnell the checks."

"Jeez," O'Neill told him. "This business is the same whether you're running for ward alderman, or whether you're running for President of the United States."[10]

O'Neill and his team performed more than capably. "Organizational activity very good," wrote Larry O'Brien, summing up Missouri in a memo on the fifty states that he sent to the Kennedy brothers on October 15. And Busch wrote to Kennedy: "The campaign is conducted with a great deal of vigor . . . the St. Louis majority will more than offset any losses in the so-called Bible Belt." Missouri went Democratic that fall.[11]

Kennedy's inauguration took place at a frigid sunlit noon, as Washington dug itself out from the previous day's blizzard. O'Neill had held an inaugural eve party in his office, and was still feeding sandwiches, drinks and coffee at midnight to Bostonians trapped by the storm. The cold kept Millie in her room at the Congressional Hotel, where she watched the ceremony on television, but O'Neill — with the help of a Boston-born Secret Service agent — slipped into the VIP section behind the podium. He found himself a seat on the aisle beside another gate-crasher: George Kara, a public relations man and political operative from West Roxbury.

"Quiet, quiet. Be quiet or they'll move us out of here," Kara said.

A moment later, the President-elect emerged from the Capitol, and stood at O'Neill's right shoulder while waiting to descend the steps. They exchanged greetings, and Kara, who had served in a minor role during the campaign, also shook Kennedy's hand. Kennedy then marched down to history, and Kara chuckled gleefully. "There goes Jack, gone to be sworn in to the most important job in the world, and he's wondering how Kara got the seat."

O'Neill laughed at Kara's conceit, but was quizzed by the President a few weeks later at a White House social event.

"Was that George Kara sitting by you the day I walked down the aisle to be sworn in?" Kennedy asked.

"Yes," O'Neill replied, and told Kennedy of Kara's prediction: how historians would wonder what grand thoughts were on the young President's mind, when in fact Kennedy was thinking, "How the hell did Kara get that seat?"

Kennedy laughed. "You know," he said, "it's absolutely true."

At the Inaugural Ball, O'Neill and Kennedy shared another ritual. In his 1952 and 1958 Senate campaigns, Kennedy had outpolled the congressman by a handful of votes in one North Cambridge precinct, and they concluded that one large French-Canadian family was cool toward O'Neill. "Hey, Tip, how many votes did you get this time in that precinct in North Cambridge?" the new President now asked him. When O'Neill told him that the results had been true to form, Kennedy grinned and said, "That Lefebvre family is still off." But despite his service to the campaign, and the fond anecdotes he took with him from the days of the New Frontier, there remained a shadow over O'Neill's relationship with the Kennedys — which grew painfully acute in the months after the inauguration.[12]

O'NEILL HAD SUFFERED another run-in with Robert Kennedy during the election. When backing out of the governor's race, he had announced that he needed to devote his time to moving progressive legislation through the Rules Committee, and to organizing congressional support for Kennedy. But before O'Neill could claim too grand a role in the Kennedy campaign, Bobby froze him out. Dick Bolling, a war veteran, intellectual and media darling, was appointed as the campaign's chief liaison to the House.

"Bobby told me he wanted me to be chairman. But all of a sudden Tip announced that he was the chairman," said Bolling. "And they just ignored Tip and announced me. As far as they were concerned, nobody had heard Tip say he was chairman. And he just disappeared. And then he knew what he was dealing with, that they were very tough folk." Nor were matters helped when a sulky O'Neill did the minimum required of him in the Kennedy-Rayburn crusade to wrest control of the Rules Committee from Howard Smith. It was more important to stay "acceptable," to the South, O'Neill said later.

O'Neill's frustration was honed by the fact that his roommate, Eddie Boland, was a close friend of Springfield's Larry O'Brien, and was often invited to White House meetings and social occasions. Boland, almost alone in the Massachusetts delegation, had consistently sided with the Kennedys in their conflicts with the McCormacks. A slim bachelor, with a fine singing voice, Boland was a popular guest at the White House, where O'Neill was blocked by Kenny O'Donnell, the gatekeeper to the Oval Office. O'Donnell was Bobby Kennedy's close friend, and a future candidate for governor of Massachusetts; he didn't want to give O'Neill, a potential rival, any access or patronage.

"You have Kenny O'Donnell, you have Larry O'Brien, you have Dick Donahue. You have those fellows all from Massachusetts who are the coterie around the President, and they're not going to let a Tip O'Neill in," said O'Neill. "I couldn't get by them. . . . I'd have had more of a chance of getting by if I came from Arkansas." O'Neill had but "half a dozen" conversations with the President during the New Frontier, generally about home state politics. So it is not so surprising that the new administration wasn't more than a few weeks old before O'Neill got into a first-class scrap with the White House over the Catholic Church and federal aid for education.[13]

EVEN BEFORE the Soviets rocked America by sending the Sputnik satellite into orbit in 1957, liberals had pushed for federal aid to the nation's public schools and colleges. The legislation, however, was always lost in the political thickets of race or religion — especially once

Representative Adam Clayton Powell of New York started attaching the "Powell amendment," which denied federal funds to segregated school districts, to the bills. In 1955, Judge Smith bricked up the education bill in his Rules Committee crypt. In 1956, the bill's Republican foes cynically voted for the Powell amendment and then, having guaranteed southern opposition to the bill, watched it die on the House floor. In 1957 the school aid bill was again killed on the floor — this time by but three votes. O'Neill angered liberals and civil rights activists by voting against the bill because, he said, it had a funding formula that short-changed Massachusetts. Of the 97 Democrats voting against the bill, only O'Neill and 4 others were from outside the South. It was one of those votes that led Bolling to declare that O'Neill was short-sightedly parochial, but it also fit O'Neill's strategy of keeping "lines open" to the South.

O'Neill was back on board in the post-Sputnik year of 1958, and Congress appropriated a billion dollars via the emergency "National Defense Education Act" to improve instruction in mathematics, foreign languages and the sciences in both public and private schools. Once Rayburn won his fight to pack the Rules Committee, liberal hopes were high for passage of an omnibus school-aid bill, which Kennedy called "the most important piece of domestic legislation" of 1961, his first year in office. To smooth the way, Powell agreed to drop his anti-segregation amendment. But then, on June 20, O'Neill and Jim Delaney joined with Smith, William Colmer and the Republicans to kill the bill in Rules. It was a stunning, costly setback for the new President, and explained why O'Neill dropped, or was dropped from, any role as a point man for the New Frontier in the House.[14]

Aside from his personal grievances with the Kennedys, O'Neill was motivated by loyalty to McCormack and the machinations of his church. The White House, after painstaking negotiations with various experts and interest groups, had proposed a $6 billion three-year package of grants and loans to public schools and colleges. The bill, however, contained no funding for religious schools because Kennedy feared a political backlash. Under the leadership of Cardinal Francis Spellman of New York, the church had made fierce, public stands in favor of aid to parochial schools throughout the 1950s. "My personal conviction is that the first Catholic President, under fire from the Catholic hierarchy, cannot now . . . support the first aid-to-parochial-schools Bill," aide Ted Sorensen advised the President.

Kennedy's stand left the Catholic clergy in the lurch. It then had 5.3 million students in more than 10,600 parochial schools, saving public school systems about $2 billion. Yet the bishops also recognized that "during the campaign our enemies alleged that the hierarchy would pressure for control of government" and that many voters "feared the potential power of the Church," according to an internal memo of the National Catholic Welfare Conference, the church's lobbying arm in Washington. While anti-Catholic feelings "were allayed to a great extent" by Kennedy's conduct during the election, the bishops decided that a "concerted action of the hierarchy would revive the fears." The church needed front men, and found them in McCormack, Delaney and O'Neill.

As a sop to the church, Kennedy had covertly agreed that the National Defense Education Act of 1958 — which contained a loan program for private and parochial schools — be extended. But McCormack was wary; he believed that once Kennedy's general school aid bill was enacted, the White House would not be able to prevent the conservative coalition from killing off the NDEA. The two bills had to be part of a package, McCormack decided: there would be no general federal aid bill without concurrent passage of the NDEA.

"Majority Leader McCormack indicates belief that the current best prospect for nonpublic school assistance by the federal government lies in pushing for an expanded National Defense Education Act . . . including within the proposed revision of that act a large semblance of the program we espouse," said a Catholic Welfare Conference memo, after a May 18 meeting with the congressman. McCormack decided to stall the Kennedy bill in Rules until the NDEA could be brought up for "simultaneous consideration." As Senator Mike Mansfield put it, the bells of St. Mary's had begun to peal. The Catholic bishops prevailed on McCormack — who then prevailed on his Rules Committee lieutenants, O'Neill and Delaney — to hold the school bill hostage. Bolling's motion to move the legislation died a 9 to 6 death on June 20. "I never thought I'd see the day when Jim and Tip would join the coalition of Republicans and Dixiecrats," Ray Madden said afterward. Rayburn informed Kennedy that aid to education was "dead as slavery."

The Kennedy administration had "only worried about the Education and Labor Committee . . . they never did worry about the Rules Committee except on a last-minute, crash, hysterical basis," said

Bolling's wife, Jim, who was lobbying for the administration at the time. "We all talked about it, but hoped it would just go away . . . that because Delaney and O'Neill were good Democrats they wouldn't leave."[15]

The pressure from the church had been wide and deep. In a letter to his sister, Mary, O'Neill confirmed that "the College of Cardinals have officially taken a position" on federal school aid, and that he had been lobbied in the course of a "personal communication to that effect from Cardinal Cushing." His office files contained correspondence from Cushing and the Catholic Welfare Conference dating back to 1955. Indeed, the conference's records reveal how McCormack, Delaney and O'Neill acted on their church's behalf throughout that spring. "Mr. Delaney and Mr. O'Neill agreed to cooperate in delaying the administration's bill in the Rules Committee," an internal memo noted in June 1961. "They have stated they want the NDEA first. This is not accidental. Their two votes in the Rules Committee are sufficient to block the administration's bill. A couple of years ago an education bill was blocked in the Rules Committee by Delaney and O'Neill at the request of NCWC."

Kennedy's supporters in Congress responded to the Delaney-O'Neill threat, and the House Education Committee gave a favorable report to extension of the NDEA, with a $275 million provision for low-interest loans to private schools. That was enough for McCormack and O'Neill — who were feeling the heat from the ADA, Massachusetts colleges and universities, the White House and the teachers' unions — but not for Delaney, whose blue-collar New York district had a militant Catholic constituency. Neither Kennedy's personal appeals, nor all the plums at Larry O'Brien's disposal, could make Delaney change his stance. "He didn't want a thing," O'Brien said later. "I wish he had." In a series of votes in mid-July, all the aid-to-education measures were killed by the Rules Committee. O'Neill switched sides and voted with the liberals, but Delaney refused to budge.

"Due chiefly to the courage of Representative Delaney (for which of course we can take at least no direct credit), it seems . . . that thus far we have done far better than we could have anticipated," the NCWC leaders happily concluded. It was not until 1965 that Lyndon Johnson — a Protestant — gave in to the church's demands, defused the church-state issue and got Congress to approve federal aid to elementary and secondary education with a dedicated share for parochial school students. He signed the bill at the site of the one-room schoolhouse in the Texas hill country where he had gone to school, with his grade school teacher at his side.[16]

KENNEDY'S REVERSALS on Capitol Hill fed what aide Richard Donahue called a "mutuality of contempt" between the White House staff and the Congress. The President "thought Tip was more than the Patsy Mulkern or Johnny Powers type, or than a great many Irish politicians," Ted Sorensen said. "He thought Tip was a man of substance." But O'Neill was often ignored as the administration consulted with a few pet legislators. When Larry O'Brien was asked by a TV producer to list some members with ten years' service who had "weight" in the House, he included Bolling and Boland but not O'Neill. His friend Tip "didn't want to apply himself to that kind of detail," Bolling said later. "He didn't want to be a technician." O'Neill was still most usefully employed by the New Frontier as a go-between with the McCormacks. In 1962, when Speaker McCormack's nephew Eddie was planning to run against Edward Kennedy for the U.S. Senate, the President sent his younger brother to O'Neill with a deal.

"I'm proposing that we have a poll," Edward Kennedy said. "They can pick the pollsters. And we will agree that if we run within five percent of each other we will oppose each other. But if he beats me I will get out of the fight. If I beat him he will run for governor and we will work as a team."

"Lookit," said O'Neill, with characteristic, and justified, wariness. "Supposing he beats you, where does that put me?"

"Let me assure you," Kennedy said to him. "My father has already said that never will a Kennedy run against Tip O'Neill. Besides, I've already taken a poll, and in the poll I lick Eddie McCormack two to one."

John McCormack, who always insisted that he advised his nephew not to run, took the offer to young Eddie, who turned it down. So the Kennedys sweetened the deal.

"We understand that Eddie is in debt over $60,000. My father can see that he can go to work for a New York law firm and get a $100,000 fee on a case, which will take care of all his expenses and his taxes and clear him out," Edward Kennedy told O'Neill. "Number two, if Eddie's looking for a job, we'll give him under secretary of the navy.

He's a navy graduate. We'll make him an ambassador to some country, if he's interested in being an ambassador."

O'Neill met with Eddie McCormack, who mused about being secretary of the navy but again decided to remain in the race. "Eddie, you're embarrassing guys like me. Your uncle . . . I'm his protégé," O'Neill said. "I don't want to be in trouble with the President of the United States. Christ, I already was with Mike Neville against him to start off with. And I don't get along with Bobby. [But] I get along with Dick Maguire and all that gang — I'm kind of a voice that they're using between [the White House and] John McCormack. And, Jesus, you're doing this to us when everything's going fine."[17]

Kennedy trounced McCormack in the primary. The White House then asked O'Neill to reprise his 1958 duties and serve as campaign manager for the Democratic gubernatorial candidate in Massachusetts, Endicott "Chub" Peabody. The wise guys in Democratic politics had handed the nomination to Peabody, thinking him a Yankee lamb to be sacrificed to incumbent Governor John Volpe, and the Kennedys were worried about a lackluster Democratic turnout. "Peabody was as loose as a Chinaman's slipper," said Dick Donahue. "He was the most naive innocent there could be. He needed some grounding."

O'Neill saw an opportunity. Peabody had assets that extended beyond his Brahmin heritage; he was an All-American football player, decorated navy war hero and likable guy. The congressman also thought Volpe was overconfident and ripe for plucking. With Peabody running as a Kennedy-style reformer, and O'Neill muscling the regulars, they used Volpe's embrace of an unpopular sales tax and the surge in pro-Kennedy sentiment that followed the Cuban missile crisis that October to score one of the great upsets of Massachusetts political history.

"The Democratic Party regulars were not actively supporting Peabody. If they failed to get out the vote, there was no chance of Chub pulling an upset," said Lester Hyman, then a top aide to Peabody. "Tip told us to call a meeting in his name at campaign headquarters of all the [Massachusetts] leaders of the Democratic Party.

"I had always known Tip as sweet, cuddly, one who would never say damn. He got up there and said, 'Listen you fuckers: you go out and work for the Democratic ticket!' The air was blue with the language. Tip told them that he didn't give a damn whether or not they liked Endicott Peabody personally. That was irrelevant. The important thing was to elect Democrats to office up and down the line. Therefore, each of them was to work for Peabody's election like their lives depended on it. And if they did not, he would know about it and they would pay a heavy price for their betrayal," Hyman recalled. "The leaders turned out the Democratic vote on Election Day. If they had not, Peabody never would have won." In the last week of the campaign, O'Neill and Peabody campaigned arm-in-arm in the Irish American wards in and around Boston. "O'Neill slipped in where others feared to tread and in the closing weeks of the Peabody campaign bolstered sagging Democratic strength," the *Globe* reported. Peabody won by 5,000 votes, out of 2 million cast.[18]

AND YET, as so often happened where O'Neill's relationship with the Kennedys was concerned, ups were followed by downs. O'Neill appeared to confirm the Kennedy clan's opinion of him in the final months of the New Frontier, when his willingness to do a favor for a friendly constituent drew him into a tarnishing flap. Martin Camacho, a Portuguese-American attorney from Cambridge, had asked O'Neill for help in a lobbying and public relations campaign he was running on behalf of some Portuguese clients. O'Neill gave him free run of his office in Washington, the aid of his staff, use of the government printing office and congressional free postage. O'Neill inserted statements by Camacho in the *Congressional Record,* introduced him to other congressmen, and joined with McCormack and other lawmakers to defend Portugal's repression of African nationalism in Angola as a necessary response to Communist aggression.

The delegation's sudden interest in Angolan affairs amused Kennedy, who teased O'Neill about his venture into foreign policy. "You've come a long way since Barry's Corner," he told the congressman. "What do you know about Angola?" The staff members of the Senate Foreign Relations Committee, which was investigating the lobbying of Congress by foreign interests, were not so amused. They discovered that Camacho had been hired by a New York public relations firm, which in turn was paid $500,000 by Portuguese industrialists with close ties to the government of Portugal. Chairman William Fulbright of Arkansas held closed-door hearings on the issue in the spring of 1963.

"I used his office the same as if I were in my own office," Camacho told the committee when asked about O'Neill. "I used his staff there the same." In a letter to the committee, O'Neill said he would let any Cambridge businessman have the run of his office, and saw no problems in letting a foreign lobbyist trade on his good name. The Camacho affair demonstrated the dangers of O'Neill's approach to politics, and ratified the fears of his friends and family over how he would have performed as governor.[19]

O'Neill turned fifty in December 1962, nagged by doubts and regrets. McCormack seemed set on serving forever, and there would be no room in the congressional leadership for another Massachusetts Catholic until old John departed. Nor could he see himself in the Senate, which he viewed from across the capitol as a haven for "the idiot sons of the rich." The job in Washington had cost him his insurance business, whose clients wanted the kind of personal service he wasn't around to provide. He was on and off his diets, gambling, shifting his money in and out of the stock market and investing in various sweetheart deals, some of which brought him grief but made him money, and others that only brought him grief. There was a President from Massachusetts, and Tip O'Neill couldn't get past the White House guard.

"They thought of my father as a Boston Irishman, and didn't want to be tinged with that," O'Neill's daughter Rosemary recalled. "He wanted something better, but he knew he could probably never be chairman of the Rules Committee, because Dick Bolling was younger than him and ahead of him in seniority. And Eddie Boland, meanwhile, is a bachelor member of Congress. Extremely eligible and, my God, every time there was an empty seat and they needed a young guy from Congress at a White House dinner they called on Eddie; he was having this fabulous time during the Kennedy years.

"I'll never forget my father and I sitting at Paul Young's having dinner and him moaning to me: 'Here I am, fifty years old, and my life is completely finished,'" Rosemary said. "'The President of the United States comes from Massachusetts and I can't even get in to see him. This only happens once in a lifetime. I've lost my chance.'"

O'Neill was in his office in the old federal building in downtown Boston on the afternoon of November 22, 1963. A secretary from Congressman Jimmy Burke's office rushed in with the news. "They shot the President. He's dead," she cried. O'Neill picked up the telephone to call Bob Healy at the *Globe.* A receptionist recognized his voice. "Is that you, Tip?" she said. "It's true." O'Neill closed the office, and he and his staff walked to the Catholic shrine on Arch Street, where the pews were filled by the shattered and the stunned.

The O'Neills went to the airport that evening to pick up Rosemary, who had rushed home from college to be with her family. "Walking through Logan, there wasn't a person speaking. Silent as death. We got in the car and I remember coming over to the entrance to the Callahan Tunnel, and the newsboys with the *Herald-Traveler* with banner headlines: 'Kennedy Dead.' And my father started to cry," she said. He was named to the official group that represented the House at the funeral, and participated in the stirring ceremonies that weekend.

O'Neill had no illusions about Jack Kennedy. They had their difficulties. He had heard the stories in Washington about the President's extramarital sex life. When his daughter Susan asked him if Kennedy would be canonized, he had assured her that the President was no saint. But he was racked by grief nonetheless. His most characteristic response to the assassination was a story he told time and again in the days that followed: how on an autumn day in 1963, the handsome young President had summoned him to the Oval Office, and how they had talked about the situation in Congress, and the upcoming trip to Dallas, and how Kennedy had vowed that he was pulling the American troops out of Vietnam once the 1964 election was over. But most of all, of how Kennedy had asked about the health and fortunes of Billy Sutton and Patsy Mulkern and Joe Healey and Peter Cloherty and Mark Dalton and all the other Boston pols who had worked to help make the career of the first Irish Catholic President, and been discarded along the way.

It is reasonable to assume that the conversation took place, though the White House logs don't reflect it. But whether or not it happened just as O'Neill said it did, it is striking that the story he took away from that prized, long-awaited moment with the President was of Prince Hal's affection for the Falstaffs, Nims and Pistols. Time and again, when asked by reporters or historians of their memories of Kennedy, these tough men returned to what they had been told by Congressman O'Neill, of how the President was still thinking about them, and inquiring about their health, just days before he died, and how he hadn't forgotten and wasn't that just like Jack. . . . And then some of them would have to pause to collect themselves.

The story was a great gift O'Neill had given them. It speaks well of his thoughtfulness and generosity. It gave them great comfort. It no doubt comforted him as well.[20]

In the days after John Kennedy's death, Lyndon Johnson made many telephone calls, seeking advice and support, to House leaders like John McCormack, Carl Albert, Adam Clayton Powell, Hale Boggs and Richard Bolling. Noticeably absent from the new President's call list was the name of Tip O'Neill. Johnson had retained Kenneth O'Donnell, Larry O'Brien and other members of the Irish Mafia. It looked like a replay of the Kennedy administration, with O'Neill once again on the outs. This time, however, O'Neill was determined that he would not be taken for granted.

Within days of Kennedy's funeral, O'Neill received a jolt when he learned that Johnson had announced to McCormack and other congressional leaders that the Pentagon was going to close the navy yards in Boston, Philadelphia, New York and San Francisco. Johnson was on an austerity drive to win votes in Congress for the pending tax cut that had been introduced but not passed by his predecessor.

"Where are you going to close them?" McCormack had asked the President, drawing on a cigar.

"Boston," said Johnson. McCormack turned, and with a mighty exhalation, blew the smoke in O'Donnell's face.

After the meeting, Johnson asked O'Donnell if he was upset about the Boston navy yard.

"No, I'm not upset about Boston, but you know Congressman O'Neill," said O'Donnell. "He's a member of the Rules Committee, which . . . any vote we won, we won by 8 to 7. . . . You'll never get a piece of legislation on the floor of the House of Representatives as long as he's there."

The New York, Philadelphia and San Francisco delegations were also rich with influential congressmen. So Johnson reconsidered. "My inclination is to do what's right," he told Secretary of Defense Robert McNamara. "I'd hate like hell, though, to be such a statesman that I didn't get elected." McNamara agreed to hold off a final decision on the navy yard closings until after the 1964 election. But the writing was on the wall, and the Pentagon's decision to shut down the army's Watertown Arsenal, where many of the employees were residents of O'Neill's district, was a taste of more to come. O'Neill asked Johnson to speak at Boston College's commencement exercises that spring, but never received a response. Then he heard from officials at BC that the President was instead speaking at Holy Cross.

"I thought you should know of Congressman O'Neill's violent displeasure," White House aide Jack Valenti wrote colleagues O'Brien, O'Donnell and Bill Moyers. "1. He was disgusted with the way the White House handled this. 2. He had initiated this request several months ago. 3. He was humiliated in the eyes of Boston College for his total failure in this matter. 4. He was waiting for an opportunity to retaliate and he would do so when the administration had a bill that it wanted to pass.

"I am relating this to you in a far milder form than it was given to me," Valenti told his colleagues.

O'Neill's chance for vengeance arrived two weeks later, when an administration-backed transportation bill reached the Rules Committee. Cashing in chits, O'Neill turned a 9 to 6 vote for passage into an 8 to 7 defeat for Johnson, and then assembled an entirely different coalition of his colleagues to defeat, 8 to 7, a motion to reconsider the bill.

"O'Neill . . . did a pretty good job on us today," O'Brien told Johnson in a postmortem telephone call. "I talked to O'Neill after the vote, said 'Tip . . . , Christ, you were against us . . . it looks to me as if you did a little effective work.'

"He said, 'I have an awful lot of work to do in my office answering the letters of 2,200 people that have been made destitute in my district by this administration. . . . As long as McNamara is screwing everybody . . . that keeps me pretty busy.' "

"Maybe we ought to close that damn navy yard," Johnson said. "If that is the way he wants to play it."

"Well, Tip . . . he plays tough. He was the first Democratic Speaker of the House in the history of Massachusetts. Boy, he didn't get that way without being a pretty tough boy," O'Brien said.

Johnson began to call around the Hill. "Tip O'Neill is belly-aching because McNamara is closing up something in Boston," the President complained to Albert. "If he's going to play that way . . . we can play rough too."

The President moved on, calling the Speaker. "This is an administration bill, and a damned important one," Johnson told McCormack.

"Tom's all right. He's a good fellow. He might bark, but his bark is worse than his bite," McCormack said. "Tom's like a big St. Bernard dog. A very fine fellow. And he'll bark. But he's just as loyal as they make them." The Rules Committee was a leadership committee, the Speaker explained, but "once in a while, they've got to do something for themselves."

Johnson's phone calls were in vain. The transportation bill died in Rules. Three weeks later, O'Neill was at it again: this time holding Johnson's "war on poverty" bill hostage. O'Neill and Delaney were upset about the navy yard closings in Brooklyn and Boston, and angry that the poverty bill channeled its federal funding through public — but not private or parochial — schools. "We sure don't want to have any match with those two boys . . . but if they want to go to the mat, well, we will," Johnson told Albert. "O'Neill is threatening us on the Boston shipyard. . . . He's threatening the wrong man when he goes threatening me."

The President again got McCormack on the telephone. He thought he had solved his Catholic problems by appointing Kennedy in-law Sargent Shriver to head the poverty crusade.

"Hell! I don't want to be President if I can't get the Rules Committee to report my stuff. It's disgraceful for Delaney and O'Neill, who won't report an administration bill," said Johnson. "I've got Sargent Shriver: I thought, by God, that would take care of the Catholics by putting him in charge of it."

Johnson was in a fix. The southerners he needed to pass the poverty bill were threatening to desert if he gave in to Delaney and O'Neill on aid to religious schools. "If you allow these crackpot preachers to get in here and say that the Pope has rewritten the bill . . . then we haven't got a stinker's chance," Johnson told McCormack. "Tip O'Neill is gutting me every minute."

O'Neill fired yet another salvo in June. "The Speaker has talked to Tip O'Neill and Tip's going to leave next Tuesday night if they don't finish that bill on Tuesday," Albert told Johnson. The President sighed in exasperation. He wanted the poverty bill passed before the 1964 Democratic convention that summer. "Well, I'll just let 'em nominate somebody else," the President said. "I ain't gonna kiss any more congressmen's ass. . . . Go tell the Speaker about it, and just tell him if he wants the poverty bill to fail because Tip O'Neill is gone, why that's all right. That's what they're going to do."

Johnson hung up the phone and immediately called O'Brien. "On the Tip O'Neill thing . . . as far as I am concerned, he can just leave and kill the bill if he feels that way about it," said the President. "I'm tired of this cheap, dirty, low-down blackmailing."

Johnson ultimately capitulated. The Boston navy yard got four new piers and remained open until 1973, when the Nixon administration finally closed it down. O'Neill was given entree to administration farm and trade officials, so he could argue on behalf of the cheap sugar imports that helped put longshoremen and the employees of two sugar refineries to work in his district. He was invited to bill-signing ceremonies. Federal money poured into Cambridge, Somerville, Boston and Charlestown. Construction of a dreaded "inner-belt" highway through Cambridge was halted after O'Neill asked Johnson to yank the reins of federal highway administrators. "This route would be a China Wall, splitting our cultural City in two," O'Neill told the President. "I am unalterably opposed to this Route and I urge your intervention."

On July 28, by a vote of 8 to 7, with O'Neill in the majority, the war-on-poverty legislation cleared the Rules Committee. It passed the House on August 8. O'Neill had finally outflanked the Irish Mafia. In August he sent O'Brien a telegram that was as specific a statement of quid pro quo as any Boston politician ever put to paper: "Dear Larry, I intend to vote one billion dollars for the Appalachian program in the House Committee on Rules. The Massachusetts delegation has been asked to vote this one billion dollars on the floor of the United States House of Representatives. We are asking that nine million dollars be allocated for competitive bid to the six private shipyards in the greater Boston area to prevent them from going into bankruptcy. Please make sure the President is shown this telegram."

"What can we do for O'Neill?" White House lobbyist Charles U. Daly wrote the Pentagon. On September 23 the congressman received a letter from the navy. Four warships and three tankers to be used by the Apollo space program were to be converted and outfitted in Boston-area shipyards.[21]

"Tip is a sensitive man who should have proper attention so that he does not get the idea he is taken for granted," wrote one Johnson aide to another.[22]

O'NEILL PLAYED no games with the other historic bill that Johnson pushed through Congress in 1964: the Civil Rights Act. The civil rights bills of 1957 and 1960 had yielded but meager success, most tangibly in a number of lawsuits filed by the Justice Department on behalf of Negro voting rights in the South. In the meantime, the brutal repression that met the civil rights marches, sit-ins and freedom rides had shamed Americans and touched the nation's conscience.

Black voters had helped elect John Kennedy, but his administration had ducked calls for another civil rights bill for fear of alienating the South.[23] The New Frontier, said Clarence Mitchell, was looking like a dude ranch with "Howard Smith as foreman." It was only after a series of bombings, shootings and vicious beatings, the prolonged and televised assaults on civil rights protesters in Birmingham, and George Wallace's unsuccessful stand at the schoolhouse door of the University of Alabama that Kennedy went on national television to speak about civil rights and declare it time for vigorous action. "The time has come for this nation to fulfill its promise," Kennedy said. It was June 12, 1963. Just a few moments after Kennedy went off the air, civil rights activist Medgar Evers was gunned down by a sniper in Jackson, Mississippi. Kennedy himself had but five months to live.

The bill that the Kennedy administration introduced that summer strengthened the Justice Department's hand in voting rights and school segregation cases, forbade discrimination by businesses, hotels, restaurants and other places of "public accommodation," established the Equal Employment Opportunity Commission, and authorized the withholding of federal funds from institutions that discriminated on the basis of race or religion. There were a number of legislative heroes in the struggle that followed — but none more so than John McCormack, whose commitment to the cause he called "the long fight; the hard fight" was absolute. Congress would not adjourn, the Speaker announced, until it had acted on Kennedy's program. "To me it was a moral question," McCormack said. "None of us are consulted when we are brought into the world. The incident of birth is an act of God . . . [as is] the color of one's skin." On August 28, in the midst of the House Judiciary Committee's hearings on the bill, a coalition of civil rights groups staged the March on Washington, which culminated on the steps of the Lincoln Memorial with King's unforgettable "I have a dream" address. O'Neill was one of some seventy-five legislators in the audience. Because the VIP area had been swallowed by the crowd, the congressmen had to march down the steps to another bloc of reserved seats. "Pass the bill," the thousands chanted. "Pass the bill." Then King began to speak.

"I remember sitting out there at the Lincoln Monument in the sweltering heat, and admiring this man, his talent, his ability. To look at him, you knew he was a leader. You knew that he had a cause. You knew that he was turning the nation around," O'Neill said. After much jockeying, the President himself convened a White House meeting of all the House principals and cut a final deal. The bill passed the Judiciary Committee on October 29, and the effort to surmount Smith's obstructionism got a tragic boost from the surge of emotion that followed Kennedy's death.

In his first address to Congress, five days after the assassination, Johnson declared that "we have talked long enough in this country about equal rights. We have talked for one hundred years or more. It is time now to write the next chapter and write it in the books of law." Smith knew when he was beaten. The Republicans on the committee, led by Representative Clarence Brown, a stout and stout-hearted newspaper publisher from small-town Ohio, had informed the chairman they would support the bill.

Liberal Democrats wondered at the supportive attitude of Brown and other Republican leaders. "They couldn't understand that once in a while a guy does something because it's right," said Republican leader Charles Halleck. "I had a few experiences. I had a black driver. We used to go down to Warm Springs, Virginia, to see friends. We'd stop at a little bit of a restaurant. I'd go in and ask if he would go in with the Hallecks. They said no but they would be glad to serve him in the car. The goddamned thing just didn't look right to me." For the party of Lincoln, it was one of its finest hours.

McCormack guaranteed that the bill would be on the House floor by mid-February. The legislation emerged from the Rules Committee by an 11 to 4 vote on January 30. Smith tried a final gambit on February 8 — attempting to love the bill to death on the House floor by adding "sex" to the kinds of discrimination (by race, color, religion or ethnicity) that were forbidden by the act. He taunted his colleagues like a Dickensian villain: "Now, what harm can you do to this bill that was so perfect yesterday and so imperfect today?"

Democratic leaders understood Smith's strategy, and opposed the amendment. It would open "a Pandora's box of revolutionary changes," said Emmanuel Celler, fearing the loss of moderate supporters. But five congresswomen came to its defense. "We are entitled to this little crumb of equality," said Representative Katherine St. George, a

Republican from New York. The House had no option but to adopt Smith's measure. It passed the bill on February 10 on a vote of 290 to 130, and the Senate followed suit. In one of the great ironies of American history, the federal prohibition against sex discrimination — which over the next three decades would help American women take giant strides toward equality — was the handiwork of an old, embittered bigot.[24]

The Johnson landslide in the 1964 election brought in a tide of Democrats, so that the party enjoyed a 2 to 1 margin over the Republicans in both the House and the Senate. Judge Smith's days of tyranny were over, as the Democrats adopted a 21-day rule, prohibiting him from locking up legislation in the Rules Committee cooler for more than three weeks. The result was the Voting Rights Act of 1965, another landmark piece of legislation, whose tough proscriptions would change the face of the South. Johnson introduced the act to a joint session of Congress, ending his speech by quoting from the civil rights anthem: "We shall overcome." O'Neill needed no prompting. He had an innate distaste for racial prejudice — daughter Susan long remembered the spanking she got on the first and only day she brought the epithet "nigger" home from the schoolyard. In February, as the battle raged in Selma, O'Neill had attended a hearing at the State House in Boston, at which a number of southern black students from Harvard testified about the violent attempts of their white southern neighbors to deny them the vote. It prompted what, for O'Neill, was a major discourse when the Rules Committee met to consider the Voting Rights Act.

"I had the opportunity of listening in on one of these depositions that a young girl from Mississippi had given," O'Neill told his colleagues. "She was a graduate of a state teacher's college. She was a graduate of the University of Texas and working for her doctorate at Harvard. She . . . wanted to register to vote in Mississippi."

O'Neill had some private reservations about the public accommodation section of the Civil Rights Act, but none about the Voting Rights Act. His whole philosophy was centered upon his belief in a political system that allowed, through the promise of education and free elections, a nation's underdogs to make better lives for themselves and their children. Racism was denying that opportunity to this young black Harvard student. "She first had to make an application to register.

After she made the application . . . the local newspaper printed her application and they asked whether there were any objections [about] moral turpitude and did she have a criminal record . . . or did anybody have any objections," he said. "Seven days later she came back and she took a literacy test. Then, seven days later, she was to return again to find out whether she passed. No answers why, she was just denied.

"She took it to court," O'Neill concluded, and "the court ordered her to be a registered voter. But of course the election had since passed."

The Voting Rights Act moved through the Rules Committee with little difficulty in early summer and passed the House on July 9. In a gesture that Clarence Mitchell always remembered, the dying congressman Clarence Brown checked himself out of the hospital to help shepherd the legislation through Judge Smith's domain. "Look out for tricks," the old newspaperman warned the great civil rights leader when they last parted; he died in August.

The Rules Committee's minutes from 1965 and 1966 reflect the newly influential role played by O'Neill in that historic Eighty-ninth Congress. Johnson and his staff regularly consulted with O'Neill, as the President and other members of Congress recognized the emergence of a new Democratic leader and an increasingly influential lieutenant to the aging Speaker. In 1966, when Johnson's foes launched a concerted attack on the war on poverty, O'Neill led the defense of the program.

Reflecting his new stature, O'Neill's horde of chits grew commensurately. "I have requested Chairman Smith to consider the bill, but with little success. I would appreciate your assistance," wrote subcommittee chairman John R. Dent of North Carolina to O'Neill, asking for help with a vocational education bill that was stalled in Rules.

"Dear Tip: Enclosed is a copy of a letter [asking for a hearing on a Michigan parks bill] I sent to Chairman Smith. I would appreciate any help you can give me with this matter," wrote Representative James O'Hara of Michigan.

O'Neill became an integral part of the coalition of Democrats (and an occasional liberal Republican) that, by one- or two-vote margins, moved the Great Society's legislation from Smith's domain to the House floor. The Appalachian redevelopment bill passed Rules by an 8 to 7 margin on February 25, 1965. The Elementary and Secondary Education Act, with O'Neill and Delaney on board, was approved 8 to

7 on March 22. The liberal coalition prevailed on the Medicare legislation by a 9 to 6 vote in April, the same month that Rules okayed the Water Quality Act. The Voting Rights bill moved from Rules in early July and the Immigration Act, which would help transform the face of America, in August.

"As the President was fond of saying, his landslide in 1964 created a reserve of capital which was to be spent and not conserved — and he spent it freely," said Johnson aide Harold "Barefoot" Sanders. O'Neill was a cosponsor of the Medicare and Immigration bills. The Medicare legislation — providing guaranteed federal health insurance for the elderly — was a triumph for Johnson and Representative Wilbur Mills of Arkansas, who chaired the Ways and Means Committee. When Medicare's conservative foes proposed to divide the House by offering rival benefits to elderly voters, Mills simply endorsed them as well: expanding the scope of the program beyond the wildest fears of its opponents. O'Neill later said that his role in cutting the poverty rate by more than half among elderly Americans (from 29 percent in 1967 to 12.4 percent by 1984) — a quantifiable result of the war on poverty, Medicare and expanded Social Security programs — was one of his proudest achievements.

The immigration legislation, on the other hand, became a textbook case of unintended consequences. The bill eliminated the "natural origins" clause and quotas, which promoted immigration from the white European nations that fed the growth of America in its first 150 years. In its place, a family preference system was adopted, allowing new citizens to bring their close relatives to the United States, who in turn were permitted to bring additional members of an extended family tree. Before the bill was passed, nine out of ten immigrants came from Europe. After the legislation was enacted, eight out of ten immigrants arrived in the United States from Asia, Africa and Latin America. At century's end, as the high-tech and market revolutions were shrinking the world, and ethnic, religious and racial tensions were replacing bipolar cold war division, the United States was reaping the benefits and serving as a symbol of multicultural cooperation.

"We have committed our nation to the preservation of freedom for all peoples of the world; not only those of Northern Europe," O'Neill told the House during the immigration bill debate. The United States would cope with the different-colored skins of the new immigrants in the same way it had dealt with the language, religion and customs of a previous class of strangers, and be better off for it, he predicted. "The pluralistic society which has resulted from the amalgamation of so many cultures has enriched the lives of all Americans and has strengthened our national character."

LYNDON JOHNSON HAD few illusions. His triumphs were not without cost. The achievements of the Great Society, and most especially its civil rights legislation, took a political toll on the Democrats, especially in the South. In doing the right thing, his party had "delivered the South to the Republican Party for a long time to come," LBJ told aide Bill Moyers.

A new tide was evident in June 1966 when the eighty-three-year-old Judge Smith (he was born just eighteen years after Lee's surrender at Appomattox) was finally brought down by the forces he so long opposed. In a Democratic primary, a record turnout of black Virginians joined moderate and liberal Democrats from the Washington suburbs to drive the Judge from office by 645 votes. Yet Smith was no doubt comforted by the fact that the liberal Democrat who beat him was defeated in November by a conservative Republican. If O'Neill looked closely he could see, in the story of that election, the first signs of a conservative reaction that would shatter the Democratic Solid South, dominate American politics for the next twenty years and bring to power the Republican antagonists with whom he would battle for the rest of his life. Their names were Nixon, Reagan and Gingrich.[25]

CHAPTER 10

Vietnam, Kooks and Commies

TIP O'NEILL HAD no cultural affinity with the delegation of Quakers and Cambridge religious leaders who called on him at his office one day in February 1966. They were pious good-government types. Goo-Goos from Brattle Street. Gown, not town. The kind who "considered me a shanty Irish politician," he'd say later. And they wanted to talk about Vietnam. As a quiet-spoken Friend made her presentation, O'Neill rudely interrupted. "I support my President," he said. "You are nothing but a bunch of Communist sympathizers." There was a moment of shock and silence and then, "We realized nothing more could be said and left," said Rosaline Herstein, a member of the delegation.[1]

O'Neill later apologized for his intemperance, but the peaceniks and academics irritated him. Like almost every other Democrat in Congress in 1966, he endorsed Johnson's expansion of the war. LBJ had inherited this cold war duty from Kennedy, as Kennedy had from Eisenhower, as Ike had from the French. O'Neill was a staunch anti-Communist. Like many other Irish Americans, he had heard the clergy tell gruesome tales of the Catholic priests and nuns in the Spanish Civil

War who, it was said, chose martyrdom before they would spit on a crucifix or give corporal pleasure to their Communist captors. "The courageous people of Spain rose up in protest against the ruthless designs of a Red government. Under the able direction of General Francisco Franco, they began their long struggle for the return of law and order and security," O'Neill said, in a 1959 tribute to the right-wing Spanish dictator. "Their battle was not an easy one as the Red menace had insidiously penetrated the nation.

"Where Communism is concerned, we cannot stand idle!" O'Neill warned.[2] He was a progressive Democrat on issues of wages and work, but clearly of that wing of party liberals that preached a muscular resistance to the Soviet system's cruelties and repression.

Vietnam had been a colony of France, conquered and occupied by the Japanese during World War II and divided into Communist North and pro-Western South at the Geneva Conference of 1954, after the French were defeated by the Communist Viet Minh. The CIA then helped spur a massive migration of Vietnamese Catholics from North to South Vietnam. Four-fifths of the million refugees who fled Ho Chi Minh's North were Catholic, and the American church rallied to their aid. Special collections were held at Sunday Masses. In Catholic orthodoxy, the villainy of the Viet Minh took its place beside the atrocities of the Spanish Communists. In an August 1954 guest column in the *Traveler,* O'Neill charged, "We have witnessed at Geneva the culmination of a perfumed 'sellout' to Communist aggression." Eisenhower had spoken that year of a "falling domino principle," and O'Neill now turned the theory against the Republican administration: "By permitting the fall of northern Vietnam we have provided a springboard from which the Communists can launch attacks for the subjugation of Laos, Cambodia and Thailand. Having penetrated and conquered these states, Indonesia and Burma would lie exposed as the next victims."[3]

Kennedy's election, and his inaugural call upon Americans to "pay any price, bear any burden, meet any hardship" in the war for freedom, clinched the matter. "The enemy is the Communist system itself—implacable, insatiable, increasing its drive for world domination," Kennedy said on the campaign trail in 1960. "This is not a struggle for supremacy of arms alone. It is also a struggle for supremacy between two conflicting ideologies: freedom under God versus ruthless, godless tyranny." Tip would back Jack. "I shall follow the recommendations of the Administration and the Department of State who have more and better sources of information than are available to me," he wrote to a constituent in September 1963.[4]

American policy had initially called only for economic and military aid, in the form of matériel and advisers. The Vietnamese were to win the war for themselves, Kennedy said. But the regime of President Ngo Dinh Diem, a monastic Catholic who had once studied at a Maryknoll seminary in New Jersey, tottered under pressure from Buddhist opponents, some of whom commanded the world's attention by dousing themselves with gasoline and committing fiery suicide before Western photographers. Kennedy, angry and frustrated at the course of the war, offered U.S. support to dissident Vietnamese generals who staged a coup d'état on November 2 during which Diem and his brother were murdered.

Four days after Kennedy's assassination, Johnson signed a national security directive pledging continued U.S. aid to South Vietnam; within two months, in response to pessimistic reports from the war zone, he authorized a series of American-supported covert attacks upon North Vietnam. Johnson wanted continuity in foreign policy and feared the Republicans might brand him as soft on Communism in the 1964 election. "They'd impeach a president . . . that would run out," Johnson told Senator Richard Russell, a Democrat from Georgia, in May. The President was also getting bad advice. Three decades later, former secretary of defense Robert McNamara described how U.S. officials blundered into tragedy, blinded by hubris and mistaking the Communist world as a monolithic bloc — in part because many of the government's Far East experts had been purged during the McCarthy years.[5]

"We were wrong, terribly wrong," McNamara wrote. "I saw Communism as monolithic . . . in hindsight, of course, it is clear that they had no unified strategy.

"We also totally underestimated the nationalistic aspect of Ho Chi Minh's movement," McNamara confessed. "We failed to analyze our assumptions critically, then or later. The foundations of our decision making were gravely flawed."[6]

The covert attacks that Johnson okayed in early 1964 included a series of commando raids launched upon the North by U.S.-supplied gunboats. On July 30, South Vietnamese commandos and their U.S. advisers raided two North Vietnamese islands in the Gulf of Tonkin, not far from where the USS *Maddox,* a destroyer, was on an intelligence-gathering mission. On the afternoon of August 2, the *Maddox* was attacked by three North Vietnamese torpedo boats and returned fire. When the USS *C. Turner Joy* joined the *Maddox* the next day, Johnson ordered both destroyers back into the Gulf.

Johnson was hosting congressional leaders at the White House on the morning of August 4 when word came that the *Turner Joy* and *Maddox* were under attack. The Pentagon began to backtrack almost immediately, acknowledging by that afternoon that no one had actually seen a torpedo wake, and that most of the sonar contacts were probably echoes from the *Maddox*'s own rudders as it took evasive action in a wild nighttime melee. Nevertheless, Johnson ordered bombing raids against North Vietnamese navy bases and oil dumps.[7]

On August 5, the White House asked Congress to enact the Gulf of Tonkin Resolution, which declared that Southeast Asia was "vital" to U.S. national interests, and authorized the President "to take all necessary steps, including the use of armed forces" to assist South Vietnam and other nations in the region. The House Foreign Affairs Committee held a forty-minute hearing when approving the resolution on August 6.

O'Neill was at McCormack's table in the House dining room on the morning of August 7 when the Speaker arrived, and the talk turned to the Gulf of Tonkin Resolution. The Democratic national convention was three weeks away; the poverty bill was coming to the floor — there were political as well as patriotic reasons to give Johnson the power he had requested. O'Neill complained to McCormack that "there was something screwy about the whole thing." The conversation at the table stopped and "everybody kind of looked at me aghast," he recalled. The Speaker said nothing, but summoned O'Neill to his office shortly before the session was to start at noon. "I don't want you to vote against Tonkin Gulf," McCormack said. "I think it would be a political disaster. Personally, I think the President is right. We can't tolerate having people shoot at our armament. . . . Tom, it will be determining that you're a traitor if you were to do a thing like that."

O'Neill quickly fell into line. "I voted more in loyalty to John McCormack as everybody knew I was his protégé and I shouldn't be breaking with him," he said. "I always looked at it as the one cowardly vote that I made . . . but he may have been right in view of the fact that it may have terminated my political career." The Gulf of Tonkin

Resolution was passed by the House after forty minutes of debate by 416 to 0. No member spoke against it.[8]

If O'Neill had fundamental doubts about Johnson's war, he kept them to himself, or — like thousands of other Americans — was lulled by LBJ's promise, made throughout that fall's election campaign, "We are not about to send American boys nine or ten thousand miles away from home to do what Asian boys ought to be doing for themselves." Besides, it was a time to rally around the Democratic president, as 1964 brought the first signs of the political polarization that would scar the next three decades.

Despite the gains of the civil rights movement, blacks in Harlem, Philadelphia and other cities rioted that summer — embittered by the length of the struggle and the unfulfilled expectations it raised. At the Democratic convention in Atlantic City, the party regulars pushed aside the Mississippi Freedom Democratic Party's challenge to the all-white Mississippi delegation, radicalizing young black and white activists who had tried, as their elders counseled, to work within the political system. In December, the free speech movement at the University of California in Berkeley challenged the state's ban on campus political rallies, launching an era of student activism. A New Left was aborning.

There was a stirring on the Right as well. The word "backlash" entered the political lexicon as George Wallace took his brand of race-baiting populism to the white ethnic neighborhoods of the North for the first time and shocked the nation by winning 34 percent of the vote in the Democratic presidential primary in Wisconsin and 43 percent of the vote in Maryland. The Republicans, meanwhile, selected conservative Arizona senator Barry Goldwater as their nominee, confirming the shift in power within the party to the Sunbelt's conservative activists. Ronald Reagan, a well-known film star and former Democrat who had embraced the conservative cause after feeling the pinch of the federal income tax on his Hollywood salary, made his political debut that year in a televised fund-raising pitch for Goldwater. Reagan, part of a new wave of modern American conservatism, believed in individualism, low taxes and the evils of big government. "You and I have a rendezvous with destiny. We will preserve for our children this, the last best hope of man on earth, or we will sentence them to take the last step into a thousand years of darkness," Reagan said, stealing liberally from both Franklin D. Roosevelt and Abraham Lincoln. He called his talk "A Time for Choosing." Among conservatives, it took on the air of scripture, known in time as "The Speech."

Still, these were but whispers of tumult to come. The economy was embarking on its greatest postwar boom, and for the most part that golden summer and fall still bore the glow of American optimism and faith in scientific progress. In the corporate pavilions of the World's Fair in New York, the O'Neills and thousands of other American families toured elaborate dioramas of the future in which model spaceships and miniature aquanauts tamed the depths of space and sea, and tiny mobile factories used lasers in the jungle to carve superhighways through the rain forests. The O'Neills viewed Michelangelo's *Pietà* in the Vatican pavilion, and laughed at the host of puppets in the Disney exhibit who songfully celebrated a "small, small world." Cold war tensions had relaxed a bit. It was the year of the first human heart transplant, the Ford Mustang, and the Beatles — for whose late summer tour O'Neill wangled tickets for his daughter Susan. The O'Neills had lingered in a seaside house he had rented for the family during the Atlantic City convention, and were there when the Beatles came to town.

On the eve of a war that would rip the nation apart, the cold war–liberal–welfare state enjoyed its greatest political triumph. Johnson won a historic landslide in November, capturing 44 states and 486 electoral votes, largely by turning Goldwater's bellicose rhetoric against him. In the relentlessly negative Democratic campaign, Goldwater was portrayed as an enemy of Social Security and, in a memorable television ad that superimposed a nuclear blast atop the image of a little girl plucking petals from a daisy, as a trigger-happy extremist. There were signs that the New Deal coalition was crumbling when LBJ failed to win a majority of white votes in nine states of the old Confederacy, but they were lost in Democratic euphoria as the party picked up 37 House seats, raising its control of the House to a 295 to 140 margin, and paving the way for the legislative triumphs of the Great Society.

Yet even as Lyndon Johnson campaigned as a peace candidate, his advisers were crafting plans for a gradual but steady increase of U.S. military pressure on the North, with bombing raids, the mining of North Vietnamese harbors and the commitment of U.S. combat forces to commence after the election. Hanoi would be convinced of U.S. resolve and reasonably conclude that its support for the Communist insurgency in the South was too costly, the White House and Pentagon planners decided. But in calculating their interests, the North Vietnamese refused to be reasonable. In January 1965, U.S. ambassador Maxwell Taylor and commander General William Westmoreland sent an urgent cable to Johnson. "We are presently on a losing track. . . . To take no positive action now is to accept defeat in the fairly near future," they said.

"The successive political upheavals and the accompanying turmoil which have followed Diem's demise upset all prior U.S. calculations," the two generals wrote. "We know now what are the basic factors responsible for this turmoil — chronic factionalism, civilian-military suspicions and distrust, absence of national spirit and motivation, lack of cohesion in the social structure, lack of experience in the conduct of govt. These are historical factors growing out of national characteristics and traditions, susceptible to change only over the long run. We Americans are not going to change them in any fundamental way in any measurable time."[9] The South Vietnamese could not do it by themselves. Taylor asked for an expanded U.S. role in the war, and for air attacks on North Vietnam. Johnson had reached a turning point.

LBJ's motives were, for the most part, honorable. Though one of America's weakest and most troubled allies, South Vietnam was nonetheless part of a global alliance that had successfully contained Communist imperialism for two decades. Johnson was now confronted with his first test as the leader of that alliance. He dreaded "another Korea," but as President of a nation that had fully embraced his martyred predecessor's vow to pay any price to resist tyranny, how could he abandon the South Vietnamese, many of whom were genuine democrats and detested Ho Chi Minh's totalitarian state? To these considerations, one must add Johnson's own political ambition, personal insecurities, Texas machismo and New Deal philosophy.

Years later, after leaving office, Johnson explained his decision to biographer Doris Kearns Goodwin in memorable terms.

"If I left the woman I really loved — the Great Society — in order to get involved with that bitch of a war on the other side of the world, then I would lose everything at home," he said. "But if I left that war and let the Communists take over South Vietnam, then I would be seen as a coward and my nation would be seen as an appeaser. . . . I'd be doing exactly what Chamberlain did in World War II.

"Once the war began, then all those conservatives in the Congress would use it as a weapon against the Great Society . . . they had never wanted to help the poor or the Negroes in the first place. But they were having a hard time figuring out how to make their opposition sound noble in a time of great prosperity," Johnson explained. "But the war: oh, they'd use it to say they were against my programs, not because they were against the poor — why, they were as generous and as charitable as the best of Americans — but because the war had to come first."

An American withdrawal, Johnson said, would cause "a mean and destructive debate . . . that would shatter my Presidency, kill my administration and damage our democracy" by engendering a fit of recrimination to match the McCarthy era. And in the front rank of critics would be his nemesis, Robert Kennedy, "telling everyone that I had betrayed John Kennedy's commitment to South Vietnam. That I had let a democracy fall into the hands of the Communists. That I was a coward. An unmanly man. A man without a spine."[10]

On February 7, 1965, the Viet Cong attacked the U.S. base at Pleiku, killing eight Americans. Johnson ordered retaliatory bombing raids on North Vietnam. On February 13, three days after the Communists raided the U.S. base at Qui Nhon, Johnson gave orders for Rolling Thunder, an ongoing bombing campaign against North Vietnam. On March 8, to protect U.S. airfields, the first U.S. Marines landed at Danang. By Christmas there were 180,000 U.S. troops in Vietnam.

As the United States slouched toward full-scale war, O'Neill remained moved by many of the same honorable impulses that motivated Johnson. "Around the globe from Berlin to Thailand are people whose well-being rests in part on the belief that they can count on us if attacked. To leave Vietnam to its fate would shake the confidence of all these people in the value of an American commitment and in the value of America's word. It would encourage other potential aggressors to think they can raid their neighbors with impunity and the result would necessarily be increased unrest, instability, and even wider war," O'Neill told a group of peace activists from Cambridge.[11]

"The president . . . has my full support and confidence," O'Neill wrote to one constituent who had complained about the February bombing raids. "I shall continue to support the policy set by Presidents Eisenhower, Kennedy and Johnson," O'Neill wrote after the marines went ashore at Danang. "I, of course, am behind the president 100 percent."[12]

There were some dissenters in Congress. In sharp contrast to Speaker McCormack, who never wavered in his support of the war,

Senate Majority Leader Mike Mansfield was willing to challenge the President in both long letters and face-to-face disagreements. Senators William Fulbright, Frank Church of Idaho, and George McGovern of South Dakota had similarly unpleasant confrontations with the President. And Vice President Hubert Humphrey wrote Johnson a long confidential memo in February 1965 warning that the war in Vietnam was unwinnable, destabilizing, too costly and unpopular. "People can't understand why we would run grave risks to support a country which is totally unable to put its own house in order," wrote Humphrey. "It is always hard to cut losses. But the Johnson administration is in a stronger position to do so now than any administration in this century. 1965 is the year of minimum political risk." His reward was to be frozen out of the administration's foreign policy decision-making for more than a year.[13]

Like Humphrey, almost all of those who disagreed conveyed their qualms about the war in private. In January 1965, the State Department assessed congressional support. "The great majority of Congressmen are neither satisfied nor dissatisfied; their thoughts are fragmented and they are genuinely perplexed," the report concluded. While a dozen senators were taking active roles, "there are fewer individuals in the House who are willing to take any precise stand; the general instinct is to keep with the herd, watch the situation, stick it out." The description aptly fit O'Neill.[14] When Johnson submitted a request for $700 million in supplemental funds to pay for U.S. activity in Vietnam and the Dominican Republic (where U.S. troops had stormed ashore in April), it took the House just two days, and a single hour of debate, to okay the appropriations bill by a 408 to 7 vote. O'Neill and the rest of the Massachusetts delegation voted with the majority. In one of the first signs of the division that would soon tear their party apart, the dissenters were all liberal Democrats, including Representatives John Conyers of Michigan, Phillip Burton and Don Edwards of California, and William Fitts Ryan of New York.

Outside of Congress, the initial signs of escalation yielded more spirited antiwar activity, with significant stirrings in O'Neill's own district. Harvard professor H. Stuart Hughes had run a quixotic campaign in the 1962 Massachusetts Senate contest on a peace and disarmament platform, and the veterans of that effort had stayed active and formed MassPAX, the Massachusetts Political Action for Peace committee.

Some four hundred faculty members from Harvard and other Boston-area colleges signed and purchased an advertisement in the *New York Times,* denouncing the bombing. There were teach-ins at college campuses that spring, and the first march on Washington on April 17, 1965, sponsored by the Students for a Democratic Society, attracted more than 15,000 participants — mostly students and professors — entertained by folk singers and led by pacifists and aging Leftists.

O'Neill responded to the antiwar forces in a speech at a testimonial dinner for William F. X. Linskey, athletic trainer for the Cambridge public schools, on April 30. "I can't understand how they were misled and got onto a wrong track," he told the working- and middle-class crowd, referring to the students and faculty members who opposed the war. He reminded the audience of how appeasement had led to war in the 1930s, and restated his belief in the domino theory.[15] "Educators with glib answers" and their student followers will "destroy the very freedom they invoke," O'Neill said in a commencement speech at Boston State College, three weeks after a May 15 teach-in was held on more than 100 college campuses. "It is up to us to contain Communism. They want to take over the world," O'Neill said.[16]

In June, 28 liberals in the House urged the Foreign Affairs Committee to hold hearings on Vietnam, and MassPAX wrote to O'Neill, asking him to add his name to the list. "With reference to the American policy in Vietnam I am in hearty agreement with the President of the United States and the great majority of Americans who concur with him," O'Neill replied. "At this time I do not intend to ask for public hearings on the matter or in any way censor the President of the United States."[17] MassPAX tried again in December, and was again brushed off. "I have your letter regarding Vietnam and I am sure you are aware of my views," O'Neill wrote to MassPAX chairman Jerome Grossman.[18]

"If you are going to put an epitaph on Tip's tombstone you are not going to put 'Liberal' you are not going to put 'Fighter' you are going to put 'Nice Guy.' He wanted to get along," Grossman said, years later.[19]

O'Neill "didn't see himself as the guy who came up with the ideas," said Judith Kurland, a Mount Holyoke college student who worked for O'Neill as an intern in 1966 and initially turned down an offer to join his staff because of his prowar stance. "He saw himself as a great

Democrat, big D, and a great Democratic legislator in terms of helping to get things through. He was on the Rules Committee — the Speaker's cabinet. He saw himself as a party man. The Speaker's man." And his church continued to support the war. "A lot of the stuff around Vietnam was Cardinal Spellman . . . and the Catholic line," Kurland remembered. "Tip was a very good Catholic. So there was a lot of tension there, too."[20] The congressman voted for another $1.8 billion appropriation for the war in August, after attending an off-the-record briefing at the White House, in which Johnson, McNamara and other administration officials pushed the case for intervention. That same month O'Neill voted to make it a federal crime, with punishment of up to five years in prison, to burn one's draft card. The vote in the House was 393 to 1.

Johnson had doubled the monthly draft calls, and there were signs that the protest movement was outgrowing the few elite campuses on which it had been nourished. But at the VFW halls in the blue-collar wards of North Cambridge and Somerville, the antiwar acts of long-haired, bell-bottomed youths were seen as disloyal, if not treasonous. The race riots that racked Chicago, the Los Angeles neighborhood of Watts and Springfield, Massachusetts, that summer only added to a growing sense of working-class vexation. In November, McNamara told Johnson that victory could require an army of 600,000 men and cost 12,000 U.S. combat deaths a year. Johnson pushed ahead.[21]

On January 8, 1966, O'Neill shared top billing with Miss USA as some 400 young people gathered in the State House in Boston for a rally to endorse the war. Nola Jane Birley, the beauty queen with a blond bouffant hairdo, posed with a bumper sticker that read: "We Support Our Boys in Vietnam." The rally was sponsored by the Massachusetts Young Democrats, Young Republicans, and the Young Americans for Freedom, an ultraconservative youth group. O'Neill's son Tommy and a group of his friends from BC were in the crowd. "The Vietnam war is not a revolution, but an invasion of the North Vietnamese into the territory of South Vietnam," O'Neill said to thunderous applause. Dismissing the war's critics, he added: "I believe in academic freedom, but not as it is expounded by kooks and commies and egghead professors."[22]

The Massachusetts chapter of the Americans for Democratic Action cried foul, chiding O'Neill in an angry letter that "elected officials such as yourself have a grave responsibility to refrain from making statements which feed hysteria and tend to encourage the suppression of legitimate debate."[23] Representatives from MassPAX and other Cambridge peace groups, who had met with O'Neill over the Christmas recess and interpreted his moving words about the wounded marines he had visited at the Chelsea Naval Hospital as evidence of concern about the war, were particularly outraged.[24] O'Neill was in no mood to apologize. He wrote to one of the rally's sponsors that "it was indeed a pleasure for me to be among so many fine young Americans. The display of genuine patriotism made me feel proud."[25]

As O'Neill sparred with the kooks and eggheads, CIA analysts in Saigon were warning Washington that the Pentagon's bombing campaign of North Vietnam was probably futile. The bombing only strengthened the hard-liners in Hanoi, who responded by sending more divisions of North Vietnamese regular troops down the Ho Chi Minh trail to the South. After the U.S. First Air Cavalry Division suffered then-record losses at the hands of North Vietnamese regulars in the course of a pyrrhic victory in the Ia Drang valley in November 1965, Johnson acceded to McNamara, briefly grounded his bombers at Christmas and sued for peace. "From now on you'll look weak," Speaker McCormack told the President.

North Vietnam rebuffed the U.S. diplomatic initiatives; the bombing resumed in January; the war escalated and the number of dead Americans doubled, then doubled again. The monthly draft quota rose from 17,000 in July to 45,000 in December. The Johnson administration never appreciated the fierce hold that nationalism had on North Vietnam's leaders, or the cruelty they were able to inflict and endure. At one point Johnson tried to buy the North's friendship with promises of a giant Mekong River Delta development plan. Hanoi was resolute, ignoring sixteen bombing pauses and seventy-two U.S. peace initiatives.[26]

Determined to have both guns and butter, and fearful that Americans would turn against the war if he raised the taxes he needed to fund it, Johnson led his administration toward a $23 billion budget deficit in 1966, triggering the start of a decade of inflation and economic stagnation that, coupled with the energy crises of the 1970s, would bring an end to the golden post–World War II era. Congress acquiesced. The year's defense appropriations and authorization bills were passed by

Congress with but a handful of dissenting votes. "Only four members of the House and two members of the Senate voted against the supplementary budget for Vietnam. Great victory for President Johnson. Your Dad carried the rule," O'Neill wrote Rosemary. A White House survey of 251 Democrats in Congress found just 9 representatives whose districts had turned against the war.[27]

O'Neill shared Johnson's deep dislike of Robert Kennedy, who was emerging as an antiwar critic and potential Democratic candidate for president. When Kennedy suggested on February 19 that the U.S. might negotiate and share power with the Viet Cong, O'Neill labeled the remark "asinine" and "dangerous." The episode caused a modest stir in Washington.[28]

The congressman had parochial concerns as well. "In the light of our continuing involvement in Southeast Asia, Cuba and Africa, as well as the almost numberless other areas where we are confronting the Communist menace, how the Department of Defense can even consider cutting back or closing the Watertown Arsenal and Boston Naval Shipyard is inconceivable," O'Neill wrote in response to an election-year questionnaire in 1966.[29]

In May, after the National Coordinating Committee to End the War in Vietnam, a national umbrella organization, had brought antiwar groups together for rallies in Boston and other cities, O'Neill addressed an AFL-CIO luncheon in Boston, renewing his support for the domino theory. "We must stop Communism there or we'll be fighting next in Thailand, Laos, Japan, Okinawa and the Philippines." As he told the *Herald,* "I feel we're in the same position today as in the time of Hitler. Had we taken a stronger stand then, there would have been no World War II." O'Neill agreed to speak on college campuses on behalf of the administration and the war; he was given briefings and reports of what questions had been asked by students at other such sessions around the country.[30]

"I have more kooks, commies, misguided students and misguided college professors on Vietnam in my district than any other member of Congress" and "quite a colony of Quakers," O'Neill told White House aide Charles Roche. But "in my district, a candidate who wants to win stays away from the college people."

LBJ was grateful. O'Neill and Millie were celebrating their twenty-fifth wedding anniversary with a fund-raising dinner at Washington's Shoreham Hotel on the night of June 15 when Johnson surprised and delighted the crowd by strolling in with majority leader Carl Albert.

"We had a terrific turnout and there was this three-piece band, and all of a sudden I look over and Peter Cloherty, this legendary rogue from Boston, is directing the band in 'Hail to the Chief.' I said, 'What the hell is going on?' And in comes Lyndon Johnson," said Terry Segal, an O'Neill aide.

Albert, at the White House, had mentioned to the President that he was due at the O'Neill fund-raiser and LBJ, in slacks and sports shirt, decided to tag along "like a little country boy who didn't get an invitation," the teasing President told the crowd. It was an impressive violation of Democratic protocol, which called on Presidents to remain neutral during primary contests. The three-piece band finished its impromptu version of "Hail to the Chief," and then the Massachusetts regulars surrounded the President and serenaded him with "Hello Lyndon," his campaign song. "I couldn't resist coming to a party for my friend Tip O'Neill," said Johnson, as the congressman beamed.[31]

IN HIS MEMOIRS, O'Neill would describe his disenchantment with the war as a relatively sudden thing, driven by moral outrage and the influence of his children, and free of most political calculation. But it is more accurately viewed as a process of erosion caused by a variety of personal, policy and political factors. Although O'Neill's replies to peace groups remained curt throughout 1966 and into 1967, his response to his working-class constituents — the key to his political heart — was always more complex. He could dismiss the generic postcards that arrived by the dozen from earnest leftist groups with names like "Individuals Against the Crime of Silence." But the handwritten letters from the working families of North Cambridge, Brighton and Somerville commanded his attention, and, sitting at his desk in his stocking feet, fiddling with the rosary beads or small change in his pocket, he struggled to send more than a form letter in reply. He still embraced the American cause in Vietnam, but he found it increasingly difficult to reassure his neighbors that the war was being waged successfully and so worth the lives of their sons.

The mail was running 18 to 1 against the war, O'Neill told White House congressional liaison Henry Hall Wilson, as they chatted after a briefing. It was too intense an issue to duck. In his June 1966 newsletter, he had tried to dodge it, devoting more space and attention to such issues as traffic safety, the humane treatment of animals and the Cape Cod National Seashore than to the conflict in Vietnam, on which he spent but three sentences. "Vietnam continues to be the overwhelming concern of all branches of our Government. Let's face the basic fact: there is no easy solution to this problem," O'Neill wrote. "As a father, a concerned citizen and your Congressman, I can only urge: we continue to pursue every avenue of peace, we continue to work for representative elections, and we continue to support President Johnson who, in my judgment, is doing what is proper and in the best interests of the Vietnamese people, the United States and the Free World."[32]

The newsletter elicited a tide of angry letters and telegrams. For the first time, O'Neill's mail was marked by mean and sarcastic attacks: sneering comments on how he seemed more worried about the treatment of dogs than of young Americans dying in combat and threats from the liberal voters of Cambridge and Brookline, who promised to retaliate at the polls.

"This is all very nice," wrote Skip Ascheim of Cambridge. "Life in Washington must be very pleasant, pretty secretaries, bright, energetic young interns — what's the weather been like? Meanwhile, what are you doing for peace?

"Perhaps your contribution is a call to the Defense Department to check on a contract for the Boston Navy Yard. Well, each does his share," Ascheim wrote. "You're running for reelection? Is that what this brochure is all about? I don't suppose you would consider it quite ethical to mention an issue or two? Just a little one? Just a little war?"[33]

Then, to his chagrin, O'Neill discovered that the campus opposition to the war was no longer limited to Harvard Yard.[34]

Boston College, in 1966, was still largely unaffected by the militant tide of resistance that had overtaken other schools. "Harvard was the antiwar campus. BC was one of the most conservative in the country," O'Neill's daughter Susan recalled. She and her brother Tom "supported the President just like every other Catholic kid in America." The big political fight on campus was waged by Patrick H. McCarthy, the iconoclastic grandson of a mayor of San Francisco. As a student leader, McCarthy successfully pushed for such revolutionary ideas as an end to the college's requirements that students attend religious retreats and wear coats and ties.[35] Alarmed by such insolence, the Jesuit administrators fought back, enlisting young Tommy O'Neill to field a slate of candidates in the campus elections to block McCarthy from becoming council president. "I was a good loser. I withdrew from school and went in the army," McCarthy said. Without the clout of the student council presidency, his grades were not good enough to keep him in school. McCarthy left BC in the fall of 1966 and, though he opposed the war, enlisted and volunteered for service in Vietnam. "I thought I had killed him," Tommy O'Neill recalled. McCarthy was still a student at BC on February 18, 1966 — the Friday that O'Neill arrived to speak in defense of the war at a Young Democrats meeting at McElroy Commons. "The questions came fast and furious from a small but articulate group of those opposed to our policy," O'Neill recounted, in a letter to Rosemary. "They gave me a rough afternoon." O'Neill had spoken on enough campuses to be confident in his ability to handle critics. "Whenever the questions grew tough, I would refer to a recent, confidential briefing," the congressman recalled. "Because I was an insider, nobody could question the accuracy of what I was saying."

O'Neill told the students how he had recently been briefed by Johnson, by McNamara, by Rusk . . . when a hand went up from the fifth or sixth row. "There was lead in my feet when I stood up," McCarthy said. But "I jutted my jaw out and asked, 'Have you been briefed by the other side?'" O'Neill was knocked off stride by the affront. After the prickly question-and-answer session, the congressman left the room scolding his children: "I can't believe you brought me into that den of thieves."

But McCarthy's question haunted him: "Nobody had ever asked that one before." That night, lying in his bed on Russell Street, O'Neill resolved to get briefed by the other side.[36] Inevitably, a card-playing buddy was among the first opponents of the war that he sought out. Retired Marine Corps commandant David Shoup, a respected critic of the war on Capitol Hill, was in a card game at the Army-Navy club one night when O'Neill leaned over and confessed his doubts. They had supper a few nights later.

"We're sending our boys over there on a mission we're not out to win," Shoup said.

Then, on August 5, 1966, in the midst of his reelection campaign, O'Neill received a letter from Raymond McNally, a professor at Boston College.

"I was approached by the Massachusetts Political Action for Peace group to run for your office," McNally wrote. "The reason why this group approached me was because of your apparent stand on the Vietnam War. This group felt that you took a rather hard line.

"It is important to note that PAX was willing to provide somewhere in the neighborhood of $5,000 to begin the financing of my campaign and to provide physical help," McNally wrote. He urged O'Neill to "think things over again in regard to the Vietnam War and to take a position similar to that of Robert Kennedy."

O'Neill was lucky. Grossman, Dr. Benjamin Spock and other leaders of the growing peace movement had organized a nationwide effort that spring to support antiwar candidates in the 1966 elections, and the congressman from Cambridge was a logical target. Fortunately, McNally was an admirer of O'Neill's and had turned MassPAX down. The professor offered instead to host a get-together at his Brookline home so that O'Neill could meet with "liberals and peace-oriented" opinion leaders. O'Neill wrote back a few days later, thanking McNally and asking him to put in a "good word" with the liberal community on his behalf.

"I am proud to stand on my record as a liberal and progressive Congressman who has fought for fourteen years for programs such as Medicare, veterans' benefits, aid to education and Civil Rights," O'Neill said. "I am distressed and saddened by what has happened and is happening in Vietnam. I think the greatest tragedy of this war is that so many lives — American and both North and South Vietnamese — are being lost.

"I support any measures that will bring this war to a peaceful and just end," O'Neill told McNally. "I see no better course than willingness to negotiate with any group or faction that has the power to end this conflict and thus end the killing of so many innocent people."

One such "faction," of course, was the Viet Cong. Six more months of war — and the MassPAX threat — had moved O'Neill to Robert Kennedy's position. He now embraced a stand that he had dismissed as "asinine" in March. He also knew that the antiwar forces were organizing politically; if he continued to dismiss their concerns, they would undoubtedly run a candidate against him in the 1968 Democratic primary.[37]

The Italian American vote — for there were now more sons of Italy than Erin in the district — added to O'Neill's worries. In 1964, O'Neill had used all of his backroom skills to keep Somerville businessman Sam Cammarata off the ballot — hiring a handwriting expert and challenging the signatures on Cammarata's filing papers before a compliant Ballot Law Commission, chaired by Bob O'Hayre, his BC classmate. In his memoirs, O'Neill described in detail how Cammarata had come to him that year and said, "For $5,000 I'll get out of the fight."

"You've got to be kidding," O'Neill said.

"No. Otherwise I'm going to raise a lot of money and make some problems for you."

"Let me tell you something, you son of a bitch. Nobody blackmails me," O'Neill said. "It might cost me $50,000, but I'm going to take you before the Ballot Law Commission and check over all your signatures." In 1966 Cammarata was back, and on the ballot, and offering to stay in or get out for a price. Jack Ricciardi, a former state public works commissioner, was O'Neill's main competition. The O'Neill camp thought that Cammarata and Ricciardi would split the Italian American vote, but just to be sure found a man named Picardi to run as well. "Picardi would appear on the ballot before Ricciardi — and confuse the Italian people," explained one resident of East Boston, who recalled how she was hired by one of Speaker McCormack's aides to orchestrate the scheme. "I got twenty twelve- to fourteen-year-olds and promised them a $500 party. We had a boiler room, with different pens and pencils, and we forged 4,200 names. Did Tip O'Neill know? Well, of course he knew. They paid me $300." It was during this campaign that O'Neill threw a "ten-strike," forging an alliance with Somerville Mayor Lawrence Bretta, a "boy wonder" elected at thirty-three and a potential rival. Instead of challenging O'Neill, Bretta would rise to the position of regional director for the General Services Administration under O'Neill's sponsorship, and in return give the congressman an invaluable Italian American ally.[38]

O'Neill "ran scared" in 1966, said Judith Kurland. "He said the nature of the voters in his district had gone from primarily Irish to primarily Italian and he believed in strong ethnic identity; it worked for him and he had seen it work against him. He ran as if this was the biggest threat in the world, as though Jack Kennedy had come back. It was the only time I had ever seen him lose his temper." O'Neill campaigned like a demon, meeting his Rules Committee duties during the week and then rushing home to attend eight or more functions at VFW and Knights of Columbus halls in his district each weekend. Kurland remembered how she found him on the phone with Tom Mullen:

giving his old friend and aide a furious, profanity-laced dressing-down over what the congressman feared was a lackadaisical organizational effort. During the campaign, Segal recalled, O'Neill "had three sets of suits. One for when he weighed 290 pounds, another for when he weighed 250 and a third for when he weighed 225. By the end of the campaign he was at 225, he had worked that hard.

"I remember saying to him, 'Hey, you look pretty good, why don't you keep it up.' And he said, 'You know, if I lose more weight people will think I have cancer and won't vote for me. So I'm going to quit at 225.' And he did," Segal said.[39]

Time magazine's Neil MacNeil recalls that O'Neill had the "large large, medium large and the relatively small large wardrobe." As Millie described it, the three sets of clothing were for "what he is, what he was, and what he wants to be."[40] Leo Diehl handled the fund-raising and ran the headquarters, as always, with competence. "God bless Leo. What a pal," O'Neill wrote Rosemary. The campaign headquarters buzzed with the energy of dozens of clean-cut college students, mostly from BC, inspired by John F. Kennedy's call to public service, many of whom were the friends or classmates of O'Neill's children. "Tommy your brother is great, what a job he is doing, out every night, making speeches, placing signs, organizing. What a great crowd he has, time has moved on your old Dad and I don't know where I would be without the kids," the candidate told Rosemary. Millie hosted a tea for 800 people, and ran 120 women volunteers, in shifts, through a phone bank of thirty telephones.

After being surprised by LBJ at the Washington, D.C., fund-raiser, the O'Neills returned to Boston for Bunker Hill Day. They again celebrated their twenty-fifth anniversary by renewing their wedding vows at a 6 o'clock Mass, and Millie surprised her husband with a wedding ring: his first after all those years. Leo Diehl and Peter Cloherty were the masters of ceremonies at the surprise party that followed, and everyone in the crowd of ninety was called upon to sing a song or tell a story. "No one was spared," O'Neill wrote Rosemary. "Everyone had a great time."

O'Neill beat Cammarata, the second-place finisher, by a 5 to 1 margin in total votes cast and did his usual best in Cambridge. The grateful dad gave son Tommy a 1965 Ford Mustang as a thank-you present. Still, there were worrisome signs in the returns. Tens of thousands of voters were "blanking" him — not voting at all for a candidate for Congress.

O'Neill worried that this was not the kind of showing that would deter future opponents and give him the kind of secure district that would let him focus on the politics of the House.[41]

Congressional redistricting after the 1960 census, meanwhile, had saddled O'Neill with the liberal, heavily Jewish bastion of Brookline, a breeding place of ambitious young reformers like state representative Michael Dukakis, whose troubled brother, Stelian, had challenged O'Neill in 1964 but failed to earn a spot on the ballot. The arithmetic was compelling: in a one-on-one match with a popular Italian American candidate, O'Neill needed the liberal votes from Cambridge and Brookline to maintain the image of invulnerability that gave him a "safe seat." After turning down the MassPAX offer to run against O'Neill in 1966, BC's McNally had sent along a voting analysis of the Eighth District. In a three-way race with the right Italian American and a young antiwar liberal, there was a chance that O'Neill could lose. Indeed, three of his old-line colleagues in the Massachusetts delegation — William Bates, Philip Philbin and Hastings Keith — would be replaced by antiwar insurgents in 1969, 1970 and 1972.

College students — those who were old enough — generally voted at home, if at all. But now many lingered on in their college communities, and saw the advantage of organizing against the war.[42] Grossman believed that "if Tip had his druthers he would have done the traditional thing. But, listen, you had a bunch of very active people opposing the war. We did a lot. In those days it wasn't money so much — you went out and spoke to people. The troops were out there."[43] MassPAX carried its antiwar petitions to every ward in the district, and presented O'Neill with the findings. They jammed his calendar with meetings. "You didn't have to defeat him to change his mind," said Grossman. "All you had to do was put something significant together, make a show of strength, demonstrate your constituency. He didn't evade. He wasn't tricky. He paid attention to his voters."[44]

O'Neill had wooed the liberals in his district with a tailored approach during the 1966 campaign. Harvard professors John Kenneth Galbraith and Samuel Beer were enlisted to top the list of the campaign's self-described "good-government group." Galbraith was O'Neill's champion on the Harvard faculty, defending him when other professors, like historian Arthur Schlesinger Jr., found the congressman too parochial. Campaign coordinator Jerry Cole reported that "a strong liberal flavor was deliberately imparted to the list" of Goo-Goos. A letter from the group was sent to 5,000 voters in the tony sections of Cambridge, hailing O'Neill's votes on civil rights and the war on poverty and praising his work bringing federal grants to the colleges and white-collar research facilities in his district. An intense voter contact campaign followed up the mailing in the "special area" — the upper-middle-class neighborhoods of Wards 4, 6, 7 and 8. The mass mailing was in turn reinforced by calls from a phone bank.

"An effort was made to recruit sophisticated young people of a liberal persuasion who could be counted on to become familiar with the material supplied them about the congressman, and to effectively present it to those who called who were less familiar with his record," wrote Cole. The percentage of O'Neill's overall vote that came from the academic neighborhoods rose from 15 percent in 1964 to 19 percent in 1966.[45]

As 1967 began, O'Neill was feeling pressure from both hawks and doves. For the next nine months he would be wrenched back and forth. At times he seemed primed to split from Johnson; at other moments he hesitated. Members of Congress were uneasy. "The President remains firm on his policy concerning Vietnam, but the Congress is wavering considerably and the American people are fed up with the war, and would like a quick end at any price," O'Neill wrote Rosemary. Interest rates were at historic highs, as the Federal Reserve sought to curb wartime inflation.

At a White House briefing, O'Neill was warned that for every 20 Americans dying in South Vietnam, 100 would die if the bombing was halted.[46] Joseph McLaughlin, who served as an intern in the congressman's office that summer, remembers frequent phone calls from the White House to his boss. In private, LBJ referred to dissenters as "chickenshits and piss-ants," and in public he was no more subtle. When awarding a posthumous Medal of Honor to the family of a marine hero, Johnson blamed the antiwar forces for his death.[47] On May 3, at O'Neill's personal request, the President reversed the decision of his scheduling staff and stopped by the Boston College Club of Washington's award dinner for John McCormack, at which O'Neill had given a warm introduction of his mentor, the Speaker.[48] "Consider the Communist ideology of hate," McCormack told a crowd of over 1,000 Eagles, almost half of whom had made the trip down from Boston. "The Communists are not only atheists, but they are atheists plus: they hate God. They not only deny God but they hate God." Communist ideology "proclaims that might is right, that the grave is the end . . . and the dignity of man is destroyed," McCormack said.[49]

Yet Johnson's government was collapsing. McNamara had concluded that the war was not winnable. The CIA reported in January 1967 that "there is no evident diminution of the Communist ability to continue the struggle." The Joint Chiefs of Staff pressed ahead with a strategy of attrition, hoping to shatter the enemy's morale and capability by amassing huge body counts. As 1967 began, there were 375,000 Americans in Vietnam, and the United States had flown 105,000 combat sorties, dropping 200,000 tons of bombs. Yet the Communists actually increased the size of their forces in the South by moving another 100,000 soldiers down the Ho Chi Minh trail, more than compensating for their 60,000 casualties that year. Meanwhile, a third of the South Vietnamese army deserted. By mid-1967, the number of Americans killed had exceeded 10,000.[50]

"We face more cost, more loss, more agony," Johnson told Americans in his January 10, 1967, State of the Union address.[51]

The antiwar movement had been torn by internal divisions and a debate over tactics for most of 1966. But as the draft calls began to swell — peaking at 364,000 that year — the Left was primed to make a political impact. "Mobilization" committees were born. Republican Senator Edward M. Brooke was elected to the Senate from Massachusetts in November 1966, in part because the peace groups endorsed and worked for him. Robert McNamara was surrounded by hundreds of protesters, who rocked his car and shouted him down and sent him fleeing through underground steam tunnels at Harvard that fall.[52]

The "youth culture stared and trembled at the enormity of what was happening on the other side of the world. By June 30, 1967 there were 448,800 American troops stationed on Vietnamese soil," wrote Todd Gitlin, a founding member of the Students for a Democratic Society (SDS). "With draft calls up, and student deferments pared down in 1966, the war moved a lot closer to the hitherto exempt, and the student antiwar movement boomed as a direct result."[53]

O'Neill's constituency included more than a dozen major colleges and universities — more academic communities than in any other congressional district — at a time when the jump in the number of college students, reflecting the arrival of the baby boom on campus, was altering the face of American society. In January 1967, the 300 medical workers, doctors and nurses who staged an antiwar demonstration at Boston City Hospital sent O'Neill a copy of their petition. In February, the Brookline Democratic Town Committee adopted a resolution calling for an immediate bombing halt. In March, angry that O'Neill had refused to attend a mass meeting on the war, MassPAX attacked him with newspaper ads that charged, "Congressman O'Neill has become the property of the War Hawks, the promoters of escalation who would extend the war for years on end." In April, the Harvard-Radcliffe Young Democrats notified O'Neill of their vote for an immediate bombing halt. In May, the East Asian department at Harvard urged O'Neill to drop "the goal of a total military victory in the South" and move instead toward "a compromise settlement and the withdrawal of American troops." In June, the antiwar forces ran an advertisement in the *Cambridge Chronicle*: "Our elected representative in Congress, Thomas P. O'Neill, has consistently supported the administration's policy in Vietnam . . . the time has come for residents of Cambridge who oppose this war TO MAKE THEIR VOICES HEARD!"[54]

O'Neill had finessed the claims of such "eggheads" for years. "I assure you that your threats do not concern me," O'Neill wrote in a combative four-page letter to MassPAX leaders that spring. In March he declined to join the eighteen liberal congressmen who voted for an antiwar amendment to a supplemental appropriations bill. But then "an interesting thing happened. I got a call from a fellow," O'Neill later recalled. It was the CIA.[55]

Of all the chapters in Tip O'Neill's life, the U.S. intelligence community's decision to use him as a clandestine back channel to Congress — conveying the agency's opposition to the President's handling of the war — was remarkable. Even in the context of the times, it was a betrayal of Johnson by high-ranking members of his own intelligence corps, justified by their belief that they in turn had been betrayed by the hawks in the administration who refused to heed the agency's warnings, and kept its reports from the President. Throughout the spring and summer of 1967, a bureaucratic war was waged between the alarmed CIA analysts and their military and White House counterparts over the size and resiliency of the Communist forces, the progress of the war and the efficacy of U.S. bombing.[56]

A CIA agent named John Walker was employed as the go-between. Walker had served on the State Department rolls as "political counselor" in the Middle East with O'Neill's daughter Rosemary, who was then in Malta with the foreign service. In reality, Walker was a spy. He had been recruited by former CIA director Allen Dulles himself and survived three assassination attempts by Palestinian terrorists. When Walker was rotated home in 1967, the CIA's experts on Vietnam asked him to set up a secret session with O'Neill.

"People were really frustrated that Johnson wasn't getting the facts, and felt that we should get out," Walker recalled. "I got a call one day. 'Johnny,' they said, 'we know you are a good friend of Tip O'Neill and we would very much like to talk to him.' This group came over one morning — it was about 10:30 A.M."[57] As he walked up the red brick sidewalk that April morning, O'Neill was startled to discover that Walker's P Street home in Georgetown was the house in which the young Jack Kennedy had lived while serving in Congress. O'Neill was further surprised when he entered the home and was greeted by a half dozen high-ranking analysts from the CIA and other U.S. intelligence agencies. They gathered in a circle in a low-ceilinged front parlor, around a cold fireplace. As Walker served coffee, they asked O'Neill to convey their opposition to the war to House Speaker McCormack.

Walker, a Middle East expert, was himself disturbed by what his colleagues now told O'Neill. "The gist was that their intelligence reports on Nam were not getting through to Johnson. They felt that there were two options: to get out, or to go all out to win. Tip listened very carefully," said Walker.[58] He set up a dinner meeting a few nights later, on April 27, with another CIA analyst — Thomas McCoy — who was gaining a reputation for his eloquent opposition to the Johnson administration's handling of the war. "McCoy had just gotten back from Nam," Walker recalled. "He felt very strongly and spoke very well. Tom's point was quite basic: we should get out, there was no way to win it, we ought to cut our losses. Tom's position was terribly influential on Tip's thinking."

"I never had any great moral objection to what we were doing in Vietnam. The thought never crossed my mind that what we were doing was immoral," McCoy said later. "My objections were purely on a pragmatic basis. That we were involved in something that we weren't winning and couldn't win."[59] O'Neill was now face-to-face with the desperate surreality of America's misadventure in Vietnam. Here was the cream of the U.S. intelligence community, confessing to him that the war was lost — but that they were powerless to end it. O'Neill's meeting with the CIA took place six months before the first major antiwar march — the October 1967 march on the Pentagon chronicled by Norman Mailer in *Armies of the Night* — and almost a year before the Tet offensive of 1968. Johnson was still assuring the American people that their sons were dying in a valiant cause, and a majority of his countrymen still supported him. Johnson's generals were asking for — and would get — more than 100,000 more troops. And 40,000 more American lives were yet to be spent on a war the nation's intelligence community had concluded was "unwinnable."

O'Neill took the CIA's message back to Capitol Hill, but McCormack wanted nothing of it. "Never could make any impression," O'Neill said. "Nobody in God's world was going to change John McCormack." O'Neill prided himself on being a "behind-the-scenes" player, but now pondered the consequences of a public break with the President.

Familial factors came into play. Like other parents of draft-aged children, O'Neill was torn between patriotic duty and the danger that a senseless war posed to his three sons. The focus of O'Neill's children, as they passed through adolescence, had moved from North Cambridge to Harvard Square, alive with the music, stylistic excess and politics of the sixties. "I had five in the age bracket, and three in college at one time," O'Neill recalled. "There was never a key to the back door. Everybody met in our house. Sunday night, it was a kind of a bull session where I'd sit around, there would be 20 kids drinking beer, and we'd talk about the war, we'd talk about the economy and we'd talk about the youth of America, we'd talk about marijuana, and talk about everything under the sun."[60]

The congressman was stung when his eldest son, Tom, who had become an increasingly militant critic of the war, spoke admiringly of the draft dodgers who had fled to Canada and Sweden to escape military service.

"You'd be breaking my heart if you did that," O'Neill told his son.

"No," Tom replied. "I wouldn't be breaking your heart. I'd be hurting you politically."[61]

Indeed, until the moment he broke with Johnson, O'Neill feared that the working-class families who formed the base of his support would never forgive him if he joined the long-haired college students who opposed the war, the despised "flag-burners in Harvard Square." Despite his mail, he was convinced that his core constituency — Irish

Americans and Italian Americans alike — supported LBJ on the war by an 8 to 1 margin. It was the sons of O'Neill's working-class constituency who were doing the fighting, and dying, in Vietnam. Of the 20,000 undergraduates who attended Harvard and MIT between 1962 and 1972, 14 were killed in action in Southeast Asia, while from South Boston High School alone, which had but 2,000 young men pass through its halls in those same years, 25 students died. Nor did O'Neill find it an appetizing prospect to go slinking into the antiwar camp with MassPAX and other self-righteous leftist groups he so ardently disliked.[62] But there were demographic realities for O'Neill to weigh. The Eighth Congressional District had changed in the fifteen years he had been in office; his base was not what it used to be. The ethnic families of North Cambridge and Somerville were moving out to the suburbs of Arlington and Malden. Replacing them were a mixture of college faculty, graduate students and other newcomers as, all across Boston, neighborhoods lost their old distinctiveness. The 1970 census would reveal that 70,000 residents of O'Neill's district had lived some place other than Massachusetts in 1965.[63]

In the late spring and early summer of 1967, O'Neill began to send a series of thinly veiled messages to his friends in the Johnson administration. These letters took the form of appeals for help, but can also be seen as warnings to the White House, as if O'Neill was trying to prepare the President for the upcoming break.

On April 27, the day of his dinner with Walker and McCoy, O'Neill wrote to W. Marvin Watson, a special assistant to Johnson, citing the MassPAX advertisements from the local newspapers as evidence of how "the termites" of the antiwar movement were "coming out of the woodwork."

O'Neill warned Watson that "The *Boston Globe,* which is the largest newspaper in New England, has of recent date become a confirmed Dove." Because "the general attitude of the *Globe* in the New England area is a strong political factor," O'Neill urged Johnson to call *Globe* editors Tom Winship and Bob Healy to the White House to try to "change the growing policy that the *Globe* is now undergoing." Watson failed to act. At the end of May the *Globe* published a series of six consecutive full-page editorials against the war, then published the series in a booklet form that went through several reprintings and was ordered by antiwar senators from around the nation to be sent to their constituents.[64]

"It was a very, very difficult summer," Joseph McLaughlin recalled. "We had a full-blown war on our hands and people were dying. Twenty here. Fifty here. We had some of those horrible battles where we lost some 200 troops in four days and it was in the news every night. It was the headline every morning. It was this body count stuff. And I think that was beginning to sink into the consciousness of even tried and true Democrats."[65]

Sensing that his colleague might be wavering, Senator Edward Kennedy sent O'Neill a copy of a June speech made by Richard Goodwin, a veteran of the Kennedy and Johnson White House, in which Goodwin called for a bombing halt and labeled the war a "triumph of the politics of inadvertence." Kennedy also lobbied O'Neill personally. O'Neill's reply to the senator offered a glimpse of his internal struggle. "Dear Ted . . . , Though I agree with Dick's statements for the most part, I do have some difficulty answering to my conscience," O'Neill wrote. Wouldn't a bombing halt expose U.S. troops to extreme danger? Weren't some of the antiwar forces "simply agitators?" But O'Neill did not mention such misgivings when passing a copy of Goodwin's speech to John P. White, the State Department's head of congressional relations. "It is an extremely well-written address and, may I add, quite convincing," O'Neill said.[66] He was also concerned about the cost of the war on the domestic programs he cherished. Detroit had erupted on July 23 into the worst race riot of the century. Johnson was forced to dispatch 5,000 federal troops when 7,000 National Guardsmen failed to restore order, and 43 people were killed. The Detroit riot followed a week of similar unrest in Newark that left 26 dead. On August 3 Johnson asked Congress for a 10 percent tax surcharge to pay for the war, stem inflation and curb rising interest rates. He also asked for 45,000 more U.S. troops for Vietnam.

O'Neill was too subtle, or the White House too harried. The Johnson administration didn't catch the hints. Both the White House and the news media missed the story when O'Neill gave his constituents the first sign of a major reappraisal in his thinking. In late June, the latest delegation of Cambridge liberals, Quakers and religious leaders met with O'Neill at his Boston office. This group was welcomed and stayed long into the evening, well past closing time, and were both touched by their congressman's account of his internal turmoil about the war and thrilled when he told them that he had come to "a new position." O'Neill said he was willing to recognize the Viet Cong for negotiations, and that he opposed any further escalation of the war. He had met and joined the group of some forty antiwar congressmen, who, led by Representative Jonathan Bingham of New York, had decided to call for a thirty-day bombing halt, he said.

Retired general James Gavin, the famed World War II paratrooper, had publicly suggested that U.S. troops consolidate their control of a series of strategic enclaves along the coast, turn over the war to the South Vietnamese army, halt the bombing and begin negotiations with the Communists. O'Neill had met and discussed the war with Gavin, he told the Cambridge delegation, and he saw the general's plan as an honorable way for the U.S. to reduce American deaths while maintaining leverage for negotiations with the Communists. The jubilant peace group wrote a letter to the *Cambridge Chronicle* hailing their meeting with O'Neill. In June, after O'Neill left with Millie for a three-week tour of Europe, his office mailed out facsimiles of the peace group's letter to constituents who wrote in about Vietnam.[67]

THE O'NEILLS VISITED Amsterdam, London and Rome and spent eight days in Malta with Rosemary and her mentor, Ambassador George Feldman.[68] O'Neill and Millie were in a Maltese restaurant one night when one of several U.S. Marines walked over from the bar and introduced himself as a native of Massachusetts. "I asked him a million questions about the war, and these kids are coming back from the war and they are totally disgusted," O'Neill remembered. "They didn't know what they were fighting for.

"Malta was a commonwealth island, and the British had a governor there and he had a big cocktail party. And the head of the U.S. fleet was there, the admiral of the fleet. There isn't a hell of a lot you can do on an island like that but have a few pops and get in a dialogue and digress, and Jesus he kicked the living hell out of the war. And here's the admiral of the fleet: 'We shouldn't be in the son of a bitch; we're not trying to win it.' The only way that we can win this war, he says, is by an invasion, by knocking out the power plants in Hanoi and by mining the coast. 'You've got to shut off the Chinese railroad. The supply lines. This is crazy. You're never going to win the war. We ought to get out of there.'"[69]

Soon after his return home, O'Neill received a letter from Christine DiGrezio of Medford. It was one of those handwritten notes from a working-class family to which O'Neill paid special attention, in this case from a woman with a draft-aged son whose daughter had attended school with the congressman's son Tommy. "I have worked very hard at stitching dresses for many years so that I could supplement my husband's salary. With this extra income we have been able to put them both through college," DiGrezio wrote of her children. "They both graduated this year, he from Northeastern and she from Boston College.

"As they were growing up I thought I would be the happiest woman in the world when their graduation day from college came. But I was wrong. I knew that either my son would be drafted or he would enlist. Yesterday, he enlisted in the Army," she wrote. "I know it is every American's duty to defend their country, but what are we defending and why are we sending many of our healthiest boys to Vietnam to be slaughtered when Vietnam doesn't even care to fight for its own cause?

"Please add my name to the thousands of American mothers who have already protested against this senseless war," DiGrezio said. "God Bless You and may He bestow the ability and know-how to enable you to present this protest to the proper authorities."[70]

DiGrezio wasn't the only backstreet constituent turning against the war that summer. On July 18, O'Neill mailed off another tortuous warning to the White House. "Upon my return home, I found the climate of my own district changing rapidly with reference to Vietnam," he said.

"Last Sunday there were about three thousand people assembled for a 'Peace Fair' in the Cambridge Common. Some members of my close personal organization attended the Fair and I, myself, drove by to get a general impression of the group," O'Neill wrote Johnson. "The one outstanding factor was that the people present were mainly from a solid middle-class social and economic status and there was no evidence of the youthful agitators as I had expected. Many of my neighbors and several community leaders were in the group."[71]

If O'Neill had needed a final push, the peace fair and its middle-class flavor was enough. On July 25, O'Neill sent the White House his final warning: a copy of his new stock reply to constituents who wrote in about Vietnam. In a brief, formal note to Johnson, O'Neill wrote that "the letters I have received since January of 1966 are overwhelmingly opposed to a continuation of the bombing of North Vietnam and favor a negotiation of the dispute as soon as possible. Some of these letters are from admittedly dissident groups in the community, the majority, however, are not. Rather, they come from average citizens who are concerned about the mounting loss of life in Vietnam and the confusion over our stated goals in Southeast Asia."[72]

The White House didn't catch on, didn't meet with the editors of the *Globe,* didn't move to rein in its new maverick. O'Neill received only a note from Barefoot Sanders, Johnson's legislative counsel: "We appreciate your keeping us informed of opinion in your district."[73] On July 28 O'Neill sent a personalized copy of his new position paper to Mrs. DiGrezio. It represented a radical break with the Johnson administration.

"As a citizen, congressman and father I am upset by the fact that we may have embarked on a limitless course of widening war which imperils thousands of lives and brings inevitably closer the danger of a massive conflict that threatens to engulf the other nations of Asia," O'Neill wrote. "Further escalation can only bring more carnage and destruction and a hardening of the bargaining positions of the combatants."[74]

AT THE START of the summer, O'Neill had set Joseph McLaughlin to work on a newsletter on foreign policy that would be mailed across the district in early September. McLaughlin, like Kurland before him, was attending antiwar protests and supporting the Movement. After graduating from BC, he had moved on to Cornell University Law School, where he was protected from military service by a student deferment. "I can't say that was irrelevant," he recalled. "It was a sobering thought, you know. Your whole new life as an adult, after you worked your tail off getting an education, and the next thing awaiting you is a trip to Vietnam. Everybody was affected by that." He spent the summer doing research on Vietnam and interviewing experts at the Pentagon and White House. By the time O'Neill returned from Europe, a rough draft of the newsletter was awaiting him.[75]

McLaughlin didn't bury the painful topic this time. "Vietnam: Solution or Stalemate?" read the headline. "Something must be done to end the growing carnage." The newsletter called for an immediate bombing halt, an end to further escalation and the withdrawal of U.S. forces into Gavin's strategic enclaves.[76]

"No, this was not administration policy," McLaughlin remembered. The congressman "took the draft when he came back and he continued his gregarious practices, taking us out to dinner and treating us like a family, not like employees. And so people were kind of curious, you know. What did he think of it? How did he react to it? But he didn't say anything. A week went by, and ten days went by, two weeks and now we are into August and everybody is thinking we got to get this newsletter out."

Finally, in mid-August, O'Neill summoned McLaughlin and gave him back the draft of the newsletter. The congressman had filled the margins with written questions, but they were questions of fact, not challenges to the newsletter's conclusions. "I thought, this is good. Ohhh, this is a good development," McLaughlin recalled. Then, after calling his staff together to warn them that "this may generate some controversy," O'Neill sent 150,000 copies of the newsletter to the post office. The meaning was clear, O'Neill later recalled: "That, ultimately, we ought to get the hell out of there as quickly as we can."[77]

"I am sending you a copy of my newsletter that I am sending out," O'Neill wrote Rosemary. "You will note I have changed my position on Vietnam. . . . Rosemary, it's a mess. We are fighting a war of stalemate, not trying to win but to drive them to their knees to force them to the conference table. It can't work."[78]

ON THE DAY that the newsletter was mailed, O'Neill told his son Tom that he feared he had signed a political "death warrant."

"He didn't expect to be reelected," Millie recalled. "I can remember particularly, I was having my hair done in Eileen's in Belmont and a neighbor of ours who had a son in Vietnam was sitting next to me and she castigated me and my husband to no end in front of everybody.

"So I finally said, 'Look, he thinks the boys should come home. Would you rather have your boy come home whole or would you rather have him stay there and be killed along the line in a foolish war?' And so it quieted her for a moment, but she was furious. And that was pretty much the case all over, until he could get out and explain things to everybody."[79]

O'Neill liked to tell a story of how an enterprising reporter from the *Washington Star* first broke the news of his split with LBJ after coming across stacks of the newsletter, waiting to be mailed, in the basement of a House office building. It was a good tale, but not accurate. The *Record American* ran segments of O'Neill's newsletter, in press release form, without further comment or analysis on September 8. The *Globe*'s James Doyle got the story right, after being tipped off by Ted Kennedy to the newsletter and its significance, on September 13.

Below headlines that heralded the bombing of Haiphong and the latest victory by the miracle Red Sox, Doyle's front-page story was topped: "Rep. O'Neill Deserts LBJ on Vietnam." O'Neill told the *Globe* that "after listening to their side of the story for a year and a half, I've decided that [Secretary of State Dean] Rusk and McNamara and the rest of them are wrong.

"The truth is that there is more infiltration than ever and the bombing hasn't changed that. The truth is that we are dropping $20,000 bombs every time somebody thinks they see four Viet Cong in a bush. And the truth is that it isn't working," O'Neill said. "My sources agree that we should either disengage or invade the North and pull out all the stops. I agree, and my answer is that we should disengage and stop the bombing."[80]

The afternoon *Star* ran a four-paragraph item on O'Neill's newsletter on page 6 of its September 14 editions. O'Neill was out playing cards that night; he came in after midnight to find his roommate, Eddie Boland, excited and upset. Johnson had phoned the apartment, demanding to talk with O'Neill.[81] "Eddie said I was to call the White House no matter what time I got in. Johnson was wild," he remembered.

O'Neill met the President in the Oval Office the next morning. "What a sonofabitch you are," Johnson told him. "I expect something like this from assholes like Fitts Ryan. But you? You're one of my own. You're my friend. I've known you since the day John McCormack brought you down . . . to the Board of Education." Johnson accused O'Neill of caving in to "the students in your area . . . all those guys at Harvard Square."

"Hey, Mr. President," he replied. "My strength is in the back streets. And when I'm out on the street I see people cross the road so they don't have to see me because of this. They look at me as if I was guilty, leaving the President of the United States. I don't want to leave you, but I think you're wrong."

O'Neill urged Johnson to withdraw or "pull out all the stops." But Johnson told him that the threat of Soviet or Chinese intervention was too great. The President shook his head. "I can't do those things. They're just too dangerous," he said. "You think you know more about this war than I do? Do you think that I don't roll and toss up in that bed every night? Don't you think I would like to get this thing over with?"

Shrewdly, Johnson salvaged what he could. He got O'Neill to promise to maintain a low profile on the war, so as not to "start the snowball running" in Congress.

"One thing, I want you to do me a favor," said Johnson.

"What is it?" asked O'Neill.

"Tip, make no statements to the press. You know, I think I'm right; you think you're right."

"Gee, Mr. President, I'm only speaking for myself. I'm not speaking for others. Let the others do what I did."[82]

O'Neill kept his low profile for months, and did not join the group of liberal congressmen who wrote to Johnson in October asking him to stop the bombing. In a subsequent conversation with White House liaison Claude Desautels, O'Neill "went to great lengths to demonstrate that had he realized the importance that would be attached to it, he, as a Democrat, would never have released such a letter," Desautels reported.

O'Neill told Desautels, "As you well know, I am a Democrat and I love the President as a brother."[83]

O'Neill's showdown with Johnson set off a modest witch-hunt within the administration, as Johnson aides sought to find what government sources had told the congressman that the war was an unwinnable proposition. Lawrence O'Brien, Desautels and White were dispatched, with orders to report back to White House adviser Walt Rostow and Johnson.

"There is no question in my mind that the various government spokesmen with whom he met privately convinced him," Desautels reported, in a September 27 memo to O'Brien and the President.[84]

On September 26, Johnson received a delegation of academic leaders from Cambridge and Boston at the White House. O'Neill's switch was fresh in his mind. "The problem is not one of communication. The problem is that Ho wants South Vietnam. He isn't going to give it up," Johnson told the professors. "Dissent encourages the enemy to think that we will bring our own government to its knees. We believe if we retire to the cities with an enclave theory it would be worse than surrender. It would get more people killed."[85]

At his regular Tuesday lunch with Rusk, McNamara and other senior advisers on October 3, Johnson scolded his aides, saying he was "astounded to find that there were several groups of people who were working to get congressmen who are in agreement with our position to make a reassessment." It was the President's "own people," Johnson complained, who had turned O'Neill against the war.[86]

On October 12, McCormack gave an "emotional, table-pounding speech" that drew a standing ovation from 100 congressmen on the House floor. The Speaker accused the war's opponents of providing comfort to the enemy and, rolling a newspaper in his hand and pounding a table, said, "If I were one of those [dissenters], my conscience would be such that it would disturb me the rest of my life."[87]

Martin Sweig, McCormack's chief of staff at the time, recalled that O'Neill and McCormack exchanged "hard words" about O'Neill's switch on Vietnam, and that the congressman had appealed to Sweig, who had his own doubts about the war, for help. O'Neill "came to me and said, 'Get your boss to calm down a bit.' But 'It's impossible,' I said. The president is calling all the time," Sweig remembered. Representative Manny Celler called O'Neill a "rat . . . deserting the ship." And there were some in Cambridge who could not forgive O'Neill.[88]

"You and Gavin and the 'enclave' — did you ever sit like a duck in an enclave and wait for 4-inch mortar fire from hit-and-run phantoms that make a shambles of your enclave in 10 minutes and when you repair and scrape the human meat off the deck let you have it all over again?" wrote a marine back from Vietnam.[89]

Nothing bothered him more, O'Neill told aide Gary Hymel twenty years later, than the accusation from working-class constituents that he had sold out the boys in Vietnam to join the peaceniks: enough so that he still harbored guilt about his decision to oppose the war.[90]

O'Neill and his friends worked hard to minimize the political damage. "Oh, Jesus, I ran through a hard period of time. . . . The Irish ladies were saying, 'Huh, after all these years of Tip, he's joined that crowd down at Harvard Square, the flag-burners.' I had to speak at every Communion breakfast, every Legion Hall, every Chamber of Commerce, every Kiwanis Club in my district. . . . And every time they burned a flag in Harvard Square, they made it tougher on me." The American Legion chapter in Cambridge called a meeting, and a move was made to censure O'Neill, until Red Fitzgerald reminded his fellow veterans of O'Neill's long years of service to their community. Johnny Melia, a state representative from Brighton, called to warn O'Neill that "Jeez, they're kicking your brains out over here. . . . I think we'd better get something together right away. . . .

How about speaking at St. Columbkille's Church, the Holy Name breakfast?"

"It drew the biggest crowd they ever had in the history of the Holy Name breakfast, and that included Jack Kennedy and Bobby Kennedy," O'Neill recalled. "I got up, gave my talk, and I was there for four hours answering questions. Four hours. And you know, I changed the people in St. Columbkille's parish."[91] If the old guard needed changing, the New Left was thrilled at the congressman's conversion. O'Neill's mail, meanwhile, ratified his decision at a rate of 1,000 to 15. Winship sent him a copy of a glowing *Globe* editorial. The Somerville Neighborhood Committee on Vietnam reported that 80 percent of the households in the working-class wards supported O'Neill's position. A dozen Harvard Law School professors cheered O'Neill's stand. Galbraith wrote to hail "another example of the good, hard-headed and practical judgment that we have all come to expect from you and which has served us so well in the past." And Katie Parker sent a card upon which she wrote simply, "Thank you."[92]

To some among the antiwar forces, O'Neill showed insufficient zeal. "We are both voters in Cambridge and it is only fair to tell you that had you not come out for a bombing pause and for immediate negotiations, we would have done everything in our power to prevent your re-election next year," wrote one Harvard couple. Actress Jane Fonda led a march up Massachusetts Avenue from Porter Square to Russell Street, where a few dozen protesters rallied outside O'Neill's home.[93] Thirty years later, Jerome Grossman — a self-described "relentless liberal" — still expressed disappointment in O'Neill's behavior that fall: "His opposition was quiet. He did not take leadership on the issue. His most vigorous response was to get Brookline eliminated from his district."[94]

But O'Neill's irritation with such left-wing churlishness was easily overcome by his relief at the response of his working-class neighbors. "I am a disabled infantry combat veteran of World War II and the holder of the Bronze Star," wrote Victor A. Campisi of Somerville. "I'll be damned if I vote for Johnson again!"[95]

"As a four-year Marine veteran of World War II and father of two present-day Marines, one in Vietnam, I was very disappointed in the Vietnam part of your report from Washington. You may be giving aid and comfort to our enemy . . . you most certainly are hurting the morale of our gallant fighting men," wrote Leo Corrigan of Cambridge.

But "if you had a fourth conclusion and it was to withdraw all of our troops the same day that you would stop the bombing and escalation, I could have some feeling for your conclusion," said Corrigan.[96]

Even McCormack finally relented. O'Neill attended the dedication of the John McCormack School in Boston "and John got up, and Jesus he flayed those flag burners and those people that are marching against the war, and I'm sitting up there and a little uncomfortable, but he never made any reference to me." In return, even as he grew to be a more vocal opponent of the war, O'Neill never confronted or criticized the Speaker.[97]

McNally, the BC professor who had tipped O'Neill off to the Mass-PAX discontent the previous year, went to work getting Brookline's political leaders to endorse O'Neill's announcement, and was "delighted" to report that a working-class audience at St. Polycarp's Church in Somerville supported the congressman's change of heart. "It took a great deal of courage to come out the way you did," McNally wrote. "The important point here is, it seems to me, that you were not obliged to make this statement. You did it on your own because of an honest change in your thinking."[98]

FOR THE REST of his life, O'Neill was highly sensitive about the suggestion that he had caved in to left-wing pressure on Vietnam, or switched sides for political profit. Popular expression against the war had caused him to pause and seek out the other side, he acknowledged. But he had never consulted his pollster, calculated the odds and flipped.

"I am insulted by your letter; I have never taken a position with regard to the war in order to pacify constituents or in order to gain votes," O'Neill wrote to one constituent who had so accused him in February 1968. "The war is too important an issue to trifle with."[99]

In the long run, O'Neill clearly faced more political danger from the Left than the Right. Antiwar activist Sam Brown, a Harvard Divinity School student, proved as much when, with Grossman and Mass-PAX support, he explored the potential for a campaign against O'Neill in 1970. The congressman's shift saved him; by then he was a prominent leader of the antiwar forces in Congress. Brown dropped the idea, moved to Colorado and won statewide office there instead, and O'Neill never faced another significant challenge for the Eighth District seat.[100]

In the near term, however, O'Neill's decision to oppose the war just as clearly jeopardized his career. When Cambridge held a municipal election in that fall of 1967, Galbraith and the peace forces overcame the opposition of city officials and placed an antiwar initiative, calling for the withdrawal of U.S. troops, on the ballot. The vote gathered national attention as a referendum on Johnson's policies in a heavily Democratic area. Despite the passions of the time, and a rush to register to vote by antiwar "students, hippies, floaters and mattress voters," the question was defeated by a 3 to 2 margin citywide, and by a 3 to 1 margin among O'Neill's backstreet neighbors.

Riding on the success of his New Hampshire victory, and running against no formidable opposition, Senator Eugene McCarthy still failed to carry O'Neill's district in the 1968 Massachusetts primary. And as late as November 1970, O'Neill's district gave twice as many votes as any other in support of a military victory in a statewide referendum on the war.[101] Clearly, O'Neill was out in front of his constituency.

The final bit of evidence of O'Neill's sincerity is contained in his papers from this period. It is a short, handwritten note to himself on Rules Committee stationery, defining what he believed his role to be.

"Many years ago I made some commitments to myself — to make the rough and unpleasant decisions as they came, to speak out at times when remaining silent may be easier — to admit my mistakes — and never be afraid of changing my views if I believed I was wrong," he wrote. "In the words of Shakespeare, 'To thine own self be true.' "[102]

PART FOUR

A Lovely Spring Rain of a Man

CHAPTER 11

A War That Can Only Be Ended

O'NEILL HAD MADE his choice. The repercussions were lasting, and consequential. "Of all the congressional changes of position on the war, perhaps the most significant politically was that of Representative Thomas ("Tip") O'Neill, Democrat of Massachusetts," said the official congressional history of the Vietnam war.[1]

Led by Mike Mansfield and William Fulbright, the Senate's inner circle had its share of outspoken opponents to the war. But the House regulars did not, and so the White House made the tactical decision to focus its efforts there. The rules and size of the House made it more difficult for an individual member to gain the public attention and press coverage allotted the more glamorous senators. The Speaker and his lieutenants were loyal to Johnson, and had more power to control the legislative agenda and block antiwar measures than their counterparts in the Senate, where any senator could offer an amendment from the floor. And the tensions of the cold war had traditionally served to enforce orthodoxy in the House, as did the disproportionate advantage that the executive branch enjoyed over its legislative counterpart in the crafting of foreign policy.

"Very likely the Congress had spent the day debating price support levels for farm commodities, or interest rates for low-cost housing," said Johnson aide Harry McPherson. "In a foreign crisis they were at a hopeless disadvantage. The difference between the parochial 'political' issues which they had debated during the day on the Hill and the cosmic events that were laid before them in the Cabinet Room was intimidating."[2]

O'Neill's announcement, then, was a startling indication that support for the war was eroding in both Congress and the nation. In August 1967, Johnson ordered his staff to conduct a secret survey of opinion on the Hill. The congressional liaison officers of some two dozen agencies were asked to fan out and host private meetings with their five best friends in Congress. Of the 169 resultant "Friendly Five" interviews, 104 were negative. Representative Julia Butler Hansen, a Democrat from Washington, spoke for many when she said, "The present course of action in Vietnam will defeat not just the president but the Democratic Party."[3]

Johnson disclosed the results of the survey to Dean Rusk, Robert McNamara and Walt Rostow at the October 3 meeting in which he scolded his aides about O'Neill's defection. As the session drew to a close, Johnson portentously told his aides that what he was about to say must not leave the room, then asked his advisers what effect it would have if he announced that he would not run for another term. For were he pressed to make a decision that day, Johnson told them, he would not seek reelection.

"You must not go down," Rusk said. "You are the Commander-in-Chief, and we are in a war."

The people would not support another four years of war, Johnson replied. "I would be 61 when I came back in, and I just don't know if I want four more years of this."

Johnson then read from the reports of the "Friendly Five" survey of Congress. "They all think that we will lose the election if we do not do something about Vietnam quick," the President said.[4] Johnson had a habit, in tough times, of stomping and pouting and threatening to retire. But LBJ meant it this time, said William Gibbons, the administration lobbyist who later wrote the congressional history of the war. "I think the president had decided not to run based on what he was getting back from Congress at that point. They gave him such poor reports, not only on Vietnam but on his presidency."[5] Other prominent

Democrats, like Representatives Morris Udall of Arizona and Claude Pepper of Florida, had followed O'Neill into the dovecote and the Washington press corps was treating O'Neill's defection as an exceptional blow to the Johnson administration and the war.

"O'Neill's conversion is significant," the *Washington Post* reported. "Unlike many doves who thrive on bucking the establishment, he is a professional politician of more than 30 years standing, a former speaker of the Massachusetts legislature, a party regular who tries to go along. The administration cannot afford to lose many such stalwarts."[6]

Members of Congress, returning from their August vacation, were "shaken up on their return" to hear of O'Neill's decision, said the *Chicago Tribune*. "O'Neill's statement in his monthly newsletter to Massachusetts voters had major repercussions. Heretofore an administration wheel horse, O'Neill was calling for the junking of administration policy. O'Neill is the buddy of Speaker John McCormack, a close friend of the president and one of the administration spokesmen on the powerful House Rules Committee."[7]

The entire episode was something of a revelation, O'Neill said later: he had not yet considered himself a leader of such import in Congress. (As late as 1966 he was still reassuring a worried Rosemary that, yes, he would run for another term.) The CIA analysts, Lyndon Johnson and the Washington press corps helped persuade him otherwise. He began to maneuver for a leadership position.[8]

Before the split with Johnson, O'Neill had seemed poorly positioned for a run at the House leadership. As long as the Boston-born McCormack was in power, there would be no room for another Massachusetts Democrat at the top, and "Mr. McCormack stayed a lot longer than I had anticipated," O'Neill said later.[9] Though he had spent fifteen years in Congress, no major legislation bore O'Neill's name. Most of the battles he had fought on the House floor were for parochial interests — the Boston utility companies, dockyards, candy companies and sugar refineries that employed the voters of his district.

"He did not see himself as a legislator, an originator of legislation," said Judith Kurland. "He would put in stuff if people asked him, like he had done a workmen's compensation bill way before I came because labor asked him to do it. Longshoremen, absolutely. Seafarers Union. Sugar . . . because of Revere Sugar." And of all the members of the Tuesday-Thursday club, few had gone home for more long weekends than O'Neill.[10] "Big and gregarious, his earliest attribute seemed to be his laziness," said Carl Albert, then the majority leader. "He always wanted to go home Thursday and he didn't want to come back until Tuesday. He likes to get away long weekends, he likes to have a lot of recesses, he doesn't like his personal business interfered with too much by work."[11]

O'Neill's staff was highly skilled at constituent service, but lacked the kinds of aides who helped propel ambitious men to higher office. There were no speechwriters, press secretaries or policy nerds on the payroll. When he had a speaking engagement, or wanted to insert remarks in the *Congressional Record,* O'Neill relied on a hodgepodge of summer interns, labor representatives, business lobbyists and Library of Congress researchers to write his speeches. Terry Segal got a job after dropping by O'Neill's Washington office one summer to catch up on the Boston sports pages. When Joseph McLaughlin applied for his summer job, he was interviewed in the O'Neill family parlor on a Sunday afternoon by Tip and Millie, who were more interested in the young law student's upbringing and deportment than in his skills. "Millie wanted to know who my mother was, and what kind of girls I went out with, and things like that," he recalled. "I guess I passed because I only dated girls from Newton College of the Sacred Heart."[12] Kurland arrived as an intern in the summer of 1966. "He took interns because he had no Washington staff. He had Dolores Snow, his office manager, and Jackie Killeen, his receptionist. He believed his office was for casework, and so he had no legislative aides," she said. "His fondest dream was to be Speaker of the House, but did he think it possible, actually? I don't think so. There were too many guys in the way. It was a dream without an expectation."[13]

When O'Neill tried to play at public relations, the results were mixed. He got great coverage for intervening with the secretary of agriculture to rescue a shipload of African wildlife, including two baby giraffes for the Franklin Park Zoo, that had been forbidden to land by customs officials because of a mixup in paperwork. And a visit to Boston by Secretary of the Interior Stuart Udall to announce a cleanup grant for the Charles River was a big success, once Ted Kennedy's press secretary showed Segal how to choreograph the scene. But an attempt to tape a television advertisement hawking O'Neill's consumer bill on generic drugs fared poorly. He repeatedly stumbled on the words "acetylsalicylic acid," the generic name for aspirin ("asacricili . . .

atselcylicick . . . fuck it") and ruined take after take. "We never did get it done," Segal said.

When O'Neill hooked up with the zealous Ralph Nader on the landmark auto safety bill of 1966, the results were disastrous. It was at the peak of the hard-run primary campaign, Segal recalled, that O'Neill — hoping to woo the liberals back home — thanked Nader for joining him in a publicity photo by promising to do "anything I can do" to help with the legislation. Nader asked if O'Neill would introduce an amendment making auto executives criminally responsible for the defects of their products. Segal urged O'Neill not to do it, and the congressman himself predicted that the amendment would not win 15 votes. But O'Neill had given his word, and on August 17 he bravely endured the rhetorical beating and 120 to 15 defeat he suffered on the House floor. When Segal and O'Neill stopped that night to get the early edition of the next day's *Washington Post,* they found a humiliating account of the day's proceedings on the front page.

"Terry, what was that slogan you designed for this campaign?" O'Neill asked.

"Keep a strong voice in Washington," Segal murmured.

"Well, we did pretty good today," O'Neill said, shattering the tension with a booming laugh. "Fifteen fucking votes!"[14]

YET HE WAS young at heart. He listened to his children. He respected the passion of the earnest young college students who continued to write or visit his office, listing their objections to the war. He foresaw the arrival of a class of new, young faces in Congress. He sensed the times were changing, and that he needed to change too. At fifty-five, an age when many of his colleagues were settling in their ways, O'Neill was still open, flexible and creative. His baby-faced interns loved him for it, and for his gentleness. On the night that LBJ appeared at his 1966 fund-raiser, O'Neill had not closed the evening in self-congratulatory celebration with his cronies, but by making sure the Shoreham's chef carved the leftover roast beef into servings that the youngsters on his staff could take home. When Kurland's classmates in Mount Holyoke College's class of '67 went off on graduation trips to Europe, O'Neill put her on the payroll over spring vacation so she could afford to go as well.[15]

"He would ask a question, and he listened. And not a lot of politicians, then or since then, listen," said McLaughlin. "He listened to his family, and he listened to the people in his office. And he observed. That was a mark of somebody who could still learn, even though he was where he was, and came from a different tradition."[16] To the young people in his office, O'Neill's claim on their loyalty was clinched by his change of position on Vietnam. "All of a sudden he wasn't the machine politician anymore," said McLaughlin. "All of a sudden he was viewed, and rightly so, as a thoughtful person. He stood behind it and never backed away, which I thought was courageous of him. He had a heroic quality — not in a charismatic, Kennedyesque sense — but, you know, a quiet hero."[17]

O'Neill discovered that his break from Johnson opened a wide range of political possibilities. As the Democratic Party was transformed by the New Left forces that first opposed and then captured it from within, O'Neill's early opposition to the war allowed him to pass the nonnegotiable litmus test of the party's liberals. Over time, he became a vital bridge in Congress between the party's warring liberal and conservative wings.[18] True to his word to LBJ, O'Neill slipped quietly into the antiwar camp. He was not among the thirty northern, liberal congressmen who met with Dean Rusk to protest the war in October, nor did he attend a massive draft resistance rally on Boston Common in mid-October, or join Norman Mailer's "armies of the night" in the march on the Pentagon. He made no effort to move the first antiwar resolutions, requiring congressional approval for additional deployments of troops to Vietnam, through the Rules Committee. When Senator Eugene McCarthy called to ask for his support in late November 1967, O'Neill told him, "I like you, Gene. You are a nice guy and we agree in principle, but I'm [with] Johnson." Well into 1968, O'Neill continued to back LBJ for President.[19]

Yet neither did O'Neill buckle or cave in when the American public showed its continued support for the war. The Harris Poll reported in late December that the "prevailing mood in America today toward the Vietnam conflict is to intensify military pressure without limits and see the war through." Escalation was favored over withdrawal by 63 to 37 percent. At home, in December, the regulars on the Massachusetts Democratic State Committee voted 45 to 3 to support the war. But O'Neill called for a bombing halt and predicted that McCarthy, who had announced his candidacy for President as a protest to Johnson's Vietnam policy, would beat LBJ in the Massachusetts primary the following April. He also made an important change in his Washington office. The civil rights era, the televised war and the threat of the draft had polarized dinner table conversations and heightened political awareness in millions of American homes. The nascent feminist and environmental movements joined the mix, as policy displaced pork barrel politics in the hearts of his constituents and colleagues. O'Neill decided he needed an "issues person," and found one in Kurland. After serving as an intern in 1966 (she had been drawn to O'Neill's office after hearing him described as a cross between Curley and Kennedy), the tiny political science major from Mount Holyoke handled ad hoc assignments for O'Neill during her senior year, writing papers on the war and other issues on a portable typewriter from her college dorm. She joined his staff after returning from her trip to Europe in September 1967. "I was Left. I was antiwar. Very active in the civil rights movement. I had organized the three-day fast against the war at Mount Holyoke," Kurland remembers. "He had me deal with the Harvard people, the Lefties, the women and the ethnics — the other ethnics."

Kurland was Jewish, and an asset when dealing with the crazed leftists in Cambridge and the Jewish liberals of Brookline. "One of the things we did in the redistricting [after the 1970 census] was get rid of Brookline. My heart was breaking," Kurland recalled. "But Mr. O'Neill said, 'Judith, all those people care about is issues. And they can't be satisfied. In North Cambridge, if I get a guy a job, he's mine for life.'"[20] In the meantime, he gave Kurland the duty of composing the form letters his office sent out on the war and other issues. After she finished a draft, she would sit down with the congressman and discuss the nuances of what she had written. Sometimes he would have to curb her enthusiasms; other times she would make a compelling case, and nudge him further to the liberal side. He also asked Kurland for short reports on issues and legislation. "Give me a paper on the moral arguments against the war," he said, in January 1968. And she banged out a two-page memo.

"Every American has been brought up believing that no matter how bad the other side, WE don't kill civilians, women and children, we don't mutilate, we don't use chemicals, we don't torture," she wrote. "No matter how good our intentions are: does the means outweigh the good intentions? Is it out of proportion to the good that is intended and all the good that could possibly be accomplished? Is it worth all the lives of Vietnamese and Americans, all the devastation and terror?" She signed such papers: "Judith. (Not a member of the military-industrial complex.)"[21]

It was in that same month, during a cease-fire honoring the Tet New Year holiday, that the North Vietnamese and Vietcong launched a series of coordinated assaults on U.S. installations throughout South Vietnam, including the embassy in Saigon. It was the worst failure of U.S. military intelligence since Pearl Harbor. The fighting went on for two months, and the Communists suffered horrible casualties — more than ten times the 4,000 Americans lost. But in its effect on American public opinion, the Tet offensive marked the turning point of the war. Television crews filmed savage street fighting in Saigon and Hue. NBC broadcast the chilling image of South Vietnamese police chief and brigadier general Nguyen Ngoc Loan pulling out a pistol and briskly executing a Vietcong prisoner with a point-blank shot to the head.

"It seems more certain than ever that the bloody experience of Vietnam is to end in a stalemate," CBS anchorman Walter Cronkite told the nation on February 27. General William Westmoreland asked for 200,000 more men. Secretary of Defense Clark Clifford, who had replaced McNamara, concluded the war was lost, and quietly began to search for a way by which the United States could withdraw.

"We hear the same hollow claims of programs and victory," McCarthy told voters in New Hampshire. "Only a few months ago we were told that 65 percent of the population was secure. Now we know that even the American embassy is not secure." O'Neill reached similar conclusions. Tet "stiffened me more than anything else . . . it was really after that that I really took off as a voice in the House that would be speaking out," he said. On March 4 he joined Eddie Boland and sixteen other members of the House in issuing a seven-point peace plan that featured recognition of the Vietcong, a cease-fire, elections and the withdrawal of "all foreign forces" from South Vietnam.[22] "The increasing scope of the conflict is eroding our manpower and diverting our resources," O'Neill told the House. "We are spending $30 billion a year in Vietnam; money which we need to educate our children, rebuild our cities, care for the sick and the elderly, and provide for the poor."[23]

That spring, O'Neill traveled to Hawaii with Representative James Wright of Texas to attend a foreign policy program. Each of the congressmen brought a daughter, who introduced them to a group of students from Asian countries they met as they toured the University of Hawaii. A Southeast Asian girl, supported by other members of the group, urged Wright and O'Neill to put an end to the war. Their people had once thought that Americans, with their own revolutionary experience, would be different from the French and British occupiers who had preceded them to the region. But the U.S. had only brought terrible war and death to their homelands, the girl told the congressmen. "Sir, we do not wish to be rude, but we wish for all the light-skinned people with uniforms and weapons to return to their homes and leave us in peace," she said. When Wright pressed her about the evils of Communism, she replied, "We know it governs Russia, and hear it said that it is bad, but we've never seen any Russian soldiers in our countries. We do not wish to be like them, not like the Americans either."[24] Johnson happened to be in Hawaii as well, meeting with military advisers, and the congressmen and their daughters were invited to a reception that night for the President. It was a thrill for Susan O'Neill, but she remembers that her dad was "conflicted" by the conversation with the Asian dissidents.[25]

On March 5, Johnson failed to file for the Massachusetts primary, thus ceding the state's 72 convention votes to McCarthy. On March 12, the voters of New Hampshire stunned the nation by giving McCarthy 42 percent of the vote in their presidential primary. Two days later, O'Neill made his appearance at St. Columbkille's Holy Name breakfast, walking his anxious and angry constituents through his decision to oppose the war. "Vietnam is no longer a place that is halfway around the world," the Brookline *Chronicle Citizen* said, reporting on the event. "It is as close as your next church breakfast, where you used to watch football films and complain about the coffee. Vietnam, gloomy, dismal and tragic as it is, has come home to America."[26]

On March 16, Bobby Kennedy announced his presidential candidacy. On the night of March 31, Johnson told a national television audience that he would not seek a second term.

THE WAR WAS not the only virulent issue that spring. O'Neill had spent much of his time in a behind-the-scenes struggle on the Rules Committee over the last of the Great Society's historic civil rights bills: the Fair Housing Act. "The real estate lobby all over America is working against the legislation," O'Neill wrote Rosemary. "Don't worry about your Dad. He'll vote right. (Champion of the underdog!)"[27] The legislation was a moral test for Northern congressmen, who had found it easier to vote to integrate Southern bus terminals and polling booths than to require that the North's suburbs and ethnic neighborhoods be opened to people of all races and creeds, and of the continued effectiveness of nonviolent tactics at a time when the Black Panther Party and other militant groups were bidding for support.[28]

The legislation passed the Senate on March 11, a few days after Martin Luther King Jr. announced that his Poor People's Campaign would invade Washington in late April to pressure the government for jobs and other economic assistance. But first, King said, he had promised to help the black garbage workers of Memphis in their strike for higher wages. He was shot and killed by a white assassin while standing on the balcony of the Lorraine Motel in Memphis at 6 P.M. on April 4. O'Neill and his staff were at the Democratic Congressional Campaign Committee's annual fund-raising dinner. The party broke up and he reluctantly left for home.

In one of his finest moments, Robert Kennedy broke the news to a rally of black supporters in Indianapolis. "I had a member of my family killed," he told the crowd, and quoted Aeschylus: "In our sleep, pain which cannot forget falls drop by drop upon the heart until, in our own despair, against our will, comes wisdom through the awful grace of God." People wept and moaned aloud.[29]

Riots broke out in more than 100 American cities that night, and Washington suffered the worst. Crowds of angry black looters set fire to white- and black-owned businesses alike. The smoke from the burning buildings on Fourteenth Street drifted toward the White House, just a few blocks away. O'Neill drove through the riot area, up Seventh Street and down Fourteenth, on April 5. "What I saw was an element in a tragedy — what anger, frustration, sorrow, and years of unredressed wrongs can produce," he recalled.[30]

King's assassination focused attention on Congress, where the housing bill was stuck in the Rules Committee. There, the old conservative coalition was revived: southern Democrats and Republicans joined with Representatives Jim Delaney of New York and B. F. Sisk of California to bottle up the legislation on an 8 to 7 vote.

"The American people will hold the Congress as a whole responsible for this legislation," O'Neill warned his committee colleagues on April 8. "I would hate to think what would possibly happen in the major cities of this country if this Congress doesn't act this week." Representative John Anderson of Illinois finally broke from the conservative bloc and let the bill go to the floor, where it passed by a 229 to 195 vote on April 10.[31] O'Neill took the floor during the debate to pay his tribute to King. "He never faltered in his faith in man; never doubted his conviction that America could be truly free; and never lost the courage it took to lead that movement toward freedom and equality for all Americans," the congressman said. "He never lost faith that men could and would learn to live as brothers. I, too, see and believe in his dream," O'Neill said. "I vote aye on the civil rights bill of 1968."[32] Johnson signed the bill into law on April 11. The next day O'Neill received a package from the White House — a pen that Johnson used to sign the legislation — with LBJ's best wishes and thanks.[33]

ALTHOUGH BOUND to McCarthy, the Massachusetts delegation to the 1968 Democratic national convention had been selected and filled by O'Neill and other party regulars that spring. He thought the gray-haired, poetry-reading McCarthy ("Mc-cah-tee" in North Cambridge) was something of a dilettante. "Things are strange," O'Neill wrote Rosemary. "All the pols are with [Vice President Hubert] Humphrey, but it looks like the people are with McCarthy. This is amazing. They don't know Gene, a great friend of mine. Brilliant, easy going, philosopher, orator, economist but a dreamer who hates work. I am surprised he is still in the contest, not only that but getting stronger every day. The people want peace. That is the big issue." O'Neill did enjoy the senator's whimsical sense of humor and independence, and they had known each other for a long time, alternating at first base on the Democratic congressional baseball team in the 1950s, when they had neighboring offices in the House office building. As Irish Catholic leaders in their own right, the two also shared a resentment of the Kennedys' sense of entitlement.[34] When asked by Allard Lowenstein and other antiwar activists to challenge Johnson in 1968, McCarthy agreed to run. It was an act of conscience and moral courage, but he also had a score to settle with Johnson, who had publicly toyed with him in 1964, dangling the vice presidential nomination before giving it to Humphrey. And McCarthy was no doubt lured by the quixotic nature of the campaign.

"Gene was difficult . . . weird," said Bob Healy, who worked briefly for McCarthy in 1968. "He loved the idea of running, loved the idea of going against the President, loved the idea of mocking the President but didn't want to be President himself. Strange, wasn't it?"[35]

O'Neill was a party regular, and didn't fit in with McCarthy's disorganized "children's crusade." "Thank God the old pros control the convention," he told Rosemary. Though some of his young office workers would answer the phones with "Keep the faith, Baby," a sixties battle cry, O'Neill never embarrassed himself by trying to be hip. His sole concession to the decade was to let his sideburns crawl a bit down his cheeks. But the change was so negligible that Rosemary, returning from Europe, failed to notice until her chagrined father pointed it out.[36]

At heart O'Neill preferred Humphrey, and hinted to reporters that he would be happy to switch to the vice president on a second ballot in Chicago. The antiwar forces back home yelped, and soon O'Neill was back in the fold, claimed by the McCarthy campaign as a solid supporter. In a letter to Rosemary, O'Neill offered her a glimpse of the trouble he would have faced had he not broken with Johnson on the war.

"This is the year of the young fellow," O'Neill wrote. "Eddie Boland is being opposed by the former mayor of Springfield, 35-year-old Mayor Ryan. Eddie is running scared and is working very hard. He goes home every weekend, walking the streets, visits the factories and shopping centers, coffee bars, rallies. He is really working, as is Ryan, whose main argument is that Eddie is too old: 56 years old . . . 34 years in public office . . . old hat . . . and stale with no new ideas or imagination. He has Eddie worried."

On June 4, Robert Kennedy was assassinated in the kitchen of the Ambassador Hotel in Los Angeles, after beating McCarthy and a stand-in for Humphrey in that day's California primary. O'Neill was a family man, with a brood of his own, and shaken by the death of a young father who had seemed to find the best in himself in the years since Dallas. "A frightful tragedy," he wrote Rosemary. O'Neill attended the funeral service in New York, and on June 26, asked for time on the House floor. "He represented the poor, the oppressed, the silent, and the ignored," O'Neill said of his old antagonist. "He saw the ills of our society, the inequities and injustices that have no place in our democracy, and with equal clarity he saw that his duty lay in trying to end them. He was tireless in working toward that goal."

Then, thinking of RFK's mother, widow and children, O'Neill quoted a bit of poetry by Padraic Pearse. While awaiting execution for his role in the Easter uprising of 1916, the doomed Irish rebel had written to his mother:

Lord, I do not grudge my two sons that I have seen go out to break their strength and die, they and a few, in bloody protest for a glorious thing.
They shall be spoken of among their people: the generations shall remember them and call them blessed.
But I will speak their names to my own heart in the long nights, the little names that were familiar once round my dead hearth. Though I grudge them not, I weary, weary of the long sorrow.
And yet, I have my joy. They were faithful, and they fought.

Kennedy "was faithful and fought," O'Neill said. "Let us pray that the few fighting for a glorious thing become many, and that the sympathy we extend to his family turns into action, so that his last child, as yet unborn, shall be born into a world that has cured itself." It was a fine, generous speech.[37]

THE TWO ASSASSINATIONS were turning points, Richard Goodwin wrote later. "The world shifted. And change, once so welcome, had taken a darker direction. The confidence of the early sixties, the belief in an inevitable destiny, the redress of old injustice and the attainment of new heights, was being replaced by insecurity; apprehension about the future; fragmenting, often angry, sometimes violent, division," he said. "The 'movements' which were the glory of the early sixties — the expression of aroused expectations for justice, relief from poverty, the triumph of more humane values — took a more ominous, ultimately self-defeating direction."[38]

Richard Nixon brushed aside challenges from Nelson Rockefeller and Ronald Reagan and claimed the Republican nomination in Miami on August 8. George Wallace, meanwhile, was climbing in the polls as southerners and blue-collar workers deserted the Democratic party in favor of "law and order" that summer. Even the party's liberal base had splintered among McCarthy's kids, the regulars and labor bosses who clustered around Humphrey and the Kennedy diehards who rallied behind Senator George McGovern of South Dakota. O'Neill believed that only one of two things could unite the party: a peace plank or Ted Kennedy.

Unity was important to O'Neill, because unity was needed to maintain a Democratic majority in the House. Though he had no opponent of his own, he worried about his Democratic colleagues, and how they would fare in a Republican landslide. As the country moved to the right, the programs O'Neill had worked for — Social Security, Medicare, the minimum wage, Civil Rights — would be threatened if the Democrats lost control of Congress. And what of his own ambition? He had served under Republican Speakers in Massachusetts, and when he first came to Congress in 1953, and he knew that all his dreams of power and advancement depended on a durable Democratic majority.

"He always understood there was a party. It wasn't just whether LBJ or Hubert Humphrey got elected, it was whether or not the Congress went Republican and whether or not everything the Democrats stood for would get roped into this morass about the war," said Judith Kurland. "He understood it well. He was always thinking about his guys. And his guys were the other House members. And that is how he got where he got, of course, because he always took care of the guys. They were his responsibility. They were the ones he thought of first."[39]

The effort to nominate Ted Kennedy died aborning, but not for lack of effort. Former Ohio governor Michael DiSalle, an old Kennedy ally, notified all delegates on July 14 that he intended to nominate the senator in Chicago. O'Neill wrote back on July 19, noting that he was bound to McCarthy on the first ballot, but promised to be "the most active Member of the Club" if DiSalle were to persuade Kennedy to run.[40] O'Neill told Rosemary that "the challenge is now up to Ted. He is worthy of it — able, talented, confident, affable, a worker and a great man." DiSalle wasn't the only worried party regular. Mayor Daley had called the compound in Hyannisport on the weekend before the convention, asking Kennedy to announce that he would accept a draft. Stephen Smith, the senator's brother-in-law, had been dispatched to Chicago to see if McCarthy might concede. Rumors swept the convention hall. Boland and O'Neill got on the telephone to Kennedy "and we both got on him, you know, kind of pleaded with him," O'Neill recalled. "But he laughed . . . no way was he going to get involved."[41]

If he couldn't have Ted Kennedy, O'Neill wanted Humphrey to run on a Democratic peace platform that would liberate the party and its standard-bearer from the burden of Johnson's war. O'Neill sent Judith Kurland to Chicago early, to join the antiwar forces in lobbying the Platform Committee. But in the chilly political climate that followed the Soviet Union's invasion of Czechoslovakia, Johnson and the party regulars prevailed, rejecting a Vietnam peace plank that called for a bombing halt, negotiations and withdrawal of American troops.

The insurgents vowed to take the issue to the convention floor. Johnson (for reasons of personal pride and foreign policy) and Humphrey (because he was firmly under Johnson's thumb) were not going to kow-tow to the peace forces in Chicago. The showdown began at Tuesday evening's session. Healy, still wearing the two hats of activist and reporter, found McCarthy in the candidate's twenty-third-floor suite with poet Robert Lowell and writer Shana Alexander.

"I said to him, 'It could really make a difference if you would go down to the convention and make the argument for the peace plank. I think it would only be fair for the kids who have busted their ass for you.' And Gene and Lowell look at each other and they start talking about the early sounds of the morning," Healy recalled. "It was like a contest. Gene says, 'The drying out of a barn.' And Lowell says, 'The opening of a flower.' And Gene says, 'When a horse gets off the ground.' And they went on and on and on. Can you imagine that? Jeez, he was something else."[42]

Johnson, sulking, was just as distanced. As the debate over the peace plank went on, Larry O'Brien, Humphrey and Representative Hale Boggs, the House whip, tried to craft some compromise language that might heal the division on the floor. But any changes in the Vietnam plank had to have Johnson's approval. "Hubert placed a call to the President. To the consternation of all of us, he was unable to get the President on the line," O'Brien said. "The vice president of the United States couldn't get the president on the line."[43]

The Massachusetts delegation voted 56 to 16 on behalf of the peace plank, but it was defeated, 1567 to 1041. O'Neill voted with the antiwar forces, and strolled the convention floor wearing a large McCarthy button. It was shortly after 10 P.M. when Senator Abraham Ribicoff of Connecticut, at the podium to put McGovern's name in nomination, told the crowd, "With George McGovern we wouldn't have Gestapo tactics on the streets of Chicago." The television cameras focused on Mayor Richard Daley, who appeared to respond with a coarse obscenity.[44] Earlier that night, the delegates learned, the Chicago police had rioted outside the Hilton Hotel, gassing and clubbing the antiwar protesters and yippie freaks who had taunted them that week. The violence took place in the full glare of the television lights, under the windows of McCarthy and Humphrey headquarters. The demonstrators shouted,

"The whole world is watching." Humphrey clinched what many thought was a worthless nomination.

O'Neill was no yippie, but neither did he fully countenance the tactics employed by the Chicago police. He believed that the police had understandably overreacted, after hearing for weeks how the antiwar forces were planning to poison the city's water supply, seize its streets and halt the convention. He argued over dinner with the outraged Kurland, and then he mischievously called on her to defend her beliefs before Representative Dan Rostenkowski, Daley's right-hand man, and a table of the mayor's henchmen at a racetrack luncheon the next day. ("Judith, tell Danny and the boys what you told me last night about the cops, and how they overreacted. . . .")[45]

O'Neill never abandoned hope. On the eve of the convention he had appeared on a Boston television news show and predicted that Humphrey would win the nomination, "become his own man" and "get us out of Vietnam." His instincts were good. Humphrey called for a halt in the bombing in a national television broadcast, and furiously closed the gap on Nixon until losing by the slimmest of margins, 43.4 to 42.7 percent, on November 5. Though Humphrey fell short in the end, his speech — and Johnson's announcement of a bombing pause on October 31 — helped the Democrats retain control of the House.[46]

Nixon's election ended any ambiguity in O'Neill's mind about the war, and had a similar effect on dozens of his Democratic colleagues in Congress. The liberal wing of the party had embraced the antiwar candidacies of McCarthy, Kennedy and McGovern, and was determined to keep the spirit of insurgency alive. If they could not stop the war with a presidential campaign, they would throttle it on Capitol Hill by cutting off its source of funds. And if McCormack and the southern Bourbons refused to go along, well, all the more reason to do away with the crusty Speaker and the seniority system that had foiled the liberals' dreams for years. So began what Mo Udall called the "November coup d'état."

McCormack's base among the southern hawks and big-city Democrats of the North and Midwest was formidable: too strong for the liberals to defeat on their own. But there were some southern Democrats who were willing to cut a deal. The usurpers, led by Representative Phillip Landrum of Georgia — "Mr. L" in the code of the cabal — liberal stalwart Representative Frank Thompson of New Jersey ("Mr.

T"), and Representative Dan Rostenkowski of Illinois ("Mr. R"), tried to assemble a ticket in which Wilbur Mills ("Mr. M") would lead the South against McCormack while Udall, representing the liberals, would run for majority leader.

"The conversation occurred on the afternoon of December 6. Mr. T opened the discussion after some preliminary greetings and friendly exchanges, by stating that he had heard from a mutual friend from Georgia about some possible action which might be taken in connection with a change of leadership in the House," Udall wrote, in a memo to his files. "T stated that he wanted to explore this with M and to see whether there is any possibility of putting something together that would be good for the party and the country."

The members of the cabal lined up 70 votes, but their alliance collapsed when Mills backed out. Udall, having gone that far, phoned McCormack on Christmas Eve to announce that he would challenge the seventy-seven-year-old Speaker when Congress convened in January. The Arizonan had a difficult time conveying his message to McCormack, who kept hooting holiday greetings on the phone — but signed off soon enough after grasping what Udall was saying. In an eight-page letter to his colleagues, Udall listed the ideological reasons for his impertinence, and promised, in the unlikely event that he should defeat McCormack, to immediately hold a second election for Speaker, open to all comers. Udall hoped to get 85 votes for his symbolic challenge, but lost by 178 to 58. Rostenkowski backed McCormack; Mills was "especially harmful," and LBJ used the Texas delegation to punish Udall for his stance against the war. Thompson offered his hand to McCormack at the caucus, but the Speaker refused to shake it.[47] The episode had lasting ramifications for O'Neill, in that it damaged two potential rivals. "Mills, by his last minute defection, wiped himself out with the men he'd failed — and lost his shot at the Speakership then and now," Neil MacNeil wrote.[48] The contest, meanwhile, left Udall with a core of loyal supporters — but a number of sworn enemies as well. Among Udall's unforgiving foes was O'Neill, who because of his loyalty to McCormack, was firmly in the Speaker's camp.

NIXON HAD PROMISED a secret plan to end the war. In the early months of his administration, he even toyed with the idea of declaring a unilateral cease-fire and withdrawing the American troops. In the end, however, his desire to demonstrate resolve to the Soviets prevailed.

To ease domestic opposition, he cut draft calls to a tenth of what they had been during the peak years of the Johnson administration, and announced a policy of "Vietnamization," in which the South Vietnamese would shoulder an increasing share of the fighting, supported by U.S. forces. The first U.S. troop withdrawals began that summer. Nixon did not tell the country that these steps toward "peace with honor" were accompanied by a secret bombing campaign against Communist bases and supply lines in Cambodia.

American liberals did not allow the declining draft calls and phased U.S. withdrawals to affect their conviction that the war had to end. Though the color of the bodies was changing, the killing went on for four more years, and so did the antiwar movement. The war's bloodiest fighting had taken place in the months after Tet, and the U.S. body count stood at 36,000 when Nixon took office. But in Nixon's first term, another 20,000 American soldiers and hundreds of thousands of Vietnamese died, and his administration was confronted by the largest, and most violent, protests of the war.

Polarization, which had begun with the first signs of backlash at mid-decade, became the dominant political motif in the late sixties. Everyone, it seemed, took a step from the center, out toward the wings. Regulars became dissenters; dissenters turned radical; radicals were revolutionaries; revolutionaries nihilists. "In the eyes of the militants, the millions who poured into the parades hoping to see their bodies count against the bloodshed mattered less than the body count in Vietnam piling up even faster. The peaceful demonstrations *had been done*," wrote Todd Gitlin, of SDS.[49] The organization spawned the Weathermen, who staged "Days of Rage" and street riots in Chicago. A wave of bombings struck ROTC halls, defense facilities and campus research centers. New Left feminists ditched the horny boys of the antiwar movement and struck out on their own search for liberation. Gays rioted in Greenwich Village. Hardhats lashed back at hippies. The drugs of choice moved from beer and dope to acid and speed; rock and roll from dreamy ballads to angry electric anthems. Hollywood lionized misfits and outlaws in *Cool Hand Luke, Bonny and Clyde, The Graduate, Midnight Cowboy* and *Easy Rider*. The press was infatuated, and the establishment outraged, by the antics of the yippies, the Black Panthers, the "flower children" in the Haight district of San Francisco. Governor Reagan ordered the National Guard to drive protesters from the Berkeley campus with tear gas, helicopters and shotguns. In July

1969, O'Neill traveled to Cape Kennedy, to watch the blastoff of the Saturn rocket carrying Neil Armstrong and the crew of *Apollo 11* to the moon. On his way back to Massachusetts, O'Neill sat next to Ted Kennedy, who looked "tired as hell" on the plane but was looking forward to a sailing weekend on Chappaquiddick Island, not knowing the tragedy that awaited.[50] The counterculture peaked at Woodstock in August, and crashed at Altamont in December. Ho Chi Minh, Ike, and old Joe Kennedy died. The Chicago Eight, the leaders of the antiwar forces at the convention, were put on trial for their role in the rioting in Chicago.[51]

O'Neill was not immune to the changing times; he was, in fact, continuing on his own transformative journey. The congressman was the honored guest when his son Michael graduated from Matignon High School on June 1, and his speech was a far cry from the cutting remarks he had made about "kooks and commies and egghead professors" at the State House rally with Miss U.S.A. in 1966.

"Every man has the right to dissent, for dissent makes those in power, in authority, in the establishment, and the people as a whole aware of our inequities," he told the graduates. "You should, in fact you must, dissent from those policies you believe to be illegal or wrong."

Vietnam was "the most tragic war in our history, even more tragic than the Civil War," he said. "We have seen how the greatest power on earth has gotten caught up and bogged down in a war that was not meant to be. For two years I have opposed this war, the senseless killing of America's youth, the devastation of the country we purport to save, and the ignoring of our nation's domestic needs. And we have learned that those who should know the most about war, the military, are often wrong. This war must end and it must not be followed by another one."

He concluded his speech on a spiritual note. He was not an introspective man, not one for self-reflection. But neither were his speeches fancy dodges; he generally spoke plain truths from the heart. On this day he showed how he had made the intellectual journey, somewhere in those long years of worship and instruction; past the catechismic dogma, the rote ceremony and the rigid rules of behavior to the Christian core of his Roman Catholic faith. He didn't tell the students to respect their elders or make sure they attended Mass each Sunday or to eat fish on Fridays — but rather to honor the Christian ideal of social justice. O'Neill may not have always lived up to his code, but here it was, condensed in a paragraph on a day in June.

"In all endeavors you must impart to others what the Church has taught us — that all men are precious individuals, loved by God," O'Neill said. "In everything you do, you must recall that Christ loved man and wished us, for our own sakes, to love Him. The method by which we exercise that love is by loving our fellow man, by seeing that justice is done, that mercy prevails."[52]

With a Republican in the White House, O'Neill now began to raise his profile in Washington, leading the liberals into battle on several fronts. In June 1969, he called for unilateral American withdrawal from Vietnam. That same summer he tangled with Wilbur Mills over tax reform, and the oil depletion allowance so prized by oil-producing states.

"I used to write him notes," Judith Kurland recalled. On tax reform, "he went to the Rules Committee and he actually read from it. I said it was a lousy bill and that the mountain had heaved and produced a mouse. And there were all these advocacy groups in the room and they gave him a hand. They clapped, and he came back and said, 'That was great!'

"And so he went to the floor and gave the same speech. Only he embellished it," she said. "He said 'the ocean roared and has produced a periwinkle.' I didn't even know what a periwinkle was. He had begun to look for issues like that."[53]

In September 1969, Kurland introduced her boss to a young reformer named David Cohen, who was lobbying with a coalition of peace groups to halt funding of the Safeguard missile system, an antiballistic missile (ABM) network that would cost $7 billion. "I was in the institutional wing of the antiwar movement, which was all about how to make the system work and be more responsive," Cohen said. "It was okay to go to the streets, but the streets are ultimately about influencing the system."[54]

The ABM had been a Johnson administration initiative. Congressional Democrats, sensing public unease with the long-standing U.S. strategy of preventing nuclear war through the threat of massive retaliation and "mutual assured destruction," had pushed Johnson and McNamara to develop a strategic defense system to protect American cities in the mid-1960s. The Soviets had already deployed a rudimentary missile defense around Moscow, and were adding hundreds of nuclear warheads to their offensive forces each year.

But liberal Democrats soured on the program by 1969 because of its high cost, and because of Nixon's decision to remove population centers from the Safeguard umbrella and to protect fields of Minutemen intercontinental ballistic missile (ICBM) silos instead. Strategic defense was inherently destabilizing, Nixon's critics decided, because it would raise Soviet fears that the U.S. was planning a surprise attack, hoping to use Safeguard to shoot down whatever Soviet warheads survived. Nixon, for his part, wanted the ABM as a bargaining chip to be used in strategic arms talks with the Soviets, and was determined to preserve it. After weeks of debate, the Senate voted in August to fund the system when Vice President Spiro Agnew's vote broke a 50 to 50 tie.[55] The action shifted to the House, where Representative L. Mendel Rivers of Mississippi, the retrograde chairman of the Armed Services Committee, was determined to ram the ABM through as part of a $21.3 billion military procurement bill that also continued funding for the first multiheaded nuclear missiles in the U.S. arsenal, the hydra-like multiple independently targetable reentry vehicles (MIRV). The MIRV program was another Johnson-era initiative that liberals now viewed as destabilizing.[56]

O'Neill the cold warrior had routinely supported the Pentagon's nuclear weapons requests. But now he and other northern Democrats in Congress were more skeptical of Defense Department claims. "I know you can't beat the rule, but we at least ought to get more time for a debate," Cohen told the congressman. "And if you don't get more time, people like you ought to vote against the rule."

"Write me a memo," O'Neill replied.[57]

O'Neill challenged the mighty Rivers in the Rules Committee, urging his colleagues to allow ten hours of debate. The panel instead okayed a rule for the procurement bill on September 30, allotting just four hours for consideration. The legislation came to the floor the next day, and O'Neill led the fight.

"The destiny of this great nation cannot be considered and disposed of in four hours," O'Neill said.

Rivers answered him with Southern spite.

"When the gentleman from New York, the beloved Manny Celler, came in here with his so-called civil rights bills and his so-called voting rights bills — aimed at only six Southern states — we could hardly get sufficient time to say good morning. But I do not recall any complaints from the voices I have heard here today," Rivers said. "The fellows south of the Mason-Dixon Line just lost their turns, that was all. I did not complain. I have been here long enough to know that this is a cold-blooded place."[58]

The rule was approved, 324 to 61. And Safeguard was preserved by a 219 to 105 vote. But "it was the beginning of challenging things procedurally," said Cohen. "This was . . . a new breakthrough."

As antiwar groups squabbled over tactics, and Nixon enjoyed the honeymoon traditionally afforded new Presidents, organized opposition to the war was episodic in the first nine months of 1969. But the movement made huge gains at Nixon's expense once the students returned to their campuses in the fall. At a MassPAX meeting in April, Jerome Grossman suggested that antiwar forces state a deadline for a U.S. withdrawal and stage an escalating series of grassroots actions and general strikes that would bring the country to a halt each month until the troops were home. Others refined the idea, and Sam Brown, the veteran of the McCarthy campaign, led the organizers of the so-named Moratorium.[59]

Massachusetts was a cauldron of antiwar activity. On September 30, State Representative Michael J. Harrington, thirty-three, mobilized antiwar troops and won a special election for a North Shore seat left open by the death of Representative William Bates. Harrington's defeat of state senator William Saltonstall, a supporter of the war, marked the first time that antiwar sentiment had scored a clear-cut triumph in state politics. In Newton and nearby liberal bastions, the movement veterans were targeting O'Neill's pal Representative Phil Philbin, a hawkish member of the House Armed Services Committee. He had won a bitter primary in 1968 when two antiwar candidates split the vote. Now, united behind the Reverend Robert Drinan, the dean of the Boston College Law School, the insurgents would dump Philbin in 1970.

Given the political climate, it was no surprise that O'Neill enthusiastically endorsed the Moratorium. On Moratorium Day, October 15, he asked for time on the House floor. "What are the choices that we have? The first choice that we have is to revert to conducting the war the way it was being fought 2 years ago. We could go back to bombing the North and heavy search and destroy missions. This was the situation in September, 1967, when I first came out in opposition to this war. At that time 12,000 men had been killed, and today 40,000 men have been killed.

"The second choice is to really try to win the war militarily as we never did. We never bombed Hanoi, we never bombed the rice paddies, we never bombed the dams, we never invaded. I think all of us realize and understand that if we were to do that we would probably cause World War III, and I do not want that, and I cannot imagine any member of this body would want that.

"There is one other choice, and if we are to be reasonable men and not want to see the war of attrition continue . . . if we do not want to bring on nuclear holocaust and the destruction of the world as we know it . . . then we must take the last course. And that is to get the boys out of there and to get the boys home."[60]

NIXON DECIDED TO "go for broke," as he later described it. "I would attempt to end the war one way or the other — either by negotiated agreement or by an increased use of force." He sent Hanoi an ultimatum: talk peace or face a devastating escalation of U.S. attacks. National security adviser Henry Kissinger met secretly with North Vietnamese envoys in Paris, but Hanoi rebuffed the U.S. peace terms. The White House moved ahead on a war plan called Duck Hook, which called for renewed bombing of Hanoi and other urban centers, the mining of Haiphong Harbor, the destruction of rural dikes and, as possible options, invasion of the north and use of low-yield nuclear weapons.[61]

The October Moratorium was a tremendous success for the antiwar forces. The largest single demonstration was in Boston, where Senator George McGovern addressed some 100,000 protesters on the Common. At churches and schoolyards and street corners around the country, smaller groups raised American flags, held teach-ins and flashed their headlights, showing that the opposition to the war was now a broad-based movement which had moved out from the elite campuses and enlisted the support of the middle class. When students and faculty members from Cambridge and Boston arrived at O'Neill's office, he told them to stop preaching to the choir, and to focus their efforts instead on their parents and on local church congregations out in middle America.

But as the marchers filed by the White House with their candles on October 15, Nixon was working on the first draft of a speech he had planned for November 3. "Don't get rattled — don't waver — don't react," he wrote across the top of his yellow legal pad. The nationally televised address, in which Nixon asked "the great silent majority of my fellow Americans" to "be united against defeat," was a political masterpiece that sent his approval ratings soaring. Agnew, meanwhile, had been dispatched as the administration hatchet man to intimidate the "effete corps of impudent snobs" who opposed the war. Led by two moderate Democrats, Representatives Jim Wright of Texas and Wayne L. Hays of Ohio, the House passed a resolution in support of Nixon's efforts by a 334 to 55 vote on December 2.[62]

O'Neill was unmoved by the "silent-majority" speech. Nor would he bend when Wright wrote to ask him to endorse the Wright-Hays resolution as "a middle-ground." He joined the 54 other representatives who voted against the measure.[63] "I am quite happy to learn from previous mistakes, and I do not choose to repeat them," O'Neill said on the floor. "This resolution can be used just as the Tonkin resolution was used."[64] In November, the army announced that it was ready to indict Lieutenant William L. Calley Jr. for participating in a massacre of up to 400 Vietnamese civilians at the village of My Lai in 1968. The news fueled passion for the November Moratorium, in which some 750,000 demonstrators arrived in the capital to march down Pennsylvania Avenue and rally on the Washington Monument grounds. They wore blue jeans and armbands, buckskin vests and boots. On a clear but breezy day, their flags, thousands of all description, waved like the colors of a Napoleonic army. "All we are saying," they sang over and over, "is give peace a chance." It was the single largest protest in U.S. history; a chapter in one of the biggest and most successful pacifist movements the world had ever seen. A group of violent protesters was cleared from the Justice Department with tear gas, increasing the sense of siege within an already embattled White House, and the televised images of long-haired youths waving Vietcong flags cost the antiwar movement support in blue-collar neighborhoods and suburban wards; but Nixon and Kissinger dropped their plans for Duck Hook, and on December 15 the President announced his third troop pullout, the largest yet.

At the request of antiwar organizers, O'Neill spent the November Moratorium in his district, speaking to enthusiastic crowds in Cambridge and Brighton. "We are now in a war that cannot be won, in a war that will not be lost, in a war that can only be ended," he told the audience at St. Bartholomew's Church in Cambridge, and announced his support for a December 1970 deadline for the withdrawal of U.S. forces.[65]

In April of 1970, Nixon announced that the U.S. would withdraw another 150,000 troops by the following spring. But to compensate for the long-term loss of manpower, Nixon moved to improve the immediate U.S. military position in Southeast Asia. The bulk of the troop withdrawals were back-ended: scheduled to take place in late 1970 and 1971. To keep the North Vietnamese from consolidating and enlarging their sanctuaries in Cambodia, and to prevent the possible fall of that country to the Communists, Nixon struck while he still had the muscle. After watching *Patton,* a gung-ho favorite movie of his, Nixon ordered U.S. and South Vietnamese troops to invade the Fishhook and the Parrot's Beak, two communist staging areas where the twisting Cambodian border protruded into South Vietnam. In a televised speech on April 30, Nixon said that he would not allow the United States to become a "second-rate power," even if it should cost him the presidency in the 1972 election. "If, when the chips are down the world's most powerful nation, the United States of America, acts like a pitiful, helpless giant, the forces of totalitarianism and anarchy will threaten free nations and institutions around the world." Then he went for a ride down the Potomac on the *Sequoia,* and as the yacht passed Mount Vernon, he ordered the crew to crank up the volume for the playing of the national anthem. He wanted it "blasted out," Nixon said, and punched the air with his fist. He and his wife, Pat, his daughter, Julie, and her husband, David Eisenhower, and Nixon's old pal Bebe Rebozo stood at rigid attention in the bow of the yacht as the anthem played.[66]

"The attack on the sanctuaries made our withdrawal from Vietnam easier; it saved lives . . . we had gained as much as two years," Kissinger concluded, but "the enormous uproar at home was profoundly unnerving." The campuses exploded; there were calls for a national student strike. After rioting and the firebombing of the ROTC building at Kent State University in Ohio, Governor James Rhodes sent in the National Guard to restore order. As students changed class on the sunny afternoon of May 4, a group of several hundred protesters confronted the Guard. Some of the young guardsmen panicked and opened fire. Four students were killed; two had merely been walking to class. "There was a shock wave that brought the nation and its leadership close to psychological exhaustion," Kissinger said.[67]

ROTC buildings were bombed. More than 400 colleges across the country shut down, many for the rest of the academic year. A hundred thousand protesters arrived on short notice in Washington on May 9, to find the White House surrounded by a barricade of sixty buses. Hard-hatted construction workers attacked antiwar protesters in New York, beating them as police looked on. Two more students were killed by police at Jackson State College in Mississippi on May 14. A hundred thousand supporters of the President, led by hardhats, rallied in New York on May 20. In a poignant predawn visit, Nixon left the White House and tried awkwardly to reach out to the youthful protesters encamped at the Lincoln Memorial. The gulf was too wide.[68]

The Cambodian invasion was a turning point for the White House, Congress and the nation. Nixon was so rattled by the protests that he ordered the federal law enforcement and national security agencies to find ways to identify, penetrate and disrupt the leftist "terrorist" groups. White House aides began to weigh the illegal tactics — bugging, break-ins — that would ultimately lead to the destruction of Nixon's presidency. It would be a Pyrrhic victory for liberals, however. The Left was itself near exhaustion. The protests had failed to end the war; the movement had splintered; the revolution had not arrived. A small segment of the radicals took up bombs and bank-robbing. Others flocked to communes and churches, self-contemplation and controlled substances or the new environmental and feminist movements. Freed by Nixon's troop withdrawals from worrying about the draft, thousands left college to try and make a living in an economy ravaged by the war's expense. The hardiest idealists kept up the pressure by organizing huge antiwar marches in 1971, and by working for McGovern's long-shot presidential candidacy in 1972. To them, the system was still viable. The real work of ending the war now moved to Capitol Hill. "The post-Cambodia uprising was the student movement's last hurrah," wrote Gitlin. "At long last, Congress took up the slack."[69]

The House, as always, was reluctant. O'Neill himself faced a dilemma. In the three years since announcing his opposition to the war, the congressman had agreed to make speeches, sponsor resolutions, support deadlines and lend his name to the antiwar cause. What he would not do, to the disappointment of many in the antiwar movement, was vote against the appropriation or authorization bills that funded the war. O'Neill had his reasons for making the distinction. The money bills often contained funds for defense jobs in his district. And congressional budgeting was long-sighted, so that a president might have years of funding in the pipeline, and the discretionary power to transfer money from other accounts. Finally, and most important, O'Neill refused to cut off funds for weapons, ammunition and other supplies that kept troops in the field, for fear he would be seen as abandoning them under fire. On May 6, the House was scheduled to take up an amendment by Representative Robert Leggett, a Democrat from California, to the military procurement bill. The Leggett amendment cut off funds for the use of U.S. troops in Laos, Cambodia and Thailand as of June 30.

In a memo, Judith Kurland begged her boss to change his position. "I think perhaps that this may be one of the most important actions of your life," she said. Leggett had crafted his amendment carefully; since Nixon was going to withdraw the troops from Cambodia by June 30 anyway, the measure would only ban future incursions, not undermine the troops then fighting in the Parrot's Beak. "Not one soldier will be deprived of a rifle or a bullet because of this," Kurland argued.[70] O'Neill's office had been jammed with protesters all day — clean-cut college students, representatives from the Massachusetts Council of Churches, matrons from Cambridge, hippies. It was a mark of his growing stature on the issue, and the significance of his decision, that when O'Neill rose on the House floor that evening, his colleagues agreed to his privileged motion and gave him five minutes of time to speak on a day when other lawmakers were limited to just forty-five seconds of debate. He endorsed Leggett's amendment.

"What good does it do if we are the most powerful and the strongest nation of the world if we are being torn apart from within?" O'Neill asked. "No nation in the world can destroy us, but it is possible that we can destroy ourselves. This will not be done by subversives, but by growing disaffection and alienation, and by the erosion of constitutional rights and guarantees.

"What we should do is bring the boys home from Cambodia immediately and bring the boys home from Vietnam immediately," O'Neill said. "We, in this body, more than any other branch of government, represent the people. If we fail to take responsibility for our actions, and fail to attempt to control the actions of the government, then we must be held accountable. We cannot abdicate our responsibility."[71]

The Leggett amendment and four other antiwar measures were killed in a series of nonrecorded votes. It wasn't the first time that the antiwar forces had lost on an unrecorded vote, and it was increasingly clear to liberal reformers that to end the war in Vietnam they would have to get the members of Congress on record. Again, they asked O'Neill to lead the charge.

IT WAS KNOWN as "teller voting." To cut down on time-consuming roll-call votes, in those days before electronic voting machines, the House members voted on most amendments by falling in line and filing down the center aisle past the "tellers" — representatives from each side of an issue who counted their colleagues, but recorded no names, as they passed. Unless a member chose to make a vote public, or reporters or lobbyists managed to count them from the gallery, the teller process let the representatives duck tough votes.

The tradition of secret voting dated back to precolonial days, when members of the British Parliament feared that the king or his agents would retaliate against those who voted against the sovereign. The British ended such secrecy in 1832, but the U.S. House had come to like the British tradition of hashing out the details of legislation, including crucial amendments, when sitting as a more informal "Committee of the Whole." Fewer members made up a quorum, and nonrecorded votes were permitted. The system was a boon to a sly or timid lawmaker, who could vote in virtual secret for amendments that gutted a bill, and then embrace the eviscerated legislation with much ado on final passage. In the case of the war, the war hawks could keep military appropriation and authorization bills free from antiwar measures like the Leggett amendment by defeating them via the teller process.

The Democratic Study Group's executive director, Richard Conlon, was determined to do away with teller voting. In the spring of 1970, the DSG had begun a letter-writing campaign to the editorial boards of major newspapers, complaining about the "secret" votes. It was the kind of safe, good-government issue that editorial writers have always loved to puff and flap about, and it pleased their liberal hearts because its first application would be against the war. The DSG and its fellow reformers packed the galleries with dozens of liberal lobbyists during a series of key arms-procurement votes; each "spotter" was charged with tracking the teller votes of four congressmen. The *Globe* and other news organizations started staking out the galleries as well. Liberal lobbyists and reporters called on the lawmakers, asking them to defend their votes on these important issues. Many members refused; some lied, some declined to answer their telephones.[72]

A legislative reorganization bill was moving through the House, and it reached the Rules Committee in the midst of the controversy over the Cambodian invasion and the latest votes on the ABM and MIRV deployments. The Safeguard system had become a major issue in Massachusetts when the army announced plans to put an interceptor base in the countryside north of Boston, and O'Neill had tried, but failed, to get a recorded vote when opposing the ABM in 1969. At a May 7 Rules hearing, he asked to be recognized.

"My next amendment is a really controversial matter," O'Neill told his colleagues. He proposed that clerks be stationed alongside the tellers to record the names and votes.

"I think the people are entitled to know how I voted, whether you are for the war or opposed to it. They now do not know how you vote. We duck the issue," said O'Neill.

"Can't a person get himself recorded if he wants to in the newspaper?" asked Representative John Young, a Democrat from Texas. "Let everybody attend to his own conscience." Other members raised procedural issues. "With 435 members in the House I just do not think this is practical," said Representative David Martin, a Republican from Nebraska. The amendment was defeated by a 6 to 6 vote. While Conlon was not a huge fan of O'Neill's, he recognized a convergence of interests. He enlisted O'Neill to lead the battle on the House floor, in bipartisan alliance with Representative Charles S. Gubser, a Republican from California. They struck on July 27, as the legislative reorganization bill was debated in the House. "The last three presidents of the United States all served in this body — Mr. Nixon, Mr. Johnson and Mr. Kennedy," O'Neill argued. "And if someone were writing the memoirs of any one of them on the important issues of the time in which they served . . . one would have to surmise or guess how they stood on the vital questions of the day, because there would be no record.

"We say whether people should go to war and the amount of taxes they must pay, but we're not willing that the people know how we vote," O'Neill said. "I wonder how Congress got away with this for so many years."[73]

The DSG had done its work well, lining up more than 180 cosponsors and pressuring Hale Boggs and other Democratic leaders to join in the cause. The O'Neill-Gubser amendment passed by a resounding voice vote; two years later, the House agreed to purchase an electronic voting system, completing its transition from the days of secrecy.

"Every time Tip did one of these things, the younger guys just loved him," said David Cohen. "Yet the older guys still trusted him. They never saw him as a reformer, in that he didn't have any of that righteousness that reformers have. He was a remarkable bridger of a guy, who could put his arm around [conservative Mississippi representative] Sonny Montgomery, and yet do well with the young, issue-oriented guys in a way that Carl Albert couldn't and John McCormack surely couldn't."[74]

O'Neill was hailed in *Time* and *Newsweek* as a national leader. It was another "big breakthrough of O'Neill being recognized now, beyond the war, around the issue of institutional change," said Cohen. Judith Kurland remembered that O'Neill "immediately saw, he knew, that this was national stuff, that he was up there in a different way.

"Was he plotting it? You know what George Washington Plunkitt says: 'I seen my opportunities and I took them,'" said Kurland. O'Neill "believed that good government was good politics. And he thought that if the opportunity presented itself, that he wanted to be majority leader."[75]

The Left was grateful: a DSG analysis of the first year of recorded voting found that "the record teller reform represented a significant gain for liberals since they rarely ever won a vote when votes were not recorded . . . not a single liberal amendment of any substance was approved during 1970 prior to the advent of record tellers."[76] The first key test came in March 1971, on a vote that determined the fate of federal funding for the SST, a supersonic transport plane that the environmental movement had targeted for defeat. The Nixon administration and the aerospace industry lobbied furiously for the new airplane, but in the glare of recorded voting it was shot down, 214 to 207.

"This will probably be the end of me," O'Neill said to Representative Henry Reuss, a Democrat from Wisconsin, as they walked down the aisle to vote.

"Or the beginning," said Reuss.[77]

CHAPTER 12

The Leadership Ladder

THE CHAIN OF events that carried O'Neill into the House leadership led back to 1954, with a decision by Representative Percy Priest of Tennessee to forfeit his job as the Democratic whip and take instead the coveted chairmanship of the House Committee on Interstate and Foreign Commerce. He weighed the percentages well: Rayburn and McCormack were in their prime and showing no signs of ill health. Why pass up the clout of a committee chair in the slim — and as it turned out, empty — hope that Old John or Mr. Sam would meet with catastrophe? In the end, they both outlived the Nashville congressman.

So Speaker Sam needed a whip. It was a choice he took quite seriously.[1] Representative Carl Albert, a tiny, short-chinned World War II veteran from Bug Tussle, Oklahoma, whose ability earned him a Rhodes scholarship in 1931 and a congressional seat in 1946, had made a deep impression on Rayburn. The Speaker was a political neighbor whose Bonham, Texas, home lay just across the Red River from Albert's Oklahoma district. The freckle-faced Albert had eagerly haunted the House chamber, soaking up the ways of the floor, and soon won a precious invitation to the Board of Education where he got to know another promising young congressman, Hale Boggs.

Louisiana has a penchant for sending colorful characters to public office and Boggs, with his sporty ties, pocket handkerchiefs and hair parted down the middle, and with his fealty to the Crescent City creed of *"Laissez les bon temps roulez,"* was no exception. "There was something of the old smoothie about him in a 1930-dance-bandleader sort of way," wrote Larry L. King, after watching him for a decade from the vantage point of administrative assistant to a Texas congressman. "Yet one sensed a hard core in the man, some sly, tough, intelligent power, an essence hinting that if times got hard and he had no other choice, then Hale Boggs might go on the road and very successfully sell lightning rods."[2] Indeed, Boggs had worked his way through Tulane University as a radio announcer and cub reporter, and by selling mail order suits on the side. As a young lawyer, he helped form a reform group called the "Peoples League" in an attempt to clean up the corruption in New Orleans politics. He was elected to Congress in 1940; at twenty-six, he was its youngest member. Though Boggs signed the Southern Manifesto and opposed the Civil Rights Act of 1964, he voted for the Voting Rights Act in 1965 and the Fair Housing Act of 1968 — two risky steps for a Southern congressman.

"Hale was very opinionated and he could smell a rat pretty good," Albert recalled years later. "He was pretty rough on members that didn't go along with the leadership."[3]

Boggs was steel and snake oil; Albert, all boyish sincerity, masking a short man's intensity. Though the five-foot-four-inch Albert was respected by his peers, and possessed the ample cravings and necessary political gifts to climb from a miner's shack in rural Oklahoma to the pinnacle of the House, there was a certain smarminess to him, a bit of the schoolhouse teacher's pet that served him well on the way up but proved little help when he was called upon to exercise power. As a leader he could be tugged every which way by more decisive personalities. Boggs, on the other hand — whose great-uncle had been a Confederate general — possessed the aristocratic surety required of a Southern Democrat who wanted to play in the turbulent ways of national Democratic politics.

Which of these two favorites would Rayburn choose as whip? Albert later insisted, no doubt disingenuously, that he had no idea what Rayburn and McCormack wanted when they called him to the majority leader's office on a January day in 1955.

"I just trotted down the hall, like any other young member summoned by Mr. McCormack," he said later. "When I got there, I was surprised to see Sam Rayburn — a very smiling Sam Rayburn — in the office. John McCormack got right to the point. Congress would convene in less than twenty-four hours, and he and Mr. Rayburn needed to name a new Democratic whip.

"They had been going down the list of Democratic members, John reading the names aloud," Albert alleged. "When he called off the name, Carl Albert, Sam Rayburn stopped him. 'That's it!' they both cried in unison."

"Who, me?" Albert asked.

"I like the kind of dirt that grows under your fingernails," Rayburn told him. And to the press Rayburn announced, "I can tell big timber from small brush."[4]

That, at least, is Albert's version of events, which closely follow the pattern of political autobiography, in which great men are invariably graced by fortune or, better yet, rewarded for their long years of diligence without suffering the telltale scars of ambition, skullduggery or cloakroom machinations. The truth is generally less noble: as a whole and in this case. For it was 1955, and Rayburn had to contend with the electorate's prejudices. McCormack was a Roman Catholic. So was Boggs. The nation, Mr. Sam concluded, could take one high-ranking Catholic atop the ladder of succession; not two. "Rayburn was as free of prejudice as any human being I've ever known, but he had been one of the loyal Democrats who had campaigned in Texas in 1928 for Governor [Al] Smith, and he had witnessed firsthand the tremendous prejudice that can be built up on that issue and he felt that it was still there," Boggs said later.[5]

Boggs's Catholicism wasn't the only factor. He would vote to reduce the oil depletion allowance, a bit of corporate welfare that was dear to the wildcatters and other oilmen who backed Rayburn and the Texas delegation; Albert, an Oklahoman, would not. Boggs was instead named deputy whip, and thus was born the leadership ladder that O'Neill sought to climb. The players changed slots but once in the following sixteen years: when Rayburn died in 1961 and McCormack, Albert and Boggs all moved up a rung. Together, they easily defeated Representative Mo Udall's 1969 challenge to the regular order.[6]

THE FIRST SIGN that the ladder was creaky came in the fall of 1969, when the taint of scandal touched Boggs and McCormack. Congress was in the midst of the bitter battles over the ABM and the Vietnam War when Boggs received a phone call from the FBI. A federal strike team in Maryland was investigating allegations of bribery involving a Baltimore contractor, Victor Frenkel, whose company had built the parking garage for the new Rayburn House Office Building. Frenkel was alleged to have offered bribes to members of Congress who supported his claim that the federal government owed him $5 million in overrun costs. The FBI interviewed Boggs twice in the fall of 1969 after witnesses told a grand jury that Frenkel's firm had performed a $45,000 remodeling job on Boggs's Bethesda home for which he was only charged $21,000. In May of 1970, prosecutor Steve Sachs wrote to Attorney General John Mitchell, asking the department for permission to prosecute Boggs and the other lawmakers. "It is Mr. Sachs's feeling that if these were ordinary citizens rather than members of Congress, a true bill would be returned in this case beyond doubt and that politics should not be used to gain favorable treatment here," the FBI's agent-in-charge reported to Director J. Edgar Hoover. But Mitchell overruled Sachs, and ordered him to limit the prosecution to Frenkel. The news did not reach the public until the following June, but it preoccupied Boggs, already reeling from a nastily close election in 1968, and no doubt contributed to an emerging pattern of erratic behavior that raised doubts about his leadership.[7]

McCormack, meanwhile, was an aging creature of habit. Though they flattered him in public, Nixon and his aides were contemptuous of the Speaker in their internal parleys. McCormack "can't deliver anything," Nixon told Republican congressional leaders in the fall of 1969.[8] "At 77, he has run out of steam," journalist Jack Anderson wrote of McCormack that fall. "He is no longer the crafty wheelhorse who delighted in shredding the enemy with knifelike sarcasm and spontaneous wit. With sunken cheeks and yellowing white hair, he is a kindly but tottering old man who looks as if he might be toppled by the next blast of congressional hot air."[9]

"Rayburn had the respect of the whole House. McCormack was always hated by the younger, college-educated liberals of his own party, who resented his Boston city-hall style of politics and his often stifling flatteries and his ties to the Catholic hierarchy," *Time* magazine's Neil MacNeil told his editors. "Politics to him was personal. It was friendship. You took care of your friends and they took care of you. Your opponents were not your enemies, they were 'Foemen worthy of your steel.'"[10]

The Speaker was a man of times past, used to the days when he would signal his boys on how to vote by pointing a cigar up or down. He refused to fly in an airplane. He never took a drink. Devoted to his aging wife, Harriet, eighty-five, McCormack left the House each evening and dined with her at night. He was a steadfast hawk on the Vietnam War. And he failed to perceive the extent to which the old ways were changing; that many Americans would find it unseemly to find lobbyists manning desks and using the telephones in the ornate Speaker's rooms, just off the House floor.[11]

One of those lobbyists — Nathan M. Voloshen — did more than borrow the phone; he allegedly conspired with Martin Sweig, McCormack's administrative assistant, to fix cases before federal commissions and agencies. McCormack did much of his business by telephone, and Sweig was a skillful mimic of his boss's voice. News of the federal investigation broke in October 1969 when *Life* magazine published an explosive article that said Sweig and Voloshen had joined to use McCormack's name, phone and offices to influence a number of agencies on contracts, paroles and regulatory affairs. McCormack suspended Sweig. Voloshen was convicted the following June of three counts of conspiracy, and Sweig of perjury.[12] The glare of attention didn't stop O'Neill from testifying as a character witness at the Sweig trial, an act of loyalty Sweig never forgot.[13]

Tremors now shook the Democratic cloakroom. Bolling had been calling for McCormack's retirement for years. In December, McCormack had an angry showdown in his office with Representative Frank Thompson and a group of other members of the liberal Democratic Study Group.[14] The old Speaker rallied one last time, and announced that he would run for reelection. But on Capitol Hill it now seemed clear that two of the three House leaders were vulnerable. As his wife's health failed, and winter turned to spring, McCormack was forced to turn down Nixon's offer to host an honorary dinner marking the day that he exceeded Henry Clay's nine-year continuous tenure as Speaker. "It would be torture for her [and] for me to receive this great honor and for her to be unable to be present," McCormack told White House lobbyist Bryce Harlow.[15] The Speaker finally bowed to the inevitable on May 20, 1970, announcing that he would not seek reelection.

McCormack's retirement triggered one of the great contested leadership races of the Democratic Party's forty-year reign of the

House: for the majority leader's post that Albert would vacate as he moved up to Speaker. The majority leader's job "is limiting only to the extent that the man holding it invokes limitations," wrote Larry L. King. The Speaker's is a constitutional office, and supposedly requires a degree of nonpartisan loftiness. Not so the leader: "His is the opportunity to push his party's or his President's programs through Congress or to ambush those of the opposition," said King. "He transmits to the President his party's viewpoint or leanings in the House, bringing back direct word of the President's mood. He is assaulted by cameras and questions and has difficulty staying out of the newspapers." And, most important, "the odds and traditions virtually assure that one sweet day the Majority Leader will become Speaker."[16]

Boggs was the titular successor, but prey for a collection of sharks that circled the foot of the leadership ladder. He tended toward arrogance, suffered from bouts of mania and mixed alcohol with pills. His behavior had become embarrassing. "Boggs was one of the really brilliant members of the House, but he was conceited and he was — he got on a dope binge for a while," said Albert. "He'd take these up and down things. He'd take something to go to sleep and to stay awake right close together."[17]

An aghast McCormack had tried to gavel Boggs down and friends had to gently pull him from the floor when he launched a nasty attack upon Wilbur Mills. Boggs held an infamous press conference that went on for two hours as he ranted from the podium; read from various news clippings, the Democratic Party platform, the Bible and his appointment book; and rushed from time to time to usher female journalists to their seats. "You know when I was growing up we used to study theology," Boggs told the startled reporters. "There was a god of the sea, a god of this, a god of that. Is there a god today?"[18]

"He worked too hard. He did drink," said Boggs's wife Lindy. "When you are tired, and you drink, after a few hours your drinks slow you more. They exhaust you. It's a vicious circle."[19] In a poll conducted by the *National Journal* in May, Democratic congressmen were asked to rate the leadership ability of various colleagues. Mills scored 104 points, Albert 68 and Boggs 11. It was clear that Boggs would be challenged when the new Congress convened after the 1970 elections, and O'Neill was occasionally mentioned in the press and among his colleagues as a possible challenger. Bolling, in fact, put his Rules Committee seatmate on a list of the top dozen contenders for majority leader.

If there were some in the House, like Albert, who thought O'Neill an amiable slacker, they underestimated him. He had used his jokes and stories, played the happy Irishman, with no small element of calculation. He had won the affection of his colleagues, while masking his ambition from potential rivals. It was a natural way for an immigrant's grandson who wanted to win hearts but — cast in the ethnic resentments of his youth and struggling to overcome the ancestral injunction that he mind his place — closely guarded his dreams and hopes. "You talk about the right place at the right time; Tip was there," said Representative Dan Rostenkowski, who would become the most prominent victim of O'Neill's strategy. Yet O'Neill's triumph was not all luck, the Chicagoan said. O'Neill knew that "if you want power, you have to reach for it."[20]

Rostenkowski was a big, blunt former car salesman with an imposing personality; a wunderkind who represented Mayor Richard Daley and the Chicago machine in Congress. "You tell me I can't do it and I'll show you I can," he liked to say, summarizing his combative creed. "Sure, I've compromised, but I always want to walk away a winner — that in my mind I'm the winner." In the 1960s he played Iago to McCormack's Othello and Dick Bolling's Cassio: filling the Speaker's head with tales of Bolling's disloyalty until McCormack was taut with fury. "Bolling thought he was Einstein and Copernicus in one person. He looked down his nose at everybody," Rostenkowski said. "He was always saying how he was with the Board of Education; he was with Rayburn. So I used to go in and tell John McCormack how Bolling was doing this and Bolling was doing that and John McCormack would be on the ceiling. I was just having fun."[21] Rostenkowski's pugnacity was his undoing. In the 1971 race he took a stumbling run at four different leadership positions, and lost them all. O'Neill profited, and for years Rosty had to look at his big Irish pal and chew on what might have been.

Rostenkowski, forty-two, triggered the political intrigue by publicly threatening to challenge Albert in the election for Speaker. When Albert wrote to each state delegation, asking its support, Illinois alone failed to R.S.V.P. Illinois representatives Melvin Price and Frank Annunzio informed on Rostenkowski — telling Albert how they wanted to support the "little giant" for Speaker but that Rosty wouldn't let them. It was a foolish bit of chest-thumping on Rostenkowski's part; he never had a prayer of beating Albert and both of them knew it. Albert quickly picked up endorsements from McCormack, Bolling, Udall and Mills.[22]

Rostenkowski's next option was to take on Boggs, but here he found he would have to stand in line. "For a time I could walk around the floor and look at any fella and say, 'Well, he's one of my opponents,'" Boggs later recalled.

In the line were:

• Representative Mo Udall of Arizona, forty-eight, the laconic one-eyed Jack Mormon of a cowboy, grandson of a polygamist (and at six feet five inches tall a former professional basketball player for the Denver Nuggets), was a hero to many House liberals and freshmen for his work in the reform-minded DSG; for engineering a congressional pay raise (at a time when hiking pay in return for limiting outside income was a prominent cause of reformers); and for his 1969 challenge of McCormack.

• Representative James O'Hara of Michigan, another DSG liberal, was the forty-five-year-old darling of organized labor, which still wielded much clout in the party and had never forgotten, or forgiven, Udall's 1965 vote against repeal of Section 14(b) of the Taft-Hartley Act, the notorious right-to-work clause. A brawler on the floor, he was aloof among his colleagues after hours, preferring to spend his time with his seven children, or sailing on weekends.

• Representative B. F. "Bernie" Sisk of California, sixty, a transplanted Texan who fled the Dust Bowl in the 1930s and represented the small towns of the San Joaquin Valley, was pushed to make the race by a group of Southern conservatives who were unhappy with Boggs over civil rights and other issues, and concerned about his behavior.

• Representative Wayne Hays of Ohio, fifty-nine, an acerbic practitioner of the inside game who would tyrannize his colleagues from his post as chairman of the House Administration Committee (until 1976, when his buxom secretary and mistress, Elizabeth Ray, told the *Washington Post* she couldn't type) rounded out the field. "The word most frequently applied to Hays was 'abrasive,'" wrote King.[23]

Rostenkowski knew there was potential support for at least one more candidate in the race — a Northern big-city Democrat. O'Neill, Eddie Boland and New York congressman Hugh Carey had also tested the thesis and believed it to be true. The problem, however, was that this candidacy came with a built-in ceiling. With Udall and O'Hara and

Boggs in the race, there were already three progressive candidates competing for the pool of liberal and labor votes that a Northern candidate would need to rise above regional status. The North's big-city votes quickly emerged as the prized uncommitted bloc and the key to the election. And so Rosty cut a deal. Illinois would support Boggs for majority leader, and Boggs would name Rostenkowski as the Democratic whip. "It was without question; without question," Rostenkowski said.

O'Neill had nursed hopes of picking up 12 to 20 votes as an unannounced candidate on the first ballot, and emerging as a compromise victor should Boggs falter. He was now a favorite among the young, issue-oriented congressmen, who saw him, with his white hair and cigars and blarney, as a symbol of middle-class opposition to the war in Vietnam. Yet he was also an old pal of the party regulars; a buddy, a safe bet, a card-playing colleague who over the years had proven true to his word, who dealt in favors and who — if the House Democrats must bend to the incessant demands for congressional reform — would be open and reasonable and not behave like some crazed child.

O'Neill had used his time to become a player in leadership politics: conferring with members, pushing the teller vote reform, leading the fight against the ABM and the Vietnam War, raising funds through the Democratic Congressional Campaign Committee and recruiting a "good following" of 12 to 20 loyalists, committed to him, primarily from New England and the Northeast. He had even taken fifty pounds off his corpulent frame by attending Weight Watchers classes at Catholic University. (He was the only man in the class, and most of the women didn't know he was a congressman. "Good for Thomas!" they said, when he had registered the loss of a few more pounds.[24])

Why didn't O'Neill mount an open challenge to Boggs? The answer has much to do with loyalty: loyalty as both a personal principle and a strategic asset. The virtue of loyalty was not merely a treasured human quality for O'Neill (though it was) but also widely recognized in the House as a valuable political commodity: a glue that helped hold the system together, brought stability and order and let politicians forge bonds with their colleagues and constituents. It was a time of necessary change in Congress. The dominance of geriatric committee chairmen was drawing to an end, and there was much about the old ways that made the House seem sclerotic. Yet reformers like Bolling and Udall, and California representative Phil Burton, paid a price among their peers even as they were lauded in the press. They were perceived as home wreckers, as having put their personal ambition before the institution. O'Neill, by disposition and design, cast his lot as a "man of the House."

"He was going to do it the way that was congenial to him," said Bolling. "By just being a nice guy. Never really pressing anybody. You had to follow your own nature."[25] Though ambition is a precious commodity in a leader, individual members, in keeping with their goals of reelection and political advancement, want the House run reliably and (to the extent that their constituents appreciate its legislative agenda) effectively. What the members don't desire, or appreciate, is a dynamic leader whose vaulting careerism threatens to send the House on a controversial crusade or otherwise put the place in turmoil, thus complicating their own careers.[26]

There are exceptions: the 1994 House takeover by Speaker Newt Gingrich's revolutionary band of brothers is an example of how years of frustration can persuade a party that it needs to put collective strategy ahead of individual security. But whether in Rayburn's era or O'Neill's, the savvy party leader generally minds the individual interests and respects the inflated egos, grandiose self-images and petty jealousies of his peers.

So O'Neill was smart, as a matter of both honor and expedience, to respect the leadership ladder, to be grateful for the benefits it gave him and to be loyal to his patron, John McCormack. And though old John was leaving office, he yet had two agendas in the struggle of succession: to promote Boggs, with whom he had been allied since 1955, and to wreak vengeance on Udall. Neither McCormack nor O'Neill would ride a sinking ship to the bottom, but they were willing to give Boggs a chance to right his foundering candidacy. McCormack made a point of allowing Boggs to preside over the House sessions. O'Neill remembered how McCormack had telephoned him one autumn day. "Tom, I hope you're not supporting Udall," the Speaker said.

"Mo Udall was a beautiful guy and a close friend, but he had made a big mistake a couple of years earlier when he had challenged McCormack for Speaker," O'Neill said. "McCormack never forgave him. I liked Mo, but I was loyal to McCormack."[27]

Loyalty, to be sure, had its drawbacks. O'Neill's plans were complicated by his friendship with Eddie Boland. In the weeks after McCormack announced his retirement, Boland had also proclaimed an interest in the majority leader race. "There is some talk around of Eddie Boland of Massachusetts," MacNeil wrote his editors. "A very liberal fellow with good credentials with all factions — a possible dark horse candidate who could make it."

Boland "just announced; told me he was going to be a candidate," O'Neill recalled. "Chances are, if he weren't a candidate, I would have been a candidate. But he announced and when he announced I had no place to go." O'Neill had gone so far as to call on Albert, carrying written pledges from the New England delegation to the new Speaker, to see if the Oklahoman would back him for majority leader. But Albert, remaining neutral, had turned him down. Now loyalty demanded that O'Neill forestall his own cause and help Boland. The awkward situation revived the rivalry that had strained their friendship during the Kennedy years.[28]

When aide Terry Segal urged him to challenge Boggs, O'Neill replied sourly, "I can't. Eddie Boland is in the race and he's going nowhere — but he is my roommate."[29]

"There was a feeling shared by both Eddie and Tip that Eddie was smarter," said Judith Kurland.[30]

O'Neill would later complain, "I didn't know how serious Eddie was about running, because he didn't do any work on his own behalf." Indeed, O'Neill suspected that Boland may have gone so far as to cut a deal with Udall, in which Boland — in return for being appointed whip — would act as a liberal stalking horse and preclude the rise of other Northern candidates. "Eddie had about 45 votes, which was an easy thing for Eddie to pick up. But Eddie never did the work. He never tried," O'Neill said.[31]

"Both of them were perceived as the next Bostonian Speaker. They both wanted it and both went after it and played it in their own way," former Representative Tony Coelho recalled. "Both were Machiavellian about it and didn't speak to each other as to what they were doing and that was what caused the break in the relationship.

"Tip was very cunning," said Coelho, who was then Bernie Sisk's administrative assistant. "He had an ability to only say what he had to say and never say more. And he didn't trust anybody, and here is a good example. Here is his roommate, supposedly his best friend, and he wasn't telling him exactly what he was doing.

"That was part of Tip's mystique. You felt you were his bosom buddy but yet he didn't tell you everything you may have wanted to know. He only told you what you needed to know, or what he felt you needed to know. That is what kept him in power as long as it did," said Coelho.[32]

Neil MacNeil remembered that "when Eddie ran, Tip revealed a humiliating thing about Eddie: that he used stuff on his hair to keep it looking black. They were roommates, so he knew. They were good pals, but now suddenly they were rivals. Now they were on edge with each other. Tip was jealous of Eddie Boland. Tip got going because of Eddie," said MacNeil.[33]

O'Neill finally announced that he too would be a fallback candidate for majority leader. It was too late. The race among the five announced contenders was reaching a climax. On January 12, the *Washington Post* proclaimed, "Udall Leads Race For Majority Leader." Udall followed that coup by announcing that Boland would nominate him before the Democratic caucus. The word spread quickly: Boland was to get the whip's job as a reward.

The contest was at a turning point. If O'Neill and the other unaligned Northerners — a number estimated at from 20 to 50 in December — followed Boland into Udall's camp, Boggs would be in serious trouble. And so Boggs had ample cause to grin when he put down his phone on January 14 and said to his aide, Gary Hymel, "I've got it won."

The man on the other end of the phone was O'Neill, and he would lead a bloc of some two dozen Northern Democrats not to Udall, but into the ranks of Boggs supporters.

"He gave me a list of 25 names or so and I reported back to him in a matter of minutes, maybe an hour or so," said O'Neill. "You got that one; you got this one."

It was then, Hymel would remember, that "Hale Boggs smiled for the first time in that race."[34]

Boggs had spent months restoring his candidacy. He brought his drinking and moodiness under control, courted leading journalists and impressed his colleagues when conducting the business of the House through that year's extended lame duck session, and at a series of huge garden parties he hosted at his remodeled Bethesda home. "The corn is ripe in my garden and the shrimp are in from Louisiana," Boggs wrote, on invitations which were sent to congressmen, lobbyists, columnists and diplomats about town. The lobbyists pressed Boggs's cause. Lindy Boggs charmed her husband's colleagues. LBJ, still complaining that Udall had "run out" on him over Vietnam, massaged members of the Texas delegation. McCormack worked the phone.[35]

To his southern elders, Boggs now made the compelling argument that if he was defeated, the former Confederate states would be without a representative in the leadership of Congress. And at last his Catholicism helped; Catholics were by now the largest single religious denomination in Congress. Though Udall was thought to be particularly strong among the incoming class of freshmen Democrats, whose interest was assumed to lie with an insurgent against the established order, Boggs had assiduously wooed the newcomers, recognizing that for all their bluster they were doubtlessly cowed by the imposing complexities of life as freshmen and therefore receptive to his reassuring offers of choice committee seats and other plums. As the ranking Democrat on the Ways and Means Committee, whose members controlled committee assignments, Boggs was in an enviable position to promise such favors.[36]

There is evidence to suggest that O'Neill, and other liberal congressmen, had falsely represented themselves to Udall. Aside from his loyalty to McCormack, O'Neill had other reasons to undercut his friend from Arizona, who was assembling a hard-core base of liberal supporters and stood in the way of O'Neill's own ambition. O'Neill strung Udall along, and as late as January 14 Udall still believed he had a shot at O'Neill's vote. In a handwritten postscript to a letter he sent to O'Neill that day, Udall wrote "Have talked to Eddie — I won't forget your help." A few hours later, O'Neill endorsed Boggs. Udall came to believe that Dick Bolling had double-crossed him as well.[37]

Boggs needed 128 votes to be elected majority leader. Starting at around 3 P.M. on Tuesday, January 19, the Democrats dropped green paper ballots into a metal wastepaper basket that had been placed on the dais. Boggs took a 95 to 69 lead over Udall on the first ballot, then won the election by a 140 to 88 margin on the second pink paper ballot after Wayne Hays and James O'Hara dropped out. Hays had urged his followers to vote for Boggs but O'Hara, to Udall's great chagrin, made no endorsement.[38]

Udall turned his campaign button upside down, so that it read "oW" instead of "Mo," and blamed his loss on defecting freshmen, congressmen from districts ruled by organized labor (still angry over his vote on right-to-work) and liberals like O'Neill and Bolling.

"In the South, the Boggs people put the heat on recalcitrants through lobbyists for various interests: oil, tobacco, textiles and so on. They snatched six or eight votes from me there. He played the freshmen like a virtuoso: he could pass out more goodies than I. The big city boys came to him through a combination of his contacts with mayors and other politicians I didn't know externally, and through such guys as Rostenkowski and Carey; and a few of the old deans," said Udall.

And "the remaining bitterness over my McCormack race surprised me. I thought I'd conducted myself as a gentleman," Udall said. But "at a critical juncture somebody brought word that Tip O'Neill had said he couldn't buy me under any circumstances. I remember trading funny stories with Tip O'Neill and once we had a marvelous time on a trip. It is easy to translate such personal experiences into potential support — easy to forget that Tip O'Neill's shared friendly moments with others and for longer."[39]

ATTENTION NOW TURNED to the appointment of a whip. O'Neill knew that bad blood existed between Albert and Rostenkowski, and that there was a good chance that Rosty's deal with Boggs would unravel in the face of the newly elected Speaker's intransigence. The whip's job was still in play. The Albert-Rostenkowski feud dated back to 1968, to the Democratic convention in Chicago and the divisive struggle over Vietnam. As the antiwar demonstrators were being beaten in the streets and driven from the city's lakeside parks by the Chicago police, a parallel battle was waged inside the convention hall. The McCarthy and Kennedy-McGovern delegates, though banished to the farthest reaches of the Stockyards auditorium, had mounted a relentless challenge to Albert, the convention chairman. The antiwar delegates "were determined to have their way on the one issue, Vietnam, that united them and gave them moral fire, the moral fire that, like the religious zealots', would be quenched with no compromise," Albert recalled. "Every attempt to transact orderly business . . . ran headlong into all of the bitterness, all of the divisions, and all of the frustrations."

The convention timetable had fallen behind schedule as scenes of the riots outside the hall were juxtaposed on national television with the equally impassioned, if not violent, Democratic Party proceedings. "If the result looked confusing to a politically inexperienced television viewer, I can only say that it looked and sounded awfully confusing to the presiding officer up there on the rostrum," Albert acknowledged. His confusion was compounded by a vicious cold and the howl of a nearby air-conditioning unit.[40]

Representing Johnson, the party establishment and the reputation of his beloved Chicago was Mayor Daley, from a seat in the second row, directly below the podium. Rostenkowski was carrying out hizzoner's instructions from an offstage command center when the telephone rang. "Lyndon Johnson was in Texas and he called me. 'Goddamn you,' he said. 'Take that . . . get up there . . . tell Carl Albert.' Oh, he was mad. Mad. The convention was so unruly and Carl wasn't, you know, banging it and really bringing it to order," Rosty recalled. "The conversation with the president was maybe 20 seconds, but Lyndon Johnson could say a lot in 20 seconds. I just said, 'Mr. President, Carl Albert is my boss — you talk to him.' He hung up, he was so goddamn mad at me."[41]

Yet, always a man of action, Rostenkowski approached Albert who — because of his ill health, he later insisted — complied and handed over the gavel. Both men agree that there were no hard feelings until a Chicago newspaper reported how a decisive Rostenkowski had restored order by wresting the gavel from a dazed, diminutive Albert. "I thought he was my friend, though hardly my brainiest one," Albert said later. "I had done him what I thought was a favor when I handed him the gavel to preside briefly and ceremoniously over the delegates assembled in his hometown. I had forgotten the whole incident by the time the story began to circulate that big Dan Rostenkowski had wrestled the gavel out of the hands of little Carl Albert because only big Dan Rostenkowski could bring order to that convention.

"If that were so, no one had told me about it at the time. But it was pretty plain who was telling it later," Albert said. "As state delegation after state delegation lined up behind me for Speaker, one state was conspicuously absent: Illinois.

"It was still the tradition that the majority leader appointed the party whip, subject only to the Speaker's veto. Hale wanted to give the job to . . . Dan Rostenkowski," Albert recalled. "He got the Speaker's veto instead."[42]

Nor was Albert finished. On the morning of the vote for majority leader, Representative Olin "Tiger" Teague of Texas trounced Rostenkowski in the balloting for caucus chairman, 155 to 91. Antiwar liberals had used the vote to settle a score with Daley, but Albert added his own bloody fingerprints to that particular dagger. "Enough of my friends shared enough of my wonder about Rostenkowski's attitude and sense to do something about it. They had come together to oust Rostenkowski as caucus chairman in favor of a man loyal to me — at least to a man with enough brains to climb on board a bandwagon while it was roaring out of the station," Albert said. "Surprised, the loser told the press, 'I got my brains beat out.' I was not surprised at all."[43]

Rostenkowski was devastated. He had managed to lose, despite all his stratagems, the races for Speaker, majority leader, whip and caucus chairman. "It was a terrible embarrassment for Rosty," said Representative Jim Wright. "He had to explain to Mayor Daley why he was not reelected, a hell of a hard thing to explain."

Rostenkowski cornered Boggs and said, "Hale, that Carl Albert didn't do a thing to help you get elected majority leader. I mean, I thought I had a commitment." And Boggs replied, "You do." But Boggs never pressed the case with sufficient "enthusiasm," Rostenkowski said later. "I didn't talk to Hale Boggs for a long time. He let me down." Of the string of defeats, Rostenkowski said: "It destroyed me. I just wanted to crawl in a hole and die." For months he came to whip meetings, sat in the front row, and glared at Albert and Boggs.

Rostenkowski wandered onto the near-empty floor of the House, and found O'Neill with a newspaper, sitting in a customary spot on the aisle. Rostenkowski sagged into the neighboring chair.

"Are they talking to you about the whip's job?" Rostenkowski asked.

"Yeah, they are mentioning it to me," O'Neill replied.

"Oh."

"Why, do you have a deal?"

"I thought I did."

"Well if you have a deal, I'm out of it," O'Neill said. "I'm out of it."

"Tip, it ain't going to work for me. It just isn't going to work for me. I know when I'm dead. Please take it."

"Jesus, Danny, if you've got some understanding . . ."

"Please, Tip, you know you can't forgo this. At least I'll have a friend as a whip. A personal friend. Please."

Rostenkowski later concluded, "I think Tip was just being nice to me. He didn't need me to tell him to take it. He was going to take it regardless. But it was a nice way for him to tell me.

"Tip was a very, very tough guy to dislike when he really put his arm around you and gave you the ol' darlin' stuff," Rostenkowski said.[44]

O'Neill had made the ranks of the mentioned, but now Albert showed why his service as Speaker would be marred by a reputation for vacillation. The whip's job has its antecedents in fox hunting, after the huntsman who was charged with keeping the fox hounds in a pack. The British applied the term to leaders in Parliament in the late eighteenth century. The American Congress adopted the custom a hundred years later, after the nation's growth had more than doubled the size of the House from the 180-odd representatives who met in the 1800s. The job took on added importance during the New Deal, when both parties struggled to keep discipline in the ranks.

"The whips are (1) responsible for the presence of their fellow party members. But they must also (2) transmit certain information to them, (3) ascertain how they will vote on selected important pieces of legislation, and (4) guide pressure to change the minds of the recalcitrant and stiffen the wills of the wavering," wrote Randall Ripley, who worked in the office while Boggs was whip.[45]

It was a job that called for loyalty. But when cornered by a group of liberal reformers on the morning after Boggs was elected leader, Albert acceded to their request that the whip's job be made an elected position. Word spread quickly. Boggs hit the ceiling; Udall hit the phones. The new majority leader didn't want as his lieutenant a foe he had just defeated; he needed a partner of unquestioned devotion. The North, meanwhile, was furious at the prospect of an Oklahoma-Louisiana-Arizona-Texas lineup in the Democratic leadership. O'Neill, Boggs and Hugh Carey cornered Albert in the Democratic cloakroom, then ushered him down the hall to an empty Ways and Means Committee room, where they were joined by Mills.

"This is absolutely ridiculous. I cannot believe it. This is wrong," O'Neill recalled saying. "How do you know who is going to win? You have to have a man for whip from your own team. He's the fella that does the errands. He's the fella that does the checking. He's the fella that stimulates the members. He's the fella that gives you accuracy. He's got to be part of your team. He's got to be hand-picked." Albert reversed himself, and the motion was tabled at that day's Democratic caucus, despite support from Udall, Boland and reformers like Bolling and Burton.[46]

The contest for whip narrowed to Carey and O'Neill, who remained atop a written list of a half dozen potential candidates after Boggs and Albert, like lawyers striking possible jurors, had exercised their preemptive vetoes. Boggs had knocked Udall, Hays, Boland and others from the list because they had not backed his candidacy.[47] O'Neill family lore inserts the Mrs. O'Brien story — "People like to be asked" — at this critical juncture. O'Neill had used the anecdote to prompt Boggs to drop the pleasantries and ask for a commitment in the course of their tide-turning phone conversation a week before the majority leader election. Now, after reading in the *Globe* that her husband was a finalist for the whip's job, Millie brought up Mrs. O'Brien to encourage him to be more aggressive.

"Tom, you haven't even asked for the position, have you?" the no-nonsense Millie demanded of her husband. "All your life you've been telling that Mrs. O'Brien story. . . . Why don't you ask Boggs for the job?" And so O'Neill went off to see Boggs, employing the Mrs. O'Brien talk yet one more time to explain why he was there. (In the months ahead, Boggs would hear the story so many times that he would roll his eyes at each hint of its coming.) When Boggs was noncommittal, O'Neill assumed that Carey had the inside track.[48]

It was here that O'Neill's loyalty and his style of "legislating by affection" had a fulsome payoff. Carey was a fine politician — he would later master the tricky currents of New York politics and be elected governor — but he possessed an imperious air, and his pretension didn't sit very well with New York representatives James Delaney and John Rooney, two prideful hacks from Queens and Brooklyn. In a fine example of the intra-ethnic nastiness and general mean-spiritedness for which many Irish-American politicians were known, they went to Albert and blackballed Carey. "It was a case of the pig-shit Irish being jealous of the lace-curtain Irish," a Carey ally would later say.[49]

It didn't take Boggs and Albert very long to make the final call; Hymel remembers that his boss returned from the new Speaker's office after only half an hour. Albert had once more vetoed Rostenkowski; Rooney and Delaney had discredited Carey. O'Neill would satisfy both the urban North and antiwar crowd and old John McCormack had intervened — yanking the strings which tied him to Boggs and Albert on O'Neill's behalf.

"I put . . . Tip . . . at the top," said Albert. "I thought of the bunch that he would be the best to come from that section of the country. He was big and blustery and likable."[50]

"You talk about being in the right place at the right time. They needed somebody North, and Tip was acceptable. And that was it," said Rostenkowski.

The events of that January "shadowed the relationship between O'Neill and Rostenkowski from that point on," said former representative James Shannon, who served with both men. "Every step of the way, Danny Rostenkowski looked at Tip O'Neill and, while he loved the guy, he looked at him and felt, 'Man, that is where I should be.'"[51]

O'Neill was named whip. He was on the ladder, and would be Speaker in just six years. It was all, said Bolling, with the icy laughter of a man who saw fate steal a prize he thought by right should be his, "by accident. By happy accident."[52]

CHAPTER 13

The Majority Leader

O'NEILL BEGAN his tenure as whip by asking how to find his new offices. He later dismissed the significance of that bit of ignorance, but it spoke volumes about his place in the House, and the leap he was about to make. He had been Rules; McCormack; Tuesday to Thursday. In 1967, he had missed more votes on Mondays and Fridays than almost any other congressman. At a backyard barbecue thrown by Lester Hyman, O'Neill had been irritated by the probing questions of a man he mistook for a newspaper reporter; it was Senator Walter Mondale. Though he had won a modest following through his favors and personality, the whip's job was O'Neill's first step into national political leadership. It was a difficult time, as Vietnam and the calls for congressional reform divided his party. He recognized immediately that he would have to lift his game.[1]

The first move O'Neill made was to upgrade his staff. Terry Segal, Judith Kurland and the other young people who worked in O'Neill's office for a summer or a season or two — most notably an intern from Yale and Brookline by the name of Ari Weiss — had boosted his effectiveness on issues of public policy. They became part of the O'Neill office family, were instructed to use the long-distance lines to call their parents once a week, and enjoyed the relaxed atmosphere of the office: "No beer-drinking until after 5 P.M. Mondays–Thursdays," read the intern rules. "Shut the door when imbibing. On Fridays you can shut the door at 4:30 or 4:45 for beer." But there was a limit on how far O'Neill could go with a staff of irreverent college students. "As the summer progressed, it became evident that the interns, although intelligent and outgoing, had much to learn in the area of courtesy. Complaints about their sarcastic remarks, their air of arrogance and over-assurance had been coming in to me regularly from other staff members," wrote Michele Ramsey, the intern coordinator in 1971.[2]

Now that he was whip, in charge of shepherding more than 200 Democratic congressman, O'Neill needed another grown-up around. Given the chill in his relationship with Boland, O'Neill also needed a pal. And, finally, having seen what Sweig and Voloshen had done to McCormack, O'Neill needed a gatekeeper. He chose Leo Diehl, then serving as a Massachusetts tax commissioner.

"He calls me," Diehl recalled. "He says, 'I'm at Paul Young's. We are celebrating.' Millie, Susan, all the kids are on the other phone. 'We just took a vote. You are going to be my administrative assistant.'

"I say, 'I'm in taxes. What the hell do I know about that?' He says, 'What the hell do I know about it? We'll learn together,'" Diehl said.

Diehl agreed to make the move, but later developed second thoughts about leaving a job he had performed for twenty-five years, and the state he had lived in all his life. "I told Tom I changed my mind," Diehl remembered. "He said, 'Good, you're unemployed. I've told [Governor Frank] Sargent you've already resigned.' I was on the 8 o'clock plane."

Diehl arrived at the Capitol on the morning of March 1. "Leo, look," O'Neill said to him, "I don't need a guy who knows everything about down here. He just has to know to protect me."[3] The danger lay in O'Neill's indulgent nature. McCormack had let lobbyists use his office phones, where they could impress clients or intimidate government officials by saying they were calling "from the Speaker's office." Despite the humiliating Camacho affair, O'Neill had offered similar courtesies to a dozen or more lobbying pals, mostly from Boston, who used his office as a place "to hang their hats" when operating on Capitol Hill. McCormack's office was dry, but O'Neill was known as a socializer; there you could get a meal, find a dinner partner, enjoy a beer or the occasional office party. If the congressman and his staff worked late, the lobbyists had carts of food and drinks sent in from Capitol Hill restaurants. And while many of O'Neill's acquaintances remember dinners at Paul Young's or Duke Zeibert's with the congressman and one or more lobbyists at the table, no one remembers him picking up the tab.[4]

Now that McCormack was gone, and O'Neill was whip, the lure of making calls "from Tip O'Neill's office" was that much stronger. "These guys thought nothing of going right to his desk, picking up his mail, using his phone and saying, 'Call me here at the whip's office.' I couldn't believe it," said Diehl. "Everyone that had been in McCormack's office, from everything imaginable. Lobbyists of all types." Diehl had the public phones removed, guarded the staff's telephone line, and closed off part of the office with a new wall. In several cases, he showed lobbyists the door and explained that they were no longer welcome. One complained to O'Neill that Diehl was "a German sonofabitch."

"Isn't he," O'Neill replied.[5]

The whip's job was an elastic responsibility that had waxed and waned in influence over the previous forty years. In Rayburn's time, the luster of the office had faded, supplanted by his private relationship with the southern committee chairmen and his cordial cooperation with Eisenhower. When confronted with the heavy legislative agendas of Kennedy and Johnson, Albert and Boggs tried with mixed success to revive the organization and improve party discipline. But the continued recalcitrance of southern Democrats limited the whip's effectiveness. "To suggest that it was an automatic pressing of the button, you'd be deluding yourself," White House lobbyist Larry O'Brien recalled.[6] Ultimately, it was O'Brien's liaison staff, and its counterparts in the various federal agencies — or LBJ himself — who directed legislative strategy, twisted arms and oversaw the whip counts during the Kennedy and Johnson years.

Nixon's victory in 1968 presented the Democratic leadership with a challenge. House Democrats could no longer rely on O'Brien's lobbyists or Johnson's "treatments" to round up votes; they would have to do it themselves. "In the Nixon years the Democrats for the first time in almost 40 years were without the executive branch; were committed to an activist platform, and also faced an aggressive, hostile, combative president," wrote Lawrence Dodd, a congressional fellow in the whip's office during the early 1970s. In the face of the Republican resurgence, O'Neill took immediate steps to strengthen the organization. He and his deputies also recognized "that the party leadership was becoming more important and that, in expanding the whip system, they might provide for themselves an avenue into the leadership," Dodd said. Liberal reformers, in particular, were demanding that their leaders take a more activist role in pushing the national Democratic agenda. Albert and Boggs each had one deputy whip; O'Neill now used two — Representatives John McFall of California and John Brademas of Indiana. In 1973, the number of deputies rose to four, and in 1975 to seven. The new deputies soon got to serve on the Steering and Policy Committee, which in 1974 was given the power to nominate committee chairmen and award committee assignments. The expanding whip operation soon had more clout, office space and staff. Within the House, O'Neill was assembling his own machine.[7]

O'Neill knew that little things mattered. It is startling to consider, but for almost all of O'Neill's first two decades in Congress, information about the coming week's schedule and the content of the legislation due up for a vote was kept secret for as long as possible by Rayburn, McCormack and the committee chairmen. "Committee chairs, in cooperation with the Rules Committee and often the party leadership, would push legislation to a floor vote before members or their staffs had an opportunity to read the bill, much less study it," Dodd recalled. "The initial assumption was that forcing members to act in the dark would produce supportive votes cast out of ignorance."[8] Indeed, one of the most valuable chores O'Neill had performed for his colleagues during the 1950s and 1960s was telling them, from his perch on the Rules Committee, what bills they could expect to see on the House floor from week to week. Now, his office published "whip packets" for the Democratic members, so that when they returned on Monday or Tuesday they found the week's expected floor schedule, with an analysis of legislation and copies of the bills and committee reports awaiting them. "A great idea and a tremendous service to the House," wrote Florida representative Sam Gibbons to the new whip. O'Neill provided his colleagues with wallet cards that carried the congressional schedule, and periodic updates on Democratic legislative accomplishments, which they could use when speaking in their districts. He worked to improve the 9 A.M. Thursday morning "whip coffees" by persuading Albert and Boggs and important committee chairmen to attend. The assistant whips and other lawmakers jumped at the opportunity to mix with the leadership in an intimate and relaxed setting.[9]

"These meetings are critical because they help ensure that the leadership will know the animosities, the passions, the rumors, the conflicts that may be sweeping through the Democratic caucus," Dodd said. The coffees served to bind the assistant whips closer to the Speaker as well; information was a valuable currency in Congress, and they could now circulate among their colleagues, impressing them with their "inside" knowledge. Even the food was a lure. In one memo to O'Neill, Judith Kurland warned him that the assistant whips had become "very spoiled" by the home-baked cakes that Lindy Boggs sent when her husband was chairing the Thursday morning coffees. When O'Neill hinted that Kurland might fill in as cook, she smiled sweetly but suggested that he find a good doughnut shop instead. Fortunately, Mrs. Boggs kept up her baking habits and O'Neill wrote to thank her for her "scrumptious" confections.[10]

Albert was happy with O'Neill's performance; even Rostenkowski admitted "he was good at it." Lobbyists and other insiders rated O'Neill as a better whip than Boggs.[11] "Members say the new leadership has kept them better informed on schedules for holidays and vacations and has communicated legislative schedules more efficiently than had been done in the 91st Congress," *Congressional Quarterly* reported. "Much of the new procedural improvement has been the work of the new Majority Whip, Rep. Thomas P. O'Neill Jr."

O'Neill was best at the instinctual chores of politics. Even with their majority, the Democratic leaders faced a constant stream of strategic and tactical decisions. Democratic leadership aide John Barriere posed a typical judgment call to Albert, Boggs and O'Neill on a public works bill: "I am confident that we have the votes to pass the bill. It would be nice to build up as big a vote as possible — it might influence the President's decision about a veto," Barriere said. "On the other hand, you may not wish to use up credit with members on a bill which we have the votes to pass anyhow. You may desire to save yourself for items where your personal intervention would make the difference between victory and defeat."[12]

The outcome of the decisions made in such cases could raise or lower a leader in the eyes of his colleagues. Rules needed to be structured to give the leaders maximum advantage in debate. Regional factions had to be considered. Trades made. Appeals extended on the basis of party, or personal, loyalty. One of the most delicate tasks was the handling of the "if" list, which was comprised of party members who had promised their votes to the whip only "if" they were absolutely necessary. "I don't show the 'if list' to anyone," said Irv Sprague, who worked for McFall and O'Neill. "At the last minute, as the count goes on, I'll tell the Speaker that 'You can talk to X and get his vote if you really need it.' But the names can't get out. We can't afford lobbyists descending on these guys before the votes. We can't embarrass them by making it appear that they are the Speaker's creatures. And we can't go after their votes unless we really need them. They may pay a high price in casting a particular vote and if a member is scarred when his vote wasn't necessary, he won't be willing to help again, or we may owe him a favor that wasn't necessary."[13] O'Neill loved to relate how Rayburn could pressure reluctant congressmen into adding their names to the "if" list, until a dozen or more sheepish representatives were crowding the front row of the House, waiting for the Speaker's nod. O'Neill was good at the flattering and schmoozing, back-scratching and vote-trading aspects of the whip's job. He inspired confidence and won friends, prodded gently and dispensed favors. Did the DSG need an extra clerk? Could a group of Catholic congressmen get an audience with the Pope in Rome? O'Neill met these and dozens of similar requests. An invitation to O'Neill's St. Patrick's Day party, a spirited affair hosted by lobbyist Paul McGowan, was a coveted ticket.[14] Dick Maguire staged a stag cookout and swim party for O'Neill in June. And in February 1972, Diehl had eighty lobsters flown down from Jimmy's Harborside Restaurant for a mid-winter clambake, which was spoiled only slightly when Wayne Hays threw a Captain Queeg–like tantrum over the kitchen help's consumption of the surplus crustaceans.

Ultimately, O'Neill was a transitional figure in his two years as whip, introducing a few important innovations that he left for McFall and others to build upon. The net effect of the changes he made — as with every reform he supported during this era — was to enhance the power of the leadership at the expense of the southern committee chairmen.

As the newest member of the Democratic leadership, O'Neill began visiting the White House for bipartisan congressional consultations in 1971. He found Richard Nixon suffering through what the

President later called "the lowest point of my first term." Unemployment had crept to 6 percent, its highest level since 1961. The problem of wartime inflation persisted. Antiwar forces had maintained their opposition, and Nixon's popular support had eroded. The North Vietnamese were intransigent in negotiations, and the painstaking diplomatic foundation that Nixon was laying with Soviet and Chinese leaders was still months away from public unveiling. By April, Nixon trailed Senator Edmund Muskie of Maine in a potential presidential match-up by 47 to 39 percent in the national polls.[15] As with the Cambodian incursion of 1970, Nixon settled on a bold military stroke to buy time: time to play great power games in Moscow and Beijing, and thus outflank Hanoi, and time for the South Vietnamese to take over their own defense through the process of "Vietnamization." The plan was for South Vietnamese troops, under the cover of U.S. air power, to invade Laos and cut off the Ho Chi Minh Trail near the town of Tchepone.

"It was a splendid project on paper," Kissinger wrote later. "Its chief drawback, as events showed, was that it in no way accorded with Vietnamese realities." U.S. military planners had pondered such a strike for years, but concluded that it would take four divisions of American troops and cost thousands of casualties. The South Vietnamese were now making the attack with just two divisions, who fought their way into Laos, suffered heavy losses, stopped and dug in. A renewed effort seized Tchepone a month later, but the South Vietnamese opted to save what was left of their best troops, declared victory and went home. Instead of cleaning out the North Vietnamese sanctuaries, the army retreated. The American news coverage focused on the retreat, with graphic news footage of panicky soldiers clinging to the skids of U.S. helicopters. Like Tet, the invasion of Laos undermined resolve in America and South Vietnam. The mood in both countries grew mean and twisted. There were now widespread reports of drug use and heroin addiction, incidents of racial violence and "fragging" attacks upon their officers among U.S. troops in Vietnam.[16]

The liberals in the Democratic caucus resolved to act. The South Vietnamese entered Laos on February 8, 1971. The next day, "Rep. Thomas P. O'Neill and 37 co-sponsors introduced legislation not only forbidding direct US intervention in Laos but also American support of any kind for any military operation in Laos," Kissinger noted in his memoirs. A furious Nixon, in a White House tape from the time, labeled O'Neill "an all-out dove and a vicious bastard."[17]

"The debate was over motives: whether an administration that was withdrawing over 150,000 troops a year might be bent on victory (a term long since turned into an epithet); whether the effort to end a war while fulfilling an obligation to an allied people was really a subterfuge for its indefinite continuation," said Kissinger. Nixon and his advisers felt the U.S. had a moral and strategic obligation to stage an orderly withdrawal from Vietnam. The war's opponents, however, "argued that by continuing the war in Vietnam we were disintegrating morally; we were destroying the chance of any healing within our society. We were contributing to the idea that human life was cheap and irrelevant, that power alone was decisive," Kissinger recalled. "We were embarked on another act in the Greek tragedy. . . . When the challenge is not only to perception but to motive, then differences take on the character of a civil war."[18]

It was a foreboding sign for the Nixon administration — and a warning that Albert's power to keep the House from cutting off funds for the war was not inexhaustible — when the new party whip took the House floor to complain, "We have opened another front in the war. We have invaded another sovereign country. We have expanded an ever widening war that is supposedly winding down."[19] Boggs and Albert tolerated O'Neill's independence on the issue because they "didn't want to hurt him," Albert said later. "I imagine that the politics of his district had something to do with his convictions." But the two Democratic leaders also needed O'Neill as their link to the growing antiwar wing of the House. The vote on the Hays-Wright resolution in December 1969 had revealed the presence of 54 doves in the Democratic ranks. That number grew to 120 after the Cambodia incursion the following June. The use of recorded teller votes now made it harder for congressmen to dodge the issue, and liberals were pressing to get the party on record against the war. A fledgling public interest group called Common Cause saw an opportunity to make a name for itself. Its newly hired Washington lobbyist, David Cohen, turned again to O'Neill.[20]

"I wanted to shift the thing to the House because the whole antiwar movement was involved in the Senate, and that was fine, but there had been no real votes in the House on the war and we wanted to stake out organizational, institutional turf," Cohen recalled. As he surveyed the

House for allies, Cohen rejected the ideological zeal of insurgents like Robert Drinan, Ron Dellums of California or New York's flamboyant Bella Abzug. "To be credible to those inside the House, and to be able to influence other members, the choice had to be a 'regular' Democrat and not a 'reform' Democrat," Cohen said. "To be credible to those outside the Congress the choice had to be someone who had publicly opposed the Vietnam War while Johnson was President. Such a person could not be dismissed as a partisan actor. There was only one natural leader: Thomas O'Neill."[21]

Cohen approached O'Neill with a "statement of principles" that called for an end to the war by the "date certain" of December 31, 1971. "O'Neill was excited about it. And the question was, who else should we hit up on it, and I thought Irish and Catholic and I said Hugh Carey, Dan Rostenkowski and James Corman of California," said Cohen.

"You'll ask them, won't you?" Cohen asked O'Neill.

"No. You have to ask them," O'Neill replied. "But you can tell them I'm for it."

Cohen blanched. Corman was a former Marine veteran who represented the largely white Los Angeles suburbs of the San Fernando Valley, packed with defense and aeronautic firms. Rostenkowski and Carey were also veterans, representing ethnic neighborhoods in Chicago and Brooklyn. But to his surprise, Cohen found that all three were agreeable, believing it was time to cut the nation's losses. In a "Dear Colleague" letter on March 29, the four Democrats mailed out their "Statement of Purpose," in which they announced their intent to vote to withdraw U.S. forces by December 31, 1971. The next day's edition of the *New York Times* announced that O'Neill was "breaking with other members of the House Democratic leadership" and that "the stand by the four influential Democrats indicated a steadily mounting antiwar sentiment in the House."[22]

Albert and Boggs agreed to let the House Democratic caucus debate the war in a closed-door session on March 31. A motion demanding that Congress set a "date certain" for withdrawal passed by a vote of 101 to 100.[23] At the White House, congressional liaison William Timmons warned Nixon that the momentum in Congress was on the side of the doves. The administration should begin to prepare for the day, coming soon, when the House would set a deadline for a U.S. withdrawal, he told the President.[24]

In negotiating sessions with North Vietnam, Kissinger began to sweeten the U.S. offers. But the leaders in Hanoi, seeing how the U.S. government was divided, were "bending all their energies toward one last test of strength," he said. "To end the war honorably we needed to present our enemy with the very margin of uncertainty about our intentions that our domestic opponents bent every effort to remove. . . . No meeting with the North Vietnamese was complete without a recitation of the statements of our domestic opposition."[25]

By June, Common Cause had over 120 signatures on its "Statement of Purpose," helped by the publication of the top-secret Pentagon Papers, which detailed America's involvement in Vietnam. Paranoia ran deep, in the Oval Office — where Nixon ordered his aides to stage break-ins at the National Archives and the Brookings Institution to obtain records that would discredit the Democrats — and on Capitol Hill, where Diehl was having the telephones in the whip's office swept for bugging devices once a week, and Judith Kurland confronted a photocopier repair man who she believed was a Nixon administration spy. When O'Neill warned Kurland to watch what she said on the office phone, she blurted in reply, "But Mr. O'Neill, that's how you call your bookmaker!"

"That's all right," O'Neill said. "That isn't what they are looking for."[26]

ON JUNE 17, the antiwar Democrats offered an amendment to a defense procurement bill to ban the use of funds in Indochina after December 31. The measure failed by a 254 to 158 vote, but for the first time a majority of House Democrats (135 to 105) had sided with their whip in support of such an amendment. "The corruption in that country makes it more and more tragic that a single American boy has given his life for this conflict," O'Neill said during debate. "It is a common expression of our soldiers in Vietnam that no one of them wants to be the last person killed in Vietnam. That is part of the tragedy — that even one more soldier should die while this nation dallies."[27] White House aides reported that Albert was now "under tremendous pressure" from antiwar forces in the caucus. The Speaker was summoned to a private breakfast meeting with Nixon on June 28, where he succumbed to presidential flattery and promised to hold the line.

Albert tried to unite his fractured party on the common ground of domestic issues, where even Nixon felt vulnerable because of the sluggish economy. The Democrats passed an emergency federal jobs measure, but lost a $10 billion public works bill when the Senate failed to override Nixon's veto. Another keystone of the party's domestic program — a raise in the minimum wage — was lost to internal bungling.[28] Albert and Boggs gave ammunition to their liberal critics when each was then caught in episodes of public drunkenness. The Speaker had suffered a heart attack in the 1960s, and was haunted by a troubled marriage. He seemed frail, at times, and meek. At a White House photographers' dinner in the spring of 1971, he looked tipsy, and in a celebrated incident in 1972 rammed his car into two parked automobiles outside the Zebra Room lounge in northwest Washington. "He has startled more than one hostess by showing up at a party, not with his wife, but with his lovely Eurasian assistant on his arm [and spent] too much time around the punch bowl," muckraker Jack Anderson reported.[29]

"Some guests on the Washington social circuit have also said that Mr. Albert has been unusually garrulous at some gatherings in recent months," said the more circumspect gentlemen of the *New York Times*.[30]

"Carl — when Carl had been in his best health and form — he could bustle into the House chamber and he had those short legs and he'd move very rapidly, he was always active on the floor of the House. You knew he was there," Gerald Ford recalled. "But later, when he got tired and physically beaten down you just saw a different person . . . he didn't seem to have the drive and the confidence that he had before. About 1966 he had a serious heart attack. . . . He lost his zip, he lost his punch," said Ford. "He had a terrible problem with his wife . . . and the unhappiness that inevitably follows in that situation . . . really forced Carl to drink more than he should."[31]

The majority leader's antics, however, made the Speaker's behavior seem tame. In the spring of 1971, Boggs suffered from a relapse of the problems that had almost cost him his post. On April 5, he startled the House and most of Washington by accusing the FBI of using electronic surveillance against members of Congress, and calling for J. Edgar Hoover's resignation. "I was informed . . . that Boggs was terribly drunk when he made that speech," Hoover wrote on April 6 to his subaltern, Clyde Tolson. "The man is an alcoholic who has gone to the dogs." The FBI began to compile a record of Boggs's aberrant behavior. The majority leader had lost a quick fistfight with a former congressman in a men's room at the Gridiron Club Dinner that spring; there were reports of another brawl in a Baton Rouge restaurant, and he was said to have put on a drunken display at a party for the congressional leadership.[32] The White House took note. "We should attack Boggs on his drunkenness and try to destroy him," Nixon told H. R. Haldeman, the White House chief of staff.[33]

Frustrated, the fiercely ideological Judith Kurland left O'Neill's staff for what she judged was a purer idealistic cause, that of the State of Israel. They had been through much, and even made a bit of history together when, early in his tenure as whip, O'Neill had summoned Kurland to the House floor to help him during a contentious debate, only to find that she was barred at the door by the crusty doorkeeper, William "Fishbait" Miller. Congresswomen were the only females allowed in the chamber, Miller told her. It was a rule that dated back to a time in the nineteenth century when courtesans had embarrassed Congress by parading through the House. O'Neill intervened, and won her floor privileges.

"Tip, God bless him, said, 'Judith is my person,'" said Kurland. But the constant defeats over Vietnam had sapped her hope. "I was really young and all these guys were getting killed and we were losing the votes," she recalled. "Here I was working for one of the most decent people I had ever met in my life and he was voting the right way and he was in the leadership and still you kept losing, losing, still kept losing."[34] Nixon, meanwhile, had broomed away his mid-winter woes with a series of bold and creative initiatives. On May 20, he announced that the U.S. and the Soviets had reached agreement on an ABM treaty, the cold war's first arms limitation agreement. On July 15 the President told a national television audience that months of secret negotiations with the Chinese had paid off, and that he would be traveling to meet with Mao Zedong and Chou En-lai on "a journey for peace." And on October 12, the President announced that he would be the first American President to visit Moscow.

Nor did Nixon neglect the domestic economy. On August 15, he announced that he was taking the United States off the gold standard and imposing wage and price controls to curb inflation. Such government adventurism was supposedly against Republican sound-money, free-market principles. But Nixon needed to goose the economy as he entered the 1972 election. Wall Street reacted with a record advance the next day and the inflation and unemployment rates dropped over the next eighteen months. The decision "was politically necessary and immensely popular in the short run," Nixon wrote in his memoirs. In the long run, he admitted, his actions merely put off the day of reckoning and resulted in "destructive double-digit inflation" in the mid-1970s.[35]

Nixon's creativity stymied the Democrats, who had hoped to recapture the White House in 1972. O'Neill's favorite was again Ted Kennedy, who he thought had the best chance to unite a party whose presidential candidates spanned the ideological spectrum from George McGovern on the left to George Wallace on the right. But, damaged by the death of Mary Jo Kopechne, a young woman who died in his car when he drove off a bridge at Chappaquiddick, Kennedy took himself out of the running. O'Neill, and most other party regulars, fell into line behind Edmund Muskie, a neighbor from Maine who had been Humphrey's running mate in 1968. But the Democratic Party was undergoing a wrenching transformation. Amid the turmoil of the 1968 convention, the New Left forces had scored a single, overlooked victory, requiring that the party change its nominating system. McGovern had chaired the subsequent reform commission, and used it to assemble his own core of devoted activists, mostly young veterans of the McCarthy and Robert Kennedy campaigns, who strove to take the delegate selection process from the hands of governors and mayors, labor leaders, state committees and ward heelers like O'Neill and give it to voters and activists via primary elections and party caucuses. For good measure, the New Left forces also demanded numerical quotas for women and minorities.

McGovern won 37 percent of the vote in the New Hampshire primary, surpassing all expectations. Wallace then whipped Muskie and the rest of the field in Florida, where the voters were inflamed by a recent federal court decision upholding mandatory busing for racial desegregation of schools. "The American people are fed up with the interference of government. They want to be left alone," Wallace said. He called busing "the most atrocious, callous, cruel, asinine thing you can do for little children." When Muskie finished fourth in Wisconsin on April 4, he no longer looked like a man who could beat McGovern, much less Nixon. The campaign turned to Massachusetts.

Muskie had led McGovern by 46 to 15 percent in the state in February, but on April 25 the insurgents beat Muskie by a two-to-one margin. The McGovernites took all 102 of the state's delegates, leaving

O'Neill without a delegate badge or a seat on the convention floor. "Did I really get licked five to one in Cambridge?" O'Neill asked plaintively.[36] Wallace was crippled by a would-be assassin in Maryland, and when McGovern beat Humphrey in California, New Jersey and New York, the New Left had triumphed. The regulars were shell-shocked. Humphrey charged that the McGovern wing was promoting the "Three A's" of acid, abortion and amnesty for Vietnam War resisters. The Massachusetts delegation to the Democratic convention in Miami "looked like the cast of *Hair,*" said O'Neill.[37]

"It was the broadest delegation the party had ever assembled," O'Neill's old antagonist Jerome Grossman said proudly. "It was 50 percent women and included black neighborhood leaders, Hispanics, radicals, liberals, professors like John Kenneth Galbraith, a few office-holders like Drinan and people who had been handing out leaflets for years without ever receiving any goodies. . . . The delegates talked issues virtually twenty-four hours a day instead of drinking whiskey and buttering up big contributors. It was an authentic people's convention that pushed aside the pros for a glorious week."

The Left seized the controls. They barred Mayor Daley and the rest of Chicago's elected delegation from the convention in favor of civil rights activist Jesse Jackson and a slate that met the party's new quota system.[38] Larry O'Brien was deposed as party chairman. The platform endorsed abortion rights, busing, an end to capital punishment and a ban on handguns. In the California delegation, 89 of the 388 delegates and alternates were on welfare. Gay liberationists made their first open appearance in national politics. During the roll call that ratified the nomination of Senator Thomas Eagleton of Missouri as the vice presidential candidate, Democratic delegates cast votes for Mao Zedong, Ralph Nader, Dr. Benjamin Spock, Archie Bunker and yippie Jerry Rubin. By the time McGovern got up to give his acceptance speech, it was 2:48 A.M. Nixon and his aides couldn't believe their good fortune. O'Neill attended the convention, talked wistfully of a Kennedy draft and, wearing a spectacularly ugly paisley sports jacket, appeared with Albert and Boggs at a press conference, where they bashed the administration's economic record and put up a brave front of unity.

DEMOCRATS IN the House were split along the same ideological fault lines. San Francisco representative Phil Burton had taken over as head of the Democratic Study Group, and married its forces to Common

Cause's effort to stop funding for the war. Together, they arrived at a scheme to have the Democratic caucus direct the Democrats on the Foreign Affairs Committee to pass end-the-war legislation and bring it to the floor. Drinan offered the caucus resolution on April 19: ordering the Foreign Affairs Democrats to move a bill to end U.S. military involvement in 30 days. The "mad monk's" proposal was too extreme, and was defeated on a 105 to 97 vote. Cohen went to Richard Conlon's office and the two of them drafted a more moderate alternative. "Then the question was, who was going to carry the ball," said Conlon. "We all went looking for Tip."[39]

Burton sent an "urgent" memo to all DSG members, urging them to attend the caucus and vote for what now was known as the O'Neill amendment. "The vote of this resolution will be close," he said. "If we succeed, it is my belief that passage of this resolution intact will — perhaps more than any other single act — force the Administration and the appropriate committees of Congress to recognize public revulsion against this war and hasten our withdrawal from it."[40] Before the caucus resumed on April 20, O'Neill met with Albert and Boggs, seeking their support for his amendment. "Whenever the issue of Vietnam came up, a small degree of tension surfaced among the three," aide Linda Melconian recalled, and O'Neill had learned to pick his spots. But he "believed this time he could sway Boggs and Albert," and succeeded. They backed his compromise.[41] The O'Neill amendment passed on a vote of 135 to 66.

The doves were overjoyed. "Let me repeat on paper what I said to you yesterday," Representative Andrew Jacobs of Indiana wrote to O'Neill. "Your frank, concise and sincere speech on American intervention in the Southeast Asian Civil War was one of the two best speeches I have ever heard in Washington. Good, very good for you." Burton, in a DSG press release, said that "adoption of the O'Neill resolution . . . [was] a magnificent victory."

More than even the war was at stake: the O'Neill amendment represented a major assault on the old ways of doing things. In an April 24 memo, Conlon told Burton that a victory on O'Neill's resolution would "have far-reaching ramifications for the future in terms of other issues and other committees." The caucus could impose its will by stripping disobedient Democrats of seniority, chairmanships and committee assignments, Conlon said, and end "the decentralization of power which hobbles Democratic leadership and prevents effective legislative action."[42]

Albert and Boggs wavered. The political winds had shifted over the summer, and chilled their feet. "Nothing in it for the Democrats politically to bring this resolution out on the floor," John Barriere wrote to Albert on June 14. "Best to let the matter rest . . . Nixon has the country with him on this at this time. . . . Tactically, it will not be politically advantageous for the party to be identified with a Vietnam defeat."[43]

When the full House voted on the O'Neill amendment on Thursday, August 10, Albert and Boggs deserted him. The end-the-war resolution was defeated, 229 to 177. Barriere had judged the political climate correctly. Middle America had rallied around Nixon and hailed his summitry with the Chinese and the Soviets. The last U.S. ground combat troops were leaving Vietnam. The embarrassments of the Democratic convention, and McGovern's subsequent clumsy handling of the news that Eagleton had received electric shock treatments for depression, sapped mainstream Democrats of their zeal.

The moralists on the Left were outraged. On "black Thursday," Drinan wrote, in an op-ed piece in the *New York Times,* "old men talked while young men died."[44] The mood in the House was nasty. The Democratic leaders, bruised by their ideological and personal battles, looked at each other with suspicion. There was "growing disenchantment among House Democrats with Carl Albert. In this connection, his private behavior and run-in with DC police adds to the rumblings," White House lobbyist Richard Cook told Nixon.[45]

There were southerners who wanted Wilbur Mills to challenge Albert. Another group of more moderate Democrats made plans to run Boggs against the Speaker, and though Boggs was not a participant in the discussions, he was aware of them. Albert "always looked over his shoulder a little bit at Hale. He thought his most likely challenger was Hale," said the Speaker's aide Mike Reed.[46] And in a third group — the antiwar liberals — there was hope that O'Neill would run for a higher office when the Ninety-third Congress convened, possibly by challenging Boggs for the post of majority leader. "The 160 Democrats who voted against their Speaker and majority leader can hardly be expected to have much confidence in the leadership of the 92nd Congress which, on the issue above all other issues, failed to lead or even to speak," Drinan said. "About the only thread of hope was the eloquent plea of Democratic Whip Thomas P. O'Neill of Massachusetts who, for the sixth time in the 92nd Congress, urged his colleagues to end the scourge of war."[47]

"Tip was in a terrible position," Lindy Boggs recalled. "He was really a leader of the liberal field. He had to express that, and yet he had all these feelings of responsibility and honor for the rest of the leadership. It was a miserable time."[48]

The Ninety-second Congress was late in drawing to a close when freshman Representative Nicholas Begich, Alaska's only congressman, approached Representative Jim Wright, an elder on the Public Works Committee, to ask a favor. "How many unemployed dog sled operators do I have to find jobs for?" Wright asked, with his wolfish grin. No, it wasn't a patronage matter, Begich said; rather, an issue of scheduling. Could Wright make a quick trip to Alaska? Boggs had promised to campaign for Begich, and events were planned for Anchorage and Juneau on October 15 and 16. But Boggs was on Ways and Means, whose members might be called to work that autumn weekend on a conference committee with the Senate. "I just know there is going to be a conference meeting on that tax bill and Hale's going to be knocked out of going," Begich said. "I hate to ask you, but I need somebody. Would it be possible, if Hale cannot go, would you?"

"Yeah, sure Nick," Wright said. "If it comes down to it." In the end, Wright didn't have to make the trip to Alaska. "There but for the grace of God," he said, with a shiver, twenty-four years later.[49]

Albert, deciding not to rush the session to a close, had the conference meeting postponed until Tuesday so that Boggs could help Begich. The forty-year-old Alaskan, a politician of some promise, was comfortably ahead in his race against a lackluster Republican opponent. Yet Boggs had his reasons for wanting to aid the nervous freshman.

"Why was Hale in Alaska? Because Begich had voted against him," said Gary Hymel. In the rough-and-tumble contest for majority leader in 1971 the young Alaskan had sided with the opposition. Now, for reasons of pride and practicality, amid talk about a shakeup in the leadership, Boggs wanted to secure Begich's allegiance.[50] "This is what a real politician does," says Hymel. "You know, you certainly help your friends — but that is not the priority — it's the guys who are your enemies, because there is always tomorrow."

Boggs had spent the fall resisting Republican attempts to capture the House, and seemed in better physical and mental shape. "From personal observations, it appears that Boggs has straightened out his personal difficulties to a significant degree during the past year," White House aide Richard Cook wrote Nixon.[51] Boggs and his wife, Lindy, had hoped to make a vacation of his Alaskan trip. Their original plans, based on the mistaken notion that Congress could complete its work on schedule, called for a leisurely, sightseeing swing through Alaska and California, where their daughter Cokie lived, and perhaps a visit to Japan and Hawaii. But the Democrats in Congress had squabbled in this election year with the White House, dragging out the closing session and keeping the lawmakers off the campaign trail. Neither Lindy Boggs nor Pegge Begich (who had six young children) had an appetite for an abbreviated trip, and so they stayed in Washington. Boggs took a Sunday morning plane from Washington National Airport on October 15 that, with the change in time zones, allowed him to speak at a fund-raising dinner for Begich in Anchorage that night.

The shrimp at the dinner was so good, Boggs told the crowd, that it must have been imported from Louisiana.[52] The majority leader called his wife several times that evening, but the line was steadily busy. An accomplished politician in her own right, Lindy was using the commercial breaks in the televised broadcast of the Sunday football games to catch Southern governors where she knew they would be — at home and in front of the TV set — to ask for their help in an upcoming Democratic campaign event.

"Hale laughed at my ingenuity," when he finally got through, she recalled. They talked about events in Washington and how Boggs and Begich were faring on the trip. "Nobody told them good-bye because everybody knew they'd be back Tuesday morning," she remembered.[53] Boggs was exhausted by the eighteen-hour days at the end of the congressional session, the flight to Alaska, jet lag and his nighttime speaking engagement. He and his hosts "decided not to get him up early to catch the commercial flight to Juneau after the dinner in Anchorage, but to hire a private plane to let him sleep in," Hymel said.[54]

Don Jonz, thirty-eight, was an accomplished pilot with 17,000 hours of flying experience. His white-and-orange twin-engined Cessna 310C was the charter of choice for those national politicians, like Ted Kennedy and Hubert Humphrey, who sometimes visited Alaska. The pilot had his plane fueled and ready on the morning of Monday, October 16. Boggs was to speak in Juneau, and then take a 7 P.M. commercial flight to Washington. Jonz took off from Anchorage with Boggs and Begich and Begich's aide, Russell Brown, thirty-seven, in fog and a steady rainstorm at around 9 A.M. after receiving a dismal weather briefing. Twelve minutes after takeoff, Jonz radioed his flight plan as he approached mountainous Turnagain Arm. It would take them through the turbulence and icing conditions of windswept, 2,500-foot Portage Pass, over the snow-peaked 5,000– to 7,000-foot Chugach Mountains to the 14-foot waves of Prince William Sound, and down the Alaskan coast to Juneau — some 560 miles away.

Lindy Boggs got the phone call from Speaker Albert at around 9 P.M. that night. "Hello," she said, distracted and laughing at the antics of her Cairn terrier, Cody, as she answered the phone. Her husband was missing; his plane had disappeared, an obviously distraught Speaker told her. "Oh, Carl!" she said. *Poor Carl, what a terrible task for you to have to do,* she thought.[55] Given the number of miles they fly in hastily chartered aircraft, their overloaded days and nights, relentless drive and congenital reluctance to disappoint a single voter (much less an expectant crowd gathered with great effort in a hotel ballroom at the next stop on the schedule), it's remarkable that more of America's political leaders aren't lost in airplane crashes. Begich had been on a seaplane that made a forced landing and was lost for nine hours with the party's candidates for senator and governor in 1970. Kennedy and Jonz had been downed by bad weather on their trip. "They push it," said Hymel. "The pilot might have said, 'It looks rough, do you want to go?' And knowing Hale, he'd say 'Go.' So he disappeared."[56] Lindy and her three children arrived in Anchorage on an air force plane on Wednesday, and stayed until the twentieth — they were struck with a feeling of dread when the searchers flew them over barren Portage Pass. "I knew what I was hearing on those radio reports. I was hearing his obituary," Cokie Roberts recalled. The search went on for thirty-nine days, until the snow and cold of the bitter Alaskan winter forced the U.S. military to give up on the day after Thanksgiving. It was said to be the most extensive search ever made for a missing aircraft. More than 140 planes and helicopters made a thousand sorties. Dozens of ships participated. In 4,000 flying hours, the searchers scanned some 325,000 square miles. The Boggs family listened to psychics, gave them bits of the missing congressman's clothing (the cummerbund to his tuxedo, in one case) and paid to fly a pair of them to Alaska. The Pentagon used airborne heat-sensing devices and the high-altitude cameras of SR-71 spy planes. The coastline maps of Alaska were later redrawn with the benefit of such detailed imagery; a missing King Cobra P-39 with a Soviet red star from World War II was found, as was orange-colored debris from passing ships. But not a sign of Boggs or his companions.[57]

"That damn bush pilot," said Hymel. "When we went up there, *Flying* magazine was on the newsstand and there was an article by Don Jonz and it's about how you can beat the icing problem but you have to learn to cheat the devil."[58] Jonz "obviously knew the weather report. An hour before they went through that pass an Army helicopter had tried to go through but the turbulence was so bad they had to turn around, go back the long way around the mountain. Jonz didn't even take his [emergency locator] beeper with him," said Hymel. Nor did the plane carry emergency survival gear.[59] "Forecasts and existing weather conditions along a significant portion of the proposed route were not conducive to flight in visual conditions," the National Transportation Safety Board later concluded. "There is ample evidence that the pilot was aware of the poor en route weather conditions, and the available evidence suggests that the disappearance may have been related to those conditions."[60]

O'Neill got the news in his Cambridge kitchen. The implication was inescapable. Because Boggs was a year younger than the fifty-nine-year-old O'Neill, and widely popular in a newly redistricted seat, only such a freak accident could give the whip a chance at the Speaker's gavel at an age young enough to make much use of it.

The election was three weeks away, and Nixon's reelection a foregone conclusion, when the House of Representatives was called to order at noon on October 17, 1972. Within the chamber the turmoil of politics had abruptly ceased — replaced by shock and concern at the grim news from Alaska. The members were huddled in small groups, swapping rumors, when O'Neill stepped into the well of the House and made the announcement: Majority leader Boggs was missing, his airplane long overdue and feared lost in bad weather. "We have been informed that the pilot who was commanding the two-motor Cessna is one of the great bush pilots of the area," O'Neill told his colleagues. "It is our hope and prayer, of course, that the men will be found safe." O'Neill was shaken; he was deeply fond of Lindy Boggs and had gotten along with her husband, traveling to New Orleans for a taste of the Crescent City on St. Patrick's Day. As the days passed, the chances faded that Boggs and Begich would someday walk out of the Alaskan wilderness.[61]

The voters of Louisiana and Alaska remained faithful to their congressmen and content to let the search go on for weeks. Though missing, presumed dead, both Boggs and Begich were reelected on Election Day, November 7. But in Washington, a town less given to noble gestures, the urge to fill the vacuum was insistent. Everyone knew that O'Neill, the majority whip and third-ranking Democrat in the House, would try to claim the office of the fallen Boggs. O'Neill was on the ladder; it was the natural way of things for him to move up to the majority leader's job. If Albert retired, as expected, after one or two more terms as Speaker, O'Neill would make the leap from the rank and file to the Speaker's chair in but half a dozen years: an amazingly brief span, in that his old mentor, McCormack, had spent twenty-two years in Rayburn's shadow, and Albert had taken sixteen years to rise from whip to Speaker.

It was all a matter of timing — of choosing the right moment to announce his intent. O'Neill had seen how Jack Kennedy's men resented Lyndon Johnson, who, no matter how courteous he tried to act in the hours and days after the assassination, was considered a usurper. Nor did O'Neill forget the charges of insensitivity leveled against Dick Bolling, who publicly challenged Albert for the job of majority leader mere hours after Rayburn died. If O'Neill moved too quickly, he might stir similar resentment. Prevarication, on the other hand, held its own risks. Contested elections for the leader's job were not new: Bolling had challenged Albert in 1962; Mo Udall had taken on Boggs in 1971. As the search in Alaska went on, Representative Sam Gibbons, a reformer, was writing letters to fellow Democrats, offering "leadership for a change." And word reached O'Neill that Wilbur Mills and other congressional barons were pondering "inside" candidacies. O'Neill couldn't let a challenger steal a march on him; couldn't let reverence be mistaken for indecision. "This was the most delicate political problem I ever encountered. As long as a legitimate hope existed that Hale Boggs was still alive, any announcement on my part would have been insensitive. But if I waited too long, somebody else might jump in," O'Neill said later.[62]

After voting in Cambridge, O'Neill and aide Leo Diehl flew to Washington on November 7 to watch the election returns on the television in the whip's office, and call around the country to congratulate the winners. Many of the victors liked him for his garrulous style, the favors he had done for them as whip or, in the case of the committee chairmen, the help he had given them as a member of the Rules Committee. And after the bitter battle between Udall and Boggs in 1971, many hoped the new leader could be chosen without a divisive contest. "He was in the job," *Time*'s Neil MacNeil said later. "To run for majority leader against Tip would be throwing a guy out who was already there."[63] But still, O'Neill faced a dilemma.

"Tip can't run for majority leader yet. There's Lindy. And Hale is still alive as far as we know in some igloo with an Eskimo. I'm sitting there in the office and people are starting to go out and get jobs," Hymel recalled. "And then Tip asked me to talk to Lindy." O'Neill got along well with Hymel, a former Louisiana newspaperman whom Boggs had brought to Washington. He asked him to approach Lindy Boggs, ascertain the depth of her grief and, if practical, find a way to obtain her assent. Hymel talked to the widow, and arranged for O'Neill to call her the next day.[64]

"The fact that the Democrats in Congress had to elect a new majority leader was disturbing to me, a tough realization," she said later, remembering that phone call. But she told O'Neill she wouldn't object because "when Hale comes back and says, 'Thanks for holding it for me while I'm gone,' I know you'd be the only person to give it back to him." Word went out to New Orleans that she would stand for election in her husband's stead.[65]

A final bit of intrigue remained when Thomas Hale Boggs Jr. — on his way to becoming one of the city's most influential lobbyists — came by the whip's office. O'Neill exploited the visit, making sure to let his fellow congressmen know that he had won the family's approval by mentioning over the phone that young Boggs was with him. But in later years O'Neill privately complained that Tommy Boggs had tried to claim credit for brokering the transfer of power. "It always galled my father," said Kip O'Neill.[66]

O'Neill "wouldn't accept Tommy Boggs, he wanted Lindy," Leo Diehl recalled. "Not Tommy or Gary or me or any other. He wanted Lindy."[67]

O'Neill now hurled himself into the race. Three secretaries placed calls at Diehl's direction to congressmen around the country. Bolling came on board quickly; Udall took himself out of contention after judging that O'Neill had most of Boggs's strengths, and few of his liabilities. Others thought about the race but hesitated. "I'm so amazed at the support I'm getting," O'Neill told the *Washington Star* on Wednesday. "It's beautiful."[68]

Mills was making phone calls too, gauging the climate in the House, and a go-between phoned to tell O'Neill that the Ways and Means chairman was considering a race for majority leader. Diehl put the call on hold and told O'Neill that they had to stop Mills then and there — this was no time for affable courtesies. Assuming that Mills was listening in, O'Neill picked up the receiver and said that Mills could do what he wished, but that he was in the race to stay, and closing in on victory. Mills publicly dropped his drive for a leadership position a week later. "Mills was a very tough guy, but he was chicken as far as taking a chance," MacNeil recalled.[69]

As he worked to lock up the majority leader's job, O'Neill had a considerable advantage over would-be challengers. To many House Democrats, O'Neill had become that most welcome of political friends, a fund-raiser. As the years in McCormack's shadow had dragged on, O'Neill had gone looking for "another door" to the leadership in the House, his daughter Rosemary recalled.[70] In 1968, when McCormack met with complaints that Mike Kirwan was too old and old-fashioned for the job, the Speaker promised to bring new blood to the task of raising money for House Democrats and chose the willing O'Neill, who took operational control of the Democratic Congressional Campaign Committee after Kirwan died in 1970. "That job really propelled me into the political lives of the members. It required that I have a detailed knowledge of every congressional district in America to decide how much money we would put into each race," O'Neill recalled. "I had to know the makeup of our candidate and of the opposition."[71]

Kirwan, who ran the DCCC in the 1960s, was a colorful character who grew up in a Pennsylvania mining town and never got past the third grade. He lived life as a steelworker, digging coal in the Heidelberg Eight coal mine, and wandering as a vagabond before settling on politics as a vocation and representing Youngstown, Ohio, in Congress. He chaired an Appropriations subcommittee that controlled pork barrel spending, and left as his monument a "national aquarium" in the basement of the Commerce Department building, a tribute to those days of his youth when, penniless but infatuated with a young lass, he would take her to the free municipal aquarium on their dates. For years

Kirwan ran the DCCC out of his coat pocket, even as the Republicans recognized that costly television advertising was replacing political clubs, labor unions and local party organizations as the best way of influencing voters, and adjusted their tactics accordingly.[72]

Representative Thomas "Lud" Ashley, a Democrat from Ohio, remembered going to Kirwan for help on a critical port project for Toledo and being told that if the city's industrialists would buy tickets to a DCCC dinner, the chairman would see what he could do. Kirwan reached into his jacket pocket, and pulling out twenty tickets, he handed them to Ashley.

"These are to the Democratic congressional campaign dinner, Mr. Chairman. The dinner was held two weeks ago," Ashley said.

"Don't make it no easier, does it?" Kirwan replied.

But, Ashley recalled, "I had the money for him by nightfall. And we had ourselves a $6 million deepening project which made us the first deep-water port on the Great Lakes."[73]

O'Neill had seen how Lyndon Johnson and Sam Rayburn used campaign contributions to pave their paths to power, and sought to modernize and revive the sleepy organization he inherited from Kirwan. He "began to move around the country as never before — attending campaign fund-raising dinners, helping fellows in their districts — and his perspective broadened and deepened," MacNeil wrote. "His attention swung more and more to the party legislative program and the work here to be done. His known talents he now addressed to a larger chore — the national party. He stayed longer each week in Washington, abandoning his old role of a Tuesday-to-Thursday fellow: he was here Mondays and Fridays too."[74]

He gave top priority to incumbents running for reelection in marginal or contested districts, and every member in this category received a minimum of $2,500 as critical seed money prior to the congressional campaign recess in September.[75] In addition to raising money, a staff of nine conducted opposition research on Republican candidates and prepared issues papers for use by Democrats and the press. A closed-circuit television seminar was conducted with candidates and party officials in eighteen major cities. And if a choice committee assignment would help a Democrat on Election Day, O'Neill interceded. Thus Representative William Cotter, representing Hartford, the capital of the U.S. insurance industry, got a seat on the Banking subcommittee that oversaw insurance.[76]

Under O'Neill, the campaign committee served as a convenient bank account through which southern Democrats could launder contributions from labor unions and other liberal benefactors, and Democrats of all stripes could filter money from special interests whose names might prove embarrassing. O'Neill did some private money laundering as well. The laws of the District of Columbia allowed congressmen to set up campaign committees that kept secret the identity of donors, and so O'Neill set up a "DC O'Neill Committee" to accept anonymous donations from labor unions and individuals (like *Globe* publisher Davis Taylor) who didn't want their contributions known.[77]

"He would tell me stories about how he got to know the chief fund-raisers across the country so he knew where the money was, and where to call to get money whenever he needed it," said Representative Tony Coelho, a Democrat from California who headed the campaign committee in the 1980s. "In those days, don't forget, there was no accounting for the monies that came in. He used to tell me how he would go around and play poker around the country and people would put money in a brown bag on a bed and you would take the brown bag home with you."[78]

The DCCC held a huge fund-raising dinner in Washington and handed out $500,000 in the 1970 elections, making contributions in 46 of 50 states. The DCCC "raised more money and expended more money for House candidates, both incumbents and nonincumbents, than ever before in the history of the committee," O'Neill reported to his colleagues.[79] Embattled House members were grateful for O'Neill's fund-raising help. Veterans like Julia Hansen of Washington, Lee Hamilton of Indiana and James O'Hara of Michigan were among those who wrote to thank O'Neill for his assistance, as did the newly elected Cotter, Bella Abzug of New York and antiwar insurgents Michael Harrington and Gerry Studds of Massachusetts.[80] O'Neill later "talked about how people became indebted to you for what you did" when raising funds, said Coelho. O'Neill told him that "there are not a lot of people in Congress who are willing to work that hard to do things for others, and so you can easily take advantage of it."[81]

The prognosis for Democratic candidates was grim in the fall of 1972. McGovern's presence at the top of the ticket was wreaking havoc in Virginia, Utah, Texas, Florida, Tennessee, Oklahoma, North Carolina, Montana, Mississippi, Michigan and other states, O'Neill's aides told him. Quietly, the DCCC commissioned a 50-state analysis on ticket splitting, and began to show Democratic congressional candidates how to disassociate themselves from the national ticket. O'Neill set to work at an exercise in political triage. Sixty Democratic incumbents were judged vulnerable, and 30 Republicans. These 90 districts formed the outline of the battleground, and he doled out money like a field commander, wasting little on safe seats.

And so Charles Wilson and Richard Hanna, in trouble in California, each received transfusions of just under $10,000. Ella Grasso, facing a tough fight in her first race for reelection, was awarded $10,300 in Connecticut. Abner Mikva got $14,650 and Frank Annunzio $7,000 in Illinois. Neal Smith received $17,000 in Iowa; Andy Jacobs $11,000 in Indiana. Hugh Carey, in a surprisingly close contest in New York, was given $16,800 — including $13,000 in the last three weeks of the election. Jack Brooks got $9,600 in Texas and Harley Staggers $16,000 in West Virginia. These were sizable contributions at a time when a race could be run for $80,000 to $100,000.

Though O'Neill consulted with other Democratic leaders before passing out funds, it was he who — as in the 1970 election — approved which names were put on the lists entitled "Candidates Deserving Top Consideration." He developed relationships with wealthy contributors in New York, California, Illinois and other states whose efforts gave them a say in the party's councils: men like Bob Strauss of Texas; George Steinbrenner of Ohio; New York's Charles P. McColough and Jim Wilmot; Irv Kovens and Jerry Cardin of Maryland; Walter Shorenstein and Gene Wyman in California and J. B. Fuqua, Irv Kaler and Phil Alston in Atlanta.[82] "If you were within 5 percent [of your opponent in the last election] you got $10,000 no matter how you voted. We never rated them on their votes. We rated them on the toughness of their fights," O'Neill said.

O'Neill's performance helped limit Democratic losses, in the Nixon landslide, to 12 House seats.[83] "The Republicans failed totally in their widely publicized drive to capture control of at least one, and perhaps both, bodies of Congress," the *Washington Star* reported. In a resolution praising O'Neill, the members of Congress who served on the DCCC said, "Our congressional victory, considering all the political adversities and the fact that our party only carried one state in the presidential contest, was nothing short of a miracle."[84]

WITHIN TWENTY-FOUR HOURS of Election Day, O'Neill had 63 commitments, more than half of the 121 he would need to be elected majority leader — mostly from his base among the northern, big-city

Democrats. The incoming freshmen were a fertile field for his solicitations of support. "He . . . raised dough and he came around. He was out working for our election; he signed the checks we got," one West Coast freshman said. On November 9, O'Neill sent out a letter to all the newly elected members of the House, promising them assistance in "the hiring of staff, obtaining office space and attending to the other incidentals in establishing your congressional office."[85] O'Neill soon found that only the most die-hard liberals and reactionary conservatives were reluctant to endorse him. And he had made enough inroads — a dozen each in the camps of some 60 southerners and 50 ultraliberals — to keep them from organizing around their own candidates.

O'Neill pressed for explicit promises of support, concluding each conversation by saying, "I'm marking you down as a hard, firm commitment — okay?" Both he and Diehl maintained lists that they double-checked against each other. As congressmen, aides and reporters wandered in and out of the whip's office, O'Neill worked the telephone, and picked up 57 more votes by the time for his departure home on the 7:40 P.M. plane to Boston on Friday, leaving him one vote short of confirmed victory.[86]

The other announced candidate was Sam Gibbons, fifty-two, a World War II paratrooper who had jumped into Normandy on the night before the D-Day landings. He and O'Neill had run across each other's telephonic tracks on the Wednesday after the election. A liberal maverick, Gibbons hoped to take advantage of the stirrings for change in the House, and throughout November wrote a series of letters to his colleagues, offering various proposals for reform.

Gibbons deplored "the escalator system" that moved leaders up through the highest ranks. He called himself "a rallying point for members who want to open up the system," yet warned that the party shouldn't elect leaders who were "too far out."[87] But there was a fatal contradiction in Gibbons's campaign: he was too southern for the liberals and too liberal for the South. O'Neill, meanwhile, was helped by the release of a Ralph Nader Congress Project report on members of Congress. O'Neill is "the ultimate Boston Irish politician," and a "Doctor of Politics," the favorable report on the congressman concluded. He "is a proud, forceful individual, so animated and vibrant in conversation that his white hair continually flops down onto his ruddy forehead as he speaks. He sprinkles his talk liberally with anecdotes, often dramatizing his stories and shifting the position of his ample body in his chair to show changes of characters." For congressional reformers who might be tempted by Gibbons's talk of change, Nader's research team reminded them that "the record teller reform is undeniably of critical import" and that "the efforts of the House Democratic caucus to make a strong, public antiwar statement . . . appeared thwarted until O'Neill offered a compromise resolution acceptable to a majority of the body."[88] Gibbons found O'Neill's "tracks all over the place. . . . I could never get any momentum going."[89] O'Neill had watched Boggs use the tools of office in 1970 to seduce his colleagues. Now O'Neill just as ably employed the choice of committee assignments and other such plums to corral votes. Freshman Charlie Rose had promised the peanut farmers in his North Carolina district that he would try to serve their interests on the House Agriculture Committee. It was a rash promise for a freshman, and he had been ridiculed by his opponents for making it. But after arriving at the Capitol, he heard that the O'Neill train was leaving the station. His elders in the North Carolina delegation had told him to stay neutral for a while, and see how the race played out, but his instincts told him to act quickly.[90]

"I went down to the whip's office and they had sort of like a dining room table, with both leaves up, sitting right over in the corner of the room with the pictures of all the freshmen. It was Leo and Tip, and I could see my picture way back in the corner," Rose recalled. "I introduced myself and said my chief ambition was to get on the Agriculture Committee."

"Well, son, I would be glad to help you get on the Agriculture Committee and if I were majority leader I would be in a really good position to help you do that," O'Neill said. Rose was the first in his class to commit. He got his seat on the Agriculture Committee.[91]

Representative J. Joseph Moakley of Boston was a special case. Moakley, a state senator, had run as an independent against Democratic congresswoman Louise Day Hicks, the famous anti-busing activist who had beaten him in a primary contest in 1970. "Louise could suck up one-third of that primary vote, and there were always four or five people in the primary. So you didn't have to be an Einstein to know that nobody was going to beat her in a Democratic primary," he said.

Though O'Neill supported busing, he was a party man, endorsed Hicks over Moakley, and joined with McCormack to make radio ads for the congresswoman. "You'll never make it. You'll disgrace yourself. You can't do it," O'Neill told Moakley, who ignored the advice, assembled a coalition of liberals, black voters and fair-minded Irish-American constituents, and beat Hicks by 5,000 votes.

"So Tip is running for majority leader and he's got all the freshmen together and he's growling, getting pledges and all that," said Moakley. "And he makes eye contact with me a couple of times and then moves on because he figures I'm going to kick him right in the balls. But finally we make contact and I put my hand out and say, 'I'm with you,' and his jaw drops.

"I said, 'Listen, Tip, I know the game. The ins are in, and the outs are out, and I'm in now.' We became very fast friends."[92]

Hymel clinched the symbolic go-ahead vote for O'Neill on the Friday after election day in New Orleans, at a wake-like gathering in the home of Archie Boggs, the brother of the missing congressman. There he ran into Representative Edward Hebert, who had been the city editor of a New Orleans newspaper where Hymel once worked as a reporter.

"You know, you always asked me to come to you if I needed help," Hymel told Hebert.

"What do you want? A job? I'll give you that," said Hebert.

"Nope. No, no. I just want you to vote for Tip for majority leader."

"Who's he running against?"

"Sam Gibbons."

"Sam Gibbons? I got no problem with that. Tell Tip I'm with him."

Hymel climbed the stairs to a bedroom and, sitting on a bed, phoned the whip's office in Washington. After learning that O'Neill and Diehl had left for Boston, he called the Delta Airlines counter at Logan Airport, and asked the airline personnel to have O'Neill call him when the plane landed. "I just talked to Hebert and he said he'll be with you," Hymel told O'Neill when he called. With Lindy Boggs and Hebert on their side, O'Neill could count on most of Louisiana, and with Louisiana and a few other inroads in the South, they could preclude a challenge from a formidable southern conservative. O'Neill and Diehl headed happily down the concourse, singing.[93]

O'Neill formally announced his candidacy on the following Monday, November 13. By Wednesday O'Neill had claimed victory. By Thursday, the 16th, the *New York Times* had anointed O'Neill as "heir apparent." On Friday, November 17, Bill Timmons notified Nixon that he had polled his House sources and touched base with O'Neill, and it was "increasingly certain" that the Massachusetts congressman had the leader's race wrapped up. "O'Neill told me he is confident any challenge can be turned back."

After O'Neill's election, "there can be no question that the House leadership will be far more liberal than before, particularly on foreign policy matters," Timmons told the President. "O'Neill is well liked and has proven to be a surprisingly able floor leader during his first two years as whip."[94] By Thanksgiving O'Neill had between 150 and 180 commitments. He went home to Boston for Christmas, where the *Washington Post*'s Myra McPherson found him at his holiday office party. "To know O'Neill for 20 years is to be a newcomer," she wrote. "With Boston shrouded in snow and Christmas cheer, there were enough Irish faces and 'dears' and 'darlins' to fill a dozen Barry Fitzgerald movies.

"A stiff brush of white hair forms a curtain over his blue eyes when he forgets to swipe at it. He does everything with ease, slipping his huge paw around a shoulder for a hug, or saying 'That's a beautiful coat, dear' or lumbering over to the serious singers in a corner and warbling, 'She's as sweet as the day she stole dad's heart awaaayyy. . . .'" McPherson wrote.[95]

The capital press corps seemed as fond of O'Neill as his colleagues. "Congress doesn't throw up cutting edges to be its leaders and Tip's a conciliatory middle man, but he's learned to temper without selling out," Abner Mikva told McPherson. "Given the system, he's the best possible choice."[96]

The *National Observer*'s Nina Totenberg called O'Neill "a white-haired beloved St. Bernard of a man who lopes around the capitol delighting his colleagues with his famous yarns," though she noted that there were traces of disapproval from some congressional colleagues who thought O'Neill "consists of delightful blarney but little substance." Totenberg quoted one anonymous congressman saying that "on the big issues — foreign trade, anti-trust, balance of payments — Tip just doesn't have it, he just doesn't have a thought in his head."[97]

Gibbons hung on, but in mid-December he wrote to his colleagues asking if they thought he should stay in the race. The message was unambiguous (despite some O'Neill backers who marked "yes" to keep Gibbons around and prevent the emergence of a stronger challenger), and Gibbons folded on December 28.[98]

MILLIE JOINED HIM for the big occasion, and the two checked into the Jefferson Hotel on Sixteenth Street. On New Year's Day, the day before the Democratic caucus, O'Neill spent time on the phone in his office, nervously making sure his pledge count was sound, with one eye on the spread of the college bowl games. The caucus convened behind closed doors at ten the next morning. As was customary, the senior member of the Massachusetts delegation, Harold Donahue, nominated O'Neill. A majority leader "should have much more than just extended legislative experience," Donahue said. "He or she should always be able to extend a full measure of genuine concern, helpfulness, tolerance and good will toward every colleague without exception. They should have an established reputation for being unwavering in their principles — and that their word is as good as their bond.

"They should have the complete understanding that the boundless ideals and energies of the younger can be joined with the prudence and wisdom of the older for the satisfaction of both and for the progress of our country," said Donahue. "Everyone who knows the man of whom I speak will testify that he exemplifies all these high qualities and convictions."[99]

Lawmakers from Missouri, Hawaii, South Carolina and Texas also seconded O'Neill's nomination. O'Neill aide Stan Brand was most impressed by the South Carolinian — Representative William Jennings Bryan Dorn — who voted with the liberals only 16 percent of the time. "I realized then that O'Neill had ties that reached into places I never knew about," said Brand. Finally, Gibbons rose to move that the nominations be closed. Only O'Neill had been nominated. "Tip, I can tell you something that nobody else in this room can. You haven't got an enemy in the place," Gibbons said. O'Neill was elected by acclamation.[100]

Lindy Boggs sent him a bottle of Dom Perignon champagne and a handwritten note that was signed "with a heart full of love."[101]

"Day we have been working for arrives," O'Neill wrote in his diary that night. "Unanimous Vote. Elected Majority Leader." He noted that he had received a "beautiful note" from Lindy, and parties in his honor at the whip's office and the International Club. "Family happy," he wrote.[102]

CHAPTER 14

Watergate

THE 535 MEN AND WOMEN of the Ninety-third Congress, who convened in Washington on January 3, 1973, were a historic bunch. For more than a decade the grumpy tenants of Capitol Hill had watched as power ran in a one-way stream down Pennsylvania Avenue to the White House, there to be exercised by imperious cold war Presidents in the conduct of foreign wars and the service of the national security state. The Ninety-third Congress would reverse that flow. In the process, the House of Representatives would bring down a President and complete a metamorphosis from a sleepy feudal culture ruled by wizened southern hawks to a "New Congress" that distributed its reclaimed powers among a host of youthful, more ideological and determinedly independent representatives. The transformation would severely test the skills of the aspirants who sought to lead Congress into this new era. In Watergate and the months that followed, as in the congressional debate over Vietnam, O'Neill would again emerge as a key transitional figure — an indispensable man.

On the House floor, that January day, O'Neill could see that the vanguard of the New had arrived — Bob Drinan, Joe Moakley, Gerry

Studds and Michael Harrington of Massachusetts; Bella Abzug and Elizabeth Holtzman and Charles Rangel of New York; Ron Dellums, Yvonne Burke and Pete Stark from California; James Jones of Oklahoma; Barbara Jordan from Texas; Patricia Schroeder of Colorado; Parren Mitchell from Maryland. On the Republican side of the aisle were Trent Lott and Thad Cochran of Mississippi; Jack Kemp of New York; Robert Bauman of Maryland. This was not a crop of courthouse pols. Republican or Democrat, they shared an impatience with the old ways. They were not willing to go along to get along; issues and ideology were as important as patronage or pork.

The polarization that gripped the country now threatened the comity of the congressional cloakroom. Most of the New Democrats traced their roots to the civil rights or antiwar movements, and the Republicans were of a new breed of militant conservatives. As the draft calls dwindled and the student movement lost its focus, the struggle over Vietnam had shifted to the halls of Congress. Along with the war, the liberal activists brought other contentious social issues to the Capitol — abortion, women's rights, busing, the degradation of the environment — and were met as fiercely by conservative resistance. With their pugnacious rhetoric, racially divisive political strategies and clandestine campaign tactics, Nixon and Agnew had sowed division; now they reaped a whirlwind. O'Neill's first critical test as a leader of this turbulent Congress would arrive within weeks of his swearing-in, when he was called upon to guide the House response to Watergate, that collection of political scandals that destroyed Nixon's presidency.

"I was born in a house my father built." With that evocative opening to the century's most revealing presidential autobiography, Richard Nixon gave a glimpse of the proud but covetous, brilliant, insecure and sometimes malicious man whose fall from power would dominate 1973 and 1974. The chip on Nixon's shoulder was monstrous. He, Richard, was no elitist; he was a son of a grocer, of the great "silent majority." He was from the frontier West, not the effete East. He was from tiny Whittier College, not the Ivy League. Driven, he rose relentlessly in politics. Nixon was a "withdrawn and shadowy" figure, said Kissinger. "His achievements were associated more with solitary discipline and remote courage than with personal inspiration" and his followers offered their support "more out of admiration for stern competence than personal affection." Loyalists, like his friend and law partner Leonard Garment,

found Nixon extraordinarily shy: a politician most at ease when he could prop his polished black wingtips on an ottoman, scrunch down in an armchair and sketch strategy on a yellow legal pad. Garment knew Nixon as an "immensely intelligent, somewhat bruised, somewhat battered pugilist" who had manufactured a "synthetic" public face to hide his considerable discomfort with the demands of public and political life. Jim Wright, to his diary, sketched a similar portrait. "He is a cold customer," Wright wrote. "He gives the impression of aloofness and austerity. His public utterances seem thoroughly considered in advance. Beyond those, he retreats behind a wall of privacy remarkable for a modern president." Yet "I think he may be, instead, a sensitive person," Wright concluded. "The public doesn't love him, and this knowledge must bother him."[1]

After returning from service in World War II, Nixon had challenged his hometown congressman — liberal representative Jerry Voorhis, a New Deal hero — and beaten him in a bitter fight by campaigning against the incumbent's "Socialistic and Communistic" voting record. Arriving in the House, Nixon took a seat on the House Un-American Activities Committee to chase accused spy Alger Hiss. He became a pet of California conservatives, and in the state's 1950 Senate race dispatched a third liberal darling — Representative Helen Gahagan Douglas — whom he labeled "the pink lady," in a notorious Red-baiting campaign. With his unctuous "Checkers" speech in 1952, he had preserved his place as vice presidential nominee on the GOP ticket, despite news reports of a political slush fund, run for his benefit by wealthy businessmen.

Nixon was a foe who united Democrats. "There was a ferocious longterm hatred of Nixon," said Garment. Even the old Democratic leadership, the get-along-go-along boys on the Hill, never much liked Nixon. "Lyndon despised Nixon, just despised Nixon. So did Sam Rayburn," said Bryce Harlow. Harry Truman called Nixon "a snakey-eyed son-of-a-bitch." Carl Albert wondered how a man of such intellectual and political gifts could also be so petty.[2]

EASY O'NEILL HARBORED no fierce hatred of Nixon, but no great affection either. The two had played poker at the University Club during the 1950s, when the then vice president had irritated the congressman by chattering during the game and whining about losses. "But that didn't fuel a Richard Nixon animus," said Stan Brand, an

O'Neill aide. "There was a time when I wrote a speech for him on something Nixon had vetoed. I ripped Nixon apart in the speech, and he came back from the floor and said, 'You know this is just too damn tough even for Nixon,' and he made me tone it down." O'Neill was a common patriot, a cold warrior, a history buff and an institutionalist, all of which left him with profound respect for the presidency. Matt Storin, then a reporter for the *Globe* in Washington, remembered how O'Neill, as a forty-year veteran of politics, had been excited to join Albert and Boggs for his first congressional leadership meeting at the White House in 1971. "He sounded like a kid who had just had his first roller-coaster ride — thrilled to be at a meeting with the leaders and the President in the Cabinet room. This was a guy who was star struck," Storin said, "though I never saw it again."

Nixon "wasn't an intimate friend, but a very bright fellow, extemely bright fellow," O'Neill said later. "But he was the wrong type of a man. He was very, very secretive. He was a loner. He was suspicious." When O'Neill and the other Democratic chieftains went to the White House for bipartisan leadership meetings, they found the President distant and formal. The President gave a presentation and then, "no questions — [Nixon] actually ran out of [the] office," O'Neill noted in his diary. It was nothing like the social hours with Ike, or the friendly cloakroom banter with Jerry Ford.

"There was a cold feeling. There was a chill in the house. You weren't there as a friend and you weren't there as an adviser. We were a majority in the House, but they ran the government and they were over there to inform us what was going to happen . . . never to ask your advice," O'Neill said. When O'Neill would call around town for favors, tapping old contacts in various departments, he found nervous federal employees on the other end of the telephone; they told him that the White House had installed Nixon loyalists in the agencies, whose job it was to watch and report on the bureaucracy, now laden with eight years of Democratic appointees. The tattling offended O'Neill's notion of loyalty. He thought of Nixon's men as informers, and called them "the Gestapo."[3]

The President and his aides, meanwhile, didn't think much about, or of, the new majority leader. Cloaked by McCormack's shadow, O'Neill was never rated among the journalists, Democratic campaign contributors, actors, liberal activists or members of Congress who made their way onto the various "enemy lists" compiled by the President's staff. "Nixon considered him a worthy ally on issues and a worthy adversary. I never heard him denigrate Tip or his abilities or character, as he did many politicians," said White House aide Chuck Colson. "While Nixon often asked for dirt on different politicians, he never asked for it on O'Neill — and I think I'm the one he would have asked."[4]

When their goals coincided, O'Neill had no qualms about working with the White House. In 1971, to preserve jobs, O'Neill ignored his staff's advice and joined only Jimmy Burke among Massachusetts Democrats in supporting an administration bailout of the Lockheed Aircraft Corporation, the nation's largest defense contractor. Their votes made the difference in a 192 to 189 vote. In 1972, when New York governor Nelson Rockefeller persuaded the White House that the time was ripe to launch an ambitious $5 billion revenue-sharing program with state and local governments, the Democratic leadership endorsed the plan, and O'Neill "counted votes and coached a lot of us on how to deal," recalled Rockefeller aide James Cannon. By the time the program was phased out in 1986, some $85 billion had been distributed.

Indeed, O'Neill praised without irony the domestic achievements of the Nixon years. It was the GOP President, cooperating with the Democratic Congress, who fully implemented the goals of the Great Society, he said. If only to keep the Congress quiescent as he pursued his geopolitical strategies, and recognizing that Americans still wanted an activist, problem-solving government at home, Nixon signed legislation to extend the Voting Rights Act and the Title IX guarantees against sex discrimination in education. He okayed the first federal affirmative action set-asides, funds for a war on cancer and increased federal spending for the arts and humanities; he went along with congressionally approved increases in Medicaid, food stamps and welfare payments. Nixon signed the Supplemental Security Income (SSI) program into law, adding new classes of the elderly, blind, poor and disabled to Social Security. In 1972, with O'Neill's vigorous support, Social Security payments were hiked by 20 percent, and cost-of-living adjustments were adopted to keep pace with inflation. Native Americans applauded Nixon's enlightened Indian policy; labor leaders hailed the new Occupational Safety and Health Administration, and environmentalists cheered when Nixon signed the Clean Air Act and the Endangered Species Act and the bill to establish the Environmental Protection Agency. Nixon even called, albeit unsuccessfully, for a national health insurance plan. Total federal spending for Social Security and other entitlement programs doubled during the Nixon years. When all was said and done, Nixon "was easily the most liberal Republican American President, excepting Theodore Roosevelt, in the 20th century," Brown University's James T. Patterson concluded.[5]

Yet Nixon's domestic achievements failed to mollify his liberal critics; many bristled at how the foundation of his political success was his ability to lure white southerners and ethnic northern working families from the ranks of the Democratic Party by tapping their fears of racial and campus unrest. The ultimate wedge between Nixon and the Left was the Vietnam War — an unquenchable source of divisiveness for Americans. There, events moved toward a denouement at the end of 1972, when peace talks in Paris failed and American B-52s plastered North Vietnam with high explosives for twelve days in punitive, high-altitude raids that were condemned by antiwar forces and newspaper editorialists as "the Christmas bombing."[6]

Nixon toughed it out. "I have the responsibility — if I fail, you can blame me," he told O'Neill and other congressional leaders at a January 5 breakfast in the White House dining room. The North Vietnamese, having expended their store of Soviet-made surface-to-air missiles, finally offered concessions. On January 23, Nixon announced the terms of "peace with honor." The fighting ceased, but South Vietnam was left surrounded and penetrated by Communist armies, and President Nguyen Van Thieu had good reason to fear that the Democratic Congress would never allow Nixon to fulfill his promise of military assistance should the North resume the offensive.

Few Americans celebrated; many struggled with shame. There was a pervasive sense that the combat was over but the bleeding was not. Supporters and opponents of the war tallied their grievances, awaiting a day of requital. The Left, particularly, craved vengeance. A third of the Americans killed in Vietnam had died on Nixon's watch, along with hundreds of thousands of Vietnamese. The U.S. could have had much the same terms — the return of POWs and a cease-fire in return for U.S. withdrawal — shortly after Nixon took office. Someone must pay.

The peace agreement went into effect on January 27, a night on which O'Neill kept a long-standing agreement to appear at a public hearing on the war at Somerville High School. "This should be a day for prayer and solace, not a time to have an antiwar rally," he told the crowd of some 800 ideologues. They booed and hissed. "This certainly isn't a praying crowd," Representative Barney Frank whispered to a reporter.

"The war is not over and will not be over until the U.S. stops aid to General Thieu," said Alice Ansara, the spokeswoman for the Eighth Congressional District Citizens Against the War. "This aid is used to continue the U.S.-supported repression of all opposition to Thieu's dictatorship."

"I didn't come here to argue," said a distressed O'Neill, sitting behind a table on the auditorium stage. "Nobody has worked harder to end this war than I have."

Later that night he wrote in his diary: "Spoke at Somerville High . . . antiwar group . . . hardest ever . . . gave me a hard time. This is the day war was supposed to stop. America will have trouble from these people."[7]

IN HIS FIRST FEW MONTHS as majority leader, O'Neill was nervous, tired, swamped by obligations and habitually tardy. Albert would start a leadership meeting at 1 P.M. and at 1:20 sigh and ask, "Has anyone seen Mr. O'Neill?" His calendar was jammed with breakfast briefings and dinners at the White House, weekly whip coffees, interview requests, strategy sessions with the Speaker and drop-bys at evening fund-raising events for Democratic congressmen on Capitol Hill; he attended seven such events one January day. There were meetings with delegations of labor leaders, the New England caucus, the DSG and the DCCC; receptions for Jordan's King Hussein and transportation secretary John Volpe; private chats with lobbyists or executives from Greyhound, Bethlehem Steel, Delta Airlines, CBS and J. C. Penney; and the Ways and Means meetings at which House members were awarded committee assignments ("Hard guys — if you don't do your homework, you lose," he told his diary).

O'Neill attended the full round of inaugural festivities, passing out his extra tickets to his lobbyist pals, but also to low-level employees of the House restaurant, document room and doorkeeper's office, and to the commandant of the Chelsea, Massachusetts, old soldiers' home. He went to a memorial service at the National Cathedral for Harry Truman (who had died in December); the National Prayer Breakfast;

the Texas delegation's quail and venison–pork sausage breakfast; the Louisiana state society's annual Mardi Gras ball and, of increasing necessity, his Weight Watchers sessions. When Representative James Symington of Missouri wrote his colleagues with an offer of free karate lessons, O'Neill admitted that his duties were taking a toll on his diet. "In my present condition," he wrote back, "I would unfortunately need more than one black belt to go around me."[8] On January 4, O'Neill and Millie traveled with the congressional delegation to New Orleans to attend the memorial service for Hale Boggs. After the Mass at Saint Louis Cathedral, O'Neill had a long talk with Lyndon Johnson, who confided that he was feeling poorly, and whose gaunt appearance shocked Millie. It was their last visit with LBJ; he died in Texas on January 22.

Much of the ceremony attendant on his new position failed to impress O'Neill. "Typical White House bore," he noted in his diary after one reception at the executive mansion. He was moved instead by a private dinner with McCormack ("a wonderful man and an enjoyable nite — I owe much to him"); by the ceremonial counting of the Electoral College votes on January 6 ("very interesting — 20 years and the first I have seen"); by the severity of the flu that had sent sons Kip and Michael to bed that month ("Millie great in a crisis, as always," he told his diary) and by his trip with Kip, Silvio Conte and friends to the Super Bowl in Los Angeles, courtesy of the National Football League. Disneyland gave the red carpet treatment to O'Neill and his crew; they were feted by movie stars at an NFL reception held on the *Queen Mary*, and mingled with big shots from Hollywood and the sporting world at Chasen's restaurant. O'Neill lost a bundle betting at the Santa Anita racetrack, and more to the bookies when the Dolphins beat the Redskins.[9]

O'Neill also bought some real estate that weekend, in a transaction celebrated in family lore. He had long hoped to purchase a home on Cape Cod, and Diehl, who owned a place in Harwichport, had been instructed to scout around for a nice vacation property. Diehl found a roomy cottage for sale, but O'Neill, fearing that Millie would resist the extravagance, schemed to bring her on board by making it seem like her idea. His plot worked too well. To Diehl's surprise, and O'Neill's subsequent shock, Millie fell in love with the place and immediately made an offer. She told her husband about it by phone while he was in Los Angeles. O'Neill had never seen the place, and he and his wife now swapped roles: he lay in bed fretting about the cost. "Millie came down and, Jesus, she bought it without telling him," Diehl recalled. "Boy, was he sore at me."

O'Neill had the $42,500 he put down for the cottage because, with the help of his political pull, he had just cashed in on a fourteen-year-old investment in the Glendale Hospital in Jamaica Plain. With Leo Diehl, Bob O'Hayre and some other pals, he had invested $10,000 in 1958 in the hospital, a private psychiatric facility. When the hospital was sold in October 1972, he earned $50,000 in cash and $60,000 in deferred payments. The sale was greased by two federal loan guarantees from agencies — the Department of Housing and Urban Development and the Small Business Administration — whose employees were well aware of the congressman's interest. With his profits, O'Neill bought a small piece of property in Chatham for $22,000; he also took out a $35,000 mortgage for the cottage in Harwichport. None of these transactions was an exorbitant reach, as he was then earning $50,000 a year in Congress, but his diary reveals that he lay awake "thinking about finances." Over time, the deal would attract the interest of government and newspaper investigators and give him many sleepless nights.[10]

O'Neill took two quick trips to Florida, got to the racetrack twice a month and dined frequently with his children, Diehl, Boland or his lobbyist pals at Paul Young's, yet the pace often left him exhausted and eating alone in a small Italian restaurant near his apartment. "Bed 10 P.M. — new record," he wrote in his diary on February 1. In the end, however, the long hours were worth it. He was winning good reviews for his performance. "A Master Politician's Silent Rise to the Top," read the headline in the *Chicago Tribune*. "Tip O'Neill is not considered the brightest man in the House, nor the shrewdest, nor the hardest working. But he may be the best politician and, what is better, the best liked," the newspaper concluded. His House colleagues, and a gang of old friends who had flown down from Boston for the occasion, gave O'Neill an early St. Patrick's Day salute at a "Saints and Sinners" roast at the Shoreham Hotel on March 8. To the tune of "Peggy O'Neill" they teased him:

If his eyes are blue as skies
That's Thomas O'Neill
If his freight is overweight
That's Thomas O'Neill

If his Pals call him Thomas the whip
If the Gals call him lovable Tip
Scourge of seniority, leads the majority
That's Thomas O'Neill.

"He made people feel safe. He took care of people. He listened to them. And he told great stories," said Judith Kurland. "I mean, who didn't want to be in his company? You would have to be such a hard-assed, cold-blooded stiff not to want to be in his company. He was just so much fun."

"He moved through the House like a ward heeler," said Ray Smock, who worked as House historian during O'Neill's tenure as Speaker. "You were loyal. You did favors. You knew who your friends were. There was a certain humility in his leadership. He knew that members had to be friends. The comity was genuine."[11] Dick Bolling, who was better at analyzing himself and his colleagues than at applying the lessons learned to his own career, said O'Neill used his genial front to mask a relentless drive.

"He gets rolling, he gets really determined, but he doesn't get ugly — ugly as I would get. He's enormously forceful and he uses a lot of Irish charm and takes the sting out of it," said Bolling. "Being friendly, personable and sociable, doing all kinds of favors for individuals — I find that about as congenial a way of living your life as walking on nails."

Christopher Lydon, a Boston newsman who worked in the Washington bureau of the *New York Times,* found O'Neill "a studied performer, polished enough to make most of us forget the years of artifice in the role," whose "whole method is indirection and blarney." A young Joe Klein, writing for an alternative newspaper in Cambridge, visited O'Neill for a profile. "To spend time with O'Neill is to be seduced subtly. The anecdotes roll out, intimate looks at people like Kennedy, Johnson, Rayburn, McCormack. The conversation travels from Washington to the old days in Cambridge and Boston, and back again," Klein wrote. "But after a while it becomes obvious that the whole show has been carefully orchestrated by O'Neill; each anecdote is calculated to enhance his appearance as a progressive, though realistic, legislator."

Loyalty, regardless of the cost, remained a paramount virtue. To the maverick Michael Harrington, who fancied himself "a crusader with piratical instincts," O'Neill would curse and say, "You're not worth a patch on your father's pants." Yet O'Neill never forgot how Harrington's dad had helped him in the 1952 showdown against Michael LoPresti. When Harrington was targeted by conservatives on the Ethics Committee for circulating classified information on U.S. efforts to depose President Salvador Allende of Chile, O'Neill came to his defense.

"He's been over the side so many times for me that his suit is all wet," Harrington told reporters in amazement. Years later he remembered "the absolute integrity of the relationship, where you never had a second thought about O'Neill's commitment. In the Chilean situation he was a pillar of pressured strength. He was the rock. They could not get around him."

There were limits to O'Neill's affability; he detested sharpies and trimmers and, Washington lobbyist Anne Wexler remembered, "he could spot a phony a mile off." His personal secretary, Eleanor Kelley, recalled how O'Neill would often form a judgment — "plus or minus" — at his first meeting with an individual. "He could read people pretty well," she said, "and you never knew it — if you were a minus. But I would know because of his body language or because he would cut them short and pretend he had something else to do."

Said aide Billie Larsen: "If you didn't tell the straight story to Tip O'Neill you never spoke to him again. Or he would appear very friendly on the exterior while taking everything with a grain of salt." Rosemary O'Neill recalls her shock at discovering, on a few occasions, her father's true feelings about a political figure she mistakenly thought he liked.

His new duties kept him away from home for greater lengths of time. The kids were growing up — and not without some troubles. Michael, the youngest, who suffered the most from his father's absences, dropped out of Boston College. And the family long remembered the Labor Day weekend that Kip managed to get jailed in upstate New York and Tommy arrested on the Cape — both for disorderly conduct. Tip and Millie made the trip to bail Kip out, and on the drive back to Massachusetts the truant youth had to dodge the intermittent blows that his father aimed at him from the front seat. It was after that ordeal that the O'Neills, trying to relax at a cookout on Cape Cod, heard from Tommy how *he* had been arrested at a loud and bawdy summer party. O'Neill knocked his son so hard that Tommy went reeling out a porch door to the lawn. O'Neill ultimately relented and quietly interceded with the judge in the case, but made Tommy pay the fines and legal fees.

Tommy straightened up and captured a seat in the state legislature in 1972. He thought, after years of hearing his father spinning tales, that he was prepared for the intrigues of Beacon Hill. "I thought I knew it all, only to learn that after sitting at the dinner table for twenty-four years of my life I had learned very little," Tommy recalled. His father had "kept the family away from the political interplay. Not from the issues . . . [but] from the political nuances, the fighting, the in-house squabbling, the daily problems. That, he never brought home."[12] Family, caucuses, funerals, the war: O'Neill's first few months in office were an intense baptism of fire for the new majority leader. And then, on March 23, Watergate burglar James McCord stood up in Judge John Sirica's courtroom and told the court that the Watergate break-in had been more than just a third-rate burglary, and that he was not about to take the rap.

THOUGH SOME of the scandalous behavior exposed in the Watergate crisis can be attributed to the venality of the President's men, the catalysts were Nixon's uncommon personality and the psychological state of siege that pervaded the White House. "Don't ever — no matter what facet of the Nixon presidency you consider — don't ever lose sight of Vietnam as the overriding factor in the first Nixon term. It overshadowed everything, all the time, in every discussion, in every decision, in every opportunity and every problem," said White House chief of staff Bob Haldeman. The barricade of buses that surrounded the White House during antiwar protests were an apt metaphor for the mood of those inside the mansion's gates.

"Strategic retreat is the hardest thing in military campaign history," said Leonard Garment, an accomplished jazz musician, riffing with a Napoleonic metaphor. In Southeast Asia, Nixon was conducting "a strategic retreat with large masses of people: men, armor, horses, snow, demonstrators, tear gas, exploding academic buildings, Russians. Tough stuff.

"Napoléon's retreat from Moscow was disorderly. He got out of there, but was savaged along the way. So Nixon managed it pretty well until the Pentagon Papers and other mounting frustrations. Then it blew up. Nixon blew up. Lost his cool. And you had a couple of people like Charles Colson and his band of merry men taking instructions that were meant to be denied and running with them like crazy," Garment said.

Watergate's precipitating event — oddly enough, given that it tarnished the reputation of Nixon's Democratic predecessors, and not his own administration — was the publication of the Pentagon Papers by the *New York Times* on June 13, 1971. The classified 7,000-page report showed how cold war zeal and secrecy had contributed to the awful misjudgments by U.S. officials about Indochina. It was leaked to the *Times* by Daniel Ellsberg, a repentant former National Security Council employee.

Nixon made a staggering blunder. Ignoring Colson's advice that "the Democrats are horribly divided on this issue . . . split, confused, angry and scrambling to get away from it," the President sent his Justice Department into federal court to ask for an emergency injunction and make the *Times* stop its publication of the papers. In doing so, he made himself the enemy, and his conduct the story. The liberal press stopped covering the historic sins of Democratic administrations and focused instead on Nixon's new threat to the First Amendment.

Nixon was prisoner of the orthodoxies of the national security state. He had relied on excessive secrecy to conduct foreign policy, whether bombing Cambodia, undermining the Allende regime, forging the rapprochement with China or holding talks with North Vietnam. And the President knew what other secrets were hidden in the vaults at the Pentagon, FBI and CIA; of coups and assassinations abroad and tapped phones and stolen mail at home. Moreover, he detested leaks, intellectuals like Ellsberg, the antiwar movement, the media in general, the *Times* in particular.[13] Nixon ordered his aides to create "a little group right here in the White House" to investigate leaks and wreak political havoc on the Democrats. So was born the White House Special Investigations Unit, with headquarters in room 16 of the Executive Office Building and a sign on the door that said Plumber. A former FBI agent, G. Gordon Liddy, and a former CIA agent, E. Howard Hunt, were hired to conduct clandestine field operations.

By the end of the summer, Hunt and Liddy had recruited a small group of anti-Castro Cubans with ties to the CIA and led them in a break-in of the southern California office of Ellsberg's psychiatrist. "We had one little operation . . . out in Los Angeles . . . we've got some dirty tricks underway," aide John Ehrlichman told Nixon. Responding to continual pressure from Nixon and his top aides for political intelligence, Hunt and Liddy concocted an ambitious plan of break-ins, surveillance, muggings, kidnappings and sexual entrapment. They launched a test version (sans muggings and kidnappings) in early 1972 with money from the Committee for the Re-election of the President (CREEP). By May, Hunt and Liddy had enlisted McCord, a retired CIA hand who had been handling security at CREEP headquarters. On the weekend of May 25–27, after two unsuccessful attempts to pick the lock at the Democratic National Committee headquarters in the Watergate Hotel, and two aborted attempts to break into the McGovern campaign headquarters, the burglars got into the DNC offices on their third try, photographing files and planting two electronic bugs. One tap produced some minor sexual and political gossip, but the other device failed: it was to fix this faulty bug that the CREEP burglars returned to the Watergate and were caught, wearing business suits and surgical gloves, in the early morning hours of June 17.[14]

"The whole thing was a silly thing. Because they were going to win the election in a walk. They had no opposition, to be perfectly truthful. And the day that the robbery took place, there was a small item in the paper, and very, very few people paid any attention to it," O'Neill said later. But federal and local law enforcement agencies traced the burglars' White House and CIA connections, and some timely leaks to the *Washington Post* and the legwork of reporters Bob Woodward and Carl Bernstein kept the story alive. Within the Oval Office, the talk turned to cover-ups and hush money. Any notion of making a clean breast of things was quashed by the participation of the Watergate burglars in the Ellsberg case and other "White House horrors." The election was three months away, and even McGovern might beat a President whose staff was revealed to have taken part in so formidable a collection of political crime and mischief. On June 23, as tape machines recorded their conversation, Nixon told Haldeman to use the CIA to intervene and prevent the FBI from learning who had hired and paid the Watergate burglars.

"My reaction to the Watergate break-in was completely pragmatic. If it was also cynical, it was a cynicism born of experience," Nixon wrote in his memoirs. "I had been in politics too long, and seen everything from dirty tricks to vote fraud. I could not muster much moral outrage over a political bugging."[15]

Because many of the ties between the burglars and the White House were being unearthed by those who "followed the money," Carl Albert turned to an old pal, Representative Wright Patman of Texas, the dogged seventy-nine-year-old prairie populist who chaired the House Banking and Currency Committee, to investigate. In a September 15 meeting, White House counsel John Dean warned Nixon of the need for "turning off" the Patman probe and set out to do some "arm-twisting." Patman convened his committee on October 3, and asked for subpoena power to investigate "the greatest political espionage case" in U.S. history. The committee defeated his motion by a 20 to 15 vote, as six Democratic defectors joined a unanimous Republican bloc. Three of the Democrats who caved in to the pressure and sided with the administration were targets of Justice Department corruption probes, and thus vulnerable to political blackmail.

The House leadership stood idly by as Patman's investigation died. Boggs was missing in Alaska, and O'Neill was busy rounding up votes for his election as majority leader. "Nobody thought that this was anything. Remember, this is pre-Watergate — this is when there is a presumption for the President," said Stan Brand. "And Tip was never one who liked investigations. He thought that was gutter stuff, mean-spirited, not his style." The House had botched its opportunity. A few months later, Patman shipped his staff's files to the Senate Select Committee on Presidential Campaign Activities, which had been established by the Senate in February with Senator Sam Ervin of North Carolina as chairman. Carl Albert was always sensitive to the criticism that the House, which had the sole constitutional authority to impeach a President, had dragged its heels. "We . . . had more jurisdiction than the Senate did," said Albert. "But . . . old man Ervin, he started giving his customary speech on constitutional law, you know, and stood up whining around about how they were violating the Constitution . . . and they let him set up a select committee. We were going to do it if they didn't, you know. But he had run out and got it."[16]

IN JANUARY, Hunt pleaded guilty to planning the Watergate break-in, and McCord and Liddy were convicted by a jury that took but 90 minutes to deliberate. "I am still not satisfied," said Judge John Sirica, "that all the pertinent facts . . . have been produced." Though Nixon's men had paid $429,000 in hush money to the defendants (Hunt insisted on funds for his children's governess and private school), the prospect of prison scared McCord. He showed up in Sirica's chambers on March 20 with a letter. "There was political pressure applied to the defendants to plead guilty and remain silent. Perjury occurred . . . others involved in the Watergate operation were not identified," McCord wrote. Sirica read the letter aloud in court, then handed down maximum sentences to Hunt and the others, with an offer of leniency if they cooperated with their prosecutors and the Ervin committee.

McCord met with committee investigators and fingered John Dean and Jeb Magruder, CREEP's deputy director, as key figures in the scandal. Within a week Dean had cracked, telling prosecutors of the break-in at the office of Ellsberg's psychiatrist and offering to link Nixon and his aides to the cover-up. On April 30, Nixon went on national television to announce that Dean, Bob Haldeman, John Ehrlichman and Attorney General Richard Kleindienst had resigned. Elliot Richardson was named to replace Kleindienst, and Archibald Cox, a Harvard Law School professor, was appointed as a special Watergate prosecutor. Alexander Haig took over as White House chief of staff.[17]

Representative John Moss of California urged Albert and O'Neill to launch a formal inquiry to see if there were grounds to impeach the President. O'Neill told reporters on April 30 that the proposal was "premature" but that "the time could come." He had privately warned the Speaker that "impeachment is going to hit this Congress and we better be ready for it." Like everyone else in Washington, O'Neill was startled by the pace of events that spring, but it cannot be said that he was totally surprised by their nature, given what he had learned as DCCC chairman, raising funds for Democratic congressional candidates in 1972.

"He was the first to think about it; the first to say it would happen," said James Cannon, a White House aide to Gerald Ford. "During the campaign of 1972, Democratic contributors were complaining, 'Look, they are draining us dry.' That was when he first thought this guy Nixon was not going to last out his second term.

"Leaders have a prescience about things. They know when something is going to happen. It's experience, instinct. Tip had some premonition. *This guy is going to go.* He mentioned it to more than one person," Cannon recalled.

It was in 1968 that Dick Maguire, O'Neill's old friend and DNC treasurer, had introduced him to several corporate executives who agreed that their businesses had done pretty well under Democratic administrations and so were willing to raise funds for the party. One of them was George Steinbrenner III, the owner of the American Ship Building Company and the New York Yankees. Steinbrenner agreed to chair the DCCC dinner in the spring of 1969. The sports-minded O'Neill hit it off with Steinbrenner: throwing a surprise luncheon party for the Ohio executive, sending him a favorite book on Irish whalers and pushing him to take the job as Democratic Party chairman in 1970. In gushy correspondence, Steinbrenner turned down that opportunity, but agreed to chair the DCCC dinner again that year. "Without you, the cause would have been lost," O'Neill wrote after the 1970 event, another successful dinner. He called Steinbrenner and his wealthy friends "golden faucets for the Democratic Party."

Steinbrenner's interest in politics was fueled by the fact that his shipbuilding firm held government contracts, that he needed the approval of the Justice Department's antitrust division to buy various competing shipbuilding interests and that he hoped to secure an ambassadorship for a member of his family. He was working both sides of the aisle, and met with Herbert Kalmbach, the president's personal lawyer and a fund-raiser for CREEP. Kalmbach, according to Steinbrenner, gave him a list of political action committees that had been set up to raise money for Nixon's 1972 reelection campaign, and instructions on how to divide $100,000 among 34 of them. To raise the money, Steinbrenner set up an illegal kickback scheme in which he gave his employees phony bonuses, which they passed on to the Nixon committees.

"We always thought it was ethical in those days because it was the customary manner in which they did things. But anyway, he was later indicted and found guilty," O'Neill said later, in a statement that pretty much summed up his casual attitude toward the campaign finance laws. The congressman wasn't bothered by what Steinbrenner did for Nixon; it was what the Yankees owner stopped doing for O'Neill that made him angry. While Steinbrenner was working for Nixon, he stopped contributing to Democrats. "I called George and I said, 'George, I can't believe it. We haven't received any contributions.'

"He said, 'I'm going to come over and see you.' So he came over and he told me the story about how they had practically blackjacked them, that he had some government work and he'd never do any government work again. He said he was being chased by investigators . . . by the IRS. And they called him and said they could straighten out his problem if he would be chairman of Democrats for Nixon in Ohio."

O'Neill called Colson at the White House and complained about how the Republicans were treating Steinbrenner. "That opened my eyes to the other Democrats out there who weren't giving," O'Neill said later. "And suddenly I saw all of these names appearing. The Democratic Committee of Massachusetts for Nixon for President. Democrats for Nixon. And I looked down the list. I talked to so many of them. They had IRS problems suddenly. Or they had business problems with the government suddenly."

"Hey, Tip," the executives told him, "they are hitting us over the head with a hammer." Sixteen corporations and dozens of individuals would eventually plead guilty to violating campaign finance laws in the 1972 campaign season, including American Airlines, Braniff Airways, Goodyear Tire and Rubber, Northrop, Gulf Oil, and Phillips Petroleum. O'Neill knew the game. To further his own drive for the Speakership, he had set up the "Thomas P. O'Neill Jr. Congress Fund," which, over the next four years, raised some $300,000 from big labor unions and wealthy contributors and passed it out to Democratic congressional candidates. So it wasn't all moral outrage that got O'Neill thinking about impeachment in early 1973: more a sense that Nixon had violated the unwritten rules of politics.

"Shoot if you must this old gray head. But don't touch my dinner chairman," said writer Jimmy Breslin. "They torched his dinner chairman. That was the fucking ballgame right there."[18]

And yet . . . impeachment! It was a dreadful idea to the men and women of O'Neill's generation, whose only exposure to the process had been John Kennedy's harrowing account, in *Profiles in Courage,* of how the Radical Republicans had impeached President Andrew Johnson in 1868 because he proposed to treat the vanquished states of the Confederacy with mercy. It was the sole time in U.S. history (until then) that a President had been impeached, and the Senate had failed to convict Johnson because Senator Edmund Ross of Kansas, a "profile in courage," and six fellow Republicans refused to join their Radical colleagues. Johnson was saved by a single vote. The disgraceful episode thoroughly tarnished the process. To contemplate an impeachment amid cold war tensions was desperate stuff indeed. "Impeach the President," a smug Richard Kleindienst dared a Senate committee in April.

Impeachment was "a frightening word to the Congress, absolutely a frightening word," O'Neill said later. He remembered meeting Representative Thaddeus J. Dulski, a Democrat from Buffalo and Navy veteran of World War II, in the cloakroom one day. "Impeachment, impeachment. Don't ever let me hear the word," Dulski said. "My father would roll over in his grave if he thought there was ever an impeachment. He came from Poland to this country. And that's how much he loves and respects the government. You could never do this to the President of the United States. It doesn't happen here."

To O'Neill's mentor, John McCormack, impeachment "was the worst thing that could happen . . . a disgrace," O'Neill said. In reply to Cambridge liberals who had begun to call for Nixon's head, O'Neill wrote, "Impeachment is a severe and final step that has never been used to remove a President of the United States from office. Impeachment could set a dangerous precedent which would seriously and permanently inhibit the powers of the Executive Branch of Government." On June 12, the House debated the need for an impeachment probe for ninety minutes, but the resolution calling for an investigation was consigned to the Judiciary Committee for a quiet burial. Then, on June 25, Dean took the stand before the Ervin committee.

The Watergate hearings had begun slowly, but the colorful testimony by McCord and various "plumbers" and burglars had been followed by the tense appearances of Magruder and other CREEP officials, attracting the nation's attention. Now Dean's self-assured, methodical testimony was bolstered by his collar-pinned manner and the faithful presence, behind him in the Senate caucus hearing room, of his prim blond wife, Maureen. He seemed the ultimate social-climbing, ambitious young executive; she the very corporate wife. With the same ferocity by which he had accumulated his White House job, sailboat, expensive suits and Porsche, now that the locus of power had shifted, Dean showed no qualms at ratting out the President who had raised him to such heights. Under questioning from Senator Howard Baker of Tennessee ("What did the President know and when did he know it?"), Dean gave a detailed description of Nixon's involvement in the Watergate cover-up.

"What turned Tip around, and he told me this at the time, was John Dean's testimony. Five days. A blinding performance. Incredible . . . he never moved a muscle," said *Time*'s Neil MacNeil. "Tip realized he was going to have to act after he heard John Dean." Dean, who had once worked as a minority aide to the Judiciary Committee, was a familiar figure in the House, and Jerry Zeifman, the committee's Democratic counsel, had listened to his old friend's testimony with great care. Zeifman was a friend of Gary Hymel's, and the two aides got O'Neill to sit down for breakfast with Judiciary Committee chairman Peter Rodino. Dean's testimony showed that Nixon had committed obstruction of justice, an impeachable offense, Zeifman argued. "Dean refuses to be the fall guy," O'Neill said. "My guess is that in fingering Nixon, he's telling the truth." With O'Neill's encouragement, Zeifman began to collect legal and historic precedents for a Judiciary Committee report on impeachment. Rodino warned his aide to keep his research at home, lest others discover that he was engaged in such politically explosive work.[19]

THE DEMOCRATIC LEADERS' stealthy preparation was disrupted by Bob Drinan, who wrote to O'Neill on July 31: "Dear Tip: I enclose for your information a statement I intend to submit on the floor of the House of Representatives today. Cordially yours, Robert F. Drinan." The accompanying resolution read simply: "Resolved, That Richard M. Nixon, President of the United States, is impeached of high crimes and misdemeanors." Drinan based his resolution on Nixon's secret bombing of Cambodia, which he outlined in a report. "I wrote 5,000 words saying this is an impeachable offense for Nixon to clandestinely bomb Cambodia with 3,800 sorties without the knowledge of Congress," said Drinan. "Tip said to me, 'This is premature.' I looked the word up; I said, 'Tip, that means it's inevitable.' "

By this relatively early date, Drinan said, O'Neill had reached a fundamental conclusion about impeachment: that the Democrats needed Republican allies. O'Neill was never one for hopeless symbolic gestures. And history, as well as pragmatic politics, demanded that an impeachment process be conducted solemnly and fairly. An unsuccessful attempt to impeach Nixon, lost on a party-line vote in the House, would leave the Democrats in the same tattered class as the Reconstruction-era Republicans.

"He did not want this to be perceived as a Democratic vendetta. If they put through that impeachment and it is four-to-one Democratic, it ain't going to work. It wouldn't wash in the Senate. And he was very fearful and understanding of that," Drinan said later.

Drinan's resolution also presented the Democratic leadership with an immediate tactical problem. "I thought that Drinan had done the wrong thing because it was a privileged motion, and anytime the Republicans wanted, they could have brought it to the floor, and it would have been overwhelmingly defeated, because the evidence wasn't there," O'Neill said later. If the Democrats lost an early test vote on the resolution, the impeachment process would be discredited. So he and his whips staked out the House floor, prepared to table Drinan's motion if minority leader Gerald Ford or another Republican should call it up.

O'Neill quickly tired of the game. He asked Ford if the Republicans planned to act. Ford checked with the White House, and told O'Neill that Nixon's men, fearing that any vote would look like a crisis of confidence in the presidency, were happy to let the matter die. O'Neill always believed that Nixon had missed an opportunity by not trying to exploit the Drinan resolution. "If they had called it up, there wouldn't have been 15 or 20 votes," he said.[20]

CHAPTER 15

Massacre

BY THE END of summer 1973, the Watergate scandal had reached a state of political equilibrium. Nixon retained the support of a citizenry that was tiring of the Ervin committee's investigation. Yet, just as clearly, the President had been wounded. It showed on the House floor where, in the wake of the April 30 resignations of Haldeman and other high-ranking administration officials, the liberal Democrats had finally clinched a long-standing goal: after nine years, the House cast its first vote against the war in Southeast Asia. By 219 to 188, on May 10, the House cut off funds for further military operations in the region.

As the House's new electronic voting system showed the time allotted for the vote running out, the happy liberals chanted "five . . . four . . . three . . . two . . . one." It was a sign of Nixon's damaged status that the President was forced to accept the legislation, which would bind his hands, and those of his successor, when Communist forces broke the cease-fire. The White House lost the votes of 35 Republicans in the showdown, and lobbyist Bill Timmons warned Nixon that though the vote reflected the strength of the antiwar forces, there was also a growing concern in the GOP cloakroom that "Watergate may defeat Republicans." Timmons told of an "every man for himself" attitude. A recent Republican poll, he said, showed "as many as 50 GOP seats [were] in jeopardy."

The administration was rocked again in July with the disclosure of the White House taping system. O'Neill remembered a leadership breakfast at the White House when Nixon's self-congratulatory, stilted conversation had led the congressman to suspect they were being taped.[1] The President's response to the Ervin committee hearings was to launch a fresh PR campaign. In a nationally televised address on August 15, he urged the country not to be "mired in Watergate." On September 5, Nixon announced that he would send a second State of the Union message to Congress, and called on the legislators to get back to work. Indeed, the White House staff was compiling evidence that the public now believed that the Democrats were piling on. Timmons reported to chief of staff Alexander Haig, "The Watergate committee is seen as partisan, biased and 'out to get' the President" and that people believed "the nation [was] being damaged by multi-investigation binge."[2] Haig received GOP polling results which showed that the economy and inflation were by far the most salient issues with the voters. The polls revealed that 42 percent of the respondents ranked inflation and the high cost of living, and only 9 percent Watergate, as the leading issues. The President's approval rating had bounced back from record lows, and two-thirds of the public said it was time to end the Ervin committee hearings and turn the matter over to the courts. When asked if Nixon should be impeached, only 17 percent said yes. "Barring some new sensational revelations, it would appear that the tempest of publicity devoted to Watergate has passed its peak," wrote pollster Thomas W. Benham. "There is no doubt that the whole issue is abating as far as public attention is concerned . . . it would appear that concern over the economy is much more fundamental to public attitudes and represents a more long-term threat to the president's standing with the public." The Democrats knew the score; they had their own polls, and O'Neill never lost sight of the fact that most voters, as his pal Joe Moakley put it, "view life through their kitchen windows." As Democratic leader, O'Neill had given just one Watergate speech on the floor that spring and summer — a May 3 response after California governor Ronald Reagan had defended the Watergate burglars as "not criminals at heart."

"This ends-justifies-the-means attitude seems to persist within the Republican philosophy of government," O'Neill said in reply to Reagan, "as if it were transmitted from one generation of candidates to the next like some malignant gene." But aside from this retort, O'Neill had chosen all year to skewer the Republican administration on economic issues: about budget cuts, the price of meat and groceries and the cost and availability of gasoline and heating oil. "Jobs. Jobs. Jobs," O'Neill wrote in his diary.

Bryce Harlow informed Haig that Representative Eddie Hebert and the rest of the Louisiana delegation were "solidly" behind Nixon. Other Nixon aides reported that lobbyists for the Catholic Church were trying to curry favor because of the "great disservice" done by Father Drinan's impeachment resolution. And Texas representative Olin Teague, jockeying for an appointment to a high-ranking job in the Veterans Administration, was said to have been increasingly "helpful" to Nixon on the Hill: Teague was chairman of the Democratic Caucus at the time. When Congress returned after Labor Day, O'Neill held out an olive branch. "House Majority Leader Thomas P. O'Neill, most partisan of congressional Democratic leaders, said yesterday that Congress and President Nixon should try to work together on legislation rather than continue battles that produce only bills that are vetoed and die," the *Washington Post* reported on September 5. Nixon noted O'Neill's words with approval at a press conference, and on September 10, O'Neill and Albert had breakfast with a relaxed and confident President. With typical attention to detail, *Time* reported the small talk about golf, the servings of scrambled eggs and sausage, and the passing around of 80-cent Flamenco No. 1 cigars and concluded the breakfast represented "the first faint stirrings of concerned men ready to sit down together and try to make things work." Alas, it was a phony peace; the autumnal era of good feelings between the Nixon administration and the Congress ended abruptly in the five tumultuous weeks that followed the breakfast — weeks that brought the nation to a series of constitutional crises, and the brink of nuclear war.[3]

This most extraordinary moment in American history was ushered in by news of a quite ordinary kind of political graft. A federal grand jury in Baltimore, probing reports that Maryland public officials collected illegal kickbacks from the architects and engineers who received no-bid contracts for suburban public works projects, found evidence of payoffs to a former Maryland governor: Vice President Spiro Agnew.

Some $10,000 had been delivered in the White House itself. The news that Agnew was under investigation broke in August, and a steady stream of prosecutorial leaks to the press soon undermined the vice president's insistence of innocence. By early September, the vice president's lawyers were engaged in plea bargain talks with Attorney General Elliot Richardson. The White House's position was "go quietly, or else," a bitter Agnew said later.

But with Nixon's blessing, the vice president tried a final gambit. To forestall indictment, he decided to submit his case to the House of Representatives, where the impeachment process could drag on for months; a subsequent trial in the Senate would require a two-thirds vote for conviction and the debate would be held on political, rather than legal, turf. "I was willing to testify in person and face my accusers," Agnew said later. "Under cross-examination, they would have had to reveal all their illegal deals with each other and their understandings with the prosecutors that they would be given light treatment in return for their testimony against me. I believe that I would have survived an impeachment hearing; if not, I would have been acquitted after a trial by the Senate." On September 25 Agnew called upon Carl Albert to formally request that the House, not the Baltimore grand jury, judge his case. As a precedent, Agnew cited the House investigation of Vice President John Calhoun, who had asked the representatives in 1826 to probe charges that he profited from a military contract while serving as secretary of war.[4] Albert had sympathy for the vice president. "Agnew was a very articulate, attractive-looking fellow that really made a good impression, you know," Albert said later. "He was very friendly to me. He always had been. He was gregarious. He knew the House leadership before he had ever met them, you know, and he did his homework on things like that."

Albert listened to Agnew complain about White House backstabbers and zealous federal prosecutors for some thirty minutes, and consulted with parliamentarian Lew Deschler. "At this point, I fully believe Albert was inclined to use that power of his office to see that I got a hearing," said Agnew in a memo he dictated that evening. But the ever-cautious Speaker then summoned O'Neill and other House leaders from the floor. Agnew repeated his request and, as O'Neill took notes, the roomful of professional politicians chewed on the matter for another hour. Judiciary Committee chairman Peter Rodino was worried about appearances — he believed that his committee should be seen as initiating an investigation, rather than acceding to Agnew's request — but most of the other congressional leaders seemed generally willing to have Congress take up the matter. Agnew and minority leader Gerald Ford later recalled that O'Neill was the lone skeptic in the group, who suggested that since the matter would ultimately be decided by the House majority, the Democratic leaders needed to confer among themselves. "I could sense that the Speaker, who was such a nice person, was a little sympathetic. I could sense that some of the other Democrats there might have been sympathetic. But Tip, almost from the outset, acted very adversely," said Ford. "I knew him so well, he couldn't disguise his feelings from me and I just knew he was opposed. He asked some questions, he made some comments and I knew Tip was against it. I knew that the vice president was not going to get what he wanted."[5]

"Dizzying, bewildering and historic," is how John Chancellor described the day on the NBC evening news. The corridor outside Albert's office was jammed by reporters, photographers, television crews, Republican senators, House employees, Secret Service agents, curious tourists and congressmen who wandered over from the floor, where the House was debating an immigration bill. Albert told Agnew they would think about it and get back to him, and all agreed that the Speaker should go to the House chamber and put Agnew's request into the record. As the vice president prepared to leave, "Tip O'Neill came over to me and said he was terribly sorry I was having all the trouble," Agnew recalled.

"Pal, it's a damn shame," O'Neill told Agnew.

"I later found out that Tip O'Neill strongly urged the Speaker to keep out of my case and let me stew in my own juice," Agnew recalled bitterly. "His sympathy apparently was not genuine."

Indeed, as the left-leaning members of the Democratic caucus increasingly called for Republican blood, O'Neill was shedding his reluctance to employ the politics of scandal. As soon as Agnew and the other Republicans left the Speaker's office, O'Neill argued that the matter should be left to the courts. As it turns out, he had not been caught by surprise when Agnew arrived at the Capitol; Jerry Zeifman had warned him of the vice president's ploy after being tipped off by a friendly newspaper reporter who had, in turn, learned of the plan from his sources at the Democratic law firm Agnew hired to conduct his defense. Zeifman had even had time to dig up contrary precedents. "So Tip had an advance warning that that was going to happen," Zeifman said.[6]

It was clear to everyone in the capital where O'Neill stood when the next morning's *Post* cited him in two front-page stories. "I don't know what we'll do," Albert was quoted as saying. But O'Neill was decisive. He told the press, "We shouldn't act at all until the court decides the question of whether he can be indicted. . . . I don't see that we have an obligation to make an inquiry on his behalf." O'Neill arrived late at work that morning, believing that the matter had been tabled until the Democratic leaders could meet again. He was startled, then, when a breathless Gary Hymel found him in the House restaurant and told him that Albert had decided to refer Agnew's request to the Judiciary Committee. O'Neill grabbed the phone behind the counter in the restaurant and rang the Speaker's office. Albert told him it was all worked out, but if he wanted, he could come on up. The Speaker was trying to please everyone. Rayburn's old friend Deschler had argued with great conviction, and sound parliamentary reasoning, that the House had a constitutional duty to honor the vice president's request, if for no other reason than that the Constitution guaranteed a citizen's right to petition the government for redress. And Rodino wanted to make sure that if the House did take action, it would be the Judiciary Committee that got the important and glamorous responsibility. So the three men had decided to refer Agnew's request to Rodino's committee, and sit on it for a while. Albert had not counted on O'Neill, who had concluded that Agnew's request was the act of a cornered cat, and thought the vice president would use any action taken by Congress as an excuse to wriggle free of an indictment. A long investigation into Agnew's affairs would at the very least tie up the Congress and keep it from turning its attention to Nixon, as concurrent impeachments of both the President and vice president were politically implausible. For all these reasons, O'Neill wanted Agnew gone. So "when O'Neill learned about the idea of it being referred to the Judiciary Committee he went ballistic," said Zeifman.

"If we refer this to the Judiciary Committee we'll be doing just what the Republicans want," O'Neill told Deschler when he reached Albert's office. "They'll try to turn the committee into a damned three-ring circus to keep Agnew from being tried in the courts."

"Carl," O'Neill said, turning to the Speaker, "if you let Agnew get off the hook . . . the boys in the Democratic caucus will skin you alive."[7]

It was a turning point for O'Neill: the first time he had forcefully issued both public and private challenges to Albert on a matter of party politics. The Speaker had been in the Democratic leadership for twenty years; O'Neill for only thirty months. But both men knew that the majority leader was better aligned with the spirit and mood of the liberal Democratic majority. Had the clash taken place a few years earlier, the formidable Deschler might have forced O'Neill to back down. The parliamentarian, however, was in the twilight of his long career. "Tip was strong about me not taking it [the Agnew investigation] over," Albert remembered. "Lew was a very conservative Ohio Republican. He was the most important single individual in the House of Representatives. A forceful kind of person . . . just by nature. [But in his] last year Lew Deschler was fading . . . in energy and he was dying."

Albert bowed to the political realities. "The Vice President's letter relates to matters before the courts. In view of that fact, I, as Speaker, will not take any action on the letter at this time," he told the press. Reports of the Speaker's decision led the evening news on all three major television networks that night. There was one final anxious moment, when Zeifman and Rodino realized that if Agnew managed to deliver his personal records to Pat Jennings, the House clerk, then the House would have to accept them, and with them some jurisdiction over the case. "I thought to myself, 'My God, once you do this, these documents are in the custody of the Clerk of the House, and in order to release them, it would need House action,' " Rodino recalled. Albert called Jennings, who at first insisted that he was duty bound to accept what Agnew might send him. "Goddamn it, I'm the Speaker of the House, and I'm ordering you to do it," an exasperated Albert said, and slammed down the telephone.

"A few minutes later the phone rings again and it's Jennings. And Albert bursts out in laughter and he says, 'Well, that was Pat again, his solution is his office is going to be closed today,' " said Zeifman.

Agnew fought on for a few more days. "I will not resign if indicted," he told a cheering crowd of California Republicans. But without the hope of a House investigation he felt pressured again by the White House to resign, and told his lawyers to resume their negotiations with Attorney General Elliot Richardson's prosecutors. On Wednesday, October 10, Agnew resigned the vice presidency and accepted a criminal sentence for federal tax evasion.[8]

O'Neill was now confronted with three unexpected developments. The first was that a Democrat — Speaker Albert — was first in the line of presidential succession. The second was that the President was heading toward a constitutional confrontation with Archibald Cox over the White House tapes. The last was that on October 6, the Jewish holy day of Yom Kippur, Syria and Egypt launched a surprise attack upon Israel.

The Arabs drove Israeli forces from the Golan Heights in the north, and back from the Suez Canal and into the Sinai Desert in the south. Both sides lost hundreds of tanks and jet airplanes in the fighting, and emptied their arsenals of missiles and ammunition. The Arabs turned to Moscow for more weaponry; the Israelis to Washington. Nixon handled the Middle East crisis with sureness. Shrugging off threats from the oil industry and its Arab clients, the President ordered a massive military airlift to resupply the battered Israeli army and air force. "There were days and hours when we needed a friend, and you came right in," Israeli prime minister Golda Meir told him later. But neither did Nixon overreact; he grasped immediately that Egyptian president Anwar Sadat's goals were to change the psychology of the Middle East as much as the cartography. Sadat had a "fundamental objective of shaking belief in Israel's invincibility and Arab impotence," Kissinger recalled. "Rare is the statesman who at the beginning of a war has so clear a perception of its political objective; rarer still is a war fought to lay the basis for moderation in its aftermath."

Israel's existence was still in doubt, and the U.S. airlift had not yet begun when Agnew resigned. The Twenty-fifth Amendment to the Constitution, which had been passed by Congress in the wake of the Kennedy assassination, gave the President the responsibility of selecting a new vice president, with the consent of Congress. The news reports of Agnew's resignation named former treasury secretary John B. Connally, Nelson Rockefeller, Ronald Reagan and former secretary of state William Rogers as the most likely replacements. Had Nixon not been caught up in Watergate, he might well have nominated Connally, a former Texas governor who fit the President's political strategy of luring southern Democrats to the GOP. But Nixon's dwindling supply of political capital narrowed his options, precluding a debilitating confirmation fight. He needed a popular choice, who could do the job and win easy approval on Capitol Hill.

"We simply cannot afford another . . . imbroglio, ending in defeat," White House aide Ray Price wrote Nixon. "I fear the nomination of John Connally could trigger a disaster. It would be bitterly divisive among Republicans and an open invitation to the Democrats on

Capitol Hill to play the crassest sort of politics, and by doing so cripple if not topple the Presidency.

"They'd comb every inch of his past and I can't believe that in 20 or whatever years of acquiring millions while in Texas politics as a protege of Lyndon Johnson, there isn't something that could be unearthed," Price wrote. "In the course of the confirmation hearings every dead cat in the Southwest would be dragged across the hearing-room floor."

On the day Agnew resigned, Nixon had invited Senator Mike Mansfield and Carl Albert to the White House. The President asked the Speaker if he had a nominee in mind, but Albert demurred, saying it was not his place to choose. Mansfield was not so humble, and quickly named two moderate Republicans, Senator John Sherman Cooper of Kentucky and Rogers. Mansfield's audacity raised Albert's hackles: if the Senate had candidates, then so would the House.

"Well, if Mike is going to make a suggestion, I'm going to make a suggestion," Albert said.

"Who is that?" Nixon guessed, "Jerry Ford?"

"He would be the easiest man that I know of to confirm in the House of Representatives," Albert said. Mansfield had to agree. The next morning, October 11, the Speaker and O'Neill shared a ride to the White House for a meeting Nixon had scheduled with a broader group of congressional leaders.

"I put a good plug in for Jerry Ford. If you get a chance before the meeting is over, put in a good word," Albert told O'Neill.

O'Neill recognized that in Nixon's eyes he was a Democratic "dart-thrower . . . and kind of an enemy," but for that very reason could speak with authority on behalf of the liberal wing of the caucus. As Nixon shook hands with the legislators at the end of the meeting, O'Neill paused at the door. "Don't send us a Democrat, Mr. President. If you want easy sledding, the guy you should have is Jerry Ford. He will get through for you without any problems," O'Neill said.

"Thank you, Tip," Nixon said sociably.

Albert, who had watched the exchange, gave O'Neill a big wink and whispered, "Good boy," as they left.

"Ford's confirmability gave him an edge which the others could not match and was the decisive factor in my final decision," Nixon said later. O'Neill and Albert were back at the White House on the evening of October 12 for the announcement that had the capital, as the *Times* reported, "nearly apoplectic with speculation, suspense and surmise."[9]

Gerald R. Ford Jr. was sixty. His blond hair and sturdy build bespoke his birth of solid Midwestern stock, but his restless drive reflected his escape from a broken home. His mother had fled her wife-beating husband when Leslie L. King Jr., as Ford had been christened, was just sixteen days old. The scandal had forced mother and son to leave Illinois and seek a new life in Grand Rapids, Michigan. There Dorothy King met and married a kinder man, Gerald R. Ford Sr. Young Jerry took his stepfather's name as a child, and adopted it legally when he was twenty-one. He attended the University of Michigan, was a star football player and worked his way through Yale Law School as an assistant athletic coach. His easy, polite manner sometimes led foes to think Ford was a dullard; they did so at their peril, as the incumbent Republican congressman whom Ford upset in a heated primary in 1948, and House minority leader Charles Halleck, whom Ford deposed in a 1964 coup, could both testify.

After twenty-four years in Congress, Ford had watched his hopes to be Speaker die in the 1972 election; if the GOP could not take the House on the coattails of a presidential landslide, there was no hope of doing so in the post-Watergate elections of 1974 or 1976. In a golf cart at the annual congressional golf tournament in the summer of 1973, he told O'Neill that he had promised his wife he would retire from politics after the 1976 elections, and offered his support to O'Neill for a bill that would increase congressional pensions. "I had tried to be Speaker five times . . . the prospects for 1976 were no more encouraging. Therefore it seemed wise to me to leave the House when I was relatively young," and could make money as a well-connected lawyer, Ford said later. He had come that close to leaving politics; now, even Nixon reckoned, Ford had a 50–50 chance of becoming President. But only if Albert and O'Neill made good on their promise that Ford would be confirmed. And there were Democrats who questioned whether that was a good idea.

There was no one Democratic position on Watergate. The New Deal coalition had stretched to encompass blacks and bigots; youthful radicals and unrepentant mossbacks; zealous reformers and stubborn traditionalists. They all had notions of what was best for them, their country and the party. The southern Democrats were easily pegged; they generally were against Nixon's impeachment and for Jerry Ford. The rest of the Democrats, from the North and West, were united in their desire to bring down Nixon, but divided on the question of timing. There were some who wanted to delay the process for maximum political gain, to increase their numbers in the House in 1974 and help Ted Kennedy or another presidential nominee in the 1976 elections. Others thought that delay served Nixon, and that he would slip the noose if the process crept toward or past the mid-term elections, because the country would not want to expend the effort of impeaching a President with just a year or two left in his term. And there was one loud liberal faction that wanted to stage an immediate coup. "Get off your goddamned ass, and we can take this presidency," Bella Abzug told Albert as she punched him in the chest. "We can get control and keep control."

The Left's plot was simple: stall on Ford and impeach Nixon. Albert would then become President and O'Neill the Speaker. If Albert didn't want the job — and he quickly learned to detest the Secret Service guards who arrived to protect him after Agnew's demise — then he could resign the presidency in favor of O'Neill, or after appointing Kennedy or some other liberal choice as his vice president. It was a juicy scenario, and not totally far-fetched: with Albert's concurrence, Ted Sorensen, the old Kennedy hand, had sent the Speaker a twenty-page "contingency plan" for a Democratic takeover. Sorensen made suggestions for an inaugural address, gave advice on transition and staffing choices, and urged Albert to take Ford as vice president as a sign of national reconciliation.

On the afternoon of October 18, the Democrats on the Judiciary Committee met behind closed doors in a dining room in the Capitol. "I think it's absolutely ludicrous for us to even be talking about going ahead with Ford when the President who made this nomination is subject to impeachment," Representative John Conyers of Michigan said. "If we go ahead with this nomination and don't move on impeachment," Bob Drinan told a colleague, "I'm going to blow the whistle on the committee. I'll call it what it is, a cover-up!"

Even if Albert had been willing, there was no way the country would stand for such a crude attempt at reversing the outcome of the 1972 elections. Over the resistance of two dozen ultraliberals, Albert, O'Neill and Rodino pushed ahead with Ford's confirmation.[10] Nixon "wasn't going to have any worry . . . where Jerry Ford was concerned," O'Neill said later. "Everything was pretty well oiled that Jerry was going to be the man." To placate the liberals, the Democratic leaders published Zeifman's 718-page report on the history of impeachment. A seemingly minor gesture, in the culture of Congress it was nonetheless a potent symbol. Few members would read it, but there it was on their desks, and there was O'Neill, praising it as if he'd memorized all 718 pages. "A loaded gun," said Jimmy Breslin. "There was now a book on impeachment. It wasn't an undefinable topic any more."[11]

NIXON NOW MADE the most damning of a series of political miscalculations. Buoyed by the bonny poll results of early autumn, and preoccupied with the Agnew and Middle East crises, he misread the mood of the country and decided to fire Archibald Cox. The special prosecutor's background, tactics and goals had gnawed at the President all summer. Cox was a Harvard law professor and Kennedy loyalist who had hired other Harvard law professors and Kennedy loyalists for his staff.[12] "If Richardson had searched specifically for the man whom I would have least trusted to conduct so politically sensitive an investigation in an unbiased way, he could hardly have done better than choose Archibald Cox," Nixon said later.

Cox and his zealous staff had gone to work with an obvious aim — to get Richard Nixon — and with an array of prosecutorial tactics that would become so familiar to Americans as a series of "independent" counsels, in collusion with Congress and the media, hounded presidents of both parties over the next twenty-five years. Like his successors, Cox did not limit his investigation to the crime at hand — the burglary and wiretapping of the Democratic headquarters. Instead, he chose a suspect first and then used a nigh-unlimited budget, his team of 150 investigators, lawyers and support personnel, and his broad subpoena power to find a crime. To generate public support for the process, Cox's office deftly leaked to the press: over the summer, the media reported that Cox's team was examining Nixon campaign fundraising; corporate favors; the President's tax returns; and government-financed improvements to Nixon's homes in Florida and California. When Nixon refused to comply with Cox's subpoena for White House tapes, the special prosecutor went to court and challenged the President's claim of executive privilege.

In early July, Nixon wrote an angry note to Haig. "Instead of following up on the Watergate investigation and either bringing indictments or indicating that there is no ground for indictment, he is deliberately going into extraneous issues," Nixon said of Cox. "He cannot be allowed to get away with this . . . as special prosecutor he is derelict in his duties [in conducting] a partisan political vendetta." Two weeks later, Haig warned Richardson that the "boss" was very "uptight" about Cox. "If we have to have a confrontation, we will have it," said Haig.[13]

The precipitating event in what came to be known as "the Saturday Night Massacre" took place on October 12, when the U.S. Court of Appeals, by a 5 to 2 vote, ordered the President to obey Cox's subpoena and deliver the tapes to Judge Sirica. It was the same day that Nixon introduced Ford to the nation as his nominee for the now vacant office of vice president, as Israeli and Arab tanks hammered each other in crucial battles on the road to Damascus and deep in the Sinai. Richardson and Haig tried to broker a compromise, which Cox declined. Nixon then ordered Richardson to have Cox drop all further demands for White House tapes and documents. The nightly news reported a "dangerous widening" of the war in the Middle East as the U.S. and Soviet Union accelerated their efforts to ship weapons to the region.

Denying that he was "out to get the President," and worrying aloud that perhaps he was getting "too big for my britches," Cox nonetheless held a press conference on Saturday, October 20, a warm Indian summer day in Washington, to announce that he would continue to press for more tapes. Nixon told Richardson to fire Cox, but Richardson resigned, after the President and his attorney general had a bitter exchange about the duties of true patriots in a time of national crisis. William Ruckelshaus, the deputy attorney general, also resigned. Finally, the solicitor general, Robert H. Bork, agreed to carry out the President's order.

It was a night of staccato news bulletins, high emotion and theatrics. White House press secretary Ron Ziegler summoned reporters at 8:25 P.M. to announce, "The office of the Watergate Special Prosecution Force has been abolished." FBI agents swept in to seal off the special prosecutor's offices and bar his staff from removing their files. The agents stopped Cox's spokesman, Jim Doyle, from taking a copy of the Declaration of Independence out the door. "Just stamp it 'Void' and let me take it home," Doyle told them. On the telephone to Cox, Richardson quoted lines from the *Iliad:* "Now, though numberless fates of death beset us which no mortal can escape or avoid, let us go forward together, and either we shall give honor to one another or another to us."

"Firestorm" is the universal, and accurate, description of what followed. The press, and the populace, erupted in anger. "The country tonight is in the midst of what may be the most serious constitutional crisis in its history," Chancellor told his audience in a special report. Democrats and journalists, in comments that Nixon fairly labeled "frantic, hysterical," compared the President's actions to those of Latin American, Communist or Nazi dictators. At stake, Cox told the nation, was "whether ours shall continue to be a government of laws and not of men." Kissinger was in Moscow, trying to keep the Middle East war from erupting into World War III. Saudi Arabia responded to the U.S. airlift of arms to Israel by announcing that it was cutting off its supply of oil to the United States; the Arabs had played their oil card for the first, and not the last, time.

"It was like a nightmare, or a dream," said Leo Diehl, never a man for hyperbolic metaphor. "Everyone was afraid. In both parties. Christ, you heard Nixon was going to commit suicide, he was going to do this, he was going to do that. Scary." Western Union's offices in the capital were swamped by 30,000 telegrams a day. A loud, continual protest began outside the White House, sparked by a sign-waving man in a Nixon mask and convict's stripes who asked drivers on Pennsylvania Avenue to honk their horns in support of impeachment; it would continue for weeks. "I was taken by surprise by the ferocious intensity," Nixon said later. "For the first time I recognized the depth of the impact Watergate had been having on America; I suddenly realized how deeply its acid had eaten into the nation's grain."[14]

After a White House briefing on the Middle East crisis on October 10, O'Neill had begun to worry about Nixon's mental health. "The President appeared to be very nervous and kept interrupting Kissinger and making silly remarks, such as referring to Kissinger as an American sex symbol and asking him when he would be appearing in the centerfold of *Cosmopolitan,*" O'Neill wrote in his diary. "The Speaker and I later remarked about the President's actions, especially since on this day at 11 A.M. Agnew resigned as vice president."

In the car on the way back to the Capitol, Representative Thomas "Doc" Morgan, a Pennsylvania physician who chaired the Foreign Affairs Committee, told O'Neill "that he thought the President was paranoid."

Years later, O'Neill recalled, "I came back and I called Mike Mansfield and I said, 'Mike, the president acted very very strange this morning. I'm frightened about things and what they are.' "

Mansfield reassured him. "Don't have any worries about it. Haig is in control over there and Haig will take pretty good care so don't worry about any button being pushed," the Senate leader said. "We are watching him very very closely."

O'Neill had been in California for a Democratic candidate's fundraiser on the Friday before the Massacre; he had flown back and was on the Cape for the three-day Veteran's Day holiday, closing up the new cottage for the season, when his phone began to ring on Saturday. He talked to reporters; he talked to Hymel, who conveyed the concerns of Zeifman and Rodino; he talked to Nixon-hating colleagues; and he talked to Albert. The Massacre, and the subsequent storm of outrage, "changed everything for him; the calculation of how this was going to go," Rosemary O'Neill said of her father. "I had been carping about Watergate: 'Nixon has got to be impeached. You have got to get rid of this guy,' " she recalled. That Sunday morning, her father "went into his bedroom; he lay down on the bed and he was figuring the whole thing. And I came in and said, 'What are you doing?' And he said, 'I'm thinking. Get out of here.' " Rosemary was startled. "He very seldom spoke harshly, but he could, when doing something like that, be very tough," she remembered. Albert was in his office that Sunday, and he and O'Neill conducted a conference call with other House leaders. They decided to gear up on impeachment and get Ford confirmed as quickly as possible. O'Neill took a chartered plane from the Cape to Washington on Sunday night. It was obvious that the calculus in the House had shifted, from whether to launch an impeachment inquiry to how it should be done. By Tuesday, 84 representatives had signed their names to resolutions calling for impeachment.

The Massacre revived the move in the Democratic caucus to stall Ford's confirmation; it almost "put Ford on the back burner," O'Neill said later. Albert and his captains quashed that idea at a press conference Tuesday. The House "should not hold the nomination of the Vice President designate hostage," Albert said. In private Albert told Rodino, "There would be riots."[15] The next challenge was to Rodino's claim to conduct the investigation in the Judiciary Committee. As the showdown over the tapes took shape that fall, members of Congress lobbied Albert to establish a select committee, like the Ervin panel, to handle an impeachment inquiry. Some in Congress wanted the glory of serving on such a body; others feared that Rodino wasn't up to the job. The New Jersey congressman was a twelve-term fixture of the House; a

World War II veteran and Democratic regular from the North Ward of Newark who specialized in immigration issues but had played important roles in the passage of civil rights legislation during Manny Celler's long tenure as Judiciary Committee chairman. It was the eighty-six-year-old Celler's age and complacency that had put Rodino in the chairman's seat — the Brooklyn legend had lost touch with his district and was defeated in a party primary in 1972 by one of the new breed of liberals, Representative Elizabeth Holtzman.

Rodino was soft-spoken, impeccably barbered and given to such stylish flourishes as Chesterfield coats, silk ties and elevator shoes. His ethnic background inevitably gave rise to rumors about corruption probes and Mafia dons, though the evidence was worse than flimsy. Rodino's close pal Hugh Addonizio, the congressman who had represented the adjoining district in New Jersey, had been convicted of racketeering and sent to prison in 1970; so had former representative Cornelius Gallagher, from nearby Bayonne. In response to such whispers, Rodino would whip out a letter from former U.S. Attorney and gangland scourge Herbert Stern, who called him "an honest man and a fine public servant." But given the tremendous stakes of an impeachment inquiry, some of Rodino's colleagues remained wary. "All I kept hearing about was Neil Gallagher and Hughie Addonizio," O'Neill recalled.

O'Neill had originally liked the idea of a select committee, but was won over by Albert's logic. Though the Speaker would handpick the Democrats on an ad hoc committee, the Republican House leaders would select the GOP representatives, and choose hard-liners. Albert, meanwhile, was sure to get intense pressure from conservative Democrats, home state newspapers and the Southwest's oil and gas interests to choose Democratic members who were supporters of the President. "When they started the investigation there were Members that didn't want the Judiciary Committee to do it. They wanted the Speaker to appoint an ad hoc committee," O'Neill recalled. "Very wisely, Carl Albert turned them down. Because he immediately was starting to get tremendous pressure." The Speaker dispatched O'Neill to the floor, the cloakroom, the House gym and the Democratic Club at the Congressional Hotel. "Peter is the perfect man for the job," he told his colleagues. "You know, Peter will do a very good job with this."

Rodino and his aides were grateful. "Rodino was seen as an Italian guy with a questionable background," said his chief of staff, Francis

O'Brien. "O'Neill played a big role in the decision to leave it to Rodino."[16]

In his public remarks that week, Albert was cautious and judicious, calling Nixon's actions "unfortunate." As the House convened on the Tuesday after the Massacre, it was left to O'Neill to rise from his seat and fire the opening shot in the impeachment battle. It was his first floor speech on Watergate. "No other President in the history of this nation has brought the highest office in the land into such low repute," O'Neill began. "His conduct must bring shame to us all." O'Neill called the resignations of Richardson and Ruckelshaus "the only course available to honorable men. And of honorable men, this administration has had few enough. Now it is poorer still by two.

"I have never seen such an avalanche of angry telegrams," the majority leader said. "Many people are demanding impeachment. They have suffered patiently through the whole sordid Watergate mess. In the American spirit of fair play and the right to a presumption of innocence, they accepted the arrangement proposed by President Nixon last April — a special prosecutor who would investigate Watergate wherever it might lead and who would make the truth known to the American public. Those were the terms fixed by President Nixon himself. Now he has chosen to violate those terms — deliberately and with premeditation. His act raises serious questions of President Nixon's ability to govern."

Nixon "has left the people no recourse. They have had enough double-dealing. In their anger and exasperation, the people have turned to the House of Representatives," O'Neill said. "It is the responsibility of the House to examine its constitutional responsibilities in this matter."

The House would begin an inquiry into the impeachment of Richard Nixon.[17]

CHAPTER 16

Impeachment

SCORCHED BY the firestorm, Nixon announced that he would release the subpoenaed tapes to Judge Sirica, and accept the appointment of another special prosecutor, Leon Jaworski of Texas. There was word of a Middle East cease-fire, brokered by the Soviet Union and the United States, and the tension in the city seemed to abate. Then, on the morning of October 25, Americans awakened to the news that the White House had ordered the U.S. military, including its nuclear weapons forces, to DEFCON III, a status of high alert and readiness. The Israeli armed forces had regained the upper hand, driving toward Damascus in the north and crossing the Suez Canal to invade Egypt and encircle the Egyptian army in the south. Israel's refusal to honor the cease-fire led to a Soviet ultimatum: if the U.S. did not rein in Israel, Moscow would intervene with its own armed forces.

The congressional leadership was called to the White House, and O'Neill's diary records Nixon's warning to Israel: " 'I told them they'd god-damned better not break the cease-fire, or break the truce, or they'd get nothing from us in the future.' " Given the mood in the city, Nixon's enemies charged that the alert had been staged to distract Americans from Watergate, and the press gave currency to the allegation. "It is a symbol of what is happening to our country that it could even be suggested that the United States would alert its forces for domestic reasons," Kissinger scolded reporters. "It is up to you ladies and gentlemen to determine whether this is the moment to try to create a crisis of confidence in the field of foreign policy as well."

O'Neill was troubled as well. He had heard about the military alert, like many Americans, in his car while driving to work that morning. Returning to the Hill from Nixon's briefing, he took the floor of the House and sought to extinguish suspicion that the White House had staged the alert for political profit. His remarks were categorical.

"The nation at this particular time is going through a very, very serious 24 or 48 hours," O'Neill said. "To my mind there is absolutely nothing political in this matter." He closed by lecturing his fellow Democrats on patriotism. "In time of crisis we stay together," he reminded them. "There is nothing political about what is going on now. It is really a deep and a serious matter."

O'Neill's speech, on a morning fraught with danger, both foreign and domestic, is illustrative of his character. He was new at this — he had been majority leader for less than a year. At a moment when the passion for impeachment ran high in the House, and corrosive innuendo could have given the Democrats further advantage, the call of honor won out. There was, no doubt, a vestige of cold war orthodoxy in O'Neill's decision to speak out: that is what Americans did in his century; at times of crisis they stuck together. But it was also a matter of conscience; a test to be passed and a quietly stirring, decent act.

The U.S. alert did its job; the Soviet intervention was scaled down from 50,000 airborne troops to a few dozen observers. The cease-fire held. Sadat had won his bet. The Egyptians and Israelis began to negotiate, setting off on the path that would bring them to Camp David. But any credit that Nixon deserved for his administration's handling of the war was lost in new furors over the White House tapes. For technical reasons, two of the nine conversations listed on Cox's subpoena had never been recorded, and even Haig admitted that there was a "sinister force" behind an eighteen-minute gap in the tape of a conversation between Nixon and Haldeman from June 20, 1972, the President's first day back in Washington after the Watergate break-in. The "missing tapes" story broke on October 30, the day the Judiciary Committee held its first meeting on impeachment. News of the eighteen-minute gap came on November 15, as Nixon was in the midst of "Operation Candor," a political offensive in which the President invited members of Congress to a series of White House breakfasts, luncheons and cocktail parties to improve his standing on the Hill. On that day, the House voted 367 to 51 on a resolution granting the Judiciary Committee a million dollars to conduct its investigation.

O'Neill led the charge. "Mr. Speaker, it is deplorable that the President should invite Members of Congress to White House luncheons in order to curry favor with his prospective grand jurors," O'Neill said, as Republicans hissed. "It is unbecoming, if not improper, of the President that he should at this time attempt to influence votes." When GOP representatives complained about the cost of the Judiciary Committee's probe, O'Neill shot back: "If it were not for the scandalous action on the part of the administration, it would not cost anything."

For the White House, the flap over the missing tape recordings extended the harmful impact of the Saturday Night Massacre for an additional month and shot Nixon's credibility with Congress, the press and the country. Even lifelong Republicans now believed that Nixon had something to hide, Governor Reagan told the White House. The *Times*, the *Globe* and such sturdy, independent voices of the heartland as the *Denver Post* called for Nixon's resignation. "I am not a crook," Nixon insisted before an audience of newspaper editors. On November 7, in what Timmons called proof of how Nixon's political standing was deteriorating, 33 House members switched sides and helped override his veto of the War Powers Act, which stripped the President's power to deploy U.S. military forces for more than sixty days without congressional approval. It was the first Nixon veto to be overriden by Congress; the House vote took place on the one-year anniversary of his landslide election victory.[1]

As Nixon's presidency tottered over the next nine months, the press took to calling O'Neill "the architect of impeachment." The recognition was proper: from the fall of 1973 until the following summer, O'Neill became a driving force behind the investigation and proposed impeachment of Richard Nixon. "Tip was a very important figure," said deputy whip John Brademas. "I remember strolling around with him at this time and he was very strong. It was clear he was in favor of nailing Agnew, and then nailing Nixon."

Yet the architectural analogy was misleading, for Nixon was the architect of his own impeachment. O'Neill's own preferred metaphor for the House's role in impeachment was that of a grand jury, weighing an indictment in which he played the role of jury foreman: firm in his own convictions but with the nuanced political task of setting a tone, arbitrating disputes, persuading doubters and nudging his fellow jurors toward a verdict.

"I'm responsible to see that the committee goes forward with its assignment, and that it doesn't lose its ardor or its zest. That's one of the duties of the majority leader of the House, to get the program to the House floor," O'Neill said. He began to shed the pretense of objectivity. On November 9, he told reporters in Boston that Nixon should resign and predicted that the President would not finish out his term. He showed journalists a list of twenty-two impeachable offenses that he carried in his wallet, and explained how the President's standing in the Republican cloakroom would crumble once Ford was confirmed. In an off-the-record session with editors and reporters in Buffalo, he spoke darkly about the President's mental health. Participants later remarked how O'Neill had taken on the voice of a "disinterested spectator." It was only in retrospect that they recognized he was going around the country, creating "an environment of inevitability" for Nixon's departure. As he hurried to the House chamber to watch Ford's swearing-in as vice president on December 6, O'Neill was asked why he rushed. "This is an historic event," he replied. "You may not see it happen again — for four or five months."[2]

The White House began to take notice of O'Neill's role. "Mr. O'Neill has decided that he would rather have an issue than the truth," said Nixon aide Ken Clawson, in a set of talking points he circulated among his colleagues on November 16. "It is . . . contrary to the time-honored, American practice of presuming innocence until one has been proven guilty." Nixon himself began to perceive O'Neill as "a very astute, tough, ruthless politician, tending toward demagoguery."

"How can we have impartiality when the whole impeachment operation is being run out of the majority leader's and Speaker's office and the chairman [Rodino] is only running errands?" Representative Harold Froehlich, a Wisconsin Republican, asked on the House floor.

As if he needed it, O'Neill was being prodded by the folks back in Cambridge. "The state was peculiarly anti-Nixon early," Michael Harrington recalled. In the four days after Cox was fired, O'Neill had received 632 letters from his district, running 630 to 2 in favor of impeachment. Two more days passed: the total was 1523 to 8. "Several things should be noted: many of these letters have multiple signatures and most of these seem to have come from people who have never contacted a government official before in their lives," said an accompanying memo from his staff. The ardent Left swung into action, carrying petitions door-to-door. On November 9, O'Neill's old MassPAX nemesis, Jerry Grossman, delivered 30,000 signatures to the majority leader at his Boston office. "We're watching you," shouted one Nixon hater, as O'Neill took his ethnic walk through North Cambridge one morning.[3]

There was snot in the response of Boston's Kennedy wannabes. "He [Nixon] has given us an administration steeped in the second-rate, a two-pairs-of-pants-with-every-suit administration," sneered *Globe* columnist George Frazier. "The awful little things he has perpetrated, the offenses he has committed against aesthetics, like the uniforms of his palace guard. No taste. Never was. Mr. No Taste. Mr. Appalling. Can you imagine how long Jackie would have allowed Martha Mitchell on the premises? Out! Back to where you belong. There's a bus leaving for Little Rock."

Throughout the impeachment saga, O'Neill kept his eye on the prize. There were advantages to a careful, deliberate course, O'Neill confided to John Kenneth Galbraith in November 1973: "There are high hopes when Jerry Ford is confirmed that some of the Republicans who are highly respected within their party may prevail upon the President to resign. This I believe would be in the best interest of the nation."[4]

O'Neill's problem in Washington was the reverse of his challenge at home: if in Cambridge he had to curb rambunction, in the House he had to spur his colleagues on. "Rodino was extremely methodical. He was just very, very slow and it drove O'Neill crazy," Francis O'Brien, Rodino's chief of staff, recalled. As an army veteran and an immigrant's son, Rodino was daunted by the notion of bringing down a President. "You know, once you begin something you can never stop it," he told O'Brien. "It doesn't mean you're going to impeach, but you have to have some end. It can't just be stopped. There is going to be some consequence."

"Nobody knew what the hell that was," O'Brien said. "Everyone was scared of it. There was a natural cautiousness on Rodino's part. O'Neill prodded him."

Rodino had his hands full, as the Judiciary Committee was also conducting its regular business; holding hearings on legislation to establish an independent counsel's office, and working on the confirmation of Jerry Ford. O'Neill could sympathize with Rodino, but grew frustrated when the chairman was slow to take such basic steps as appointing a chief counsel for the impeachment inquiry. It was up to O'Neill to nag and nudge and send Rodino lists of Ivy League deans and law professors and prominent Boston attorneys, all of whom Rodino discarded as partisans or "deadwood." Finally, in a somewhat heated exchange on the House floor, O'Neill gave Rodino a deadline: they had to have a chief counsel in place by the time Congress left town for the Christmas recess. It wasn't until December 20, on the eve of the recess, that Rodino announced that John Doar, who had served with distinction and courage in the Justice Department's civil rights division during the 1960s, would be the committee's special counsel.

Rodino and O'Neill shared a history in the House; an appreciation for backroom politics and the gritty demands of urban precincts, and the sensibilities of ethnic pols. And Rodino owed O'Neill. Redistricting and "white flight" had cut the Italian vote in Rodino's district in half after the 1970 census, and doubled the number of African American voters, giving the Tenth a black majority. When Rodino was challenged by a popular black mayor in 1972, DCCC chairman O'Neill broke with party protocol and intervened in the Democratic primary, raising funds for the incumbent. The Judiciary chairman's reliance on the man he called "Tippy" was compounded by Albert's decision to stay out of the impeachment fray. The Speakership was a constitutional office that required a nonpartisan stance, Albert decided. "I have told the committee I won't take the initiative," Albert told an aide. The White House considered Albert a "silent ally."

"The members didn't go to Carl. The Speaker's office had kind of a sanctity. Your problems were brought to the majority leader. So everybody would be coming in to me: 'We ought to be doing something on impeachment. The American people are calling for impeachment.' And the polls this and the polls that. And I'd go to Peter," O'Neill said.[5]

"Albert and Rodino were very, very hesitant. Scared. They very much felt the weight of history on their backs, in the sense of believing they could get creamed politically for being involved in something like this," said O'Neill's aide Ari Weiss. O'Neill helped the two leaders, and his fellow members, "get over their fears." As more and more House Democrats looked to O'Neill for guidance, the press began to catch on. "It is fair to say now that if Richard Nixon is impeached this year by the House of Representatives, it will be Thomas P. O'Neill, Jr., more than any other man in the House, who will have brought about that result," MacNeil wrote in a file to his editors. On February 4 *Time* put O'Neill on its cover: "The Impeachment Congress," read the headline.

"The man who is charged with guaranteeing the probity of the impeachment steps in the House is hardly a household name. Congressman Tip O'Neill, the majority leader, has always preferred to work behind the scenes during his 21 years on the Hill," *Time* said. "How the question of impeaching the President reaches the floor of the House this session, when, in what form and with what support, are all his duties. They are the sort best executed in the back offices and cloakrooms of the House, where the bargains are struck . . . , where persuasion can take root."

Albert and Rodino now shared O'Neill's inviolable conviction: that any viable impeachment resolution would have to have the support of some House Republicans. After spending part of the Christmas recess with O'Neill in Massachusetts, MacNeil reported to his editors that "the best hope for Nixon now to escape — perhaps the only way — is for the congressional Democrats to give Nixon the chance to argue that this is a partisan, Democratic attack on a Republican president. O'Neill knows this as well as anybody — and he knows also that he, of all members in Congress, is the fellow who, blundering, could most give Nixon his chance to escape by confusing the issue into partisan politics."

In the weeks after the Saturday Night Massacre, O'Neill guessed that there were some 50 House Republicans who would vote for impeachment. A letter from Representative Charles Sandman, the New Jersey Republican who would become one of Nixon's staunchest supporters on the Judiciary Committee, showed why the GOP ranks had fractured. New Jersey held an off-year election in 1973, and Sandman wrote to Republican National Committee chairman George Bush with the results. "Every Republican in New Jersey was severely punished. Thirteen incumbent state senators were defeated. Twenty-five incumbent assemblymen were defeated. Almost every county courthouse fell as did some of the strong municipal leaders," Sandman wrote. "None of this was due to our local issue or any state issue. To the contrary, our candidates were far better than their conquerors, and we were on the strong side of every issue.

"The resignation of the Vice President was the beginning of our great decline. The firing of Cox, followed by the resignations of Richardson and Ruckelshaus, were devastating. The loss of the Watergate tapes was the crowning blow," Sandman wrote.[6]

In his State of the Union speech in January, the President told the Congress that "one year of Watergate is enough." Bill Timmons urged his boss to take advantage of the budget process "when there is strong congressional interest in pork projects. These hometown goodies are most important to many. . . . This is not the time to save nickels and dimes!" Jerry Ford issued a challenge to the Democrats: hold an impeachment vote by spring, or plead guilty to extending the nation's ordeal for partisan gain. The White House, Bryce Harlow advised, needed to make the argument that "everyone's fed up with it and the country can't stand it much longer . . . so make your committee move quickly with the impeachment inquiry. Get this over with, one way or the other."

O'Neill responded to Nixon's counteroffensive by promoting a solution that many a worried Republican found appealing, particularly after Ford was confirmed as vice president. On January 21, the day that Congress returned from its winter break, O'Neill told newsmen that "it would be in the best interest of the nation" if Nixon resigned, and pointedly added, "It's the job of Republicans to advise the President." Dangling the elements of a deal, O'Neill said he would cosponsor legislation to grant the President immunity from criminal prosecution if that was what it would take to get Nixon to leave office.

"There is speculation on Capitol Hill that Tip O'Neill is pulling the strings behind the House Judiciary Committee and that the Democrat's strategy is to force a confrontation quickly on the President's tapes and papers, contempt citation and impeachment," Timmons wrote Haig on March 8.

"I knew that with the opposition worrying, they'd put in their first team and believe me they did," Nixon said in his memoirs. "They gave the job to Tip O'Neill. He was the majority leader. Now I've known every Speaker since World War II including Sam Rayburn, one of the great ones. I would say that Tip O'Neill is certainly one of the ablest, but without question he is the most ruthless and most partisan . . . we have had in my lifetime. The only time he's bipartisan is when it will serve his partisan interests. He plays hardball, he doesn't know what a softball is. So under the circumstances when I heard that he was taking over shaping up the Democrats I knew that we were in trouble."[7]

THOUGH THE WHITE HOUSE attributed such behind-the-scenes magic to O'Neill, it was hard to see it in the initial performance of the Judiciary Committee. By early March, the number of lawyers and support personnel on the committee's impeachment staff exceeded 100, and they had almost spent their million dollars. But internally, the committee was divided, and the staff had little to show for its efforts. "Tip spent a lot of time with Rodino, sitting him down, giving him courage. There was a lot of hand-holding on the decision whether or not to subpoena the President of the United States. Tip played a big role," said Francis O'Brien. "Rodino and O'Neill would go to the Capitol and talk for hours. O'Neill was a center of strength for him. There were a lot of dark times. There were many days and nights of fear."

Nixon's contribution was more tangible. On April 29, the President appeared on national television with a stack of blue notebooks embossed with the gold presidential seal, and announced that he was turning over 1,300 pages of transcripts from 46 tapes to the Judiciary Committee. The move backfired, awfully. The public was fascinated by the opportunity to eavesdrop on a President and his aides. Newspapers and wire services published huge verbatim supplements; two paperback editions sold 3 million copies in a week. And few Americans liked what they heard: the raw, profanity-strewn, cynical exchanges of professional politicians, and in the Oval Office. "Sheer flesh-crawling repulsion. The back room of a second-rate advertising agency in a suburb of hell," wrote columnist Joseph Alsop. Senator Hugh Scott of Pennsylvania, the Republican Senate leader, derided the taped conversations as "deplorable, disgusting, shabby, immoral." New words and phrases muscled their way into the American vocabulary. "Expletive deleted." "Stonewall." "Modified limited hang-out." One statement by Nixon to Mitchell would prove particularly memorable: "I don't give a shit what happens. I want you all to stonewall it, let them plead the Fifth Amendment, cover-up, or anything else, if it'll save it — save the plan."

The damage was grievous. The committee subpoenaed more tapes. "This thing is hemorrhaging terribly," Pat Buchanan wrote to Haig. Leading Republicans in the House and Senate joined the chorus urging Nixon to resign. "The political foundation of Richard M. Nixon's presidency seemed to split apart beneath him in the second week of May," *Congressional Quarterly* reported. In early June, the White House was rocked again by reports that Jaworski's grand jury had secretly named Nixon an "unindicted co-conspirator."[8]

O'Neill told reporters he was "shocked, chagrined and ashamed as an American citizen," when he saw what was in the transcripts. Now, as the Judiciary Committee reviewed Doar's compendium of the facts, O'Neill served as the envoy between the committee members and the Democratic majority. It was a delicate task. Though House chairmen like Rodino were given great leeway to run their committees, impeachment was too big an issue and the stakes too high for the party leaders not to play a supervisory role. On the other hand, O'Neill's goal of winning bipartisan support would be lost if the House Republicans came to believe that it was all a partisan plot, being choreographed by the majority leader. And so O'Neill did what he did best. For months, he talked. He talked to John Rhodes. He talked to Jack Brooks. He talked to Jerry Zeifman. He talked to Carl Albert. He talked in the House restaurant at breakfast. He talked in the steam bath in the House gym. He talked in hurried exchanges in the well of the House, behind the rail, or in the Speaker's lobby during votes and quorum calls. He talked, in leisurely conversations, while in his customary seat on the right-hand side of the chamber, or over doughnuts or sandwiches in the cloakroom. He talked, with a drink in his hand, at receptions in the Rayburn Building, or during fund-raisers at the Democratic Club. He talked in the House barber shop. On at least one occasion, he talked with Zeifman in the men's room. "It was always informal. They never had meetings; that was not his style. It was the gym or the steam room. I can remember him calling me over there and I'm going in with my clothes in the steam room and he's telling me stuff and I'm walking out soaking wet," Stan Brand recalled.

There was more than a little bluff in O'Neill's performance. Journalist Jimmy Breslin had arrived in Washington in March, and by June had taken up residence at O'Neill's elbow. "All political power is primarily an illusion," Breslin concluded in *How the Good Guys Finally Won: Notes from an Impeachment Summer*. "The ability to create the illusion of power, to use mirrors and blue smoke, is one found in unusual people. They reach their objectives through overstatement or understatement, through silent agreements and, always, the use of language at the most opportune moments.

"When a Tip O'Neill began using the word impeachment on the floor of the House of Representatives, this changed the issue. For he was no frivolous dreamer," Breslin wrote. "This was a bone politician, a man with a word, and he gave great believability to the prospects of impeachment merely by saying it."

Breslin chose to follow O'Neill at the urging of Charles Daly, who had worked the Hill for the Kennedy administration and had a house near the O'Neill cottage on the Cape. "We used to hang out at the same bar, the old Wayside down there," Daly said.

One day, in early 1974, Breslin called Daly and asked him, "Where the hell is O'Neill going with this? Nixon will eat him up."

"Why don't you come up?" Daly suggested.

Breslin and his wife, Rosemary, arrived, played around on Daly's boat and joined the O'Neill clan at Tip and Millie's thirty-third wedding anniversary party that June.

"Will you drink a Manhattan?" O'Neill asked the journalist. Breslin pondered the question. "I asked you, will you drink a Manhattan?" O'Neill persisted. "The reason I'm asking you if you take a Manhattan is that there's no bar here and it takes them too long to bring us back a drink. So I ordered two Manhattans for myself and you can have one of them if you want."

Breslin liked the big man's style. He liked it even more when, after the party ended, O'Neill led the stragglers into the nearby taproom and took the bandstand's microphone.

"My name is Tip O'Neill and I fool around in politics, and I just want to sing a song for my wife, Millie, on our thirty-third wedding anniversary. I want to sing the song I sang to her the day we were married," O'Neill said. He launched into a version of "Apple Blossom Time," and ended with a sandlot cheer: "Millie Miller O'Neill! Yeah!"

Breslin, struck by how Haldeman or Ehrlichman would smirk at such "open, old-fashioned people," leaned over to Daly. "That fucking Nixon doesn't have a chance," he said.

"You got it," Daly told him.

With the admonition "I'll tell you how it happened, but of course you can't use any of this" (which Breslin immediately ignored), O'Neill accepted the writer into his inner circle, took him to the Massachusetts Handicap at Suffolk Downs, for meals with Carl Yastrzemski and other ballplayers when the Red Sox were playing in Baltimore, and to dinner with the gang at Duke Zeibert's or Paul Young's. "Tip spent a lot of time at Duke's with him, let him into the inner sanctum, included him in the family. Rosemary got close to him and Ari [Weiss] went to his house and played with his kid. You know how a reporter can do it: they can pretend to be a good friend of yours. He was Irish and bullshit and you know it all fit," said Gary Hymel.

"Actually we never sat down and had an interview head to head, or anything of that nature. And when I read the book I was amazed that he had all the details," O'Neill recalled. "We went over to see the Red Sox play two or three times over in Baltimore and after the game we'd go out with Yaz and he'd be with us, and then Yaz and the ball players would ask different questions as to what was happening on the impeachment proceedings and I'd give them the answers and Breslin would never write anything down, but he had direct quotes in the book. It was really amazing."

Not so amazing, Breslin recalled later. He was afraid O'Neill would suspect he had digestive problems, as he repeatedly ran to the bathroom to scribble down notes in the privacy of a stall.[9]

O'Neill liked to flash a public opinion survey, taken by pollster William Hamilton, which showed that just 7 percent of the nation's Democrats would support a candidate who opposed impeachment. "Danny, old pal, did you see this poll yet?" he asked Rostenkowski. "A Republican could beat a Democrat in a city if the Republican is for impeachment and the Democrat is against it. Can you imagine that? Say . . . , you represent a city, don't you, Danny?

"Hey, Angie, old pal. Geez, but you really love it down here, don't you?" O'Neill asked Representative Angelo Roncallo, a New York Republican. "To show you how much I think of you, Angie, my door is still going to be open to you next year when you're not going to be in the Congress because of this impeachment."

"It was a bullshit poll. It wasn't worth $30. But they would get scared to death," Breslin recalled. O'Neill also made great use of "the list" he supposedly kept of congressmen ready to vote for impeachment. "He made the list seem ominous, like if you were not on the list you would be beheaded. He spooked them. There was no list. The list was in his head," Breslin recalled. "He rumored them to death."

As Doar's researchers did their work, huge stacks of paper began to arrive in each congressman's office: some bound, some tied in stacks with white string. Ari Weiss would take the material, read it, and prepare a summary. "They would arrive late, these books, and Ari would sit down and start reading. In the meantime we were heading for Duke Zeibert's. Ari would walk out in the morning, no shoes on, same clothes. He had never gone home," Breslin remembered. "And O'Neill would go out on the floor and say to somebody, 'Jesus, did you read page 25 of volume 9?' And they would nod solemnly. Not one of them ever read a page — and O'Neill, the only thing he read is gangster stories in the paper."

In the House dining room, O'Neill gave Breslin a lesson on the politics of impeachment, contrasting Joe Moakley's exuberance (the South Boston congressman had learned that Louise Day Hicks would not challenge him in the Democratic primary that year) with Jimmy Burke's reticence (Burke had a primary opponent).

"James, you look disturbed," O'Neill told Burke.

"Not at all, I'm fine."

"What are you going to be doing this weekend?"

"I've got to go home. I've got a couple of parades I've got to go to."

"When was the last time you went home for a parade?"

"Oh, I don't know."

"It doesn't matter, because this year you'll be carrying the flag the whole time." O'Neill laughed.

"You see what an opponent can do to you?" O'Neill said to Breslin after the morose Burke had left. "I think Jim can win all right. But the money kills you. Cost you a hundred thousand dollars. Now if an opponent you can beat is this disturbing, imagine what it's like to face one that you might not be able to beat. Imagine what it must be like for some of these Republicans. You're facing an election in November and the only issue in the country is how you stand on impeaching the President?"[10]

Most important of all, O'Neill talked to Rodino, who was taking fire as the impeachment timetable slid from winter, to spring, to summer, and toward fall. Many in Washington came to believe, as May swung into June, that Doar and Rodino were missing their moment. As O'Brien ate lunch in the Rayburn cafeteria one day, a reporter from the *New York Daily News* threw a chair at his table and shouted, "You lousy bastard, you are letting him off." Wayne Hays said much the same thing to Doar as they passed each other in the Capitol. With O'Neill's blessing, the pugnacious Jack Brooks and other senior committee members began to put the spurs to Doar and Rodino. "There was a lot of pressure. There were a lot of press stories about it dragging on. And Brooks was a terror," said O'Brien. "Once he took me by my tie and dragged me across my desk to the floor as I just kept saying, 'Yessir. Yessir.' Feelings could not have run higher. There was a lot of conflict between Brooks and Rodino. A lot of conflict. The press had no idea of the depths of animosity."[11]

Brooks would tell O'Neill: "This thing is getting nowhere. It's falling apart. There isn't any movement."

"The investigation dragged and dragged and the members got greatly concerned," O'Neill remembered. The public's patience began to run thin as well. On June 25, Representative Jim Stanton of Ohio came up to O'Neill, who was hearing "confessions" on the House floor, and said, "We need action one way or the other . . . instead of the impeachment being an asset to us, now it's starting to hurt us."

O'Neill sat down next to Rodino.

"When are you going to move?"

"Get off my back," Rodino said.

"Get off your back? I got 240 guys on my back. When are you going to move?"

The next day, Rodino rebuked O'Neill for interfering in the affairs of a committee chairman, but handed him a timetable for completing the impeachment process.[12]

Despite their mutual frustration, O'Neill and Rodino were colleagues of long standing, and drew closer as they tugged and tusseled over how best to proceed. Rodino, who as a younger man had worked for a newspaper, written an unpublished novel and peddled songs on Tin Pan Alley, would say, "Tip, I should have been a poet — it would have been so much easier." But O'Neill never lost his respect for the man of whom, after it was all over, he would say: "He has done more to preserve the integrity of our constitutional process than anyone else in our nation's history."

"I got on Peter's back and he resents it. He should," O'Neill told Breslin and his other dining companions at Duke Zeibert's on the night of the "Get off my back" exchange. "When the rest of us are all forgotten, Peter is the guy who is going to be in history."

"Peter Rodino never took his suit jacket off — never. You could never meet a more polite man," O'Brien recalled. But behind that soft-spoken demeanor, "you couldn't move him. There were many of these sessions where Tip O'Neill, this large human being, was sitting next to this small man with perfect hair — threatening him! Rodino would come back and make some minor changes to appease him.

"He would come back and all he would say to us was, 'You know, this process cannot be rushed.' And in the end they let him do it at his pace," said O'Brien.

"But to be fair," he added, "if they had left him alone, we'd still be doing it."[13]

WORD OF O'NEILL'S actions reached the White House. Timmons informed the President that O'Neill was "putting pressure on Rodino which Rodino was passing along to Doar to do something to get impeachment back on the track," Nixon recalled. In his diary the President wrote: "I would have to say that O'Neill's bunch is going to be able certainly to get a majority vote out of the committee and a very damn close vote in the House." Nixon now rated the chance of impeachment as "very possible."

Rodino knew that his position made him a target. He had electronics experts come down from Newark regularly to sweep his phones. There was a tense moment at the end of June when "it became very serious to Peter. We had knowledge and information they were going over Peter with a fine-toothed comb seeing if there was anything in the woodwork and the background that they could humiliate and insult and bring him down," O'Neill recalled later.

"Peter, there is an awful lot going on. There is nothing that can come out of the woodwork on us, is there?" O'Neill asked Rodino.

"Absolutely nothing," Rodino replied.

Breslin asked O'Neill: "That's all you had to say to him?"

"Yes," O'Neill replied. "We had to believe each other. He knew what we were into as well as I did."[14]

AS THE JUDICIARY COMMITTEE prepared to vote, both sides focused their attention on three southern Democrats and a half dozen moderate Republicans. If they voted for impeachment, the bipartisan verdict of the Judiciary Committee would likely swing the House; if they opposed impeachment, the process would be seen as a partisan vendetta. Pat Buchanan urged Nixon to "polarize the sides politically" with vetoes and anti-busing rhetoric. White House aide Ken Khachigian told Haig on July 18, "Now is the time to draw the partisan lines . . . speculate on the roles of Tip O'Neill and Carl Albert. Hit the orchestration of the partisan aspects here.

"All that we do in the next few days must have one purpose and only one purpose: to discredit the work product of the House Judiciary Committee — to show that it has no impeachment case — that it is partisan motivated — that its procedures regularly denied due process to the president — and that the impeachment agony must rest on their shoulders," said Khachigian. "We cannot allow the articles of impeachment to be enshrined in respectability and legitimacy. They are producing a bastard product of dubious parentage conceived in clandestine, backroom trysts."

O'Neill interceded on several occasions when partisan squabbling broke out in the committee over Doar's attempts to bar Nixon's lawyers from the hearing room, to limit the number of witnesses that the Republicans could call and to circumscribe the questions that members of the committee could ask. When, in a rare lapse, Rodino told reporters in late June that the three southern Democrats were in the impeachment fold with their more liberal colleagues, O'Neill gave Rodino a harsh dressing-down and scrambled to soothe the feelings of the irate trio, whose conservative constituencies had been riled by the story. But aside from the reassurance he provided to the three southern Democrats, O'Neill largely gave way to Rodino when it came to assembling the bipartisan coalition that would vote on the impeachment resolutions. It was Rodino who courted Representative William Cohen, the Republican from Maine, and Representative Walter Flowers, the Democrat of Alabama, and urged them to assemble like-minded members of what came to be known as the "fragile coalition." As the day of the impeachment debate neared, Flowers was walking down the corridor in the Rayburn Building when, turning to Representative Thomas Railsback, a Republican from Illinois, he said, "I have a couple of guys. Why don't you get your guys and we'll get together and talk about it." As so often proved the case in the House of Representatives, it was easier to jump off a cliff holding hands with others than to make the leap alone. The three Democrats — Flowers

Thomas P. O'Neill Jr. as a baby in his mother's lap, with brother, Bill, and sister, Mary, behind them. (*Courtesy of the O'Neill family*)

Tip, age five. (*Courtesy of the O'Neill family*)

At Boston College.
(*Courtesy of the O'Neill family*)

DEMOCRATS RE-ELECT

THOMAS P.

O'NEILL, Jr.

REPRESENTATIVE

WARDS 9 - 10 - 11 CAMBRIDGE

PRECINCTS 1 - 2 WATERTOWN

PRIMARIES: TUESDAY, SEPT. 17, 1940

74 (over)

1940 campaign card. (*Courtesy of the O'Neill family*)

HE SERVED WELL

IMPORTANT BILLS INTRODUCED OR SUPPORTED

(1) Reducing Old Age Assistance from 70 to 65 years of age.
(2) Veterans Hospitalization Bill.
(3) Opposed the Sales Tax.
(4) Opposed the Cigarette Tax.
(5) Voted for all Unemployment Relief Measures.
(6) Voted for all Bills to reduce power and light rates.

ENDORSED BY LABOR

COMMITTEES:

Committee on Education
Committee on Power and Light

EDUCATION:

St. John's Grammar School
St. John's High School
Boston College

RE-ELECT

Representative

THOMAS P.

O'NEILL, JR.

74 ORCHARD STREET

A Proven Democrat

Three generations of O'Neills. Thomas P. O'Neill Sr. with his son Tip, the newly elected Speaker of the Massachusetts House; Tip's wife, Millie, and children (left to right), Tommy, Rosemary and Susan. (*Courtesy of the O'Neill family*)

State representative Tip O'Neill and James Michael Curley. (*Courtesy of the O'Neill family*)

President Eisenhower meets with new members of Congress, 1953. O'Neill is at far right in front row. Edward Boland is second from left in front row. (*Courtesy of the O'Neill family*)

Freshman congressman Tip O'Neill and new senator John F. Kennedy stand behind O'Neill's family and friends at the old Capitol subway in 1953. (*Courtesy of the O'Neill family*)

St. Patrick's Day with (left to right) entertainer Phil Reagan, Congressman Mike Kirwan, Speaker Sam Rayburn, O'Neill and Congressman Edward Boland. (*Courtesy of the O'Neill family*)

Tip with JFK in 1961, joined by (left to right) Congressmen Hugh Addonizio, Wayne Hays, Peter Rodino and James Roosevelt. (*Courtesy of the O'Neill family*)

Tip O'Neill and Lyndon Johnson. (*Courtesy of the O'Neill family*)

President Nixon meets with congressional leaders (left to right) Senator Hugh Scott, majority leader O'Neill, Speaker Carl Albert, Senator Mike Mansfield and minority leader Gerald Ford. (*National Archives*)

Tip O'Neill, Les Arends, Carl Albert, John Volpe and Hale Boggs in 1971. (*Courtesy of Boston College*)

Democratic whip Tip O'Neill with Leo Diehl (third from left) and members of the Massachusetts congressional delegation in the early 1970s. (*Courtesy of the O'Neill family*)

John McCormack and Tip O'Neill. The photograph is inscribed "To Speaker Tom O'Neill, with my deep friendship and respect. John McCormack." *(Courtesy of the O'Neill family)*

O'Neill, Senator Edward M. Kennedy and President Jimmy Carter at the dedication of the John F. Kennedy Library in 1979. (*Courtesy of the O'Neill family*)

Speaker Thomas P. O'Neill Jr. at the Reagan White House. (*Courtesy of the Ronald Reagan Library*)

O'Neill welcomes the new President at Reagan's birthday party, February 6, 1981. Nancy Reagan is at right. (*Courtesy of the Ronald Reagan Library*)

O'Neill aides Chris Matthews, Gary Hymel and Kirk O'Donnell in 1981. (*Courtesy of Chris Matthews*)

Daniel Rostenkowski, O'Neill and Reagan. (*Courtesy of the Ronald Reagan Library*)

Reagan, George Bush and O'Neill. (*Courtesy of the Ronald Reagan Library*)

Tempers flying: Reagan and O'Neill. (*Courtesy of the Ronald Reagan Library*)

O'Neill family portrait, with friends, Harwichport, 1984. Tommy is in front row with Tip and Millie. Kip (second from left), Susan (fourth from left), Michael (fifth from left) and Rosemary (far right) are standing behind them. (*Courtesy of the O'Neill family*)

The Shirtsleeve Summit, 1985. (*Courtesy of the Ronald Reagan Library*)

Reagan inscribed this photograph: "Dear Tip—Just two Irish smiles on the day the Anglo-Irish Agreement was announced. Best Regards, Ron." (*Courtesy of the O'Neill family*)

Mikhail Gorbachev and Tip O'Neill, April 10, 1985. (*Courtesy of the O'Neill family*)

Congressmen Silvio Conte, Dan Rostenkowski, O'Neill and Bob Michel at a Moscow meeting, April 1985. (*Courtesy of the O'Neill family*)

Reagan appears at O'Neill's farewell dinner, March 17, 1986. (*Courtesy of the Ronald Reagan Library*)

Tip O'Neill in Ireland, 1985. (*Thomas Quinn*)

was joined by Representatives Raymond Thornton of Arkansas and James Mann of South Carolina — found Railsback, Cohen and two other Republicans waiting for them in Railsback's office the next morning, July 23. They agreed that Nixon had undermined the Constitution by abusing power and obstructing justice in the Watergate cover-up, and deserved to be impeached.

Timmons conveyed the bad news to Nixon. "Wilbur Mills was said to be getting to his fellow Arkansan Thornton, while Rodino was reportedly having private sessions with Flowers, and O'Neill was rumored to be putting the strong arm on Mann," Nixon wrote. "The political consensus had already been reached and the political consensus was to impeach." Nixon phoned George Wallace, to ask the governor to intercede with Flowers. Wallace told Nixon he would pray for him, but that he didn't think it was proper to intercede. "Well, Al," Nixon told Haig after hanging up the phone, "there goes the presidency."

The Judiciary Committee began its debate on the evening of July 24, the day the Supreme Court ruled that Nixon must relinquish the White House tapes. In an extraordinary performance, Rodino and his colleagues rose to the challenge. The world was treated to a contemporary validation of the revolutionary ideal that Madison, Jefferson and the rest had proposed two hundred years before: that the power to govern flows from the consent of the governed, and that an enlightened people will invariably triumph over leaders who trifle with the rights of man and the rule of law. Barbara Jordan, a black congresswoman from Texas, noted that though she and her kinsmen had not been included in "we, the people" in 1787, "my faith in the Constitution is whole, it is complete, it is total, and I am not going to sit here and be an idle spectator to the diminution, the subversion, the destruction of the Constitution." And Jim Mann of South Carolina, whose district had given 79 percent of its votes to Nixon in 1972, memorably warned, "If there be no accountability, another President will feel free to do as he chooses. But the next time there may be no watchman in the night."[15] The country was captivated. The White House estimated that between 35 and 40 million Americans watched as two articles of impeachment were passed with the votes of the southern Democrats and a half dozen or more Republicans; a third article was passed by a narrow, more partisan margin. O'Neill's office began to make preparations for the House debate. But at the White House, Nixon's lawyers and aides were listening to a tape that the President had told them was "a problem."

The tape was from June 23, 1972. On it, Haldeman had complained to Nixon that the FBI was successfully tracing the money found on the Watergate burglars. Haldeman wanted Nixon's approval to call in the CIA, and have the agency falsely inform the FBI that the money trail led to a U.S. intelligence operation vital to national security. "Call them in. Good. Good deal. Play it tough. That's the way they play it and that's the way we are going to play it," Nixon said. It was "the smoking gun," that proved Nixon had obstructed justice.

As Haig and Nixon discussed the incriminating tape on July 31, Jerry Ford was scheduled to fly to Massachusetts and play in the Pleasant Valley Golf Classic, a charity golf tournament near Worcester. O'Neill and a handful of pals from the Hill — Dan Rostenkowski, Les Arends, Silvio Conte and Timmons — waited for the vice president on Air Force II. Naturally, the talk turned to the upcoming debate.

"Tip, you don't have the votes to impeach," Arends said.

"Not only do we have the votes there; you people haven't been paying attention. You haven't been counting," said O'Neill. "Because he's going to be impeached [and] he's going to lose in the Senate."

The vice president's entourage arrived and, because the press was sure to ask whether they had talked about impeachment on the way, Ford's aides asked the congressmen not to raise the topic. The vice president then came aboard, and apologized for being late. His wife, Betty, had summoned him to the new vice presidential mansion to consult with the decorators.

"Why are you worrying about that, Jerry? You'll never live a day in that house anyhow," O'Neill said.

O'Neill's sense of satisfaction swelled as he watched Arends summon Ford into a private onboard compartment and then, through the flimsy walls, heard Arends warn the vice president, "Tip says that Nixon's done; that they've got the votes. He's got the votes in the Senate."

"I don't believe that," said Ford.

"You know Tip. He can count," said Arends.

O'Neill and Ford played in the same foursome as professional golfer Dave Stockton and Richard Hanselman, a Samsonite executive. Ford wore a gold shirt and Hush Puppies golf shoes. O'Neill wore a maroon shirt and pants and a narrow-brimmed golf hat, and chewed on a cigar;

he had stocked his bag with eight woods and thirteen irons, far in excess of what the rules allowed. To the delight of the 15,000 people in attendance, Ford's opening shot hit a stand of trees. But Ford was thrilled by the warm reception he got in Massachusetts that day, and photographers caught him with his arm around O'Neill's waist, as the majority leader patted him on the back. The photograph was carried by newspapers across the country; few thought it boded well for Nixon.[16]

On August 1, after he returned to Washington from Pleasant Valley, Ford was summoned to the White House by Haig and told to be prepared to assume the presidency. On August 5, the White House released the transcript of the June 23, 1972, tape. O'Neill received his copy on the House floor, where he read it aloud to a small group of colleagues who had gathered around, and then took it to his office. "Well, here it is," he said. "Confession is good for the soul, but it doesn't save the body."

A delegation of Republican elders — minority leader John Rhodes and Senators Barry Goldwater and Hugh Scott — called at the White House and urged Nixon to resign. "Everybody climbed aboard the good ship Let's Get Rid of Nixon," said Leonard Garment. "He could have said various things — impeach me, come and get me — but for that mixture of a kind of sense of the office and the idealistic side of the crummy, bumpkin, frustrated, starred side. The witch was for burning. Who knows, he may have even wanted to be gotten. First president to resign. First in the heart of his enemies. First one to make his comeback."

Rhodes came to O'Neill and asked, "Tip, can we censor him?"

"Too late. The votes aren't there. There is nothing you can do about it," O'Neill replied.

On August 7, Timmons reported to Nixon that the Democratic leadership had "absolutely no interest in pursuing any kind of criminal action against the President should he elect to resign." O'Neill's deal was still available. That night, Nixon told his family the end was at hand, and on August 9, he resigned.[17]

O'Neill had received the news in a phone call from Rhodes at mid-morning on August 8. He spent part of the morning trying to persuade Millie to come down to Washington for Jerry Ford's inauguration. Rosemary had been deputized.

"Mother," she said over the phone, "Dad says you better get dressed and come down here. He's got a room for you at the Jefferson."

"A suite," someone called out.

"A nice suite," Rosemary told her mother. She hung up and told her father, "Dad, she says she has to drive to Cambridge to get a dress. She doesn't have any with her at the Cape. . . . She'll be on the first plane in the morning."

Ford called that afternoon, shortly before 3 P.M.

"Tip, I want you at my swearing-in," he said.

"Are wives invited, Jerry? The reason I'm asking is that I've already told Millie to pack and get down here."

"Wives were not invited," Ford said, "but they are now."

O'Neill read Ford the brief statement he was about to make to the press, promising cooperation if the new President treated the Congress with candor and respect. He warned Ford not to appoint a Democrat as vice president. "The country doesn't work that way." There was a moment of silence. "Christ, Jerry, isn't this a wonderful country?" O'Neill said. "Here we can talk like this and you and I can be friends, and eighteen months from now I'll be going around the country kicking your ass in."

Ford laughed. "That's a hell of a way to speak to the next President of the United States."[18]

O'Neill was not invited down to the White House with Albert, Rhodes and other congressional leaders to get the news from Nixon's own mouth. "I want you to know, Mr. President, that I have nothing to do with this whole resignation business," Albert blurted out as Nixon entered the room. "I understand, Carl," Nixon said. From there, the President moved to a meeting in the Cabinet Room at the White House, where many of his old congressional colleagues had gathered. Hearing Arends sobbing, Nixon broke into tears as well. "I just hope that I haven't let you down," he said.

O'Neill remained in his office, in shirtsleeves, with Leo Diehl, Breslin and other friends and family, and watched Nixon's speech to the nation that night on television. "This is not a banana republic. The rest of the world will look on with wonder at our orderly transition of power," O'Neill told the press afterward. "The Founding Fathers — such wisdom they had." But there was little glee. O'Neill told friends he was hurt by the congratulations of a Democratic congressman who approached him and admiringly asked, "How does it feel to bring down a President?"

Ford took the oath of office the next day at noon, then told his countrymen, "Our long national nightmare is over.

"Our Constitution works; our great Republic is a government of laws and not of men. Here the people rule," Ford said.

On their way to dinner on the night of Nixon's speech, O'Neill had been struck by much the same thought. As his car passed the White House, he and his companions noticed that there was only one motorcycle policeman directing traffic; no tanks, no mobs, no ranks of riot squads. *In America, we change the government with one cop,* Jimmy Breslin thought.

"Isn't this the damnedest thing you ever saw?" O'Neill said. "You couldn't imagine this."[19]

WHEN NIXON ANNOUNCED his resignation, O'Neill tried to console Breslin, who had come to Washington to witness the House debate on impeachment, and a Senate trial.

"Well, Jimmy, there's no book apparently, because the resignation has taken place. There's no impeachment in the House," O'Neill said.

"Oh," said Breslin, "I've got a few thoughts on my mind."[20]

When published in the spring of 1975, *How the Good Guys Finally Won* was a critical and commercial success, boosting the reputations of its subject and author.

"There will be other, more definitive accounts of impeachment, although none could be more romantic," wrote Mary McGrory in the *Washington Star*. Yet for all the book's blarney, she wrote, "there's no question that O'Neill smelt the rat early, spoke the word impeachment first, conditioned the nervous members to the sound of it, goaded Peter Rodino to get a counsel, prodded him to set a deadline and worked the cloakrooms like a day laborer when the members were snarling and whining about the burden of it all."[21]

The most noteworthy passage conveyed Breslin's assessment of O'Neill's character. "If you see in a man and say of a man only that he is a big, overweight, cigar-smoking, whisky-drinking, back-pounding Boston politician, then somewhere over the years the man himself, somewhere deep down under the winces, could begin believing some of this himself," Breslin wrote. O'Neill suffered from his insecurities, resented the fact that his looks and background would never allow him to reach heights like Jack Kennedy or dazzle the Harvard faculty.

"So much of his life has demanded caution, waiting in line behind others, that he can often make going along sound like accomplishment,"

Breslin went on. "His talent was betrayed by the life he had lived." What redeemed O'Neill, and helped save the nation when it most needed a 'good guy' to step forward, was his generous, genuine heart. The old pol was more than the caricature.

"For if you see Tom O'Neill as he is," said Breslin, "there is coming into the room a lovely spring rain of a man."[22]

CHAPTER 17

Reform

O'Neill was in Cambridge on September 8; having just returned from Sunday Mass, he was getting ready to go play golf, when the phone rang on Russell Street. "Tip? Jerry," the caller said. "I'm calling to tell you: I talked to Mike and I talked to Carl and I'm telling you I am going to pardon the President."

"You're not asking my advice."

"The decision has already been made."

"You're never going to get reelected if you do that," O'Neill told his friend.

"Listen, I can't run the government the way it is and I think he has suffered," said Ford. "I have got to get it behind me."

"Jerry . . . , I hope you didn't make a deal."

"Tip, I give you my word I made no deal."[1]

At heart, O'Neill agreed with Ford's decision. At a local political event that evening, he joked to Walter Sullivan that the two of them were the only ones in the room who didn't want Richard Nixon put on trial. But for political reasons — the liberals in his district and across the country raised hell about the pardon — he had to condemn it.

"It is one thing to pardon someone after the prosecution has run its course," said O'Neill, in the statement that his office released. "But in this case we see one President pardoning a former one before all the facts are known to the American public." Historical scholarship, and the release of Nixon's tapes, would confirm the parameters of the former President's sins, but in the fall of 1974 the Democrats feared that Nixon and his loyalists would make the claim that he had been railroaded from office.

Immediately upon taking office, Ford had shuddered at the "degrading spectacle" of a former President in the dock, and at the endless media attention that would salt the wounds of Watergate. He was also touched by Julie Nixon's appeals on her father's behalf. "Can you imagine, as some people said to me, 'Why don't you wait until he is indicted? Why don't you wait until he is convicted? Why don't you wait until he has an appeal?' Those headlines would have been across every newspaper for my two and a half years," said Ford. "It would have been the most undercutting, disruptive thing. If you were going to do it, you had to do it then, period."

It was a merciful decision, which cost Ford dearly. His honeymoon ended at thirty days, and his rating in the Gallup Poll dropped 22 points. The Democratic leadership in the House was afraid that the country might be facing another failed presidency. When Ford offered to go to Capitol Hill and tell Congress and the nation why and how he had acted, Albert, O'Neill and Rodino gave him their full support. They drew the ground rules for his October 17 appearance before a Judiciary subcommittee as favorably as possible. Ford's show of candor stifled talk that he had made a deal to trade a pardon for the presidency. But the political fallout lingered. Three weeks later, on Election Day, the nation extracted its price from the Republicans, and the GOP lost 43 seats in the House. Many other incumbents, of both parties, had decided to retire. All told, there would be 92 fresh faces — 75 new Democrats and 17 new Republicans — in the Ninety-fourth Congress.[2]

"The group that came in 1974, the Watergate babies, were a bunch of mavericks," said Jim Wright. "All of them had run on reform platforms intent on changing anything and everything they found that needed changing." Indeed. The turbulence of the sixties, the Vietnam War and the years of Watergate had led millions of young Americans to abandon the political process and turn inward — to the wide-tie, double-knit, mood-ring, disco-dancing days of the 1970s, the "Me Decade." But those who persisted in Democratic politics were highly committed activists who had cut their teeth on civil rights, the antiwar movement or the McCarthy, Kennedy and McGovern campaigns and now viewed Washington as a capital in need of purging.

"These youthful, able, talented people — they didn't like the Establishment, they didn't like Washington. They didn't like the seniority system. They didn't like the closeness of it and they came down here with new ideas. They wanted to change the Congress of the United States; which they did," O'Neill said.

The old politics had fallen into disrepair and disrepute. The Democratic members of the class of 1974 — and 1970 and 1972 and 1976 — were prototypes of a new kind of senator and representative. They were comfortable with their ideological allies in a press corps that was undergoing similar changes, conversant in the politics of televised imagery and campaign commercials and generally beholden to few party leaders. They were independent political entrepreneurs, who raised their own funds, hired professional advisers and reached out to the voters via direct mail appeals, single-issue interest groups and radio and TV advertising. "About 50 percent of these people had never served in public life before," said O'Neill. "When I came to Congress the average man had been to the legislature, had been a mayor or district attorney or served on the local city council, and grew up knowing what party discipline was about. These new people came in as individuals.

"They got elected criticizing Washington," O'Neill said. "They said, 'Hey, we never got any help from the Democratic Party. We won on our own and we are going to be independent.' That started in 1974 and it broke the discipline." For the majority leader, who hoped to rise in two or four years to be Speaker, the new breed posed a serious test to even his vaunted adaptability. O'Neill had risen through the ranks by cultivating friendships and building relationships over twenty years of service in the House. Now half his fellow Democrats had served three terms or less. They were eager to dump O'Neill's card-playing buddies from the ranks of committee chairmen. Moreover, the sudden flux in the regular order offered an opportunity to a shrewd strategist who could forge an alliance between the class of 1974 and their older liberal counterparts in the Democratic Study Group; an ambitious man who had no qualms about shoving his elders off the leadership ladder; someone who had already earned a place in the hearts of the Watergate babies by channeling funds to their campaigns. His name was Phil Burton, and he would emerge in 1974 and 1975 as O'Neill's final obstacle on the path to the Speaker's office. For more than two years, O'Neill and Burton waged a gritty, often nasty war in the cloakroom for the ultimate House prize. "Tip really felt that Burton was his biggest threat," said Representative Jack Murtha. Every vote, every friendship, every long-standing jealousy, unforgotten grievance or parliamentary maneuver became potential grist in their political struggle. When it was over, O'Neill would stand alone above the vanquished titans whose political standing in the House of Representatives had been destroyed in the course of the battle: Phil Burton, Wilbur Mills, Wayne Hays, Dick Bolling, Frank Thompson, Eddie Hebert, Wright Patman. It was an arduous task and no sure thing. In the last fierce push from majority leader to Speaker, O'Neill's gifts and flaws and bloodless ambition were put on stark display. Such were the changes wrought by the class of 1974. "It was brutal, I tell you, absolute murder," O'Neill himself said.[3]

The leadership's wary regard for the newcomers was best captured by Carl Albert. "This was a group that could do some plowing," he recalled. "It was also a group that could kick over the traces." The Democratic caucus was the field of conflict. John McCormack had made one significant concession when defeating Mo Udall in the 1969 Speaker's race: he agreed to schedule monthly meetings of the caucus. Sam Rayburn hated the notion of a regular caucus. Knowing the ideological gulf that existed between the northern and southern wings of his party, he preferred to broker differences in the privacy of his office. Yet the caucus had considerable latent power under the party rules, and so was a most opportune place for the so-called "national" Democrats — who on many issues could claim a majority of the majority — to vent their deep-seated differences with the southern barons. Richard Conlon, the Democratic Study Group's staff director, joined Representatives Donald Fraser of Minnesota and James O'Hara in devising a strategy of sequential change. Representative Thomas Foley of Washington likened it to slicing a salami, with a slice or two taken at the start of every Congress.

Both Burton and O'Neill were early advocates of congressional reform. Both had sincere reasons to try and dismantle the seniority system, which they identified as an obstacle to their goal of aiding the working guy, and society's sick and downtrodden: a DSG study in 1969 showed that a third of the Democratic chairmen exceeded the average Republican in opposing the Democratic Party's programs on the House floor. Burton was a skilled and tireless advocate, always in search of a way around, or through, the resistance put up by the southern bulls. O'Neill, meanwhile, had been cast by the Massachusetts system — in which strong leaders exercised their mandate, controlled legislative committees and could dump a balking state rep from a prize panel if he did not toe the line. As far back as 1965, O'Neill had told his colleagues on the Rules Committee that the House leadership should "have more control over the members in the party" and "a chairman ought to be able to be removed, and the Speaker should have enough power to be able to put the administration's program through." In a January 1967 reply to a Cambridge constituent, O'Neill agreed that "the seniority system should be abolished."

And long before the arrival of the class of 1974, O'Neill and Burton concluded that the reform impulse must be factored into any of their strategies for advancement; if properly reined and ridden, the desire for change might well propel a man to power. Months before he was chosen as whip, and while his patron John McCormack still ruled the House, O'Neill had established his bona fides with the reformers through his dealings with David Cohen and Common Cause, and his alliance with Conlon (who had come on as DSG director in 1968) in the battle against unrecorded teller voting. "I remember wondering, could we persuade Tip to do this?" said Linda Kamm, the DSG legislative director under Conlon. "It was going out on a limb for him, taking on the chairmen, and was regarded more as an act of courage than of political opportunism."

"I suspect it was both," said O'Neill's son Kip. "I would like to say he was motivated by the good of it, but I suspect it was both."[4]

Burton mapped his own path to power through the revived DSG and caucus. He and his liberal cohorts were stymied in 1971 when Albert first embraced, but then abandoned, their proposal that the Democratic whip be elected. Though not seen at the time as a direct Burton versus O'Neill clash (Udall would have been the presumed beneficiary), the episode foretold their future rivalry. O'Neill became whip, and got control of the Democratic Congressional Campaign Committee. Burton just as quickly sought and claimed his own party platform: mounting a vigorous and determined campaign to succeed Fraser as DSG chairman in 1971. If O'Neill's appeal was as a regular who could work with reformers, Burton played the flip side, casting himself as a reformer who could work with the regulars.

As O'Neill was using the DCCC's war chest to win the gratitude of endangered Democrats during the Nixon landslide of 1972, Burton mounted a similar effort from the offices of the DSG. Unlike O'Neill, Burton didn't reserve his $200,000 campaign kitty for incumbents — he looked for liberal challengers like Joe Moakley, Charlie Rose and Colorado's Pat Schroeder, or embattled mavericks like Robert Drinan and Washington's Mike McCormack. "He's got the personality of a Brillo pad," Udall said. "But he gets a lot done." Burton was forty-six in 1972, fourteen years younger than O'Neill and a decade behind him on the seniority list. His hometown of San Francisco was a notorious seat of the sixties counterculture. But along with his die-hard liberal philosophy and irascible nature, Burton brought to Congress a political savvy to make things happen. He had an encyclopedic knowledge of the nation's political terrain and an ability to find common ground among disparate foes.

"He overwhelmed people with knowledge of their districts," said Burton aide Ben Palumbo. "He would study them, and in some cases know more than even the member did. He spent an inordinate amount of time studying the demographics, election results and history of the district until he could say to someone, 'You know, you had a problem with people in that one ward, and this will be for them.' "

In 1969, Burton had single-handedly held a Nixon tax bill hostage and so killed a freeze on aid to dependent children. No coal miners lived in his California district, but Burton bartered northern votes for peanut, tobacco and cotton subsidies in return for southern support of a historic coal mine safety bill, creating in the process a federal compensation program for miners who suffered from black lung disease. He played leading roles in the establishment of the Occupational Health and Safety Administration and in passage of the Supplemental Security Income program, which boosted Social Security payments for aged, blind and disabled Americans. Conlon, a bearded crusader who came from the moralistic tradition of Minnesota liberalism, got over his initial fears about Burton, and the two joined in a formidable collaboration.

• • •

Yet, as invariably is the case in politics, Burton's strengths were his weaknesses. His volcanic passion was not limited to liberal causes; his appetites included unfiltered cigarettes, liquor and women. He had an explosive temper and a crude, profane manner. "I admired him: whatever he was doing was for the good of humanity, and you knew it," said Gary Hymel. "But his personality . . . his bug eyes, talking a mile a minute, and he'd start spitting at you."

"I thought he was a wild man, that he believed in himself more than anything else," said Bolling. "Burton was very physical . . . very much a bully. Very uncouth. I heard all kinds of things about women and when he was drunk. The only person I ever compared him to was LBJ. I had a problem with both for the same reason. Ultimately, they were domineering. They expected you to have a complete willingness to obey. . . . A dictatorial personality." Drinan and other liberal allies remembered dinner parties or strategy sessions that would abruptly break up when Burton, after hours of drinking vodka, erupted in an abrasive, insulting manner. At times Burton's outbursts were calculated — to determine if an opponent or an ally could be intimidated. "Phil loved machinations, finding little wires to make people jump," Udall said.

Burton got along well with Albert, who thought he was "a real operator" if "far out in left field," and "the buddy of the homos and all that stuff." In later years, Albert fondly remembered that Burton "took me around to show what kind of a town San Francisco had become and they had these topless and bottomless stuff [and] wherever we would go everybody would stand up and yell for the congressman." At one joint in North Beach, topless icon Carol Doda slipped into a flimsy robe and joined Burton, his wife, Sala, and Albert at their table. Apparently thinking that Doda was Jewish, Albert told her of his friendship with Golda Meir. Doda turned, puzzled, to Sala. "Who is this little man and why is he talking to me about Golda Meir?" the majestic dancer asked.

But among those whom Burton alienated was O'Neill. "They had words more than once," Stan Brand recalled. "Burton was a guy who would take a drink. I was in the whip's office one night when he just went crazy on Tip in a completely ungentlemanly-like way. He was cursing and screaming about something he didn't like, or wanted done and it had not been done." Hymel remembers another angry exchange between Burton and O'Neill at the bar of the Democratic Club, and how the staff then warned O'Neill to stay away from the place, one of Burton's haunts.

The Massachusetts congressman was no Boy Scout; he patronized bookies, cut deals, liked a drink and, in a private gathering of his pals, could cuss a blue streak. But O'Neill was of the old school when it came to being polite, and mannerly, in public — especially when women were in the room. Billie Larsen, who took notes at leadership meetings for O'Neill, would shrink from the attention when, after her boss let slip a four-letter word, he would interrupt the gathering and apologize to her for his minor use of profanity. "Tip had an old-fashioned rectitude about women. He never liked guys who were screwing around; screwing their secretaries. He did not like women who talked dirty or guys who talked dirty in front of women," said the *Globe*'s David Nyhan.

O'Neill recognized Burton's talent, and devotion to liberal ideals. "The two brightest individuals I ever saw in Congress were Bolling and Wilbur Mills, for sheer ability. The next three were Foley, Burton and Brademas for knowledge of what was going on in the House and the depth with regards to issues and knowledge of legislation. They were masters," said O'Neill. "The most abiding Democrat, the one who the Democratic Party was most in depth in his heart and mind, was Phil." Yet in the fall of 1972, in a hotel lounge in Los Angeles, an ugly confrontation left an irreparable schism.

O'Neill had gone to California for a Democratic fund-raising dinner in Beverly Hills, and afterwards joined Burton and his wife, and party donors John and Betty Stephens, in the bar at the Beverly Hills Hotel. Burton had been drinking, and now he sprinkled his remarks with repetitious use, and imaginative variations, of the reliable Anglo-Saxon expletive.

"Phil kept using the word 'fuck.' I said, 'Phil, we're in mixed company.' He was saying, 'Fuck this' and 'Fuck that,' " O'Neill recalled.

O'Neill at first cautioned Burton, telling him that Millie would wash out a child's mouth for using such language. When Burton continued, O'Neill bluntly told him to "Curb your tongue." Burton lost it; went "berserk," started to rant. "He challenged me to a fight," O'Neill recalled. "I said, 'That's the silliest thing I ever heard. We'd both be defeated.' I was the whip at the time: the idea, of two leaders fighting."

Before Betty Stephens could help Sala Burton restrain her husband, he had threatened O'Neill. "I'll never forget this. I'll never forgive you," Burton said. "I'll run against you."

Years later, O'Neill said, "There should have been a close affinity between Phil and myself. We were friends to a degree. I had knowledge of him, and he had knowledge of me. But that night we broke apart completely.

"I don't know if Phil thought I could interfere with him and his rise to power. I was ambitious, as well as he was," O'Neill said. "When I used the words, 'Curb your tongue,' that was the opportunity to really pounce on me. He was going to take me out of the leadership, so on and so forth. That's where the break came, and there was a terrific coolness."[5]

FOR BURTON, the timing of the argument was awful. Just a few weeks later, Hale Boggs disappeared in Alaska and O'Neill clinched the vote for majority leader. Even before Boggs went to Alaska, O'Neill believed that Burton would try to make whip an elected position and challenge him in the January caucus. Now that the whip's job was going to be open, Burton announced his campaign. If the leadership ladder was going to move men like Albert and O'Neill inevitably toward the Speaker's chair, Burton asked, shouldn't the first rung be filled by the popular consent of the caucus? O'Neill warned Albert that Burton was "crazy" and "a revolutionary."

The caucus opened at 10 A.M. on January 2, with Burton believing he had the votes. But after listening to nominating and seconding speeches, and electing Albert and O'Neill, the Democrats broke for lunch. It was not until the afternoon session that the resolution for an elected whip was introduced. Bolling, who thought that the plan would atomize the leadership into rival camps of "Speaker, a junior Speaker and a junior junior Speaker," rose in opposition and moved to table the resolution, but lost on a 115 to 110 vote. Approval of Burton's plan now seemed a mere formality.

O'Neill then took a risk that even Burton, in retrospect, appreciated as "an enormous gamble." Just as the caucus was about to vote, the new majority leader stood and asked for unanimous consent to speak. No one could object, and O'Neill outlined his opposition to Burton's plan. As O'Neill's deputies — John Brademas, John McFall and Jim Wright — worked the cloakroom for the votes that would kill the resolution, rallying the troops as they drifted back from lunch, O'Neill put "his prestige on the line," said Burton. The speech was particularly effective among O'Neill's closest allies in New England and the South.

The caucus was loath to repudiate its newly elected leader, and southerners now began to grumble that the whole idea was a DSG plot. As the debate went on, Burton could only fret. O'Neill and his allies found the votes they needed to kill the plan, 123 to 114. O'Neill selected McFall, a Burton rival, as the new whip. Burton had been so sure of victory that he had issued a press release, which the *San Francisco Examiner* touted under the headline, "Burton Elected Whip." He was deeply embarrassed, and never forgot.[6]

Having played the master role in defeating Burton, O'Neill covered his bet by joining the reformers in their latest attack upon the seniority system. In keeping with its strategy of incremental change, the DSG had advanced a proposal to require that the caucus elect, by secret ballot, all committee chairmen. A 1971 reform contained a provision by which ten Democrats needed to challenge a chairman before a vote was held; but it was loathed by many Democrats as a "kamikaze" system because it left the upstarts open to retribution. "It was like Sodom and Gomorrah, where Abraham is pleading with God: What if I find 40 good men? 30 good men? What if I can get 10? Will you save the people?" David Cohen recalled.

The battle would have to be won on the caucus floor. The DSG needed a champion, and persuaded O'Neill to sponsor a resolution drafted by Representative Jonathan Bingham of New York. The key was to make a secret ballot seem comfortable and routine. So Bingham mimicked the familiar format by which congressmen could request a recorded teller vote: if a fifth of the caucus stood up, a chairman would face a secret ballot. "You were just sort of standing, anonymously," Cohen remembered. O'Neill's resolution was easily adopted, 117 to 58, and the caucus went on to consider its chairmen.

Alphabetically, the first committee up was Agriculture, whose chairman, Representative Bob Poage of Texas, favored subsidies for planters over food stamps for indigents. Burton and the requisite fifth rose to ask for a secret ballot, and though Poage had 169 supporters, 48 Democrats voted in secret to oust him. Poage was still a chairman, but his ego was bruised, and now he played into the liberals' hands. Appropriations chairman George Mahon, another Texan, was next in line. "Mahon was popular," Cohen recalled, "but Bob Poage decided that if they voted on him they would vote on everyone, and so he had his guys stand up and Mahon got voted on. That was pretty fantastic: talk about the law of unintended consequences. Nobody could have scripted it that way." All of the chairmen got elected, but "some of them had some votes against them. It was an early warning that they all had to face the electorate: the caucus," said Cohen. "Had fight for change," O'Neill noted in his diary. "Committee chairmen really disturbed." Albert was more expansive. "The seniority system — for sixty-two years the path to legislative domination — died that day," he said later. The triumphant liberals went on to adopt a "subcommittee Bill of Rights" to protect themselves from autocratic chairmen, and passed an end-the-war resolution. They also voted to add the Speaker, the majority leader and the whip to the "Committee on Committees" that made committee assignments.[7]

O'Neill got a healthy share of the credit. "The gloom had deepened" in the Democratic caucus until "fortunately, new Majority Leader Tip O'Neill . . . offered a procedural resolution permitting votes on chairmen . . . turning a seeming defeat into victory," an Americans for Democratic Action newsletter told its members. "The mood of the reformers slid from astonishment into jubilation as the caucus then proceeded to vote, one by one, on the . . . 21 chairmen. The way is open for future attempts to defeat chairmen who fail the test of ability, fairness and sensitivity to national needs." *Congressional Quarterly* noted that "only a last-minute intercession by Majority Leader O'Neill gave the DSG a victory."

O'Neill was, once again, serving as an important bridge between the liberals and the old guard. "Tip O'Neill was a regular. He always saw himself as a regular. But he was a regular who had the capacity to lead regulars and reformers and the credibility to do it," said Fred Wertheimer, a longtime Common Cause official. Some in Burton's camp wondered whether O'Neill was not merely an opportunist. "I think he smelled a new way of doing business in Congress that was coming down the road. It was different from the way he had been trained . . . but he wanted to be the leader," said Representative Charlie Rose. "He wanted to learn how to adapt to the new times and the new ideas. Sometimes he did it smoothly and with grace and style; other times it was a little awkward for him . . . and the liberals would holler that maybe his heart wasn't really in it."

From the vantage point of the Speaker's office, Albert's aides saw the confluence of interests in O'Neill's actions, and chose a railroad metaphor. "Tip was pushing reform: he was philosophically aligned with Burton," said Mike Reed, an aide to Albert. "But that train was going down the track, and being the engineer was a good place to be."[8]

The Nixon White House had no doubts about where O'Neill's heart was. It looked on the changes of January 1973 with distinct unease. Bill Timmons and Dick Cook wrote to Nixon on February 23 to warn him that the Democrats were "McGovernizing the House."

"The ultra-liberal House Democratic Study Group (DSG) has won a series of impressive victories in the House Democratic Caucus," Timmons and Cook said. "These caucus changes threaten to radicalize House procedures . . . [and] institutionalize the liberals' total control over Speaker Albert" and "intimidate moderates and conservatives." His aides informed Nixon that "the elevation of 'Tip' O'Neill to whip and then to majority leader . . . further insured [the liberals'] success." In April, Timmons warned Nixon, "Albert continues to display generally weak leadership" and that "the caucus controls the Speaker." O'Neill, said Timmons, "continues to emerge as the key House Democrat."

The Democratic reform impulse was not constrained to matters of their caucus. Just as momentous were the steps the Congress took to cut the "imperial presidency" down to size. "Since Teddy Roosevelt, the first three-quarters of the century had seen the ascendancy of the executive," said Michael Harrington. "Tip was there for the emergence of a legislative branch that was clearly not just reactive and parochial." A popular President who had conducted the war in Southeast Asia with seeming impunity now watched helplessly when, in the wake of the Saturday Night Massacre, the Congress overrode his veto of the War Powers Act. The Congress reasserted itself in domestic policy as well. From 1970 to 1973, Nixon had encroached upon congressional authority by refusing to spend billions of dollars Congress had appropriated for popular domestic programs. The ramshackle congressional spending process — in which the tax-writing, authorizing and appropriating committees all worked from separate spreadsheets — gave Nixon a sound basis to blast the Democrats for fiscal irresponsibility. The DSG liberals didn't much care about their image as budget-busters, and wanted to force Nixon to spend the impounded funds. Conservative Democrats, however, wanted to adopt budget restraints that would show the party could be fiscally responsible. Albert's solution — which O'Neill later called the crowning achievement of the Speaker's reign —

was the Budget Reform and Impoundment Control Act of 1974, which merged the two goals and established the modern congressional budget process.[9]

The Burton-O'Neill rivalry did not surface in the war powers and budget debates, but was a critical factor in other important reforms concerning the committee system and campaign finance. Dick Bolling had emerged as one of Albert's top advisers. He was widely recognized as the intellectual father of congressional reform, having spelled out with noteworthy prescience, in two early books on the subject, the need for a strong Speaker and a muscular caucus. He viewed Burton's success with suspicion and envy and had worked in vain to deny him the DSG chair (O'Neill had also sided against Burton, according to Bolling's whip count), and helped O'Neill defeat the Californian's campaign to be elected whip.

Burton saw his chance for vengeance when Bolling sought to open up a new front in the reform movement in 1973. With Albert's approval, Bolling led a bipartisan committee given the task of bringing order to the chaotic maze of overlapping and obsolete committee jurisdictions. More than thirty congressional committees asserted their jurisdiction over energy matters; eighteen of the twenty-two standing House committees claimed a piece of the education pie. Some of the turf wars seemed ludicrous: two committees claimed jurisdiction over the national forests, depending on whether the trees were growing to the east or west of the Mississippi River. The Bolling committee, staffed with academic specialists and manned by thoughtful members of both parties, worked for more than a year. "They came out with a pretty good solution," Albert said, "but he stepped on too many toes. It became the bitterest fight we had in years."

Bolling's strong opinions on several jurisdictional issues, it turned out, were closely related to his personal enmity for the men — Burton and Mills, primarily — who exercised that particular jurisdiction. At a March 27, 1974, meeting called by Mills, Bolling's opponents vented their anger and agreed that "the whole package must be attacked and defeated." Bolling struck back with characteristic scorn; in a speech before the National Press Club, he criticized "dunghill" liberals who would obstruct reform to preserve their fiefdoms.

Burton saw his opportunity when the maritime trade unions, objecting to the abolition of the Merchant Marine Committee, came to him to complain. He soon tore the rest of the AFL-CIO (where other member unions were worried about losing clout in the partition of the Education and Labor Committee) away from Bolling's side as well. After months of debate, the Bolling plan was killed by the House. O'Neill thought that the whole process, moving things from box to box, wasn't worth the trouble it caused. Just to make sure, he ordered Ari Weiss to compile a member-by-member analysis of how power in the House was distributed, and where it would flow under Bolling's proposal. When Republican John Anderson of Illinois tried to revive the issue on the House floor, O'Neill raised the critical point of order that put an end to Anderson's efforts.[10] O'Neill's summary of the dispute was quoted time and time again, until it came to serve as an epitaph for Bolling's defeat: "The name of the game is power, and the boys don't want to give it up."

Burton had won, but at a cost. "Bolling was never able to recover psychologically, and bore a hatred for Burton all out of proportion," said Burton aide Ben Palumbo. From that point on, "It was personal. It was very personal. Almost to the point of being vicious."[11]

Burton's two years as DSG chairman ended in 1973, and he set his sights on the next highest elective position — caucus chairman — hoping to then run for either Speaker or majority leader when Albert retired.[12] To do so, he formed an alliance with Wayne Hays, the chairman of the House Administration Committee and the DCCC. As such, Hays controlled the allocation of office funds, staff allowances and other congressional perks, and supervised the collection and distribution of campaign contributions. He also had a reputation as one of the meanest men in Congress. "He was so selfish. . . . It was nothing for him to cuss out an elevator operator. Fire them right on the spot," Albert recalled. And "he hated Tip. Absolutely hated him."

The feeling was reciprocal. It was Hays who convinced the caucus that O'Neill, once majority leader, should relinquish control of the DCCC. "He made my father's skin crawl, quite frankly," Kip O'Neill remembered. "He was an arrogant, cocky little guy who was sort of an operator moving around to feather his own nest." The poisonous feelings spilled into the path of public policy in early August 1974, as Nixon was preparing to resign and the House fought over another of the great Watergate-era reforms: public financing of elections. Common Cause and other reform groups were pushing a bill that extended public financing to congressional candidates as well as presidential campaigns, but the idea met fierce resistance in the House. "Tip was very hostile to it; an adamant opponent," said Cohen. "He said, 'I'm not going to subsidize my opponent.' "

Hays was managing the bill, hoping to avoid an embarrassing loss at the hands of the reformers, when Burton stepped in with a quiet deal. He and Hays would push a Common Cause amendment for public financing of congressional campaigns if the public money would be controlled and distributed by the two congressional campaign committees: the DCCC, which Hays chaired, and its Republican counterpart.

There was only one obstacle — a requirement that the amendment be published in the *Congressional Record* 24 hours in advance of the vote. Burton did his best to shroud the deal by having Representative Frank Annunzio, a Chicago regular, sponsor the amendment. "But light bulbs went off all over the city," Wertheimer recalled. O'Neill and Bolling, aghast at the notion that Hays would be controlling the funds, erupted. "Annunzio withdrew from the deal. Hays withdrew from the deal. It was chaos, happening in this totally isolated and unnoticed cauldron because the entire country was focused on Nixon," Wertheimer recalled. The campaign finance legislation was signed into law by President Ford without the provision for public financing of congressional elections. "Tip is more responsible than anyone for our bifurcated campaign finance system," Cohen said. "We had all the reformers — the old-timers who were reformers and Phil Burton and all of them — but we didn't get O'Neill." Wealthy interests continued to foot the bill for congressional contests. And as the costs of campaigns mounted, and the influence of corporate, labor and single-interest political action committees (PACs) grew, O'Neill came to regret his role in torpedoing public financing for the House. "He came to see the PAC system as a threat," said Wertheimer.

As they skirmished over public financing, O'Neill competed against Burton and Hays in the art of buying friends with political contributions. The great inherent flaw of the Watergate era reforms was that the changes which enabled a candidate to assert independence from a corrupt machine or courthouse gang were quite expensive. The new breed of politician quickly became addicted to money. With no precinct captains or ward heelers to vouch for a candidate, distribute literature or round up voters for the polls, a politician had to hire pollsters and campaign consultants and purchase huge swaths of television time. It didn't take long for corporate chieftains, labor unions, wealthy individuals and trade associations to recognize and exploit this addiction. Nor did it fail to register with Burton, Hays or O'Neill.

"What people didn't realize is that whether you were an incumbent, or a candidate out there doing your thing, is that when somebody gives you a helping hand, no matter how big it is, you are appreciative," said Tony Coelho. "It took a dedication, a willingness to be on the road, going around the country. But it was amazing the impact you could have with so little. Tip understood that. Tip understood you could give somebody $500 and have a major impact."

O'Neill set up his own campaign committee. He couldn't put on a gala to match the DCCC's $500-a-plate event, but he staged a buffet supper at the Potomac home of lobbyist Bill Ragan for some eighty people and came away with $52,550 for the "Thomas P. O'Neill, Jr. Congress Fund." The AFL-CIO, ironworkers, seafarers and other unions contributed, as did wealthy donors like Xerox's Charles McColough, philanthropist Mary Lasker and developer James Wilmot. In the summer and fall of 1974, O'Neill campaigned in over 30 states and distributed some $90,000 among more than 90 candidates.

Burton and Hays did even better. The DCCC coffers had traditionally been filled by the sale of tickets to the grand party gala, a process in which all Democratic congressmen participated. For just that reason, the lion's share of the committee's war chest had always been earmarked for incumbents. Now Hays, arguing that the veteran Democrats were in good shape and that the party had an extraordinary opportunity to steal Republican seats, changed the rules. When he was chairman of the DCCC, "we used to give to members of Congress. We would never give to anyone from the outside who was running for the job," O'Neill recalled years later. But "Phil talked to Hays and said, 'You know, a fellow in Congress ought to be able to raise money himself. We shouldn't be raising money for him. We should go out to the hinterland and see the candidates who have a chance of winning, and finance *their* campaigns. Get labor to support them. That was an innovative idea. And the timing was perfect."

Burton, working closely with Hays, called on Democratic challengers around the country, offering help. Many candidates were left with the impression that it was Burton who raised and gave them the money. "Burton and Hays had an arrangement in which, before Wayne Hays sent out a check to one of our contenders, he would notify Phil Burton," Jim Wright recalled. "Burton would get on the phone and call the recipient and would say, 'This is Phil Burton. By golly, how are you doing? How's the election coming?' And he'd feel him out and he'd say, 'Well, you need a little help. I'm going to see if I can't get my friend Wayne Hays to send you a check from the congressional campaign committee.' Now then, the fellow in a couple of days would receive a check and he would give credit to Phil Burton for having gotten him a contribution."

Jim Wright and others were furious because the DCCC money had been raised through the sale of tickets by Democratic incumbents. O'Neill was incensed because he had done much of the yeoman's work for the gala that raised the funds. But years later, he admitted that Burton and Hays had "seen the sweep coming that a lot of us, including myself, didn't see." Burton traveled to forty districts and helped supervise the distribution of more than a quarter of a million dollars from the DSG and DCCC, over half of which went to the incoming class of seventy-five Democratic freshmen. It was a watershed election for the House, in terms of quality as well as quantity. The Watergate babies — George Miller, Norm Mineta, Henry Waxman, Tim Wirth, Chris Dodd, Marty Russo, Paul Simon, Phil Sharp, Tom Harkin, Paul Tsongas, Jim Oberstar, Max Baucus, Jim Florio, Thomas Downey, Steve Solarz, to name a few — would join with their counterparts from 1970, 1972 and 1976 to form a corps that ruled the House for another twenty years. Largely on the strength of his relationship with this class, Burton was elected chairman of the Democratic caucus.

"Since becoming heir apparent to Speaker Carl Albert, Representative O'Neill has grown cautious," the *Wall Street Journal* reported. "If Phil Burton becomes chairman of the Democratic caucus, there's a good chance he'll try to use the position to fill the power vacuum in the House . . . [and] someday he could be Speaker." The *National Journal* sought out Dan Rostenkowski, who predicted, "Phil Burton's going to set the pace" and (pointing to the Speaker's office) "take giant steps toward that door."[13]

O'NEILL WAS TAKEN by surprise by the militancy of the freshmen, who grouped together as the grandly named "Class of the Ninety-fourth," hired staff and opened a Washington office before any of them had been sworn in. He was stunned even more by the sudden fall from power of Wilbur Mills. At 2 A.M. on October 7, the U.S. Park Police had fished Annabella Battistella, a.k.a. striptease dancer "Fanne Foxe —

the Argentine Firecracker," from the Tidal Basin. She had jumped from Mills's Lincoln Continental, leaving the boozy Ways and Means chairman with scratches on his face.

The reformers had expected a tough fight in the December 1974 caucuses over their plan to strip Ways and Means of some of its powers. But the liberals won in a walkover when Mills self-destructed. He chartered a private plane to catch his girlfriend's act in Boston and, on the night of November 30, strolled onstage at the Pilgrim Theater, where he was photographed by the *Herald* holding hands with the comely brunette, who had billed herself as the "Tidal Basin Bombshell," and was clad in naught but a black G-string and a feathered pink peignoir. The power to make committee assignments was taken from Ways and Means and given to the newly restructured steering and policy committee, led by Albert. Mills checked into Bethesda Naval Hospital, and resigned his chairmanship a week later.[14]

As caucus chairman, Burton strove to fill the leadership vacuum in the House. "Power is when people think you have power," O'Neill liked to say. He worried about perceptions, and resolved to weaken the Hays-Burton alliance. The opportunity presented itself when the steering and policy committee gathered on January 15 to vote on the nominees for committee chairmen. Bob Poage, George Mahon and Eddie Hebert were nominated by surprisingly narrow margins: Wright Patman was rejected. Up came Hays. Through three ballots the committee was deadlocked. Then someone switched their vote. Hays was rejected.

O'Neill always denied that he had helped organize the coup. Few believed him. It was the perfect place for an ambush. Here was Albert, whom Hays threatened. Here were John McFall and Jim Wright and John Brademas, their status endangered by Burton and Hays. And here was Bolling, in his fury. Years later, Albert confirmed the plot, and acknowledged that he was the one who switched his vote and cost Hays the nomination. "Tip said, 'Let's get rid of this son of a bitch while we can,' " Albert recalled. "After Tip asked me to, I said 'Okay.' "[15] When Hays got the news, he was thunderstruck. "I'm beat. Screw it," he told Burton. But they rallied to try and reverse the vote when it reached the full caucus.

The alliance of liberals and freshmen held a formidable majority in the caucus, and they were not sated by the defrocking of Wilbur Mills. In early January, the freshmen had summoned the Democratic committee chairmen back to Washington from their holiday vacations and demanded that they justify their continued usefulness. Some of the chairmen were respectful and congenial — like Mahon — but others declined to knuckle under. Hebert called the newcomers "boys and girls," and expressed his regret that the U.S. had not more aggressively conducted the Vietnam War. Representative Les Aspin, who was Hebert's chief critic on the committee, helped the freshmen Armed Services appointees organize in opposition. Word went around of how Hebert had declined to hold hearings on the bombing of Cambodia, refused to sign a travel voucher so that Representative Pat Schroeder could attend a NATO meeting in Europe and had given a single chair to Schroeder and Representative Ron Dellums so that they had to perch at hearings "cheek to cheek," as Schroeder put it.

On January 16, the caucus met to take up the steering and policy nominations for committee chairmen. Poage, first up, was defeated 146 to 141. Mahon survived. Then Hebert was rejected, 152 to 133. "We got him. We got him. Man, oh, man," Aspin exclaimed. Patman would also be defeated. The old South's grip on the House was broken. The *Washington Post* called it "a stunning abandonment of tradition . . . the first occasion in modern times that the party caucus had abandoned the seniority system to remove a chairman."

To O'Neill's dismay, Hays survived. The *Post* and the *Times* had called for his removal. Ralph Nader sent a letter to every representative, calling Hays "a continuing disgrace to the entire House." Common Cause had singled him out as an example of everything that was wrong with Congress. But the DCCC had handed out $202,000 in 1974, including $87,000 to 69 members of the freshman class. Hays promised to boost the members' per diem and to work to get them a pay raise; he okayed their new desks and draperies, and defended their perks when they came under attack from the media or Common Cause.

The debate raged in a closed-door caucus session. "I want to play a 100 percent part in reform, but I wash my hands of revenge," said Representative John LaFalce, a thirty-five-year-old Watergate baby from Buffalo, speaking on Hays's behalf. "This man has done me no harm; he has done you no harm, he has done us no harm. He has been our lawyer, our advocate, he has been the man who has stood up to the [press] galleries and defended us. Defend him." Representative Jim Stanton of Ohio, the floor manager for Hays, closed the debate for his side. "Wayne Hays is a son of a bitch — but he is our son of a bitch,"

Stanton said. The caucus approved Hays, 161 to 111, in a clear rebuff to Albert and O'Neill.

"Ladies and gentlemen, I approach you with a good deal of humility and a great deal of thankfulness for your vote of confidence in me," Hays told his colleagues after the results were announced. "Obviously from everything that has been said in the newspapers and quite a few things have been said in the corridors, and a few things said publicly, I am a miserable SOB.

"I will try to be a nicer SOB."[16]

The struggle between O'Neill and Burton was interrupted by the last, dreadful act of the Vietnam War. There was no illusion on either end of Pennsylvania Avenue as to the ultimate result of the Communist spring offenses: South Vietnam and Cambodia would fall. Ford had no wish to go to war, and Congress would not let him. "It is high time we got out completely and let this civil war resolve itself," O'Neill told the House. Warily, the White House and Congress jockeyed to avoid the blame as, for two months, television showed Americans the shameful denouement of their misadventure in Indochina: the armored personnel carriers carrying defeated ARVN troops from Hue and Danang, the helicopters removing refugees from the U.S. embassy's roof in Saigon. "I have only committed this mistake of believing in you, the Americans," Cambodian leader Sirk Matak said, in turning down a U.S. offer to flee Phnom Penh with the American evacuation. He was captured, tortured and beheaded by the Khmer Rouge.

The U.S. government was paralyzed. "The fear being expressed is that if we make a definitive decision in the Congress over the next few days to cut off all further military aid, the South Vietnamese will turn against the Americans, feeling we sold them down the river, and perhaps start killing or threatening those Americans left in Vietnam," Ari Weiss wrote O'Neill. "This could mean, if stretched to its most horrible dimension, U.S. military intervention would be necessary to quell a South Vietnamese rebellion against all Americans in Saigon. The question is being asked: do we have more to fear from the South Vietnamese than the North Vietnamese?"

In the end, the United States made no attempt to stop the North Vietnamese advance. "America can regain the sense of pride that existed before Vietnam," Ford said in a speech at Tulane University on April 23. "But it cannot be achieved by refighting a war that is finished as far as America is concerned." Saigon fell on April 30, 1975, but Americans never stopped refighting Vietnam. The cultural divide caused by the war narrowed but did not close; it would scar American politics for the next twenty-five years, until it seemed that only the passing of the generations who lived through the experience would cauterize the wound.[17]

With a 291 to 144 "veto proof" majority in the Ninety-fourth Congress, the House Democrats were supposed to have command of national policy. But as spring turned toward summer, Ford exploited the division between the party's liberals and conservatives, and employed his veto to neutralize the Democratic advantage. The Democrats found it easy to pass a bill, but quite difficult to muster the two-thirds vote needed to overcome a presidential veto. By Election Day, 1976, Ford would veto 59 bills and have but 12 vetoes overridden. If the Democrats were serious about passing legislation, it was a time that called for bipartisan cooperation — or at least the kind of compromises that guaranteed Democratic unity. But liberals in the caucus were bent on ideological purity, while conservatives were feeling spiteful and neglected. In the early months of 1975, the party splintered over military spending, energy policy, environmental protection and other measures. "I tried to be the leader of this group that refused to be led," Albert said. "Sometimes they had more muscle than heart or brains."

In the short run, the liberals were successful: they got a Democratic President in 1976 (though not the one they wanted) and preserved their jobs (only three of the 75 freshmen lost in 1976) and majority status. But in the long run, the stalemate between Ford and the Congress over pressing issues like energy, unemployment and inflation helped feed the disgust that many voters felt for Washington. Nor was it much fun, at the time, for Albert and O'Neill. "Defeats Split Bitter House Democrats," read the front-page headline in the *Times*. The House Democrats were "fractured today by rancor of an intensity seldom seen," the *Times* said. "Rarely has a party in Congress promised so much and accomplished so little." The paper described Albert as "the diminutive Speaker" and O'Neill as "a shaggy, 300-pound politician of the old school." *Newsweek* called the Democrats "marshmallows."

The freshmen panicked when Ford's standing in the public opinion polls was bolstered by his veto victories and the recapture of the U.S. merchant ship *Mayaguez* from the Cambodians in May. On June 18, Representative William Brodhead of Michigan, who represented the class of 1974 on the steering and policy committee (and was a committed Burton supporter), sent a memo to the leadership complaining of the "intense dissatisfaction among Democrats about the performance of Congress." Albert and O'Neill were not effectively leading, communicating, rounding up votes or enforcing party discipline, the thirty-three-year-old Brodhead complained.

As he had promised the previous January, Hays pushed a $10 million increase in fringe benefits and travel allowances for his colleagues. He called on Albert.

"Don't you think I ought to succeed you as Speaker?" Hays asked. The caucus needed to show its muscle. "By God, I'll give them power."

"Well, you might give them the wrong kind," Albert replied.

Albert and O'Neill met with the freshmen to calm them down. "If we were any other nation of the world, the Democratic Party would be five splinter parties," O'Neill told the caucus at its June 18 meeting. "We have in the confines of our party about 7 to 10 percent of you people who are way out to the left. We have about 7 to 10 percent of this party who are way out to the right conservative. The balance of the party is in the middle, left of middle or right of middle.

"Since the time of Socrates, politics has been the art of compromise," O'Neill told his troops, but for the ultraliberals, "no matter what we do, we don't go far enough," and for the ultraconservatives "no matter what we do, we go too far." O'Neill defended the 40-odd conservative Democrats from charges that they should be disciplined for failing to toe the party line. "Let's forget about punishment or anything of that nature. I have seen Congresses when we needed those 40," O'Neill said. "They are in our party, and there is room for everybody in our party, and always remember that. . . . They have to think, too, of the next election."[18]

THOUGH BURTON AND HAYS had prevailed in the caucus warfare that winter, they were caught off guard by the depth and range of hard feelings they evoked. The members of the House were increasingly irritated when even the most minor decisions became grist for the struggle between the Hays-Burton forces and the House leadership. Moderates worried that Burton's image as a liberal Robespierre — or "leftist oddity," as the *San Francisco Chronicle* put it — was leaving the party vulnerable to Republican efforts to portray the Democrats as looney liberals. Burton sought to cool things a bit at a meeting of the

Women's National Democratic Club in late February. After making sure the *Globe*'s Marty Nolan was in attendance, the Californian gave a gushy introduction of O'Neill as "the next Speaker." In interviews with other reporters, Burton said he would not challenge O'Neill, but would run for majority leader after Albert retired. Hays did his part as well, sending four bottles of Irish whiskey to O'Neill. The crusty Ohioan "has a heart as soft as the foggy dew," O'Neill told Nolan.

But the entente didn't last for long. On the day after Burton's speech to the Democratic women, the caucus ignored Albert and O'Neill and voted to kill the oil depletion allowance. Columnists Rowland Evans and Robert Novak noted tartly that the vote "exposed the impotency . . . of the nominal Democratic leadership, Speaker Carl Albert and Majority Leader Thomas P. O'Neill." Shirley Elder noted in the *Democratic Review* that O'Neill "seems to have faded into the institutional bureaucracy, a hulking white-haired shadow of the tiny Albert." The two leaders lost again in March when the caucus voted 189 to 49 on a resolution, pushed by Burton, to reject Ford's request for emergency aid for Cambodia and Vietnam. Doc Morgan, who chaired the newly renamed House International Relations Committee, angrily told the caucus, "If this is the way we're going to operate, let's abolish the committee system, open up the caucus and call witnesses."

The Washington press corps gave O'Neill another rash of bad reviews. The *Star* noted that O'Neill, "for the second time in a month, went to bat for a committee chairman and lost." Though O'Neill and his staff did a better job than most in ignoring the speculation of Capitol Hill reporters, they knew that at some point the perception that he was slipping could become a self-fulfilling prophecy. The always acute James Naughton wrote in the *Times* that "Mr. O'Neill, who has waited patiently, traditionally, for two dozen years to succeed to the Speaker's position, has been told so often by Mr. Burton that no challenge is intended that, Mr. O'Neill's associates say, he is beginning to expect a challenge."

Yet despite their setbacks, Albert and O'Neill had shown skill at balancing the demands of reformers and the old guard in a large, unruly party, Naughton wrote. O'Neill had been "swept along" but "not . . . swallowed," he concluded, and would be well positioned when the revolutionary fever inevitably faded. Though he continued to defend the Speaker, O'Neill thought it was time to exert more influence as heir apparent. It was a delicate thing — to nudge Albert into retirement without seeming to be doing any nudging. But the last thing O'Neill wanted was to be bound to Albert as the Speaker waged a campaign against Burton or Hays or some other vigorous challenger in 1977. O'Neill began to speak out more, to argue more forcibly in leadership councils, and he dropped the coyness with which he had previously answered questions about his own ambition.

"He's my friend. I'm not going to breathe down his neck," O'Neill said of Albert. But in private he pressed the Speaker, who finally told him to go ahead and prepare for the race. In late July, O'Neill leaked two choice pieces of self-promotional gossip to the *Globe:* that he had collected 70 unsolicited commitments should he run for Speaker, and that he had confronted Burton about the reports that the Californian would challenge him.

"Phil, I see some of these stories that say you're thinking of running for Speaker," O'Neill claimed to have said.

"Tip," said Burton, "I not only said I wouldn't before 400 women, but I told the same thing to my wife, Sala. I will not be a candidate for Speaker against you."

O'Neill planned a birthday bash that would net his "Congress Fund" about $75,000 at a $1,000-a-plate dinner at the Madison Hotel in December. His larger-than-life personality and approachability began to win the younger members over. They learned how he had challenged the seniority system and led the fight against secret voting, the Vietnam War and Nixon. The issues began to break O'Neill's way as well. When Ford's proposal to lift controls on gas and oil prices reached the House floor in July, Albert was muted by oil patch loyalty. O'Neill took over and led the Democratic opposition to victory. And when New York City lingered on the verge of bankruptcy that autumn, O'Neill steered the loan guarantee package through the House. Joseph Kraft wrote a favorable column about "The Emergence of Tip O'Neill." O'Neill's "unsolicited" pledge count rose to 75 by Labor Day, and to 144, a near majority, by Christmas.

Then, O'Neill got a gift of fate. He was in a car, being driven from Logan Airport to his home in North Cambridge, when he heard in early November that Burton had been stricken by a heart problem and was hospitalized at Bethesda Naval Hospital. O'Neill could not imagine that Burton would now have the stamina to challenge him. "He said later that this was the moment when he knew he was going to be Speaker," said driver Pat McCarthy, who had given O'Neill the news.

By April 1976, O'Neill was claiming 164 votes and the *Times* was back in his corner. His image had noticeably improved from the dark days of early 1975, when the paper had described him as the "shaggy 300-pound politician of the old school." Now that he was "virtually certain to become Speaker" the *Times* found him "an amiable bear of a man who combines the charm of the Boston pol that he is with a strong liberal bent."[19]

Nor had fortune finished smiling on O'Neill. On May 23 the capital awoke to find a story in the morning's *Washington Post* about Wayne Hays and twenty-seven-year-old blond Elizabeth Ray, who served on his staff and "says she is paid $14,000 a year in public money to serve as his mistress." Alongside a Hollywood publicity photograph of the bosomy Ray was her confession, "I can't type. I can't file. I can't even answer the phone." Hays had divorced his wife of twenty-five years in 1975 to marry another of his office secretaries; Ray was miffed she wasn't the one.

Albert had warned Hays to be more discreet in his womanizing. "I don't give a shit," Hays told him. Now the FBI, the House Ethics Committee and the Washington press corps began to investigate. Hysteria commenced. A half dozen more congressmen were named as lotharios. There were stories about hookers, sex parties on houseboats and orgies in the Board of Education room. "The place has never been popular," *Time*'s Neil MacNeil wrote his editors, "but now the daily newspapers and the TV broadcasters come proof in hand that the Members of Congress have been just what they suspected all along — freeloaders, snouts in the public troughs, boozing and screwing up a storm. Day after day. Night after night. All at the public expense."

The members of the House were justifiably fearful of what the raging sex scandal could do to their reelection prospects. Democratic pollsters told O'Neill that the fallout from the Ray affair was wiping out any advantages on the issues of trust and ethics that the party had gained from Watergate. The Democrats turned to their leaders, demanding that Hays be punished. Albert met with Hays but wavered, announcing that he had "taken no position" on the case and would give the chairman time to work things out. It was up to O'Neill, later that same day, to summon Hays to the majority leader's office and demand that he surrender chairmanship of the DCCC and the House Administration Committee. Hays said he would be willing to appoint two temporary substitutes. "No way can I buy that," O'Neill told him.

"You're not nominating anybody." O'Neill threatened to take the issue to the caucus where, he told Hays, the Ohioan would get but 30 votes. Hays approached Leo Diehl at a Democratic event at a downtown hotel. "Wayne Hays never spoke to me in all those years," Diehl said. "Now he comes up to me and says, 'Leo, I got problems. You can help. Can you speak to Tip for me?' I said, 'I can like hell.' "

"It all had to do with the Burton threat. When Hays got in trouble with the Elizabeth Ray stuff, O'Neill was ready to use the guillotine," David Cohen recalled. "O'Neill was the toughest one, far tougher than anyone else in the House. When Phil Burton went to plead for Wayne Hays, Tip said, 'No dice,' and Hays was out of there. There was no amount of plea bargaining Phil could do." The pressure mounted, and on June 3 Hays resigned as DCCC chairman. A week later, he took an overdose of sleeping pills. He left the Congress in September. Hays "told me the only reason he hated to get out of Congress was that he wanted to give Tip O'Neill one god-durned blow to hell," Albert recalled. "He wanted to knife him if he could."

On June 23, in a rare public session, O'Neill pushed a series of reforms, including a provision that banned the popular practice of pocketing expense funds for personal use, through the Democratic caucus over Burton's resistance. O'Neill also leaked word that Burton had been maneuvering behind the scenes to save Hays.[20] In their search for scandal, the city's investigative reporters had happened upon Albert's name, and were asking ugly questions about after-hours parties in the Board of Education room. Albert announced on June 5 that he would retire at the end of his term. O'Neill was in California, putting in an eighteen-hour day campaigning for Representative Norm Mineta, and got caught by surprise. He quickly declared his own candidacy and announced within a week that he had the votes to win.[21]

Having clinched the Speakership and banished Hays, O'Neill now took on the risky task of snuffing Burton's hopes to succeed him as majority leader. To Burton and anyone else who asked, O'Neill vowed that he would remain neutral in the evolving fight for the majority leader post. He had several reasons to keep that promise. All three of Burton's rivals in the race — John McFall, Dick Bolling and Jim Wright — had claims on O'Neill's allegiance: McFall and Wright were part of the leadership team, and Bolling had sat beside him on the Rules Committee for almost two decades. Nor was it seemly, or smart, for a prospective Speaker to antagonize any of the factions that formed around the various candidates: they could decide that they might as well run their man for Speaker instead. So O'Neill took the safest course. Out of respect for the regular order, he said, he signaled his intention to vote for McFall, his whip.

The problem, for O'Neill, was that McFall could not win. McFall had admitted in early November that he had accepted $4,000 for his office expense fund, most of it in a package of $100 bills, from Korean lobbyist Tongsun Park. McFall admitted that he had used the fund for political expenses and no-interest loans for himself and his staff. His candidacy withered with autumn's leaves.

O'Neill knew Bolling well, and would have tolerated him as majority leader. With the help of his ebullient, attractive, cigar-smoking tomboy of a second wife, Jim, Bolling had worked hard (and for Bolling, it was hard work) at schmoozing and glad-handing. He made deep inroads in the class of 1974, which was Burton's base, and he drew like a magnet from around the House the other members of the Anyone but Burton club. When asked in a joint appearance with the other candidates on *Meet the Press* on the eve of the vote if he were not running to keep Burton from the post, Bolling replied, "That's no secret."

But if Bolling was a dose that O'Neill could swallow to ward off a Burton victory, part of him wondered if the antidote would be more harmful than the poison. O'Neill did not relish the idea of serving with a haughty know-it-all at his side. "Bolling was too enamored of his own intellect. He didn't know guys by their first name; wouldn't hang out with them; was seen as aloof, seen as an intellectual," said Stan Brand. "Not someone you want to rub elbows with."

O'Neill liked to tell the story of how, one night in 1956, he had been dining with Philadelphia's Bill Green at the Democratic Club and decided that they needed to put a House member forward as a vice presidential candidate, if only to bedevil all the arrogant senators who were lusting for the job. O'Neill and Green had quickly settled on Bolling as the handsome young star who could carry the House banner when the Missouri congressman, quite coincidentally, entered the dining room. Bolling walked by his two colleagues, without acknowledging their presence. O'Neill and Green knew when they had been cut. Thus ended aborning the Bolling boomlet.

"His colleague Gillis Long told me twenty times if he told me once, that Bolling did not suffer fools gladly," said Charlie Rose, a Burton supporter. "And in my humble opinion there were a lot of us fools in the House that had been duly elected by the folks back home."

That left Jim Wright. To the handicappers who viewed the race, Wright had several weaknesses. He was supported by oil and gas interests and the remaining southern mossbacks; had voted against the 1964 Civil Rights Act; defended the Vietnam War well into the 1970s; and never participated in the reform movement. Yet O'Neill found qualities in Wright that were attractive. The Fort Worth congressman, a decorated World War II bomber pilot, was quite liberal for Texas. He was one of only five congressmen from the region who refused to sign the Southern Manifesto. Though he had ideological and regional differences with Wright over energy issues, O'Neill nonetheless valued the Northeast's forty-year-old alliance with Texas — the so-called Boston-Austin axis — which had allowed the Democrats to bridge the ideological differences that threatened to divide the party. And, unlike Bolling, Wright would feel a sense of obligation to O'Neill. He could neither overshadow the new Speaker nor afford to be disloyal. Wright was also the vehicle Dan Rostenkowski had chosen to make a comeback. In the spring of 1976, while working with Diehl and other loyalists at nailing down the Speaker's race for O'Neill, Rostenkowski began to nag Wright about running for majority leader. Then O'Neill came to call.

O'Neill told Wright that he heard the Texan was thinking about the race. Wright, recently remarried, replied that he was indeed contemplating the effort, but was worried that the responsibilities of the leader's job would consume his waking hours. "It doesn't take any more time than it would take to be chairman of that committee on Public Works," O'Neill said.

It was all O'Neill needed to say. *Never write when you can speak; never speak when you can nod.* He had conveyed his blessing, while retaining his ability to look the others in the face and insist he was neutral. "He began the conversation, and he was encouraging," Wright recalled. "So I began to meet with little groups of members who were not committed to any of the others and the first thing you know I had 25 or 30 commitments."

As a subcommittee chairman and high-ranking member of Public Works, Wright had been accumulating chits from the nation's urban congressmen for twenty-two years. Rostenkowski got him a November audience with Mayor Daley, who, after hearing about the favors that Wright had performed for Chicago, endorsed him and began to work the phone among his fellow mayors. Wright tapped wealthy Texans for a war chest of $50,000, which he used to mail out checks, with modest notes and best wishes, to challengers and incumbents. Liberals, like Baltimore's Barbara Mikulski, found checks in the mail from Texas industrialists they had never heard of — and who had never heard of them. A conservative mood had seized the nation: Jimmy Carter was driving to victory that fall, and a disproportionate number of the incoming freshmen were from the South. Wright wore a gold peanut in his lapel.

And when it came to cloakroom machinations, Wright took full advantage of the Bolling-Burton feud. At different points in the fall campaign, Wright's camp reached separate understandings with the two feuding titans, thus undermining them both. First, Rostenkowski met with Burton, and the two agreed that since neither could beat Bolling in a one-on-one showdown, they should share information and work together to knock him from the race in an early round. "Nobody, head to head against Bolling, could win," Rostenkowski said. "We had to eliminate Bolling." The Bolling camp suspected as much, but their hatred of Burton was still such that Bolling's campaign manager, Gillis Long, followed with a promise to Wright: if Bolling lost in an early round, Wright could count on his troops in a face-off against Burton.[22]

THE CANDIDATES could count on three rounds of voting, with the low man dropping from the race after each stage. As the balloting neared, the conventional wisdom on Capitol Hill was based upon ideology. If Burton faced Bolling in the final showdown, the wise money said, Bolling would take Wright's conservative supporters and defeat the Californian. But if Burton faced Wright, most everyone agreed, there was no way Wright could pick up Bolling's liberals: they would have to go to Burton, their ideological kinsman.

As is often the case, the conventional wisdom was wrong. Ideology mattered, but this was payback time for every friendship, grievance, rowdy junket, legislative alliance, campaign contribution, double-cross, insult or Tuesday night poker game of the preceding twenty years. These intangibles might account for only 5 or 10 percent of the votes cast in a leadership election — but this one was going to be that close. And Burton, for one, was worried about O'Neill. "His strength is not issues, it's chemistry. Nobody has a better understanding of the members and what is important to them and what makes them tick than Tip," Burton told a subaltern.

Burton used Diehl as an envoy. "I was friendly with Burton and he used to come to me. He never talked to Tom. He would give me a message," Diehl said. One night, at the Monocle restaurant, Burton cornered Diehl in the upstairs hallway. "O'Neill is waiting for me downstairs, and here is Burton: 'Leo, this is important.' I told him I had to go. So I reach for my crutches and he takes them from me. He took my crutches way the hell down the other end of the hall. And I couldn't move. I had to listen to him. And O'Neill is down there calling, 'Leo! Where the hell are you?' "[23]

To convince himself, or perhaps because he believed it, Burton told all who asked that O'Neill was remaining neutral in the race. But "Rostenkowski was Wright's right-hand man on that thing," Diehl said. "He was getting the votes for him, you know, and he would report to Tom on what was going on." In the days before the vote, Diehl joined the Wright campaign. He made calls and was available whenever Rostenkowski or another of Wright's captains told an uncertain member to "Call Leo."

"Guys would call me," Diehl recalled. "And I would say, 'Well, you know, Tom likes Jim Wright, a guy that can try to keep the temper.' We didn't want [Burton] to be kicking the crap out of O'Neill on everything. I wanted O'Neill to be protected."

The caucus convened at noon on December 6. For the first time, the election of the Democratic leaders was open to the public, and the galleries were jammed with families, aides and reporters. Everyone knew what was at stake: the last ten Speakers had been elevated to the chair from the post of party leader. It was to be "the closest, most volatile and least predictable contest for the office of House majority leader in the two-hundred-year history of Congress," as two prominent historians later put it.

The first ballot was no surprise. O'Neill wrote "McFall" on one of the yellow 3-by-5 cards that had been distributed, showed it to his whip, and walked to the well of the chamber to cast his vote in one of four wooden boxes. The results: Burton 106; Bolling 81; Wright 77; and McFall 31. McFall dropped out; the next round would be key.

O'Neill retreated to a corner of the House chamber, where he filled out his ballot with what one observer thought was the crossing of a "T," but may well have been the concluding swirl, in his parochial school handwriting, of a cursive "G." (Diehl, for one, believed that O'Neill voted for Bolling.) Bolling slouched low in the front row, his fingertips touching like a schoolboy in prayer. The tellers returned: Burton 107; Wright 95; Bolling 93.

The House chamber slid into controlled pandemonium: it was inconceivable that Burton had picked up only one vote from McFall's supporters. Indeed, assuming that Wright would be easier to beat in the final round, Burton's troops said later they had thrown votes to the Texan to drive Bolling from the race. If so, it was an audacious, manipulative tactic, too clever by half. It angered Bolling's supporters and gave weight to Wright's contention that Burton was too slippery to trust.

Had they but time, Ben Palumbo thought, Burton's lieutenants might have been able to soothe some of the irate congressmen. But the announcement of the results from the second round of voting was immediately followed by the call for the final ballot. This was Burton's doing: he had emerged from his unsuccessful attempt to win the Democratic whip's job in 1973 with the conviction that O'Neill had beaten him by extending the debate and scrounging for votes. For the majority leader's race, Burton had insisted on immediate rounds of voting. "It was evidence of his concern that once O'Neill had the speakership in hand, Tip would try to affect the outcome," said Palumbo.

Wright's troops "fanned out like a bunch of June bugs," the Texan later recalled, with lists of Bolling and McFall supporters. Gillis Long and the other members of Bolling's high command joined them, fulfilling their promise. "If Phil Burton had been his next in command, Tip would have had to hire a food taster," Wright said later, recalling the argument his team used that day.

Bill Cable, a Bolling aide who assumed the House liberals would now vote their ideology, bumped into New Jersey's Frank Thompson.

"So, are we going all out for Burton?" Cable asked.

"Fuck Burton," Thompson replied. "I'm looking to make our deal right now." All but two of New Jersey's votes went to Wright.

O'Neill "had his little brood gathered around him over there, and was sending them in different directions" on Wright's behalf, Representative Charlie Wilson recalled. Eddie Boland lobbied his fellow New Englanders. "This one's for Tip," Burton's supporters heard O'Neill's pals say. O'Neill would later guess that he and his allies swung some 12 liberal votes, primarily from the Northeast, to Wright.

Lud Ashley, a buddy of O'Neill's and Rostenkowski's, had voted for Bolling in the first and second rounds but had never been asked about, or given much thought to, the possibility that the final showdown might be Burton vs. Wright. As he returned to the chamber for the third ballot, Ashley fell in with Rostenkowski.

"I guess it's going to be Burton," Ashley said.

"Well, you're not going to vote for him, are you?" Rostenkowski replied.

"Yeah. I like the guy. He's kind of mouthy. But he's a hell of a Democrat. I think Tip wants him more than he does Wright."

Rostenkowski stopped, grabbed Ashley by the arm, and spun him around. "No, you're wrong," he told his friend. "You are absolutely full of shit on that."

"Don't give me that," Ashley said. "I've been with Tip as much as you have. Why Wright? He hasn't done jackshit. He's a nice guy, but why would Tip want Wright?"

"I know goddamn well who he's for," Rostenkowski said. "Christ, take my word for it. No doubt about it. Lud, he wants Wright."

Ashley had his ballot in his hand. He was prepared to write "Burton." Instead, he wrote "Wright."

The voting took some fifteen minutes, and then the boxes were carried to the lobby to be counted. Wilson, a Wright supporter from Texas, was tallying the final box when he realized that the two opponents were, to that point, tied. A lone, uncounted, face-down card before him would make the difference. "I reached out like my hand was deadweight and turned up the last card. It was Jim Wright," he said later.

"Two fellows came in the door holding up one finger with smiles on their faces," said Wright. "I didn't know what it meant . . . whether there was one more vote to be counted or that one finger means w-o-n or what." Across the floor, the word spread. Wright. Wright by a vote. "It dawned on others a bit before it did me, I think, because I was suddenly surrounded by people reaching over shaking hands and congratulating me," he remembered.

O'Neill broke into a big, wide grin. Burton grimaced and looked up to where his wife sat in the gallery; he shook his head. The final vote was 148 to 147. Bolling, who had been near tears just moments before, embraced Wright in the well of the House. Bolling and his wife went home that night and had two drinks: one in consolation, and one in celebration. Rostenkowski, who had suffered a similar disaster six years earlier, was overcome with emotion when he saw Burton's dejected demeanor. But Rosty was back. And when Mayor Daley died of heart failure later that month, among the old man's possessions was a piece of paper with the vote totals from the House majority leader's race. "Look, we've been through the war, we've been through Watergate, we've been through fighting with two Republican presidents. We're tired of contention, confrontation," a senior Democrat told the *Post* in as good a postmortem as any. "The thought of infighting between O'Neill and Burton and divisiveness among House Democrats now was just too much."

Years later, Sala Burton would ask O'Neill if the argument in the Beverly Hills hotel lounge, as she suspected, was the event that cost her husband the majority leadership. O'Neill said it had. But Burton had no shortage of enemies who dipped their sleeves in his blood that day. Burton was "the only man who lost the speakership of the House because of style," O'Neill said. "There were an awful lot of people that, when the chips were down and Phil needed them, they weren't with him."

"Frankly, O'Neill was probably right," said Palumbo. "If I were Tip, would I have a Phil Burton, hard-driving, driven, with a desire to run things? He would put me in an early grave."

Like Rostenkowski, O'Neill was awed by the scope of Burton's fall. In his remarks at a reception at Ford's Theater that night, O'Neill singled out Wright and Bolling for praise and then said softly, gently of Burton: "My feelings go to the others, so lonely in their defeat."[24]

PART FIVE | *Old Pal*

CHAPTER 18

Mr. Speaker

THE HOUSE OVER WHICH Speaker Thomas P. O'Neill Jr. would now preside had been thoroughly remade from the sleepy institution of his early years in Congress. The southern autocracy had been broken; the shuffling old bulls had been swept from the Capitol's halls. Of 289 Democrats that January, only 15 had served in Congress longer than O'Neill, and 168 had been elected in the decade of the 1970s. The average age in the House had dropped to 49.3, the youngest since World War II. The regional distribution of the two parties had begun to reflect the transformative success of the Republican "southern strategy." And the old urban strongholds of ethnic white Democrats had been washed away by the great postwar migration of black Americans from the South and the subsequent white flight to the suburbs. The new breed of Democratic officeholders — Tim Wirth, Gary Hart, Paul Tsongas, Michael Dukakis and the rest — were "neoliberals" who had sold the notion of political reform, and their own personalities, to suburbanites who gathered political information from television, not the local block captain. Ticket-splitting was more common: the percentage of voters who chose the party line dropped in

House elections from 84 percent to 69 percent in the twenty years after 1958. Without an old-time machine to distribute winter coats and Christmas turkeys, these new political entrepreneurs invested considerable resources in sophisticated constituent service operations: answering mail and telephone calls, staffing satellite and mobile field offices, chasing down wayward Social Security checks and conveying requests to the federal bureaucracy. Between 1971 and 1981, the volume of incoming mail to Congress more than tripled. WATS lines, word processors and computerized mailing systems were commonplace features in congressional offices.

Members of the "New Congress," dependent on televised imagery, required telegenic forums, and so the number of committee and subcommittee chairmen had doubled to some 200 in the time O'Neill had been in Congress. The duties of constituent service and the work of the proliferating subcommittees fueled the demand for more staff, as did the need for greater congressional expertise to keep tabs on the growing federal budget and to counter the imperial executive. The 435 members of the House had some 2,000 employees on their office payrolls when O'Neill arrived in 1953; there were 7,000 such employees in 1977, and another 3,000 working for committees, subcommittees, service organizations and the party leadership.[1] The Rules Committee served as a prime illustration of how the congressional establishment had grown: Howard Smith had 2 committee aides in 1960; twenty years later there were 42.

Congress was now a billion-dollar business[2] with a commensurate demand for more lobbyists, special-interest groups, trade associations and journalists. The average number of days in session jumped from 230 in the Eisenhower years to 323 in the Ninety-fifth Congress, and the number of recorded votes from 71 in O'Neill's first year to 834 in 1978. Members spent more of their time raising money for their increasingly more expensive campaigns, or hurriedly shuttling back and forth between their offices and the House floor, where they would plug their plastic cards into the new electronic voting system, knowing that each vote would be scrutinized by the growing number of interest groups.

Gone were the days when Carl Albert, following Sam Rayburn's advice, would spend his days in the House chamber, soaking up knowledge and forging collegial relationships; gone as well were the hours that Harold Donahue and Phil Philbin could slump in the soft leather chairs of the House chamber each afternoon like aged hotel detectives, whiling away the hours with gossip and the occasional rousing snore. A 1977 study by a House committee found that members worked eleven-hour days, of which only thirty-three minutes were spent at contemplative tasks like reading, thinking, or writing. The House became a place to cast a vote and flee, not as much to mingle, converse or enjoy the debate.

For many, it was hard not to harken back to George Washington Plunkitt, the legendary sage of Tammany Hall, who asked in 1905: "Have you ever thought what would become of the country if the bosses were put out of business, and their places were taken by a lot of cart-tail orators and college graduates? It would mean chaos."[3]

O'Neill had a variety of tools with which to command this new, chaotic and still-evolving political creature — the postreform House. When the reform movement stripped the committee chairmen of their clout, it had distributed the power both up, to the leadership, and down, to the rank and file. In the Democratic caucus, the Speaker led a revived steering and policy committee, which awarded committee assignments and declared what legislation was a matter of party policy. He appointed the members of the conference committees that would negotiate with the Senate, and the select committees that were from time to time formed to take on special issues. He got to nominate the members of the Rules Committee, thus making it an arm of the leadership. (To clinch this power, he faced down the huge California delegation, which demanded the right to name its own choice to the "California seat" on Rules.) O'Neill also had the authority to schedule legislation: calling the party's favored bills to the floor at opportune moments, or bottling unwanted measures in committee until support faded. He could refer bills to more than one committee and set reporting deadlines to force recalcitrant chairmen to deal with legislation they would just as soon neglect. He controlled the agenda on the House floor through his authority to recognize members who rose to speak and his power to rule on points of order. He could gavel a roll call to a close if his side was on top, or let it stretch for precious minutes as his lieutenants scoured the cloakrooms or cut last-minute deals when his side was behind. He could find a job for a congresswoman's kid, or pick up a phone and spur a White House aide or agency head to respond to a member's request. He had a limousine and corporate airplanes at his disposal; a "hotline" connecting his suite with the Rules Committee and the majority leader's office and an automatic paging system to summon members to the floor. He had a staff of two dozen employees to run his office, to conduct policy research, monitor the committees and keep him in touch with the legislative machine over which he presided — so that he could intervene at the subcommittee level, if need be, on a matter of importance. And, though it exacted a personal cost, O'Neill knew that his appearance at a political fund-raiser was a prized plum to dangle before the members.

Reform had its drawbacks. The old system, "in which a handful of senior members could make all of the important decisions, and where legislation was virtually unamendable on the House floor, was obviously more efficient," Dick Conlon acknowledged. It was the Speaker's job to make the place efficient now. In contrast to his predecessors, who could lurk in their bourboned and cigar-smoked lairs and cut deals with a handful of oligarchs, O'Neill was expected to supervise almost every aspect and stage of the party's program — from the identification of priorities to the management of legislation to the marketing of political ideas on the national stage. The new Speaker would have his work cut out for him, and in some quarters, the early line was not good. "O'Neill's age and his slowing pace are painfully obvious . . . he will probably be Speaker for a maximum of two terms or four years, hardly long enough to become one of the titans in the history of the House," one spectacularly mistaken commentator predicted in the pages of Boston's own *Atlantic* magazine. "There are rumors he will retire."[4]

Hardly. Tip O'Neill had not invested forty years in politics only to serve a few ceremonial months as the Speaker of the U.S. House of Representatives. He summoned the energy and the good qualities that had carried him that far and went to work. Despite his new perks and title, the essence of his style was based on personal relationships. His principal power was what his new deputy, Jim Wright, called "a hunting license to persuade."

O'Neill "had a way," Joe Moakley recalled. "He just had a way of putting his arm around somebody and putting that Irish face in your face and just making a friend out of you." The sociable times and favors he shared with them fostered a feeling of obligation among the members of Congress, until they found it difficult to say no. Linda

Melconian, who went on to her own successful career in politics, would not forget how her boss would gather a group of antagonists in his office and sit back as they blew off steam. Gradually, O'Neill would enter the debate, asking for their cooperation, sketching out potential areas of compromise, urging recalcitrant members to bend. "It was his powers of persuasion," she said. "You wanted to satisfy him. He would always look you in the eye. It was not intimidating, but very powerful, almost hypnotic." The windows in that room were always shut, the lights dim, cigars lit and the stifling air itself enough to break down a reluctant compromiser. "A typical Tip room. Once he was in there with Rostenkowski and some others and there was a big storm and the power went out," said aide Chris Matthews. "They never left the room. They sat there talking in the dark."

The personal touch. When the Chrysler Corporation needed a government-secured loan to survive the structural revolution that struck the automobile industry in the 1970s, O'Neill gave Chrysler Chairman Lee Iacocca's entourage of lobbyists and experts a frosty reception. He passed the word that he wanted to see Iacocca in a one-on-one meeting.

"How many people in my district work for Chrysler or one of its suppliers?" O'Neill asked Iacocca, who confessed that he had no idea. The Speaker told the baffled Chrysler chairman to find out, and to do the same for every other congressional district. "He was the point man," Iacocca recalled. "He said, 'Lookit. I fight for my constituents for 50 jobs: you've got 600,000.' " The younger breed of Democrats were philosophically opposed to big-government intervention in a dying Rust Belt industry. But, following O'Neill's prescription, Iacocca went to work, Chrysler got its loan, survived and prospered.

Charlie Rose saw O'Neill as a patriarch. "Tip and Leo ran a family operation. And they did it with great style, and with a strong hand. You hardly ever felt you were standing out in the rain waiting to be recognized, and if you did, you told him about it and he would give you a big bear hug and make sure you felt you were back in the family," Rose said.

"There was more to Tip O'Neill than ambition. There was compassion. There was affection. You didn't see Tip standing over there in the corner looking like a little boy all eaten up with ambition," said Rose. "There are leaders who wait for you to come and kiss their ring and body parts and then there are leaders who are out there in front, hugging and kissing you and bestowing their blessings on you without you having to do anything. Tip was a compassionate giver of everything that he had: advice, warmth, friendship. And never perceived as huddling in the corner conniving and crafting secret meetings to make his next power grab."

The members of Congress felt a sense of obligation to their Speaker, one so strong it sometimes overrode their political self-interest. Moakley recalled one instance when a bill on abortion had come before the Rules Committee and, given the tension between his conservative South Boston Catholic constituency and the prevailing liberal orthodoxy of the Democratic Party on the issue, "I didn't want to vote. And it was close."

Moakley sought out the Speaker.

"Tip, uh, the vote on abortion — Jesus, that's a tough one. Can I get released?"

O'Neill looked at him and said, "Joesy, I don't need you on the easy ones."

Disarmed, Moakley voted with O'Neill. "Sonofabitch," he told himself, "that's the last time I ever ask him any questions like that."[5]

O'Neill gave no quarter in his combat with the Republican Party, but he usually fought fair, and fostered friendships with individual Republicans. House minority leader Robert Michel joined O'Neill at globe trotting and golf. Representative John Anderson may have chaired the Republican caucus, but that didn't stop O'Neill from phoning the president of Boston College when Anderson's son was seeking admission.

As in the Massachusetts legislature, O'Neill strove in his first term as Speaker to demonstrate impartiality. Toward the end of the 1977 session, O'Neill ruled that a bill that was dear to the maritime industry — and so the port of Boston — had passed by a voice vote. Representative Paul McCloskey of California, a Republican foe of the bill, negligently failed to rise and demand a roll call. McCloskey soon sputtered in embarrassment and claimed that he had been cheated. "The chair will not stand for that: nobody rose," O'Neill said. But the maritime interests were stunned when O'Neill then urged the bill's Democratic sponsor, in the interest of fairness, to allow a roll call. The bill was defeated; the maritime industry squealed, but O'Neill had decided that it wasn't worth winning on a technicality.

"While we may have disagreed on policies etc. at no time did I ever have any reason to question your loyalty to our country, or your word," wrote right-wing representative John Ashbrook, an Ohio Republican, at the end of the 1978 session. "We had many dealings and as I have told many on our side who do not understand all of the goings-on, in every dealing with you, you did absolutely what you said you would do. In the last days, I may have been a little tough on some things and hope I did not in any way unduly add to your problems, although I am clearly a thorn. It is gratifying to know I serve with a Speaker whose word I implicitly can trust."

It was the kind of praise that touched O'Neill. "A personal commitment . . . in politics is very sacred, not to be given without deep and pensive concentration of thought, and from which there can be no change of position once the commitment is made," said aide Linda Melconian, reciting the O'Neill creed. "For if a politician breaks a commitment, his word means nothing to his colleagues from that day forward."

If trust was a virtue, so was loyalty. "With O'Neill, everything was personal relationships," said Chris Matthews. When Representative Joseph F. Smith of Philadelphia was elected in 1981, O'Neill knew that Smith had been a trusted aide to the late Representative William "Digger" Byrne.

"So, how's the Digger?" O'Neill asked Smith.

"Oh, he died two years ago," Smith replied.

"Yes, I heard," said O'Neill.

The conversation sounded "like the dialogue from an Abbott and Costello routine," Matthews recalled. "But to an ear more finely attuned to the basic protocol of the street-corner politician, Tip O'Neill was not inquiring about a dead man's health. He was saluting another man's coat of arms. 'How's the Digger?' was his way of saying, 'I know where you come from. I know your loyalties.' "

At one point in his tenure, O'Neill turned down the formal requests for an interview made by John Mulligan, the Washington bureau chief of the *Providence Journal-Bulletin*. "Tell him you know somebody," Matthews advised Mulligan.

And so Mulligan, finding an opportunity, said to O'Neill: "I was wondering, Mr. Speaker, if you remember a guy from Holy Cross who once pitched for the Red Sox. His name is Joe Mulligan and he's my uncle."

"Not only do I remember Joe Mulligan," O'Neill said. "I remember his lifetime record. He was 1 and 0 in 1934. He won the ball game about 15 to nothing, and they sent him down to Syracuse! He's your uncle? C'mon into the office tomorrow."

"Once you were friends with Tip, you were friends for life," said Jim Dinneen. "I had three kids. All became lawyers. Each of them had the thrill of being an intern in Tip's offices." Once, when O'Neill was criticized for employing two of the lobbyist's kids, the Speaker replied in high dudgeon, informing the critic that he hired three Dinneens, not two.

Yet O'Neill was no pushover. He made sure that loyalty worked both ways, and had ways of reminding his vassals to pay duty to the lord. O'Neill interceded to get Representative Barbara Kennelly of Connecticut a coveted seat on the Ways and Means Committee, and Kennelly recalled how the Speaker thereafter would sit down beside her and powerfully squeeze her wrist when he needed her to change her vote during a tight roll call. After Lud Ashley had lost a close election for the chairmanship of the Budget Committee, he happened upon O'Neill, who said, "Ah, Jesus, Lud. To lose by 10 votes: 139 to 129. Oh Christ. Six votes would have done it."

Ashley had a sinking feeling in the pit of his stomach. "Do you think you were good for six votes, Tip?"

With a scornful look, O'Neill let Ashley know that he thought the question was insulting. "Next time, ask," he told Ashley.

"Oh, Jesus. I wish I had asked," Ashley said.

A few weeks later, Ashley was approached by Ari Weiss, who told him that the Speaker was looking for someone to chair a select committee that would be in charge of pushing the Carter administration's energy bill through the House. The stakes were enormous: the energy package was one of two or three high-profile measures by which the new Speaker and President had declared they should be judged. Ashley had never chaired a full committee, and he thought Weiss was asking him to nominate a colleague for the post. No, said Weiss, "the Speaker thinks you might be good for the job." Through such gestures, O'Neill bound men to his side.

Even the Goo-Goos were not immune. Common Cause lobbyist David Cohen won O'Neill's highest accolade when a deal he had cut with the new Speaker (to support a pay raise that would relieve the House of aging conservatives by sweetening their pensions) came under fire from the *Washington Post*. Cohen didn't much care for the covert methods that O'Neill had used to pass the measure — the Speaker broomed it through without hearings or notice — but he defended it under fire. "You stuck. You stuck," O'Neill told him when their paths crossed a few weeks later.

"It was a great moment," said Cohen. "He said, 'You stuck.' I felt great about that." Cohen later learned that O'Neill's old pal Jimmy Burke, seriously ill and retiring from Congress, was a beneficiary of the bill.[6]

O'NEILL SAVED SOME of his best performances for the all-day meetings of the steering and policy committee, where the top Democrats would gather to swap favors, push their protégés or frustrate foes while making committee assignments. The Speaker usually had a handful of favorites, generally from New England, to be planted on the most important committees when veterans from the region retired. "It was like crop rotation," said Representative James Shannon, who was planted on the Ways and Means Committee.

O'Neill held the steering committee reins lightly, letting individual congressmen wheel and deal. "You get a Rostenkowski, a Murtha, a John Breaux, an amiable fellow," said O'Neill. "John can go to Dan and a Murtha, who are putting together cliques, and say, 'We can give you three votes for yours if you give us votes for our guy.' Rostenkowski, Murtha and Frank Thompson were experts at that, once the leadership was taken care of." They voted by casting pink slips of paper into a cigar box.

"There Tip sat with his cigar and his coat off and short-sleeved shirt, you know, sort of presiding," said Charlie Rose. "He just rolled the cigar in his mouth and gave everybody a kind of hazy stare as if to say, 'All right, go at it.' " For the calorie-counting O'Neill, the steering committee meetings were fraught with temptation. "Morgan Murphy and I sat next to each other, and we're both fat boys who've had trouble watching our weight and we know exactly what's going on in Tip's mind because he has the same problem," said Rose. "They had this beautiful Danish pastry and coffee there in the morning. And then for lunch they'd bring in ham sandwiches, turkey sandwiches and tuna sandwiches and potato chips and late in the afternoon they'd bring in pie.

"Tip would resist. He would drink his coffee with no sugar in it, he would try and try, and then he couldn't stand it anymore and he'd come back in the room with a doughnut in each hand," said Rose.

"Thank you very much for your letter of February 12," O'Neill wrote to one colleague. "I went off the Weight Watchers diet between Thanksgiving and Christmas and gained 18 pounds in two months. I have gone back on the diet this week and am attending my first Weight Watchers meeting tonight. I still have kept off 27 out of the 55 pounds I originally lost, but still feel disgusted with myself."

During one tense session of the steering committee, Tom Foley's dog sneaked up and snatched the Speaker's doughnut from his plate. The explosion that followed had no small element of calculation, Representative Brian Donnelly concluded. "Left and Right are at each other's throats, the party is about to be ripped asunder, and Foley's dog steals O'Neill's doughnut. 'It's not funny,' the Speaker shouts, really steamed. 'Tom, get that goddamn dog out of here. It ate my doughnut!' He didn't talk to Foley for two weeks, but in the laughter, the party became harmonious again."

O'Neill kept personal control over the seats on the Ethics Committee, whose duty it was to police the House for ethical infractions. "Nobody who ever wants to serve on the Ethics Committee should ever be appointed. They should be drafted," he told Jim Wright.

Good Time Charlie Wilson, the east Texas rogue who found time from his gallivanting to help bring down the Soviet Union by securing U.S. aid for Afghanistan rebels, was one such draftee. Wilson had made it known that he craved an appointment to the board of trustees of the Kennedy Center, Washington's temple of the arts, so he could impress his dates with good seats. One day, after listening to O'Neill announce the new members of the Ethics Committee, Wilson turned to Udall and said, "My God, Mo, this is horrible! Tip didn't put one damn member on there who appreciates good pussy or whiskey!" Udall laughed so loudly that O'Neill motioned him up to the podium where, upon hearing what Wilson said, the Speaker was chortling too.

A few months later, O'Neill called Wilson to his office. "I was scared to death . . . trying to figure what I had done lately to embarrass the House of Representatives."

"Chollie, Mo Udall told me what you said about the makeup of that Ethics Committee," said the Speaker. "I agree. So I'm going to put you on the Ethics Committee."

"They'd laugh us both out of town!" Wilson protested. "I'm a live-and-let-live kind of guy."

"You still want to get on that Kennedy Center board?" O'Neill said. "It's a package deal."[7]

But if O'Neill could play for laughs when it suited him, he had a deft, sentimental touch as well. When Bolling's wife, Jim, suddenly grew ill and died, O'Neill's House tribute was kind, heartfelt and moving. "I've been fond of Tip for a long time," Bolling said, "but it didn't hurt with me what he said about my late wife, I'll tell you that. That's the kind of thing he is master at, and he meant it."

O'Neill's staff remembered many such kindnesses. To Barbara Sutton, who had asked him for an afternoon off, explaining that she could only afford to buy furniture at a midweek discount warehouse sale, O'Neill slipped an envelope filled with ten $100 bills. He sent her father, Billy Sutton, to an expensive black-tie dinner, honoring their old friend JFK. "He was the kindest man I ever met in politics," said Billy Sutton. "I met him one day at the Kennedy Library. Out of the blue he said, 'I understand your daughter Barbara goes to Trinity in Washington.' I said, 'Yeah.' He said, 'Isn't that a tough nut for you to crack?' And I said, 'For chrissake, Tip, I haven't had a good meal since she's been there.' " At O'Neill's instruction, Barbara called the Speaker's office when she graduated. "I know your father: he's a champion," O'Neill told her. "You come work in my office."

The year that Boston College quarterback Doug Flutie won the Heisman Trophy, O'Neill gave away his tickets to the award dinner to the sports-loving husbands of the women who worked in his Boston office. Pam Jackson's widowed mother ran a cleaning shop where O'Neill and Boland took their laundry, and where Pam would work the counter, doing her homework, after school. At the widow's request, O'Neill broke one of the unwritten rules of patronage — reward your own — and found Pam a job in his office, where she rose through the ranks as intern, receptionist and legislative aide. When John McFall was beaten in 1978, his career spoiled by the "Koreagate" scandal, Irv Sprague wanted to put one of the defeated congressman's aides on the Speaker's payroll for six months so that the man could have a salary and a respectable title on his résumé while looking for a job. "Here is a kid who is smart and has four children and one kidney and has been destroyed by this McFall thing through no fault of his own," said Sprague.

"One kidney and four children? Okay," O'Neill said.

The Speaker ordered Stan Brand to take afternoons off to study for the bar exam, and the other Hill aides in his law school class, dragging their bodies into the library after a ten-hour day in a congressman's office, thought O'Neill a candidate for sainthood.

O'Neill relished one perk of his prominence: the invitation to play golf at the Burning Tree and Congressional Country Clubs in suburban Washington, and the opportunities he got to participate in celebrity pro-am tournaments at some of the country's finest golf resorts. He was chagrined when one such tournament was held on a day that an important appropriations bill was scheduled to hit the House floor, and Gary Hymel was dispatched to see the tall, courtly George Mahon, the chairman of the committee.

"Mr. Chairman, the Speaker sent me over here and he knows you got that bill scheduled on Monday and he respects your schedule but he has got a golf tournament that day," said Hymel.

"Well," said Mahon, after a momentary pause, "it is a royal and ancient game."

In 1974, Nelson Rockefeller established a "Commission on Critical Choices" to "save the country and Western civilization, and lay the foundation for his campaign for President in 1976," as Jim Cannon, then an aide to the New York governor, recalled. O'Neill happily accepted membership on the panel after hearing he would have funds for a part-time aide to represent him in its work.

"Several months later the commission had its first meeting in New York City, and Tip sent word that his representative would be, as I recall the name, Edward Donovan, of Cambridge," said Cannon. "Some staff worrier began to wonder if Mr. Donovan might be an intellectual liberal from Harvard who would come in and try to impose his ideas."

Rockefeller ordered Cannon to discover who Donovan was, and learned only that the mystery man was one of O'Neill's lifelong friends. Cannon invited him to drop by his office the morning before the first commission meeting. "He was amiable, and older than I expected. I described the methodology of the commission's work, the studies we were undertaking, and tried to convey Rockefeller's seriousness of purpose in the enterprise," Cannon recalled.

Donovan had but one question. "Do you think Governor Rockefeller will object if I leave the meeting in time to make the third race at Belmont today?" he asked. "I've got a little inside information."

No problem, said Cannon, trying to keep a straight face. He got a state car to take Donovan of Cambridge to the racetrack for the third.

Francine Gannon, who worked in the Speaker's Boston office, could spin a series of anecdotes about her boss. How he refused to cut in line in restaurants. How he called Lee Iacocca on the telephone when an elderly constituent had problems with her car's undercoating. How, when Gannon called him to chortle about the fact that one of his vanquished Democratic primary opponents was trying to get a job as a probation officer, O'Neill told her to help the man secure the job because "he's got a slew of kids." Long after he could safely function as a driver, the aged Ralph Granara was kept on the office payroll.

O'Neill had a "diabolical" way of teasing his staff, said parliamentarian Charles Johnson, who was driving to work in a drop-top sports car one day when O'Neill pulled up beside him at a Massachusetts Avenue stoplight. Johnson waited for the inevitable needle; it came as the House was ready to go into session and, in the presence of the House chaplain, O'Neill asked Johnson if he had been successful that morning, cruising for co-eds at American University.

Eleanor Kelley rolled her eyes at all the priests and nuns who dropped by over the years, and shattered the Speaker's schedule or were dispatched to lunch with the handiest available aide. And Charlie Rose recalled, "I think it was Jimmie Burke who came in to Tip one day and said, 'I want you to meet the Lord Mayor of Shannon.' They all patted each other on the back and told a bunch of stories and maybe one or two other Irishmen came into Tip's office and then eventually somebody said, 'Why don't we go down to the White House and say hello to the President?' And they all piled in a car and go down to the White House and Carter brings them into the Oval Office and they take the picture.

"Well, about two weeks later one of them called [Bill] Cable and said, 'Cable, where are the pictures of the President with the Lord Mayor of Shannon?' And Cable said, 'Hey. There ain't going to be no pictures because there ain't no Lord Mayor of Shannon. Shannon is not a city, it's an airport. And we have all been mightily flamboozled.' "[8]

Looking back, most members of O'Neill's staff remembered how his management style — characterized by huge and frequent delegations of authority — further bound them to their boss. "Once you worked for him and once he trusted you, that was it. Nothing could sever the bond. That was his code," said Brand. "In fact, you would be reticent to use all the rope he gave you because it was, in a sense, the check that he designed to keep you from going too far astray. I never saw anybody delegate like him in my life. Just do it. That's it. Report back to me. I'll see ya. And he did it a thousand times a day."

So it was in the House. For the most part, O'Neill let the committee and subcommittee chairmen set the agenda, and used his staff to track what the committees were working on. It was quite a responsibility for young men like Ari Weiss and his deputy, Jack Lew. "He expected us to be interacting with the committees at a very high level. He expected us to keep him abreast, not of every little detail, but of all the major big moving pieces he needed to know about and he expected us to reserve for him the ability to make the political judgments and the tough choices," said Lew.

"He liked young people. He wasn't afraid of them like a lot of old politicians. He loved young pols and he let you in," said Brian Donnelly, who had won Jimmy Burke's old Dorchester-based seat over an O'Neill favorite in 1978. Donnelly's uncle was a Boston city councilman who had lost his chance to become mayor in 1947, when O'Neill had conspired with Governor Robert Bradford to give John Hynes the job.

"I'm sorry about what I did to your uncle," O'Neill told Donnelly when the freshman from Dorchester arrived in Washington.

"Yeah, and thanks for trying to keep me from getting here," Donnelly replied.

But Donnelly quickly succumbed to the "ol' pal" routine, and O'Neill's flattering solicitation: "C'mere Brian, whattya think?"

The Speaker's openness to youth was attributed to the influence of his five children, and a tale about O'Neill and Lyndon Johnson was typically used to make the point. According to the story, Johnson had received a new stereo system as a gift in the early 1960s[9] but could not make it work. While on the phone with the President, John McCormack — similarly isolated from the emerging consumer culture — confessed that he too was baffled by the device, but said he would ask O'Neill, who happened to be sitting there. Having endured his share of rock and roll on Russell Street, O'Neill explained the principles of stereophonic sound. Different noise from two different speakers? It sounded too far-fetched to Old John. "Tom doesn't know either, Mr. President," he told LBJ.

The stereo story made the rounds because O'Neill's ability to bridge the gap between the old hands in Congress and the anti-Vietnam and post-Watergate generations was widely respected on Capitol Hill.

O'Neill "was very good with change and changing times," Lud Ashley recalled. "He wasn't judgmental, like many of the older fellas were, about the new guys. He didn't make snap judgments about people that were unkind. He let a person speak or develop or show what they were." The Speaker had young friends everywhere. When debate in the House droned on, he would lean from the chair and chat with the House pages about the respective quality of motion pictures like *Star Wars* ("I don't get it," O'Neill said) and *Rocky* ("Now that's a movie"). One of the House pages had celebrated so hard on the night before reporting to his new position that he spent most of the morning lying down in the cloakroom, the victim of a mighty hangover. The Speaker never said a word. But on the page's next-to-last day months later, O'Neill asked him if he would be there on his final day. "Sure, Mr. Speaker. Why?" the page asked. "Because you sure weren't here on your first day," O'Neill said.[10]

O'Neill was a matchless barometer of the mood of the House because he kept himself available. "He would just sit there in his chair on the floor and members would come over to him and without moving he would get what a pretty good cross section of the House was thinking," said Lew. If O'Neill was coming from H-209, the Speaker's ceremonial office, he would park his cigar on the railing by the door and sit in one of the first few rows on the side; if he wandered in from H-204, his hideaway office, he would lumber down the aisle from the cloakroom and take a seat up front. "There weren't a lot of places to look for him," Lew remembered. The constant complaints of his colleagues could irritate O'Neill, but he took the job quite seriously, and quickly grew restless when sensing he was away from the floor for too long. "I hear confession," he would explain.

As the pace of turnover in the House increased, O'Neill augmented his personal relationships with "the book," a computerized record of the loyalty of each House Democrat that was compiled, refined and maintained by aide Billie Larsen. When Representative Sam B. Hall of Texas wanted a seat on Ways and Means, the contest came down to Hall and Representative Martin Russo of Illinois. O'Neill said, "Let's have the book," and showed the steering committee how Hall had consistently failed to support the Democratic leadership. Russo got the seat.

Yet O'Neill's long career had taught O'Neill about the tides of politics. He did not gloat, and generally was gracious in victory. There would always be another day, another need to round up 218 votes, he told Weiss. In the weeks that followed Jim Wright's election as majority leader, O'Neill reached out to the losers. He appointed Phil Burton to head the House delegation to NATO's North Atlantic Assembly, a prestigious job which required yearly junkets to Europe. O'Neill placed Charlie Rose, a Burton lieutenant, on the steering and policy committee. And Bolling was rewarded with a shrewdly chosen gift: the keys to H-128, the old Board of Education room. Such moves paid off: Bolling became a staunch O'Neill ally.

Nor did O'Neill neglect Wright. In early 1978, after Burton used a speech at an AFL-CIO convention to signal his intent to challenge Wright in the next Congress, the Texan's response was to launch a preemptive strike — to sign up enough early supporters that Burton would be dissuaded. To end any doubts about where he stood on the matter, the Speaker embraced Wright at his St. Patrick's Day party. "It was pure O'Neill. He had insisted that I come," Wright told his diary. "When I arrived he was singing Irish songs. He spotted my arrival, called me up publicly and asked me to sing . . . I'm sure he wanted to make such a gesture." Within two days, with O'Neill loyalists like Joe Moakley and Jack Murtha working on his behalf, Wright had 191 pledges of support and Burton's insurrection was over.[11]

To the extent that O'Neill rose to be captain by being a good ship's engineer — keeping the engines oiled and running smoothly — he suffered as a navigator. His adaptability was a gift, but it could cut both ways.

"Dick Bolling didn't get to be Speaker because Bolling took these fairly hard stands, which were not consensus stands," said Bill Cable, who served on Carter's legislative affairs staff. "O'Neill didn't do that very often. It wasn't that Mr. O'Neill wasn't a principled person, but he only took stands when they were seriously important, or where there was a consensus that this is where the institution was going to go: where the water had found its path. And in that sense he was a great survivor. He could read the institution and he understood it and loved it and could lead it from that point."

"Tip was a guy who had his finger up a lot and he understood where the House was going or wanted to go and he got ahead of the bandwagon. I don't think Tip ever got out ahead of the team too much," said Tony Coelho. "Burton wanted to educate. Burton wanted to convince. Tip was more . . . he wanted to lead the troops, and help you accomplish things as opposed to having his own ideas of what needed to be done.

"The reason that Tip stayed in power as long as he did was he always had an ability to keep moving," said Coelho. "He would make modifications. He would make adjustments in order to pacify certain dissident elements."

O'Neill was "a broad-brush guy" who left the finer details of legislation to the experts, said Gary Hymel. He remembered how O'Neill informed two reporters, in some detail, how the House was about to tackle prison reform. But the Speaker had misread the briefing sheet Hymel prepared; the House was in fact going to take up pension reform. Hymel chased the newsmen down in the hall, and successfully begged them to spare his boss — which they did. Neil MacNeil was flabbergasted to discover, in the course of a Sunday morning talk show, that O'Neill did not realize that a package passed by Congress to keep Social Security solvent included so massive a hike in the payroll tax for working Americans. "Did we do that?" O'Neill asked the aide who had accompanied him. "Tip O'Neill was like Lyndon Johnson — he let the generals operate," said Rostenkowski. And sometimes O'Neill's hands-off approach to his committee chairmen had serious consequences. The soaring interest rates of the late 1970s prompted the nation's savings and loan lobby to ask Congress to deregulate the industry, and the House banking committee was quick to comply. The resultant legislation abolished usury laws, lifted regulations and opened sleepy rural thrifts to takeovers. At the same time, the House raised the amount of each account that the U.S. government would guarantee from $40,000 to $100,000, virtually inviting the thrift owners to gamble with federally insured deposits. It was a dreadful combination that the Democratic Congress — in league with the Carter and Reagan administrations and the nation's dozing press — casually accepted. The new hotshot S&L owners exploited the "greed is good" values of the 1980s, and threw money into bad real estate deals, inflated operating expenses, political campaign contributions and their own lavish lifestyles. The lack of due dilligence by the U.S. government cost the American people more than $150 billion.

Yet only a smart, savvy and well-grounded individual could navigate these times, as O'Neill did, without betraying either his conscience or ambition. "Instinct" and "intuition" and "great staff" could sometimes be used as euphemistic put-downs by critics who wanted to cast doubt on O'Neill's intellectual gifts, but it is useful to consider how many obstacles he had successfully dealt with — simultaneously — in the years leading up to his election as Speaker. A smooth narrative requires that the reform movement, Watergate, the end of the Vietnam War, the Ford administration, his competition with Burton, the Mills and Hays scandals, American economic stagnation, the 1976 presidential election and the Speaker and majority leader's races be addressed in some sort of sequential pattern. Life wasn't nearly so tidy. For O'Neill, all these daunting problems broke at once, affecting each other's course like rebounding balls on a pool table and increasing, geometrically, the complexity of his task.

"Underneath the guise of a gentle, friendly giant lay a substantial intellect O'Neill would not want to expose to everybody," said former Cambridge school committeeman Glenn Koocher. Barney Frank found O'Neill "much smarter than people gave him credit for," and intellectually the equal of most college professors. Bolling said O'Neill was "highly intelligent" and, while not an intellectual, quite comfortable in their company and able to use them for his political aims. Daughter Susan recalled how her dad would pull her through the art museums of Europe to view the Old Masters.

O'Neill didn't read novels or go to the movies or the theater; his favorite motion picture was *Gone With the Wind* and on TV he watched comedies (*All in the Family*), sports (*Monday Night Football*) and news. Yet he loved verse and studied and underlined books on public policy. He was an unrepentant city boy, whose idea of a wide-open space was a manicured golf course, but O'Neill kept a pair of binoculars handy in his Cape Cod house so he could watch the native wildfowl and he read and reread *The Outermost House,* by Henry Beston, a naturalist's tale about the Cape.

Jack Lew, who went on to serve as budget director for President Bill Clinton, said that the grillings he would get from O'Neill were different — more plainly put — but no less vigorous than those he got from Clinton, a noted policy wonk. "The President has an enormous grasp of policy detail. He is enormously, not just smart, but well read and well versed. But I can't tell you I felt appreciably more able to trim the edges going in to brief Tip O'Neill," said Lew. "In his own way he got right to the heart of the matter very, very quickly. He had an extremely keen intellect and extremely keen sense of how people, and particularly congressional institutions, function."

"He was smart enough to get there: that is the real measure of smartness," said Breslin. "He would say of his staff, 'Leave 'em alone. Let them work. They're making me look like a million fuckin' dollars.' That ain't a dumb guy."[12]

FOR ALL HIS GOOD TIMES and blarney, O'Neill never lacked the cold-blooded will to do what was necessary. When required, he could bring the hammer down, and astonish people with his cruel calculation.

"As I continue as a stalwart, providing the margin of success for your leadership, I can't help but be perplexed by your hostility," Representative Richard Ottinger of New York wrote in 1979, after angering O'Neill. "You've denied my every request, all really important to me . . . what on earth did I ever do to earn such animosity? You've hurt me to the core — and I'm flabbergasted to know why."

Ottinger had voted against O'Neill at the most critical stage of the House's consideration of Jimmy Carter's energy package. The Speaker had punished him by rejecting his requests for plum committee assignments, and by opposing his candidacy to chair the Democratic Study Group. "I understand the necessity for independence," O'Neill replied brutally, "the kind of independence that assures us a majority on the Floor."

"He played you off people," said Coelho. "He played Rosty off people and other people off Rosty and so forth. You were never quite sure what else was going on.

"He invited my wife and me on all those Speaker's trips. That was very important to him. He only had certain people on those trips. But he would say to me, 'Lookit, your ass is here only because of your wife, Phyllis. I can't stand you, but I love Phyllis.' And that is the way he talked to you," said Coelho. "He was always trying to put you off a bit, to be tough on you, knowing you would be wanting to come back in."

THE WEEK BEFORE JERRY FORD left the presidency, he invited some of his closest friends in Washington to one last White House breakfast. The bittersweet morning was capped when O'Neill gave the political benediction, speaking eloquently of Ford's decency and patriotism and invaluable service in the dark time after Watergate. Ford always regarded that morning as a very special moment; he remembered O'Neill's brief words as "one of the nicest, very emotional, couldn't have been a finer, tribute."

Ford's aides were nowhere near as generous. Years later, they recounted how O'Neill, leaving the mansion after the breakfast, had savaged Ford and his presidency when asked by the White House press corps to rate the president's performance. "Tip defamed and excoriated him," Jim Cannon said.

The Speaker was "the most partisan sonofabitch in town," said Ford aide Terry O'Donnell, who had seen O'Neill play a similar trick. "I had been out on the golf course with the President and Tip, and they have the great banter . . . terrific interchange . . . kid each other, have more damn fun than monkeys," O'Donnell recalled. A few days later, O'Donnell was stunned to watch O'Neill slash at Ford on a Sunday television talk show. Upset, O'Donnell had taken the rare step of asking for a private meeting with the President. "I simply cannot abide by this guy who purports to be your friend and golfing buddy going out and calling you dumb and just taking off unshirted hell, you know, just blasting you," he told Ford.

"You don't understand, we're old adversaries," said the President. "This is all part of the game."

In large part because of the President's affection, O'Neill had been treated with deference by the Ford administration, and his requests for favors or patronage had been honored. "I got pissed off. I think Tip took advantage of him," said O'Donnell. "There's an understanding in the political game of a little quid pro quo. . . . I don't think Tip abided by it and Tip was never a friend in my book."

Indeed, by mid-1975 O'Neill had proclaimed Ford "a lovely guy but a lousy President" and "worse than Harding and Hoover put together." In public, O'Neill showed little sympathy for his friend, who was trying to govern amid the shambles of Watergate, and facing a fierce primary campaign challenge from Ronald Reagan. "The record of his two years shows the nation will be better served by his departure," O'Neill said of Ford. "His accomplishments are minuscule, his place in history is secure as Richard Nixon's hand-picked successor."

"Tip would cut your heart out when it comes to politics. . . . He was terribly abusive," said White House lobbyist Max Friedersdorf. He was "the most partisan congressman up here, an extreme Democrat partisan, and he wanted Ford to look bad on as many things as he could," said Friedersdorf. "He wanted to elect a Democrat President in 1976. That was his goal, and to do that he had to make Ford look bad."

So Tip savaged a pal. And Jimmy Carter beat Ford by a narrow margin on Election Day 1976. And the new Democratic Speaker got his wish; he would have a Democratic President with whom to work in common purpose. Or so he thought.[13]

CHAPTER 19

Jimmy

IN LATE NOVEMBER 1976, President-elect Jimmy Carter asked his chief advisers to write strategic plans for his new administration. What he got from pollster Patrick Caddell was less a step-by-step blueprint for governing than a bleak description of the crisis within the Democratic Party. Carter's 1976 election was a gift of fortune, Caddell said, an individual victory and one-time event. After years of political polarization, and a series of national failures — the shortcomings of the Great Society, the folly of Vietnam, the Watergate scandals — the country had chosen Carter as its President because the voters wanted to feel good about America again, and had liked his promise of a cleansed, decent government. "I will never lie to you," Carter had said, and promised "a government that is as honest and truthful and fair and idealistic and compassionate and filled with love as are the American people."

Carter was perceived as an innocent, a skilled outsider untainted by the corruption in Washington — an "anti-politician" — Caddell noted. In the Democratic primaries, the one-term Georgia governor had wooed the young, and just enough liberals, by offering a hip brand of piety. He salted his speeches with quotations from "my friend" Bob

Dylan and philosopher Reinhold Niebuhr. He could fairly claim that, over the course of his career, he had taken the banner of the progressive "New South" into battle and vanquished George Wallace. And with the ongoing shift in population to the Sun Belt, a southern governor seemed a sensible bet to the many Democrats who were starved for a winner. "A vote for Carter requires a certain leap of faith," wrote counterculture journalist Hunter S. Thompson in *Rolling Stone* magazine, "but on the evidence I don't mind taking it."

Once Carter clinched the Democratic nomination, however, his aides found that the New Deal coalition he inherited was a shambles. The party machinery was a shell. "Look at the role the Democratic party played twenty-five or thirty years ago in the life of a person living in Chicago or New York," said Hamilton Jordan, the leader of Carter's young team of advisers. "The party helped people. If you had a sick child or a problem, and you and your family regularly voted Democratic, you had a precinct captain who could get your child in the hospital or would bring you a turkey for Christmas or Thanksgiving. It did things for people. It also served the role of informing people about candidates and issues. The party stood for something.

"Today all the party does is serve the mechanical functions in nominating. The Democratic or Republican Party doesn't really help people anymore and it doesn't inform people anymore. With the advent of television, it doesn't stand for anything anymore," said Jordan.

During the national convention in New York, it seemed that Carter spent all his time trudging from one hotel meeting room to the next, offering concessions to haughty single-interest caucuses representing labor bosses, women, Hispanics and blacks. Carter remembered it as a "horrible" experience, and later that fall complained after one campaign foray into New Jersey that half the hacks on the podium were under indictment. Ford closed a 33-point gap, but just enough low- and moderate-income southerners had joined black voters and northern liberals to give Carter victory. There were no guarantees that the South would continue to support him: Ford had actually outpolled Carter among white southerners.

Carter's men were not alone in their analysis. After the sobering experience of serving as George McGovern's campaign manager, Gary Hart had retreated to Colorado to analyze the defeat and concluded in 1973 that the "fields of liberalism" were barren, "the soil [was] worn out" and "the traditional sources of invigorating, inspiring and creative ideas were dissipated." Hart was elected to the Senate in 1974, and soon he and a group of like-minded Democratic politicians — Senators Joseph Biden of Delaware and Bill Bradley of New Jersey; Representatives Timothy Wirth of Colorado, Paul Tsongas of Massachusetts and Governors Michael Dukakis of Massachusetts, Jerry Brown of California and Bruce Babbitt of Arizona — were identified as "neoliberals" for their willingness to reach out to better-educated suburbanites by recasting traditional Democratic positions on busing, taxes, crime, government waste, economic growth and national defense.

"We were the children of Vietnam, not children of World War II. We were products of television, not of print. We were products of computer politics, not courthouse politics. And we were reflections of JFK as President, not FDR," said Wirth. In many respects, the neoliberal philosophy tracked the ideas of the breed of Southern moderates who rose along with Carter: Arkansas governor William Clinton and senator Dale Bumpers; Georgia senator Sam Nunn; Florida senator Lawton Chiles; Tennessee representative Albert Gore and Missouri representative Richard Gephardt. Such "young Turks" could be trouble "if not handled properly," Caddell warned Carter. Still, the real danger to the Carter administration, the pollster predicted, would come from the the old Democratic establishment.

"Although Jimmy Carter is the successful nominee of his party, his support from the activist levels of that party has come more because he imposed victory on them than because they chose him," said Caddell. "To be frank, Jimmy Carter is not particularly popular with major elements of the Democratic Party, whether it be activists, the Congress, labor leaders or the political bosses." Indeed, Eugene McCarthy had run as an independent that year and drained enough liberal votes to tip four states out of Carter's column on Election Day.

The new President would find few friends among the newly elected leaders on Capitol Hill. "A Democratic President diminishes the importance of the leadership in Congress. Carter's quick rise from relative obscurity to the White House is by its very nature a direct threat to the style and experience of the men who make up the leadership of Congress," said Caddell. "While they intend to cooperate, they are anxious to be independent. Their recent years of opposition have done nothing for their willingness to cooperate with the Executive Branch."

Though he negligently dismissed the political potential of the "antiquated and anachronistic" conservative movement that had coalesced around Ronald Reagan in the 1976 primaries, Caddell offered the new President an otherwise prescient look at the dangers he would face in the next four years. Many of the new administration's goals were contradictory. Carter needed to spur economic growth — but not with big-government spending programs, and while controlling inflation and fulfilling his campaign promise to balance the federal budget. Carter needed to court the South, the middle class, and independent voters — but by all means avoid a primary challenge from the Left in 1980. And, perhaps most difficult of all, Carter needed to produce a tangible record of achievement in Congress, while always remembering that "it is crucial that President Carter keep the image that he is not part of the traditional political establishment, that he is not satisfied with what he finds in Washington, that he is, as he has said, 'disgusted with the laxity and looseness of approach in Washington' and has really come to clean house."

Even Caddell — never at a loss for provocative ideas — was daunted by the challenge. "What we require is not stew, composed of bits and pieces of old policies, but a fundamentally new ideology," he told Carter. "Unfortunately, the clear formulation of such an ideology is beyond the intellectual grasp of your pollster."[1]

STEW. TIP O'NEILL was comfortable with stew: he ate it, by tradition, on Election Night. But Caddell was right: after raising him to the highest office to which he had ever aspired, O'Neill's timing was deserting him. This unreconstructed New Deal Democrat was cast to preside over the final dissolution of the noble coalition for which he had served, as soldier and captain, since 1936.

The strains, surely, had always been there. Despite the successes of half a century, no coalition that included southern rednecks, Jews and African Americans, working families of ethnic stock and silk stocking liberals was safe from rifts and tears. And O'Neill had seen too many North Cambridge kids go to college on the GI bill or with the aid of Pell grants, watched too many Irish and Italian households use an FHA mortgage to make the leap to the outer suburbs, known too many families whose standard of living had soared in the postwar period, to think that a political strategy based only around the have-nots would succeed. The Democratic Party's own success was part of what threatened to put it out of business.

And so the new Speaker faced a very different challenge than the ones that had confronted Sam Rayburn and John McCormack. They had helped build the American middle class; his job was to preserve it. He would need to consolidate the achievements of the New Deal, while still promoting the interests of that minority of Americans — which by capitalism's own logic must by now consist of the nation's weakest and most forlorn citizens — who'd been left behind.

Carter had not been Tip O'Neill's favorite candidate for President in 1976. "What I had done as a candidate in 1976 was basically to run as a nonpolitician, as a southerner, as a farmer, and as someone outside the Beltway who criticized the Congress. And Tip, when I would criticize the federal government as being overly bureaucratic and so forth, I think Tip took that as kind of a personal reflection on him and on the House," Carter recalled.

Until Senator Ted Kennedy renounced the race in September 1974, O'Neill had been — publicly, at least — a Kennedy man. After the senator left the field, O'Neill offered his allegiance to Mo Udall, among the most liberal of the crop of candidates and a fellow House member. A Udall campaign had an additional benefit for O'Neill in that it removed a potential challenger for the speakership. O'Neill worked hard on Udall's behalf, and the Arizonan's good showing in the Massachusetts primary could be partly attributed to O'Neill's help. After Carter had clinched the nomination, some of Udall's aides wanted the congressman to return to the House and enter the race to succeed Albert. "I couldn't do that to Tip," Udall told them.[2]

The Georgians had begun the race with chips on their shoulders. "We were sitting down in Atlanta in 1972 and saw all these, I was going to say clowns — we had seen all these gentlemen come through that were running for President. It was not an overwhelming experience," said Jordan. "President Carter used to say when he was governor that he could never think of himself in terms of Abraham Lincoln or Thomas Jefferson or George Washington, but he had no difficulty comparing himself to Scoop Jackson and George Wallace."[3]

James Earl Carter had been born in tiny Plains, Georgia, the son of a prosperous grocer and farmer. In 1943, in keeping with an American tradition by which small towns promote boys of exceptional promise to serve the nation, Carter won appointment to the U.S. Naval Academy, where he served on wartime navy cruises and, after graduating in 1946, was accepted in Admiral Hyman Rickover's nuclear submarine program. In 1953, his father's death brought him home to Georgia where, despite his refusal to join the segregationist White Citizens Council and his subsequent expulsion from the segregated local country club, he entered public service. In an episode that helped cast his later attitude toward politics, he challenged fraudulent election results, beat a courthouse gang, and won election to the state Senate in 1962.

Carter was one of the more exasperating men ever to claim the White House. His tenacity, so admirable, could shift to stubbornness; his religious faith and personal commitment could lead to self-righteousness. His brilliant mind could be bound up by intricate details. He was a master practitioner of the new politics, who often showed disdain for the conventions of his craft. "You know, even when you are working together on a project, he makes you feel somehow or another that everything you are doing is dirty," Jim Wright told his colleagues.

It was to be expected that a self-proclaimed outsider who beat a half dozen members of Congress in the Democratic primaries and feared "the appearance of establishing strong ties to the 'old' Washington," as one campaign aide put it, would stir resentment. The members of Carter's staff were justly proud — in fact downright cocky — about the political miracle they had just pulled off. And it would have been personally difficult, and politically dubious, for Carter and the Georgians to suddenly transform themselves into Washington insiders. The President and his aides knew to dance with the one who brung ya: that the country had elected Jimmy Who? precisely because he was an outsider.

"Sure there was a little arrogance. Did we reach out enough to these people? Probably not. Did they give us as much of a chance as they should have? Probably not. So there were mistakes made, and there was some paranoia on both sides," Jordan said. Years later, several of the Georgians would confess to their fear — eminently justified, it turned out — that the Washington establishment looked down on them as rude rednecks, arriving in town from the piney woods of Yoknapatawpha County. And though Carter had fudged tough ideological questions like abortion and busing during the campaign, showing just enough ankle to liberals to get by, he was at heart a herald of the "new Democrats" who would recast the party to serve middle-class dreams in the decades ahead. There were serious ideological rifts between the old liberal gang on Capitol Hill and the new crowd at the White House.

Not surprisingly, the awkward relationship between the President and the Speaker became the reigning metaphor for the problems in the

Democratic family. "I'm sure there are things that we did that we could have done stylistically differently, that would have patched over some of these differences. But the thing that was unavoidable and inescapable was that Tip O'Neill and Jimmy Carter disagreed," said Jordan.

"Carter had a different sense of what the Democratic Party was all about," Jordan said. "I can remember in 1975 and 1976 going to eighty-eight conferences around the country. They had these godawful forums with 99.9 percent screaming, unrealistic, doctrinaire liberals. . . . Jimmy Carter would stand up and talk about trying to balance the budget . . . [and] people would hiss or boo him.

"There was hostility toward Carter preaching this new message, but in fact that new message was much more in tune with what the American people wanted in 1976 and 1980," Jordan said. "Carter's reading of the American mood was more accurate and perceptive than that of Speaker O'Neill. So there was a basic cleavage that started from the outset.

"One of a number of great myths about the Carter presidency is that he and Tip O'Neill developed a deep affection for one another," said Jordan. "I remember the times I would see Carter in meetings with the legislative leadership talking about cutting the budget and reducing jobs programs. O'Neill's eyes would just roll back in his head. It was like a bad dream. He'd spent all of his life waiting to be Speaker of the House and to have a Democratic President."

O'Neill's perception of the Georgians wasn't much different. "They ran against the Tip O'Neills — the cigar-smoking, whiskey-drinking Irish politicians," he recalled. "They were all parochial. They were incompetent. They came with a chip on their shoulder against the entrenched politicians. Washington to them was evil. They were going to change everything and didn't understand the rudiments of it."[4]

THE ILL-FATED CARTER inherited a backlog of intractable issues. Foremost among the pending problems were the related demons of economic stagnation and energy, but there were other stubborn matters like welfare reform, tax simplification, soaring health care costs, inflation and environmental protection on the national agenda. On the international front, Carter was handed the fragile Middle East peace process, the job of crafting new relationships with the Soviet Union and China, and a revival of anti-Americanism in Nicaragua and Panama. Many of these issues exposed the fractures in the Democratic

Party. "We had no unifying Democratic consensus, no program, no set of principles on which a majority of Democrats agreed," said Landon Butler, another of the original Georgians. "As we addressed this myriad of issues we had to have an ad hoc approach to every issue. If we dealt with the natural gas problem, we put together one coalition; if we dealt with the Panama Canal, we'd put together an entirely different coalition. We would wind up with a hodge-podge, ad hoc approach." Throughout the Nixon years, the Democrats in Congress had dreamed of a kindred partner who would join them in releasing a pent-up font of patronage and costly social programs. Instead, they got a crusty moralist who disdained the spoils system and loaded their plates with the spinach of governing. "Carter didn't have a political mind that looked at the Congress as trying to assemble and sustain a governing majority," said Jordan. "He looked at Congress and said, 'Okay, deregulation or whatever is the right thing to do. I'm going to draft a good bill. I'm going to send it up there. I'm going to talk to the American people and based on the merits we are going to have it passed — and, oh yeah, ol' Tip is going to help us.'

"He didn't think, well, we just sent two really hot potatoes up there for them to handle, let's send something that helps Democrats in the 1978 congressional races," said Jordan.

"The President disdained political calculations for major decisions," said aide Anne Wexler. "I would say, on several occasions, that there were political consequences to be faced by making a decision, and he would say he didn't want to hear about that. He wanted to do what was right. And, as you know, he was tenacious. It probably drove Tip crazy. . . . It was a matter of some frustration to all of us who tended to feel that politics is an honorable profession." Indeed, Carter later decried the "insidious legal bribery . . . that is pervasive in Congress" in which "a committee chairman can get a $40,000 contribution from a lobbying group . . . providing he's subservient to the lobbying group's interest."

The final challenge for the new President was the nature of the postreform Congress. "If a previous President wanted to pass a bill in Congress, he'd get Speaker Sam Rayburn and Majority Leader Lyndon Johnson and George Meany and maybe somebody from the business community. They could sit down in the Oval Office and write a tax bill and leave with a high degree of confidence that it would pass pretty much in the form they had agreed on," said Jordan. "Our experience was that you could have the President and the Speaker and the committee chairs putting a full-court press on a piece of legislation on the Hill, and you could get defeated in subcommittee by a group of people whose names were barely recognizable to you."[5]

It was against this difficult backdrop that Carter and O'Neill conducted their courtship, and the differences were manifest from the start. When O'Neill told Ari Weiss to poll the House committees and draw up a plan for early legislative activity, it included such liberal totems as a public service jobs program, a federal pay raise, expansion of Social Security, establishment of a Consumer Protection Agency and a number of other measures dear to labor and environmentalists. O'Neill's own wish list was topped by his desire to take the first steps toward federalizing health insurance — perhaps by creating a new Medicare-style program to cover catastrophic care. But when O'Neill's aides contacted Carter's domestic affairs adviser, Stuart Eizenstat, they discovered their dreams were not shared by the President-elect. Carter was thinking instead about tax cuts, curbing government spending, reforming regulatory agencies, relief for small businesses and putting welfare recipients to work. In bold letters the memo warned O'Neill: "NOTE: CARTER IS COMMITTED TO A BALANCED BUDGET BY THE END OF HIS FIRST TERM."

O'Neill traveled to Lovejoy, Georgia, with other members of the leadership on November 17, two weeks after the election, to meet with Carter at the 3,000-acre estate of Senator Herman Talmadge. The Speaker noted with interest a display case holding bullets pried from the walls of the property; they had been fired by troops under the command of Union General William Tecumseh Sherman during their famous march to the sea. Carter began the meeting by requesting congressional authority to reorganize the executive branch. He then asked O'Neill and others for their advice on setting up the White House congressional liaison office. All went well until Carter turned the subject to foreign affairs ("I couldn't understand why he was getting into something of this nature," O'Neill told his diary) and the need for a balanced budget. "New programs have got to be phased in slowly," Carter said.

The President-elect began to close the meeting when O'Neill spoke up about the high unemployment rate: "Gee, wait a minute — I think we'd be terribly remiss if we left this meeting without discussion of some kind of stimulus package to move the economy of the country. That's what people are interested in.

"We've talked about reorganization, liaison, foreign affairs, funding, economy and a balanced budget. But we haven't talked about a stimulus package," O'Neill told Carter. "I think you've got to have something going."

Everyone sat back down and the conversation was revived. O'Neill later summed it up as a "very friendly and amiable meeting," but the gulf in attitudes was clear. In a subsequent meeting with his committee chairmen, O'Neill warned them that he was going to be firm in scheduling the Carter program for consideration in the House, but that he would not be "a rubber stamp."

On January 7, Carter had another meeting with the leadership of Congress — this time in Plains. After helping themselves to a make-your-own-sandwich bar, the President-elect and the senators and congressmen sat in a circle in the living room of Pond House, the President's mother's home. During one break in the discussions, Carter told O'Neill and Jim Wright that if Jack Brooks or any other House chairman tried to stall the administration's agenda — in this case the reorganization plan — he would use the powers of the Presidency to take his case to the people. Wright later recalled that O'Neill looked as if he had been handed "strychnine on the rocks" to drink.

"That would be the worst thing you could do, Mr. President," said the Speaker. "Particularly with a fellow like Brooks. Jack doesn't get mad; he gets even. You don't know your throat is cut until you try to turn your head."

Carter and the congressional leaders agreed on a two-year, $30 billion stimulus program. At the President-elect's insistence, the plan gave short shrift to a federal jobs program but included a tax rebate of $200 for a family of four. O'Neill's mood was not improved by the steady pain he felt in his bladder as the long day progressed. Though he frequently excused himself to go to the bathroom, he could not find relief. On the way to the airport from Plains, his car left the motorcade and headed to a nearby hospital, where he was catheterized, and "I felt like a racehorse; they took about a quart of piss," he told his aides. He had been having prostate problems for some time, and would suffer throughout his speakership, but put off any time-consuming surgery for fear it would make him look old and vulnerable. He flew back to

Washington that night and rested for four days, taking medication, in the Bethesda Naval Medical Center.

Nor did O'Neill much care for Carter's reliance on political symbolism. The President cut back the White House use of limousines, enrolled his daughter, Amy, in public school, sold the presidential yacht *Sequoia* and stopped the bands from playing "Hail to the Chief." The Speaker "resented very much the Carter campaign" and Carter's subsequent decision "to be Roosevelt — going to have fireside chats with those sweaters and all that bullshit," said Leo Diehl. In a break from past practice, Carter had the congressional leaders say grace before their White House breakfast. At a steering committee breakfast soon thereafter, O'Neill astonished his colleagues by opening their meeting with a prayer. But then he looked up with a twinkle and said, "That ought to last us for the year."[6]

The differences between O'Neill and the Carter administration were compounded by a series of confrontations over petty, trivial matters. "Tip took great offense to little things," said Jody Powell, the White House press secretary. In retrospect, most of the early clashes can be attributed to the Georgians' inexperience, or to lapses in communication. O'Neill and his staff, however, chose to chew on each episode as an intentional slight, and then leaked their own version to the press as a parable of Carter's ineptness. Leading the list was the Rashomon-like saga of the Inaugural Gala tickets.

This much was undeniable: as part of the preinaugural festivities there was an inaugural gala with famous performers at the Kennedy Center. It is known that the Speaker and his wife attended, and had excellent seats. It is also true that a block of seats which the Speaker's office had ordered at the last minute from the White House for the O'Neill family and friends, including Eddie Boland and his wife, Mary, were in the back row of a balcony. It was a mistake, Carter conceded years later, that his staff should not have made.

But if the basic facts were indisputable, the details, hows and whys were not. O'Neill claimed that the "lousy" seats were a calculated insult, designed to show the Speaker that the new team wouldn't kowtow to Congress. When he called the White House to complain, O'Neill said, he got a brush-off from Jordan, who flippantly offered to refund the Speaker's money. "I'll ream your ass, you sonofabitch," O'Neill reportedly thundered.

No way, the Georgians insisted: it was all a fantasy concocted by O'Neill. Jordan insisted that the infamous "ream-your-ass" exchange never took place. "I have heard the story. It assumes that I am stupid and it assumes that I am rude," Jordan said. "It never happened." According to Moore, the Speaker's office had been sent a pair of good tickets to the VIP section, which O'Neill's staff — knowing he detested formal affairs — had given away to two pals from North Cambridge. When the O'Neills expressed their interest at the eleventh hour, Frank Moore, Carter's head of congressional liaison, said, members of Carter's staff gave up their own tickets so that Tip and Millie could have good seats and the members of the Speaker's party could be fitted into the hall at all. "And looking down to the VIP section, among all the senators and Supreme Court justices, were these two guys from Cambridge, waving at everybody and having a good time," Moore said.

O'Neill did call Jordan, who was distracted by the work of staffing the government and perplexed because he thought the White House had actually done quite well at fulfilling the Speaker's last-minute requests. Eleanor Kelley recalled that after talking to the White House, her boss was indeed "livid." But she said that O'Neill was more astounded by Jordan's insensitivity than angry at his rudeness. "Do you know what he said to me? 'If you want your money back we will send back a check.' He missed my point entirely," O'Neill told Kelley.

The "ream-your-ass" remark may actually have been made a week later, when Jordan paid a visit to the Hill. By then, the White House had further infuriated O'Neill by rejecting two of his suggested appointments — James Gavin for CIA director and Robert Griffin to head the General Services Administration — and compounded the insult by not consulting O'Neill before naming two Massachusetts Republicans to administration posts: Elliot Richardson as ambassador to a United Nations conference on maritime law and Evan Dobelle, the former mayor of Pittsfield, as head of protocol at the State Department. The Speaker saw Richardson as a potential obstacle to his son Tommy's hopes of running for governor. Marty Nolan reported that O'Neill "spoke in surgical metaphors, suggesting painful and indelicate rearrangement of Hamilton Jordan's anatomy" when they met in late January.

Years later, Diehl said that O'Neill staged the ticket flap for a purpose. "O'Neill went down to Georgia and he found Carter real standoffish. Anti-Washington. That was his whole campaign. And how they were going to stay away from the Washington crowd, including O'Neill and his staff," Diehl said. And so O'Neill was primed for any slight, and ready to retaliate when his family wound up in the rear of the hall. "They stuck the whole family in the upper deck of the balcony or somewhere. And Jesus, that started it — Tom would let you know if he thought you screwed him," said Diehl. "Really, he didn't care about the tickets. This was a message. This is the way he wanted to be treated. He used it to send the message."

O'Neill's tantrum spoke of petulance and pride. The White House staff clearly had other things on their mind; indeed, after leaving the gala, Carter had gotten briefed by the Joint Chiefs of Staff on the procedures for launching a nuclear war. But it was equally true that "the Carter people didn't understand Tip O'Neill; they regarded him as a horse's ass," said Mark Siegel, who worked in the administration but was not a member of the Georgia Mafia. And "if you call someone a horse's ass in the White House, do you know how fast that gets back to someone?" In private, but around enough friends in the press to be sure it got around, O'Neill began to refer to Jordan as "Hannibal Jerkin."[7]

O'NEILL'S RELATIONSHIP with Frank Moore was no better. The members of Congress had not waited until Carter's inauguration to complain about Moore's office: a front-page piece in the *Washington Post* on November 5 had announced to the world, "Hill Democrats Unhappy With Carter's Emissary." Moore was forty, a native of Dahlonega, Georgia, and a longtime member of Carter's inner circle. He had direct access to the Oval Office, the President's confidence and the freedom to be brutally candid when informing Carter about the administration's status on the Hill. Moore believed that his job was to serve Carter, not the Congress. His office would, in time, compile an enviable legislative record and employ some of the most effective members of the White House staff, but Moore's reputation was damaged by a rocky start. He was typecast as a bumbler; the *Post* story portrayed him as a dimwitted "good ol' boy" who could not keep track of more than one problem at a time. In a memo to Carter that day, Moore assured his boss, "We simply didn't play games with some of the members" during the campaign "and as a result some disgruntled persons are putting you on notice by attacking me.

"Some members' egos are hurt that they weren't calling the signals in your campaign, and [are] asserting their independence to see how far they can go with you now that you have won," Moore wrote. Moore had indeed ducked O'Neill's phone calls on a voter registration bill — but on Carter's instructions, as the candidate had not wanted to take a stand on the measure. "The first impression just stuck with the press: Frank Moore doesn't return telephone calls. Well, it was true. I was worried about us getting elected; I wasn't worried about kissing some freshman congressman's ass," Moore said.[8]

But even Moore admitted that his office was undermanned and overwhelmed throughout the crucial time when the new President was introduced to the Congress. He made some questionable personnel decisions as well: Rick Merrill, a deputy who worked the House, was a former aide to Phil Burton whose presence irritated O'Neill and Wright. "Recent announcements of the death of the Democratic Caucus in the House (and its replacement by a powerful Speaker) may have been premature," Merrill told Moore. And, "the Wright election was a fluke."

As it struggled to find its legs, the Carter administration found it nigh impossible to pull off some of the most basic political tasks. Representative Herman Badillo of New York was outraged when he heard on the radio only that very day that Carter was touring his district. Republican representative Jack Kemp got to announce the visit of a White House delegation to Buffalo; the city's two Democratic congressmen did not learn about the event until twelve hours before it happened. Carter turned down an invitation from Dan Rostenkowski to address the annual Cook County Democratic Dinner. Peter Rodino griped that the new Attorney General was ignoring him. O'Neill walked out of the White House when Carter kept him and other members of the Massachusetts delegation waiting. "I arrived with my friends and I'm leaving with my friends," he said. Wright asked the White House for three jobs with which to reward supporters; he got one part-time position. O'Neill was angered at the administration's reluctance to clear out Republican holdovers in the regional federal offices in Boston. And no one at the White House bothered to inform Rules Committee chairman Jim Delaney when his son was dumped from a list of nominees to the Securities and Exchange Commission.

"How can I forget the cold treatment I received from you at that event?" Representative Henry Gonzalez of Texas wrote Carter after a rally in San Antonio. "How can I forget being shouldered aside by your entourage? How can I forget the nearly systematic exclusion I got from your staff on political matters that are tremendously important to me? All this is enough to test the loyalty and dampen the enthusiasm of even the most loyal Democrat."

"Two months ago . . . I wrote the President asking him to join with us in honoring Speaker O'Neill at a DSG dinner," Representative Abner Mikva wrote to Moore. "The only response we received to that letter was in the form of remarks . . . regarding a possible problem with respect to the Democratic Party dinner to be held in mid-March." The DSG had addressed those concerns and sent a second invitation, Mikva said. "There was no acknowledgement or response whatsoever to this letter." Mikva had pressed the White House by phone, and had been told that a decision would be made within a week. That deadline came and went as well. "A week has now elapsed . . . during which we have heard nothing — despite four telephone calls . . . which have gone unanswered," Mikva wrote. "We can only conclude, therefore, that the President does not wish to participate in the salute to Speaker O'Neill and that we are not to be accorded the courtesy of a response informing us of that decision."[9]

On January 25, Carter held his first White House meeting with the congressional leadership. The President told the Democratic congressmen, "I hope to have a tight budget." O'Neill responded as a good soldier, vowing to pass legislation on energy, ethics, the economic stimulus plan and government reorganization by the August recess. "Mr. President, the word 'confrontation' is not in our lexicon, at least for another six months," he said. But when Carter economist Charles Schultze met with the steering and policy committee on February 2 to brief the members on the final stimulus package, O'Neill led the complaints: there just weren't enough funds for public service jobs to satisfy the Democratic caucus, which had endorsed the package by a single vote the night before. "I want to explain the cold facts of political life up here," O'Neill told Schultze. "You came up from Pennsylvania Avenue. We walk down Pennsylvania Avenue. Where we want to meet is in the 800 block. I can't sell, as leader of this House, your program. . . . It has to be increased.

"We don't want the frustrations of a Nixon administration or a Ford administration," O'Neill said. "I am giving you warning, Charlie, that we are going to increase these things along the line." After Schultze left, the steering committee discussed its options and O'Neill told his colleagues that there was "grave dissatisfaction" in the caucus with Carter's conservative approach to federal spending. The Democratic consensus was cracking, and the new President had been in office less than two weeks.

At the next leadership breakfast, on February 8, Carter apologized to "a number of you in Congress [who] have been embarrassed by reading in the newspapers that somebody in your state was appointed to a position that you had not known about. . . . I'm aware of when I make a mistake." But then the President complained that his cabinet officers (who had irritated members of Congress by canceling appointments to appear before the Appropriations Committee and other important panels) were spending too much time preparing and giving testimony to the new, hydra-headed Congress.

"It's been damaging to the government," Carter said.

"This is a part of congressional life that we have always had," O'Neill said. "I have not heard this kind of complaint before, Mr. President." O'Neill's colleagues tried to explain to Carter how the new budget process made such appearances necessary, and how committees jealously vied for the most important cabinet officers to attract television coverage.

"I'll speak frankly if you don't mind. I don't want to stroke you," Carter replied. "You say that you will get television attention with the appearance of a cabinet officer but with one appearance he can get television attention — some of those meetings and appearances by cabinet officers happen seven different times."

The Speaker felt the need to guard congressional prerogatives. "Mr. President," said O'Neill. "The history, the style, the dignity of the Congress must be preserved. We are an equal branch. When we need your cabinet secretaries we will send for them and we will not do so unnecessarily."[10]

Both sides tried to bridge the gap. When O'Neill complained to the press about the skimpy continental breakfasts that the Carter White House served, the table was groaning under plates of eggs, breakfast meat, breads and sweet rolls at the next meeting. "I'll try one," O'Neill said, when the waiter offered him grits. O'Neill also complimented the Baptist President on the quality and fervor of the Protestant prayers at grace, and was struck by the thought that Carter would call on a

Catholic at the next leadership meeting. The Speaker phoned Rostenkowski, and told him to be prepared. Sure enough, at the next breakfast the President called upon Rosty, who responded with "a stream of eloquence that would have done justice to the Archbishop of Canterbury," Wright recalled. O'Neill jabbed Wright in the ribs with an elbow: "Didn't think he could do it, did you?" he said. Yet the differences in their background were always evident, as when O'Neill warned Carter that when dealing with one sly congressman it was good to "keep your left up," and then had to explain it was a boxing metaphor.

"To Jimmy Carter, political machines meant sleepy southern courthouses, corrupt organizations, the sort of thing that almost stole his first election, and Tip O'Neill was the kind of crony-loving, patronage-oriented politician he had fought his entire political life," wrote Martin Tolchin in the *Times*. "To Tip O'Neill, the Democratic Party was like family, loyalty was a commandment and liberalism was a way of life; and this President who had no base in the party, who had won the party's nomination as an outsider, reminded him of the bloodless, moralistic, self-contained Yankees of his childhood."

Carter "spent more time with members of Congress than any other recent President," said Vice President Walter Mondale's chief of staff, Richard Moe. "But he spent the time with them in fairly formal sessions, trying to sell them a specific piece of legislation. It was very seldom spent in a relaxed social setting where these relationships are often cemented. He would never call somebody down from the Hill just to put the feet up on the desk and bring out a bottle of Scotch and have a cigar. And he seldom called them down for advice. It was usually to tell them what he wanted. . . . He hated small talk of any form. He felt that every waking moment should be spent at work, and if you were going to relax, you planned your relaxations, you went out and jogged. But you never sat down and just chatted with members of Congress."

Said Carter: "We had them over . . . in groups of thirty or forty ad nauseam. I mean, it was horrible. Night after night after night after night going through the same basic questions when I was absolutely convinced that the House members knew they ought to support the legislation."[11]

Government reorganization had been one of Carter's campaign themes, and he pressed the congressional leadership hard on the matter.

"This is a question of honor to me," he told O'Neill and the other leaders at a February 8 meeting. Yet Carter got little credit for his triumph when his plan passed the House that spring. It was a recurring phenomenon: no matter how successful the Carter administration was, it rarely (the Camp David peace accord being the major exception) received its due in the media. The news of Carter's success on one front invariably had to compete with developments or defeats in the other battles he had started.

Much of the problem was Carter's fault. He saw himself as a trustee, and when confronted by a problem felt compelled to try and solve it. "The President has been taking a checklist approach to legislation. He sends proposals to the Hill without having had his people lay the proper foundation. Members feel that they are being surprised with legislation and pressured to move faster than common sense dictates," Ari Weiss told O'Neill in a memo. "Just as members are no longer blindly obedient to the leadership, they are no longer especially impressed with the presidential label. . . . The President should not exhaust his store of goodwill on non-priority fights."

It was not a thing to ask of Jimmy Carter. Jordan recalled how, in the closing hours of the congressional session, O'Neill asked Mondale to come up with a list of four or five priorities from the twenty-odd pieces of legislation still pending on the Hill. Mondale and Jordan and Moore went over the list, and named five priorities. Carter reviewed the list, and added eleven more "and so the list we sent back to the Speaker had sixteen instead of twenty," Jordan recalled.

Carter couldn't help himself. "Everybody has warned me not to take on too many projects so early in the administration, but it's almost impossible for me to delay something that I see needs to be done," he told his diary. The committee system was bent to the point of breaking. In Carter's first seven months in office, he asked the Ways and Means Committee alone to craft a package of energy taxes, a stand-by gas tax, the economic stimulus plan, income tax reform, health care cost containment and welfare reform — any one of which, in a normal year, could be considered a singular accomplishment. "You have an awful lot of balls in the air at the same time," O'Neill warned him at a leadership breakfast.[12]

The pent-up tensions between Carter and the Congress erupted that spring. One of Carter's first chores had been to revise the Ford administration's budgets for the 1977 and 1978 fiscal years. In doing so, the new President made a decision to eliminate 19 federal water projects and reconsider some 300 others. These were prized chunks of congressional pork that, in many cases, had been nurtured for years by senior members of the House and Senate. Lawmakers waited their turn for the big dams, irrigation canals and reservoirs, which boosted the local economy and made the congressmen heroes in newspapers, barber shops and Rotary Clubs back home. "This is motherhood," said one congressional aide. "In a democracy," Mondale counseled Carter, "someone's waste is another person's treasure."

But Carter concluded that many of the water projects were economically wasteful and environmentally unsound. Word that he had a "hit list" spread across Capitol Hill in late February. "The problem was a lack of notification and consultation," said Moore. "I remember [Public Works Committee chairman Harold] Biz Johnson [of California] calling me. He said, 'I just got up and I've never been so upset in my whole life. I just read it in the paper.'" Many of the water projects were indeed outdated boondoggles, but if Carter had deliberately set out to alienate Congress he could hardly have done a better job.

"I can't tell you, Mr. President, how much damage the water project list is doing to our efforts," Senate majority leader Robert Byrd told Carter when the Democratic leaders gathered to discuss passage of Carter's economic program in early April. Carter refused a proffered deal. He would not, he told the congressional leaders, trade votes on water projects for his economic plan. It was not right.

Then "we don't have a prayer," said Senator Hubert Humphrey. The Congress quickly passed a measure that prohibited the administration from cutting funding for the water projects from the 1977 budget, but Carter pressed on, adding to the hit list for the 1978 budget. The President's refusal to deal on the water projects had "confirmed the fears of those senators in attendance that you are all take and no give, that your decisions are irrevocable, and your demands are non-negotiable," White House aide Dan Tate wrote the President. "The concern around the Senate is that you are naive or selfish or stubborn, perhaps all three. Most senators already see you as hard-nosed and they respect that, but they also see some signs which, to them, indicate that you are hard-headed and, even worse, high-handed."

As he sparred with them about water, Carter was demanding that the congressional leaders push through his proposal for a $50-per-

person tax rebate. O'Neill and others thought it was useless, but steered the tax cut through the House. At Carter's insistence, Bob Byrd and Edmund Muskie of Maine, the chairman of the Senate Budget Committee, twisted arms and got four Democrats on the panel to change their votes and support the tax rebate. Nine days later, Carter announced that he had changed his mind and was dumping it. Frank Moore told Carter that Muskie "feels that we have . . . made a fool of him. . . . He believes he went to the wall for us . . . tearing his Committee apart along party lines . . . and making several speeches in support of the rebate . . . only to have us pull the rug out from under him."

Byrd met privately with Dan Tate, the White House liaison to the Senate. "Senator Byrd asked twice if you and your advisers . . . really recognized that a President cannot deal with the Congress in the same fashion that a governor deals with a state legislature," Tate reported. "He said that the way you handled the rebate situation could have serious repercussions. When you again ask congressional leaders to carry the ball on a controversial issue, some might not be willing to go to the wall, fearing that you might change your mind and leave them high and dry, embarrassed and battered politically."[13]

CARTER'S ABANDONMENT of the $50 rebate was evidence that the President had changed his economic priorities. He had concluded that the unemployment he warned about during the 1976 campaign was not as important as the threat of inflation, which was back to double digits that spring. A tax cut would be inflationary, as would further spending programs. In an April 19 breakfast with the leadership, Carter complained that Congress had added $61 billion to his budget. "It is almost impossible to stop spending programs once they get started," Carter said. The Democratic Party needed to "remove the stigma of unjustified spending." In the shorthand of the Hill, the word went out: the President had ordered "No new programs."

Four days later, Carter invited Federal Reserve Board chairman Arthur Burns to make the case against inflation at a summit meeting of administration and congressional officials. Burns and Charles Schultze lectured the Congress on the need for restraint, and Schultze said that the national economy would grow by 5 percent a year if American businessmen only had more confidence that the Democrats in Washington were fiscally prudent. O'Neill was mostly silent, but he went home that day, talked with his colleagues, and weighed the competing causes of cooperation and compassion. He returned to the White House for breakfast the next morning.

O'Neill reminded the President that they were Democrats: "The champions of the poor and the indigent." The nation's Democratic mayors and the Congressional Black Caucus were in arms. Liberals worried about the 7 million children on welfare and the 7 percent unemployment rate. "I can read this Congress," O'Neill told Carter. "If there is no move to serve those who need compassion, we'll run into a bag of troubles." O'Neill was particularly angry that Carter was taking advice from Burns, a Nixon appointee.

"When Arthur Burns starts praising" the economic policy of a Democratic President, "somebody has changed along the line and it isn't me," said the Speaker.

"Mr. President," O'Neill said. "There was no dialogue yesterday. Please don't think that silence meant consent. I wouldn't want to lead you down that road."[14]

BUT CARTER WAS DETERMINED, and now threatened to veto three costly bills, including the water projects legislation. O'Neill, the ultimate party loyalist, faced the ugly prospect of having a Democratic House try to override a Democratic President's vetoes. Avoiding a first-term veto was the "goal which the Speaker has uppermost in his mind," Carter's staff told him. O'Neill decided to make a personal appeal to the President.

Despite their sharp words in the privacy of the White House leadership meetings, Carter appreciated the fact that O'Neill was such a strong and vocal defender of the President in public. Carter had been pleased and surprised when O'Neill had gone on *Face the Nation* in late February and defended the administration's economic policy. "I really appreciated the comments you made yesterday," Carter told the Speaker, in a handwritten thank-you note.

In March, Jimmy and Rosalynn Carter invited Tip and Millie O'Neill to a private supper at the White House. "The Speaker is committed to making the administration look good. He is intensely partisan and still views himself as majority leader," Moore said to Carter in a briefing paper. "He has gone to the wall with us a number of times in the past two months." The supper went well. O'Neill entertained Carter with his stock of stories, and gave him advice on how to handle the Congress. The relationship warmed further when, on May 22,

Carter took O'Neill on Air Force One to Notre Dame University, where the President gave a commencement address and both he and the Speaker were awarded honorary Doctor of Law degrees. "I am proud that we received together the honor," Carter wrote him. The next day, back in Washington, O'Neill dropped by the *New York Times* bureau for a long interview with editors and reporters. The President was a "beautiful" man, O'Neill declared.

On June 1, O'Neill went to the White House for another dinner with Carter, to talk to the President about the vetoes. Millie bowed out because Rosalynn was away on a tour of South America. So Carter and his children and O'Neill joined hands and said grace; they sipped Frescas and dug into lamb curry, salad and pie; the Speaker told stories about Sam Rayburn, JFK and John McCormack, and then the President and O'Neill had their private chat. O'Neill conceded that the President could probably sustain a veto of the water projects and other measures. He showed Carter the results of a poll conducted for Joe Moakley, which gave the President an 86.2 approval rating in Massachusetts. But he asked Carter to step back from the brink. "We don't want any vetoes," he said. "We've got seven and a half years to go. Let's keep our eye on the main priorities. Don't waste your store of goodwill on secondary matters. Let's concentrate on what's important." The two shared cigars on the Truman balcony.

"He was reluctant, like most people, to confront me directly and say, 'Mr. President, you are making a serious mistake. There is a better way to do this.' Instead, he would tell me about his relationship with previous Presidents, and get a very closely paralleled situation and say, 'This is the way we worked it out before, and we were successful,'" Carter remembered. "He didn't even spell out how he had worked it out. He just left that thought with me and the next day, or maybe the same night, I would be saying, 'Now why don't we try this same thing, Tip? It's already been successful in your dealings with other Presidents.' There was a subtlety there, but a very great strength, and a wisdom that was beneficial to me."[15]

Carter was moved. To improve relations, he dispatched Jordan and two other aides to sit in at a June 14 session of the steering committee and listen to the gripes about patronage. "We appreciated the frank way in which these concerns were presented," Jordan wrote O'Neill in a follow-up note. On that same day, the House voted to fund all but one of the water projects, but as O'Neill predicted, the margin was not big enough to overturn a presidential veto. Carter was inclined to hang tough, but O'Neill pleaded with the President to accept a compromise, in which just nine water projects would be eliminated, and so end the divisive battle.

"We had the water projects won, but Tip undercut us by calling Carter with a 'compromise' that saved some of them," Moore said. Over time, Carter came to doubt his decision. In his memoirs, one of his chief regrets was that he listened to O'Neill on "those worthless dam projects." The compromise "was accurately interpreted as a sign of weakness on my part, and I regretted it as much as any budget decision I made as President," he wrote.

O'Neill, however, heaved a sigh of relief. The White House might not have been able to arrive at priorities, but he surely could.[16]

CHAPTER 20

The Politics of Inclusion

CARTER MAY HAVE RUED the deal on water, but O'Neill was convinced that the squabble was an unnecessary diversion from what the President had listed as his top priority: addressing America's energy crisis. In the most memorable televised address of his first year in office, Carter had donned a cardigan sweater on February 2 and promised to deliver a comprehensive energy program to Congress within ninety days. In April, having met his deadline, he asked the American people to enlist in a cause of sacrifice and discipline that was "the moral equivalent of war."

The energy crisis traced its roots to the Arab-Israeli war of 1973, and the subsequent emergence of OPEC — the cartel of oil-producing nations — as a muscular player in international affairs. In many ways, it was one more price the U.S. paid for the disastrous intervention in Vietnam. As the price of oil doubled, then doubled again, Presidents Nixon and Ford found their hands tied by their weak political standing at home and the decline of American prestige in the wake of the U.S. retreat from Southeast Asia. The energy crunch further fed the stagflation that so frustrated U.S. Presidents throughout the 1970s, as the bill for the duplicitous financing of the Vietnam War came due. Japan and Germany were emerging as economic rivals, forcing U.S. industry into a painful retrenchment, and the Soviets still posed a cold war check on whatever notions the United States might have had, as a great power, to intimidate the oil-producing nations.

Oil consumption of the United States and other industrial nations had risen by about 8 percent a year during the 1960s. In 1970, U.S. oil production reached its high-water mark — 11.3 million barrels a day — and still just barely met domestic demand. As demand continued to increase, American reserves were depleted, domestic production dropped and the nation grew increasingly reliant on foreign supplies. "Demand is increasing fantastically," Ari Weiss warned O'Neill in 1974. "Domestic production has been declining by some 300,000 barrels per day each year."

The U.S. looked to the Persian Gulf states, particularly Saudi Arabia, to meet the need for oil, and by the time Carter took office, American dependence on foreign reserves had risen from 25 percent to 50 percent. The demand was met, but the cost of oil rose from under $2 a barrel in 1970 to more than $11 in December 1973. The hour-long lines at gas stations in the winter of 1973–74 seemed to confirm the rhetoric of politicians like California governor Jerry Brown, who talked about a time of limits. Indeed, the oil shock of 1973 was a contributing factor to both the drop in the U.S. gross domestic product by 1.7 percent in 1974 and 1.9 percent in 1975, and to the simultaneous arrival of double-digit inflation.

The Ford and Nixon years had not passed without some successful efforts to deal with the problem. A strategic petroleum reserve was established, the huge Alaskan pipeline was approved and motor vehicles were required to meet fuel-efficiency standards. The economic squeeze eased in 1976, with growth in GDP of 5 percent, and candidate Carter had not found it necessary to include energy as a major issue in either his acceptance speech at the Democratic convention, or his inaugural address. Most Americans had grown accustomed to paying up to $1 per gallon for gas. Yet Jimmy Carter felt the obligation to be a good steward, and found it impossible to ignore the inadequacies of U.S. energy policy.

"Nobody ever had the courage to bite the bullet," O'Neill had told the members of the Democratic caucus in 1975. "President Eisenhower, President Kennedy, President Johnson, President Nixon or

President Ford: all along the line. All the Congresses and all the people of America . . . it was like the ostriches sticking their heads in the sand."

The political problem — which had so thoroughly frustrated the Nixon and Ford administrations — was both ideological and geographic. The producing states of the South and West were increasingly more Republican and conservative; they had proportionately more power in the Senate than the House, and believed that the nation could close the gap between production and consumption if the government would only deregulate the energy industry and allow rising prices to spur exploration and production. The House, on the other hand, was controlled by a liberal Democratic leadership that embraced the views of the energy-consuming states of the Northeast and Midwest and environmentalists from around the nation; it favored conservation, wanted to keep prices tightly regulated and suspected that the energy industry was itself a cause, not a cure, of the crisis.

Carter had proposed to lift controls of oil and gas during the campaign. If the White House had only coupled decontrol with new windfall profits taxes, Carter's domestic policy advisor, Stuart Eizenstat said later, the President might have steered the package through Congress quickly, been hailed as a miracle worker and won a second term. But the new administration shied away from decontrol because Gerald Ford had failed to get deregulation of gas and oil through Congress. "We did not realize the currents were changing," said Eizenstat. Carter instead struck a middle course as President, with a baffling program of 113 interlocking provisions that was designed to raise prices, encourage conservation and capture excess profits via a series of energy taxes. It was an "utter and tragic catastrophe," said Eizenstat. "We turned out to be on the wrong side."[1]

O'Neill, handed the President's plan, recognized that he and Carter had some honeymoon capital to spend, but that it would vanish over time. He also knew that the lobbyist's best friend was delay — that the oil companies and other opponents would try to tie up Carter's plan in the House committees, where a few friends of the energy industry could spin the strands that would strangle it to death. Lobbyists for Exxon and other energy giants had told him as much. Convinced that nothing good could come from the Democratic administration, the industry would exploit the "conflict of jurisdiction" to "maintain the status quo," they said.

The Speaker's solution was bold and innovative: he would appoint an ad hoc committee on energy, and use his power of scheduling legislation to set a deadline that would counter the clout of the committees of jurisdiction.[2] O'Neill had decided on his strategy long before Carter donned his cardigan sweater; he had announced plans for an energy committee when meeting with the House freshmen in December 1976, and told his staff to come up with a format. The energy industry could be counted on to oppose anything that threatened its intricate relationship, cultivated over the years, with the jurisdictional matrix that governed energy. And the committee chairmen would passionately fight any attempt to give an ad hoc committee the power of drafting the legislation. But there was room for some sort of superseding authority — what Mo Udall called a "council of elders" and John Dingell an "umbrella committee" or "super Rules Committee" — to make sure that Congress didn't botch the highly visible duty it had been given by the new President.

Inclusion was the key, O'Neill decided. If influential members of the authorizing committees were appointed to the ad hoc panel, they would contribute their expertise and prestige to its deliberations. With a stake in the panel's success, they would feel no need to gut its handiwork. And by including them in the process, O'Neill would ease their fears about losing influence. Because they were included, the chairmen were willing to cede to the ad hoc panel (in effect, to cede to themselves) the authority to sit as a final arbiter of disputes.

"Our past energy failures have most often resulted because disagreements were left to be worked out on the floor. This proposal has the virtue of establishing a forum, and a new pressure, to work out disagreements ahead of time," Weiss wrote O'Neill. To keep the process moving in the face of the industry's delaying tactics, O'Neill used his power as Speaker to set firm deadlines. The package would be passed before the August recess, and if any standing committee failed to meet the July 13 deadline of reporting legislation, it would forfeit the right to draft its segment of the bill. And since O'Neill would appoint the members of the ad hoc committee, he could stack it in favor of the President's plan.

"The issue is terrifically parochial, but this is as severe as a war. The crisis is upon us, and by 1985 we could be stripped of our defense as a nation," O'Neill said on April 20, the day that Carter brought his proposal to the Hill. The President's other run-ins with Congress were "mere skirmishes," said O'Neill. "This is a battle."

O'Neill selected Lud Ashley to chair the 37-member ad hoc committee on energy. It was a good choice. Ashley was a Yale graduate who represented the industrial city and ethnic wards of Toledo, Ohio. He had voted with industry to postpone clean air standards, yet had the guts to vote for a higher gas tax in 1975. He had shown his popularity in running a close, though unsuccessful, race for the chairmanship of the Budget Committee. Though he was not a member of any of the standing committees that routinely struggled for jurisdiction over energy, neither was he captive of the industry lobbyists that infiltrated their offices. He was no O'Neill sycophant, but got along well with the Speaker and was more than grateful for the appointment. In choosing the members of the panel, O'Neill deftly exploited the fact that the selection process for the ad hoc committee was organized along committee, and not regional, turf. As the House focused its attention on how many seats each committee would get, O'Neill quietly shortchanged the oil-producing states. And when it came to selecting representatives from the Sunbelt, the Speaker picked flexible wheeler-dealers like Texan Charlie Wilson over industry champions.[3]

As MIGHT BE EXPECTED with rookies in both the Oval Office and the Speaker's chair, the passage of the energy package through the House had its share of suspenseful moments. Carter's efforts to sell the package suffered from inconsistency, and from competition with other White House initiatives. The program suffered immediate reversals when the standing committees began to vote: a standby gasoline tax was shot down in Ways and Means, and the Commerce Committee approved an amendment to deregulate natural gas. Carter stewed, and blasted the Commerce Committee's action as a "ripoff of the American consumer."

But, as in the water projects fight, Carter took O'Neill's counsel and backed off. "I've worked very hard on this," the Speaker told *Newsweek*. "If it fails, I'm not as good as I think I am." Foes tried to stall, but O'Neill laid down the law. "I'll be biting your ass," he warned members of the ad hoc panel. "We will not go home without an energy bill," he told the Rules Committee. When Dingell objected to the pace, the Speaker responded, "John, you know when I was speaker of the Massachusetts House and told a committee chairman to report out a bill by a certain date, if he didn't I'd have a new chairman the next day." With a smile O'Neill added, "I don't have that power here." But Dingell got the message. O'Neill intervened in the Commerce Committee, lobbying members until they reversed the vote to deregulate natural gas.

Personnel changes helped as well. The Speaker installed Irv Sprague, who had lobbied the Hill for Lyndon Johnson and worked in the House whip's office, as head of the steering committee staff. Sprague had the invaluable perspective of someone who worked at both ends of Pennsylvania Avenue and liked Frank Moore and understood his problems. When O'Neill wanted to send a message to the White House about the need for a shakeup of Moore's staff, he told Sprague to "straighten it out." That day, over lunch, Sprague told Moore that he needed to find a lobbyist to work the House who spoke the Speaker's language and understood the institution. Bill Cable, said Sprague, fit the bill. Cable, then thirty-two, was a burly, tall congressional aide who looked a little like a young O'Neill, shared the Speaker's love of sports and spent much of his time hanging out in O'Neill's office. It was no accident that Carter's influence in the House grew with his appointment.[4]

The regular committees met their deadlines, and the action moved to the ad hoc panel. Again, O'Neill made a critical move to keep the debate away from where it had always wound up: with parochial differences shattering party unity. He took the ad hoc committee's original authority — to ensure consistency — and expanded it beyond all recognition. Ashley, with the ever-present Weiss by his side, called the Democratic members of the energy committee into closed-door caucuses, where they virtually rewrote the bill. At a breakfast meeting with the ad hoc panel's Democrats, O'Neill reminded them that their seats on the committee had been prized assignments. For every congressman who was appointed, four supplicants had been rejected. "I selected you. My reputation, our party's reputation, and the House's reputation are tied up with this legislation," he told them.

Carter's "Energy Crusade has been transformed into Tip O'Neill's Party Caucus," the *National Journal* concluded. The Commerce Committee had been bitterly divided on the question of deregulating natural gas — so under a deal worked out by O'Neill and a handful of Texas Democrats, the ad hoc committee sweetened the price structure, but only for independent producers of newly discovered gas, and so secured enough votes from the South and Southwest. Republicans gnashed their teeth, but on one party line vote after another, the Democrats stuck together. A process that might have taken weeks was over in three days, and the package moved to the floor on schedule.

On July 26, O'Neill addressed the steering committee. To avoid mischief on the floor, the Speaker said, he would employ another of his enhanced powers. "In the last week, the ad hoc committee, selected by me, has met to reconcile the legislation reported from the standing committees and shape a comprehensive energy policy," O'Neill told his colleagues. "To the surprise and disappointment of the Republicans, the Democratic members of the ad hoc committee worked together like Democrats. They caucused on all issues, reached consensuses and voted them through the committee.

"So now, with the ad hoc committee's completion of its business, what we have is a Democratic energy bill. This is as it should be. The President is a Democrat. The clear majority of the Congress is Democratic. We cannot, nor should we want to, rely on Republican votes to put through the energy package," he said. "The issues are difficult; all of us are interested in them. In the past, opponents of energy legislation have logrolled and nitpicked them into disarray. To avoid this danger, I will support a rule that limits amendments to major, national and regional, germane issues. The vote on the rule will be a party vote."

Over lunch the next day, O'Neill gave the Rules Committee its orders. "Never before have I been pushed like this by the leadership," said Rules chairman Jim Delaney. The committee members bridled at the Speaker's orders, so O'Neill cleared his calendar and spent hours with them, stroking their egos and arguing his cause.

For the House floor, O'Neill had yet another innovation in mind. The ad hoc committee had rewritten the bill in the form of three major amendments to the work of the standing committees; for each amendment O'Neill now organized a "task force" that would be led by a respected member of Congress — Phil Sharp, Abner Mikva and Dan Rostenkowski. With Ashley's ad hoc committee, the three task forces, the steering committee, the Rules Committee and John Brademas's whip organization, O'Neill now had some 100 members of Congress with a leadership role — and a personal stake — in passing the energy legislation. When combined with those liberal and northern Democrats who were philosophically aligned with O'Neill, he had a formidable starting block of some 150 votes from which to build on any critical roll call.

"The energy bill that comes before the House of Representatives tomorrow has, in the three months since it was unveiled by President Carter, come to bear most dramatically the imprint of House Speaker Thomas P. O'Neill Jr.," the *Times* reported on the eve of debate. "Mr. Carter's real problem will be the Senate, where he lacks as good a friend and as strong a friend as Speaker O'Neill."

The key battle on the House floor — the potential deal breaker — was over deregulation of natural gas. O'Neill and Ashley had bet that, in making the natural gas pricing rules more generous for independent producers of new gas, they could satisfy enough southern and border state Democrats without alienating the northern and midwestern liberals. But to show they were fair, the Democratic leaders allowed the oil states a vote on an amendment to deregulate all natural gas, including the existing reserves controlled by the big oil companies. It was a crucial vote; if the amendment passed, the northerners would turn against the entire package. "I am fearful that if this amendment is adopted, the bill will not pass," O'Neill told the House, as he closed debate on August 3. "I am wondering what America will think. America is watching this legislation more than it has watched any legislation in years. Will the House fail? Can the House act? Can the House put together an energy policy?

"On one side are the people of America [and] the independent producers — the little man from Texas or Oklahoma or Louisiana who invests his money and truly goes out and looks for new gas," said O'Neill. "On the other side is big oil . . . never have I ever seen such an influx of lobbyists in this town as from big oil on this amendment.

"Do you want to go home on Saturday of this week and say that the Congress has failed? As between the people and the independent gas producers working together on one side and big oil on the other: Where do you come down?

"The future of America . . . the economy of this country, the defense of this nation, are at stake," O'Neill said. He won. The deal-killing decontrol amendment was defeated by a 227 to 199 vote. The final package passed the House on a 244 to 177 vote on August 5. "If it wasn't for Mr. O'Neill's decision to create the energy committee, President Carter never would have gotten an energy bill. Never would have happened. There isn't a chance in the world. We never would have gotten those six committees to report," said Cable. "It was another example of Mr. O'Neill's understanding of the machine, and of his craftiness. He understood how the machine worked and where the power levers were and how to push one against the other and make things happen." An ebullient, emotional Carter called O'Neill from Air Force One to thank him. "Jeez, Mr. President, you're bringing tears to my eyes," O'Neill said.[5]

IN THE LONG RUN, the House passage of the energy bill was as important for what it said about the new Speaker and the strategy he employed than for what it actually did to reduce American energy consumption. O'Neill had pioneered the process by which he would govern the House for the next ten years. It came to be known as the politics of inclusion. The idea was to rope your colleagues in, to secure their allegiance by giving them a stake in the results, to share the responsibility and the spoils, and to co-opt resistance. Did the new breed of congressmen and congresswomen, the political entrepreneurs, demand a piece of the action, input and a ticket to the 5 o'clock news? Then O'Neill would give it to them, in return for their loyalty. The ad hoc energy committee and the three energy task forces were just the beginning. Soon every major issue had a task force, and a bright young member to chair it, willing to trade his or her independence for the power and celebrity of serving the leadership. O'Neill didn't "direct" his colleagues to do his bidding, said Philip Sharp, an Indiana Democrat; he "entrusted" them.

The rise of Representative Richard Gephardt, elected in 1976, was illustrative. Soon after taking office, the Carter administration had discovered that the cost-of-living increases were soaring in this time of high inflation, and threatening to bankrupt the Social Security trust fund. After toying with minor cuts in benefits, the Democrats ultimately concluded that a massive hike in the payroll tax was the best way to keep the system solvent. To head the Social Security task force, O'Neill selected the thirty-six-year-old Gephardt, and they pushed the bill through the House before the 1978 election season. It passed on December 15, 1977, by a 189 to 163 margin. It was the largest increase in payroll taxes in history — $227 billion over ten years — but Gephardt and his task force had gotten it done. He moved into the leadership's favor and was soon being hailed in the press as "a force to be reckoned with" because of "his ability to deal with a cross section of House members."

In a written report on the task force system, Irv Sprague said it triumphed because it involved "as many people as possible" and gave them "a personal stake" in the outcome. "We have the policy committee working, we have the whip organization working, we got the Rules Committee working and we get the chairmen all working together," O'Neill told the *National Journal* in June. "I keep myself free. I keep myself open. I listen to them.

"They're part and parcel of the organization. They're part and parcel of making decisions," O'Neill said. "There are more people in the decision making. That's the way I like it, and I'm sure that's the way the members like it."

Listening. The new Speaker met daily with his leadership team — Jim Wright, John Brademas, Tom Foley and Dan Rostenkowski — and weekly with the whips. Two or three times a month, he held meetings of the steering and policy committee — which put its imprimatur on important bills by declaring them matters of party policy. He invited committee chairmen to his office. Outside-interest groups were brought in to endorse legislation and lobby members. The task forces were called together a week to ten days before a bill hit the floor to plot tactics. On the day before a bill was scheduled, O'Neill typically summoned Wright, Brademas, Bill Cable and the task force chairman and made final assignments.[6] "Talk to your assignment in person, in depth. After you spend some time with the member, report your findings. . . . The Speaker and the President will be following up on the information you report. This is an all-out Democratic Party effort. We have to win big. We need commitments we can depend on," read one instruction sheet.

On the day the vote was held, the whips and task force members would work the doors of the chamber, while the party leaders and their aides walked the aisles and the wells, trading favors or making pleas for help. "Outside the chamber, in somewhat gauntlet fashion, lobbyists of one sort and another line the aisle from the elevator to the chamber door, importuning members pro and con," Wright told his diary. "I stand, on critical votes, just inside the door. Usually I take the west door, through which more senior members enter from the elevator which opens upon the Rayburn building subway. John Brademas often mans the east door, entrance for more junior members whose offices are in the Longworth and Cannon buildings. . . . It is a contest in sloganeering.

"It is in one sense a bit frightening — the whole process seems juvenile — but it is absolutely essential on the close ones," Wright wrote.

"The Speaker's task force system you developed in the 95th Congress proved to be the most important single factor in getting critical legislation enacted," Sprague wrote O'Neill. "You named 15 task forces. All were successful. In the process 116 different members were brought into the leadership orbit — some of them a number of times. The task force members, particularly the chairmen, got an awareness of the problems of leadership and a feeling of meaningful participation that paid dividends on later legislation, as they felt some obligation to cooperate with other task forces. Many of the task force members, like [Representative John] Murtha, became emotionally involved with the leadership."[7]

"An old dog can learn new tricks, if he wants to learn," O'Neill liked to say. The politics of inclusion was a new trick. But that didn't mean that some old tricks couldn't work as well. O'Neill showed that much when pushing a new code of ethics through the House.

For a period after Watergate, the House had basked in the glow left by the Judiciary Committee's performance during the Nixon impeachment hearings. But then Wilbur Mills and Wayne Hays self-destructed, and the House squirmed through its own scoundrel time. And so, when promising to break the logjam on energy, O'Neill had also vowed to enact a new ethics code. For this reform he built support in a quite old-fashioned way: he bought his colleagues off with a pay raise.

"The thing Tip did when he became Speaker that was really fabulous was in the area of ethics. And the way he did it was through money," *Time*'s Neil MacNeil remembered. "McCormack told me a hundred times that in 1946, when they had passed a reorganization of Congress, that the reason the members went for it was to get a pay raise he had dangled. Tip knew that from McCormack. It was bait and switch. But it was a terrific thing to do and you wouldn't expect it from a machine politician. That was the first sign of his grandeur as Speaker."

The strategy on ethics was, like the energy scheme, an innovative assembling of off-the-shelf components. In the months since the Hays disaster, a commission led by Representative David Obey of Wisconsin had been studying the House rules with an eye toward reform. Among the matters that the Obey commission recommended were proposals to cap the sources of outside income that members of Congress could earn, and to require that they disclose, in far greater detail, their personal finances. Both ideas were very unpopular among the members of the House, as were proposals to restrict speaking fees, gifts from lobbyists and use of campaign funds for personal obligations. But when Obey asked O'Neill if he should draft a "hard" code or a "soft" one, the Speaker asked, "Which one is best for the House?"

"The hard one," Obey said.

"Then do it," said O'Neill.

O'Neill had some honeymoon capital to spend, but he didn't intend to rely on that alone. In December of 1976, a presidential commission on government salaries had reached the conclusion that members of Congress, federal judges and executive officials deserved more money. The confluence of events was fortuitous. I'll get you your raise, O'Neill told his colleagues, if you accept the new ethics code.

It was a simple strategy, but a complicated plan. Under law, the higher pay was automatic unless Congress voted to turn it down, and critics now called on the Senate and House to reject the "backdoor" raise. O'Neill could not delay a vote forever, but he could stall, betting that the public clamor would die down once the new ethics rules were in place, and that the members would find more resolve (having sampled the fruits of their bigger paychecks) as time went on. The Speaker refused to schedule a vote, and the raise — which hiked congressional salaries to $57,500 and the Speaker's own pay to $75,000 — went into effect on February 20, 1977.

Now O'Neill moved on the ethics code. On February 23, having rammed the measure through the House Ethics and Administration Committees, O'Neill had breakfast with the Rules Committee Democrats. It was Ash Wednesday, a day of fasting for Catholics, and the Speaker picked a taboo piece of bacon from his plate, and tossed it aside as he laid down the law. There were just enough members of the Rules Committee opposed to the limits on outside earnings to endanger the proposed ethics code. O'Neill let them vent, but then he threatened to banish the ringleader, Morgan Murphy of Illinois, to the District of Columbia Committee.

"I've committed myself as the leader of the party to the strongest ethics bill in the history of the country," O'Neill said. "You're my handpicked people, and you all serve on this committee at my behest. . . . When this bill gets to the floor you can vote your own conscience, but I need your support now to get it out of Rules." O'Neill called it "dialoguing people." The package moved from Rules with the votes of all 11 Democrats and the rule survived by a 267 to 153 vote. On one test ballot, fifteen Democrats voted against their leadership. O'Neill told Hymel, "I want their names," and made sure that the press reported his comment.

"I fought for a pay raise for my colleagues," O'Neill told the House, stepping down from the neutrality of the Speaker's chair to close the debate on final passage. "I know some members will have to make a financial sacrifice now. But it's a sacrifice we have to make. America demands a strong code of ethics." The bill passed 402 to 22. "Tip O'Neill was calling in his chips. The tally was a foregone conclusion," the *Times* reported. "That was the day the House knew it had a Speaker."

O'Neill stalled as long as he could, until July, to schedule the vote on repealing the pay raise. In the cloakrooms and hallways, he and his lieutenants portrayed the vote as an act of solidarity.[8] "You were told you were weak and cowardly if you didn't vote for it," Pat Schroeder, an opponent, complained. "There were none of us who didn't get leaned on." O'Neill even put the heat on Boland — or pretended to do so to intimidate other members — by postponing consideration of the measure creating a House Intelligence Committee, which Boland was to chair, until after the vote. When the yeas and nays were called, supporters of the pay raise rushed toward the electronic voting machine with their plastic cards, building a quick lead on the scoreboard and establishing a momentum that never let up. The Democratic leaders stood shoulder-to-shoulder in the well to browbeat anyone who thought about switching. The pay raise survived, 241 to 181.

"In a carefully orchestrated plan to assure that the pay increase would be upheld, House Speaker Thomas P. O'Neill Jr. of Massachusetts had probably his greatest day as the leader of the House, overcoming strong fears of voter reprisal," the *Star* reported.

ENERGY. ETHICS. A pay raise. It was, all in all, a remarkable start for Speaker O'Neill. The Washington press corps had a new hero. To the *Star,* he was a "Strongman." To the *Herald,* "A Winner as House-keeper." To the *Post,* "A Powerful Speaker" and "A Legend Being Born."

"With the gavel in his grip, O'Neill is no longer the shambling, forgetful leprechaun," wrote Marty Nolan in the *Globe.* "He is all business." The *Post* said that "Tip O'Neill wears the speakership like a glove. He and the office were meant for each other."

"Tip O'Neill, in sharp contrast to his two lackadaisical predecessors, rides herd on the House of Representatives these days . . . the most dominant figure in the House since Speaker Sam Rayburn died," wrote Al Hunt in the *Wall Street Journal*. "By almost any standard, the O'Neill leadership so far gets pretty high marks. The Speaker pushed a tough ethics code past some lethal landmines planted by colleagues; the economic stimulus package and government reorganization authority breezed through . . . and Mr. O'Neill, almost routinely, superimposed a special energy committee over the established legislative panels."

"The President views him as a more formidable figure, and desirable ally, than he thought he would be," a White House aide told Hunt. "A lot of people have been crying for leadership," said Representative Anthony "Toby" Moffett of Connecticut. "Now they've got it."

The *Post*'s Mary Russell was a bit more skeptical. "What is so amazing is that he moves like lightning to keep the odor of defeat from rubbing off on him," she wrote. "Albert feared the press. O'Neill plays with it like a cat with a mouse. He has killed the tough, post-Watergate press with candor and charm." It was, a dismayed O'Neill was about to discover, a premature conclusion.[9]

CHAPTER 21

Trouble

YEARS AFTER Richard Nixon resigned, Tip O'Neill told Stan Brand that "Watergate ruined politics." He no doubt reached this conclusion in the difficult period from the fall of 1977 to the spring of 1981, when many of the same forces that he had helped set in motion as the stage manager of impeachment were now directed at him: the prosecutorial press, the congressional investigators, the FBI inquisitors. He would escape his collision with post-Watergate morality by the narrowest of margins.[1]

O'Neill's attitude toward ethics was forged in an earlier era. He always maintained that his career in public service required a financial sacrifice. He was burdened throughout his life by the costs of keeping homes in Washington and Cambridge; the expenses (fruit baskets, charitable contributions, fund-raising tickets, Mass cards and the occasional cash handouts) of a career in politics; and his duty as sole provider for Millie and five children whose tuition costs began with Catholic elementary school and continued through college.[2] "It was a living, but he was very nervous financially," Neil MacNeil recalled.

Legislative salaries were woefully meager for most of O'Neill's time in politics. When he started out in the 1930s, it was expected that politicians of his class would partake in a buffet of accepted perks to supplement their paychecks. O'Neill's standing as a Massachusetts representative with statewide aspirations surely boosted his career as an insurance, real estate and advertising salesman in the 1930s and 1940s. The automobile, piano and cash "purses" given him at the "times" that were thrown in his honor helped O'Neill get by, and the public and press were content with the knowledge that statehouse lobbyists were buying many of the tickets to these affairs. Nor, in those days, were there strict controls on the use of cash to pay for campaign expenses, or rigid definitions of what qualified as an expense.

"I remember when he was elected Speaker of the Massachusetts House they had a party for him in South Boston. A testimonial. And I went down with a fellow from Lowell," said Richard Donahue, who worked in the Kennedy White House. "It was $25 a ticket and the way we figured it out, at the most it would cost five bucks for the overhead. And at the cash bar he was making more money. And you couldn't get in — they had sold more tickets than the place could hold. What was that?

"Well, as another Massachusetts Speaker — David Bartley — once said when they asked him what he was going to do with his campaign money: 'You know, I am driving back and forth on the turnpike to the State House all the time. I could drive off the road, and who is going to take care of the little Bartleys?' Those are the types of funds that may indeed have been accumulated. You operated out of one pocket in those days," said Donahue. "But was Tip a guy out for dough? Absolutely not."

The Kennedy administration "tried to be sensitive about that, and we had some identifiable rogues and rascals we zeroed in on. Fired guys right off the bat," said Donahue. There was no such taint to O'Neill. Eliot Spalding was a reporter and editor at the *Cambridge Chronicle* for the entire length of O'Neill's career — from his first legislative race to his retirement as Speaker of the House. "I never heard his honesty questioned in all that time," Spalding said. Elliot Richardson, the most famous foe of graft and corruption in Massachusetts, made a name for himself by investigating and prosecuting several of O'Neill's close associates, and found nothing that led him to doubt the Speaker's character.[3]

In later years, O'Neill used a political action committee to subsidize his salary. The PAC raised more than $250,000 between 1972 and 1976, of which some $23,000 was spent on car repairs, meals, parties and personal gifts. As a congressman — until he pushed through the changes in the ethics rules in 1977 — O'Neill was allowed to "cash out" his stationery and $500 monthly expense accounts and accept donations to his "office account," an all-purpose fund which could finance travel, meals and other political expenses. At government expense, he leased a $300-a-month automobile.

O'Neill never worried much about the conflicts of interest that reform organizations like Common Cause found so objectionable. In 1976 for instance, he interceded with Georgia state officials to obtain favorable treatment for an insurance company in which, according to that year's financial disclosure form, he owned 4,000 shares of stock.[4] He took meals from lobbyists, used corporate jets and "when he bought the home down here, he told me how proud he was of the low-interest mortgage he got through the mortgage bankers lobby, via the aides on the Banking Committee staff, and never thought twice about saying it," MacNeil said. Nor was O'Neill ever shy about performing "favors" for constituents, campaign contributors, pals and allies. "Sure, he'd pick up a phone for you," said Diehl. "He opened the doors for everyone. He didn't deny you. He was your friend," said Francine Gannon. "You had to sell your product, but he opened the door for you."[5]

Boston-born Jim Wilmot offered a typical example. Wilmot was a financial angel for O'Neill throughout the congressman's rise to power — co-chairing the Democratic congressional dinner in 1974 and assembling an $8,000 bundle of contributions from friends and family for O'Neill's PAC in 1975. Carl Albert called Wilmot "a real good man to know when you have one-third as much money as the Republicans." Hubert Humphrey and Hugh Carey topped a list of other prominent Democrats whom Wilmot called friends, and one of his firms won a $10 million contract to service and fuel all private aircraft at Washington's two federally run airports, which was extended five times without competitive bidding. In 1976, when one of Wilmot's apartment projects was stalled by the Department of Housing and Urban Development, O'Neill telephoned HUD Secretary Carla Hills in an effort to nudge an $88 million federal rent subsidy along.

Word of O'Neill's intervention reached the *New York Times,* and Marty Tolchin called Hymel, who was told by O'Neill to deny that any calls were made on Wilmot's behalf. Only when told that Hills had confirmed Tolchin's account did O'Neill change his story. "Did I make a call for him? Yes. He's my friend. He said he was being pushed around by the department. An inequity and an injustice was happening to him. I'd do it for anyone," O'Neill said. "I don't pressure people. I open the door. I think I have a right and an obligation, when a substantial businessman comes and says an inequity is being done, to call the department head and ask that it be looked into."[6]

O'Neill extended that reasoning to the judicial system. He admitted to calling judges on behalf of defendants. He pestered the federal prison system to get inmates who were represented by politically connected lawyers transferred to more comfortable quarters. Records from the Johnson White House show that, on behalf of one associate, O'Neill tried to get LBJ to pressure the Attorney General to intercede "in a case where the Justice Department and the U.S. Attorney's office [in Boston] are in disagreement," as White House aide Barefoot Sanders wrote the President.[7] The White House refused.

It was up to O'Neill to ask the favor, yet he would not always rage if someone, for good reason, turned him down. Lester Hyman recalled how he and newly elected governor Chub Peabody quaked at the thought of giving one of the congressman's cronies a judgeship. O'Neill's pal "was a real yo-yo. Totally unqualified," said Hyman. "I told Chub, 'You can't appoint him!' but Chub said, 'I can't say no to Tip. We owe him.'" After days of dodging an increasingly irate O'Neill, Hyman was finally ordered to break the bad news.

"What is the problem?" O'Neill demanded.

"He is totally unqualified," said Hyman.

"Why didn't you say so, Les?" O'Neill asked.

As for reporters, O'Neill had two categories. There were the good guys and gals who protected him, who forgave or delighted in the blarney and with whom he shared valuable snatches of an insider's perspective on Congress. And then there were those who "broke the faith," parsed his words and strove to hold him accountable to the post-Watergate standards. Tolchin, a friend and admirer at the *Times,* was banished from O'Neill's office for writing about the Wilmot affair. To Tolchin's amazement, the sentence lasted for an exact year, down to the day — as if O'Neill had circled a date on the calendar, with no time off for good behavior.

"You know, Marty, I'm Irish, and we Irish never carry grudges," said O'Neill, after inviting Tolchin back into the inner sanctum.

"The thought never occurred to me, Mr. Speaker," said Tolchin.

"But that story you wrote about Jim Wilmot was a piece of shit," O'Neill said.

Years later, Tolchin explained, "What I had done was violate Tip's idea of what a newspaper friend did. A newspaper friend was part of the gang, and in exchange for the fellowship and the occasional leaks or tips, you didn't take off on him." Neil MacNeil got the "broke the faith" treatment when O'Neill heard — mistakenly, MacNeil told him — that *Time* was digging into the Speaker's financial affairs in 1978. Their break was permanent. O'Neill's was a strange moral compass: breaking his word to fellow politicians was a mortal sin, but lying to his friends in the press was a part of doing business.

Jack Murtha recalled one episode in which O'Neill agreed to help double the amount of money each congressman could keep from the lucrative speaking fees — "honorariums" — that were paid them by special interests. Murtha waited until Representative Robert Walker, a GOP watchdog from Pennsylvania, was off the floor and they summoned O'Neill to the chamber. "Tip didn't like the interruption at all. But I told him we had to have him in the chair. He didn't duck it," said Murtha.

"So I made the motion for unanimous consent and it went through," Murtha recalled. "Well, afterwards they confronted Tip and he said, 'I didn't know what the hell Murtha was doing.' But he had not pushed the button that cut off the sound at the rostrum, and so they played him the tape of it. I had gone up to him and said, 'Okay, Walker's off the floor. Let's do it right now.' And that was on tape. So he had to admit, 'Okay, I lied.' "

O'Neill was asking for trouble when he carried this attitude into the post-Watergate era. The old breed of reporter would have accepted O'Neill's confessions with a laugh, teasing him for getting caught. The new breed took O'Neill's willingness to lie and twist the truth as proof of deeper dishonesty, and chased him that much harder.[8]

THE CATALYST FOR O'Neill's troubles was Tongsun Park, an ambitious young Korean businessman. Park was a likable, chubby-faced socialite who came from a well-to-do Korean family. He attended Georgetown University's School of Foreign Service in the early 1960s and opened the George Town Club in a nineteenth-century townhouse on Wisconsin Avenue in 1966, worming his way into the cheeseparing heart of Washington society by distributing free memberships and hosting gaudy parties. Among Park's new friends were several members of Nixon's cabinet and justices of the U.S. Supreme Court.

Because of Korea's strict currency laws, Park was chronically short of cash in America. From 1967 on, after Lyndon Johnson dropped by a party that the club had hosted for John McCormack, impressing the powers-that-be in Korea, Park worked as a clandestine agent. He was subsidized by the Korean Central Intelligence Agency, shared his home with a KCIA contact and sent reports on his lobbying efforts back to Seoul, where the government of South Korean president Park Chung Hee was frantic at the prospect that the United States, in the post-Vietnam era, would cut back its military and economic aid to Seoul. Other Korean agents worked on Albert's staff and for a key foreign aid committee, and helped arrange a series of reciprocal visits between Korean legislators and their U.S. counterparts.[9]

The Korean lawmakers got to see the Apollo moon shot take off from Cape Kennedy in 1969 (O'Neill was put in charge of buying gold congressional cufflinks for them to take home as souvenirs), and an American delegation of two dozen congressmen — led by Albert and including Representatives O'Neill, Boland, Tom Foley and Lee Hamilton — was received in Seoul, with visits to a plush casino and a *kee saeng* house, the Korean equivalent of a Japanese geisha house. O'Neill was smitten. "I am overjoyed to report to the Congress that our aid to the Republic of Korea is one of the most worthwhile investments ever made," O'Neill told his colleagues after his return home.

O'Neill tried, generally with success, to stay true to his North Cambridge roots. But he loved the foreign trips he took as a member of Congress. The trips had genuine foreign policy benefits, and aided O'Neill as a leader of the House by generating a spirit of camaraderie among the members. They were quite pleasant junkets, with guided jaunts to tourist attractions, embassy receptions, duty-free shopping, visits to nightclubs and golf clubs and other perks. In 1975, an O'Neill delegation of two dozen members spent more than $70,000 on a tour of Greece, Israel, Egypt and Spain. "They gazed upon the Pyramids, communed with the Sphinx, visited the Egyptian Middle Kingdom capital of Thebes and the tomb of King Tutankhamen. They dined and drank on the barge *Omar Khayyam*," the *Post* reported. Many took along their wives.

"As near as I can tell, they are mostly interested in large expanses of green with tiny holes in them," wrote one ambassador to his staff, when O'Neill and Rostenkowski and ten other members traveled to Yugoslavia, Morocco and Portugal in 1980. O'Neill would tour Ireland, England, France, Italy, Greece, Egypt, Israel, Australia, China, Spain, the Soviet Union and South America in the course of his career, and state representative Edward Galotti, who ran against him in 1976, ran commercials that lampooned him as "Trip O'Neill." Albert, who as Speaker controlled the foreign travel budget for the House, complained that O'Neill was "constantly wanting to go on a trip."

The journeys to South Korea stood out, however, for their frequency to a nation of such relative unimportance. It was understandable that O'Neill would make a sentimental visit to Ireland, or take a diplomatic mission to cold war rivals like the Soviet Union and China; but Korea four times? The Koreans had gotten in on the ground floor of O'Neill's globetrotting, correctly identifying his yearning for travel and making his journeys memorable. To close friends, O'Neill and Boland told of a night they found themselves invincible at the tables of the Seoul casino to which their Korean hosts had steered them. They guessed the games were fixed and fearing a set-up, they dumped their winnings on their flabbergasted driver, who told them they had given him enough to buy a house.[10]

As O'Neill rose in the leadership, Brademas and others urged him to step out on the Washington social circuit — to meet the movers and shakers of capital society, and get his picture in the Style section of the *Post*. "I got him, inadvertently, into trouble," said Brademas, an energetic bachelor at the time. But the gregarious O'Neill was happy to oblige. He was fifty-seven when he first hooked up with the Koreans, trying to keep up as Washington took on a hipper, looser atmosphere in the late sixties and the early "Me Decade." It was the one time he forgot from whence he came, and he paid a dear price. Brademas had told him, "You know, you're the Speaker of the House. You go to Duke's, you go to Paul Young's, you go to the Democratic Club — you don't meet the nicer people in town. You don't meet the Cabinet members. You don't meet the society people," O'Neill later recalled.

So, in December 1973, then majority leader O'Neill attended a party at the George Town Club, at which he was given two pewter hurricane lamps as birthday presents. He was by no means alone: Vice President Gerald Ford, Speaker Albert, Senate majority leader Mike Mansfield and five members of Nixon's cabinet were on the guest list.

The party cost Park around $2,000. "Against the desires of my staff, I reluctantly said yes, and I went and I had a hell of a time, to be perfectly true," O'Neill said. "My two daughters went with me and we had a good time. We enjoyed it. We had some laughs and we had our own little group. Park didn't pay any more attention to me than the man in the moon. He was happy Jerry Ford was there. And the big man was [secretary of defense] Mel Laird."

In April 1974, Park threw a party at his home on embassy row for the two dozen members of a congressional delegation that O'Neill was taking to Korea that spring. O'Neill and Attorney General William Saxbe dominated the evening, standing at the piano singing "Ten Little Fingers and Ten Little Toes," and "Nobody Knows What Happened to McCarthy." Park told the *Star* that "all these congressmen are my close friends. They know they can come here and let their hair down." And on December 16, 1974, Park underwrote yet another party for O'Neill — this time at the Madison Hotel, where some 150 people, including thirty-four members of Congress, mingled in black tie and ate roast wild goose. Silvio Conte was toastmaster. Comedian Mark Russell told jokes, and a photograph of O'Neill and Park graced the next day's Style section. The majority leader was given a bag of golf clubs as a birthday present, but left the party with a sour taste in his mouth. O'Neill had watched Park's face drop when he learned the news that President Ford would not be coming. "It was as though I had hit Tongsun Park over the head with a baseball bat," O'Neill said. "I was bait for Jerry Ford." The party had cost Park $5,597.

Ford had intended to go to the party, but at the last minute Donald Rumsfeld, his chief of staff, warned him not to leave the White House: Park was under investigation by the Justice Department. "'The nicer people in town'!" O'Neill said later. "Jeez, I never got in any trouble hanging around with my own crowd in my life."

"When Tip got in trouble over this Korea thing, I said to him, 'You see your problem: you're with the demitasse — instead of the scotch or the whisky and the beer chaser. You're having fondue instead of a good steak.' And Tip was innocent as the day was long, but they overwhelmed him with that stuff," said Rostenkowski.[11]

Park's work for the KCIA had not been limited to entertaining. He and Representative Richard Hanna, an impish Californian, had schemed to corner the market in federally financed U.S. rice sales to

Korea. As the sole agent for U.S. rice sales to his homeland, Park earned $9 million in commissions, of which at least $850,000 was spent to buy influence in Washington.

The scandal did not break until April 1975, when James Howe, whose wife was an assistant to First Lady Betty Ford, committed suicide as the *Post* prepared a story on a Caribbean vacation that the Howes had taken with Park. O'Neill, loyal to a fault, at first defended Park in the press. "I know of no dealings he has with the government; I know of no dealings he has with the Hill; I know of no campaign contributions he has given. . . . He has never asked me for a single thing," O'Neill said. The statement was demonstrably false. According to the two men's daily diaries, there had been nine scheduled meetings between Park and O'Neill in the five-year period between 1969 and 1974. And O'Neill's office schedules, as well as notes that federal agents would later confiscate from Park, show that the young Korean had indeed asked O'Neill and his colleagues for introductions to federal officials and other favors.[12]

The U.S. government launched a full-scale probe in October 1975, that the *Post* reported the following February. For O'Neill, the "Koreagate" scandal was like water torture. Park "never gave me money and it wouldn't have been accepted," O'Neill told the *Globe* in November 1976. "If Park came up to me with $3,000 I'd hit him in the puss with it." But Watergate had changed Washington. Woodward and Bernstein had become wealthy celebrities, and been portrayed in a movie by Robert Redford and Dustin Hoffman. Thousands of young people dropped their plans for law school and instead became journalists, many with a prosecutorial attitude. For this new breed of reporter, the relationship between O'Neill and Park was suggestive: the *Congressional Record* showed that O'Neill had praised President Park's regime and voted in the early 1970s for military and economic aid.

It was no clear-cut case, however. The record also showed that O'Neill's support for the South Korean government cooled once President Park took repressive measures to end dissent in 1972, arresting Roman Catholic clergymen and other critics of his regime. State Department records show that O'Neill confronted South Korean officials — at the embassy in Washington and on his trip to South Korea in 1974 — about their country's dismal human rights record. A State Department report on the "CODEL O'NEILL" visit that he led to Korea in April 1974 reported how the Park government was chagrined because it "did not derive from the visit the implication of full understanding and support for its domestic policies it undoubtedly had hoped for.

"In course of visit Congressman O'Neill included in toasts and other formal remarks observation that Americans are watching developments in Korea and are 'concerned with measures that seem incompatible with a free and open society.' He also made this point in private meeting with President Park," wrote U.S. Ambassador Philip Habib in a confidential report to Washington. O'Neill met with the persecuted American missionaries and signed a letter to President Ford warning that "the destruction of democracy in Korea" could lead to a cutoff of aid by Congress. Indeed, in December of that year O'Neill voted to halt military aid to Park's regime. And so, in the end, there was nothing tangible — just a shadow. But O'Neill compounded his own troubles with his blithe denials, which he invariably had to revise or correct.[13]

As Speaker, O'Neill also had to chart the House response to the Koreagate affair, and did so by having the House Ethics Committee conduct an investigation. The chairman, Representative John Flynt of Georgia, hired Watergate prosecutor Philip Lacovara to direct the probe, but the two had a falling out by the summer of 1977 over the counsel's aggressive pursuit of John Brademas and John McFall, among other things. Lacovara resigned in protest, and told an ABC news reporter that O'Neill and Jim Wright had their own "reason to be concerned" by what the Ethics Committee's investigators had unearthed. Lacovara's words were badly translated by the network, which reported on July 17 that "Speaker Thomas 'Tip' O'Neill and Majority Leader Jim Wright have been linked with the alleged influence peddling scheme." The network tracked down O'Neill at his Cape Cod home.

"I refuse to answer that. That's an insult and such a thing I can't believe came up," O'Neill told the reporter. The irate Speaker said the report was "a complete lie" and called the reporter "a cheap bum" before hanging up. But within forty-eight hours, O'Neill had a full-fledged crisis on his hands. Common Cause was demanding Flynt's resignation, and anxious congressmen were threatening to call an emergency session of the Democratic caucus. O'Neill and Wright put a phone call through to Texas and asked Leon Jaworski, the Watergate prosecutor, to come and take over the investigation. The Texan ultimately agreed, after getting a guarantee of complete freedom.

Jaworski's appointment satisfied O'Neill's colleagues, but the press would not let up. *Times* columnist William Safire, a former Nixon aide, taunted O'Neill for months. Nicholas Von Hoffman, a liberal columnist, was just as tough. "Tip has been in the business a long time and he knows damn well that Oriental rice dealers don't spend thousands of dollars on your birthday party because they love your shaggy, white-haired self," Von Hoffman wrote. "Tip's defense is that he never reciprocated, never used the power of the Speaker's office to do anything for Park. That'll keep you out of the grand jury room, perhaps. . . . But when a man like O'Neill allows a fast buck guy like Park to give him a birthday party it's a huge favor.

"O'Neill, who has only been around politics since the days they put Boss Tweed in jail, knows exactly how those who sleaze and wheeze through the porous membranes of the corruption statutes can cash in on giving the Speaker a perfectly legal and perfectly foul birthday party," Von Hoffman wrote.

It was fair criticism, and O'Neill was stung again in August of 1977 when the Ethics Committee heard closed-door testimony from Albert aide Suzi Thomson, who said she had seen Park in O'Neill's office on two or three occasions. The information was leaked to the *Los Angeles Times,* which reported that Park "frequently operated" out of O'Neill's office. The story was dubious on its face — Jimmy Breslin, Marty Nolan, David Nyhan, Neil MacNeil and other reporters had virtual run of the place and would have remembered such a distinctive presence — but it added to the Speaker's troubles. Park had been indicted for bribery and conspiracy and officially charged with being a South Korean agent. "I was the victim of a terrific smear," O'Neill told the House on September 7, 1977. "All I have is my reputation. I have been in public life for forty-three years, and the only thing I want to leave with is the satisfaction that I have done a good job; that I leave a heritage to my family, and I do not want anybody tearing my reputation apart."[14]

The torment went on for months. In March 1978, NBC ran an interview with Tandy Dickinson, Park's American girlfriend, in which she displayed snapshots of the now famous parties and gave a blithe running commentary. "The name Park meant a good party, a relaxing time, lavish food, the best wines," Dickinson said. "After dinner we went into the living room and sang some songs and laughed and joked and clapped and sat on the floor and just had a wonderful time, relaxing. . . . Everybody let their hair down." It was innocuous stuff—exonerating, even—but embarrassing nonetheless. *People* magazine ran an article on the pretty, blond Dickinson, illustrated with a photo of O'Neill telling stories in Park's living room as the Korean sat by his side. The women in the photograph looked twenty years younger than the men.

Then, in the last week of March, as the Ethics Committee prepared for Park's public testimony, one of Jaworski's investigators unearthed an unsigned document, written in Korean, entitled: "United States Congressional Delegation's Visit to Korea." The report had been seized at Park's house, and appeared to be an update of his efforts to buy influence on the eve of O'Neill's April 1974 trip to Korea. The visit was noteworthy, the document said, because O'Neill was "de facto Speaker due to the waning political influence of the present Speaker" and "commander-in-chief of the impeach-Nixon movement." One section, entitled "Congressman O'Neill's Request for Funds," seemed particularly damaging. "The fellow congressmen who have accompanied O'Neill, the delegation leader, to Korea, contributed decisively in installing him as the majority leader and, therefore, Mr. O'Neill specifically requested us to provide those congressmen with election campaign funds and their wives with necessary expenses. This will be an ideal opportunity to hand them the funds, but should it not be possible, we recommend that you pay them in the near future," the report said.

FBI investigators had already concluded that Park liked to lie and exaggerate to puff himself up for his KCIA handlers. Yet there was much in the report that had the ring of truth. It would be in keeping with O'Neill's character for him to ask for favors for loyal friends. If properly reported, campaign contributions from foreign nationals would, in fact, have been legal in 1974. And in an August 1975 visit by a subsequent congressional delegation to Korea, the Koreans did indeed try to give thousands of dollars in cash to the wives of two members of Congress. On Saturday, April 1, O'Neill traveled unanounced to Washington to be deposed by the Ethics Committee staff. Under oath, he insisted that he had never made the request for campaign contributions, or taken any money. Park made his debut two days later when, impeccably dressed, wearing tinted eyeglasses and taking notes with a Cartier pen, he testified before the committee. On his first day of testimony

Park admitted that he gave more than $850,000 in gifts, cash and campaign contributions to thirty-four House members. He described the O'Neill parties and acknowledged that they had cost him more than $6,000, plus $200 for the lamps and $300 for the golf clubs, but said that Hanna and other congressmen had posed as hosts to lure O'Neill to the events.

"Tip looked unusually worn and worried yesterday," Wright wrote in his diary. "The Boston newspapers have been featuring big black headlined stories rehashing the tenuous claims of some connection with Tongsun Park . . . now they're claiming Tip asked Park to raise money for some colleagues.

"I feel for the Speaker," Wright wrote. "I have smarted under several unfair stories in my local papers since becoming majority leader, but nothing quite as bad as the roughing up Tip has to take, with some regularity."[15]

Under oath, Park told the committee that the report discovered in his house was a fake. Though he claimed that he had a "great friendship" with O'Neill, Park admitted that they had had but a handful of face-to-face meetings. The only time any money was exchanged, said Park, was when O'Neill sold him a block of baseball tickets. In late April, the Justice Department revealed that Park's testimony had been buttressed by the results of a lie detector test. And the Justice Department concluded that the document found in Park's house was probably a work of fiction, as its "authenticity is not established and its accuracy is contradicted on substantial points by the evidence." On July 13, 1978, the Ethics Committee lodged charges against four representatives, but absolved O'Neill, Brademas and seven other congressmen of ethical misconduct. Listing the impressive lengths to which it had gone to track down every allegation, the Ethics Committee staff announced that it was "unable to find any evidence that in his dealings with Tongsun Park Mr. O'Neill violated the Code of Official Conduct of the House of Representatives, or any law, rule, regulation or other standard of conduct." After listening to tape recordings that Park had made of the parties, the committee investigators concluded that anyone there — especially O'Neill — would have thought that the gifts came from his congressional colleagues. "The only thing the evidence shows Mr. O'Neill to have done of questionable propriety is to accept two parties in his honor paid for by Tongsun Park. The value of the parties to O'Neill is difficult to measure. He (as well as the other guests) received food and drink worth about $50 plus the psychic pleasure of being the guest of honor," the committee investigators concluded. "The parties were well publicized at the time, however, and were obviously not considered improper by the participants, who included prestigious persons from the legislative and executive branches, including, in 1973, the then Vice President of the United States. The evidence that the parties were given indirectly by the government of Korea, or that O'Neill was aware of it, is slim. Although, judged by today's standards it may be unwise for an important congressman to permit either a foreigner or a suspected lobbyist to give him a party, there appears to be no warrant for disciplinary proceedings." A relieved O'Neill told reporters: "No man in the history of Congress has ever been investigated as thoroughly as I have."

The Speaker, meanwhile, had kept his promise to support the Ethics Committee. In a good-bye letter to O'Neill, Jaworski wrote, "I wish to repeat in words of genuine appreciation: you stood steadfastly by me and my colleagues in the investigation we undertook and never failed in the slightest to come to our assistance when we called on you.

"Without your strong and determined help, I do not believe that we would have obtained the testimony of Tongsun Park on American soil, under oath and in public so that the American people could hear the story of what occurred," Jaworski wrote. "The investigation was not without its frustrations and its traumas. It also had its bright spots and one of these is the experience I had in observing a great American leader unwaveringly and completely keep his promise of cooperation and assistance made to me when I entered this investigation."[16]

In the end, what really stung the Speaker was a comic strip. In June 1978, O'Neill's office was contacted by the *Los Angeles Times*, which wanted to check out the accuracy of assertions made in two upcoming episodes of "Doonesbury." Gary Hymel phoned cartoonist Garry Trudeau to try and stop the strips; Kirk O'Donnell, the Speaker's new counsel, reviewed the libel law, but to no avail. The "Doonesbury" strips were printed, and more than 4,000 letters and postcards arrived in response at the Speaker's office. In one strip "Congresswoman Lacey Davenport" was asked by reporter "Mark Slackmeyer" to comment on "the lavish parties thrown by Korean businessman Park for House Speaker O'Neill."

"Well, dear, I wouldn't make too much of that. You see, Tip's a very popular man, and people simply like to do things for him," Davenport replied. "For instance, some banking pals of his once offered him a free interest in a nursing home. Rather than offend his friends over a silly principle, he graciously accepted."

"Just lets people walk all over him, eh?" Slackmeyer asked.

"Quite right. He just doesn't seem to know how to say no," said Davenport.[17]

IF O'NEILL'S EXPERIENCE with Tongsun Park was purgatory, the "nursing home" saga was hell. On Sunday, April 8, in the midst of the Park controversy, the *New York Times* ran a front-page story: "O'Neill's Business Dealings Raise Questions of Conflict and Candor." A long, well-documented investigation had found that the Speaker made misleading representations about his assets on financial disclosure forms, and benefited from investments in the Glenside Hospital and the Bristol Nursing Home in Massachusetts. Other investigators were at work as well. O'Neill was now a target of the Boston media, the *Times* and the *Washington Post,* the House Ethics Committee, the FBI, the U.S. attorney's office in Boston and the Montgomery County, Maryland, police department. FBI agents were interviewing his staff; his Bethesda, Maryland, condominium was under surveillance, and detectives were combing through the trash of his former aides.

What the *Times* and other investigators had unearthed are best described as sweetheart deals. A promising elected Irish American official, in O'Neill's formative years in politics, was the pride of a community of similarly proud and aspiring lawyers, contractors and businessmen. His ability to provide favors — jobs, contracts, judgeships, immigration papers — was a valued service. His fellow Boston College alumni or Knights of Columbus treated him with respect and viewed his tiny government salary as a mark of Yankee myopia. In the ethos of Boston politics, it was viewed as nothing more than a fortunate confluence of interests if a group of investors chose a local pol to complete their circle, gave him a cut-rate share in the real estate deal or business project, and profited from his pull.

In O'Neill's case, the deals involved a nursing home in Bristol, Massachusetts, and a psychiatric hospital in Jamaica Plain, a neighborhood of Boston. After being elected to Congress in 1952, O'Neill discovered that his new duties prevented him from properly tending his insurance business. In 1958, he took $10,000 and invested it in Glenside Hospital. He bought 24 of the 346 shares in the corporation, and became a member of its board of directors. A decade later, O'Neill made a $100,000 profit when the hospital and its assets were sold in three related transactions, two of which were made possible by federal loan guarantees.[18] In a similar, though not nearly as lucrative, deal, O'Neill invested in the Bristol Nursing Home, which also received a federally guaranteed loan.[19]

There were obvious questions in both transactions. Did federal agencies offer special treatment to the investors because O'Neill's name was included on the application? Did he violate conflict-of-interest laws? Did he put his own capital at risk, or was his only investment his name and office? Did he pressure the bureaucracy for favorable action? The Speaker's counsels said later that O'Neill pushed and bent the law, but never broke it. "Glenside . . . the personal stuff . . . was hard," said Stan Brand. "Look, I'm a realist, but his situations were penny ante compared to what came down the road and the record is no one ever found anything actionable. This was a time of tremendous changes of what the ethics governing elected officials were going to be." Kirk O'Donnell said that O'Neill's partners no doubt "assumed that having him in there would certainly be helpful in the process. That is natural. But the deal stood up on its own."[20]

The genesis for the *Times* exposé dated back to December 1976, when, as O'Neill prepared to take over as Speaker, he had been pressed by the newspaper to disclose his net worth. Smarting from the paper's demands — he later said that it offended his "street pride" — O'Neill took the phone call in the House gym and casually rattled off a series of numbers that added up to $125,000: thereby underestimating his holdings by a third. "There are people who think I've made a lot of money in public life, but it just isn't so," O'Neill said. There were indeed such people, and the *Times* was talking to them. The newspaper reported that there were "widespread rumors that he had accumulated wealth during his 40 years of public office" being spread by "some of his political foes in Boston." Republican William Barnstead, whom O'Neill had brushed aside in the 1976 election, aimed to run against O'Neill again and had assembled a team of youthful Republican sleuths to comb through public records. "Anybody above the moral stature of Attila the Hun is infinitely preferable to O'Neill," he told reporters.

Barnstead, then fifty-six, was a World War II veteran, inventor and entrepreneur who had built his own successful business. He was a former chairman of the Republican State Committee and state organizer for Ronald Reagan. He called himself "Battlin' Bill" and prided himself on publicity stunts — setting up a four-foot wooden carnival wheel in Harvard Square to illustrate "how a big wheel named O'Neill has made a fortune at the taxpayer's expense."

As news of O'Neill's dealings with Park dribbled out, Barnstead became convinced that O'Neill had bought his Cape Cod land and cottage with cash from the Koreans. He combed the Registries of Deeds and assembled a bulky packet which he mailed or delivered to reporters, charging that " 'Poor man' O'Neill paid out some $64,500 CASH for two separate choice parcels of real estate on Cape Cod within 5 months, around time that Park held birthday party. Also, O'Neill made a hush-hush request for information about Swiss bank accounts to the Library of Congress." Barnstead even found it sinister that O'Neill's name was misspelled in the Cape Cod telephone directory for "the second consecutive year."

Barnstead looked clairvoyant in the fall of 1977, when the news broke of a federal-state investigation into the misuse of federal vocational education grants in Massachusetts. Maurice Shear, a banker and political ally of the Speaker's, was among those indicted. Now reporters from the *Times* and "a dozen" other news organizations were scurrying about Massachusetts to investigate his affairs. "They are out to get Pulitzers in the wake of Woodward and Bernstein, and their editors want to get me because I'm a Boston Irish politician," O'Neill griped. Barnstead was in his glory, now claiming authorship of the mysterious packets and predicting that "O'Neill may not be there next year."[21]

Once again, O'Neill's denials only served to set him up for the next punch. Gary Hymel had told the press that O'Neill "has had no business association" with Shear. But the *Herald* soon reported that Shear was a partner with O'Neill in the Bristol Nursing Home. When asked to reconcile the facts, O'Neill explained, unpersuasively, that he never knew Shear was his partner. The *Herald* pressed on, and embarrassed the Speaker by confronting him with the minutes of meetings that both O'Neill and Shear had attended, at which a partnership agreement had been signed. The *Herald,* at the time, was benefiting from a Hearst Corporation decision to reinvigorate its aging afternoon dailies in Boston, Baltimore and other cities with the addition of new editors and bright young reporters. To the fresh faces in the *Herald* newsroom, O'Neill looked like the stereotypical Irish American hack, and his troubles a ticket to glory. A few weeks later, the paper was back with a front-page story detailing O'Neill's involvement in Glenside Hospital that claimed that he and his partners had received a $1.3 million HUD loan guarantee. The gist of the story was correct: O'Neill had indeed been a partner when Glenside applied for and won preliminary approval for the loan guarantee — but the *Herald* missed the fact that the Speaker and his partners had sold the property a few days before HUD's approval was final. The mistake gave O'Neill just enough room to wriggle off the hook. He wrote a long letter, threatening to sue and demanding itemized corrections, which the *Herald* was forced to publish on its front page in November.[22]

The *Herald* backed off a bit, but the reports from Boston had convinced *Times* reporter Wendell Rawls that O'Neill was hiding something. His April 8 story covered the Glenside loan guarantee, showed how O'Neill had failed to mention various stocks when disclosing his finances at the end of 1976 and opened a new investigative front.

O'Neill had not merely owned stock in the Industrial Bank and Trust Company when Shear was president and chairman of the board in 1970, Rawls wrote. The congressman had borrowed $73,100 in seven loans from the bank, of which $56,100 was unsecured, and then used a middleman to borrow still another $15,000.[23]

The news of the bank loans was troubling. O'Neill had obviously been in severe financial trouble, and had turned to his pals for help. Rawls got his hands on a transcript of the secret grand jury testimony of Burton Faulkner, a Somerville businessman and pol who served as the middleman in the deal, who had been called to testify in a federal investigation of Shear's bank.[24] Faulkner said he served as the straw because O'Neill had reached the legal limit of what he could borrow in unsecured funds. O'Neill aide "Jim Rowan asked me. He told me Tip needed it and he'd pay me back in a few months," Faulkner told the grand jury.

Faulkner borrowed $15,000 from Shear's bank and $15,000 from another bank and wrote O'Neill a check for $30,000. The new House ethics rules that went into effect in January 1971 required that O'Neill list any unsecured loans in excess of $10,000 — but he had not done so. The *Times* story posed a new round of questions: Why did O'Neill neglect to list any unsecured loans when he filed his ethics report in 1971 or 1972? What did he need all that money for? How was he able, just two years later, to buy the Cape property with so much cash?[25]

The Speaker was rocked by the accusations. "Tip is very upset over a front-page story that was printed in yesterday's *New York Times*," Frank Moore reported to President Carter. O'Neill told reporters that "there's never been a more honorable man to be seated in this chair, nor a poorer." And then, without being asked, he denied that he had needed the money to pay off gambling debts.[26]

IT MAY NOT HAVE BEEN HIS gambling that got O'Neill in trouble, but it was the side of him that loved taking chances, loved risk and craved action: he had been speculating in the stock market.

O'Neill was an inveterate gambler. He bet at card games and on sporting events and liked to patronize craps tables and racetracks. At Fenway Park or Braves Field, Leo Diehl recalled, O'Neill would sit in sections favored by gamblers, where they could make instant side bets on whether a batter would get a hit or strike out, or how many more innings a pitcher would last.

The Korean casino episode offered one example of the risks posed by O'Neill's gambling. Billy Sutton recalled another. "We were at the Breeders' Cup. And this guy from Providence came by — all well-dressed, I knew he was a wiseguy," said Sutton. "And he says, 'Mr. Speaker. We're partners.' And puts down a ticket on the Number 9 horse. I look up at the board — 100-to-1 — pretty good odds. I said, 'Don't take that frigging ticket, Mr. O'Neill. He's looking for something, believe me.' And so he walked over and said, 'Ol' pal, I can't be your partner. The only partner I have is Millie.' And he gave him back the ticket. Don't you know I was right. The horse ended up winning. That guy wanted to get somebody out of Danbury federal prison or something."

Over the years, journalists Jimmy Breslin and Tom Winship each received warnings that O'Neill's gambling habit had reached dangerous levels. "I heard from guys I knew in the gambling business that O'Neill was all over the wire," said Breslin. "Betting forty-two football games a weekend. He was in town, and I said, 'Look, they keep telling me you're all over the wire. It'll be no good.' But 'Jeez, I'll never make another bet in my life,' he told me. And when he said that I knew he hadn't heard a word I said." O'Neill gave a similarly empty assurance to Winship. And he told reporters in 1977, "I'm not a gambler; I engage in games of skill."

O'Neill stayed out of serious trouble because he had the discipline to structure, and compartmentalize, his financial affairs. He had a small checking account in Washington, from which to fund his political obligations and card games, and the no-nonsense Millie took his paycheck to run the house in North Cambridge. She served to curb his impulsive enthusiasms ("I know no one who could spend money faster than Tip O'Neill. I had to keep the bills in the apartment that we shared," said Eddie Boland, who faced the same challenges) and demanded that he be home, and be a father, on weekends. Millie frowned on the invitations he received to go junketing with his congressional buddies and, with a very few exceptions, she or one of her children accompanied him on foreign trips. And "he was very careful, and told me once how when he finished his income tax each year he added an extra $2,000 [in income] and sent it in just to cover himself," said MacNeil. "It was a protective thing."

For much of O'Neill's life gambling had a Runyonesque respectability, and was accepted in Boston's Irish Catholic neighborhoods as not so destructive a vice as alcoholism, nor so evil a sin as the use of birth control. Indeed, the evening *Globe* would print the results of the afternoon's races on the front page, and state governments vied to steal the daily numbers business from the Mob. As an adult, O'Neill competed against his children at card games and board games. After dinner on Thanksgiving, it was not unusual for a dozen or more members of the extended O'Neill family to join in a raucous penny ante card game. In his later years, he and Millie played bridge with Silvio and Corinne Conte, and in retirement he was said to be a killer in the poolside gin games in Florida. "We all played at different things. He played gin. He loved a football game. Loved to win at everything he did," said son Tommy. "It was not that he was an addictive gambler; he just loved the action." Nor did O'Neill ever hide his fondness for the sporting life: his racetrack companions over the years included journalists like Breslin, JFK's brother Joe, Boston police commissioner Joseph Timilty, FBI Director J. Edgar Hoover and Millie and the kids. O'Neill liked to bet his wife's age in the daily double, patronizing the $5 and $10 windows.[27]

Cards were an instrument of his rise to power in Congress. "When I went to Washington I played cards probably every night of the week," O'Neill recalled. "Some fellas like women. Some fellas like booze. Other fellas like cards. Cards keep you out of trouble.

"You would be in town Monday, Tuesday and Wednesday night, playing poker each one of the three nights. You'd go to the University Club and they'd have twenty-five fellows from Congress there and from six to nine you eat, and at nine you cut cards for who was going to get in the poker game and who was going to play gin," O'Neill recalled. "It was like a routine. On Monday night you played poker at John Bell Williams's office, on Tuesday you went to the Army-Navy Club, on Wednesday you went to the University Club." They played endless variations of seven-card poker, with just three raises per hand allowed. A good night's winnings was $400. "Nobody ever got hurt," O'Neill said.

Bigger losses might lead to bruised feelings, and that would defeat the purpose of the game. "They would be here Tuesday to Thursday, and he would be in that game with the southerners and real rednecks," said Richard Donahue. "So he was a fount of information. And he knew it was information that was extraordinarily valuable." Members of O'Neill's staff remembered the boss, after a bad night at the card table, bumming a ride to the airport because he didn't have the cab fare. But the stakes at these games were generally modest, and there were occasional big nights (family lore has O'Neill and Boland winning a couple of years' rent at one game) to compensate for the losing streaks. "Gambling is a problem if you lose. He won," O'Neill's son Tommy insisted. "You memorize the deck and you understand the game and the odds of the game and you manage your money. So if you are losing and you can't win one night, you get out of the game. That is how you stay ahead of it."

"McCormack had a pretty high-stakes game, and Tip told me that he sat in on one game, and if McCormack had not seen to it that he broke even before the night was over, he would have lost his shirt," Jim Wright recalled. "McCormack told him, 'Tip, this is too high-stakes a game. Don't come back.' " McCormack aide Martin Sweig remembered the occasion as well. O'Neill "saw me in the hallway, and said 'Boy, oh boy. They play for keeps.' I said, 'Watch out Mr. O'Neill. They'll take your seat away,' " said Sweig.

"I'm a man of extremely moderate means. I could never sit into a $500 no-limit game," O'Neill said years later, explaining why he shunned McCormack's table in favor of a lower-stakes circuit.[28]

In explaining the financial transactions outlined in the *Times* article, O'Neill acknowledged that a different kind of gamble had caught up to him: he had lost big playing the stock market. "I remember sitting in his office and the phone would ring, and it would be his broker, and he would spend a few bucks, buy some stock, start worrying and sell it three weeks later," said Neil MacNeil. "He was a speculator;

he would be in and out of stocks every three or four weeks. Very, very nervous."

"He didn't really have a good sense what to invest in and what not to invest in," said Stan Brand. Dinneen remembered how O'Neill, in those days before overdraft protection, would fret about the balance in his checkbook, worrying about being overdrawn. O'Neill was the victim of at least two major stock market losses, when he mistakenly put his trust in a Boston College football coach's get-rich scheme in 1959, and when he was confronted — he now explained — with a margin call in 1970.[29]

The $73,100 in secured and unsecured loans from Shear's bank, O'Neill said, were taken in 1968 when he wanted to make a large purchase of stock in the Del Webb real estate firm. "I was a member of Congress, no pauper in the street," O'Neill said. "I could get unsecured loans easily." To qualify for the secured loans and demonstrate net worth for the unsecured loans, O'Neill had offered his Cambridge house and Glenside stock as security. But when the Del Webb stock collapsed in value, he had to scrape together enough cash to cover his losses. That, he said, was when he went to Faulkner — whose $30,000 loan kept O'Neill afloat until he could sell the Glenside stock and pay off the bank. He had paid off his debts before the House reporting deadline required him to disclose the unsecured loan, O'Neill said, and had been "cleared" by the federal grand jury.

As for the Bristol Nursing Home, O'Neill said he entered that deal as a favor to John Shea, who was in danger of losing his investment and needed prominent partners to persuade the banks to keep loaning him money. Shea was in charge of all the patronage in the state when I was Speaker of the Massachusetts House. Don't you think I was friendly with him?" O'Neill said. "That is how I got involved in the thing. Because his money was about to go down the drain."

As the press hammered away at O'Neill over the Korea scandal, his children and staff had persuaded him that he needed a full-time counsel to handle the demands of the post-Watergate environment. Kirk O'Donnell, a former aide to Boston Mayor Kevin White, arrived in the spring of 1978, and was immediately confronted with the *Times* story. O'Donnell quickly proved his worth; he hired an accounting firm to audit O'Neill's finances and invited the press to a detailed briefing at the end of April. As far as the national press was concerned, the audit — which uncovered no wrongdoing and showed that O'Neill's net worth was $181,000 — put an end to the mysterious loans story. "All these documents show he has been honest," the *Star* reported.[30]

The Rawls story, however, caught the attention of investigators elsewhere. Officials at the Small Business Administration (SBA) knew something that the press had not yet discovered: that the Bristol Nursing Home partners had applied for a $150,000 SBA-guaranteed loan. The agency's investigators combed through their records and interviewed participants in the deal throughout the spring and summer of 1978.[31] Nor was the *Herald* finished. It heard about the SBA loan guarantee, and thought it had hit gold. "O'Neill Firm Had SBA Aid" said the October 22, 1978, headline. "Under the federal conflict of interest law, a congressman may not be a partner in a business at any time during the life of a federal contract," the *Herald* said. In fact, O'Neill had checked this provision before signing the SBA loan guarantee, and found two legal loopholes. He had not broken the law; the *Herald* had overreached again, and finally abandoned the chase.[32]

At the *Washington Post,* society columnist Maxine Cheshire had won a reputation as a determined reporter with her digging on the Korean scandal. In late 1977 she concluded that O'Neill and Park were involved in a convoluted plot involving seafood, Korean fishing fleets, Richard Nixon, the Mafia, the Republic of Ireland and the popular Miami restaurant named Joe's Stone Crabs. Like many of the rumors about O'Neill, there was a kernel of truth at the core of Cheshire's theory. While searching through Park's file cabinets, the House Ethics Committee investigators had found a folder which showed that both Tongsun Park and the Speaker's son Tommy were on the board of directors of McLaughlin Fisheries, Ltd., an enterprise owned by O'Neill's friend and former aide Frank McLaughlin. The discovery was "a matter of immediate concern" to the Ethics Committee staff because the Speaker had denied any business dealings with Park. The committee subpoenaed McLaughlin's bank records, dispatched an investigator to Ireland, and combed through Massachusetts corporate filings.

"The investigation established that neither Mr. O'Neill nor his son received any financial benefit from the younger O'Neill's association with McLaughlin Fisheries," the Ethics Committee concluded. The Speaker told the investigators he had no idea that Tommy served on the firm's board, and Tommy told them that he never knew Park was a fellow director.[33]

Nevertheless, when Cheshire brought the story to the attention of the Montgomery County Police Department's new organized crime strike force in late 1977, it launched an investigation of O'Neill, with the help of the FBI. Cheshire told the police "that McLaughlin supplied Irish stonecrabs to Joe's Stonecrabs of Miami, Florida; and an unidentified La Cosa Nostra money courier delivered Irish stonecrabs to ex-President Richard M. Nixon in San Clemente on Nixon's first birthday after leaving office," according to the police records. It was ludicrous, but the police searched McLaughlin's trash and, for four months, kept O'Neill's condominium under surveillance. In a "Dear Ed" letter to *Post* lawyer Edward Bennett Williams, McLaughlin offered to take a lie detector test. "Ms. Cheshire has expanded her theory beyond the Park aspect and is now stating (not asking) that I am not only the 'bagman' for the 'other Boston Irish Catholic crook, Tip O'Neill' but I am the liaison between leaders of organized crime and the Speaker," he wrote. "The Speaker and I, as would most decent people, deeply resent such bigoted, prejudiced and expressed hatred.

"The Speaker has authorized me to say that he joins with me in denying (1) that he has ever received, directly or indirectly, money or anything of value, from or through me or any company with which I have been associated; (2) that I was ever designated to receive any money or thing of value for him, or to act as a so-called 'bagman' for him; (3) that I ever served as liaison between him and any group, much less leaders of organized crime," he wrote. The *Post* and the Montgomery County police dropped their investigations.[34]

The press had abandoned the chase. So had the House Ethics Committee, the local police and the SBA. But O'Neill had one last investigation to weather, and this would be the most exhaustive, nerve-racking and thorough of them all: the FBI was interested in his affairs. In the summer of 1979, an informant contacted the FBI's Washington field office. The name of the individual remains a secret, guarded by federal privacy statutes, yet from the bureau's files it appears that she was an acquaintance with one degree of separation from the Speaker: a pal of a pal. She spun a tale of corruption, alleging that Jim Rowan and others had acted as "straws" for the Speaker, disguising his financial interests with their names. The Glenside and Bristol deals were at the center of her story. "O'Neill has received payoffs for his assistance in obtaining these loans," the initial FBI memorandum on the case alleged, quoting its mata hari. She agreed to infiltrate the Speaker's inner circle while wearing a hidden transmitter.[35] Agents were dispatched to comb Registries of Deeds and other depositories of public records. The probe was given a series of code names — "Phoenix Bird" and "Quarterback" — and its records secured in the FBI's "top secret file" vault. The investigation began at a key moment in O'Neill's relationship with the Carter administration, just as the White House successfully pressed the Speaker to remain neutral in the 1980 presidential primaries between Carter and Edward Kennedy. But Jimmy Carter and Hamilton Jordan, when asked years later, said they had not known about the FBI's actions, nor used it to twist O'Neill's arm, and the bureau's records do not reflect any White House knowledge or interference.

The FBI opened a second front in its investigation of O'Neill in October 1979, when a braggadocious New Jersey building consultant named Joseph R. Silvestri offered to serve as the bait in a federal sting operation targeting O'Neill, Edward Kennedy, Peter Rodino and other prominent Democrats. Silvestri was politically well connected in his home state, and had played a role in the FBI's successful attempt to entrap New Jersey congressmen in the Abscam case — in which federal agents disguised themselves as wealthy Arab sheiks and offered huge bribes to members of Congress and local politicians. Silvestri didn't know O'Neill, but was able to persuade the FBI that he was quite friendly with the Speaker. The Abscam agents were given permission by Washington to have Silvestri offer a $75,000 bribe to O'Neill, and were disappointed when their informant failed to follow through. The news of the Abscam scandal, with its videotapes of U.S. congressmen taking cash bribes, broke in February 1980. The FBI "sheiks" had trapped a U.S. senator and seven representatives. In private, the Speaker roared, "It was a setup, a goddamn setup."

The Justice Department now resolved to bring its probe of O'Neill's finances to a head. Orders were dispatched to agents in ten or more states in the summer and fall of 1980, and interviews were conducted regarding the Glenside and Bristol deals, Maurice Shear, O'Neill's intercession for Wilmot and other, fanciful allegations concerning organized crime. In February 1981 alone, the G-men conducted two dozen interviews in Boston. The probe netted some minor fish, including the indictment on unrelated bribery charges of the SBA case officer who had approved the Bristol Nursing Home loan. But "all interviews conducted met with negative results regarding allegations concerning Congressman O'Neill and the misuse of his office," the Washington field office informed the FBI director in late March. A month later, the director's office ordered the D.C. field office to close its investigation.[36] White House chief of staff James Baker, like Jordan before him, said the White House had not known of the federal investigation, nor used it to harass O'Neill. It was, nonetheless, a burden for the Speaker, weighing on his mind. It is no coincidence that his leadership and political performance suffered badly throughout this period of time.[37]

In the end, his colleagues and inquisitors concluded that O'Neill was an honest man. His taste and lifestyle were profoundly middle-class, and he knew the price of a monthly mortgage payment for most of his adult life. O'Neill's sole apparent splurge was the purchase of his retirement home on the Cape, which he did not buy until he was sixty. The Cape home was comfortable, but no Kennedy compound or Newport mansion; thousands of other New England working or middle-class families bought similar "cottages" on the region's ocean shores or lakes in the postwar years.

"He got overwhelmed by the fact he is a very good natured man who likes to say yes," said Bolling, in an off-the-record conversation after the Koreagate affair. "To be perfectly honest, I worried about whether he was honest for a long time. But I haven't seen a sign that he was not. They tried like hell to put the gloves on him, but they never could."

His experience with the new political morality wore O'Neill down, soured his good nature, fed his mistrust. He could only take solace in the reaction of the folks back home. In October 1978, O'Neill had pollster Bill Hamilton conduct a survey of his district. Over three-fourths of his constituents gave the Speaker a positive rating, and only 14 percent had negative things to say of him. "The overall rating is healthy; indeed robust," Hamilton wrote. "It suggests that very little damage has been done to the Speaker by the barrage of negative press."

In the spring of 1980, a Notre Dame professor stopped by the Speaker's office to interview him about the relationship between religion and politics. The FBI was then combing through O'Neill's financial affairs, and the Speaker's thoughts were with his pal Dan Flood, who had just resigned from the House after being found guilty of corruption. The professor's questions inspired an off-the-record riff from O'Neill on political, and his personal, morality.

"I have never had the thirst for money," O'Neill said, assured the interview would not be made public. "Have I done things in my course of my career you would not possibly do today? No question about it. I've done a million favors. And in that million favors I helped the poor, the needy, and the indigent and the underprivileged and I had to twist the law a little bit sometimes to be able to do it.

"Today you wouldn't be able to do things like that: to save a family man from disgrace or ruination by talking to a judge. You thought nothing of it in those days. Thirty-five years ago it was a legitimate thing to do. But when you go over that history in the light of today you ask, 'What the hell kind of a scoundrel was he? A typical Irish politician?'

"I lived my times as the times were," O'Neill said. "Always in mind that the day I leave that I hold up my head and say, hey, I left a good family name, and never betrayed my God or my country."

Over time, even the Goo-Goos came to see it that way. "He may have done favors for his friends. He may have cut corners. But he didn't leave here with TV stations, a bank account or a large stock portfolio," said Common Cause's Fred Wertheimer. "He wasn't in this for his personal financial gain. He didn't even do it in a marginal way. Power? Yes, he had power. But that was tied to his political and philosophical goals. His character reflected an awful lot of what is good in politics and too rarely seen today."[38]

CHAPTER 22

An Uncertain Trumpet

O'Neill's troubles with the press and prosecutors were not the only events to cast a shadow on his early achievements as Speaker. The denouement of the energy saga offered a far different story line than he had written in the House during the summer of 1977, and other catastrophes followed. Almost everyone in Washington agreed that the federal controls on the cost of oil, gas and other resources needed to be lifted so that Americans felt the pinch of the real market price. Consumers would then conserve by buying fuel-efficient cars, using mass transit, weatherizing their homes and taking other energy-saving steps. And aside from a few free-market zealots, almost everyone in the capital recognized that the complete and sudden decontrol of oil and gas would give an undeserved windfall to the energy companies, even if it did spur production. So the question was: how to get to market price? The House had adopted the Carter administration's plan to raise the price of energy via taxes, so that the government could capture the windfall and redistribute the money for the common good. The House plan would have raised $40 billion in new taxes, restored $28 billion to the consumer via rebates, invested in research and development and still left the Treasury with a $9 billion surplus.

The Senate had a different idea: it wanted to set the country on a glide path toward decontrol, gradually permitting the oil and gas companies to raise the price of energy to the point where consumers would conserve. Instead of taxing the industry's windfall profits, the Senate hoped that the incentive of higher prices would result in more production. To secure the votes for decontrol, Senate Finance Committee chairman Russell Long of Louisiana bought off his colleagues by offering to include their pet projects — mass transit, shale-oil development, tax credits for the elderly, solar research — in the legislation. And so the Senate plan levied only $774 million in new taxes, gave back $41 billion in tax breaks and cost the Treasury $64 billion.

"Well, Senator Byrd, how quick will the Senate pass the administration's energy plan?" Carter asked the majority leader at their September 27, 1977, breakfast.

"The Senate is a place of shifting moods," Byrd answered. "It is a rough ship and sails through some unstable seas."

House liberals were furious. "The members know that Senator Long is trying to buy off individual groups of members by subsidizing their favorite hobby horses," a White House aide warned Frank Moore. But Byrd was as intent on preserving the prerogatives of individual senators as O'Neill had been at running roughshod over the House. He was also jealous of O'Neill's success and, unlike the Speaker, represented an energy-producing state. Moore urged the Carters to invite Byrd and his wife to dinner "to deal with the senator's considerable, and, as of now, bruised ego. Byrd feels neglected when he considers how much he has done for you and your administration and sees that the Speaker and Senator Humphrey are getting most of the publicity. . . . If we can make progress in getting Byrd's nose back in joint, then the evening will have been well spent."[1]

Byrd delivered for the White House in its difficult but successful efforts to craft a new treaty that would turn over control of the Panama Canal to Panama. But on energy he was hesitant and conflicted and confronted by Long. "The Finance Committee has a stranglehold on many of the major elements of the administration's legislative program," Moore told Carter, and "Long has the trading stock within his committee's jurisdiction to actually run the Senate if he chose to do so." Long assembled a bloc that postponed final passage of the Carter plan for more than a year, while constantly assuring the White House that he was laboring in its interest. Long said that he would pass a "skeleton" bill, which he would then flesh out when the House and Senate went to conference. But the House leaders had little faith that Long would ever put meat on the bones. "As the Senate moves along in its consideration of the energy bill," Lud Ashley wrote O'Neill in the fall of 1977, "it is becoming increasingly clear that only the bare skeleton of a national energy policy will emerge from that body. And that skeleton will save very little oil or natural gas."[2]

Carter was not the popular President he had been in midsummer. His hopes for fundamental welfare reform and tax simplification had collapsed amid the public squabbling of cabinet secretaries and interest groups, and he suffered when Bert Lance, an old pal from Georgia who was serving as budget director, got hauled before a Senate committee for a series of questionable banking transactions and was forced to resign.[3] The reports of financial misdeeds struck directly at Carter's reputation for propriety, eroding his standing with the public. He had "mortgaged a piece of his own simon-pure reputation to Lance," said *Newsweek*.

It was not until October 1978 that an eviscerated version of Carter's energy program — shorn of most of its taxes, rebates and reforms and including deregulation of newly produced natural gas — got the approval of House and Senate conferees and passed the Ninety-fifth Congress. "I understand what Hell is. Hell is endless and eternal sessions of the natural gas conference," said James Schlesinger, Carter's energy czar.[4]

O'Neill had tried to bluff and bluster, but the enthusiasm in the House for Carter's tax-heavy plan melted away as the process dragged into the election year of 1978. The Senate's tax breaks were far more appealing, and sentiment in the House for decontrol of natural gas had always been strong, if not predominant. The coordination between the House and the White House still left something to be desired. "I called Carter on one occasion," Lud Ashley recalled. "I said, 'Mr. President, . . . I'm going to lose this natural gas bill unless I can get some guys to change their vote. And I have a list of ten people that we can work with but we got to get 'em and we got to get 'em today.' He said, 'It will be done. Thanks, Lud. Good-bye.' So I went to Tip with the same list. I got back to my office and there was a call from the White House and it was the President. I said, 'What is it, Mr. President?' He said, 'There is a natural gas title that is being considered in the energy bill and I have got to have your vote on it.' I said, 'Does this sound familiar by any chance, Mr. President? For crissakes. I called you twenty-five minutes ago. How about crossing off the fellow at the top of the list and going from there? I think you got me.'"[5]

In the end, in order to get any part of the Carter plan through Congress in the weeks before the election, O'Neill had to assemble a task force and scrounge for the votes to pass Long's bill to decontrol natural gas — the same measure the Speaker had struggled to defeat in 1977. Since the Senate had gutted the rest of the plan, deregulation had now become the centerpiece of Carter's package.

"This is the symbol and the substance of our program," O'Neill told the steering committee in late September. "It must be passed." It was no easy sell. Representative Edward Markey of Massachusetts was one of a group of young liberal congressmen, mostly from the Northeast, who opposed deregulation. O'Neill sympathized with their position, but believed that Congress had to deliver something it could call an energy plan in 1978.

"Now we came down to whether it was going to pass by one vote or not on the floor, and he came to me up there in the back, and he said, 'Eddie, I really need your vote. We are very close. I have to get it done,'" Markey recalled.

"Tip, I just don't think I can be with you," said Markey.

"I really need your vote," said O'Neill.

"I don't know how I can," Markey replied. "When you are right, I'll be with you."

"Eddie, I don't think you understand," O'Neill said. "When I'm right I don't need you." It was a tough vote for a Northeastern congressman. Among those who voted no was O'Neill's old roommate, Eddie Boland.

As in 1977, O'Neill's strategy called for an omnibus bill that lumped together the various surviving provisions, and could be sold as a package in the national interest. He and Carter twisted arms and traded favors when the rule for the bill appeared lost in the waning moments of the vote, and switched just enough votes until the vote was deadlocked at 206. In the well, Toby Moffett pleaded with Michigan representative Robert Carr, "Don't do it." But under O'Neill's watchful eye, Carr voted for the rule, making the tally 207 to 206. O'Neill immediately brought down the gavel and "gave a sigh of relief." He said later, "My most embarrassing moment as Speaker would have been if we lost by one vote." Moffett was devastated. He walked out on the Capitol grounds and wept. The final package passed on October 15, 1978.

There was a footnote to the natural gas debate that spoke volumes about how O'Neill ran the House. As the rule was being debated on the floor, Ari Weiss walked up to where O'Neill was presiding. "How we doing? Where are we?" the Speaker said, and Weiss told him that they had a problem. Representative John Young had agreed to vote for the rule after getting assurances that a matter of importance to his Texas colleagues was included in the bill. The problem, Weiss said, was that Young was mistaken — his fix had not made it into the final version of the legislation. "If he switches we are in big trouble," Weiss told the Speaker: Young and his fellow Texans would desert.

Just then, Young joined them. "Tip, I'm really happy about this," he told O'Neill. "I got my problem worked out."

Without hesitation, the Speaker told his old Rules Committee colleague: "John, you better check on that again. I'm not sure you have got it right."

Young left in a hurry. "We don't want to win by misleading people," O'Neill told the stunned Weiss. After a moment the Texan was back.

"Tip, you're right. It isn't the way I thought it was," the congressman said. Weiss went to work, and put Young on the phone with the White House, and they managed to put Humpty Dumpty together again. But in the wake of the one-vote victory, when so much had been at stake, Weiss marveled at O'Neill's sense of fair play and obligation. The Speaker's young aide would never forget it. Neither, no doubt, would Young.

Critics noted that the acronym for "moral equivalent of war" was MEOW, and the best that can be said for Carter's efforts is that, though his original policy prescription was lost, he successfully forced Congress and the nation to confront and upgrade its flawed, outmoded and heavily regulated system of producing and delivering energy. "The road was set to free market prices," said Eizenstat. In the long term, as rising prices made oil from the North Sea and other sources more economically attractive, the market would leave the world awash in petroleum. But politically, it was hard not to believe that the Democrats had failed. The final passage of Carter's plan was an ugly spectacle in both the House and the Senate, as members used the opportunity to take revenge on the White House for the water projects fight, sold their votes for pork and patronage, or scurried to make sure that their hometown interests were spared any sacrifice.[6]

O'NEILL'S LOVE AFFAIR with the President continued to blow hot and cold. Both sides made efforts to assuage their differences. The Speaker and his wife were on hand when former President Nixon returned to the White House for a state dinner honoring Chinese leader Deng Xiaoping — once Millie was assured that she would not have to sit at the same table with Nixon. In a meeting with O'Neill and Jim Wright, Deng expressed his deep mistrust of the Vietnamese, an irony that was not lost on the two leaders, who recalled how the war had been sold to Americans as a holding action against Chinese aggression. At a DSG "roast" of O'Neill in February, Carter cracked a few jokes and then became serious. He called the Speaker one of "my closest friends," and a man who "can make the masculine reference to 'love' be sincerely meaningful." Then the President stepped down from the dais and met O'Neill in the middle of the ballroom for a very public bear hug.

O'Neill pitched in (and got a personal thank-you note from Carter) in a successful effort to cut funds for the proposed B-1 bomber. It was a tough fight, because the Air Force had parceled out work on the airplane to dozens of congressional districts. "The B-1 vote is very important to me. I hope you will help personally," Carter wrote to the Speaker. "O'Neill made an impassioned plea, walked the aisles, changed votes in the well — to give you a 204 to 194 victory on B-1," Moore told the President a few days later. The B-1's proponents struck back, and won approval to build two of the expensive bombers in December. But O'Neill approached a gang of lobbyists and supporters at Trader Vic's restaurant and, pretending to read a fortune cookie, said, "What is done today can be undone tomorrow." The rubber match was played in February, and the Speaker and the President prevailed. "We all know the weapon of the future is the cruise missile," O'Neill told his colleagues, closing debate on the floor.

"Tip helped to kill it; he took the floor even though GE made the engines in Massachusetts," Moore remembered. "He thought about it and thought about it and decided it was right. We took the money and put it elsewhere and in the Persian Gulf War the Stealth aircraft and cruise missiles proved themselves."

O'Neill was a firm supporter of Carter's Middle East initiatives as well. The accord that the President had helped craft with Israel and Egypt at Camp David the previous autumn was in danger of falling apart when Carter called O'Neill and Byrd to a meeting at the White House in March. The president looked "drawn" and "extremely nervous," O'Neill told his diary. Israel and Egypt were both demanding U.S.-guaranteed security treaties, and up to $8 billion in economic and military aid over the next four years.

"Byrd . . . and I agreed we thought we could sell this to Congress," O'Neill wrote. Then Carter, a devout Baptist whose Secret Service code name was "Deacon," climbed into his helicopter for a daring journey to the Holy Land. "I may come back without a peace treaty, and it would be a terrible blow to my Presidency and to our nation," Carter told O'Neill before he left, and as they watched Marine One take off, Mondale and the Speaker had to agree.

"Every time the pieces are together Israel gets tougher," O'Neill confided to his diary. "VP and I both agree, terrific political gamble. If he comes back empty handed — he had better go back to Plains." Carter came home with his treaty, and phoned O'Neill from Air Force One. "You're no longer a deacon — you're a Pope!" O'Neill told him.[7]

For the most part, the Speaker left foreign policy to the White House and the State Department. But there was one nation whose affairs O'Neill understood in considerable detail, and in whose interest he acted with bold imagination: Ireland. As far back as 1949, when he was Speaker of the Massachusetts House, O'Neill had corresponded with Irish officials, and as a freshman congressman he had spoken on behalf of unification of the southern Republic with the six counties of Northern Ireland. Years later, O'Neill told a group of British journalists that he had supported the Irish Republican Army's attempts to bring about reunification through force of arms in the late 1950s. Then, in the late 1960s, Ulster's Catholic minority — inspired by the example of Martin Luther King and other black leaders in America — began their own civil rights movement. Many of the Catholic complaints about discriminatory gerrymandering, housing opportunities and employment practices struck chords in Irish American communities. Television cameras captured the violent scenes of Protestant repression: police using water cannons and clubbing Catholics who sang "We Shall Overcome." A series of such scenes from the Northern Ireland town of Derry in 1969 stirred O'Neill to action. "The policy of the government of Ulster is one of absolute discrimination and deprivation of rights of the Catholic minority," he wrote to U.S. secretary of state William Rogers. "The present course of the Unionist government can only lead to civil war." In June, as a "battle of the Bogside" raged in riot-torn Derry, O'Neill helped gather signatures from 102 of his colleagues and asked President Nixon to intercede on behalf of the Catholic marchers with the British and Northern Ireland governments. "Intolerance and discrimination are encouraged by and rooted in the laws of Northern Ireland," O'Neill told the House. "When discrimination is founded in law, intolerance is fed and flourishes." The Nixon administration, however, rejected the congressmen's request. "The government of the United States is outside the area of constructive influence as well as sovereign responsibility," wrote Bryce Harlow, on Nixon's behalf, in reply. The United Kingdom "has taken a number of valuable steps to resolve its internal tensions," Harlow said.

Irish nationalists organized a new, militant branch of the IRA: the Provisionals, or Provos, as they were known. Two decades of street barricades, Molotov cocktails, bombings, hunger strikes and assassinations followed, as the Provos proved themselves as adept at the political use of murder and terror as their Protestant counterparts. After fourteen Catholics were killed by British paratroopers on "Bloody Sunday" in Derry in 1972, O'Neill — now the Democratic whip — introduced a House resolution calling for an international inquiry into the shootings, the immediate withdrawal of British troops and an end to the practice of internment without trial.

Remarkably, O'Neill and the other House members who took an interest in Irish affairs acted on their own initiative: the Irish government had allowed its ties to Irish America to wither at the precise moment when Irish American politicians were reaching their zenith in national politics. It was only after republican hard-liners capitalized on that vacuum, raising humanitarian aid through the Northern Irish Aid organization (NORAID) and money and arms for IRA gunrunners, that a handful of younger Irish and Northern Ireland political leaders devised a counterstrategy. In the mid-1970s, O'Neill became a key link in two initiatives launched by these young statesmen.

In Dublin, the Irish government was awakening to the dangers posed by a resurgent IRA, armed and financed by misdirected Americans. Sean Donlon, who headed Anglo-Irish relations under foreign affairs minister Garret FitzGerald and was later to serve as the Irish ambassador in Washington, was determined to counter the IRA influence by reaching out to Irish American political leaders. The genial Donlon (who had been serving in Boston as Irish consul general when "the Troubles" erupted) was assisted by the embassy's equally personable political counselor, Michael Lillis, who approached O'Neill in 1976 with a two-step plan to weaken the IRA, and use the U.S. government to pressure the British. "One of Ireland's greatest exports to the United States has been politics," Donlon said. "We are one of the world's experts in politics, and we will solve this problem through politics, not through political violence." O'Neill was also listening to Derry's John Hume, an inexhaustible schoolteacher turned politician who had participated in the Northern Ireland civil rights movement, believed in the power of creative nonviolence and opposed the Provos. Early in the Troubles, Hume made pilgrimages to the United States to visit Irish American political leaders, and used a stay at Harvard in 1976 to forge strong relationships with Kennedy, O'Neill and others.

The Irish missionary work yielded impressive results on St. Patrick's Day 1977, when O'Neill and Kennedy, joined by New York's Senator Pat Moynihan and Governor Hugh Carey, issued a statement calling on Americans to renounce "any action that promotes the current violence or provides support or encouragement for organizations engaged in violence." The "Four Horsemen," as they came to be known, told their fellow Irish Americans that "continued violence cannot assist the achievement of a settlement but can only exacerbate the wounds." The "St. Patrick's Day declaration" dispersed the romantic mists of nationalism and made clear to Irish Americans the consequence of their actions. In the Irish neighborhoods of Boston and its environs, where the local bars often sported NORAID's fund-raising jars, O'Neill's actions were frequently met with scorn. His old pal Monsignor John "Speed" Carroll warned O'Neill in October that at a NORAID dinner "you became the target of a number of the speakers — at times, a bitter target." On a visit to New York that year, O'Neill was accosted by a mob of protesters. "The political courage of Kennedy, Carey, Moynihan and O'Neill in going public on St. Patrick's Day . . . should never be underestimated nor should it be forgotten," Donlon wrote later. "The message they delivered was not popular."

Five months later, the horsemen had another breakthrough, after O'Neill successfully intervened at the White House and got Carter to drop the "hands-off" U.S. policy toward Northern Ireland. "It would be simplistic to expect early dramatic developments," O'Neill wrote Secretary of State Cyrus Vance in a confidential note on behalf of the horsemen. "But we believe that, with due regard for the complexities and sensitivities that underlie the politics of Northern Ireland, the United States should take whatever helpful initiatives that lie within its power." O'Neill's seemed a modest request, but met with resistance from the British government, whose lobbying in Washington had kept the United States from voicing any opinion on Northern Ireland for fifty years, and the State Department's Northern European desk, which was famously protective of America's cold war partnership with Great Britain. Nevertheless, when combined with the President's own sympathies for the human rights of besieged minorities, O'Neill's pull was such that Carter took a public stand against the violence in Ulster, urged the Irish and British governments to work toward a settlement and offered U.S. economic aid to help rebuild the strife-torn province.

A precedent had been set for American involvement in the Troubles. "The first and really strategically important break was the Carter initiative on Northern Ireland. And Tip O'Neill was the person who delivered it," said Lillis. "The United States was no longer on the sidelines."[8]

As THEY APPROACHED the 1978 mid-term election, many House Democrats began to worry that the Carter administration's troubles could cost them at the polls. A steering committee analysis accused the White House of "simplistic economic analysis . . . ignorance [of] historic background of current problems . . . naivete . . . inability to master congressional process . . . shallowness in subject matter grasp . . . gross miscomprehension of US economy, history and society . . . [and] amateurism." The White House recognized its problem as well. Moore warned Carter that "many on the Hill perceive us as uninspiring, indecisive, disorganized and undisciplined."

Among some on Carter's staff, there were sore feelings about the credit O'Neill had reaped for their success in 1977, his insistent demands for favors — like continued production of the F-18 fighter plane, because its engines were built in Massachusetts — and his role in a series of patronage disputes that bruised Carter's image. White House aides got severe indigestion when O'Neill insisted on appointing John McGarry to the Federal Election Commission. McGarry was a House counsel, longtime pal and BC alumnus whose tavern-owning family had helped O'Neill in his 1952 race for Congress. His brother, wrote columnist William Safire, was a "noted philanthropist, loan executive and participant in games of chance," who, Kirk O'Donnell later acknowledged, had sometimes served as O'Neill's bookie. The Senate Rules Committee postponed its hearings and demanded a more thorough background investigation, and Common Cause fought the appointment in court.

O'Neill and the White House found another silly thing to spar about when the Speaker tried to get Red Sox great Carl Yastrzemski in to see Carter after the outfielder had ripped hit number 3,000 in his Hall of Fame career. The White House had already invited St. Louis Cardinal great Lou Brock, who had his own 3,000th hit in August, and a small flap occurred over, as Missouri Senator Thomas Eagleton put it, "who the White House loves most."[9]

In June, the President and his wife, Rosalynn, joined U.S. trade representative Bob Strauss and his wife, Helen, and Bob Byrd and his wife, Erma, at Paul Young's. The table was set for eight, and as the President ate his roast duckling it became increasingly apparent that the Speaker and his wife, Millie, were not going to show. There was a flurry of bows and scrapes the next day, as O'Neill's office explained that Leo Diehl had told Christine Sullivan, the appointments secretary, to reserve the wrong night. "O'Neill is heartbroken," an aide assured Carter. But, strangely — or not so strangely — the Speaker never chewed out Diehl for the mistake, and Diehl gave a knowing wink to Sullivan. Diehl didn't like Carter, and was treating Strauss just like any other lawyer or lobbyist who might claim to "deliver" Tip O'Neill.

O'Neill's relationship with the White House reached its nadir in August 1978, with the firing of Bob Griffin from the number two slot at the General Services Administration. Griffin, then sixty-one, was a college pal of the Speaker's, a BC graduate who had grown up in Somerville and had taken part in the D-Day landings in Normandy and at Iwo Jima and Okinawa. He worked in the early Kennedy campaigns, and joined the GSA in 1949. Through a stint as congressional liaison, and as a prominent member of the circle of Massachusetts natives who arrived in Washington with John McCormack and the Kennedys, Griffin grew to know O'Neill quite well.

When the Georgians arrived in 1977, O'Neill had pushed Carter to appoint Griffin to head the GSA, the agency which secures and administers the properties and office space and services used by the federal government around the country. To the dismay of the Speaker and many in Congress (who loved to help the GSA make its purchasing decisions) Carter chose to retain Jack Eckerd, a Florida Republican who held the job during the Ford administration. O'Neill insisted that Griffin get the number two slot — deputy administrator — and the White House concurred. Eckerd eventually quit, alleging that Carter had set back his efforts to "remove politics" from the GSA's decisions.

Griffin served as acting administrator until the White House appointed Jay Solomon, a wealthy and self-important Tennessee real estate developer who was an early supporter of Carter's presidential campaign in 1976. Solomon arrived in the spring of 1977 to discover that the GSA had come under the scrutiny of congressional investigators and federal grand juries. Griffin had, in fact, uncovered some of the corruption that Solomon now condemned, but he had also been with GSA from its inception and had dozens of friends and friendly coworkers whom he now tried to protect from his new boss. Griffin, as he himself later acknowledged, was a company man. "You can stay on a job too long," he recalled. "I had fallen into the culture of the agency. Rather than make broad changes, I was trying to see if we could make it work if we tried it the old way for three more months."

Solomon complained to the White House that he couldn't run an agency whose executives had divided loyalties, and resolved to fire his deputy — not caring that dismissal amid a season of scandal would unfairly taint Griffin as corrupt. Carter and his staff approved the dismissal. In a statement released by the White House press office on July 26, Carter gave Solomon a vote of confidence, decrying "a pattern of misconduct extending over many years" at GSA and informing Solomon that "I will back you fully in whatever procedural, personnel, organizational and other actions are needed." That afternoon, the press called Gary Hymel and asked him to comment on a report that Griffin was about to be sacked.

O'Neill asked Frank Moore about Griffin's status. He acknowledged to O'Neill that "a showdown" was coming and that Carter would back Solomon. But Moore told the Speaker that no action was imminent. Back at the White House, Moore urged Carter to postpone the confrontation, but Carter's media adviser, Gerald Rafshoon, was telling the President he needed to look tough. The next morning's *Post* carried the news that Griffin would be fired.

"The feeling had developed that Tip was running the government as opposed to Carter and that Carter had to change the relationship. They created an incident so Carter could manifest his ascendency," Griffin recalled. "I felt at the time I had been Rafshooned." When Moore arrived at work on the 27th, he found a note waiting for him from his secretary: "The Speaker first learned of the Griffin decision in this morning's paper. He's furious." It was an understatement. O'Neill was ballistic, nuclear, volcanic in his anger. The dismissal had confirmed and aggravated all his grievances with the Georgians. They had sacked his buddy. Had not consulted him. Lied to him. Sucked up to the press. Blackened a good man's name. Broken the rules of patronage. Shown their scorn for Congress. And revealed their true hypocrisy, for who was Jay Solomon but some rich campaign contributor anyway? O'Neill called the decision "cruel . . . one of the worst things I have ever seen."

The press feasted on the news, and it was not until the end of the day that the White House recognized the situation was out of control, and Carter told Solomon to issue a statement saying that the firing was unrelated to the ongoing scandals. After reaching O'Neill at his son Kip's house, Carter invited the Speaker to breakfast at the White House the following morning. As he entered the Executive Mansion, O'Neill's mood was not brightened by the story in that day's *Post,* in which members of the White House staff were quoted as viewing Griffin's firing as "a small but significant test of strength between Carter and Capitol Hill." Twenty years later, Moore recalled with awe how O'Neill was so wrought with anger that he wept, his head bent to his knee, as he lashed out at Carter. "It's just one of those things," the President told O'Neill. "It's the way you did it," O'Neill said, "in the middle of a scandal!"

The Speaker left the White House decidedly unsoothed. "I am deeply hurt," a flush-faced O'Neill told the Capitol Hill press corps, when they asked him about Griffin. "Not only was he treated in a shabby manner, I was treated in a shabby manner." O'Neill then did something he never did: he called a staff meeting. To his assembled aides, O'Neill gave the strict order that Moore was theretofore banned from the Speaker's offices. "He didn't tell me the truth," O'Neill said. "I don't think he had the guts to tell me."

Carter was shaken. When Jim Wright met with the President, southerner to southerner, to explain the North Cambridge rules of political fealty, Carter said that the breakfast with O'Neill had been his single most painful moment as President. The White House retreated; Griffin got a job with the U.S. trade representative, and Moore wrote an abject letter of apology. Well, O'Neill said, the Irish are a forgiving race. At a memorial service for Pope Paul VI, Carter joined O'Neill in the front pew at St. Matthew's and offered a warm handshake as a "gift of peace." O'Neill let Moore back into the Speaker's lobby. "The Speaker told me he was sorry this whole misunderstanding happened and wanted to put it behind him. He doesn't want to talk about it anymore and wants things to be like they were. He still doesn't feel like there is any warmth on the part of the White House and that people down here just don't like him, but doesn't feel that I am in that group now," a relieved Moore told Carter. "The Speaker also has some private warnings about Solomon which I will pass on to you verbally."

Carter was the ultimate loser in the Griffin affair, as the press split into two camps: those who criticized the administration for political ineptness, and those who ripped the White House for backing down and rehiring an O'Neill "crony." (An aide to Griffin later noted how "politicians of the old school like Tip O'Neill have cronies," while Common Cause presidents have "associates.") Jordan, much later, said the White House had been dragged into a fight it didn't want by the headline-hunting Solomon, who was shoved out of his job the following spring, and heard of it when a reporter informed him that the White House was looking for a successor. But it was just as true that the controversy took place as the administration launched a "veto strategy" that was designed to make the President seem "tough."[10]

In early April, Carter had been handed a memo from James McIntyre, his new budget director. Bolstering his case with statistics from past presidencies, Democratic as well as Republican, McIntyre argued that "the administration's presumptions and implicit rules regarding vetoes are too constraining for our own good.

"We seem now to consider vetoes as major exercises of Presidential power: Presidential actions which signify extraordinarily significant differences between the Congress and the Administration and which, therefore, are almost inappropriate actions by a Democratic President with a Democratic Congress," McIntyre complained. "The Hill perceives our extreme reluctance to use the veto, and predictably, is less willing to negotiate over a wide range of issues."

The "no-veto" philosophy, of course, had been drummed into Carter's head by O'Neill — who was aghast at the notion of leading his troops in an effort to override the wishes of a Democratic President, but surely recognized that he was also depriving Carter of a potent constitutional check on the Congress. McIntyre's office drew up a list of thirty objectionable bills as candidates for a veto. In June, Moore signed on. "Both in the halls of Congress and among the public at large runs a quietly spoken but nonetheless dangerous theme: that Jimmy Carter isn't tough enough to be President," Moore wrote. "We believe, as do others within the administration, that this feeling is at the root of our continuing problems with Congress . . . that you simply do not enjoy the level of respect to which you legitimately are entitled.

"In many respects, the modern Congress is like the proverbial, stubborn jackass — you have to hit it beween the eyes with a 2 x 4 to get its attention," Moore said. "We should identify six to ten especially bad, expensive and/or symbolic bills and begin now to orchestrate a veto campaign." Carter issued his veto threat at a nationally televised press conference ten days later. Water projects, social spending and a defense authorization bill topped the new hit list. Jim Wright wrote to Carter, quoting an exchange from the Broadway musical *Camelot.*

Lancelot (unbelievingly): "It's your wish, Arthur, that this dread battle go on?"

Arthur: "No, it's not my wish, Lance. But I can think no longer what to do but ride the tide of events."

Wright added in a postscript: "Happily we deal in water and in money, not in blood. I believe I understand the necessity of your position. I hope you can understand mine."

Carter replied the same day, sending Wright a quotation from First Corinthians: "For if the trumpet give an uncertain sound, who shall prepare himself for the battle?"

The trumpets sounded on October 5, over the infamous water projects. O'Neill and Wright led the efforts to override the President's veto. "Tip is working hard on all members. . . . Tip is pushing," Moore told the President. But the White House, trading in presidential phone calls and favors — a bridge in Arkansas, an Army base in New York, a presidential photo opportunity for one congressman, some public works pork for the New Jersey delegation — defeated O'Neill by 53 votes. Carter's stature had soared after his diplomatic triumph at Camp David that fall, and he had the invaluable help of Phil Burton, who still harbored hopes of challenging Wright for majority leader, and used the vote as an opportunity to humiliate his rival. "We could not have won the public works veto without Phil," Moore informed the President. At Carter's invitation, O'Neill showed up at the White House on the evening after the vote, prepared to hear the President ask for his resignation as Speaker. "Do you want me to throw in the towel?" he asked Carter. Don't be silly, Carter told him, and worked to close the breach, choosing O'Neill to lead the U.S. delegation to the installation of Pope John Paul II in Rome.[11] Some 50,000 people heard Carter hail O'Neill as "the greatest Speaker of any Congress" when the President made a campaign swing to Massachusetts in October. John McGarry got his appointment ("We used up a lot of chits on that one," Moore recalled), O'Neill counsel Charles Ferris was chairman of the Federal Communications Commission, and Irv Sprague was about to be appointed chairman of the Federal Deposit Insurance Corporation. O'Neill tried harder too, charming the President's mother, and Jody Powell's mother, when they visited the Capitol.[12]

THE PETTY SQUABBLING between the White House and the Hill was an indulgence that the Democrats thought they could afford, but it was a mistaken belief, born of recklessness. The New Deal and the Great Society had transformed America, but the intellectual vigor and popular support behind those great social movements had crested in the 1960s. The Democrats had been riven by the civil rights movement and the war in Vietnam. The Solid South was shattered and the working class alienated by the cultural revolution of the sixties. O'Neill's own experience should have warned him. For though he came from one of the most Democratic districts and states in the nation, he had seen firsthand how the party's rights-based policies, when pushed to their logical extremes, had divided his working-class constituency. On issues like abortion, school busing, affirmative action, welfare and taxes, which the Republicans used to drive wedges between the liberal and working-class wings of the Democratic Party, O'Neill saw his own people torn by the party's agenda.

O'Neill was a religious man, a church-going Catholic who almost always fulfilled his obligation to attend Mass on Sunday or Holy Days of Obligation and who scheduled the House so he could get ashes on Ash

Wednesday. His philosophical lodestone was the Sermon on the Mount, and he gave more than passing credence to the belief that the Declaration of Independence and the U.S. Constitution were the result of Divine intervention. Though he later bowed to liberal pressure and reversed his stand, he had voted to bring a constitutional amendment to restore prayer in schools to the floor in 1971. And throughout the sixties, he clung to his church's teachings on abortion.

"It is not simply an issue of equal rights for women respecting 'their right to control their own bodies.' It involves profound legal precepts, as to the independent viability of the fetus and the status of an unborn infant," O'Neill wrote to one of his McGovernite constituents in the summer of 1972. "It is my deep personal conviction that abortion is wrong. . . . It is for this reason that I cannot endorse liberalized abortion."

O'Neill dropped his opposition to abortion in 1973, after the U.S. Supreme Court, in the case of *Roe v. Wade,* upheld a woman's right to terminate a pregnancy. He was an institutionalist, and the Court had spoken. He was also the majority leader, the champion of the liberals in the caucus, flanked on the left by Burton and from a district that had overwhelmingly endorsed McGovern. "The command of the Supreme Court is clear," O'Neill wrote, just a few days after *Roe* had been decided. "Federal action at this time would further confuse the issue, adding yet another variable to the already volatile combination of forces." It didn't take long for his church to respond. Boston archbishop Humberto Medeiros and the Massachusetts Catholic Conference were resolute in their opposition to abortion and pushed O'Neill to support a proposed constitutional amendment banning the practice. So did his old pals in the clergy, who wrote to him in blistering terms about "the inviolability of innocent life from conception to natural death" and "the developing national policy of genocide of the unborn."

O'Neill, at first, stuck to his guns. Abortion was a highly personal issue, he said, and in a pluralistic society an elected official must separate his Catholic faith from his duties to a heterogeneous constituency. A BC professor, the Reverend Paul Murphy, accused him of "an unexpected moral and political immaturity.

"You simply opt for the personal moral arbitrament of the individual conscience. That is a plea of avoidance," Murphy wrote. "The issue is not, as you mistakenly affirm, the separation of powers but the actual slaughter of the innocent."

"Let's be candid about this, shall we? It is a hot political question and your facade of rationalization is a weak, thin and cowardly approach," wrote the Reverend Michael Bowab, of St. Camillus in Arlington. O'Neill asked his staff to count the mail. The ratio was better than 5 to 1 in favor of a constitutional amendment.

Ultimately, the combination of private qualms and public and priestly pressure was compelling. Before *Roe* was a year old, O'Neill switched back to his original position and announced that he would support a constitutional amendment banning abortion, which he now declared "morally indefensible." By 1976, the Massachusetts Citizens for Life were thanking him for his "continued pro-life support." When the House passed an amendment in 1977 offered by Representative Henry Hyde, a Republican from Illinois, to bar the use of Medicaid funding for abortions, O'Neill voted for it. "Tip couldn't take a hand in this one, because of the hard line position of the Catholic bishops in Massachusetts. Brademas can't get out front because of Notre Dame," Wright confided to his diary. "That leaves me."

"In my heart I say it's a mortal sin, it's against my religion, it's a question of the death of a living person," O'Neill said. "But, hey, do I have a right to deny you, who don't believe like I do? I've voted both ways on the subject. Sometimes I say to myself I can't vote that way because my religion won't allow me. Next time I say to myself even though I don't believe it, I don't have the right to prevent somebody else. I don't satisfy either group. Sometimes I have to think how my conscience is acting on the day the vote comes up, truly."[13]

ANOTHER ISSUE THAT splintered the Democrats, and caused unending pain to O'Neill and Boston, was the plan to bus students across neighborhood boundaries to desegregate the city's public schools. Violent battles around South Boston High School commanded most of the attention of the national news media, but the Townies of Charlestown — in the heart of O'Neill's district, in whose Bunker Hill Day parade he had marched, whose navy yard jobs he had labored to protect for years — were as furiously opposed to the court-ordered busing plan as the residents of Southie.

The controversy dated back to 1965, when a coalition of blacks and liberals pushed a law banning racial imbalance in public schools through the Massachusetts legislature. By 1967, Louise Day Hicks, a doughty foe of desegregation who chaired the Boston School Committee, had run a close second to Kevin White in the Boston mayoral election on a platform of neighborhood autonomy. "You know where I stand," she said, and posed a strong enough threat to the liberal consensus that the *Globe* had broken an eighty-six-year tradition of neutrality in municipal elections to endorse White. Cambridge was known for its tolerance, and at first O'Neill had no trouble endorsing busing and defending the practice in Congress. In 1970, in a departure from his usual taciturn presence on the Rules Committee, he had blasted Appropriations chairman George Mahon for including an anti-busing amendment in an appropriations bill.

"I do not believe you ought to pick them up and send them way across town to some other schools in order to commingle the races. I just do not believe in that," Mahon said.

"Regardless of what the law of the land is?" O'Neill asked.

"I just cannot believe that that is the law of the land," Mahon replied. "It is so preposterous and unreasonable. . . . It ought not to be tolerated."

"Regardless of whether in one section there is a better type of school program? Teacher program? School facilities? You do not believe that as opposed to a second section, where you have a rundown school, you have inadequate teachers . . . you do not think it is fair to bus a certain percentage of them?" O'Neill asked. "The object of this desegregation program, of trying to bus children around [is to] equalize the school opportunities."

Mahon's amendment, O'Neill charged, was "for the purpose of scuttling whatever has been done in the area of civil rights for the last 10, 12, 15 years."[14]

Busing achieved the status of certified liberal dogma. In August 1972, O'Neill placed a study on the practice, prepared by his staff, in the *Congressional Record*. "Busing is . . . the only tool which can overcome segregation which occurs through housing, dual educational systems, and discriminatory school assignment based on the mythical neighborhood concept," said the report. Opposition to busing "is an insult to the record of civil rights legislation accumulated in the last decade, and represents a return to the doctrine of separate but equal, a system of apartheid which has been ruled unconstitutional."

But as O'Neill supported busing in Washington, events were moving toward confrontation in Boston. In June 1974, U.S. District Court judge Arthur Garrity found Boston's school system guilty of segregation and ordered the adoption of a busing plan for 18,000 students. The School Committee refused to comply, so the judge devised a Phase I plan to integrate schools from neighboring communities. Poor black Roxbury was paired with poor white Southie. Anti-busing groups like ROAR — Restore Our Alienated Rights — took to the streets. The schools opened, but boycotts and intermittent violence marred the year. At one point Mayor White called O'Neill and asked him to intercede for the city at the White House, and President Ford put the 82nd Airborne on alert. Phase II of the plan was put into effect in 1975, and included Charlestown and East Boston, both in O'Neill's congressional district. A *Herald* photographer captured the searing image of a black attorney being speared by a mob with the pointed staff of an American flag.

The anti-busing protesters were blue-collar Democrats. They were the kind of people O'Neill had grown up with, on whose votes he had counted throughout his career. They played by the rules, they prized their turf and cherished their neighborhood high schools. Their sons fought the nation's wars. Then the sixties wreaked havoc with their values of country and community. They asked why the *Globe,* Arthur Garrity and Tip O'Neill cared more about unwed welfare mothers than the families of their God-fearing, hard-working constituents. They elected bigots to the School Committee, and let those bigots manipulate their fears. They were Irish in Southie and Charlestown; Italian in Eastie. And their sense of siege was heightened by economics. As the suburbs lining Route 128 bloomed with new industries and tens of thousands of well-paying jobs, the white residents of Boston competed with an influx of black arrivals for the city's aged, shrinking industrial base. The wealthier white families fled to the suburbs, while the percentage of Boston's residents who were black rose from 3 to 16 percent. And everyone knew that most of the experts, editors and judges who supported busing sent their children to private schools or lived in affluent white suburbs that were fiercely opposed to, and legally protected from, any cross-jurisdictional, metropolitan busing plan.

In Charlestown the local ROAR chapter was called "Powder Keg," and represented a tight-knit urban village of 15,000 people who lived on the slopes of Bunker Hill, hemmed in on their peninsula by elevated highways and massive bridges, beneath the obelisk that commemorated one of the American Revolution's most famous battles. In scenes right out of Belfast, youths from the town's large housing project set up barricades and threw bottles and stones at the police, and mothers clashed with the helmeted riot troops of the Tactical Patrol Force. Charlestown's inclusion in the Phase II plan put the Powder Keg on O'Neill's doorstep. ROAR announced that it would hold a March on Washington in March 1975, and in the weeks leading up to the protest, feeling pressured, O'Neill mangled his previously consistent stand. During a meeting with Southie's state representative Raymond Flynn and two dozen other busing foes on March 4, O'Neill said he would intercede with Peter Rodino and bring a constitutional amendment to the floor. O'Neill's switch was news — Flynn hailed it as a "breakthrough" — and the then majority leader was asked by the press if he would support the amendment if it were brought to the floor. "I'd vote for it," O'Neill said.

The liberals in Boston and Cambridge yelped, and 200 people picketed O'Neill's home, chanting, "Kids can't learn in racist schools" and asking, "Which side are you on?" The NAACP's Clarence Mitchell said O'Neill's stand was "disgraceful . . . fakery." By the story's third day, O'Neill was furiously backpedaling. He took out his anger on *Globe* reporter Stephen Wermiel, whom he accused of breaking "the faith" and "trying to manufacture news stories," and banned him from the Speaker's office. At a showdown in October, the Powder Keg representatives brushed aside O'Neill's equivocations and put the question to him: "If you really want to help the people of Charlestown, you can do it. The question is, do you want to help or don't you?" O'Neill responded with studied indirection, by talking about his efforts over the years to keep the navy yard open. His brief rapprochement with the anti-busing forces was over. In December, the Democratic caucus debated a motion to instruct the Judiciary Committee to bring the anti-busing amendment to the floor. Speaker Albert urged the caucus to table the anti-busing motion, and O'Neill voted "aye." The Charlestown contingent hooted and shouted, and were cleared from the gallery. For more than a year, the Powder Keg troops dogged O'Neill, holding sit-downs in his office, picketing his house, and chanting "Dump Tip!" as he made the rounds for his 1976 campaign. Ed Galotti ran an anti-busing, anti-abortion campaign against O'Neill, and Leo Diehl and other advisers warned the congressman not to venture into Charlestown. O'Neill breezed past Galotti, but lost Charlestown by a 3 to 2 margin.

The motives of its supporters may have been noble, but as a tool for desegregation, and a matter of political or educational policy, school busing was a titanic failure for Boston and its schools. In four years, the white population of Boston's schools dropped by 20,000, as almost half of the city's white pupils fled the nation's first free public school system for private, parochial or suburban classrooms. Middle-class black families followed suit, and by 1985, nine out of every ten students in the Boston schools qualified for government low-income lunch plans.[15]

THE LIBERAL AND conservative wings of the Democratic Party had traditionally bridged divisive issues like abortion and civil rights by promoting broad themes of economic justice and class-based politics. But in the Carter years, the Democrats ceded these lunch bucket issues as well. There was no shortage of causes for the miserable performance of the U.S. economy in the 1970s: the deferred bill for the Vietnam War came due at the same time that the oil shock rocked the industrial nations. Germany and Japan emerged as disciplined competitors to U.S. industries that had grown soft in the postwar years, and whose workers paid for that softness in storied factory towns like Flint, Michigan; Bethlehem, Pennsylvania; or Youngstown, Ohio. The industrial age was coming to a close, and the tools of the information society that would replace it — personal computers, VCRs, fax machines, cable television, cellular telephones — were still in their infancy.

The Democratic Party's intellectual exhaustion coincided with America's economic decline. The postwar economy was such a mighty machine that Democrats mistakenly viewed it as invulnerable, and thought it could easily handle the host of rules and regulations they enacted to clean up the air and water; protect workers and consumers; improve schools; regulate the energy, transportation and manufacturing industries; enhance the bargaining power of labor; desegregate society; build new housing; improve fuel efficiency; restore inner cities; and federalize the farm economy. Nor, the Democrats believed, would the taxpayers balk at the cost of supporting the bureaucracies that were needed to administer and comply with these efforts — even though, in O'Neill's time in Congress, the number of civilians employed by government had grown from 6.5 million to 14.5 million, all of whom needed offices and desks and filing cabinets for the swollen tide of paperwork that kept them busy. In 1977, the U.S. Department of

Health, Education and Welfare was demanding 44.5 million hours of paperwork from its grantees and contractors. The budget of the federal Equal Employment Opportunity Commission, which handled job discrimination cases, jumped from $3.25 million in 1966 to $111.4 million in 1979.

There were only good intentions behind the Democratic Party's decision to adopt cost-of-living increases for Social Security benefits in 1972 and a huge hike in the payroll tax to keep the system from going bankrupt in 1977; to gradually but steadily broaden the reach of Medicare, Medicaid, Aid to Families with Dependent Children, Supplemental Security Income and other "entitlements"; and to expand, geometrically, the budgets for new domestic programs like school lunches ($338 million in 1967 to $3.1 billion in 1980) or food stamps ($13 million in 1961 to $12 billion in 1980). The number of families receiving benefits under the federal welfare program jumped from 787,000 in 1960 to 3.5 million in 1975. But racial division added to the Democratic dilemma. The party had constructed two tiers of social programs, and while it still profited from widespread support for the larger tier, which funneled Social Security, Medicare, college loans and unemployment checks to working and middle-class families of all races, the benefits from the smaller tier of programs — food stamps, Medicaid and welfare among them — went by disproportionate rates to minorities, who failed to vote, and whose dependence on welfare aggrieved many working-class families. Though black Americans made up 12 percent of the population, they received 35 percent of the food stamps and 43 percent of the welfare payments.

By the end of Carter's term, as much as half the population relied to some degree on some sort of federal entitlement payment, rent subsidy, subsidized mortgage, education or small business loan, free or discounted meal, veterans' benefit, welfare check or farm program. Was New York broke, Chrysler failing and retired Americans demanding higher Social Security payments? The Democrats would find the money. Their answer to the decade's economic woes was to create the waste-ridden Comprehensive Education and Training Act (CETA) jobs program in 1973. CETA grew from a $1.5 billion to an $11 billion program in four years. "For much of the third quarter of the twentieth century, Americans, in choices actually made, had more or less consistently opted for more government and less growth," said Daniel Patrick Moynihan. "Extrapolated, as mathematicians say, these curves could only lead to a condition of no growth and total government. Before that . . . there would be a reaction."

The reaction was ignited in 1978 by a new wave of stagflation. The economy stalled and the ranks of the jobless grew, yet the annual inflation rate soared into double digits, where it stayed for most of the rest of Carter's term. Hamburger rose from 88 cents a pound in 1970 to $1.86 a pound in 1980; coffee from 91 cents a pound to $3.69; and milk from 28 cents to 59 cents a quart. Middle-income voters were finding that inflation had moved them into higher federal income tax brackets and hiked their Social Security payroll taxes, while local property tax bills doubled as the value of homes surged from inflationary appreciation.

In California, retired businessman Howard Jarvis led the effort to collect a million signatures and put Proposition 13 — a $7 billion tax-cutting referendum — on the ballot. In June, the state's voters stunned both themselves and politicians across the country by approving Proposition 13 by a 2 to 1 margin. More than a dozen other states followed California's lead in the next four years, including Massachusetts. The tax revolt was a factor of math: the bite of federal taxation grew from 13 percent in 1958 to 19 percent in 1976. Since the growth in hourly wages was stagnant and family income stalled, people were paying their taxes from a shrinking household budget: in the two years before the 1980 election, the average weekly paycheck dropped by 8.8 percent — and even the increasing number of mothers and wives who joined the workforce could not keep median family income from falling by 4.6 percent.[16]

A quarter of a century had passed since O'Neill arrived in Congress, and the Democratic Party's liberals and conservatives had reversed their roles. Now it was the liberals who controlled the House, clung to old ways, stopped change and frustrated a restless minority in their party. Now it was the conservatives who represented the national mood, but found their way blocked by sclerotic barons and stale and tired doctrine. "I wish you could have seen the stricken expression on the faces of those Democratic leaders when I talked about balancing the budget: John Brademas and Shirley Chisholm and Tip O'Neill," said Carter. "I mean it was an anathema to them to be talking about balancing the budget. That wasn't something a Democratic president was supposed to do. . . . All they knew about it was stimulus and Great Society programs."[17]

Tax-cut fever fractured the Democrats. Representative Jack Kemp, a Republican from Buffalo, proposed a 33 percent, across-the-board tax cut in late 1977, and got 177 votes for it when it first came up in August 1978 — including those of 37 Democrats. In November, the GOP picked up 15 House seats in the congressional elections. O'Neill shrugged it off, but Carter and his aides were concerned. When the Democrats held their mid-term convention in Memphis in December, Carter invited O'Neill to join him on Air Force One for the flight to Tennessee so he could lobby the Speaker about the need for fiscal prudence. Carter told the convention that "it is an illusion to believe we can preserve a commitment to compassionate, progressive government if we fail to bring inflation under control. . . . Short-term sacrifices must be made." But Ted Kennedy gave the liberals red meat. "Sometimes a party must sail against the wind," Kennedy told the cheering delegates, "we cannot heed the call of those who say that it is time to furl the sail." Kennedy urged the delegates to reject "drastic slashes in the federal budget at the expense of the elderly, the poor, the sick, the cities and the unemployed."

O'Neill had some private concerns about bloated government, especially when he heard of able-bodied workers lounging on unemployment. But he lined up behind Kennedy. Ari Weiss had told him that Carter's austerity would not "do much in economic terms to curb inflation," but instead reflected the administration's attempt to appease the business community. When the President delivered his budget in January, O'Neill chafed at the cuts in CETA, Social Security, food stamps and other programs. "I did not become Speaker of the House to dismantle the programs that I've fought for all my life, or the philosophy I believe in," he told reporters. "I'm not going to allow people to go to bed hungry for an austerity program." Though Carter's proposed cutbacks were quite modest, O'Neill summoned the Budget Committee Democrats and urged them to protect the party's legacy.[18]

The Democratic fumbling over energy then returned to haunt O'Neill and his party. In January 1979, a fundamentalist Islamic revolution forced the shah of Iran to flee his country. Iran was the second-largest exporter of oil, in part because the shah had defied his OPEC brethren and kept the flow of oil running to the West. Now Iranian exports were cut off. A few weeks later, the future of nuclear energy was called into question by an accident at the Three Mile Island nuclear power plant near Harrisburg, Pennsylvania. Panic swept the energy industry, and those who depended upon it. The price of oil jumped from $13 to $34 a barrel. Motorists stood in line for gas in California and Florida in the spring and across the nation by mid-summer. Gasoline had cost 37 cents a gallon in the summer of 1970. Now, when you could get it — what with the odd-even days and closed-down stations, long lines of hundreds of cars and fistfights at the pump — it was three times as much. On that first summer weekend of June 23, 1979, some 70 percent of the gas stations in America were closed. "People are absolutely irrational when they don't get gas. The average purchase in California is three gallons. They are topping off their tanks," the President griped to the congressional leaders. "Eighty percent of all the cars I saw on the way to the airport had one passenger. . . . We waste too damn much oil."

In April, Carter had responded to the energy shock with a nationally televised speech in which he asked Congress to lift control of the price of oil and to pass a windfall profits tax so consumers would not be gouged. The plan had the effect, once again, of dividing the Democrats along geographic and philosophical lines. Oil patch conservatives wanted decontrol without the tax, and Northern liberals the tax without decontrol. "The energy situation that's developing in the Congress, with almost everybody trying to demagogue decontrol and the windfall-profits tax . . . is disgusting," Carter wrote in his diary. O'Neill chose to be parochial — siding with northern liberals for a stiffer windfall tax and leaving the lobbying on energy to the White House. More than 100 Democrats deserted Carter and killed a standby gas rationing plan. Bolling called them "gutless," but Carter's popularity had crashed, to a Nixonian 25 percent approval level, and an every-man-for-himself mood seized the Hill. Editorial cartoonists always had fun with Carter's Southern ancestry and toothy grin; now he began to shrink in size in their strips, to a tiny yappy figure. "Things are falling apart," O'Neill told Carter at the May 1 leadership breakfast. When the Democrats refused to lift the controls on oil, Carter looked impotent. "The President was in a mood almost approaching despondency this morning. I've never seen him so discouraged. He blames himself for the failure to do anything adequate on energy," Wright told his diary.

Then things got worse. Pat Caddell had come to the conclusion that the United States had reached "a crisis of confidence marked by a dwindling faith in the future." The frantic state of affairs was not due to

Carter's poor leadership, the President's pollster told him; it was the American people who were plagued by a debilitating "psychological crisis of the first order." Mondale, Eizenstat and others objected, but the analysis fit well with prevailing Democratic dogma, that the U.S. had entered an age of limits, and had better start conducting itself with more restraint — like England after the loss of empire. Preoccupied with the task of dividing a shrinking pie, convinced by its liberal elite that capitalists were wolves and economic growth was environmentally destructive, the Democrats focused on miles per gallon and mandatory seat belts in a country whose mythos was built around liberty or death, and wide-open highways. Two days before he was to speak to the nation on the unfolding energy crisis, Carter postponed his address and retreated to Camp David, where for eleven days he met with aides, members of Congress, intellectuals, religious leaders and representatives from business and labor to consult about the "crisis of spirit." Although it was never used in his subsequent speech, the word "malaise" was bandied about in the discussions at Camp David, and emerged as shorthand for the entire episode.

Carter's speech was a success; his standing in the polls improved. Then, two days after the July 15 address, the President called on his entire cabinet to resign. "It went from sugar to shit right there," Mondale remembered. Carter accepted the resignations of five cabinet secretaries, and news of the purge reawakened whatever doubts about his leadership that his speech was able to dispel. The President tried to rescue his administration. Jordan was given the title of chief of staff and, clad in a dark pin-striped suit, went to the Hill, a supposedly chastened penitent, to make peace with the Speaker. "I hope you know that all of us here recognize and appreciate the total support you have given the President and our legislative programs," Jordan wrote to O'Neill after the visit. "We Georgia boys will never be Irish politicians, but we are going to try to learn to meet you half-way." Tommy O'Neill's name was floated by the White House as a potential cabinet secretary and, after Silvio Conte had thrown a backyard barbecue so Jordan could better get to know the congressional leaders, the chief of staff wrote O'Neill again. "You have really opened the door for me on the Hill, and I already realize the great mistake I made in not establishing some relationships there the past two years," Jordan said. It wasn't enough. In September, chaos struck the House floor when spooked Democrats bolted in a self-protective stampede and O'Neill lost four major votes on the 1979 budget resolution, an extension of the national debt ceiling, the implementing legislation for the Panama Canal treaty and a spending resolution. "The train is off the track," O'Neill told reporters. "You are looking at a guy who has nothing but troubles."

There were some successes that fall: Congress created a Department of Education and approved the $3.5 billion aid package for the Chrysler Corporation. But one of Carter's top inflation-fighting initiatives — a bill to cap soaring health care costs — was defeated at the hands of the hospital and medical lobbies. Carter had placed his hopes on the bill with Rostenkowski, but the Chicagoan was angry over a patronage matter and "betrayed" him, the President claimed. To retaliate, the President left Rosty off the official U.S. delegation to the installation of the first Polish Pope, until O'Neill interceded. "This is the vote to fight inflation," the President had written to O'Neill. "We are going all out. . . . If we fail on this I'll just be a deacon again." The health care lobbies prevailed, and the approval rating for the President's handling of the economy drooped to 16 percent.[19]

Carter had made one very important appointment as a result of his cabinet shuffle: he installed Paul Volcker, an inflation hawk, as chairman of the Federal Reserve Board. Volcker was determined to bring the inflationary spiral to a halt, and in a series of steps in the fall of 1979, the Fed raised interest rates and tightened credit. Then, with the Middle East in turmoil, an economic crisis and their President besieged on all sides, the Democrats concluded that the true path to success was to stage a civil war: to rip off all the scabs and choose up sides behind the moderate Carter or the liberal Kennedy. Even before his Memphis speech set down his philosophical grounds for running, the Massachusetts senator had been dropping hints that he might challenge the President in the Democratic primaries. Carter's performance in the spring and summer of 1979 caused many an anxious Democrat to look at Kennedy as a savior, and they urged him to run. O'Neill did his share, with a series of off-the-cuff comments to the press that helped maintain interest in a Kennedy candidacy after the senator had whispered to him, "Keep me alive, Tip. Keep me alive."

At heart, the Speaker was "thrashing about . . . like a wounded whale," wrote Mary McGrory. He was torn between his ideological ties and home-state allegiance to Kennedy, and his duty as the party's leader in the House. In the end, he had a long "fatherly" talk with Kennedy, warning him about the lingering fallout from Chappaquiddick and the

President's ability to use the power of incumbency to pass out favors and quell rebellion. He never came right out and told Kennedy not to run, but "was of the you-ought-to-wait-your-turn-school," the senator recalled.

Kennedy had made the decision to challenge Carter by the time the President invited O'Neill to attend the seventh game of the World Series in Baltimore on October 17. The event didn't start off too well for the two Democratic leaders: O'Neill wanted to eat peanuts and pizza, drink beer, keep his box score and enjoy the game, while Carter insisted on talking business. But a foul ball that ricocheted off the presidential box, and a towering home run by Willie Stargell broke the ice. During the fifth inning, Carter asked O'Neill to chair the national convention in New York in 1980. Both men knew that the President was offering the Speaker a way out, since the chairman of the convention had to be neutral. After the game, Carter headed for the victorious Pirates' locker room. O'Neill, an American League fan, ducked the celebration and went over to console the losing Orioles. No one else was hungry, so he helped himself to a couple of crab cakes from the players' postgame spread.

"Carter set you up," said Jack Murtha.

"He didn't set me up," O'Neill replied.

"He's got you neutral. There's no way you can be for Ted."

"I don't intend to be for Ted," O'Neill said.

Twenty years later, when asked about O'Neill's neutrality, both Carter and Kennedy had the same answer. Tip had generally played it straight, they said, but each complained that O'Neill had leaned just a little bit toward the other guy. Kennedy's candidacy was doomed by the senator's inability to articulate his reasons for running, by his lack of preparation and disorganized campaign, by lingering doubts about Chappaquiddick, and by events in Iran. On November 4 — the same day that CBS broadcast a damaging documentary on Kennedy, in which he flubbed a series of questions posed by newsman Roger Mudd — Iranian militants seized the U.S. embassy in Tehran and took sixty-three hostages. Americans rallied around their President in a time of crisis, and Carter's job approval rating doubled.[20]

In late winter and spring, Kennedy lost twenty-four of thirty-four primaries, and O'Neill tried to nudge him from the race. But the onslaught of recession and the endless televised crisis — "Americans Held Hostage: Day 103" — began to erode Carter's standing. The televised images of taunting Muslim militants struck a chord in the post-Vietnam era. The hostage crisis seemed to symbolize all that was wrong with Carter's leadership, particularly when a rescue mission failed in April, and eight men were killed in a fiery collision in the desert night. "You seem to be snake bit," O'Neill told the President. "You get a good hand and the dealer drops the deck." Of the hostage crisis, Carter said later: "It was a gnawing away at your guts."[21]

Nor was Carter helped when inflation soared to an annual rate of 18 percent in February, causing the White House to convene emergency meetings with House and Senate leaders to try and eliminate a $16 billion deficit in the just-released FY 1981 budget. "There was a very real crisis, an economic crisis," said one of the House negotiators. "It had a threat of doom like I haven't seen since I was a child. The markets were going to hell, the bond markets, the investment markets, everything was going to hell. There was real fear in the land." Again, O'Neill flunked the test of leadership. He boycotted the emergency negotiations, leaving Jim Wright to represent the House. "I am a traditional Democrat, I guess. I vote for traditional aid programs and I can't see casting all those people aside," the Speaker told the press.

For Wright, it was a dismal assignment. "America cannot survive as a viable economy with 18 percent interest rates. And so we try," he told his diary. "We find some cuts on which we can agree. It is tedious. It is painful. We're swimming against the current. . . . The experience was excruciating at times, tearing at the fabric of Democratic Party unity."

The taxpayers were rebelling at home. The two wings of the party were fighting it out in a series of bloody primaries. The average congressman, many of whom were elected in suburban districts that had not seen Democrats since the Civil War, shifted with each change of the prevailing wind. Votes on the budget were postponed until the fall, and O'Neill had to use all the bluster and threats he had — he stood by the whip's door, then ostentatiously posted himself by the electronic monitor, letting the members know he was looking at how each vote was cast — before an initial budget resolution finally passed the House in September. Some of his oldest friends — Jamie Whitten and Lindy Boggs among them — were with the 44 Democrats who deserted O'Neill on a series of procedural votes, declining to support the rulings of the chair. They earned his wrath and a written reprimand. "It is elementary to our procedural control of the House that the chair be supported by members of our party," O'Neill wrote. "In other countries, if such a vote were lost, the government would fall."

As a political statement, the House response to the economic crisis — final passage of the FY 1981 budget did not occur until a lame duck session in December — was far too little and late. When Carter and the Democrats needed to demonstrate unity and resolve in the spring and summer, they had instead showed pettiness and disarray. Once the Carter administration finished distributing a host of election-year goodies, and unemployment payments soared in response to the recession, the final budget was $60 billion in the red. The Republicans taunted O'Neill, carrying stuffed, lamed ducks onto the House floor to illustrate the Democratic failures. As part of a $4 million ad campaign the GOP ran, throughout the year, a popular commercial that showed a fat, white-haired, cigar-smoking O'Neill lookalike driving a big black Lincoln and running out of gas on a deserted New Jersey highway. The budget battle was "a case study of the legislative chaos that can occur in today's House without strong unified leadership, which House Speaker Thomas P. O'Neill Jr. was slow to provide," wrote *Newsweek*'s Gloria Borger. The *National Journal*'s Richard E. Cohen said O'Neill "sometimes appears terribly vulnerable."

"It has not been a fun-filled session," O'Neill told reporters. "There is no more fun around here anymore. Those days are gone."[22]

O'Neill did a little better as chairman of the Democratic convention, where he at least had a family model in his efforts to keep peace between the Kennedy and Carter factions. Tommy and Kip were supporting Kennedy; Susan backed Carter. The only time the O'Neills stood together, said one wisecracking pol, was during the Sunday Gospel. Because Carter had such a strong lead in delegates, the Kennedy camp's only real weapon was its threat to disrupt the convention and spoil the party's image on prime-time television. In a memo to his boss, Kirk O'Donnell warned the Speaker that the Carter forces were "playing hardball . . . refusing to give an inch," and that Kennedy's men were responding by demanding time-consuming and divisive floor votes on forty contested issues. "If there isn't a compromise here you are going to be the one holding the gavel at two in the morning with a wild convention in your hand and the press finding fault with your stewardship," O'Donnell told O'Neill. The Speaker remembered the humiliating experience that Albert had suffered in Chicago in 1968, and the chaotic conditions of Miami in 1972, and wanted none of it. "We're not going to have people walking out of my convention," he vowed. Kennedy was invited to the House side of the Capitol, where O'Neill picked up O'Donnell's memo and began to read it aloud. Kennedy shot daggers at O'Donnell, but eventually agreed to drop most of his demands in return for some face-saving tributes and dignities, including a nationally televised speaking appearance.

"The work goes on, the cause endures, the hope still lives and the dream shall never die," Kennedy told the convention, in an electrifying speech. As the delegates chanted, "We want Ted!" the Speaker decided that he had had enough hardball from the Carter forces, who "ought not to paralyze his convention any longer." O'Neill marched toward the microphone, threatening to call the roll on three liberal amendments to the Democratic platform, which Carter opposed. Jordan knew the President's troops would lose a roll call in the midst of the pro-Kennedy din, and capitulated. A "compromise" was struck, and O'Neill quickly gaveled the liberal planks into the party platform. On the closing night of the convention, O'Neill stood on the podium between Carter and Kennedy. He "had worked hard for that moment in an effort to salvage the party he loved and to prevent both the President and some vulnerable congressional candidates from going down to defeat. And although the outcome may have been dictated by the political realities, it was the Speaker who brought those realities home to both camps," the *Times* reported. "He had told Senator Kennedy repeatedly that if the senator expected to have a future in the Democratic Party he should be on the podium with President Carter at the close of the convention. He had warned the President that he needed the party's Kennedy wing. He had urged Mr. Carter to be conciliatory."

Yet many in the hall noted how, in a final bit of peevishness, Kennedy dodged the traditional arms-raised embrace of the victor, and how Carter thus looked like an unsuccessful supplicant as he chased the senator around the podium. O'Neill left the convention with few illusions about Carter, but totally underestimated the Republican candidate. "The best thing he's got going for him is his opponent, Ronald Reagan," O'Neill said.[23]

The Speaker entered the fall campaign with the belief that the House Democrats might lose from 10 to 25 seats, but that the nation would reject Reagan's right-wing philosophy. Reagan held a lead all fall, and put the election away on October 28, in his only debate with

Carter. A national TV audience saw no snorting Neanderthal, but a warm, charming guy who teased, "There you go again," after Carter launched a rhetorical attack. Reagan's closing question to the American people — "Are you better off than you were four years ago?" — was answered resoundingly on Election Day.

Carter was informed of his impending loss by his staff as he flew back to Plains to vote on the morning of Election Day. "It's gone," said Caddell. The President, Jody Powell and others strove to keep the news from the media, but it was too painful a charade. Carter conceded an hour before the polls closed in California, and O'Neill was convinced that the early surrender cost James Corman of California and other West Coast congressmen their seats. "Everybody was calling it and the networks were saying big landslide for Reagan," Jordan recalled. "Carter said, 'Everybody knows. It's obvious. Let's go in and get it over with.'

"It's one of those things if you do over again you would do it differently," said Jordan. "I remember Jim Corman, what a good guy he was. It's bad. It's bad."

Said O'Neill: "I'm sitting here and my men are tumbling and falling. My men are checking the returns, and pollsters are coming in and saying, 'You're hitting an avalanche.' I get a phone call from Frank Moore. He says, 'The President ten minutes from now is going to say he's conceding and he wants you to come down.' I told him, 'I can't, and he's doing the wrong thing.' " But there was nothing Moore could do.

"You guys came in like a bunch of pricks," O'Neill told him. "And you're going out the same way."[24]

PART SIX

From Whence He Came

CHAPTER 23

Reeling on the Ropes

THE CARTER YEARS had been a political disaster for Tip O'Neill's Democratic Party. And justly so. When handing the Democrats control of both the White House and the Congress in 1976, the voters had looked to the party for competence, resolve and the promise of national revival. Handed that opportunity, the Democrats had staged a thoroughly miserable performance. They had been petty, selfish and spiteful. They had looked beholden to the oil companies, the health care industry and other special interests. They had refused to curb their insistent liberal base, and chosen to fight a destructive, self-indulgent civil war in the presidential primaries. They had been intellectually clueless and politically inept.

O'Neill stood as a symbol of their failure. The Republican TV commercial that showed the burly white-haired actor who ran out of gas clicked not because it represented just any generic big-city pol, but because it lampooned the Speaker of the clownish House in Washington. After a fine first year as Speaker, with the passage of the ethics and energy packages, O'Neill's performance had lapsed to adequate in 1978, and then to piteous in 1979 and 1980. There were good reasons for the disaster, and few in Washington were more adept than O'Neill at deflecting the blame toward the White House, the centrifugal effects of congressional reform or the ideological incohesion of his party. But in a time of economic, international and political crisis, when his party and countrymen looked to Tip O'Neill for leadership, he had failed. His was the party of Tongsun Park and CETA, of 18 percent inflation and gas lines. When they should have been addressing the problems of America's malfunctioning economy, the Democrats had spent their time squabbling over pork barrel dams, their prideful prerogatives and patronage jobs for their pals. They had failed to respond to the tax revolt. "We'd run out of ideas," said Representative Gillis Long of Louisiana, the chairman of the Democratic caucus. "For four years we've been living in a dream world."

The electorate's retribution had been just and severe. It was not just what the Republicans won: the White House, the Senate and a 33-seat gain in the House of Representatives. It was who had won: Ronald Reagan. And who had lost: liberal icons like John Brademas, Frank Thompson, Lud Ashley, Senators George McGovern, Birch Bayh of Indiana and Frank Church of Idaho. In the Senate, conservative Senator Jesse Helms of North Carolina and Strom Thurmond of South Carolina became committee chairmen. Carter was gone, Kennedy dismayed and Bob Byrd a minority leader. "The House will become the national Democratic Party, to the extent that it exists," the *Post* concluded.

"Until such time as we nominate a new presidential candidate, you are the leader of the Democratic Party as well as the highest public official of that party," leadership aide Burt Hoffman wrote the Speaker. "You are also, more than ever, the only person in a position to continue representing the ideals of justice and compassion." It would be the final battle, the defining historic moment, for this bruised old white-haired man, and O'Neill knew it. He would sit, alone, in his darkened office, brooding over each day's reversals. He would be betrayed by captains, scored by old foes, challenged by young rebels in his ranks. His name, his pride, were on the line, but so, more important, was what he believed. If Tip O'Neill bungled this job, if he failed to hold the bridge, the hill, the last foothold, he knew that his place in history would suffer, but so would Roosevelt's legacy. The elderly whose fears of poverty and illness had been eased by Social Security and Medicare. The working-class kids, carrying their families' dreams, going to college with the help of Pell grants and federal loans. The water and the air that were getting cleaner, and the wilderness preserved from development. The single mother or the motherless child who still, in his abundant nation, knew the pain of hunger, the cost of ignorance or the rags of poverty.

He was no saint. Win or lose, there would be no canonization of Thomas P. O'Neill Jr. In a lifetime in politics he'd gouged eyes, thrown elbows, bent the law and befriended rogues and thieves. He could be mean and small-minded. But at his core there lay a magnificence of spirit, deep compassion and a rock-hard set of beliefs. He had a sense of duty that he refused to abandon for those whom Heaven's grace forgot — and he would sooner die on the floor of the House, or watch his party be vanquished and dispersed, than desert them. "You know you're right?" Millie would ask him, as he adjusted his tie at the door in the morning. "Yes," he would say, and he knew it — *knew it* — knew it like he knew the sidewalks of Cambridge, the liturgy of Sunday Mass or how to stack a conference committee. "Then do your best," she would say, and off he would go.

He may not have had the looks of a movie star, but he had great instincts and sound judgment and a joy for life that could match Reagan's charm and, like the new President, an innocence that had survived many years in a cynical game and would, given time and enough exposure, allow Americans to come to love him. Indeed, Reagan and O'Neill had much in common. They were broad-brush types who liked a joke and never let the facts get in the way of a good story. They could take a punch and come back swinging. They prized their downtime, loved to be loved and bore without complaint, or much interest in correcting, the liabilities of their parties: Reagan the greed of laissez-faire and O'Neill the complacency of bureaucrats and hacks. They each had spectacularly talented staffs. Most important, and despite their acting talents, they stood out — among the sharpies and trimmers of the nation's capital — as men of deep conviction. Each was sustained, in much the same way, by his own distinctive mythology. Reagan was a son of the small-town Midwest, a lifeguard and radio announcer who had made his way to the Golden State and become a wealthy movie star. He revered individual liberty, and his icons were the cowboy, the entrepreneur, the singular heroes of sporting fields and war. His speeches rarely failed to cite the American

Revolution, which had thrown down the government of a rotten tyranny and claimed the freedom and rights of man. O'Neill was the product of the East, of the great crowded cities. He reveled in the collectivity of purpose, in the fruits of charity, neighborhood and fellowship. His was the creed of Honey Fitz and Curley, of snow buttons, Roosevelt and the Sermon on the Mount. He too revered the Founding Fathers, but for the magnificent system of government they had built, which had proven so adaptable and addressed so many social ills.

Tip O'Neill versus Ronald Reagan. Theirs was no sophistic debate: these were world views clashing, hot lava meeting thundering surf. And good it was, for the country, to have the debate — to stake the claim of a "more perfect union" against the demand for "life, liberty and the pursuit of happiness" once again. History was happening. The heritage of the New Deal, a philosophy of governing that had lasted for half a century, was at stake. Reagan didn't want to trim the sails — he wanted to turn the ship around and head back to port. For more than fifty years, Republicans had argued that the country had taken a horribly wrong turn in the 1930s — that Roosevelt's social insurance programs and the taxes that supported them were seductively undermining the American way, and breeding lethargy, dependence and corruption of the spirit. Nor was there ambivalence in the Speaker's lobby — O'Neill was free of the conflicting loyalties that had hindered his performance during the Carter administration.

O'Neill and Reagan. Their struggle would bring out the best in them. Each would have his victories, and grimace in defeat. They would be ranked among the greatest Presidents and Speakers of the century, their stature underscored by the flaws of those who followed them. Yet to equate them in November 1980 is to leap ahead of the story. Reagan was tasting his first triumphs, and O'Neill had still to serve a season in political hell.[1]

O'NEILL DIDN'T STAND amid the wreckage of Election Day and claim the title of Mr. Democrat. But he recognized his new responsibility, and said so with a number of strategic decisions. The first concerned his personal plans. He had toyed with the notion of retiring, of going home and making a little money. If Carter had been reelected, O'Neill would have resigned in 1982, at the age of seventy, he told his family and friends. Now he banished such thoughts. There could be no uncertainty. The decision was public, and unequivocal. "I'm not going to retire until there's a Democrat back in the White House," he told *Newsweek*.

The next step was to establish the Democratic priorities, and there was no doubt in the Speaker's mind what the number one priority was: "To save the House." Maintaining his party's control of the chamber was, even in the best of times, a Speaker's prime political obligation. And now, with the White House and the Senate in Republican hands (and the Supreme Court embarking on its own rightward course), the House was the last redoubt. "Save the House. That was his goal. He went out and worked like a sonofabitch. He killed himself going out around the country for guys," said Leo Diehl. Lose the House in 1982 and there would, indeed, be a revolution. Lose the House and lose most of the Great Society, and much of the New Deal. Lose the House and there could, in fact, be realignment. The idea had caught fire among journalists and political scientists: the electorate might be dividing itself along new ideological fault lines. The Republicans might dominate in the Reagan years, and after, as they had in the Gilded Age or Roaring Twenties. "The Republicans had a real chance in 1982 to realign the parties," said Kirk O'Donnell, and O'Neill concluded that "what you had to do was organize a successful retreat so that your troops would be, morale-wise and weapon-wise, ready to battle" when the critical campaign of 1982 began.

That done, O'Neill set out to analyze the Democratic defeat. He had to acknowledge that the country was tilting to the right, and that the Republicans had outspent and outfought the Democrats in the 1980 election. But he also believed there was insufficient evidence to call Reagan's election a revolution. The voters, after all, had given Democratic House candidates 51 percent of the vote. There were, instead, politically quantifiable reasons for that November's disaster: the voters' disdain for Carter; the lurching economy; lapses in Democratic unity in the wake of the Carter-Kennedy fight; and, above all, the deep feelings of anger and frustration caused by the Iranian hostage crisis. And though the Democratic vote slipped in northern bastions like Massachusetts, many of the defectors voted for the liberal Republican, John Anderson, who was on the ballot as an independent. The Democratic chieftains, surveying the wreckage in November, felt they could have picked up Massachusetts, Connecticut, Michigan, New York and several other states had Anderson not run.

Another glaring factor in the 1980 results was Democratic turnout. Reagan had capitalized on issues like crime, busing, taxes and abortion and scored quite well among blue-collar Democrats and Jewish Americans, but reports of his inroads were exaggerated by the low turnout in these groups, which hurt Carter as much as or more than Reagan's gains. Catholics and blue-collar families and poor southerners were leaving the New Deal coalition, that was for sure — what was yet to be proved was that they had permanently fastened themselves to the Republican core, or shared its fervent disdain for middle-class social insurance programs. O'Neill recognized that Reagan was a far more formidable foe than "the matinee idol . . . from another time" he had ridiculed during the campaign, and whose name he had purposely mispronounced as "Reegan." But he also knew that the voters were more disgusted with Democratic ineptness than with the party's long-standing commitment to the needs of Americans with modest incomes. In the short run, O'Neill had to respect the new President's popularity. In the long run, the Speaker believed the voters still saw themselves as a goodhearted people, supported the middle-class entitlement programs, relied upon what had come to be called the "social safety net" — and would resist attempts to dismantle it.[2]

Liberals in the Democratic caucus believed that the political situation was now clarified — that the accommodating Jimmy Carter had gotten what he deserved, that the party should regroup under the New Deal banner and that the demands of both conscience and politics dictated the need for a righteous scorched-earth campaign against Reagan. Though O'Neill might have been sympathetic to their goals, as a leader he had other factors to consider — particularly the political needs of the 50-odd moderate and conservative Democrats whose districts had gone heavily to Reagan and were already the target of a plausible recruiting drive by congressional Republicans. The stark arithmetic confronted O'Neill: if just 27 southern Democrats were to vote with the Republicans when Congress was organized in January, he would be out as Speaker. And 40 conservative Democrats, led by Representative Charles Stenholm of Texas, had already organized themselves as the "Democratic Conservative Forum," and met with O'Neill to demand better committee assignments and more input on party policy. "It could well have been that they have been ignored along the line — on the basis that the squeaky wheel gets the grease," the Speaker admitted. Now the conservative Democrats, if for no other reason than self-preservation, were determined to be squeaky. They came to be known as the "boll weevils," and when they voted with the Republicans would dictate the decisions of the House. "The plain fact is that the House is Democratic, but only nominally," Mo Udall said. "Technically, I'll be in control of one of the key House committees, but I won't have the votes there or on the floor."

O'Neill was also, at heart, a patriot. He honored the verdicts of Election Days and believed that Reagan deserved his honeymoon. "He felt strongly that the institution of the Presidency was in trouble," O'Donnell said. "And he didn't want another failed Presidency. He worried about it." Nor did O'Neill believe, especially after the display that the Democrats had staged in 1979 and 1980, that the public would forgive him if he kept Reagan's program from the floor of the House. Even if he could round up the votes to support a strategy of obstruction — a dubious prospect in itself — the Speaker knew he would only be handing Reagan and his allies a potent campaign issue for 1982.[3] "The American people wanted to give Reagan a chance . . . and they had voted for change. There had been a strong repudiation of Democratic leadership. So O'Neill decided to give Reagan a chance to offer his legislation and not play games with it, and to do it in a very public way so that we couldn't become the scapegoat, and would not take the blame," O'Donnell said.

The Speaker had the parliamentary power over scheduling to delay the process, but chose not to. "O'Neill guaranteed the President a schedule of consideration of the President's economic and budget and tax programs," said O'Donnell. "It gave the upper hand to Reagan because it lay within the honeymoon period. He actually made big calendar charts that he put up in the Speaker's office, which was very uncharacteristic of him. This gave a tremendous advantage to the Republicans and the administration."

O'Neill recalled his days as the minority leader in the Massachusetts House, when he had worked to develop an agenda — veterans' housing, opposition to birth control, labor reform — that gave the Democrats a winning platform for the 1948 election. The key, he told his aides, was to set up issues in 1980 for Democrats to run on in 1982. "He wasn't looking for legislative victories," O'Donnell recalled. "He was looking for the opposition to make errors: namely, to really develop hubris, so that they thought they could do anything they wanted to . . . in that arrogance of success." O'Neill would let Reagan have his day.

He would give Reagan rope. Sooner or later, O'Neill believed, the economy and the electorate would turn on Reagan — and Democrats would ride that reaction back to power. Within days of the election O'Neill had selected the basic strategy by which he and his party would operate in the next two years.

"We're going to cooperate with the President. It's America first and party second," O'Neill said in mid-November. "We're going to give 'em enough rope. They can use it either to herd cattle or make a mistake. . . . They've got to deliver." Of all the decisions O'Neill made in the aftermath of the 1980 election, giving Reagan the rope was the most significant. It was also the most painful, as it virtually ensured that O'Neill and his party would take a grievous beating in the first year of Reagan's presidency.[4]

Reagan toured the Capitol on November 18 and met with O'Neill, who warned him (as he had warned Carter) that now he was playing in the "big leagues." The lecture rubbed Reagan and his aides the wrong way, but they bit their tongues and smiled when O'Neill promised the new President a six-month honeymoon. O'Neill told the old movie actor that though he didn't go to the pictures often, he had enjoyed the poolroom scene in the Reagan film *Knute Rockne, All American*. Reagan was puzzled — he remembered no poolroom scene in that movie. "I liked him," O'Neill told the press. "A very personable fellow."

A week later the Speaker faced the sad duty of speaking at John McCormack's funeral Mass. The lame duck session of the Ninety-sixth Congress adjourned on December 16. "It was the Congress in which liberals and Democrats finally ran out of gas," said the *Times.* "Many ruefully acknowledged that the programs and philosophy that had sustained them for a quarter of a century ceased to work." The Ninety-seventh Congress started no better for the sixty-eight-year-old Speaker. On January 6, the day after he was formally elected Speaker, O'Neill was rushed in great pain by helicopter to Bethesda Naval Hospital. His prostate had swollen and blocked his urinary tract again.[5]

"We find him very charismatic, with a lot of charisma and a lot of duende and flair and class and knowledgeable, and he's got a good political sense and he's got a lot of experience. Don't undersell him. He's a sharp fellow," O'Neill told the *Globe* when Congress reconvened in January. Reagan was a lucky fellow, too. The release of the fifty-two hostages from Iran, after 444 days in captivity, on a warm and sunlit Inauguration Day seemed to underscore his call for a new order, and heightened the feeling of celebration. "We are too great a nation to limit ourselves to small dreams," the new President said. "We are not, as some would have us believe, doomed to an inevitable decline."

The new President was in a good mood when, stopping by O'Neill's office that day, he agreed to sign a series of commemorative stamped envelopes for the Speaker, jokingly offering to trade his autograph for a few votes. O'Neill and other House leaders were decked out in rented striped pants and cutaways, after Eleanor Kelley had scoured the countryside for a shop that stocked size 52 "stout." When O'Neill mentioned that his office desk had been used by Grover Cleveland, it triggered a non sequitur from Reagan.

"I have some affection for him. I played Grover Cleveland Alexander in the movies," Reagan said.

"He was one of fourteen pitchers to win three hundred games," O'Neill replied.

"Yes, and that was the 1926 World Series," the President said. The Speaker malevolently bent the anecdote to make it seem that a vacuous Reagan had mistaken a President for a pitcher, and he told it often to disparage his foe.

O'Neill and Wright had initially selected Sam Rayburn and Lyndon Johnson as their role models, recalling how the two Texas Democrats, during the Eisenhower administration, would sit down for drinks and cut deals with Ike. Reagan and his aides, for their part, had been seductive: asking if the Speaker had enough tickets and accommodations for the inaugural events and making other gestures of respect. "It was very nice of them to call," the Speaker said, after the White House phoned to make sure his family had gotten good seats for the inaugural gala. "Compared to some administrations they are off on the right foot."

O'Neill expected to get a budget from Reagan that would cut a mere $18 billion from domestic spending, and then be adjusted by Congress to reflect a "broad middle-ground consensus." It was a wildly optimistic assessment. Years later, Wright admitted that "Tip and I got rolled. We said, 'Let's treat him well. Let's try to deal with him as Rayburn and Johnson were to Eisenhower. Let's show him around and help him learn the ropes.' You know, we were going to be father advisers and all that smart stuff. Little did we know. That sonofabitch rolled us. God, did Reagan ever. If you quote me, I didn't say sonofabitch — I said that charming old thespian rolled us. But God, did he ever."

Reagan had warned in his inaugural address, "Government is not the solution to our problem: government is the problem." And he meant it. While running for President, he had endorsed the Kemp-Roth tax plan, with its across-the-board tax cuts of 30 percent, spread over three years. He believed that the U.S. needed to boost defense spending to counter Soviet aggression. And he promised to balance the federal budget by cutting wasteful (but unnamed) government programs until spending was less than 20 percent of the gross national product. Within a day of his swearing-in, the Republican Party mailed out a national fund-raising letter, under the new President's signature, asking for contributions to make the House Republican in 1982. "There was a hard-core group around Reagan who not only wanted to reverse the Great Society, but also the New Deal," Gary Hart recalled. "If they thought they could get away with it, they would go after Social Security, Medicare and the core programs. There was some hard-core pre-Rooseveltian thought that had gone underground and waited for its day, and believed that day had come with the 1980 election."

When opponents asked how Reagan could increase defense spending, cut taxes and still keep his promise to balance the budget, he told them he was counting on a "supply side" dividend. His tax and budget cuts would spur economic growth and renew Wall Street's confidence, Reagan said, and the government would recoup its lost revenue by taking a smaller percentage of a bigger gross. Sort of like a retailer, cutting prices, and making up in volume what he lost per sale. As a theory, supply side economics appeared to make sense — and its appeal was certainly real enough in a climate of double-digit inflation, in which taxpayers found themselves shifted to higher tax brackets as their cost-of-living raises kicked in. In practice, however, it would represent a huge experiment, with a host of unknown variables. George Bush had scorned it, during the Republican primary campaign, as "voodoo economics." The new Senate majority leader, Howard Baker, more accurately called it a "riverboat gamble."

Well, "'nothing happens unless first a dream,'" Reagan told Congress, quoting Carl Sandburg. The Reagan regime, in the person of budget director David Stockman, devised an economic shock plan. Reagan had promised a 5 percent hike in defense spending during the campaign: Stockman and defense secretary Caspar Weinberger doubled it. The Republicans had been torn between the Kemp-Roth tax plan and a Ways and Means scheme to give business tax breaks: Reagan embraced them both. The White House put a long list of federal programs on the chopping block as it reached for $74 billion in proposed savings from CETA public service jobs; water projects; subsidies for airlines, railroads and farmers; urban development grants; federal aid to education; synthetic fuels development; Amtrak and mass transit funds; clean water programs; low-income housing; middle-income college grants and loans; foreign aid; and school lunch subsidies for middle-class children.[6]

Stockman was a true believer who, over the course of his career, found many truths in which to believe. He was at heart a libertarian, but had moved from the left-wing halls of the Harvard Divinity School to the right-wing circles of supply side theology. "I remember when he was running around Cambridge as a way-out liberal opposed to the war," O'Neill said. "I'm a progressive liberal myself, but he was three mouths to the left of me. Now he is a conservative, and as I say, when you convert to a party you go from one extreme to the other." Stockman was inexhaustible, and dedicated to the task of dismantling as much as he could of the New Deal and Great Society, to liberate people and financial capital from oppressive bureaucracy. Most of official Washington was snowed. Even O'Neill could be sidetracked by a compelling anecdote. After hearing Stockman argue that wealthy children in posh suburban schools didn't deserve to get federally subsidized lunches, the Speaker "and other members of the Politburo expressed both gratitude and amazement. They hadn't even known that the subsidy was going to children whose parents earned over $18,000 a year," Stockman recalled.

"We don't agree with everything, but this young fellow sure knows what he's talking about," O'Neill told his lieutenants, as that February meeting broke up.

There was early evidence that Reaganomics, as it came to be called, was set upon shifting sands. The target date for a balanced budget was quietly moved from 1983 to 1984. Stockman's plan depended on a "rosy scenario" that called for 5 percent real annual growth. And there was a "magic asterisk," in the plan for $44 billion in "future savings to be identified." A preliminary analysis by the staff of the House steering committee warned O'Neill that Stockman's plans were "frequently incomplete and vague. There are proposals with purported savings without an indication of the specific programs that are included in the proposed reduction."

But if there were holes in Stockman's calculations, there were few omissions in the White House strategy for pushing the economic plan through Congress. The Reaganauts had gone to school on their predecessors' failures. The early White House strategic memos contain a number of cautionary references to Carter's scattershot performance. "The record of the last four years is instructive," read one memo to Edwin Meese, Reagan's trusted counselor. "Jimmy Carter announced seven major economic programs, on average a new one almost every six months. No consistent signals were transmitted from the White House. The administration shifted course several times without ever communicating a sense of direction or a destination. Both the policies and the articulation of these policies were characterized by vacillation, indecision, inconsistency and confusion."

Reagan and his aides resolved to be focused and consistent — and to launch a blitzkrieg upon the the welfare state before its creators could organize a defense. There would be no tide of initiatives, or confused priorities. Foreign policy was, for the moment, pushed aside.

"Over time, the honeymoon period will end, organized interest groups will regain their strength and aggressiveness, and the clock will move inexorably toward another campaign season for the Congress. Politically, the time is now to attempt the most difficult tasks," the memo to Meese said. "If the administration's four-year spending control battle is to be won, a plan to permanently reduce the size of the federal budget must be launched within two or three weeks of the Inauguration and must be the lead element in the total economic package."

Baker, Meese and the others believed that the presidential honeymoon was a crucial period, because it molded a President's image as someone who could or could not get things done. "We were single-minded in those first six to eight months," said Baker. "We kept our eye on the ball. We had a 100-day plan. We courted the Congress assiduously."

"There were several meetings where we talked about the need to go forward expeditiously, while you were at the heart of your power, the height of your influence," said Kenneth Duberstein, a member of Reagan's congressional liaison office. "The Carter administration had not had a strong sense of priorities and had overloaded the system and there was gridlock and there was inertia and deadlock."

A "Legislative Strategy Group" was created at the White House, chaired by Baker and including the President's top economic and political advisers and the congressional liaison team. Duberstein and his boss, Max Friedersdorf, believed that Congress "for four years had felt by and large ignored" and so they sought "to set up a relationship with Congress where there was mutual respect. Harmony. Even if philosophically there were differences," said Duberstein, who led the White House lobbying team in the House. Richard Bolling, running into Duberstein at the White House, told him that it had taken two years to get into the Oval Office in the Carter administration, but just two months to be invited to see Reagan.

"We stroked and we stroked and we stroked and we stroked and we stroked and we traded, and the President was very good at that, and willing to do it all day and all night," said Baker. The Speaker was not immune from the attention: he and other congressional leaders were invited to the Oval Office for Reagan's seventieth birthday party in February, and O'Neill and Millie were hosted at the White House for a private dinner with the Reagans. The President's staff made careful note of O'Neill's favorite brand of cigars, and did all they could to avoid the kind of petty incidents that had caused ill will between the Speaker and the Carter White House.[7]

Opposing the single-purposed White House lobbying team was a Democratic Party that was, ideologically, all over the map. In notes prepared for a March 4 leadership meeting, O'Neill listed seven different groups of Democrats, spanning the ideological spectrum, that were working on responses to Reagan's proposals. On the right were the boll weevils. Two groups shared the middle: a caucus committee led by Gillis Long and the Democrats on the House Budget Committee, led by Jim Jones. ("Defending programs for the poor will not sell," Jones told his colleagues. "We have to speak to middle-class voters.") On the left were four more factions: the Black Caucus; the Democratic Study Group; an ad hoc group of liberals affiliated with Phil Burton; and a group of younger Democrats from the classes of 1974 and 1976.

"How do we try to keep all these groups under the same umbrella, and discourage them from going public, which only serves to divide and weaken us?" O'Neill asked his lieutenants. By early March, he was taking fire from liberals in the Democratic caucus who believed he should be leading a more forceful resistance to Reagan and accused him of "running for cover." But, after reviewing the President's popularity in Lou Harris's polls, O'Neill had decided that he should swallow up to $25 and $30 billion in budget cuts. "Now is not the time to attack," he said. "The Senate and House Republicans are trying to brand us as obstructionist." In a March 10 decision, O'Neill guaranteed Reagan a vote on his tax and budget proposals by the August recess.

Reagan and his aides were cheered: the clock was always their most worrisome foe. The action shifted to the Budget Committee, where a group of centrists led by chairman Jim Jones, with the Speaker's acquiescence, thought they could reach an accommodation with the White House by trading support for Reagan's budget cutbacks if he would scale back his three-year tax cut. Stockman scoffed at the deal, betting that it would be easier for Reagan to pick off the boll weevils than for the Democrats to craft a budget that could span the ideological distance between the Burtons and Stenholms in their caucus. On February 18, the night that Reagan had presented his plan to a joint session of Congress and a national television audience, Stenholm had sidled up to Duberstein and said, "I think the President is being a bit chintzy. I think we can go another $8 to $10 billion in cuts." It was all or nothing, Stockman announced. The showdown was set, and the Democrats' hopes rose with the first indications that news of Reagan's cuts was beginning to affect his ratings in the polls. "The Democratic spirit, so long subdued by the obvious Reagan popularity, is showing signs of life," Wright told his diary. "It soon must become clear to even the most benighted Reagan fan among America's average people that his budget cutters really have gone too far." Then, early in the afternoon of March 30, a deranged Coloradan named John Hinckley shot Reagan on the sidewalk outside the Washington Hilton.[8]

Reagan was hit in the chest by a bullet that bounced off his limousine and lodged in his lung, just behind his heart. He collapsed as he walked into the hospital emergency room. "Honey," he told his wife as they prepped him for surgery, "I forgot to duck." As they put him on the operating table, the President told his doctors, "Please tell me you're all Republicans."

Vice president George Bush was in an airplane, flying from Fort Worth to Austin, when he got the news.[9] O'Neill, who was second in the line of succession to the presidency, was in his office in the Capitol, having lunch with Jones and a lobbyist when Gary Hymel interrupted to tell them of the shooting. O'Neill got an update on the President's condition from Secretary of State Alexander Haig — shortly before Haig breathlessly interrupted a White House press briefing to declare, "I am in control."

For the rest of the evening, O'Neill and his staff sat helplessly in the office, watching the news on television like the rest of America. Three days later, the Speaker was the first outsider to visit Reagan in the hospital, and was shocked at the President's condition. Though the media had been supplied with optimistic reports about Reagan's recovery, the President was weak, in pain, doped up, feverish and suffering from pneumonia when the Speaker stopped by to say a few words and give him a book of Irish jokes. "He was in terrific pain. Much more serious than anybody thought," O'Neill recalled. "I thought, 'This is no place for me.' He thanked me for coming and we squeezed each other's hands."

"He was probably closer to death than most of us realized," O'Neill said later.

Reagan's gallantry, and the brio he brought to his recovery, moved his "revolution" to a higher plane. The country had endured almost two decades of assassinations, scandal, social turmoil, economic stagnancy and unhappy presidencies. Now the old movie star, in the best Hollywood tradition, had taken a bullet, shrugged it off, and risen more determined than ever. He was no longer just an adept herald of mythic America, he was a part of it. The people had offered unanswered prayers for the recovery of the era's other victims of political violence; now here was a man for whom the heavens had rewarded their appeals. He must have been spared for a reason, Reagan concluded. Millions admired his pluck. And his recovery fitted with the sunny, idealistic optimism of supply side theory and individual freedom. Within a week, Reagan's public approval had leaped by 10 points, then jumped again.

"Just when the honeymoon might ordinarily have been expected to begin to fade, it was deepened and extended," said aide Richard Darman. The White House shrewdly tied Reagan's return to action to the budget and tax debate, scheduling an April 28 comeback speech before a joint session of Congress. It was a triumph, and people began to call him the "Great Communicator."

"We've just been outflanked and outgunned," Wright wrote in his diary after Reagan's speech. "The aura of heroism which has attended him since his wounding, deserved in large part by his demeanor under the extreme duress of his physical ordeal, assured a tumultuous welcome.

"It was a very deceptive, extremely partisan and probably very effective presentation," Wright said. "So Tip and I and the mainstream Democrats are embattled, trying to stem the flow of conservative sands through the sieve." Stockman and Jones now engaged in a bidding war for the hearts of the boll weevils. "One gimmick followed another," Stockman recalled. "More importantly, once the numbers and policy choices became nearly meaningless, the decisive battle for the Reagan Revolution got reduced to an image contest between the Speaker and the President, a question of hope versus nostalgia. Would you go with the President's brave new gamble or stick with the Speaker's failed tax-and-spend policies of the past? That's what the members were finally called upon to decide."[10]

Another matter plagued O'Neill and Wright: their decision to put Representative Phil Gramm of Texas on the Budget Committee. Gramm was a conservative economist from Texas A&M University who, after being elected to the House as a Democrat in 1978, had joined Stockman in offering balanced budgets as alternatives to those drafted by the Democratic White House and Congress. At the start of 1981, Gramm pressed the leadership for a seat on the Budget panel, and tugged at the ties of loyalty with his fellow Texan.

"I must serve to look out for 'our own.' Sam Rayburn always did," Wright wrote in his diary. "I had mixed emotions about Phil. He is such a gadfly. He will make waves. He'll grandstand. He'll get in the papers. He is a fly in my Fort Worth soup. No victory for moderation will be sufficient for him . . . but he is, after all, one of 'our own.'" Wright extracted a written promise from Gramm, who vowed to support the Budget Committee's budget on the floor of the House. Instead, Gramm joined with Stockman and Representative Delbert Latta, an Ohio Republican, to draft a budget resolution that could capture the votes of the 40-odd boll weevils and other conservative Democrats. Gramm had been his "spy" in the Budget Committee, Stockman said later, providing the Reaganauts with inside information on the Democratic plans. "His blatant open split with the Democrats had made me look a bit like a fool," Wright told his diary.

Liberals blamed O'Neill for Gramm's appointment, and yelped even louder when the Speaker and a delegation of fourteen pals in Congress headed for Australia, New Zealand and Hawaii on a two-week junket over the Easter recess. The trip, which was taken at the invitation of the

Australian and New Zealand governments, had been planned for months and was a legitimate diplomatic mission to those two far-distant U.S. allies. But the timing was terrible. While O'Neill was caught by TV cameras sampling the pleasures of the South Seas, Reagan was furiously lobbying the boll weevils.

Later in his presidency, Reagan was to become the target of critics for his supposed laziness. But while still recovering from a gunshot wound in April of 1981, there was no mistaking his zeal and hard work on the budget plan. He stunned O'Neill by phoning Tom Bevill, a Democrat from Alabama who was with the Speaker in New Zealand, in the middle of the night.[11] Reagan called Representative Eugene Atkinson, a Democrat from Pennsylvania, when the congressman was appearing on a radio talk show. It was the first time the public had heard Reagan's voice since he got out of the hospital, and Atkinson promised the President his vote while they were on the air. After a conversation with Reagan, Representative James Jeffords, a moderate Republican from Vermont, was spirited out of the White House so that the press could not report his wavering presence to his liberal constituency. Representative Carroll Hubbard of Kentucky was so moved by a presidential phone call (and offers of box seats at the Kennedy Center and an invitation to a state dinner) that he immediately called the Speaker's office, and his local Chamber of Commerce, to tell them he was backing Reagan. "We were back in Washington working," said House Republican floor aide Bill Pitts, "and Tip was in Pago Pago."

O'Neill later ranked the South Seas trip as the biggest mistake he made that year. "Who the hell knew all that was going to happen while I was in New Zealand?" he grumbled. The Speaker compounded his difficulties when, tired and feeling jet lagged on the day after his arrival home, as Congress gathered to debate the Reagan budget, he told reporters that the battle was lost. "The Congress goes with the will of the people, and the will of the people is to go along with the President," O'Neill said. "I know when to fight and when not to fight.

"Time is the cure of all evil," the Speaker said.

It was an honest statement of the Speaker's "Give him rope" strategy, the wisdom of which was being underscored by the red ink then pooling at Stockman's feet. To save the House, O'Neill believed, it was better to lose now than win. "For all his sins, the foxy old Speaker knew something I didn't," Stockman decided later. *"We'll wait this thing out,* he was saying, *then we'll get back to business as usual."* O'Neill also knew that he didn't have the votes — his aides and intuition had told him that, barring some climactic change, Reagan was going to get the 30-odd votes he needed from the boll weevils to pass Gramm-Latta. During Reagan's comeback speech on April 28, the Speaker had looked out on the chamber and counted the boll weevils who rose to applaud the President's endorsement of Gramm-Latta. "Here's your forty votes," he whispered to Bush, who sat beside him. Reagan was approaching divine status in the public opinion polls in the South and Southwest, and in many ethnic neighborhoods in the North, and White House political aides Lyn Nofziger and Lee Atwater had effectively targeted media outlets and mobilized legions of corporate executives, civic leaders and other Reagan supporters in 54 swing districts. The outreach campaign "tightened the screws pretty good" on wavering boll weevils, said Atwater. "I guess you could say we intimidated them."

"Because of the attempted assassination, the President has become a hero," O'Neill said. "We can't argue with a man as popular as he is." Not all the boll weevils would remain in the Democratic Party, and not all would survive the 1982 election even if they voted for Gramm-Latta. But if the party was going to save those 40 to 50 seats in 1982, O'Neill decided, he had to give the members of "Redneck Row," as their customary place in the rear of the chamber was called, a pass on this vote.[12]

Huge chunks of the Democratic caucus — impulsive liberals and the younger moderates who were working with Jones — were furious at O'Neill's capitulation. Jones said it would now be impossible to capture the votes of liberal Republicans. The most damaging aspect of the Speaker's statement, California representative Leon Panetta said, was that it sent a signal to undecided Democrats that they could vote for Gramm-Latta without fear of reprisal. "The morale of House Democrats plummeted," said *Congressional Quarterly.* A Democratic whip told the magazine: "We have no game plan. We're just going to get killed. It's pathetic." Some thought Reagan had psyched the Speaker out. Others, who guessed his strategy, accused O'Neill of betraying, for cold-blooded political gain, the Americans who would suffer if Reagan's plan was adopted. In a newsletter that was passed around the Hill like samizdat, Les Aspin summed up the prevailing mood.

"Tip is reeling on the ropes," said Aspin. "Tip doesn't understand the explosions that have been going off since November. He's in a fog."

The Speaker's strategy was a cynical violation of Democratic principles, Aspin wrote. "Approving a package on the assumption that it will fail would be a violation of my oath of office," he said. "Welfare is due for the ax; the tax deduction for the three-martini lunch is due to stay. Medicaid is to be chopped down; Big Oil's depletion allowance will remain.

"The Democratic Party needs some new leadership and needs it badly," Aspin concluded.

Hopeful foes began to spread rumors that O'Neill would retire in 1982, forcing him to issue denials. In matching columns in the *Globe,* Bob Healy and Mary McGrory torched their old pal. "The malaise speaks for itself. Reagan is trampling our leadership," Phil Burton told the press. Jones and his supporters offered every bouquet — higher defense spending, a balanced budget, the indexing of taxes to end bracket creep — to corral the southern Democrats and a group of liberal Republicans from the north that were known as "gypsy moths." But as he went through the motions of opposing Gramm-Latta, O'Neill knew Reagan was destined for victory. "This is only the first skirmish in the war. The war is the election of 1982," he said. "A horse that runs fast doesn't always run long."

"He was getting the shit kicked out of him," said Joe Moakley. "Les Aspin and the guys were saying, 'Why don't you step down? You're too old. You're dragging us down.' I'd go in the office and he'd be sitting there smoking a cigar, really morose. There were a lot of days Tip didn't want to get out of bed and put on his shoes. He was getting beaten up pretty good."

On May 5, an embattled O'Neill spoke at a closed session of the Democratic caucus. His whip counts had forecast a severe defeat.

"There is an old saying that an old dog . . . cannot learn new tricks. An old dog can learn new tricks if he wants to learn new tricks. This old dog wants to learn," O'Neill said. "Where did we go wrong? We went wrong when we overregulated. We have too much red tape, we have too much idealism in the running of the programs, and we have not paid enough attention to problems of production. And so in 1980 we suffered the consequences."

But there was only "a small minority, 10 or 15 percent, who voted for Reagan who really wanted to deliver a mandate," the Speaker reasoned. "We know why we lost the election. We had an unpopular presidential candidate, inflation was too high and so was unemployment.

"I do not know how you are going to get yourselves off the hook," he warned the boll weevils. "I want you to remember this. The opinions of the man in the street change faster than anything in this world. Today he does not know what is in this program and he is influenced by a President with charisma and class and [who] is a national hero because of events that have taken place."

But "the Stockman program is going to falter along the line," O'Neill predicted. "America is not going to be happy or satisfied with cuts that don't reduce inflation. You have an opportunity to vote for an alternative program, and so when they come back to you and say, you know, the program is not working . . . the onus is on the President of the United States."

It was not enough. "The really important number is 31780: that's the Zip code for Plains, Georgia, the address of the Democratic candidate who opposed the Reagan program," said minority leader Bob Michel as the House opened debate. In the end, Reagan carried every one of the 190 Republicans and 63 of O'Neill's Democrats. The Speaker looked rumpled and distracted in his emotional closing argument. Its logic and diction were as disheveled as his clothes. "Do you want to meat ax the programs that have made America great?" he asked. It was a stunning triumph for Reaganomics. As he left the *Globe* the following day, after meeting with the editorial board, a pressman from North Cambridge asked O'Neill what was happening in Washington. "What's happening to me? What's happening to me in Washington? Dick, what's happening to me is, I'm getting the shit whaled out of me."[13]

The Speaker took his whipping. And a week later he appeared on a public television show and recited the words he had suffered long to say. "From now on, it's Reagan's budget. From now on, it's Reagan's unemployment rate. From now on, it's Reagan's inflation rate.

"You can't criticize the Democrats," O'Neill said. "It's Reagan's ball game."

The Speaker now adjusted his tactics. Stung by the criticism he had received from within his party, and determining that the "Reagan" brand had been sufficiently stamped upon whatever fiscal ills and economic pain might follow, he decided that the Democrats needed to post some victories. When the next, and final, budget resolution hit the floor, he vowed, the Republicans would face amendments that would isolate and highlight the most unpopular budget cuts, and be forced to cast politically damaging votes. And when Dan Rostenkowski's efforts to try and reach a compromise with Reagan on the Kemp-Roth tax cut collapsed, O'Neill ordered the Ways and Means chairman to craft a Democratic alternative that could beat the White House tax bill on the floor.[14]

But there was no way that Reagan and Stockman were going to let their boll weevils and gypsy moths face O'Neill's array of politically painful amendments. So was born Gramm-Latta II, a substitute package that put all the painful cuts in one massive "reconciliation" bill to give Reagan an opportunity to argue that O'Neill was denying him "an up-or-down vote."

"If you are successful with Gramm-Latta II, the perception of your leadership and commitment will be strengthened, the traditional House Democratic leadership will be weakened, and the prospects of building upon the new bipartisan coalition will be enhanced," Darman wrote Reagan. But "the strategy is risky. If it does not succeed it will play as a major administration loss." Reagan didn't blink. The President called the Speaker and asked for permission to offer Gramm-Latta II. O'Neill interrupted him, saying, "Didn't you ever hear about the separation of powers? The Congress of the United States will be responsible for spending. You're not supposed to be writing legislation."

"I know the Constitution," Reagan snapped.

The debate on Gramm-Latta II began in late June with both sides determined to win. O'Neill openly taunted Michel and the other Republicans, claiming that they had mortgaged their manhood to Stockman. The nervous gypsy moths responded by forcing the White House to restore a multibillion-dollar array of spending for programs like Amtrak, federal aid to education and low-income heating assistance. The boll weevils, the target once more of Reagan's phone calls and personal lobbying, then extracted their own porky price. "The Democratic cloakroom had all the earmarks of a tobacco auction," said Jim Jones. After the White House had caved in and restored sugar subsidies demanded by John Breaux and three other Louisiana congressmen, Breaux joked that while his vote was not for sale, "It can be rented." The bargaining went down to the final moments, and because of a bit of skulduggery by Phil Burton — he pried the resolution from the House printers and kept them from delivering a polished version to the chamber — the final law included scratched-out clauses and penciled inserts and the phone number of Rita Seymour, a congressional aide.

Irate over O'Neill's tactics, and not wanting to face the politically difficult amendments he had in store for them, 29 boll weevils deserted their leadership, sided with the Republicans, and defeated the Democratic rule. O'Neill had lost control of the House floor. There would be one, up-or-down vote, as Reagan wanted. Bolling called the defectors "chickenshit bastards." Ari Weiss recalled it as the low point of the Reagan years. "These are the times that try men's souls, and make no mistake about it," the Speaker said. Gramm-Latta II was passed the next day, June 26, on a 217 to 211 vote.

After losing on Gramm-Latta I and II, O'Neill stood by as Rostenkowski and the White House engaged in an expensive bidding war over the final element of the Reagan economic package: the tax cut.

"In my frantic endeavor to get the Democrat-dominated House to reduce spending, I had (a) not succeeded, (b) annoyed them, and (c) produced in them an irrational, desperate sense that they were engaged in a life-or-death struggle for power with the executive branch. As a consequence, the Democrats abandoned every principle, policy, prejudice or even mushy sentiment they possessed about the federal tax code," Stockman said.

"Win now, fix later," became the unofficial mantra at both ends of Pennsylvania Avenue. Big oil, savings and loans, securities, small business, utilities, the high-tech industry, realtors, home builders, cattlemen and other special interests won plum concessions by playing one side off against the other. Seeking support from the Georgia delegation, the White House promised to curb peanut imports. Even the oil depreciation allowance, which liberals had labored so long and so hard to reduce, was enriched, as was the inheritance allowance for wealthy families.

Reagan rallied the voters in a televised national address on July 27, and the Hill was flooded with 40,000 phone calls and telegrams a day. The President met with 58 wavering congressmen (39 voted with him), including the dozen who joined him for Bloody Marys and hamburgers at Camp David and were given commemorative pewter beer mugs.[15] The President called another 26 on the phone, converting 17. "With us all the way," Reagan noted, after calling Representative Doug Barnard of Georgia. "Assured him I will remember come election time," Reagan wrote, after talking to Representative William Boner, a

Democrat from Tennessee. ("Notify missing persons," Reagan wrote, after Representative Robert Young, a Democrat from Missouri, repeatedly ducked the President's phone calls.) O'Neill lost 48 Democrats, and the key vote on the legislation by 238 to 195 on July 29. O'Neill slumped in a sixth-row seat next to Jim Shannon. Charlie Wilson strolled over to Rostenkowski to convey his condolences and express his awe at the Great Communicator's talents: "I sure as hell hope that sonofabitch doesn't come out against fucking," Wilson said. It was a tremendous victory for the still-wounded President. "Now, if I can only find my walker," Reagan told his staff as they sipped champagne in the Oval Office. "Not bad for a lazy President," said Nofziger.

"We really haven't laid a glove on him," Wright told his diary. "It is odd. In conversations over programs he has seemed terribly shallow, albeit charming. He isn't able, nor willing, to discuss programs in detail. His philosophical approach is superficial, overly simplistic, one dimensional. What he preaches is pure economic pap glossed over with uplifting homilies and inspirational chatter. Yet so far the guy is making it work. Appalled by what seems to me a lack of depth, I stand in awe nevertheless of his political skill. I am not sure that I have seen its equal."

O'Neill called to congratulate the President. "No hard feelings, ol' pal," he said. "It's a great two-party system we have. We gave our best and you outdid us. As a matter of fact you stunned us. I never figured you could beat us that badly." Said Reagan: "We're stunned too."

The final bill contained the $983 billion Kemp-Roth cut, the $402 billion accelerated depreciation break for business and an additional half-trillion dollars in special interest "ornaments" from the bidding war. The cost of the tax cut had almost doubled in the process, to $1.853 trillion over nine years.

O'Neill's reviews were grim. "Thanks in part to Speaker O'Neill, Michel may be Speaker in 1983," said *Newsweek*.

"The way things are going in the House and the country," said the *Times,* "the suggestion that he may face a challenge for re-election as Speaker in 1983 may be academic. Democrats in the House of Representatives may not be electing anything higher than a minority leader."

O'Neill coped as best he could. "Remember Smoot and Hawley," he told Stan Brand, referring to the authors of the punitive 1930 tariff act that helped plunge the world into the Depression. "People thought they were heroes once, too. Everything changes and comes around."

But in a mid-August piece in the *New York Times Magazine,* Martin Tolchin summed up the summer. "The President, in his six months in office, has engineered a revolutionary change in the direction of government, reducing its size, powers and appetites. He had effectively taken control of the Congress, raising questions about the ability of the House and Senate to compete on anything like an equal footing with a popular President who knows how to use the power of his office.

"The Reagan victories had led many in Congress to entertain doubts about Tip O'Neill and his leadership. Was this the Speaker's last hurrah?" Tolchin asked. "Next year, with congressional redistricting cutting into the Democratic bastions of the Northeast and Middle West, the party will be in danger of losing even nominal control of the House.

"Is Tip O'Neill ready to join his old cronies in retirement?" Tolchin wrote. "The Speaker is a proud man who will not easily be driven from office. But he knows that he is considered a burden by many Democrats, too large a target in the legislative battles and on Election Day."

Years later, O'Neill analyzed his season of discontent like this: "There was a hatred toward the have-nots of America — whether you were old, whether you were black, whether you were an infant.

"I screeched and hollered and fought every way I could by retrenching and holding and holding until the people of America would say, 'Hey, we are going too far and it's wrong.' But I was overrun. I was a voice crying in the wilderness. I was old hat. I was a square. Members of my own party said I ought to quit, that we needed new leadership, we needed new ideas. And I said that we shouldn't run away from the things we can be most proud of.

"I had certain visions, from the day I was a kid, that the American system, while it was great, had its faults. And the faults were that there was an upper tier and there was the rest of us. And I had played a part, been part of the America that developed middle America," he said.

"I never had any doubts. I firmly believed in it," O'Neill said. "I guess I was an idealist — that was it."[16]

CHAPTER 24

An Old Dog Can Learn New Tricks

THE *Christian Science Monitor* breakfast was a Washington institution. A half-dozen times a month, generally when Congress was in session, some ten to twenty reporters from the capital's press corps would join a "man in the news" for bacon and eggs in the dining room of a stately downtown hotel. On April 7, 1981, O'Neill was the featured guest. The Speaker was taking the plunge into the type of media politics at which Reagan excelled; O'Neill, Dan Rostenkowski and Jim Jones had scheduled public events in an orchestrated attempt to sell the Democratic alternative to the President's economic plan. His staff had prepared a six-page briefing packet with a suggested theme: "Democrats in the House have their act together. They have adjusted to the new economic — and political — realities." But for O'Neill, the morning did not go well. He was too much himself. As the reporters snickered, he defended, in most memorable terms, the big-spending days of the Great Society.

"I've been one of the big spenders of all time," O'Neill confessed. "Ah, I've been a big spender.

"I remember when a doctor came in and told us the average dwarf was twenty-six inches high. He said he could increase that to fifty-two inches. He brought in six dwarfs," O'Neill said. "Over the years I sneaked into the budget $45 million." There was the money for sickle-cell anemia. And $12 million for turned-in ankles. "I remember putting in $18 million for knock knees. I put in $160 million for research on cancer of the breast. I put in money for research on spinal injuries . . . whales can fuse their spines, China and the Soviet Union were doing research, and the greatest nation on earth wasn't. There are thousands of veterans who need it.

"We used to be able to sneak these in. Nobody knew. But nobody is going to be able to do that anymore," O'Neill lamented. "There are 150,000 dwarfs in America. Does anyone have an obligation? Is it the obligation of the federal government? I think it is.

"I'm just giving my philosophy," O'Neill said. He spoke with reverence of the days of Roosevelt. "That day is gone now. The people are more interested in a second home, better recreation, more education. . . . with affluence, people change." As the meeting broke up, and the reporters rushed to their bureaus to write about Tip O'Neill and the dwarfs, he looked ruefully at his cold, hardly touched plate and said: "I want to thank you for that one piece of bacon."

As an initial foray into media politics, O'Neill's performance at the Sperling breakfast was "off-message" at best. "One of the things that made him remarkable was that this was a person driven in large measure by his sense of compassion — his sense of trying to help people who were suffering for one reason or another," Ari Weiss recalled. "And he started to make this speech which reflected his deepest commitments and emotions. Of how this was something that the families of those children could not provide, and wasn't it the role of government. And as he began to talk about it, straight from the heart, the reporters started to guffaw." Back on the Hill, the boll weevils groaned, thinking what sport the Republicans would make in their one-minute speeches and televised ads of big Tip O'Neill and his federal funding for the dwarfs and the knock-kneed. "He was quite serious," the *Washington Star* felt the need to inform its readers.

Yet lost in the jokes about Tip and the dwarfs was an important development. The old dog was trying new tricks. The Speaker was fighting back, and on Reagan's turf, in a battle for popular opinion. The decision had been made: it was Tip O'Neill who would step out of the cloakroom to challenge Ronald Reagan, not some telegenic young stand-in of a congressman. O'Neill would not lead the Democratic Party from the confines of the Speaker's lobby. He would serve as its public spokesman and symbol. He would make the Speakership the forum from where the Democrats issued their response to Reagan. It was an audacious idea. No twentieth-century Speaker had attempted such a thing: to challenge a Presidency so.

"The Republicans wanted him to be the symbol of all that was wrong with government," said Representative Richard Gephardt. "He could have just retreated into his office. To his credit, he realized he couldn't do that. He had to stand his ground and fight, or not be Speaker. He chose to stand his ground, and he won. By the end of it all, the American people came to respect his character, and he became a folk hero."

Not every reporter at the Sperling breakfast had laughed at O'Neill; a few softies found him disarming, admirable and genuine. The Democrats were wagering that the public could be made to feel that way too. In truth, he had little choice. "He had to do it," said Chris Matthews. "If he tried to be silent Carl Albert or quiet Mike Mansfield it wouldn't have worked. The Republicans were already running ads with his picture. They had spotted him as a target, and so now his only choice was whether he was going to be a moving target or a sitting duck.

"He knew we needed to do something. And he did it," said Matthews. "He took on the role."

MATTHEWS WAS HIMSELF proof of O'Neill's willingness to try new tricks. As Reagan proved himself so formidable a foe, the Democrats had scrambled to reinforce their Speaker. Tony Coelho was recruited to take over as chairman of the Democratic Congressional Campaign Committee, and one of his first acts was to put Matthews on the payroll, detached to the Speaker to help, as O'Neill put it, "with the media stuff." A cheerful Holy Cross graduate from Philadelphia, Matthews had served in the Peace Corps in Africa, made an unsuccessful run for Congress and worked in the Carter White House as a speechwriter. He spent months on Coelho's payroll, writing statements for the Speaker and offering advice on how to craft a simple, repeatable Democratic message. O'Neill finally felt comfortable enough to hire Matthews as his administrative assistant and official spokesman in July, when Gary Hymel, who had half a dozen children to send through college, left to find more lucrative work as a lobbyist.

Matthews was a spinmeister, the first ever employed by a Speaker of the House. "This young, flamboyant guy . . . he's high strung and he moves fast," O'Neill said. He cautioned Matthews that "everything has to be cleared through Ari and Kirk and Leo because they are family." But "I like the guy. He is able and talented," said the Speaker. "He's done a great job. He's a good writer and he has good political sense." And though he rarely showed it, O'Neill even sympathized with Matthews: "It's hard to move into the little inner circle and sometimes I think he feels it," the Speaker said.

Once again, O'Neill's great sense of timing had extended to his selection of staff: he had an uncanny ability to discover someone whose talents fit the moment. Diehl was the indispensable pal and protector who had notified the wiseguys that times had changed. Judith Kurland was a prototypical Democratic policy wonk. Gary Hymel had been a bridge to the southern barons and an envoy to the pencil press, and had run the House floor when O'Neill was majority leader. Kirk O'Donnell was hired in 1977 when the post-Watergate era called for a legal counsel with well-honed political instincts.[1] Now Matthews came aboard, at the dawn of an age of artifice, to stage a war of words against the Great Communicator. "I have never seen a staff like Tip O'Neill's. There is not even a close second," said Al Hunt, a reporter and bureau chief for the *Wall Street Journal*. "It said a lot about O'Neill, that he was an incredibly secure man."

O'Donnell was the first among equals. "Kirk is a brilliant tactician. A guy who was hard as a rock. Surrounded by scaredy-cats and bullshitters, Kirk was the best," Matthews said. O'Donnell had left Kevin White's staff and was setting up a law business in Boston when O'Neill first called; he was reluctant to move to Washington. But the Speaker set to work on O'Donnell's wife, Kathy, a North Carolinian who didn't much care for New England's cold climate. "Haven't you ever heard of pillow talk?" O'Neill asked her on the dance floor one night. Her husband agreed to take the job, and quickly became the Speaker's trusted consigliere. Besides his legal duties, O'Donnell wrote the Speaker's speeches, specialized in foreign policy and served as O'Neill's envoy to the national Democratic Party.

Diehl continued to handle patronage, fund-raising and the other nuts and bolts of the old politics. "He's the watchdog," O'Neill said. Weiss was the Speaker's chief policy analyst; the main liaison with the House committees and O'Neill's eyes and ears on the floor. "Ari is the nearest thing I've ever seen to a legislative genius. He understands the legislative process better than 95 percent of the members," Dick Bolling said. "He knows everything there is to know about the subject and . . . everything to know on that subject about the members. He's a very good analyzer and he's completely loyal to the Speaker. He's stepped on lots and lots of toes in the interest of the Speaker. But he's the best I ever saw as a staffer."

"Ari came down. Oh, was he shy. But terrifically bright. He was absolutely marvelous. Well, the father-son relationship grew. Jeez. I loved the kid," O'Neill recalled. "I'm not a legislator, to be perfectly truthful. Ari is my legislator. He explains everything that's in the bill, the inequities, what I ought to know, what I shouldn't know. I'm the doer. I know how to get things done. I know how to move people."

The Speaker and his four top advisers — O'Donnell, Diehl, Weiss and Matthews — were assisted by a skilled and loyal supporting cast who could be counted on to follow his agenda, not their own. "We don't want any activists around here," O'Neill would say. Nobody ever wrote a kiss-and-tell memoir about their days with Tip O'Neill.[2]

As Matthews went about explaining the grammar of television to his boss — keep it simple and symbolic and *repeat, repeat, repeat* — he found that O'Neill was self-conscious about his looks and dubious about competing with the movie star in the White House. "He was scared to death of it. Because it was live television. He was so afraid he would say something wrong. He was afraid of being embarrassed. He lacked confidence," Eleanor Kelley, his secretary said. For years, O'Neill had resisted the invitation of the Sunday talk shows. He said it was because he wanted his Sunday with his family, but "Tom kept away from those things on purpose," said Diehl. "Because you could only get killed. You can die on those things on a Sunday morning."

"Tip didn't get it, at first," said Matthews. "He hadn't seen it coming. He and his buddies were out at dinner every night [while the] American people . . . were home watching TV. The old-timers didn't appreciate the TV culture because they weren't in on it. They didn't know this is how the country communicates in the 1980s. The hardest part was just getting him out there every day — pushing.

"Leo and Eleanor had the theory that TV cameras are like vacuum cleaner salesmen — if you ignore them, they'll go away," said Matthews. "Well, hey, they don't go away. They can hire actors to portray you.

"He was never sure of his looks, he was always talking about cabbage ears and his big nose. He was very mean to himself," Matthews said. "And that amazed me, because I thought he looked fabulous on television. The first time I saw him, I said to myself, 'This guy's got all his hair, he has an incredible image. A lot of guys his age would love to look as good as him.'" Indeed, even when they disagreed with his politics, Americans appreciated O'Neill's authenticity: at the height of the Reagan honeymoon, 52 percent of his countrymen thought favorably of the Speaker, and just 17 percent unfavorably.

Television news likes simple stories. Reagan was a skilled performer, and his media adviser Michael Deaver and his colleagues were exceptionally good at crafting scripted "moments" in which the President could perform. "Cable TV had not really come in. You could target the three networks and talk to 80 percent of the public," Deaver recalled. "And we really believed that you had to get a simple message and repeat it over and over and over again.

"And I used to have a table in the Roosevelt Room and all the department heads would come in for scheduling meetings once a week. I would sit up front and they would have to give me a one-page summary for every request they had for the President's schedule that showed me what the visual would be for the evening news," said Deaver. "I was absolutely arbitrary about it."

O'Neill could never hope to match such superb Reagan moments as the fortieth anniversary of the D-Day landings, or the President's rallying address to a stunned nation after the space shuttle *Challenger* exploded. But a sturdy journalistic imperative — *Get the other side of the story* — provided O'Neill with an opening, as did the media's unquenchable thirst for controversy. Reporters from the networks and other national news organizations needed a Reagan foil, someone they could go to and get the other side, and that was a role the Speaker could fill. But it was a tough, evolutionary process — especially for a man who had just endured three years of pummeling from the press.

"You had to beg him to do interviews, and when you did your butt was on the line. If you strung two bad interviews in a row, you were dead," Matthews recalled. "He assumed you were screwing him. There was always this assumption that the reporter was a pal of yours and why did you let him in?

"And I wanted desperately to say, I let him in because I came here to help you become who you can become. And the way to do it is to be publicized. And the only way to be publicized is to let people write about you. And the only way to let them write about you is to let them take some shots at you. That is the only way to become a figure in American politics. You cannot customize it. You cannot come in and tailor it. All you can do is go in, let them see who you are and let them make their own judgments about you. It's a distillation, not an accumulation. You can have twenty brickbats thrown at you and what matters is what comes through.

"And what came through for him was this big guy with a good heart and a lot of guts," said Matthews. "And Kirk was always behind me. He always believed in it. It was the main reason I was in there: Kirk believed in the cause."

O'Donnell backed Matthews; so did Coelho. And in his efforts to make O'Neill more comfortable with television, Matthews was helped by TV producer Jerry Colbert, who staged televised holiday concerts on the Capitol grounds and enjoyed O'Neill's confidence. The Speaker "was a pre-TV guy. He was scared to death of it," Colbert recalled, and his memos echoed what Matthews was preaching. "The Democratic leadership in the House has used television sparingly and with little effect in countering the Reagan TV onslaught," Colbert wrote his friend the Speaker. "Considering the fact that today 70 percent of the news received by Americans comes through television, the Democratic Party and the Congress are put at a distinct disadvantage." He urged O'Neill to perform for the cameras on congressional turf, where he would feel more comfortable, with carefully tailored speeches on the House floor or choreographed responses from the Speaker's formal office, where his big desk would "cover up your midsection." To overcome O'Neill's skepticism about the use of cosmetics, dark suits and scripted sound bites, Colbert appealed to his ethnic pride. "When you are appearing before 100 million people for a one-minute speech or a five-minute press conference, it is worth twenty to twenty-five minutes of preparation to package it correctly," Colbert scolded. "In the final analysis, it is the image of the Speaker, the Irish people and the Democratic Party that you will be projecting and upon which you will be judged." Over time, the little things helped. Kelley learned which cosmetics were best for television, and how to make up her boss. O'Neill dropped forty pounds ("laying off beer and bread"). He worked on his wardrobe — left the powder blue suit that made him look like William Howard Taft in the closet, and let Matthews brush the Vesuvian flow of dandruff from his shoulders. O'Neill had smirked, at first, when he ostentatiously read the sound bites that Matthews pounded out on an electric typewriter before each morning press conference. But as he saw it all work, he began to get a kick out of his new role as TV star. "Whaddya got for me?" he began to ask Matthews in the morning.

It was a tough assignment for Matthews. Because he was the newcomer in the Speaker's office, he was expected to "bat 1.000 all the time," a sympathetic O'Donnell told him. And O'Neill sometimes wondered just who Matthews was promoting. Once, when Matthews had been a mite too self-congratulatory in an interview with an obscure men's magazine, O'Neill chewed him out. "I've got more political sense in half my ass than you have in your whole body," O'Neill said. "Do it again and I'll get rid of you." But the Speaker who railed against the "royal" Reagan tax bill in July was a far better tailored, scripted and prepared politician than the befuddled bear who had opposed Gramm-Latta in May, or who had replied, "What kind of fool do they think I am?" when House Democrats urged him to seek network time to respond to Reagan's triumphant April blitzkrieg.

"If you were to study Tip in his last year as Speaker, and compare him to the first year he was Speaker, you saw a man who had learned a great deal about television as the dominant medium in the game," said Representative Newt Gingrich.[3]

"THE PENDULUM SWINGS," O'Neill kept telling his staff and colleagues. He and the Democrats were flailing about, searching for a political opening when, in May, the Reagan administration made its first political blunder. It was an issue that was custom-made for O'Neill: the Republicans were scheming to cut back Social Security. The President's problems could be traced to Stockman's rosy scenarios and the $44 billion magic asterisk. If the defense budget was untouchable, and the tax cut sacrosanct, the Reagan administration would face massive budget deficits unless it reduced the soaring costs of Social Security and other so-called entitlements, like Medicare, unemployment insurance and veterans' pensions, where double-digit inflation had led to mammoth cost-of-living hikes. The Social Security program alone cost some $200 billion a year, about a third of the nondefense budget. Stockman thought it "a giant Ponzi scheme," and once the first round of budget and tax cuts were enacted, the entitlements became the administration's next target. Could the Reagan era truly be revolutionary if it gave a free pass to such social insurance programs — failed even to take a swipe at the heart of Franklin Roosevelt's legacy? "If not us, who? If not now, when?" Reagan asked.

Republicans in the House and Senate were game for the campaign, which Stockman described as "a frontal assault on the very inner fortress of the American welfare state." But an attack of that magnitude demanded time, planning, preparation and unanimity — qualities that, during the frantic and frenetic days of spring, the White House found in short supply. Instead, the GOP launched its assault in a wavering, piecemeal fashion. Within his early rounds of budget cuts, Stockman had proposed that Congress chip away at some extraneous Social Security benefits, like the minimum monthly payment, and was lulled by his initial success. Indeed, a Ways and Means subcommittee led by Democratic Representative J. J. "Jake" Pickle of Texas had introduced its own Social Security reform bill, with several billion dollars in savings, as a first step toward meeting an anticipated shortfall of $75 billion over the next four or five years. Pickle even invited the administration to join him in the search for a bipartisan solution.

In early May, Stockman made his move, proposing to cut back Social Security benefits for beneficiaries who chose early retirement. It was a logical step, to cut first among those who left the workforce voluntarily. The system had been created to guarantee dignity and security, not an extra decade on the golf course in Florida. To his credit, Reagan signed on. But Jim Baker and Richard Darman, quaking when they heard the news, insisted that HEW secretary Richard Schweiker, not the White House, announce the cuts. The President got the worst of both worlds: as the White House switchboard was jammed with calls from panicky retirees, Democrats caught the whiff of Republican hesitancy. "Someone planning to retire in nine months who thought he was going to be getting $650 per month would now be getting $450. The cut was tough — but the lack of warning was devastating," Stockman admitted. "I just hadn't thought through the impact of making it effective immediately." As the news spread on Capitol Hill, the press revealed that the administration was also planning to delay that summer's cost-of-living increase.

It was a critical turning point, O'Donnell recalled. "This was right from O'Neill, right from his gut. He was on his way to work, reading the paper, and he read about Stockman's cuts and he came into the morning conference we had and asked, 'What do you know about these proposals?' And nobody knew anything about them," he remembered.

"Call Danny," O'Neill said.

O'Donnell spoke to the Ways and Means staff, and discovered that Rostenkowski and Pickle were playing down the controversy because they felt a fiduciary responsibility, as good Democrats, to work with the White House to make Social Security solvent. "Danny doesn't want to play politics with it," O'Donnell told the Speaker. Though O'Neill generally let his committee chairmen make such calls, this time the knife was too close to bone. "Danny wanted to deal with it in a responsible, nonpolitical way. But O'Neill saw the Reagan administration overreaching and at that point he just jumped on it. And that was him. All him. Totally him. And he never let it go," O'Donnell recalled.

"I have a statement on the Social Security," O'Neill said at his May 13 press conference, reading from a typed page. "A lot of people approaching that age have either already retired on pensions or have made irreversible plans to retire very soon. These people have been promised substantial Social Security benefits at age sixty-two. I consider it a breach of faith to renege on that promise. For the first time since 1935 people would suffer because they trusted in the Social Security system."

"Are you saying that is a serious political mistake?" a reporter asked.

"I'm not talking about politics. I'm talking about decency. It is a rotten thing to do," O'Neill said. "It is a despicable thing."

The Speaker stunned the Capitol press corps by arriving in the House radio and television gallery a few days later to announce the results of that morning's Democratic caucus. To no one's surprise, the caucus had condemned Reagan's plans for Social Security. To everyone's surprise, here was the Speaker looking to get on television. He also invited crews from CBS and NBC to interview him in his office. He made all three network news shows that night, and clips from the interviews were used throughout the following week. "I will be fighting this every inch of the way," the Speaker promised. It was the first time he had drawn a line at Reagan's feet.

"Reagan finally has made a wretched mistake," Jim Wright told his diary. "The administration is badly stung by the wrath of millions of aging Americans." The Republican-controlled Senate voted 96 to 0 on May 20 to repudiate any solution that would "precipitously and unfairly penalize early retirees." In a letter to the Speaker, Reagan sued for peace, saying he was "not wedded to any single solution," and calling for a bipartisan approach.[4]

THE NEXT CLASH came in June. Departing the White House after a meeting with Reagan, O'Neill told Rostenkowski he was ready to "beat the bejesus" out of the President, and then informed the scrum of reporters that the Reagan tax plan was a "windfall for the rich." The following weekend, after getting the producers of ABC's *Issues and Answers* show to tape his appearance from the Speaker's office, O'Neill broke a three-year drought and appeared on a Sunday talk show. The first question was a softball about the President's tax bill. "I'm opposed to the Reagan tax bill, number one, because it's geared for the wealthy of the nation instead of being spread out among the working class of America and the poor people. Number two, it's going to send inflation through the roof. The deficits are going to be so high that I fear for America," O'Neill said.

He stumbled a bit when trying to explain the technical differences between the White House tax bill and the Democratic alternative, but then went for Reagan's throat. "He has no concern, no regard, no care for the little man of America. And I understand that. Because of his lifestyle, he never meets those people. And so consequently, he doesn't understand their problems. He's only been able to meet the wealthy," O'Neill said.

"You're saying he's callous," said ABC's Charles Gibson.

"I think that he has very, very selfish people around him, very selfish people around him, people only of the upper echelon of the wealth of this nation, and they are his advisers," O'Neill said. "I think he'd do much better if he had brought in some people close to him who are from the working force of America, who have suffered along the line, not those who have made it along the line and forgotten from where they've come."

Forgotten from where they've come. Breach of faith. Windfall for the rich. These were the ultimate epithets in the O'Neill canon, not freshly minted sound bites. What made the Speaker's performance so effective was that his rhetoric so reflected his personal beliefs. The viewers at home could taste the authenticity. So could Reagan, who went into a slow burn. "Ronnie," his wife, Nancy, recalled, "was very hurt by the harsh criticism that Tip had leveled."

After ending a nationally televised news conference on June 16, Reagan retook the podium when ABC's Sam Donaldson shouted a final challenge: "Tip O'Neill says you don't understand about the working people, that you have just a bunch of wealthy and selfish advisers."

Reagan growled, "One more," and returned to the microphone. "Tip O'Neill has said that I don't know anything about the working man. I'm trying to find out about his boyhood, because we didn't live on the wrong side of the railroad tracks, but we lived so close to them we could hear the whistle real loud," he said.

"And I know very much about the working group. I grew up in poverty and got what education I got all by myself and so forth, and I think it is sheer demagoguery to pretend that this economic program which we've submitted is not aimed at helping the great cross-section of people in this country that have been burdened for too long by big government and high taxes."

Sheer demagoguery. The ball was back in O'Neill's court. Taking an occasional shot at Reagan was all part of playing the loyal opposition. But staging a public, man-to-man quarrel with an American President was something else. It was time to fight or flee. He could cement his new claim of being Reagan's foil, or retreat to the cloakroom. In the Speaker's office, as the press clamored for a response, his staff was divided. The older hands urged O'Neill to duck it — that it was unseemly to make it personal. "Let it pass, Tom," said Diehl. The younger guys told O'Neill he had to respond. In fact, they relished the opportunity.

"I'm going up to the gallery," O'Neill decided.

"He went into the bathroom, combed his hair, straightened his tie, left the sanctuary of the Speaker's rooms behind," Matthews recalled.

Upstairs, as the camera lights blinked red, O'Neill took the high road, but didn't back down.

"I would never accuse a President, whoever he was, of being a demagogue," O'Neill said. He had "too much respect for the President, for the institution . . . [and] I assume that in the future he would have the same feeling for the Speakership."

But what about Reagan's tax bill? he was asked. "The Reagan program speaks for itself," O'Neill said. "It is geared toward the wealthy."

Reagan phoned the next day to make peace. "Ronnie called him to clear the air, and Tip told him right then, 'Old buddy, that's politics —

after 6 o'clock we can be friends; but before 6 it's politics.'" Nancy Reagan recalled. That night, June 17, was the DCCC's annual fund-raising dinner. It was a subdued event, in the midst of Reagan's honeymoon blitz. But O'Neill brought the crowd to its feet, not with his customary stories or red-meat rhetoric, but by saying something about the long view of things with a song. He crooned "Apple Blossom Time" to Millie, for their fortieth anniversary. Even the *Post*'s sardonic Style section was impressed. "He sang in a voice clear and true and tender and he sang with all the sweet sentiment an Irishman can bring to a song, this big rough-hewn politician who knows how to go the distance," Lynn Darling wrote. The following morning, when O'Neill walked into the regularly scheduled whips' meeting, they rose in unison and sang, "We'll be with you, in apple blossom time. . . ."[5]

THE BATTLE RAGED all summer. "Tip took him on. Rostenkowski didn't take him on. The rest of them wouldn't take him on. Jim Wright was scared to death of Reagan in 1981," said Dick Bolling. "Everybody was running. Tip was getting no support from Democratic chairmen, except the black ones." In late June, O'Neill stirred a United Steelworkers of America meeting, saying Reagan's program was "for the selfish, the greedy and the affluent." On July 7, O'Neill told another union convention, "Let's face it. This is a callous, right-wing administration committed to repealing the Great Society, the New Frontier, the Fair Deal and the New Deal. It has made a target of the politically weak, the poor, the working people."

He called Reagan "a tightwad" and "a real Ebenezer Scrooge." But "when it comes to giving tax breaks to the wealthy of this country, this President has a heart of gold," O'Neill said.

Two days after the "Scrooge" speech, the Democrats were cheered by a minor miracle — a Democrat beat a Reagan Republican in an off-term congressional election in a GOP district in Mississippi. The party as a whole was doing a little better. An economic "truth squad" was named, with Dick Gephardt as its leader. Gillis Long led the caucus "Committee on Party Effectiveness." Weekly leadership packets were sent to every Democratic member. Democratic administrative assistants and press secretaries met to coordinate their efforts. The whips set up a schedule of one-minute speeches for the floor. O'Neill began to stop for interviews with the TV crews that gathered to catch him as he arrived at the Capitol each day. At the steering committee, Ari Weiss and Jack Lew pioneered the tactic of drawing up "distributional analyses" that measured the effects of each of Reagan's proposals on the middle-class, blue-collar Americans, the poor and other income groups. The DCCC began to target the districts of moderate Republicans, especially those whose constituencies had low median family incomes. The Speaker himself sat down with Ways and Means aides and helped draw up the tax tables for a Democratic alternative to the Kemp-Roth tax cut, targeting relief to those who earned $50,000 or less a year.

"They would trot out the wheelchairs, as they always do, and trot out the women with aid to dependent children and all that sort of thing — the poor and the old," Deaver said dismissively. But it was a far different Tip O'Neill who stood on the House floor on July 29, to close debate on the Reagan tax plan. Wright and Rostenkowski had wanted to compromise with the President — perhaps trade some Social Security cutbacks for reductions in Reagan's tax bill. But "in all this, Tip [was] the hardest boulder to budge," Wright told his diary. "He instinctively mistrusts Reagan and his whole crew, wants instead to offer House members a clear choice." O'Neill was trim, well coiffed, and armed with a succinct set of remarks, printed in large type on 4-by-6 index cards. It was the day of Princess Diana's wedding, O'Neill noted. "If the President has his way, this could be a big day for the aristocracy of the world," O'Neill began. "This morning there was quite a royal wedding. This afternoon President Reagan is proposing a royal tax cut."

The Republicans laughed aloud at O'Neill, taunting him with calls of "Vote! Vote!"

"You can snicker. . . . I recognize the breeding," he said, staring them down across the aisle.

"This proposition has no precedent. It is a terrible gamble. If it fails, the consequences for the nation will be horrible. Deficits will soar, inflation will persist, budgets will be cut. Amongst the casualties will be the Social Security program, health care and education programs, and possibly a reduced defense program," he said.[6]

Given the Democratic losses on Gramm-Latta II and the tax plan, most of the press decided that the summer's hottest feud was proof of Deaver's genius. "Reagan must see how useful it is to be opposed by O'Neill, a cartoonist's caricature of urban liberalism on its last legs," *Newsweek* guessed. "Surely Reagan keeps zinging O'Neill to keep him in the public eye." When the battle over taxes entered its final days, the Republican Party spent $600,000 on radio ads depicting O'Neill as a phony Santa Claus, tormenting a little girl by giving her empty Christmas packages. Indeed, Jim Baker said later that they found O'Neill the "perfect foil," and much preferred to wage war with him than with a younger face like Dick Gephardt or Gary Hart. "I really have fond memories of Tip and I had respect for Tip O'Neill and he was the genuine article, but he wasn't any match for Ronald Reagan," Baker said. "Why would we have wanted somebody different carrying the baton on the other side?"

But a few began to challenge the conventional wisdom. On August 7 Mark Shields wrote a defense of O'Neill on the *Post*'s op-ed page. "For six months now, the criticism of the man has been as inconsistent as it has been insistent. Take your pick: he is either a hopeless liberal, out of touch with the times, or he is too quick to cave in to, or cooperate with, the conservative opposition," Shields wrote. "He has been called too old and too heavy, and you know that some of the knocks have to hurt.

"But not once . . . did the Speaker of the House complain. The Speaker is a professional and he cares about his craft," Shields warned. "He should not be underestimated."

"If — as they think likely — our economic policies fail, they could become the ultimate winners," Darman privately warned Reagan. It was a prospect that, amid all the celebrations that summer, was increasingly worrying David Stockman.

The problem was in the math, for the White House was losing its riverboat gamble. As the Washington press corps hailed the victorious "revolution," the nation's financial community was scrutinizing Stockman's balance sheet. Wall Street traders don't believe in rosy scenarios, and wanted to know what cuts would be made to replace the magic asterisk. The political victories of the Reagan revolution had not set off the bull market that Stockman had predicted when making his economic assumptions, while over at the Federal Reserve, Chairman Volcker had embarked on a tight-money course to wring inflation from the economy. The bidding wars on the tax and budget bills further fed the tide of red ink. There was no way around it: Stockman needed more cuts. He turned once again to Social Security, where a relatively obscure section of Gramm-Latta II did away with Social Security's monthly minimum payment. Stockman thought the benefit was wasteful because it primarily benefited "double-dippers," who could get by quite nicely with their income from other pension plans. And, in truth, the truly impoverished elderly were still fully protected. But in a neat bit of demagoguery, O'Neill and his lieutenants used the abolition of the monthly minimum to fan the glowing embers of that spring's firestorm over early retirement. In a letter to Reagan, the Speaker attacked the President for promoting "ill-advised, unacceptable . . . unconscionable" cuts in benefits.

"The eighty-two-year-old woman sitting by her television set doesn't hear all the details — what comes through is they're cutting Social Security," Senator Pat Moynihan acknowledged. National seniors' groups staged a rally of 5,000 people at the Capitol. Moynihan and Wright introduced resolutions, promising to restore the minimum monthly payment, and charging the White House with a "breach of faith." The House passed it by a 405 to 13 vote.

"At the time, I dismissed the vote as a gesture, a symbolic sense-of-the-House resolution. I believed, incredibly, that the 405 stampeding congressmen could be corralled," Stockman wrote later. "Now I see it in a different light. The vote was historically significant: it was the *coup de grace.* If the politicians could not bring themselves to make even that adjustment to Social Security, then the $44 billion magic asterisk was just that: magic."

On August 3, fresh from their summer of legislative triumphs, Reagan and his aides gathered in the cabinet room at the White House for a working lunch, and Stockman showed Reagan the consequence of that summer's victories: they would need from $250 billion to $500 billion in further spending cuts over the next four years, or face triple-digit budget deficits. "Dave, if what you are saying is true," said Reagan, "then Tip O'Neill was right all along."

"Oh, no," said Stockman quickly. Why, he had plans for a "September offensive." But in the Speaker's office, they were planning an offensive of their own.[7]

On August 4, as the press continued to sing of Reagan's victories and Stockman and his colleagues paged through their black budget books, earmarking proposed cuts in Social Security, veterans' pensions, food stamps, farm subsidies, mass-transit grants and other popular federal programs, Kirk O'Donnell delivered an eleven-page memo to his boss. O'Neill would come to call it "The Plan."

"Out of the triumph of the Republican Economic Program, Democrats have some consolation. The economy is no longer our burden; it is a Republican economy. The economic program is uniquely Reagan's and his party's. By not choosing to compromise with House Democrats, Reagan has assumed total responsibility," O'Donnell wrote. Democratic pollster Peter Hart had identified a soft spot in Reagan's popularity, O'Donnell noted: stagflation persisted, and the voters were getting impatient. The heroics of the spring were fading in memory; people wanted results and "solutions, not heroes," said Hart. The Federal Reserve's effort to wring inflation from the economy would only increase the pain of working families. "A recession brought about by tight money is at hand," O'Donnell wrote. "It is an ideal time to expose the weaknesses of the Reagan economic program." The Democratic committee and subcommittee chairmen should fan out across the country, holding hearings in their hometowns to demonstrate the effects of Reaganomics. "We cannot assume that the cuts will be felt," O'Donnell said. "We must identify where they are going to occur and who is going to be hurt. The House, through its committees and hearings, must inform Americans about what is happening.

"Control of Congress will be the issue in 1982. We have to give Democratic voters a sense that they have something at stake in 1982: their jobs, their homes, their children's future, their retirement. Republican congressmen have tied their fortunes to Reagan's policies almost without exception," O'Donnell wrote. "It is time to take the offensive."

The first issue that O'Neill confronted was Social Security. Jake Pickle's subcommittee had worked long and hard at being good stewards of the New Deal's brightest jewel. And there was no doubt about it, Pickle was right: Social Security was in trouble. O'Neill's own steering committee analysts had been privately warning him for two years that the main trust fund was in "truly alarming" and "critical" shape and likely to run out of money in 1982. Reagan had shown his willingness to hold hands with the Democrats and make the painful changes that were required to restore the system's solvency. But to save the House, O'Neill needed an issue, and Social Security promised to be one. Support for Reagan's economic program had been at 61 percent in the polls in January and 58 percent in May, but after the flap over early retirement benefits only 38 percent of the voters supported

Reaganomics in July. Reagan's own pollster, Richard Wirthlin, warned the White House in July that "an issue which was not even mentioned from January through March of this year appeared at one percent in April, five percent in May and now stands at eight percent" when respondents were asked to name the nation's leading problem.

"The motives of the administration must remain suspect and their entreaties for bipartisanship rejected," O'Donnell wrote O'Neill. "Democrats need not be defensive or accommodating in our defense of the system. This debate offers a real opportunity to demonstrate the genuine differences between the two parties." Representative Claude Pepper of Florida, champion of senior citizens, also urged O'Neill to exploit the Social Security issue. In a private note, Pepper asked the Speaker to "restrain Jake Pickle's efforts" to strike a deal with the White House. The government could postpone the fiscal reckoning by giving the old-age trust fund a transfusion of money from the system's other accounts, he said. "Opposition to the President's efforts to cut Social Security benefits is rising enormously," Pepper said happily.

And so O'Neill made a far-reaching decision to politicize Social Security, ordering his Democrats to withdraw from the bipartisan alliance with Republican moderates that had guarded the social insurance programs from conservative attacks in the postwar era. For the next twenty years, whenever Reagan or his heirs would mount a fresh offensive on the American welfare state, Democrats would follow O'Neill's lead and cry, "Save Social Security!" or "They want to cut Medicare!"

"O'Neill took Social Security and just drove it home ruthlessly and in some respects dishonestly, but with great effectiveness," Newt Gingrich recalled. From a political standpoint, it was a brilliant short-term tactic. "The Republicans, to this day, haven't gotten over it," O'Donnell said in 1998. "O'Neill and his actions had made an entitlement, probably the most significant New Deal entitlement that exists, untouchable."

Yet Pickle had a point. Social Security was then on an iconic shelf — removed from partisan give-and-take. By folding Social Security and the other social insurance programs into the political mix, O'Neill was exposing them to assault — indeed, daring Republicans to make the attack. The Democratic scare tactics upset senior citizens, exposed the party to the charge of demagoguery, and fed the growing cynicism about politics and government. It all began to look like a game, and Social Security and Medicare became but pieces on the board. "The Republicans will never trust the Democrats again on Social Security. It was made clear to them, indelibly and lastingly, that this is the third rail and if you touch it you get burned. It will never be anything other now, because nobody will ever trust each other again, and that was almost totally Tip's doing," said Lud Ashley.[8]

O'NEILL BROUGHT THE curtain down on Pickle's efforts in typically sly fashion. On September 17, after the House had returned from its five-week summer recess, Pickle was summoned to a conference of war in O'Neill's office. The Speaker "had a cigar and he put it in his mouth and he let Pickle make his appeal," said Jim Shannon, who served on Pickle's subcommittee. "Pickle made a very impassioned speech, saying this is a bedrock issue . . . the Democratic Party . . . we have to solve this. And Tip didn't say a word. He didn't take the cigar out of his mouth. Twirling it. Puffing it. Pickle finished his pitch and Tip still didn't say anything."

Bolling cleared his throat. "Mr. Speaker, can I say something?" the Rules Committee chairman asked.

"Sure, Dick," said O'Neill.

"Jake, we are all proud of your work," Bolling told Pickle. "But I want to say one thing. As long as I am chairman of the Rules Committee there won't be any Social Security legislation in this Congress."

There was silence for a moment. Pickle looked at Bolling, then to an implacable O'Neill.

"I know when I'm licked," Pickle said.

The Reagan administration was out to "wreck the system," O'Neill told the press when the doors were opened. The Democrats would not cooperate with Reagan's efforts to pare back Social Security. Pickle's subcommittee "does not intend to go forward at the present time," O'Neill said, as its muzzled chairman stood by his side.

For insurance, the Speaker ordered Shannon to serve as a saboteur. "You don't let him move a bill," O'Neill told his young protégé.

"Pickle wants to write the bill. Danny agrees. We're Democrats. We're responsible," Shannon recalled. "But Kirk's view is that Social Security is all we got. I had to spend a year throwing sand in the gears."

Reagan had no hand to hold. The House Republicans lost their stomach for the fight, and sent a message to the President via conservative representative Trent Lott of Mississippi. Without political cover from the Democrats, Lott told Reagan, "not a corporal's guard" would vote for further cuts in Social Security. The Senate caved in next. "Tip O'Neill has blown the prospect of any major Social Security legislation out of the water. We were having quite a lot of success working towards a bipartisan coalition, but after what he said this week, there's just no way to do it," said Republican senator William Armstrong of Colorado, chairman of the Senate's Social Security subcommittee. On September 24, Reagan capitulated. In a letter to O'Neill, the President renounced the assortment of cutbacks he had proposed and called for the establishment of a bipartisan commission to seek a permanent solution. A month later the Senate, following the House's lead, restored the minimum monthly benefit that had been cut in Gramm-Latta II.[9]

Stockman's "September offensive" had failed. As the economy slowed under Volcker's tight rein, unemployment rose to 8 percent and interest rates hit 20 percent. The President chose an option from Stockman's briefing papers that was called "Muddle Through." Finally, in mid-October, Reagan admitted the truth. There would be no robust supply side dividend, no 5 percent or better annual growth. The economy was in recession. "The new consensus economic forecast resulted in a budget which showed cumulative red ink over five years of more than *$700 billion,*" Stockman said. "That was nearly as much national debt as it had taken America two hundred years to accumulate. It just took your breath away."

The 1982 election was a year and change away when O'Neill rose to say I-told-you-so on the House floor October 21. "Today the government made it official. We are in a recession and it's a real recession.

"For months we have been told just the opposite. We have been told that everything was going to be all right, that we were headed for prosperity, for an economic renaissance. The President on August 5 said he had everything that he wanted. He had his rich man's tax cut. He had his budget cuts. Yes, indeed, now we are facing economic reality. We are in a recession.

"For months we have been told we would have huge tax cuts for the rich, huge new defense systems, brutal cuts in social programs and cruel interest rates, and that we could have all these things and still reach a balanced budget, we could still have economic prosperity," the Speaker said, turning to the Republicans. "Today we have the Reagan nonsense, economic nonsense, which you people voted on, and we have seen what that really is here in America."

For almost a year, O'Neill had worked toward this moment. He had given Reagan rope, and now the rope had become a noose. The terrible pounding that O'Neill had taken was the price he paid so he could this day saddle Reagan with the blame for the recession. "If he had delayed Gramm-Latta II, he would have been in a position of not being able to get the tax bill out by the first of August," O'Donnell recalled. "Then, in the crisis the nation was in, in the sense that there was an overwhelming need for change, that there was an overwhelming sentiment that the President should be given a chance, the Democrats would have been blamed for obstructionism. . . . Democrats would have been blamed for the recession.

"The genius of what the Speaker did is that he went out and became the leading opponent to a program that he was putting on the fast track. It was a brilliant tactic," said O'Donnell.

The Speaker's "Plan" now called for Democratic unity and O'Neill's invisibility. He called a closed-door caucus in September, at which the Democratic leadership announced a general amnesty for its wayward boll weevils. Then, as the committee chairmen fanned out across America to document the effects of Stockman's budget cuts, O'Neill let the recession do his work for him. "Republicans are fighting with Wall Street; Republicans are fighting with themselves — I think I'll sit on the sidelines for a while," he said.

There were some opportunities too good to pass up: interior secretary James Watt's assault on the environment; Stockman's notorious confessions in the *Atlantic Monthly* ("None of us really understand what's going on with all these numbers. . . . We didn't think it all the way through. . . . The whole thing is premised on faith. . . . The hogs are really feeding. The greed level, the level of opportunism, just got out of control"), and the administration's ill-fated policy to categorize ketchup as a vegetable to cut costs for school lunches. The AFL-CIO put 260,000 protesters — the largest such crowd since the Vietnam War demonstrations — on the Mall for a "Solidarity Day" in mid-September. A showdown between the President and Congress over the appropriations process closed the federal government for a day in November. And there was one sweet bit of payback when the Democrats from Georgia and Louisiana, who had voted with Reagan in the spring and summer in return for his commitment to maintain peanut and sugar subsidies, lost their price supports when the farm bill hit the House floor in the fall. Charlie Rose and the North Carolinians who had stuck with the Democratic leadership throughout the budget battles, received the Speaker's blessing and were able to preserve their tobacco subsidies. "They have been loyal," O'Neill told the press.

Yet for the most part, hard times did the work. The recession of 1982 was the worst economic downturn since the Great Depression, and the jobless rate rose to 10.8 percent, putting millions of Americans out of work, before it ended in 1983. Many of those jobs never came back. Unlike previous cyclical slowdowns, the soaring interest rates and the ravages of recession gave a final, fatal shove to many American companies and industries, already in deep trouble from Japanese and European competition. In the industrial East and Midwest, a whole way of life ended. No longer could a young man graduate from his hometown high school and confidently follow his father to a $17-an-hour union job, plus overtime, at the local steel mill or auto plant in Allentown, Baltimore or Youngstown. The new factory jobs were in nonunion plants in the South. The computer boom was still a decade away, and the newly created jobs up North were in the lower-paying service sector. And small businesses were failing at a rate unmatched since 1933.

The press, which O'Neill had repeatedly chided as Reagan apologists in 1981, began to roast the administration with months of headlines and TV news reports about plant closings and layoffs as more than 60 House committee hearings were scheduled, most in major media markets across the nation, in the last three months of 1981. In April, CBS aired a much-imitated Bill Moyers documentary that showed how the cutbacks in federal programs affected the poor, the crippled and the hungry. The return of a Depression-era phenomenon — homelessness — made an appearance on the network news. Hundreds of local editors sent reporters out in their communities to chronicle the effects of Reaganomics.

"The trouble with this TV story . . . was that it bore little resemblance to the real world of budget cuts. For all the furor and anguish in Congress over paring social spending for 1982 by $35 billion, the cuts were hardly apocalyptic," wrote conservative columnist Fred Barnes. "One reason was the cuts were often not cuts *per se;* rather they were cuts from the 'baseline' level of spending for a program. In other words, the program got less than was projected if it had been allowed normal growth."

But the media's relentless pounding got to Reagan. "It's an entertainment medium, and they are looking for what's eyecatching and spectacular," the President complained, the irony lost on the old actor. "Is it news that some fellow out in South Succotash someplace has just been laid off, that he should be interviewed nationwide?" To his credit, Reagan stayed the course, declining to pressure Volcker or criticize the Federal Reserve's war on inflation, though it would cost his party dearly in 1982.[10]

Democratic reinforcements, meanwhile, were arriving on Capitol Hill. In September 1981, Coelho invited a team of the party's best political consultants to meet with the Speaker. O'Neill's son Kip, O'Donnell and Charlie Ferris joined consultants Anne Wexler, Bob Squier, Michael Berman and pollsters Pat Caddell, Bill Hamilton and Peter Hart on a free-flowing campaign team whose goal was Democratic victory in the 1982 elections. Their efforts were augmented by a core of Democratic aides: Matthews, Weiss, Jack Lew and Kevin Peterson from O'Neill's office; Al From from the Democratic caucus; George Kundanis from the whip organization and Dotty Lynch from the Democratic National Committee. The DNC and the House and Senate campaign committees pooled their resources and ordered the pollsters to conduct in-depth interviews with 1,265 registered voters in late November 1981. The respondents were interviewed by a pollster who visited them in their homes, for a session that lasted as long as an hour. Caddell, with his unique hyperbole, summarized the results. "The partisan struggle for political supremacy has reached a new and critical phase. The Republican offensive, seemingly relentless and irrepressible in the spring and summer of 1981, has stalled," Caddell wrote. "The political battle has arrived on a changed landscape of public opinion. The flat lowlands, so amenable to spring's Republican juggernaut have given way to the rocky, broken, dark marshlands and shrouded wilderness so conducive to political guerilla sweeps and large force issue ambush. In such terrain oppositions thrive."

Reagan was still personally popular. The voters believed he was trying hard, and hoped he would succeed. But the electorate was now more receptive to Democratic initiatives. The apparent failure of Reagan's economic prescriptions was beginning to erode support for the President's party and policy. "The Democrats are granted an opportunity, nothing more, to fill the vacuum," Caddell said. Women and blue-collar Democrats were returning to the fold. Social Security and unemployment were rising to the top of the public's concerns. The Democrats should attack Reagan over the failure of his economic nostrums, pound his Republican flanks about the dangerous budget deficits and force the President to take the first step toward reimposing taxes on the wealthy, the pollsters concluded. The House needed to use the budget wars to educate the public about the failure of Reaganomics and the unfair advantages it gave to the wealthy: that the rich got tax breaks while working people lost their jobs. The interests of "fairness" required, as the consultants put it, a "mid-course correction."

It is a mark of O'Neill's intuitive skills that as far back as early February 1981 — many months before the pollsters sent out their surveys — he had repeatedly cited "fairness" as the ultimate test of Reagan's policies. Now the Democratic consultants took their polling data and produced a prepackaged television show that served as the party's response to Reagan's State of the Union Address. In a documentary style, man-in-the-street interviews were mixed with statements by Walter Mondale, Ted Kennedy and other prominent Democrats. O'Neill closed the program with a strong summation of its central theme: fairness. Reagan's aides would come to hate the word "fairness," and by June 1982 had compiled an extensive internal briefing book on the topic.[11]

The skirmishes continued in the back rooms as well. When Reagan presented the FY 1983 budget to congressional leaders in early February, O'Neill grew impatient with the President's anecdotes of how greedy poor families were ripping off the school lunch, college grants and food stamp programs. "I disagree with about 80 percent of what you said," O'Neill said, and the two went at it for close to half an hour. O'Neill told Reagan about Debby Davis, a seventeen-year-old high school honor student from Georgia who could not afford to go to college because Gramm-Latta II had cut Social Security's postsecondary survivor benefits. The President was so taken that he ordered his staff to try and help the girl. "No, no, Mr. President. I'm not talking about one individual," O'Neill said. "I'm talking about thousands who expected to go to college on their parents' Social Security."

After he left the White House, O'Neill complained to the press corps that the President "has forgotten his roots. He associates with that country-club style of people." Reagan, knowing O'Neill had just returned from playing in a celebrity golf tournament, retaliated by telling reporters that "I've only played golf once since I've been President. . . . He's an inveterate golfer." The microphones and notebooks swung back to the Hill, and O'Neill obliged: Reagan's was a "Beverly Hills budget."

But it was easier for the Democratic dream team to prescribe a unified Democratic response than it was for the members of the House to deliver it. The White House had one chief to set the tone of the day; the House of Representatives had 435. Some members wanted to hang tough and let the White House "stew in its own juices," as O'Neill put it. Others wanted to show that the party could offer sensible alternatives, and favored a package proposed by Senate Democrats to defer implementation of some of Reagan's tax cuts, reduce cost-of-living increases in Social Security and pare defense spending. The Senate plan would have brought down the swollen budget deficit, but the House leadership dismissed it, in Matthews's memorable analogy, as a "River Kwai" approach, after the World War II movie in which allied prisoners grew so enamored of building a bridge they forgot it would benefit the enemy.

Reports of a $180 billion budget deficit led to negotiations by leaders of both parties after Jim Baker broke the ice in a secret visit to O'Neill's home on March 20. The negotiators called themselves "the Gang of 17," and their peace talks ultimately led to a face-to-face session between O'Neill and Reagan. The Speaker was willing to negotiate, but under one condition: that the White House be the first to propose any changes in Social Security. "He has to go first. . . . They're trying to set me up," O'Neill warned. The President traveled to the Hill on April 28, and sat down for three hours with O'Neill, Howard Baker and other leaders in the President's Room, off the Senate floor. The squabbling started immediately, as O'Neill objected to the seating chart, which put him next to Reagan instead of across the mahogany table with the other Democrats. He also demanded that Weiss be allowed into the room, since the President had Jim Baker. The White House then added Stockman and Treasury secretary Donald Regan to the group; it was quite a compliment to Weiss.

O'Neill was persuaded that the White House just wanted a photo opportunity so that the blame for the resultant deadlock would fall on both parties, and his instincts were correct. Darman's game plan was for Reagan to make a "thoroughly reasonable offer — that O'Neill will nonetheless reject." Indeed, the White House speechwriters had already drafted the President's subsequent speech, blaming the Speaker for slamming "the gate . . . on all those hours and weeks of effort to work out an official, bipartisan settlement." Reagan tried to lighten the mood with a joke. When Mary had the morning sickness back in

Ireland, the President told the summitteers, her doctor had asked her for a specimen. Not wanting to appear as ignorant as she was, Mary kept mum but stopped on the way home to ask her neighbor Dierdre what a specimen was. When she got back to her house that evening, her eye was blackened and her face was bloody. "What happened?" asked Mike, her husband. "I stopped to ask Dierdre what a specimen was. She told me to piss in a bottle. I told her to shit in her hat, and the fight was on."

The fight, indeed, was on. O'Neill gave Reagan a lecture about tax cuts for the rich, massive deficits and the historic achievements of the New Deal. "I know you people don't like to hear it, but you're just advocating trickle-down economics," the Speaker said. Nevertheless, the Democrats would accept another $35 billion in domestic spending cuts, O'Neill said.

Reagan responded by blaming the Democrats for waste and taxes and inflation. "Our defense spending as a percentage of the budget is much lower than in John F. Kennedy's day," said Reagan. He cited the Kennedy tax cut as well. "I'm just advocating President Kennedy's program," Reagan said. "We haven't thrown anybody out in the street to die." He wanted $60 billion in cutbacks.

Each side tried to maneuver the other into offering cutbacks in Social Security.

"Mr. President, are you putting Social Security on the table or not?" O'Neill asked.

"You're not going to trap me on that," said Reagan. "I didn't put this proposal on the table."

"It's not coming from us," O'Neill said. Jim Wright offered an alternative deal: the Democrats would accept more domestic spending cuts if Reagan would cut the third year of his tax cut by half, from 10 to 5 percent.

"You can get me to crap a pineapple," Reagan said, "but you can't get me to crap a cactus."

The efforts at reaching a compromise ended. At the end of the meeting the participants shifted uneasily in their seats, wanting to leave but worried that the other side would accuse them of breaking off the talks.

"I think we're all waiting for you to get up, Mr. President," said O'Neill.

"Let's all stand up together," Baker suggested. And so they did.

Reagan addressed the nation on television the following night, claiming that the Democrats wanted "more and more spending and more and more taxes." O'Neill passed out bumper stickers that said, "Vote Democratic — Save Social Security." Bolling was chosen to make the Democratic response to Reagan on television. "The key issue is fairness," he said. "If we are going to have an enormous increase in defense, everybody in the country should help do it — the rich and the poor alike."[12]

THE FAILURE OF the Gang of 17 negotiations brought the parties back to where they were in 1981, with each side bidding for the support of the GOP's gypsy moths and the Democrats' boll weevils. The White House whipped O'Neill in June when a Republican budget garnered enough votes to pass the House. But the old lifeguard in the Oval Office finally had to admit that a river of red ink was too dangerous a place for the country to swim. O'Neill's revenge came late in the summer, when he forced Reagan to accept a $98.3 billion tax hike, the largest such increase ever, crafted by Senator Robert Dole and passed by Senate Republicans. "I want him to use his smiley countenance and that sweet-sounding voice and hard knuckles with his Republicans," O'Neill said with satisfaction. The bill repealed some of the egregious tax benefits given to business in the 1981 bidding war, and hiked taxes on dividends, cigarettes, phone calls, and airline travel. To pass TEFRA, as it was known (the Tax Equity and Fiscal Responsibility Act), Reagan had to take on Jack Kemp and Newt Gingrich and other reluctant conservatives, and use the airwaves to round up the 100 Republican votes O'Neill demanded. "Are you going to follow the leader who brought you here or are you going to run?" O'Neill said, taunting his foes in the House. With Reagan providing political cover, and the Speaker's backroom help and fine closing speech, TEFRA passed the House by a 226 to 207 vote.

Reagan phoned to thank O'Neill, and found the Speaker armed with a quip about the double-edged nature of the Democratic gift. "Did you hear that the Irish gave the bagpipe to the Scots — and they took it seriously?" O'Neill said. Indeed, in the preelection jockeying it was hard to tell who was more cynical: O'Neill, who ducked the House's constitutional responsibility to initiate revenue measures to make sure the GOP bore the blame ("It's their recession . . . and it's going to be their tax bill"), or Reagan, who proposed that a balanced budget amendment to the Constitution was the proper cure for his own administration's deficits.[13]

With the fiscal housekeeping behind them, the two parties turned their attention to the November election where, thanks to Tony Coelho, the Democrats had cut into the Republican advantage in fund-raising. The thirty-nine-year-old Coelho had been elected to Congress for the first time in 1978. The DCCC chair seemed quite a leap for a second-term congressman, but he had a demonstrated talent for raising money. In his first two years in the House, Coelho had hustled up some $400,000 for his Democratic colleagues. Coelho wanted the job, and vowed to raise $5 million for the 1982 elections.

O'Neill's Democrats were in need of Coelho's confidence and determination. In the two-year cycle before the 1980 campaign, the NRCC had raised $20 million to the DCCC's $2.8 million, and the Republican national party and its Senate committee had enjoyed similarly huge advantages over their Democratic counterparts. All told, the GOP had raised $110 million, John Anderson $19 million and the Democrats $15 million in 1980 — a prime reason why the Republican gains had been so far-reaching. The GOP had used the money to pay for sophisticated direct mail, television, computing, polling and fund-raising operations. The NRCC had ended 1980 with $4 million in the bank; the DCCC was $200,000 in debt. Coelho got the job.

The new chairman approached his work with the zeal he had shown as a prospective Jesuit in his youth. The previous campaign committee chairmen had limited their appeals to big labor unions and the relatively few rich, progressive businessmen. Coelho went to where the money was — to the wallets of the corporate PACs, independent oilmen and other business interests who were regulated by the Ways and Means, Commerce, Banking and other House committees. His message was a not-so-subtle form of political blackmail. "In the past, this committee hasn't actively sought business PAC contributions. Now we intend to go after them, so they won't have an excuse," Coelho said. "And we're going to keep a record."

O'Neill had never thought to try it. "His view had always been that if the business community gave 75 percent to the Republicans and 25 percent to the Democrats we were doing pretty good. What did we have to complain about? They were Republicans, and representing the business interests," Lud Ashley recalled. But now the Speaker endorsed

Coelho's strategy. "If the Democrats are to retain control of the House in 1982, we must compete with the Republican campaign committee machinery," O'Neill told the organizing meeting of the DCCC in January 1981. "I am personally going to invest a considerable amount of time and effort in making sure that the campaign committee is competitive." Coelho plunged into his work, appointing Ways and Means chairman Rostenkowski as DCCC vice chairman and establishing seventeen task forces on every aspect — direct mail, PACs, issues, reapportionment, candidate recruitment, opposition research, and so on — of the 1982 campaign. They drew up a list of 80 contested seats, and vowed to give each of the Democratic candidates in those districts $25,000.

"What Tip told me when I became committee chair was, 'Lookit. You are going to have to be one of the tough guys. You are going to have to make the enemies. You are going to have to give the money to people who really need it.' He was good to me about that, because I got attacked a lot," said Coelho. One of Coelho's key innovations was the Speaker's Club, a device through which big contributors could buy access to O'Neill and the rest of the House Democratic leaders and committee chairmen. "As a member of the Speaker's Club: You will have many opportunities to meet personally with the Democratic Leadership and Committee Chairmen of the House of Representatives and share with them your interests and concerns," the promotional material told prospective donors. "Whether it's playing a round of golf with the Speaker, having dinner with the House Leadership, or sharing our ideas with other prominent Club members you will be broadening your circle of friends and contacts among the Senior Members of the House. When you come to Washington you will be assured courteous and direct access to those whom you wish to meet." The yearly cost was $5,000 for individuals and $15,000 for PACs. "In my fifty years in politics, I have learned to listen," O'Neill told the fat cats in another piece of promotional literature. "Tell us what you think — at a time and in a place where we can really hear what you have to say."

In late October 1981, O'Neill participated in a typical round of Speaker's Club events on a trip to Texas. Accompanying O'Neill on the private jet to Austin were his son Kip, Coelho and two club members — Sam Stone of the Associated Milk Producers and Bill McGowan, the chief executive officer of MCI Telecommunications. "McGowan is contributing $5,000 and promising to raise additional members," said a memo from the DCCC to the Speaker's office. "MCI is interested in telecommunication regulation."

The group picked up a couple of oilmen and another dairyman in Austin, where O'Neill played golf with the businessmen at the Onion Creek Country Club. More contributors joined the Speaker's party on the flight to Dallas, where O'Neill was the guest of honor at a cocktail party hosted by A. Starke Taylor, the chief stockholder of US Telephone Communications, another firm the DCCC was romancing. At the Taylor home they were joined by Tim Wirth, the chairman of the House telecommunications subcommittee, and some 120 people who paid $1,000 per couple to attend. After the party, O'Neill and Coelho and Wirth were to get together with US Tel CEO James Devlin and other stockholders and executives at a private dinner, followed by "brandy and cigars" and a cozy, private "business talk on communications issues," according to the itinerary. At a Speaker's Club breakfast the next day, O'Neill broke bread with twenty oil, high-tech and communications executives who had paid their $5,000 Speaker's Club dues.

Brandy and cigars and corporate jets didn't fit the image of the Democratic Party as defender of the working man. Yet the Democrats had to expand their lists of donors in order to compete with the Republicans, who were assembling a staggering $215 million war chest for an off-year election. It was a classic question of ethics versus power, and the Speaker and Coelho had no reservations about choosing power.

O'Neill "not only encouraged me but came up with ideas. He never expressed any concerns," said Coelho. "The thing he understood is that the Republicans were coming after us. It was a real danger; we could lose the House. Tip understood that he had to do something to stop it, and the only way you could do it was by raising money."

"I don't have any qualms," said the Speaker. "Do they have access? Yes, I would say they have access. But we run an open shop. Practically everybody has access."

By any other standard but Coelho's own expectations, his leadership at the DCCC for the 1982 election cycle was successful. In July 1982, he wrote to O'Neill to thank him for "giving so generously of your time and patience" to the Speaker's Club, and reported that in its first year it attracted 150 members and raised $800,000. Coelho met and surpassed his $5 million goal, raising $6.5 million for the DCCC, then an all-time record. At the annual DCCC dinner in April 1982, there was a festive atmosphere that contrasted markedly with the previous year's event. Rather than rallying his colleagues with a song, O'Neill was serenaded by Becky Snyder, the twelve-year-old lead in the Broadway musical *Annie,* who, after assuring the Democrats, "The sun will come out tomorrow," called the Speaker onstage amid cheers and applause and sang him her ode to Daddy Warbucks, "Together forever. We're tying the knot they never can sever."

Only the Republican Party's far deeper pockets threatened Coelho's sense of accomplishment. The NRCC alone raised an astonishing $58 million in its effort to seize the House. In May, Coelho had to warn O'Neill, "We can expect the Republicans to outspend us by more than $50 million this year," and that the Democrats, faced with that disparity, would be lucky to pick up a dozen seats. Still the Democrats could count on in-kind contributions from labor PACs, and the proven ability of incumbent Democratic congressmen to raise their own funds, and so stayed in the game.[14]

THE ECONOMY CONTINUED to be O'Neill's great ally. In January, an administration analysis of Reagan's tax plan had concluded, "The job creation push of the tax cuts is actually far less than thought and will cause a serious shortfall in new jobs created. Tens of billions of dollars in tax benefits now flow to firms who will make only minor contributions to our jobs goals." Volcker, meanwhile, had succeeded where Nixon and Ford and Carter had failed: by April 1982, the recession brought the consumer price index down to 2.4 percent, and the years of the Great Inflation were over. But after so many years of battling so formidable a foe, the economic policymakers at the Fed decided it was better to be safe than sorry, and the huge budget deficits gave Volcker whatever excuse he needed to keep wringing the economy. He relented only when a series of U.S. bank failures threatened the international monetary system that summer. Reagan had wanted to whip inflation, and get the resultant recession out of the way by the time he ran for reelection in 1984. He would achieve both goals. But for Republican congressional candidates in 1982, the first sign of recovery — that fall's surge in the stock market — came too late.

The recession would not end until 1983, and it savaged Republicans in the fall election season. The downturn brought 20 percent unemployment rates to construction, steel and other manufacturing industries, and led blue-collar workers to put aside their reservations about abortion, school prayer or busing and come home to the Democratic party. "Social conservatives are the part of the Reagan coalition which is wavering," one anxious White House memo reported. "Its core is the blue-collar ethnic voter." The Democratic base — labor unions, liberals, environmentalists, minorities and women — were energized as they recognized the threat Reagan posed.

On Capitol Hill, amid clear signs that the political tide was turning, each side pressed to make the other look bad. During a White House foreign policy briefing, the President excused himself to have his photograph taken with some handicapped children. "Your heart would die for them," Reagan said as he got up to leave. "Tell them Tip O'Neill is fighting for their budget," O'Neill responded. When a group of Young Republicans unveiled a seventeen-foot pie at the Washington Monument to celebrate the start of the second year of Reagan's tax cut, Matthews tipped off a group of anti-poverty activists, who surrounded the pie with hungry homeless people, spoiling the GOP media event. In a rare appearance on NBC's *Today Show,* O'Neill said Reagan had "ice water for blood." Reagan responded by comparing the Speaker to Pac-Man, the video game character who was "a round thing that gobbled up money." At a campaign appearance, Reagan inserted O'Neill's name in the list of nine planets, replacing Uranus.

After months of prodding by O'Neill, the press began to highlight and criticize Reagan's selective use of facts, his gaffes and apocryphal anecdotes. Before leaving Washington for the campaign recess, the House overrode the President's veto of an appropriations measure and passed an old-fashioned jobs bill, designating $1 billion for 200,000 public works jobs. Thirty-two nervous gypsy moths voted for the legislation, spurred by the news that the unemployment rate had topped 10 percent for the first time since the Depression.

The Democrats had entered the election cycle with a case of nerves about the 1980 redistricting — the necessary reapportionment of House seats to reflect population trends after each census. Americans were moving to the South and West, into Reagan country, and away from the East and Midwest. All told, seventeen new congressional districts would shift with them.[15] The Republicans had dreams of capturing the lion's share of those new seats but, with a determined effort, Democratic legislators and governors frustrated the GOP. All told, the Democrats picked up 10 of the 17 newly created seats. To make friends among the state legislators who would approve redistricting plans, O'Neill had helped craft an amendment to the Reagan tax bill, exempting state legislators' per diem allowances from the federal income tax. Phil Burton, displaying his genius once again, took command of the California mapmaking and — by putting his own seat and those of other secure Democrats more at risk — helped turn the state's 22 to 21 Democratic split into a 28 to 17 Democratic advantage, despite a million-dollar, computerized GOP campaign designed to foil him. "As we ran around with all of our computer sheets — we were going to show him — he'd whip out a Mobil gasoline station map and a crayon," Reagan aide Ed Rollins remembered.[16] In the numerical manipulation of his own seat, Burton went too far, putting his own reelection in jeopardy. But O'Neill responded by making a campaign swing through San Francisco for his old rival, boosting him in the Irish American community and helping him nail down an important endorsement from the city's police union.[17]

THE SPEAKER AND his staff took a personal interest in the race for a Long Island congressional seat held by freshman Republican representative John LeBoutillier, a twenty-seven-year-old, blue-blooded conservative who had, to the delight of the media, labeled O'Neill as "big, fat and out of control — just like the federal government." The Speaker "personifies everything the public hates about politics in America," said LeBoutillier, and the wealthy young congressman helped bankroll and lead a "Repeal O'Neill" campaign with the goal of unseating O'Neill and 26 other liberal Democrats. "I wouldn't know him from a cord of wood," O'Neill shrugged, but Leo Diehl was assigned the task of exacting revenge, which he did by raising tens of thousands of dollars in campaign contributions for Democratic state representative Robert Mrazek, who was running against LeBoutillier. The UAW, the NEA and the communications workers unions were among those who gave the maximum $10,000 contribution to Mrazek, but the fund-raising drive also brought O'Neill into contact with Long Island's aerospace industry and its lobbyist in Washington, a corrupt defense subcontractor, James Kane. The Reagan defense buildup had set off a frenzy in the industry, and Kane concluded that "the skids needed to be greased" in Washington. He was a wisecracking Irish American, known for wearing white sneakers with his suits, who loved cigars and golf and Georgetown University and wormed his way into the Speaker's orbit by helping Diehl raise money for Mrazek's campaign.

Kane played golf with the Speaker, invited him to fund-raisers on Long Island, introduced him to the executives and special needs of Grumman and other big defense firms and invested in business and real estate deals with O'Neill's sons Tommy and Kip. He became a "patron" of the Speaker's Club and hosted a DCCC event. O'Neill was just one of Kane's list of targets, which included a dozen members of the House Armed Services and Appropriations Committees. Kane collected kickbacks from defense subcontractors, and he and his associates offered congressmen plane rides, clothes, dinners and tickets to Broadway shows and sporting events. Through Georgetown University, which piggy-backed its lobbying efforts with Kane, he gave out $20,000 in scholarships to an aide to Jim Wright and the children of three congressmen. Kane's activities caught the attention of federal investigators in 1988, and their electronic eavesdropping revealed "a culture where political favoritism and influence-peddling [were] the accepted norms . . . a world where bribes, political favors and the like were an accepted and necessary element to survival," said U.S. prosecutor Joseph Aronica. Kane died of cancer in 1990, before he could be prosecuted, and the O'Neills were eventually cleared of any wrongdoing by the federal investigation into Kane's activities. But several of O'Neill's best buddies in Congress resigned when their connection to Kane came under investigation.[18]

With Kane's help and the slumping economy as an issue, Mrazek upset LeBoutillier in the heavily Republican district. A grateful Speaker hugged Mrazek at a congressional dinner, said "You're a beautiful guy, Mazursky," and helped him to a seat on the Appropriations Committee. "The Repeal O'Neill kid got repealed," Diehl crowed on Election Night.

AS THE 1982 balloting neared, the White House predicted that the Republicans would lose just 8 to 15 seats — about average for the midterm election of a new President's first term. The Democrats needed to pick up 20 seats to regain ideological control of the House chamber. Then a Republican mistake allowed O'Neill to revive the Social Security issue on the eve of the election.

From a reporter, Matthews heard about a Republican Party fundraising letter, which asked donors if they wouldn't like to make Social Security a voluntary pension system. O'Donnell urged Matthews to push the story, *hard,* and Matthews wrote and released a statement by O'Neill, calling on Reagan to "repudiate" the idea. The GOP had labored mightily to inoculate its candidates on the issue, with a TV ad campaign that showed a happy mailman delivering Social Security checks "with the 7.4 percent cost-of-living raise that President Reagan promised." Now the Democrats, who had alleged all summer and fall that the Republicans were scheming to cut Social Security benefits, had a fresh hook. Reporters confronted Reagan at a campaign appearance, where he denounced the Democratic charges as a "dishonest canard." The media seized on the controversy, and the story led all three network news shows that night. "They used it against us and killed us with it. Absolutely killed us," Jim Baker recalled. O'Neill campaigned among seniors with a blown-up copy of the GOP fund-raising letter, and Democrats across the nation bought TV time that weekend to drive the issue home. The voters went to the polls on November 2 and gave O'Neill an impressive victory. The Democrats picked up 26 seats in the House of Representatives — a total that exceeded both expectations and historical precedents.[19]

O'Neill received the news in his office in the Capitol. "Hi, Mom," he told Millie on the telephone. "Everything is going great." He kept track of the won and lost seats on a yellow legal pad, breaking away from the phone at his desk for a plate of beef stew and a Canadian Club and water. "God bless ya," he told Representative Phil Sharp. "You had us scared. It was the old Hail Marys that did it. I guess they work."

"You know," the Speaker told a *Newsweek* reporter, "the good Lord said to Solomon, 'You have great power and beautiful wisdom, what can I do for you?' And Solomon said, 'Give me a heart that hears.' That is what the President doesn't have. I think it's because of the company he keeps. This man is unbelievable. He has forgotten where he comes from."

Of special interest to the Speaker was the fate of Gene Atkinson, the Pennsylvanian who had switched parties and become Republican in the blush of Reagan's popularity. O'Neill had campaigned for Atkinson's Democratic challenger, and in private called the congressman "Gyppo Nolan," after the turncoat in the movie *The Informer.* The Speaker grinned with satisfaction when O'Donnell brought in the news. "Gyppo has gone down the tubes," O'Neill said.[20]

O'NEILL HAD SAVED the House. "The one clear winner election night was Thomas P. O'Neill," wrote the *Wall Street Journal*'s Al Hunt.

"He had suffered more than any other political leader in the past two years. But his strategy . . . paid off on election night."

"Everybody's favorite scapegoat doesn't look so bad anymore," the *Post* declared. And "Tip O'Neill, labeled a political bumbler hopelessly out of step with the times, spoke on election night as the undisputed leader of the House," wrote Michael Barone.

It had been a remarkable two years for the two septuagenarians. "There was no Democratic leader," O'Neill recalled. "I was the highest elected Democratic official. The President took me as the symbol of the Democratic Party — that I was fat and big and out of shape and a big spender. He thrust me into the prominence of the most important Democrat in America because he thought I was going to be easy to handle. But he kind of misjudged.

"He and I both came from the same side of the railroad tracks. I never forgot from where I came. He kind of forgot.

"You know God gave him a handsome face, a great physique, the ability to act and present pathos, sentiment, happiness, which he is able to do on the media — and all of a sudden from a radio announcer making $35 or $40 a week he is a movie star earning a half a million and he's paying the 85 percent tax, he's shocked. He wants to get into politics and change it. And maybe the taxes were too high.

"But those taxes: they changed America. We changed America. Made middle-class America."[21]

O'Neill had won elections before. Knowing what to do with such a victory was as important a test. He was determined to use his mandate well. Until the economy fully emerged from its tailspin in late 1983 and the increasing preoccupation with the presidential election year of 1984 closed off most avenues of compromise in Washington, the Speaker had a brief window in which hard times and a chastened Republican Party would give him some freedom to maneuver. In his first honeymoon, in 1977, O'Neill had spent his political capital on jobs, ethics and energy — important short-term goals, but with little historic importance. The Speaker would use his second honeymoon on a more lasting mission: protecting the legacy of the New Deal and the Great Society.

Reagan feared the worst. "It will be a brand new ballgame; one in which we are not now prepared to play . . . going on bended knee to Tip O'Neill for his support on issue after issue," a White House analysis decided. "Given the previous situation, it would surprise no one if O'Neill told us all to get lost." But O'Neill recognized the limited mandate of the 1982 election. Peter Hart and his other advisers had warned the Speaker that the voters had opted for a "mid-course correction," not a counterrevolution. And though the balloting had brought him a militant group of freshmen, most of whom had run against the excesses of Reaganomics, and many of whom admired his Horatio-at-the-bridge act, they were, by style and philosophy, more akin to Gephardt, Coelho and the other young Democratic chieftains than to the old-fashioned liberalism of Tip O'Neill. Nor did the Speaker have any illusions that Reagan's postelection offers of accommodation were more than a temporary phenomenon, brought on by the politics of the moment.

So as he assembled his priorities for 1983, O'Neill followed the advice he had given to Jimmy Carter, and kept the list short. First up, the Speaker knew, was relief for the victims of the recession, especially the hard-hit blue-collar families that had returned to the Democratic fold. He promised to "take the offensive for jobs, jobs and more jobs." With unemployment at 10.8 percent, Howard Baker made the walk from the Senate to the House, cut a deal with O'Neill and (after Bob Byrd spent some time fuming) joined the Democrats in passing a nickel hike in the federal gasoline tax to pay for a job-generating highway and transit construction bill. The President grimaced but signed the $27 billion gas tax hike and by March, with Reagan's support, Congress passed a $4.9 billion public works bill as well. A turning point in that debate occurred when Reagan and O'Neill had another verbal brawl in the Oval Office in January. White House aides and congressional leaders watched mutely as O'Neill and Reagan wrangled for forty minutes.

It was "the toughest going-over I've ever heard a President subjected to," Wright told his diary. "The Speaker, asked by Reagan to support the budget request, told the President very plainly that Democrats could not acquiesce in good conscience to this passive acceptance of high unemployment and its attendent evils without making every effort to amend such a budget. Reagan's face grew red and he swore, 'God damn it, Tip, we do care about those people.' But the Speaker was not assuaged. 'It's easy to say that you care but you aren't willing to do anything about it,' he said."

Reagan ultimately turned the meeting over to Regan and Stockman, but before leaving he calmed down, and walked up to O'Neill and said, "Dave tells me we're really not that far apart."

"Clearly the Speaker had scored," Wright wrote.

Next up was the budget, and here the Democrats had several goals: to demonstrate to the voters that they could handle the responsibility; to reduce the size of the budget deficit (which many of the freshmen had used as a campaign issue); to chip away at the Reagan defense buildup; and to sap the administration's ongoing attack on domestic programs. This was no time for liberal self-indulgence, O'Neill told his troops: "We're going to be moderate. We couldn't pass a bill if we go the liberal route."

Reagan and O'Neill engaged in their usual shenanigans. The Democrats pardoned most of the boll weevils, but kicked Gramm off the Budget Committee; he manfully resigned his seat, switched parties, and won reelection as a Republican. "I had to choose between Tip O'Neill and y'all," Gramm told the voters, "and I decided to stand with y'all." The President promoted his State of the Union speech with a stop at the Eire Pub, in an Irish American neighborhood in Dorchester, a section of Boston, but muddied his message later that day by telling a group of businessmen that corporate taxes should be abolished. O'Neill did a drop-by at a bar too — this one on Reagan's turf, in Hollywood, where the son of Delores Snow, his longtime assistant, was the casting director for the new NBC show *Cheers,* and had persuaded the Speaker to do a guest appearance. The set was patterned after the Bull & Finch on Beacon Street in Boston, where O'Neill admitted to have "quaffed a few" himself over the years. He donated his acting pay and residuals to the Cambridge Boys and Girls Club, which bought six new tires and repaired the clutch on its bus.

After cutting a little bit more from defense and a little bit less from domestic programs than the Republican Senate, the House passed a budget resolution on March 23. O'Neill lost only 36 boll weevils and got 4 Republican crossovers in a 229 to 196 victory. The budget called for $30 billion in higher tax revenues, and restored funds to food stamps, Medicaid, welfare and other social programs. O'Neill won more kudos from the press, and announced that he would run for another term in 1984. But he felt the brush of mortality when, on April 11, Phil Burton died of a ruptured artery.[22]

O'Neill lost one big fight in 1983, when the House Democrats failed in their attempt to reduce or delay the third year of Reagan's tax cut. The Speaker pushed a $700 cap on the Reagan tax plan through the House; it would have preserved the tax cut for families earning under $50,000 a year and just lightly penalized the wealthy, but was rejected by the Senate Republicans. O'Neill decreed that from then on his Democrats would not do the GOP dirty work — any hike in taxes would have to be proposed by Reagan. Since neither party was willing to raise taxes, and both had shown that they didn't have the stomach for the huge cuts in domestic and military spending it would take to balance the budget, the result, as Stockman put it, was that "there will be $200 billion deficits as far as the eye can see."[23]

He had won on jobs and the budget, but the real cornerstone of O'Neill's second honeymoon — and one of his lasting achievements as Speaker — was the deal he struck with Reagan to preserve Social Security. In 1981, when O'Neill had taken the calculated risk to politicize the Social Security debate, his staff and colleagues warned him that the system teetered on the brink of insolvency. Reagan proposed to let a commission led by his economic adviser Alan Greenspan come up with necessary "reforms." O'Neill was wary of a trap, but the quality of the appointees — who included Bob Dole, Pat Moynihan, Claude Pepper and AFL-CIO president Lane Kirkland — eased his concerns. The Speaker's most important appointee was former Social Security commissioner Robert Ball, O'Neill's personal guru on the issue. "Bob didn't make a move that we weren't aware of," said Jack Lew. "He would leave the meeting and call me, or if I needed to I would call the Speaker. And it was all very safe in the sense that we were never negotiating anything directly." For most of 1982, the commissioners struck public poses while their staff researched the problems and drafted possible solutions. "We weren't going to put our head back in that noose, and the Speaker wasn't going to come forward unless the President came forward, and so we just danced around and danced around," Ken Duberstein recalled. Then, over the course of several weeks following the 1982 election, Greenspan convened a series of secret meetings with Dole, Moynihan and Ball — and White House staffers Baker, Duberstein, Darman and Stockman. "Are we going to let this commission die without giving it one more try?" Moynihan asked Dole on the Senate floor, when stalemate seemed all but certain.

Meeting at Baker's house on Foxhall Road in Washington and in other out-of-the-way locations, the small group of negotiators arrived at a formula: any bailout plan would consist of both benefit cuts and tax hikes, on a 50-50 basis. Ball and Baker were the two essential players, for they represented O'Neill and Reagan. From the first days of May 1981, when O'Neill had bludgeoned the GOP over early-retirement benefits, Baker had been determined to neutralize Social Security as a political issue before the President's 1984 reelection campaign. The chief of staff, as Stockman put it, prowled the White House corridors as if armed with a bazooka, ready to blow up any budget proposal that had cuts in Social Security. The major conceptual breakthrough was a trial balloon that Ball proposed: to apply the federal income tax to the Social Security benefits of wealthier recipients. To this the commission added a postponement of COLA raises, acceleration of previously scheduled payroll taxes and other cost-saving measures. Reagan's victory over inflation had eased the pressure on the trust funds, and Pickle and Rostenkowski — getting revenge for the way O'Neill had taken the issue from Ways and Means — engineered a gradual increase in the retirement age, despite O'Neill's objections. (Physically worn blue-collar workers, the Speaker argued in vain, could not extend their working years as easily as their higher-income white-collar counterparts.) The friction with Rostenkowski was to be expected: the Speaker was spreading the word in the cloakroom that Jim Wright, not Rosty, was his preferred choice as a successor.

The final negotiations on Social Security were held at Blair House, from where the President's aides would shuttle across Pennsylvania Avenue in the frigid cold to brief Reagan, and Ball or O'Donnell would telephone O'Neill — who was playing golf at the Bob Hope Tournament in Palm Springs, California. With Reagan, O'Neill and Pepper on board, even the powerful senior citizen interest groups couldn't derail the train. The Speaker rarely attended such ceremonies, but he was there at the White House on a cold April day when Reagan signed the bill into law. O'Neill had shown a remarkable sense of the moment. Roosevelt's jewel had been saved, for at least another two decades.[24]

With the signing of the Social Security bill the Reagan Revolution came, with the scratch of souvenir pens, to an end. For the true conservative revolutionaries, those who wanted Reagan to dismantle the core of the welfare state, the President might just as well have signed a treaty of surrender. Indeed, Stockman would argue that a brief historic window for radical change had been slammed shut by O'Neill's ruthless use of the Social Security issue as early as the spring and summer of 1981.

The real Reagan "revolution" was attitudinal. For students of politics and public policy, the Reagan era is a remarkably creative and liberating time — an explosive episode in U.S. history when a half-century's assumptions and theory were ripped raw and opened to reexamination. When it ended, Reagan could justly claim to have ended the nation's drift toward a Western European–style social democracy. Americans had reaffirmed their love of risk and freedom, of markets and entrepreneurs. In the twenty years after Reagan's election there would be no new federal agencies or departments; the U.S. government workforce would shrink; Reagan-Bush appointees to the Supreme Court would dismantle chunks of the Warren Court's legacy; and the one Democratic effort to create a new federal entitlement — the doomed push for national health care in 1993 — would lead to a Republican takeover of the House of Representatives. To win reelection in 1996, Democrat Bill Clinton would promise that "the era of big government is over." Reagan couldn't have said it better himself.

"If you define the 'revolution' to mean that you are going to eliminate the departments of Commerce and Energy and Education, get rid of Legal Services and all that, then you can say, I suppose, that part hasn't gone over," said Jim Baker, in a 1998 interview. "But given his druthers, Tip would never have wanted to see that 70 percent tax rate go down, and we did it. Tax reductions, the impetus to the economy, free trade, the elimination of a lot of regulations, downsizing of government — that is all still working today, and you don't hear anybody out there arguing to go back."

Jimmy Carter, in his inaugural address, had told Americans that "we have learned that 'more' is not necessarily 'better,' that even our great nation has recognized limits, and that we can neither answer all questions nor solve all problems." Reagan, in his inaugural, had challenged Americans "to believe in ourselves and to believe in our capacity to perform great deeds, to believe that together with God's help we can and will resolve the problems which now confront us.

"And after all, why shouldn't we believe that? We are Americans," Reagan said.

By the end of the Reagan years, his nation's faith in itself, which had been shattered in the 1970s, was restored. "Ronald Reagan picked a very limited number of very important ideas: cutting taxes, rebuilding our defenses, reasserting American morale," Gingrich said. "On most things Ronald Reagan focused on, O'Neill lost. He slowed it down, but lost."

Yet, in no small part because of Tip O'Neill, who staggered against the ropes in the summer of 1981 and bled for the dwarfs and the knock-kneed and the elderly and the rest of those millions of Americans whose voices were stilled by lack of talent or money or education or health or by the color of their skin or their accents or ancestry, the Reagan "revolution" remained attitudinal. Slowly, but largely because this bleeding, pained old man kept hollering "fairness" and "justice" as Reagan pounded him around the ring, the American people stopped to consider those principles, began the long dialogue of democracy, considered what was too costly and what was unfair, and put the revolution on hold.

"There should be no doubt about what experience has demonstrated: The specific ideas necessary to make radical cuts in modern American government consistently fail the test of public acceptability," Dick Darman concluded, after Newt Gingrich's attempt to reprise the "revolution" failed in 1995. "The reality is that the American government is as big as it is, acting in the areas that it does, primarily because a substantial majority of Americans wants it roughly so."

O'Neill may have sensed it, as he huddled in his overcoat on the White House lawn, watching Reagan sign the Social Security bill on a raw April day. It was exactly fifty years since Roosevelt's 100 days. The Democrats' biggest loss during the Reagan revolution was the gravy of the welfare state — the supplements and hikes in benefits that O'Neill and his colleagues had spooned out, with presidential help, during the Nixon, Ford and Carter years.

Of the $110 billion that Reagan and Stockman had chopped from the baseline budget of the Carter years in their first thirty months in office, about $26 billion was from retirement programs like Social Security and veterans' benefits; $25 billion from public works jobs programs like CETA; $27 billion in welfare payments, food stamps, unemployment insurance and other income security programs; $18.5 million from Medicare and other health care programs; and $13.7 billion in education and social services. Projected domestic spending had been cut from $1.63 trillion to $1.52 trillion over four years — about 7 percent. Real people had been affected — 325,000 families lost their welfare payments, 3 million students lost school lunches, 1 million people lost their food stamps and 700,000 college students lost guaranteed federal loans. But because the war had been fought over *tightening eligibility* for such things as college scholarships, food stamps and school lunches, the authorizing legislation remained on the books.

"The budget cuts brought about a halt in the growth of spending on programs for the near-poor and poor. They were achieved largely by trimming around the edges. Requirements were tightened and rules were made more stringent," Barnes reported. "Except for public service jobs (and, eventually, revenue sharing and urban development grants) no major program was eliminated."

It was the near-poor that suffered: the working folk whose incomes were just enough to push them past the federal poverty level or state welfare standard. About 850,000 people, for example, were dropped from the food stamp program in 1981, leaving 22 million recipients, as the food stamp budget dropped from $11.4 billion in 1981 to $11.3 billion the following year. Reagan's budget cuts may have been debatable public policy, in that cutting benefits like food stamps and Medicaid for the working poor may have removed the incentive for staying off welfare, but they were hardly cataclysmic.

The Reagan tax cuts, on the other hand, were indeed revolutionary. They benefited the very wealthy, held the middle class harmless and penalized the poor. Yet taxes can be raised and adjusted, and were — seven times under Reagan and by congressional Democrats acting in concert with George Bush in 1990 and Bill Clinton in 1993. In the meantime, the muscle and bone — and even some flab — of the New Deal and the Great Society survived.

"All the indications were that 1982 should have been a realignment year. But O'Neill led a strategic retreat that turned into a successful offensive," said O'Donnell. "In the process he probably saved the New Deal welfare state. In the final analysis it is the laws that make the difference. Reagan was able to de-fund some programs, but he wasn't able to de-authorize them. Head Start. AFDC. They stayed and the environmental laws stayed and the Voting Rights Act stayed. Unless you get the laws off the books you do not dismantle the New Deal state."

Much of what Reagan claimed as victories — cutbacks in public works jobs, tax cuts and increased defense spending — were already features, albeit more modestly, of Carter's budgets. In 1980, Carter had promised a 25 percent hike in defense spending, over five years. Reagan was never to cut enough to match the low 20.6 percent spending to GNP ratio of Carter's FY 1979 budget, and by the time Reagan left office, and the Congress had finished adding TEFRA and a host of smaller tax hikes, the percentage of taxes to GNP was just about where Carter had left it.

The Great Society was bruised, yet breathing. And the New Deal? Franklin Roosevelt's legacy was untouched. The souvenir pen in O'Neill's hand was proof. "This is a happy day for America," the Speaker said. He had remembered where he came from. He had kept the faith.[25]

CHAPTER 25

Maryknolls and Marines

REAGAN'S REVOLUTION was not limited to domestic affairs; the President also had a revolutionary insight about the Soviet Union, the foe he branded as an "evil empire." In a meeting with the congressional leadership in March 1982, Howard Baker asked Reagan if, given the size of the federal budget deficit, they should not pare back the defense buildup. Reagan responded by recounting how Lenin had once spelled out the Communist strategy for worldwide domination. Europe and Asia and South America would fall to revolution, and then the United States would drop into Communist hands "like overripe fruit," Reagan said, quoting the old bolshevik. It was one of the President's favorite anecdotes, and he was determined it would never come true. "We must keep the heat on these people. What I want is to bring them to their knees so that they will disarm and let us disarm; but we have got to do it by keeping the heat on," Reagan said. "We can do it. We have them on the ropes economically. They are selling rat meat in the markets in Russia today."

Wright and the other congressional leaders were stunned by Reagan's outlook. U.S. Sovietologists and intelligence analysts were nowhere near as sanguine about the USSR's fate. But there was no doubt that the President believed it: that Communism was tottering and that the United States could, with a final burst of military spending and resolve, make the whole rotten tyrannical structure collapse upon itself. Reagan adamantly refused to scale back his plans for a trillion dollars' worth of new intermediate and intercontinental nuclear missiles, fighters and bombers, high-tech tanks and weaponry, a 700-ship Navy and a space-based strategic defense system that was dismissively tagged "Star Wars" by its critics. The Pentagon spent $21 million *an hour* in 1982, the first year of the buildup, and almost doubled that by the end of the decade. If a few hundred-billion-dollar deficits were what it would take to invigorate the American spirit, revive the U.S. economy and win the cold war, well, "the man on the street" would forgive him, Reagan said.

"I remember Reagan blowing up at Baker and Stockman saying, 'You know, those bastards in Congress are never going to give me a budget and I'm not going to play the game with them. I will accept responsibility for the deficits, but I am going to get the Soviets to the table and we will still go ahead on defense spending,'" said Michael Deaver. "It was a conscientious decision that historically he would accept the deficits — for that reason."[1]

Looking back, having witnessed the astounding speed with which the Soviet empire disintegrated, it may be hard to appreciate just how radical Reagan's vision was in its time. Americans had been raised on the notion of a "long twilight struggle" in which periods of "detente" or "peaceful coexistence" might at best grant some moments of reprieve from the dread of thermonuclear annihilation. No one seriously spoke of *winning* the cold war, or of the Soviet Union's collapse, or of mutual disarmament, or the fall of the Berlin Wall — until Ronald Reagan. O'Neill, for one, thought Reagan was merely reciting the anti-Communist spiel he had peddled on the rubber-chicken circuit. But Reagan believed that victory in the cold war and the overthrow of Communism were real, achievable goals — not merely words to be mouthed. The President saw, and grasped, a historic opportunity.

When Reagan traveled to Berlin, stood at the Brandenburg Gate and said, "Mr. Gorbachev, tear down this wall," he meant it. When Reagan told O'Neill and Wright and the others that the Soviet economy was on the ropes and that one more good push could bring the whole rotten structure down, he meant it. When Reagan spoke of a space-based shield that would free children from the terror of mutally assured destruction, he meant it. When Reagan compared the evils of nuclear war to the horrors mentioned in the Biblical tale of Armageddon, he meant it. And when Reagan suggested that Providence had spared his life for some momentous reason, he meant it. There was more than a little augur in Ronald Wilson Reagan.

If O'Neill did not share Reagan's vision, neither did he employ his powers to foil it. With a few key exceptions — most notably the U.S. intervention in Central America — the Speaker approached the President's foreign policy from the mushy bipartisan center. "Reagan felt that if he had a sound foreign policy Tip would be with him," said Deaver. Assistant Secretary of State Elliott Abrams said, "I wouldn't give him a hell of a lot of credit, but O'Neill was part of the very broad consensus.

"And he didn't have red hots on his staff — aides far to the left of what a member would show the voters — like other members of Congress did," said Abrams.

O'Neill had been surprised and angered by the Soviet invasion of Afghanistan, and endorsed Jimmy Carter's subsequent call for an increase in American military spending. He had backed Carter on the development of the MX intercontinental ballistic missile, cruise missiles and other "smart" weaponry — and the deployment of nuclear-tipped cruise and Pershing II intermediate-range missiles in Europe. In the hope of trapping the Soviets in their "own Vietnam," O'Neill was happy to support covert U.S. assistance to the mujahedin resistance forces in Afghanistan. Nor did the budgets approved by O'Neill's House ever propose to gut Reagan's defense buildup. In 1983, flush from their triumph at the polls the previous November, the resurgent House Democrats voted for a budget that gave the Pentagon a 4 percent real annual increase, as opposed to the 6 percent increase adopted by the Republican Senate. In conference, the two houses split the difference and awarded the Pentagon $269 billion — not much less than the $280 billion that Reagan had asked for. In supporting such a robust defense budget, O'Neill was bowing to political reality. Given his druthers, the Speaker would certainly have spent less and negotiated more. "Our position was peace through strength. The Democrats' was negotiate, negotiate, negotiate," said Baker. And O'Neill never hesitated to criticize the Reagan defense buildup as excessive, to ridicule "Star Wars" or to back such symbolic liberal causes as the nuclear "freeze" resolution, which urged the great powers to freeze the size of their nuclear arsenals. But O'Neill was too much a consensus politician, and cold warrior, to challenge a President's fundamental authority to conduct foreign policy. The peaceniks in his Cambridge district seethed when the Speaker promoted Raytheon's development of the Patriot missile, personally intervened to continue production of the F-18 jet fighter (whose engines were made in the General Electric plant near Boston) and strenuously, albeit unsuccessfully, lobbied to get Boston named as the home port for a new navy battle group built around the refurbished battleship the USS *Iowa*. The head of the freeze movement publicly labeled O'Neill a hypocrite.

O'Neill's parochial approach to Pentagon spending was illustrated by his intervention on behalf of the GTE Corporation, which was bidding for a military communications system called MSE (Mobile Subscriber Equipment) in 1984. GTE was the low bidder, but its main competitor was a British subsidiary of Rockwell International, whose interests were being represented at the White House and the Pentagon by no less an advocate than British prime minister Margaret Thatcher. With Rockwell fielding that kind of clout, Armen Der Marderosian, the GTE executive in charge of the project, thought his firm had a one-in-ten chance of landing the deal. Then Der Marderosian promised Representative Joe Moakley that the company would put the main manufacturing plant — and 1,000 jobs — in Taunton, Massachusetts, if GTE won the contract.

"Taunton was in my district. It had a 15 percent unemployment rate. So I went up to see Tip," Moakley recalled.

"Tip, here is a company in Massachusetts that bid this thing, got it fair and square, and every time it comes to award the project, Cap Weinberger pulls it back. It's worth a thousand jobs and it will be in Massachusetts," Moakley said.

"Really? A thousand jobs?" said O'Neill. "Nothing else about it, is there?"

"So help me God. They got Rockwell tied in with an English company and they are trying to make the deal and I think Cappy is playing with Thatcher over the Star Wars thing," said Moakley.

Soon the Speaker was on the telephone to the Defense Department. "He says: 'You're not playing politics with this fucking thing!' He really gave it his best South Boston lingo and let him have it. And backed them off," Moakley said.

"And did I tell you how much the contract was worth? Four billion dollars. GTE goes in there and then boom, boom, boom. The unemployment rate in Taunton dropped to 3.5 percent," Moakley said.[2]

THE SINGLE GREAT exception to O'Neill's conviction that politics stopped at the water's edge was Central America, where the Reagan administration chose to make a stand against Soviet-financed and Cuban-assisted wars of liberation. "The war in Central America was the Holy Grail both for the far Left in the United States and the far Right," Jim Baker recalled. "It was *the* divisive foreign policy issue." In 1979, cold war tensions in the region rose when the Marxist-Leninist "Sandinista National Liberation Front" overthrew Nicaraguan dictator Anastasio Somoza, whose family had ruled the country for four decades. The Democrats, in keeping with Jimmy Carter's promise to support human rights around the globe, had withheld aid from Somoza and hoped the Sandinistas would bring political freedom and economic reform. With O'Neill's help, Congress had passed Carter's request for $75 million in U.S. aid for Nicaragua in 1980.

"I am not ready to give up trying to help Nicaragua to recover from its civil war and pursue a path toward democracy," the Speaker said. But the Marxists in the Nicaraguan junta pushed their centrist allies aside, built ties with the Soviets and funneled arms and assistance to leftist rebels in neighboring El Salvador. O'Neill and other congressional Democrats tried to moderate the Nicaraguan behavior, to no avail. As one of his final acts in office, Carter reauthorized military aid for the right-wing Salvadoran government in January 1981.

Incoming secretary of state Alexander Haig, and others in the new Reagan administration, believed that the United States had to send a clear signal to the Cubans, who were backing the leftist forces in Nicaragua and El Salvador. But Baker, Deaver and Meese knew — and Reagan understood, after seeing the results of surveys by pollster Richard Wirthlin — that military conflict in Central America in the spring of 1981 would alienate Congress and the electorate, reinforce perceptions of the President as a warmonger and doom the administration's economic and political initiatives before they got off the ground. So the Holy War was put on hold. "I look back at that as one of the best decisions we made in terms of that presidency succeeding, because that is how we do judge our Presidents: Are they able to work with the Congress? Are they able to get things done?" Baker recalled.

"The fact that we were able to do that was one of the things responsible for his solid job-approval ratings after we began to come out of the 1981–82 recession. We were all justifiably worried, but by then we had gotten our program through. And Reagan had proved he wasn't a rigidly ideological cowboy who couldn't accomplish anything in Washington, D.C." The CIA was instead authorized to provide covert support to the counterrevolutionary — *Contra* — forces in Nicaragua. The White House had put Central America on a back burner, for a time.

At the other end of Pennsylvania Avenue, O'Neill insistently viewed Central America through the prism of America's disastrous experience in Vietnam: here were more revolutionary armies, supported by a peasant population, ready to lure American boys to death in impenetrable jungles. He would speak of Eddie Kelly, a kid from old Cambridge who had joined the marines and come home in a wheelchair after being stabbed by Nicaraguan rebels during the U.S. military intervention in the 1920s, which had been urged on Washington by the United Fruit Company and other corporate interests. "Why are we there?" O'Neill had asked Kelly. "We're taking care of the property and rights of United Fruit," Kelly told him. O'Neill was also profoundly influenced by the left-leaning Jesuit priests and Maryknoll missionaries who labored in the region and were among the most vocal critics of its repressive right-wing oligarchies. O'Neill's ninety-one-year-old aunt, Sister Eunice "Annie" Tolan, had been a high-ranking member of the Maryknoll order and was a "strong and penetrating influence" on the Speaker, Jim Wright recalled.

For years, on the floor of the House and in other venues, O'Neill cited reports from the Maryknoll missionaries when calling for "a reappraisal of our policy in Latin America" and a shift in emphasis from military confrontation to economic and social justice. "I hope all my colleagues will pay close attention to Sister Marian's well-documented, thorough statement," O'Neill said on April 23, 1968, inserting a statement on conditions in Central America by Maryknoll Sister Marian Pahl into the *Congressional Record*. "To disregard her advice is to invite another Vietnam." Wright recalled how another Nicaragua-based Maryknoll missionary, Sister Peggy Healy, maintained a steady correspondence with the Speaker throughout the early 1980s. "Sister Healy felt keenly that the CIA's support of the Contras was wicked," the majority leader recalled. Wright, whose centrist views on Central

America were later to play a key role in U.S. policy, met with Healy at O'Neill's urging and found her "outspoken in her denunciation of the terror, bullying and needless violence perpetrated by the growing bands of armed resistance." After listening to Healy, O'Neill told his aides, "I believe every word."

"I have a lot of friends in the Maryknoll Order, and they keep me highly informed," O'Neill told reporters. "They look at it . . . like Vietnam.

"With the mountains and the terrain there, our boys would be enmeshed for years. Our policy is wrong. I told the White House that, but they think I get my policy from the little old ladies there, the nuns. And in part I do. They are women of God who are doing His work. They, as I do, believe in the holy word and are carrying it out," O'Neill said. "I have had nuns and humanitarians in who tell us that the people in the villages of Nicaragua do not know what Communism is. But they know they are living a better life — with food and health care — for the first time."

Elliott Abrams, who supervised Latin American affairs during the Reagan years, said, "The basis of his substantive view was ludicrous: this Maryknoll nun. The Speaker's information base was irresponsibly narrow. You couldn't argue with him like you could with other determined opponents like, say Chris Dodd. O'Neill, one had the feeling, had reached his view, God knows how, and you could not argue with him."[3]

In December 1980, O'Neill was outraged at the news that four female American missionaries — two Maryknoll nuns, an Ursuline nun and a lay worker — had been abducted and murdered as they drove from the airport to San Salvador, and their bodies dumped in shallow graves. There were signs that at least one of the women had been sexually abused before they were killed by members of one of El Salvador's notorious right-wing death squads. In that the incident permanently colored the Speaker's already antagonistic view of right-wing forces in the region, and confirmed the reports he was getting from the Maryknolls, it was a profoundly counterproductive act of terror by the Right. Given O'Neill's subsequent relentless and powerful opposition to right-wing forces in the region, it is no exaggeration to say that lay missionary Jean Donovan and Sisters Ita Ford, Maura Clarke and Dorothy Kazel, through their martyrdom, indeed changed the future for the people they had come to help.[4]

In November 1982, the Speaker's attention moved from El Salvador to Nicaragua when *Newsweek* published a cover story: "America's Secret War: Nicaragua." The magazine detailed the ongoing efforts by the CIA to undermine the Sandinista regime, and inspired a *Globe* editorial that harshly criticized the administration's policy. Eddie Boland read and was impressed by the editorial, and furious that his Select Committee on Intelligence had to rely upon the press to learn the scope of the CIA's operations. A month later, with O'Neill's encouragement, the House passed the first "Boland amendment," which prohibited the CIA and the Pentagon from using funds for the purpose of overthrowing the Nicaraguan government. Reagan signed it into law, though the CIA's counsel, Stanley Sporkin, presciently warned that "this thing is going to come back and bite us in the ass like nothing you've ever seen."

Six months later, Reagan was back before Congress asking for hundreds of millions of dollars in economic and military aid for the Contras, El Salvador and other Central American governments. He ordered the navy to conduct military exercises in the region and raised the specter of Soviet influence; the House met in a rare secret session to consider classified reports about Nicaragua. But on July 28, O'Neill and Boland did it again. The House approved a Boland-sponsored measure to cut off all covert aid by September 30. The Senate did not follow suit, so the House passed yet another Boland initiative in October, and finally succeeded at capping funding for the Contra war at $24 million when the measure went to the House-Senate conference. Reagan "thinks he's John Wayne," O'Neill told Mary McGrory. Focusing on El Salvador and Nicaragua, the House Democrats overlooked the warnings that had begun to appear in Reagan's speeches about the Cuban labor battalion building a military-sized airport with a cooperative Marxist government on the tiny Caribbean island of Grenada.[5]

As the jousting between O'Neill and Reagan over both domestic politics and Central America stuttered toward stalemate, the pace of the debate over the administration's foreign policy in another region was accelerating. In 1982, in the aftermath of Israel's disastrous invasion of Lebanon and the massacre of 700 Palestinians at the Sabra and Shatila refugee camps, Reagan had dispatched a small contingent of 800 marines to Beirut as part of an international peacekeeping force. O'Neill tried to be supportive, even as it became clear that the peacekeepers had walked into a raging war zone; the U.S. force grew to 1,600 marines and half a dozen were killed.

In September 1983, after Reagan called him to the White House and appealed to his sense of patriotism, O'Neill worked to defuse a mutiny by House liberals, who were ready to give Reagan a ninety-day deadline to withdraw the marines. The President and the Speaker reached an agreement: Reagan would acknowledge that the restrictions of the War Powers Act applied to Lebanon and, in return, the House would agree to let the marines stay for another eighteen months. "We can't cut bait and run in Beirut. The people of the world would lose faith, because we are the last bastion of freedom in the world," O'Neill said.

"I believe that the Commander-in-Chief's first concern is for the safety of the fighting men in Lebanon," O'Neill promised a solemn, hushed House. It was one of those rare occasions, members of Congress said later, that a speech from the floor changed many votes. The resolution passed. After a summer in which he battled a painful sinus infection, and hit an impasse on the budget, the Speaker felt on top of his game. Reagan was grateful. "I know you were as gratified as I with Sunday's announcement of a cease fire in Lebanon," Reagan wrote O'Neill in a personal note on September 27. "While there were many things that contributed to the cease fire, it is my belief that your agreement to advance the compromise resolution on war powers . . . [was] particularly important."

Reagan's optimism was tragically misplaced. Early in the morning of Sunday October 23, a suicidal terrorist driving a truck packed with high explosives rammed his way into the courtyard of the building used as a barracks by the marines in Beirut. The building was obliterated, and 241 marines died. Isolated among warring, well-armed militias, the young Americans had been sitting ducks. O'Neill was alerted by the State Department, which called him at home at 6 A.M. that Sunday. He was publicly supportive — to withdraw precipitously "would be the worst possible thing we could do," he said — and privately shaken. The President was the commander in chief, but in this case the Speaker, as leader of the opposition, had shared the responsibility of sending young men to die. In his press conference that Monday, he looked pained and defensive as he put down his cigar, took off his glasses, and tried to explain things to the crowd of reporters.

"When we discussed this at various briefings at the White House, we never took into consideration that a terrorist movement of this type would take place," O'Neill confessed. "It is easy to say, 'Bring the boys home.' But what is the depth behind the whole thing? Do we want to split Lebanon and have it taken over by the Syrians?

"What would happen to free Europe in the event they would lose the [Middle East] oil fields to Russia?" he said. "I think, personally, to pick up and run would send a terrible message, particularly to moderate Arabs of that area who are depending on us, and to the terrorists of the world who have said they could drive us out.

"I don't see this to be a political issue. I hope my party, which is asking for a caucus, believes that we are Americans first and Democrats second," the Speaker said. He was faithful to his agreement with Reagan, and giving the President valuable political cover in the wake of the disaster.

That afternoon, as O'Neill and other House leaders were being briefed on the events in Lebanon by Cap Weinberger and Secretary of State George Shultz (who had replaced Haig), a White House car carrying Jim Baker and Ken Duberstein sneaked onto the Capitol grounds. Using back staircases and little-known connecting doors, the two Reagan aides evaded the press and arrived in the Speaker's office. Kirk O'Donnell sent a note in to O'Neill, telling him to excuse himself without saying why. Baker then asked the Speaker to attend an urgent, secret meeting at the White House that night. At 7 P.M., O'Neill and O'Donnell entered the White House via a roundabout route through the Executive Office Building. In the mess they found Bob Michel, Bob Byrd, Jim Wright and Howard Baker waiting. They drank coffee and watched a cockroach scuttle across a table. After sneaking through the empty Oval Office and the Rose Garden to avoid reporters, the silent procession arrived in the President's private residence, where members of the Joint Chiefs of Staff and the cabinet had gathered. Reagan told the congressmen what O'Neill had predicted to O'Donnell in the car on the way over: the meeting was not about Lebanon, it was about Grenada.

"There was an awful lot of seriousness at that meeting," Duberstein recalled. "This was a fundamental decision for the U.S. government. Somber. Quiet. No rhetoric. No posturing." O'Neill sat next to Reagan. "You are informing us, not asking us," O'Neill said, and Reagan acknowledged that was true. But from time to time, O'Neill would reach over and reassuringly touch the President on the arm. Reagan had made the decision to invade Grenada to protect a group of several hundred American medical students who attended school there from being injured or taken hostage in an ongoing coup d'état, and to end the Cuban threat. O'Neill passed around a letter that had been written to him by Representative Michael Barnes of Maryland, which argued that the administration needed to build a better public case for its intervention in Lebanon by having Reagan address a joint session of Congress. "I need some help. The President has to do something like this," O'Neill said, extending the reasoning to Grenada as well. Wright was quite supportive, saying that he hoped the U.S. would use massive force, having learned a lesson from the Bay of Pigs and Carter's failed Iranian rescue mission. Privately, O'Neill and Wright worried that Reagan's vision of American GIs "greeted by crowds waving little American flags and throwing flowers" smacked a little too much of a World War II movie. Reagan left the meeting at one point to talk to Thatcher, who opposed the invasion but could not change his mind.

As the meeting came to a close, O'Neill "kept his own counsel," said Duberstein, but told Reagan, "Good luck." Reagan and Duberstein thought O'Neill meant to be comforting and supportive, but Baker later interpreted the Speaker's words as telling the President, "You're on your own." The invasion began a few hours later. O'Neill was back at the White House for a more general briefing with a wider array of congressmen that morning, then met the press before the day's session. Again, he was supportive. "This is no time for the press, or we in public life, to be critical of our government," said O'Neill. "In trying moments, it's no time for the leadership, when we have the Marines there at the present time, for me to be criticizing my country."[6]

After unexpectedly bloody fighting, in which 115 Americans were wounded and 19 were killed, the U.S. troops restored order and discovered a cache of arms that included rocket launchers, armored vehicles and artillery. The surviving Cubans were sent home, and TV crews filmed the medical students, who arrived in the U.S. the day after the invasion, kissing American soil in gratitude. The public overwhelmingly supported the mission, and Reagan's approval rating in the polls shot up to 63 percent.

A restless Democratic caucus met behind closed doors on October 26. O'Neill once again took on his liberal critics and, with yet another passionate speech, deflected efforts to pass a resolution calling for a U.S. withdrawal from Lebanon by the end of the year. "Have we got a reason to be there? You bet we have a reason to be there, and make no mistake about it," O'Neill said. "Russia . . . has her eyes on that Persian Gulf. It is an opportunity and it is a means. Syria is her satellite and make no mistake about it.

"As the leader of your party, elected by you, I am not talking as a Democrat. Yes, I love partisans. They say I am the toughest partisan that has ever been in this House. I love politics. They say I am one of the toughest politicians in America, and I am proud of people like that."

But "I am an American, and at a time of patriotism . . . I think what is in the best interest of this nation and I try to lead my party down that road. I don't look to the next election. I don't look to the fear of being defeated in the ballot box," the Speaker said. His face was red and he spoke with emotion.

And then, after all this effort, the alliance between the Speaker and the President fell apart. The cause of the split was Reagan's decision, when addressing Congress and the nation on the night of October 27, to include Nicaragua in the list of targets of Soviet expansionism. O'Neill erupted, furious at how the President's speech had not been limited to Lebanon and Grenada, but had also singled out Nicaragua as a target of Soviet expansionism. That wasn't part of the deal. Reagan was now exploiting the Speaker's patriotism to promote a policy that O'Neill detested.

"He is wrong. To be perfectly truthful, he frightens me. I think he was looking for a reason to go there and he found the opportunity last week," O'Neill told the press, as it all came pouring out on October 28. "We can't go with gunboat diplomacy. The Marines did a tremendous job down there, but we can't continue that route — going into Nicaragua and places like that. His policy is wrong and frightening." The Speaker's outburst sounded, and was so reported in the press, like criticism of Reagan's invasion of Grenada. When *Times* columnist James Reston visited a few days later, O'Neill unloaded again. It was "sinful" that such a shortsighted and lazy man was President, O'Neill said. Reagan should pass up the chance to run for reelection, said the Speaker, and return to California where the First Lady could be "queen of Beverly Hills."[7]

The weeks dragged on, and the situation in Lebanon slipped into chaos. In the aftermath of the Reagan administration's own scathing investigation of what had gone wrong in Beirut, and after hearing from White House officials that a change in policy was in store, O'Neill announced that he was rethinking his position and might support an

American pullout. "He may be ready to surrender, but I'm not," Reagan told the press. It was a cheap shot, since the White House had already made the decision to withdraw. In April, Reagan used a prime-time news conference to accuse O'Neill and other congressional critics of undermining the marine mission and providing comfort to terrorists. The Speaker lashed back with his toughest language yet. "The deaths of the U.S. Marines are the responsibility of the President of the United States," O'Neill told the press. "He is looking for a scapegoat. The deaths lie on him and the defeat in Lebanon lies on him and him alone."

After all he had done for the President, O'Neill thought that Reagan's attack on his patriotism was "despicable." But the White House had skillfully manipulated the Speaker — getting him to endorse an unpopular and unwise exercise in Lebanon, employing him for cover when it went sour, and then using Grenada to make the case for an intervention that O'Neill opposed in Nicaragua. At each step of the way, O'Neill had allowed the White House to snooker him on the politics. "They hoodwinked me," he admitted.

"Tip never got over that. He felt he had been misled. He never forgave them," said Murtha. "His personal relationship with Reagan changed." O'Neill resolved to not let it happen again, and soon got a chance to retaliate.[8]

THE MX NUCLEAR missile system was a legacy of the Carter administration, whose military planners had decided they could protect the hydra-headed missile from Soviet attack by applying the principles of the age-old shell and pea game, with 200 missiles shuttled among 4,600 launch sites via underground rail systems, so an enemy would never be sure where they were. Though Reagan rejected Carter's underground rail system in 1981, he pressed Congress for the funds to build and deploy MX missiles in existing silos.

To the Reagan strategic arms buildup, O'Neill had offered a multi-pronged response. He endorsed and spoke out for the public movement to "freeze" the U.S. and Soviet nuclear arsenals, but also supported funding for the MX, if only so the system could be used as a bargaining chip in strategic arms negotiations. And, worried that his party would be tainted as soft on defense, the Speaker gave his blessing to efforts led by Les Aspin and Representative Albert Gore to develop a Democratic strategy that could meet Reagan halfway on nuclear arms issues. With O'Neill's approval, Aspin and Gore pushed a compromise in which

100 MX missiles would be built in return for development of a less-destabilizing, single-warhead "Midgetman" missile.

That, at least, is where events stood when O'Neill got hoodwinked on Lebanon and Grenada. After Reagan accused him of cowardice and of coddling terrorists, the Speaker joined the MX opponents, led by Dick Gephardt and Tony Coelho, and in a series of close votes in late May stopped production of the missile. "The leadership decided they wanted to win this one," said a disappointed Aspin. "The MX will never be deployed," the Speaker crowed.

O'Neill got another opportunity for vengeance when, in the months before the 1984 election, news broke that the CIA was mining Nicaraguan harbors and distributing guerrilla-training manuals that offered tips on terrorism and assassination to right-wing forces in Central America. The Contras were "marauders, murderers and rapists," O'Neill said, as he joined again with Boland to cut off U.S. funds to the Contra army. The measure passed the House, and on October 12, 1984, Reagan was compelled to sign the second of Boland's funding bans into law. Known as "Boland II," it was far more restrictive than its predecessor, and forbade the expenditure of funds, by any U.S. government agency, to help the Contras. Reagan administration officials, looking for a loophole, decided that the White House's own National Security Council did not fit the legal definition of a government "agency," and was thus exempt from Boland II. At the NSC, a boyish, gap-toothed marine lieutenant colonel was given the Contra brief. His name was Oliver North.[9]

"Tip was an old-fashioned pol: He could be sincere and friendly when he wanted to be, but when it came to the things he believed in, he could turn off his charm and friendship like a light switch and become as bloodthirsty as a piranha," Reagan wrote in his memoirs. "Until six o'clock, I was the enemy and he never let me forget it."

"Tip has joined that chorus back here that's bent on a lynching, with me in the noose," Reagan wrote to Frank Sinatra when, toward the end of the President's term, the famed singer suggested that O'Neill be appointed ambassador to Ireland.

And yet, despite their profound differences, O'Neill and Reagan had a begrudging regard for each other, recognized each other as professionals and were not averse to some mutual political back-scratching. "Kenny Duberstein and I were the only two guys who were there when Reagan had Tip upstairs, in the family dining room, for his seventieth birthday," said Deaver. "And God it was just amazing. Kenny and I sat there with these two old Irishmen, and they told Irish jokes back and forth, and about 1 P.M. Reagan, who really didn't drink — I mean he would have a screwdriver occasionally or a glass of wine — rings the buzzer for the butler and orders a bottle of champagne."

The butler poured the champagne and the President said, "Tip, if I had a ticket to heaven and you didn't have one too, I would give mine away and go to hell with you."

Said Deaver: "It was an old Irish toast he had heard somewhere. Well, Tip's eyes were all filled up, you know, it was just incredible. And they left the dining room with their arms around each other's waist and Reagan took him down to the elevator and Tip went out on the South Lawn and beat the shit out of Reagan with the press.

"Reagan thought Tip was absolutely wrong, and pigheaded. And Tip thought Reagan didn't understand anything about this country except the rich," said Deaver. "But there was a lot of respect that both of them had for each other." O'Neill later wrote Reagan, thanking him for "a birthday I will never forget."

In 1981, O'Neill showed up at the White House with a present for the President: the gavel with which the Speaker had failed to block passage of the Reagan tax and budget plan that summer. When a liberal Christian activist named Mitch Snyder went on a protest fast because the navy was going to name an attack submarine the *Corpus Christi,* which in Latin means "Body of Christ," O'Neill called the White House, and warned them that he and the Roman Catholic hierarchy weren't happy with the name either. Reagan ordered the Pentagon to change it to *The City of Corpus Christi*.

O'Neill was more than merciful with Reagan appointees who ran into ethics scrapes; the Speaker didn't much like media feeding frenzies and worked to rein in House Democrats who were investigating Jim Baker and Environmental Protection Agency administrator Anne Gorsuch. When all was said and done, Reagan and O'Neill liked each other just enough to be hurt, and angered, by the other's actions. A 1984 letter from Reagan to a New York man captured the tension in the relationship, and might just as easily have been written by O'Neill about the President.

"I don't think you've seen me embracing or being embraced by Speaker O'Neill recently. And, yes, I find some of his personal attacks hard to forgive," Reagan wrote a supporter in 1984. "He's an old time politico. Earlier in my term and before recent events, he explained away some of his partisan attacks as politics and that after 6 P.M. we were friends. Well, that's more than a little difficult for me to accept lately.

"But . . . there are certain things I cannot do if I'm to carry out my responsibilities," said Reagan. "I can't publicly refuse to be civil, nor can I show anger and resentment."[10]

Their Irish ancestry was one thing that O'Neill and Reagan had in common. Throughout the Reagan years, they worked together on a secret diplomatic initiative on Northern Ireland that had far-reaching results. The Speaker, ably assisted by O'Donnell, had now eclipsed Ted Kennedy as a central figure in Irish American affairs. Great Britain needed to seize the moment, O'Neill believed, but Margaret Thatcher was preoccupied with her own Conservative revolution — a historic dismantling of the British welfare state — as the awful cycle of violence and retribution in Northern Ireland continued.[11] When Belfast Catholics elected Bobby Sands, an IRA hunger striker, to an open seat in the British House of Commons in the spring of 1981, Thatcher refused to make even symbolic concessions to terrorists. She had lost close friends and countrymen at the hands of the IRA and seen the grieving faces of their widows and children. In a telegram, the Four Horsemen questioned her "inflexibility." Thatcher wrote back: "The government will not compromise." O'Neill turned to Reagan.

"Intense media coverage of the hunger strike in the United States has dramatically improved the image of the Provisional IRA among 35 million Irish-Americans and reversed a five-year trend of declining financial support of the IRA," O'Neill wrote the President on May 19, 1981. "Members of the IRA are terrorists and should be treated as such. But by refusing to negotiate regarding prison rules, Mrs. Thatcher is permitting the terrorists to undo significant political progress." But Reagan turned down O'Neill's request that he intercede. Sands and nine other hunger strikers died.

So matters stood in November 1982, when O'Donnell met with James Sharkey, who had replaced Michael Lillis as the Irish embassy's political counselor, to see what could be done to salvage the situation. The hunger strike and its violent aftermath had set back the prospects for peace, they decided, and the Four Horsemen were too identifiably Democratic. With a Republican President who had a close relationship with Thatcher, and who had explored his own Irish roots in a visit to his ancestral town of Ballyporeen during the summer of 1984 (O'Neill delighted in telling Reagan that the name meant "valley of the small potatoes"), it was time to make Ireland a bipartisan issue.

The key figure was Judge William Clark, a former California supreme court justice who served as deputy secretary of state and Reagan's national security adviser before becoming secretary of the interior. Clark was one of those rare Irish Americans who, like O'Neill, maintained an educated interest in Irish affairs. Clark knew how the indefatigable John Hume, with the help of the Irish government, was trying to revive the peace process. But Thatcher, who had just narrowly escaped harm when the IRA bombed a Conservative Party conference in October, had rejected proposals for Catholic and Protestant power-sharing with "out . . . out . . . out." The Irish decided to play the American card. Appeals were made to Clark and O'Neill, who once more appealed to Reagan.

A month after her "out . . . out . . . out" press conference, when Thatcher was due to visit Washington, O'Neill asked Reagan — Irishman to Irishman — to prod the prime minister on the Irish question. "The negotiations between the Irish and the British government were very difficult, largely because Mrs. Thatcher was extremely, viscerally uncomfortable with the notion of giving the Irish government any role whatsoever in her sovereign territory of Northern Ireland," Lillis recalled. "O'Neill was very active and effective in mobilizing the President. And there is no doubt whatsoever that Reagan's regular references to this in his interaction with Thatcher helped us in a major way."

"I want to personally share with you my deep concern," O'Neill wrote to Reagan on December 13, 1984. "The best hope for a peaceful, lawful and constitutional resolution to the tragedy of Northern Ireland may be in serious jeopardy as a result of Mrs. Thatcher's public statements."

After meeting with Thatcher at the presidential retreat at Camp David on December 22, Reagan replied to the Speaker on January 9, 1985. "I made a special effort to bring your letter to her personal attention and to convey your message of concern," the President wrote. "I also personally emphasized the need for progress in resolving the complex situation in Northern Ireland, and the desirability for flexibility on the part of all the involved parties."

(Reagan's intervention wasn't totally altruistic; the White House was displeased with the Speaker and the Republic of Ireland for their leftist stands on Nicaragua and "we hoped to use this as a lever against Tip in order to get Contra aid moving," wrote one National Security Council official in a memo.)

O'Neill pressed the issue when Thatcher visited Washington again in February, and she was granted the privilege of addressing Congress only after the Speaker was satisfied she was being more receptive on Northern Ireland. O'Neill received her in his private office, which was decorated with a photograph of his ancestral home in Ireland, a painting of Jefferson and Adams collaborating on the Declaration of Independence, a painting of Washington taking command of the Continental Army on Cambridge Common, and the model of Old Ironsides. "There wasn't a single thing in there that wasn't an irritant to the United Kingdom," O'Donnell recalled. "The only diplomatic thing that Thatcher could do was seize on a photograph of an O'Neill family reunion and say, 'Who is this?' and 'Who is this?'"

Thatcher's instincts and advisers told her she was being too intransigent, and she bent to Reagan's appeals. In November 1985, after months of negotiations, Thatcher and Irish prime minister Garret FitzGerald signed the Anglo-Irish agreement, in which their two governments recognized each other's interest in Northern Ireland; agreed that any change in status would have to be made by the majority of the people of Ulster; and promised to work together to end the violence. O'Neill had won Reagan's support for a $250 million package of aid for Ireland, to be announced that same day. When the State Department dragged its heels, O'Neill called the President. A few moments later, the White House called back. "Okay, we'll go along," said Reagan. "We politicians don't break our word."

Thatcher "didn't want to get on the wrong track with Reagan," said FitzGerald. He called O'Neill "the consistently most helpful ally Ireland has ever had in Washington." Sean Donlon recalled that "the intervention by Reagan was vital, and it was made possible by Tip."

In her memoirs, Thatcher assessed the results of the Anglo-Irish agreement as "disappointing." Yet it provided a framework for discussions and kept the peace process alive until Hume (again with the help of Irish Americans, and an American President) could convince Sinn

Fein and the IRA to seek a political resolution of the Troubles and come to the bargaining table in the 1990s. The Carter and Reagan initiatives, which O'Neill had helped bring about, were "the beginning," said Donlon. "The American involvement continued, and was highlighted once President Clinton came to office and advanced it to a whole new phase."[12]

CHAPTER 26

Newt

UNLIKE REAGAN and O'Neill, Newt Gingrich's political beliefs had not been cast in the Depression and World War II eras. He was a baby boomer, nerdy, the insecure product of a broken home, but bright and precocious, with a bent for public life. "I think you can write a psychological profile of me that says I found a way to immerse my insecurities in a cause large enough to justify whatever I wanted it to," he said. After unsuccessfully challenging the local Democratic machine in a suburban Atlanta district in 1974 and 1976, Gingrich finally triumphed and was elected to Congress in 1978. He was thirty-five, a college professor by then — a glib and audacious libertarian with a personal sense of destiny and a vision of the great revolution he would lead against the evil welfare state. He allied himself with Republican Young Turks like Representative Robert Walker of Pennsylvania, Jack Kemp, and David Stockman, predicted he would one day be Speaker and quickly made a mark in the House with his mop of graying hair, preternatural confidence and provocative sound bites.

Gingrich chafed at the air of resignation he found among House

Republicans — many of whom had concluded that their minority status was a permanent affliction, and that their most achievable ambition was to become the ranking Republican members of committees like Public Works or Appropriations, where they could cut deals with the Democratic chairmen. "This party does not need another generation of cautious, prudent, careful, bland, irrelevant, quasi-leaders who are willing as people to drift into positions because nobody else is available. What we really need are people who are tough, hard-working, energetic, willing to take risks, willing to stand up in a slug fest and match it out with their opponent," he said.

"One of the great problems we have in the Republican Party is that we don't encourage you to be nasty. We encourage you to be neat, obedient and loyal and faithful and all those Boy Scout words, which would be great around a campfire but are lousy in politics," Gingrich said. He set out to get nasty.

Reagan's election gave the young conservatives hope and a cause, but after the setback of 1982 they concluded that the House Republicans needed a more militant and aggressive strategy. Bob Michel, the GOP leader, was O'Neill's friend and golfing partner. Though Michel and the Speaker had their run-ins, and the Republican leader had given no quarter in the budget and tax wars of 1981, he was still a man of the old school, in which courtesy and friendship were important values. The Speaker respected Michel, and when hard economic times in his Peoria, Illinois, district threatened to cost the GOP leader his seat in 1982 and 1984, O'Neill had reined in the Democratic dogs.

So Gingrich, nothing if not audacious, set out to create his own majority. One of his first steps was to organize, with Walker, Representative Vin Weber of Minnesota and several dozen like-minded Republicans, a "Conservative Opportunity Society" (COS) to wage guerrilla warfare against O'Neill's Democrats. These were not mossbacks — they listened to futurists like Alvin Toffler, who told them that the "second wave" industrial era, conducive to massive, collectivistic, bureaucratic New Deal–style solutions, was being replaced by the entrepreneurial, quick-footed, information-based "third wave." Said Gingrich: "We are all a band of brothers and sisters in a genuine revolutionary movement. . . . What I want to do is replace a decaying, out-of-touch second-wave system with a 21st century, information age citizen-led system."

Armed with the power of their ideas, and an unquenchable esprit de corps, the Republican backbenchers had one other formidable weapon in their arsenal: television. "We had ended up with an activist corps, optimistic about our agenda but frustrated with the process and increasingly frustrated with the Republican leadership that seemed to be more accommodationist," said Walker. "There were a lot of us running off doing various things in various ways. I was on the floor. Newt was doing the visionary stuff. Weber was working with new members. You had a group of people who began to meet in Newt's office, talking through Newt's ideas of saving the Western World. But we faced the question of how we were going to make an impact." Walker told the others of an interesting phenomenon: at party conventions, the Republican faithful knew who he was, and came up to thank him, because they had seen him on C-SPAN.

"I was amazed at the outside impact of my tactics on the floor," he recalled. "The C-SPAN coverage of Congress was reaching the country. And we realized that there were times — early in the day with the one-minute speeches or late in the day with special orders — when we could actually take control of the floor agenda. We could actually control very large blocks of time."[1]

It was O'Neill who had brought the television cameras into the House, albeit under steady pressure from the broadcast industry, congressional barons like Bernie Sisk and Jack Brooks, and media-hip reformers like John Anderson and Al Gore. Although televised Senate hearings had helped make national celebrities of Jack Kennedy and Estes Kefauver (and helped ruin Joe McCarthy), the House had a traumatic formative experience with the medium. In 1957, the House Committee on Un-American Activities, off on one of its witch hunts, had ignored Sam Rayburn's ban on televised hearings and a terrified witness committed suicide rather than face the cameras. It was not until 1970 that, in the course of deliberations over the same legislative reorganization act that ended teller voting, O'Neill offered a compromise to a Rules Committee that was divided over Sisk's motion to televise the House and its committees. Younger House Democrats were frustrated by Richard Nixon's near monopoly of television, which the President effectively employed to defend his conduct of the Vietnam War. Traditionalists, however, correctly foresaw that the installation of TV cameras would radically alter the culture of the House. "To see if we can get somewhere on this — the old axiom you have to creep before you walk — why not strike out the House but go along with the committees?" O'Neill said. "If in the wisdom of the House it is felt it has worked well in committees, at a later date we can amend it to put in the House." His compromise passed the Rules Committee and was preserved on the floor by a 96 to 93 vote. The Judiciary Committee's star turn during the televised Watergate impeachment hearings then eased the fears of many members. But others — citing the networks' captious coverage of national political conventions — continued to resist. "Some of our brothers think better with their eyes closed, and if they were so perceived on the television set it might be misunderstood back home," Brooks said.

In 1976, Sisk was back with a resolution to permit a pool of network cameras to broadcast sessions of the House. "Supporters of the House floor television coverage argue that since the majority of the American people rely upon the electronic media as their major source of information, televised House floor debates will expose the people to the process in which their laws are created and thus develop a more informed electorate. Supporters also feel that broadcasting the proceedings will help to counter the advantage the President has in television and radio coverage," Jerry Colbert, O'Neill's media adviser, told him. "Opponents of the measure fear a destruction of the legislative process on the floor" and the transformation of the House into "a TV stage." But Colbert warned O'Neill that under Sisk's plan for a network pool, Congress would "enter the communication revolution with the means of communicating its message to the American public surrendered to a few network individuals in New York." He urged O'Neill to allow televised sessions, but to keep tight control of the cameras, and to limit the coverage to one major debate each week because that "would go a long way towards controlling what the leadership wanted communicated."

In early 1976, having been handed the issue by the retiring Carl Albert, O'Neill announced that he would let the cameras in, but that they would be owned and operated by the House and under the control of the Speaker. In June 1978, the House defeated a last stand by the pro-network forces and voted by 235 to 150 to proceed with its own cameras. Al Gore gave the first televised speech, a one-minute tribute to the occasion, on March 19, 1979. O'Neill wore a blue suit, had his hair trimmed and lost weight (this time on a high-protein, no-carbohydrate diet) for the occasion.

At first, the televised sessions were a novelty, useful mainly for showing members and staff what was happening on the floor. But

Brian Lamb, a journalist and former disc jockey, had concocted a plan to assemble a network of cable television companies, which he called the Cable-Satellite Public Affairs Network, to carry the House broadcast into the nation's living rooms. Lamb's father had run a tavern in Lafayette, Indiana, that was a hangout for local newspapermen and helped make his boy a news junkie. When the navy stationed him in Washington during the Vietnam War era, Lamb used his off-duty hours to drop in on famous trials, protest marches and congressional debates. He stayed on to work in the Nixon White House and as a press secretary for a Republican senator. When Lamb got in to see the Speaker, "I was a nervous wreck. I was shaking," he recalled. But he persuaded O'Neill the idea had merit. "I don't think, to this day, that he understood what was going to happen," Lamb said. "And I'll never understand why he did what he did. He had nothing to win in the process, except a little openness."

O'Neill gave his blessing, and the House signal, to C-SPAN. Though the initial feed went out to only 3.5 million cable-fitted households, it served the Speaker's need for a public outlet that he could use to counter the demands of the three big broadcast networks. "He was not real excited about televising the House floor proceedings," said Charlie Rose. "But he thought it was something that was coming, and his weathervane told him this was something he ought to get out in front of, and not get overrun by, so he could in fact control it."

Over time, C-SPAN picked up viewers. Conservatives, always wary of the liberal media, especially prized C-SPAN's neutrality. The exciting stakes of the Reagan revolution, much of which was fought out on the House floor, helped build the audience. Soon the one-minute speeches that began each day and the longer special orders that ended them, in which any representative could take the floor and speak about any subject, became valuable and inviolate rights for members of the postreform House. By 1986 the Senate, fearful that the televised House was becoming the predominant congressional body, followed with its own electronic era.

Television was a perfect vehicle for Gingrich's plans: it poorly conveyed the subtleties of compromise and instead rewarded controversy, polarization, symbolic amendments and the repetitious presentment of partisan themes. "C-SPAN does work best for the minority party. The majority controls the process — and looks like it's closing things down," Walker said. When he challenged the Democratic leaders on the floor, "the phones in my office would light up," he recalled. By 1984, C-SPAN's potential audience had spread to 16 million homes and included some 200,000 devoted viewers. "Newt immediately understood this was a great opportunity," Walker said.[2]

As early as his freshman term, Gingrich had earned O'Neill's scorn as a "radical." Then, in the weeks after the 1980 election, Gingrich had dispatched emissaries to the boll weevils — asking them to join in a conservative coalition that would strip O'Neill of the Speaker's office. The Democratic leadership had been forced to hustle, and make concessions that later drew fire from the ranks of House liberals, to end the threat. "The coalition project has already racked up several important achievements," Gingrich wrote to conservative activist Paul Weyrich that December. "We have forced O'Neill to use strong arm tactics on his own people . . . set into motion the weakening of O'Neill's power . . . made our future attacks on O'Neill credible." Gingrich always kept the long-term goal, of a Republican House, foremost in mind. "That we haven't removed O'Neill yet should not discourage us. While the temptation to despair because of this short-term 'failure' may be overwhelming, our people must see that we have achieved much, much more than we had a right to expect." O'Neill and Gingrich had tangled in the fight over TEFRA in 1982 and when the Speaker had lost his temper on the floor in 1981 and made the crack about the Republicans' lack of "breeding." When Representative Gerry Studds was censured by the House in 1983 for having sex with a seventeen-year-old male congressional page, Gingrich had tried to have him expelled from the House. O'Neill was a homophobe, but Studds was, after all, a Massachusetts Democrat.[3]

Gingrich was at his most effective when stoking Republican resentment of Democratic tactics. The House Democrats viewed themselves as an imperiled minority during the Reagan era and so felt justified in taking a hardball approach. During O'Neill's terms as Speaker, a compliant Rules Committee began to make restrictive rules the norm. The GOP's power to offer amendments, move to recommit legislation and raise points of order was restrained. In committee, the chairmen used proxy voting to bottle up Republican bills and otherwise frustrate the GOP, and majority staffs exploited their power to "correct" the record by rewriting hearing transcripts to the Democrats' advantage. The

Democratic attitude was "Hey, we've got the votes. Let's vote. Screw you," said Joe Moakley.

Writing to his fellow Republicans, Gingrich charged that O'Neill's "savage liberal partisanship" led to high-handed efforts to "stack and rig the game." The GOP members, who were in the distinctly stressful psychological state of being under the thumb of a besieged minority, were increasingly receptive to Gingrich's message. Matters came to a head in May 1984 when O'Neill used his power over House television to incite a Republican revolt.[4]

"Camscam," as it was called, began routinely on May 8 when Gingrich and Walker used special-order time to present a report, written by Gingrich aide Frank Gregorsky, accusing the Democrats of being apologists for Communist regimes. Gregorsky had gone back to the Vietnam era and assembled a list of dovish statements made by Democrats over the years, and one of those targeted was Eddie Boland, the bane of the Contra armies. O'Neill was already under pressure from the Democratic caucus to rein in Gingrich and crew, when he chanced to hear the attack on Boland. "Tip felt he could ignore Gingrich like a mosquito," New York congresswoman Geraldine Ferraro recalled, "but after a period of time people began to tell him that he better be careful because the mosquito was carrying malaria."

The Speaker was particularly angered by Gingrich's suggestion that Boland and the other Democrats cited in his speech did not have the courage to rise and defend themselves. The House rules governing television required that the camera remain fixed on whoever was talking, and O'Neill reckoned that the viewers at home did not realize that the day's legislative session was over, that people had gone home, and that Gingrich was speaking to an empty chamber.

"Tip thought Newt was calling people Communists. What Newt had said was that they sounded like Communists and he challenged them to tell the difference," said Walker. "We occasionally made the assertion: If anybody disagrees, why don't you come down here and disagree with us. We would do it rhetorically. We wanted to get the debate on."

O'Neill didn't see it that way. The Speaker called Charlie Rose, whose subcommittee administered the television system, and told him to have a caption written to inform the audience that the House had completed its legislative work and was in special-order time. To drive the message home, O'Neill told Rose to have the cameras pan the chamber and show the empty House. "Tip was fed up," said House parliamentarian Charles Johnson.

Though O'Neill's orders were within his authority, he purposely neglected to inform the Republicans. On Thursday night, May 10, as Walker spoke on the floor during another special order, the House cameras showed him speaking to an empty room. "Walker looked like a fool," O'Neill recalled, with satisfaction, years later. The camera trick was spotted immediately in the Republican cloakroom, and Walker — still on television — was handed a note. "It is my understanding that as I deliver this special order here this evening, the cameras are panning this chamber, demonstrating that there is no one here," he said. "It is one more example of how this body is run: the kind of arrogance of power that the members are given that kind of change with absolutely no warning."

Minority leader Michel and GOP whip Trent Lott, who had a hands-off relationship with the COS brigands, were bound by Republican solidarity to support their injured brethren. Michel accused O'Neill of an "act of dictatorial retribution." The debate was renewed when the House returned on Monday, and Walker and Michel and O'Neill tangled on the floor. The Speaker said he took action because Gingrich had misled viewers by "stepping aside, debating and pointing — as if there were people on this floor — asking, 'Why don't you get up and answer?'

"A more low thing I have never seen," O'Neill said. "The prerogative of the rules of this House give me the right to stop that, give me the right to say when there will be a wide lens and when there should not be a wide lens. . . . Nothing in the rules says that I have to notify you. Courtesy probably said that I should have. That is a courtesy your member never gave to the 20 members he accused on the floor of the House."

Lott reached Gingrich at lunch in Georgia. "You better get up here," Lott said. "Tip O'Neill just attacked you." Gingrich demanded a "point of personal privilege" on Tuesday, May 15, to respond to the Speaker's assault.

"Mr. Speaker, yesterday in my absence the Speaker made certain allegations which are inaccurate and which require correction," Gingrich said.

"The chair recognizes the gentleman," O'Neill replied. "The House will be in order. Members will take their seats. The chair wants to listen with keen interest to the gentleman from Georgia."

As Gingrich began to talk, he was interrupted by Democrats who asked him to yield for questions. After Jim Wright had used one such opening to lecture Gingrich about "impugning one another's patriotism," the Georgia congressman refused to yield any further.

"He is willing to engage in debate when the members are not here whose patriotism he impugns, but he is not willing to engage in debate when we are here," Wright responded.

At this point, Gingrich was faring poorly. The Democrats should have let him finish his speech and sit down. But O'Neill now interrupted. The Speaker had made the mistake of staying on the floor, his anger building. "The madder he got, the cooler I got. And I was supposed to cower or apologize or kowtow because he was the Speaker and I did not," said Gingrich.

"Let us look at the truth," O'Neill said.

"I reclaim my time . . ." said Gingrich.

"I would like to have a dialog on what happened. You are making accusations. . . . ," O'Neill said.

The Speaker was raising his voice now and shaking his finger at Gingrich. Across the aisle, the Republicans were shouting and laughing.

O'Neill lost it. "My personal opinion is this: You deliberately stood in that well before an empty House and challenged these people, and you challenged their Americanism, and it is the lowest thing that I have ever seen in my 32 years in Congress," the Speaker said.

Personal insults are not allowed on the House floor. "He can't say that," Republican floor aide Billy Pitts told Lott, who stood up and asked to be recognized. "I demand that the Speaker's words be taken down," the whip said, citing the House rule against offensive language that dated back to Thomas Jefferson. Everything came to a sudden halt. The press galleries were abuzz. Ari Weiss rushed over to Lott's desk. "Can't we work something out? Can't he withdraw it?" he asked. "It's out of my hands," said Pitts.

As fate (and O'Neill) would have it, Moakley was in the chair. Moakley turned to parliamentarian Bill Brown. "I have heard a lot worse in the Massachusetts House," the South Boston Democrat said. But the conclusion was inescapable: O'Neill had crossed the line. The Speaker had gotten away with calling Gingrich "low" the previous day, but only because no one had challenged him. Over the years, the House had banned such gentle epithets as "snoop," "canard" and "hypocritical." In 1946, Sam Rayburn had stricken the statement of a New York congressman who noted mildly, "I cannot respect the actions or even the sincerity of some of the committee members." When Brown and Charles Johnson assured Moakley that O'Neill would want a fair decision, Moakley suspected they were overstating the Speaker's thirst for justice. But in the end he had little choice.

"The chair feels that that type of characterization should not be used in debate," Moakley said.

By rights, O'Neill should have been banned from speaking for the rest of the day. Lott, with gleeful magnanimity, asked that the Speaker be absolved of that humiliating punishment. Triumphantly wounded, Gingrich declared, "In many ways, it is my patriotism being impugned. I am as sincerely committed to the survival of this country, Mr. Speaker, as you are."

"I am not questioning the gentleman's patriotism. I am questioning his judgment. I also question the judgment of the chair," O'Neill said, glaring at the morose Moakley. "I was expressing an opinion. As a matter of fact, I was expressing my opinion very mildly, because I think much worse than what I said."

Jim Wright, David Obey and other Democrats came to O'Neill's aid. But it was too late. Gingrich had carried the day, and House Republicans gave him a standing ovation as he packed up his papers and relinquished the floor. "Gingrich . . . really is a shrill and shameless little demagogue," Wright wrote in his diary that night. O'Neill had been "less offensive by far than the rotten, self-serving claptrap of Gingrich, Walker and Weber." The fact remained: O'Neill had been the first Speaker since 1795 to have his words taken down by the House. "I looked at O'Neill and whacked the gavel. He looked back at me and just shook his head. Boy, he could have killed me," said Moakley. "For two days he didn't speak to me. He was bullshit. Every once in a while he would look down at me and say, 'My pal Joe.'"

The confrontation "anointed Newt Gingrich and his special order tactics and made him a household name," said Pitts. The exchange made the news on all three networks that night, the front page of the *Post* — and Newt Gingrich's career. "It was a huge breakthrough. It was just huge for us," Walker remembered. "What made the moment was Trent Lott. When the whip came to Newt's defense, not only did we move from the back bench to the national spotlight, we were defended by our leadership and legitimized."

"It moved us from wild young guys to serious partisan contenders," Gingrich recalled.

"You could see the passing of the old order and the honing of this new, confrontational spirit," said former House historian Ray Smock. "Tip contributed to that by his crude manner. He was pissed. He was mad when he came out on the floor, and he was not prepared. And Gingrich was: this was a chance to cut the Speaker down.

"O'Neill was outgunned by a whippersnapper. He expected them to have more reverence for his office, and they didn't. Instead, they attacked, effectively. It was only a symbolic setback, but it put Gingrich on the map," Smock said.[5]

"Walker, you and Gingrich owe me," O'Neill would later grumble. "When I came out on the floor and attacked you, you were nothing but backbench-rabble rousers. I made you."

Because it so contributed to Gingrich's success, the Camscam incident is often cited as a seminal moment in a subsequent loss of "civility" in Washington. Encouraged by their victory, the COS group did indeed turn up the heat, producing an edited tape of "Tip's Greatest Hits" and two TV commercials to capitalize on the ruckus.

O'Neill "is an extremely partisan old-style machine politician," Gingrich told the press. "He is teaching a younger generation the tactics of public thuggery." The Democratic leadership was "corrupt," said Gingrich, and needed to be purged. Weber said the Speaker was "a petty, second-class Boston politician [and] one of the cheapest, meanest politicians to occupy that office in this century."

But O'Neill and his Democrats gave as good as they got, and share the blame for what civility was lost. Coelho hired a private research firm to collect derogatory information on Gingrich and, after the leftist journal *Mother Jones* published a story on the congressman's troubled marital affairs, the DCCC distributed copies to House Democrats. O'Neill called Gingrich and Walker and Weber "weirdos" and referred to them as "the Three Stooges."[6] In O'Neill's view, this was the rough-and-tumble of politics. Of Reagan, O'Neill once said: "The evil is in the White House at the present time. And that evil is a man who has no care and no concern for the working class of America and the future generations of America, and who likes to ride a horse. He's cold. He's mean. He's got ice water for blood."

For conservatives, O'Neill was now a certified enemy. When he allowed a Boston orchestra to offer "Lunch with the Speaker" as one of the prizes in its fund-raising auction, the winning man and wife were feted in his office. "And he'd start to say something and his wife would say, 'Not now dear. Not now,'" O'Neill recalled. Finally, at the end of a cordial conversation, the husband could contain himself no longer. Why had he made the winning bid? "To tell you I think you're a dirty, no-good sonofabitch for being so mean to the President of the United States," the man said.

On another occasion, Dan Rostenkowski had to thrust his considerable bulk between the Speaker and a belligerent "big, blond-haired buck" who accosted them at the Chicago airport. It happened all the time, O'Neill told his pal. "From now on," Rostenkowski said, "you're getting a police escort from the moment you step off a plane in Chicago." When O'Neill arrived in Boston one night to hear that there had been threats made on his life, he took the state police escort along to Joe Tecce's, where the nervous restaurant owner put his staff on alert as well. "I'm not going to have you shot here, and blow my liquor license," he told O'Neill.

The Democrats got revenge for the Camscam incident the following year, when the House Republicans tried, with a surprise motion, to have a GOP congressional candidate declared the winner in a disputed Indiana election. The Speaker stalled, holding the clock and the vote open until enough Democrats had arrived at the Capitol to table the measure. A committee dominated by Democrats then disallowed a pack of absentee ballots and declared the incumbent Democrat, Representative Frank McCloskey, the winner of the seat by four votes. "You know how to win votes the old-fashioned way, Mr. Speaker — you steal them," said Representative Robert McEwen, a Republican from Ohio. When the matter was brought before the House, Representative Barney Frank and 18 other Democrats voted with the GOP, but McCloskey was seated. The Republicans staged a symbolic walkout, and there were two near-fistfights on the floor that summer. The episode strengthened Gingrich's hand, by further polarizing the House and discrediting those Republicans who argued for moderation. "It validated Newt's thesis: the Democrats are corrupt, they are making us look like fools, and we are idiots to co-operate with them," said Weber. Four years later, Gingrich was elected Republican whip. In 1994 his little band of brothers would end four decades of Democratic control of the House, and elect him Speaker.[7]

The Gingrich debacle was not the only indication that the seventy-two-year-old O'Neill was losing his touch, and nearing the end of his remarkable political career. There were reminders of mortality: the funerals of old pals, Dick Bolling's heart surgery and retirement, the respiratory illness that put Millie in an American military hospital in West Germany, interrupting a trip that was to have taken the Speaker and his wife to the wildlife preserves of Africa. Time brought other changes. Tommy's political career ended, after two terms as lieutenant governor, with an unsuccessful gubernatorial campaign in 1982. And Michael, the Speaker's youngest son, struggled in the grip of drugs and alcohol.

As the namesake and oldest son of one of America's most beloved, canny and powerful politicians, Tommy O'Neill carried an extra burden into public life. He might have done better by building an independent persona before entering politics at the early age of twenty-eight, for he labored always in his father's shadow. The sharks on Beacon Hill taunted him with cruel nicknames, and the State House press corps wondered if there was substance behind the famous name and familiar profile. In fact, young Tommy was an adept street-corner politician, a sensitive man with strong liberal beliefs and proof of the Nietzschean dictum that what fails to destroy you makes you strong: in a lifetime he would have a respectable political career and make, lose and regain a fortune. What Tommy did not have was his father's spectacular shrewdness, luck, and timing. After being elected a state rep from Cambridge in 1972, Tommy immediately launched a successful campaign for lieutenant governor, and his name on the ticket helped elect Governor Michael Dukakis in 1974. Dukakis, a reformer from Brookline, was grateful for the help that Tip O'Neill gave the new team in the campaign, and in Washington, and the partnership at first flourished.

Tommy's misfortunes began in 1978, when Republican senator Edward Brooke was wounded by ethics problems, and the young lieutenant governor with the famous name was pronounced by his friends, the press and many leading Democrats the favorite to take the Senate seat back for the party. He wavered, endorsed another candidate, changed his mind, then reversed himself again and withdrew from the race, leaving the voters and his fellow pols with the impression that he was indecisive; not ready for the big time. Tommy won reelection in 1978, but the aloof Dukakis lost the Democratic primary to conservative Edward King, a former BC football player and Massport director who had clinched the governorship with an infamous recipe — you put all the hate groups in one big pot and let it boil.[8]

Leo Diehl was a pal of Eddie King's. And Tip O'Neill shared another close friend and fund-raiser with King in the politically well connected Dick Thissen, whose architectural firm was investigated by the Ward commission, a public corruption–fighting panel, for his uncanny knack at winning government contracts from friends in public office. Nor did either O'Neill feel completely comfortable with the Dukakis brand of holier-than-thou political rectitude. The O'Neills worked hard and supported King as loyal Democrats in the general election, and the Speaker lured Jimmy Carter to Massachusetts to campaign for the ticket. But if they thought Dukakis was arrogant, the O'Neills had no illusions about King. They knew him as a bully, and one who stood in Tommy's way. In 1982, Tommy ran for governor against both Dukakis and King.

"Mike Dukakis was an arrogant guy," the Speaker later recalled. "And it hurt him tremendously. King also had an attitudinal problem. He thought he was elected like Ronald Reagan. He didn't appreciate the fact he was a political accident. King thought he had a mandate which was not there. He went after the people who have been the backbone of the party — the poor and the needy."

Tommy's strategy was to portray his two rivals as tired has-beens, and to try and stake out the middle ground. But Dukakis won "The Rematch" with King after forcing Tommy to withdraw from the race by whipping him in the party caucuses. "We felt from the beginning we had to have a head-on-head with King. We needed a two-way race desperately," said John Sasso, the Dukakis campaign manager. "The Rematch idea was an attempt to energize the Dukakis base. Everybody likes a fight. But it also marginalized Tommy."

In 1982, as throughout Tommy's career, the Speaker helped his son in fund-raising, and with the old-line neighborhood political organizations in the Eighth Congressional District. But, for personal and political reasons, the Speaker never put all his clout and resources behind his son. He was no Joseph Kennedy, twisting arms and stomping people to get Jack and Bobby and Teddy their careers. "Tip did not go to the wall for Tommy," Sasso said. "I don't think he put the hammer to anybody for Tommy," said Jim Shannon.

O'Neill "never felt comfortable being on the ballot with his son. It was as if he was asking too much — to create a dynasty," said the Speaker's Boston-based aide Francine Gannon. Nor, for the same potent mix of the political and personal, did Tommy ever ask. "I want to be my own man," he told reporters. It was a classic story of a powerful father, and the son who loved him and sought his approval, yet all the while struggled to escape his gravitational pull.

Tommy wanted and needed to make it on his own, and did. So too, facing many of the same challenges, did Kip and Susan and Rosemary. But Michael was not so strong, and was crushed by the circumstances of his life. He didn't like the pests from the press, the nighttime phone calls from his father's constituents, the demands that were placed on him as a famous person's son or the toll that politics took on the family, and on Millie. "I'm thoroughly disillusioned with it," Michael told a reporter from the *New York Times,* who was doing a profile of the new majority leader in December 1972. "I saw my mom answering those calls from drunks at 2 A.M. Who needs it?" Michael shunned politics, drove a cab, helped out in a nursing home, married and worked in the insurance and investment businesses, trying to fit in.

"Michael was a smart, warm, loving guy who was not inspired by my father's line of business. He chafed under the notoriety. But these were more symptoms of a greater problem," said his brother Kip. "I think the bottom line was, there were emotional and psychological problems that probably were never recognized properly, or treated."

Michael was fascinated by gambling and gamblers. He read books on gaming and fancied himself a Runyonesque character, dominating a card game, a pool hall, or the Las Vegas demimonde. He liked the nightlife, and abused alcohol and cocaine, and his addictions brought him personal, financial and legal troubles. It wasn't that Michael didn't try the straight and narrow. In the late 1970s and early 1980s, he worked as an insurance broker, and looked as if he could make a go of it. But his afflictions ruined his marriage, career and health. He barely outlived his father.

Tip O'Neill had certain expectations of his children. Though he assured them of his love, he also instructed them to meet their social obligations, to be scrubbed and presentable in public, and to remember that their actions reflected upon the family and his career. Then he left them for days at a time. O'Neill had always felt some guilt about his absentee status, but when he learned of Michael's problems he was ashamed, angry and stricken. "It was a question of being around more. Of guilt. Of whether love or more attention in itself could have made a difference. Who knew? Michael was the youngest. He may have needed more love or more attention or more psychological help," said Kip.

"Oceans of tears fell," said Susan O'Neill. The storms would periodically sweep through O'Neill's office, when Michael dropped out of Boston College, lost his health insurance, or admitted a dependency. Eleanor Kelley recalled one painful moment when the Speaker stopped her from sending Michael a gift of aftershave. It had alcohol in it, O'Neill explained. "He always felt he didn't give Michael enough time," said Gannon. "All the other kids, he was home, it was Tuesday–Thursday, he was at their ballgames. Michael, he wasn't. That was when he was in the leadership. When the Speaker was home, Michael would answer the door and say, 'Go away. My father's having dinner.' With the other kids it was, 'Hey, c'mon in.' But not Michael."

Tommy shouldered much of the burden of bailing Michael out from his troubles, and shielded their parents as best he could. Michael's difficulties never made the newspapers, and so the public was puzzled when, in an interview in the spring of 1984, the Speaker — a longtime foe of the death penalty — suddenly endorsed its use on cocaine dealers. "My God, if they are going to destroy America with these drugs, they ought to be publicly horse-whipped," he said. He began to urge young congressmen to buy a house in Washington, and raise their families there, so they could know their children as they grew up.

"My heart goes back to those days when I could not give my love and affection and time to those children," O'Neill said. "I gave it to my job."[9]

THE 1984 PRESIDENTIAL campaign offered further signs that the Speaker was showing his age. After failing to persuade Walter Mondale to give Reagan a free ride and run in 1988 instead, O'Neill made an early endorsement of the Minnesotan, a kindred believer in old-time liberal values and solutions. Then Gary Hart, one of the "New Democrats" whom O'Neill tried to cope with, but never completely understood, whipped Mondale in the New Hampshire primary. "He was not a fan of Hart. He couldn't understand the Hart part of the party, what that was all about. We all looked like boat-rockers to him," said Representative Pat Schroeder.

To clear the way for the party's presidential nominee, who would take over O'Neill's duties as the national Democratic spokesman, the Speaker announced on February 29, 1984, that he would retire at the end of 1986, or sooner if the Democrats elected a President that November. He dreamed of capping his career with a stint as U.S. ambassador to Ireland in a Democratic administration. In typical fashion, O'Neill made the much-awaited and speculated-upon announcement in one of those casual conversations he had been having with friendly reporters, in this case Marty Tolchin from the *Times,* for nigh on fifty years. The *Times* blew its exclusive by insisting that O'Neill pose for a formal portrait for its front page. The commotion caused a stir in the Speaker's office, and it didn't take long before the *Globe*'s Bob Healy and the *Journal*'s David Rogers were on the phone. "What kind of friend are you, telling Tolchin you're leaving and that you want to become an ambassador?" Healy barked.

"Married forty-three years, and you never had enough sense to keep your mouth shut," Millie told her husband. O'Neill had handled the big decision as impulsively, and clumsily, as Carl Albert had ten years before; perhaps it was the only way that heroes could relinquish the ring of power. O'Neill phoned Jim Wright and apologized for the surprise, and then tried to make it up to his majority leader by anointing him the likely successor. "I would be very much disappointed if anybody was to oppose him," the Speaker said. Still, O'Neill appeared content with his decision and happy to have it made. He met the press the next day crooning, "Sure Ireland must be heaven, my mother came from there." Rostenkowski, who still harbored thoughts about challenging Wright, was furious.

Hart's success in that spring's primaries further helped persuade O'Neill that his time was nearing its end.[10] The Colorado senator was a charter member of the New Democrats, the candidate of "New Ideas" and an early herald of the neoliberal creed of more economic growth and less regulation; a more efficient military; and a government that invested in schools, young industries and skilled workers instead of worrying about redistributing income. "Democrats have been concerned for too long with the distribution of golden eggs," said Paul Tsongas. "Now it's time to worry about the health of the goose." Hart's prescription for reforming the Pentagon was characteristic of the new generation's attempt to find a "third way" that freed them from the old

Left-Right dichotomy. When it came to the U.S. military, said Hart, "More isn't better. Less isn't better. Better is better."

Many in the Democratic electorate, particularly Westerners, middle-class suburbanites and young professionals who disagreed with Reagan, were champing for a better alternative. O'Neill's pollster, Bill Hamilton, warned the Speaker, "It is clear that the message of the Hart campaign, not the Mondale campaign, is much more dangerous to Ronald Reagan, probably more helpful to other Democratic candidates, and more likely to be successful in the fall." But the minority interest groups, labor unions, fat-cat contributors and dogmatic liberals who formed the backbone of the party were a few conceptual steps behind the New Democrats and could not yet be persuaded that Hart's "new" direction stood for anything more than political malleability. The nation's political reporters were similarly mired in Left-Right orthodoxy, and embarrassed when Hart began to ride a wave they had missed. By the narrowest of margins in the big round of "Super Tuesday" primaries, Hart failed to apply a knockout blow. He and Mondale and Jesse Jackson clawed and scratched their way through the spring. Though Mondale finally clinched the nomination in June, he had been exposed to the nation as dull, cautious and beholden to the Democratic interest groups.[11]

The Democrats had plenty of potential issues in 1984. There were real, wrenching changes in the heartland. The median family income in America had doubled from 1947 to 1973 but had been stagnant ever since, despite the increasing number of working wives and mothers. The loss of manufacturing jobs, and the demise of the unions, drove the median wage for young men from $10 an hour in 1973 down to $9 in 1984. The cost of college doubled in the 1980s, and housing prices soared. A worker turning thirty in 1949 found he could pay the mortgage of a median-priced home with 14 percent of his monthly pay. By 1984, that same young worker would have to dedicate 44 percent of his paycheck to buy a house. But Mondale's proposed solutions to these problems, and his approach to trenchant issues like crime and defense, were decidedly second wave. He offered the voters higher taxes, a diminished military, protectionist trade policies and more government spending programs. O'Neill was partly to blame. One of the trade-offs of the Speaker's 1982 success, said Mondale pollster Peter Hart, was that it gave one last shot in the arm to the old Democratic Party, and forestalled an inevitable reckoning.

O'Neill did his best to help Mondale, despite complaints from the candidate's staff that the Speaker was not fading into the background. "Get me some new ideas, will ya?" the Speaker asked his staff, and urged Mondale to use tax reform as an issue. When Hart dropped by to consult with O'Neill in June, the Speaker threw his arm around him and said, "You'll make a great President — but not this year." And it was O'Neill who bestowed one historic, if mixed, blessing on the Mondale campaign: the selection of Representative Geraldine Ferraro of New York as the first woman to be nominated for the vice presidency by a major political party. A cool former prosecutor from the tough Queens neighborhoods that had given the nation Jim Delaney and Archie Bunker, Ferraro had been raised by a widowed mother who worked as a seamstress to make sure that Geraldine attended college. Ferraro herself worked as a teacher, and earned her law degree at night school. She first caught O'Neill's fancy when she ran for the House in 1978, after scaring the aging Delaney into retirement. O'Neill was so impressed that he pressured the regulars in the borough's Democratic organization to support her candidacy.

"I was ethnic. I had come up the hard way. He respected that fact. And I had lost my father when I was eight, and never had a father figure since then. He was very much like my father. A teddy bear. He would put his arms around me and say, 'What's going on?'" Ferraro remembered. "He was willing to take the role as mentor and father figure." She was the Speaker's kind of gal, much to the dismay of more senior Democratic congresswomen like Lindy Boggs and Pat Schroeder. "I don't think he understood me, and I clearly didn't understand him," said Schroeder, who was once asked by O'Neill why she, and not her husband, had run for Congress. The Speaker was "appalled" when Schroeder brought her small children to the floor. "It was the planet of the guys around here," she said.

Ferraro, on the other hand, wasn't "a threat," said Tony Coelho. "She is not a feminist with wounds." Unlike most eager freshmen, who craved the prestigious Ways and Means or Appropriations Committees, Ferraro had requested a seat on the lowly Post Office and Civil Service panel. Why? All politics is local, she told O'Neill: there were 38,000 families in her district who were riled about the postal service's decision to keep them in a Brooklyn zip code, where insurance rates were higher. She got her committee assignment, secured a Queens postal zone for her constituents (and thus her reelection) and O'Neill continued to look out for her. "I want to thank you so much for having my Donna work as an intern in your office during the first part of the summer. I am most anxious for my children to have the best and meet the best," Ferraro wrote him in 1980. "I consider the opportunity an opportunity for Donna to get to know one of the finest men this country has produced."

O'Neill helped Ferraro retire her campaign debt and, in only her second term, backed her successful effort to become secretary to the Democratic caucus and a member of the steering and policy committee. When Public Works chairman James Howard of New Jersey ignored her efforts to ban tractor-trailer trucks from the Brooklyn-Queens Expressway, O'Neill interceded on her behalf. She got a prize seat on the Budget Committee as well. In 1983, Mondale's aides had asked Ferraro to take a leading role in the campaign. O'Neill told her to keep her options open and play hard-to-get. She chaired the party's platform committee instead. In early May 1984, when talk of a Mondale-Hart ticket began to circulate, O'Neill made a preemptive strike. "I have a candidate. Her name is Geraldine Ferraro. She's from New York. She's a Catholic. She's been an effective member and she's very smart," he announced.

It was a breakthrough for women. Another "need not apply" sign was down. O'Neill himself did not fully appreciate the contribution he had made until he saw his daughter's tears as Ferraro was nominated in San Francisco.

"What is the matter, Susan?" O'Neill asked.

"You know, in all the years you said to Tommy and Kip and Mike that they could grow up to be President of the United States, never once did you say it to Rosemary or me," said Susan. "Now Geraldine has broken the barrier, and I can say to my daughter Michaela that someday she can be President."

"Tip very clearly saw the need for a little bit of pizzazz. He also recognized it was time," said Ferraro. She asked him to stand beside her on the podium. "He said, 'No. I don't want to hurt you. You are the new politics and I am the old.' It came from his heart and his gut. What you saw is what you got with Tip."

O'Neill had come a long way from the Speaker who, when the federal Title IX protections for female athletes and scholars were first proposed in 1979, had asked HEW Secretary Joseph Califano, "Joe, how can you do this to your alma mater — Holy Cross? The Jesuits will never speak to you again. This is not the time." Christine Sullivan Daly, who handled women's issues for O'Neill, recalled how her boss's consciousness had been raised by the time, just a few years later, he rejected the pleas of a room full of university presidents and college athletic directors — Jesuits, old pals and sporting legends alike — who wanted to gut Title IX. "Here they thought they were going to have a pal, a guy's guy, a sports lover to tell that Title IX was killing their programs. But 'Sorry, guys. That's the law and it's going to happen,' he told them, and they got nowhere with him," Daly said.

The convention was a bittersweet finale for O'Neill. "If the Democratic convention were a massive family reunion, Thomas P. O'Neill would be the aging patriarch, moving fondly through a brood that adores him, is irritated by him, knows his stories by heart, wishes he would get out of the way and hopes he will go on forever," wrote the *Post*'s Cynthia Gorney. In his own speech to the convention, O'Neill had blasted the Reaganites for their "private planes, limousines and chinchilla coats," but he had a grand time being chauffered around San Francisco in the stretch limo he had ordered from the DNC — "the bigger the better" — and staying in the 6,500-square-foot VIP suite at the Fairmont Hotel, with its three bedrooms and private game room.

Disaster struck two weeks later. O'Neill had warned Ferraro, "I want you to be prepared for the onslaught that will hit you . . . about everything that can possibly be dug up about you." What got dug up were her family's real estate dealings, and the way that she and her husband pushed the ethical envelope when financing her 1978 campaign. "There is nothing wrong in what she did whatsoever," O'Neill insisted, and Ferraro gave a bravura performance in a no-holds-barred press conference. But the pizzazz was gone from the Mondale campaign, and 1984 was shaping up as another Democratic disaster.

In June, Dick Darman had written a memo to his White House colleagues about the fall campaign. "Paint Mondale as: a) weak, b) a creature of special interests, c) old-style, d) unprincipled, e) soft in his defense of freedom, patriotic values, American interests, f) in short, Carter II," Darman wrote. "Paint RR as the personification of all that is right with, or heroized by, America. Leave Mondale in a position where an attack on Reagan is tantamount to an attack on America's idealized image of itself — where a vote against Reagan is, in some subliminal sense, a vote against a mythic 'AMERICA.'"

Reagan did just that. It was a seamless performance. From his stirring address about "the boys of Pointe de Hoc" at the fortieth anniversary of the D-Day landings in Normandy to his artful association with the triumphant "U-S-A! U-S-A!" cheers at that summer's Olympics in Los Angeles, to his "It's morning in America . . ." TV commercials, it was an election year in which it was hard to tell where the news footage ended and the Republican television campaign began. Reagan also collected on his bet that getting the recession out of the way in 1982 would mean good times for his reelection campaign. As Mondale talked about taxes and deficits, the cod liver oil of politics, Reagan was basking in the glow of 6.2 percent economic growth in the first three-quarters of 1984, and a record of having tamed inflation. "You ain't seen nothing yet," he promised.

O'Neill urged Mondale on, publicly complaining that the Minnesotan was "too much of a gentleman" and should "come out slugging and come out fighting." Mondale's one opportunity occurred when Reagan looked old and confused in the course of their first nationally televised debate. O'Neill questioned the President's fitness for a second term, and Reagan adviser Ed Rollins fired back: "Tip O'Neill, who's overweight and has never shown any moderation of food, drink or anything else — to compare himself to Ronald Reagan, who's fit — is just crap." Indeed, a few days later O'Neill was hospitalized for bronchitis. Then Reagan responded with a skilled performance in the second debate. "I will not make age an issue in this campaign," he said with a twinkle. "I am not going to exploit, for political purposes, my opponent's youth and inexperience." It was clear sailing for the President from that point on. Reagan crushed Mondale by a margin of 59 to 41 percent, with a record 525 electoral votes. The Democrats lost every state but Minnesota and the District of Columbia. On election night, as the results came in, a pained and shaken O'Neill asked his aides: "Can we lose the House?" In the end, the Democrats lost but 14 seats, and retained their numerical and philosophical control of the House. But the long knives were out.[12]

A CHIEF CONNIVER was Coelho, whose continuing efforts to raise money for House Democrats (he spent 150 days a year on the road) had met with even greater success in 1984. His investments in political technology — computers, direct-mail campaigns and a million-dollar Democratic media center with television and radio production studios — pleased the grateful young technocrats in the party. Coelho's not so subtle arm-twisting had raised the Democratic share of corporate PAC donations to 44 percent in 1984, and he was so effective that by 1988 the Democrats would actually get a majority of the corporate PAC funds. Coelho put O'Neill, Wright and influential committee chairmen like Dan Rostenkowski and John Dingell of Michigan on a national fund-raising circuit and doubled the overall DCCC take: to $11 million for the 1983–84 cycle. The "Speaker's Club" alone brought in $1.7 million — more than 60 percent of it from corporate executives, lobbyists and trade associations. In the twenty-five closest congressional races in 1984, PAC funds went to the Democrats by a better than 2 to 1 margin.

Yet all was not well within the Democratic leadership. "Tony at this stage was like an athlete in his prime. His ability, his instincts, his cunning — all those things — he was there," said Peter Hart. "Tip liked Tony, and felt that Tony was unbelievably good as a politician, but Tony made Tip uncomfortable. Tony pushed him. Tony was always on the edge. Tony was always looking for something."

"I think Tip despised Coelho. I don't think so, I know so," said Lud Ashley. "He considered him for years to be a two-faced sonofabitch."

In 1982, Coelho had challenged the Speaker by supporting language in the TEFRA tax bill that gave tax breaks to independent oilmen. They were a promising source of money that Coelho was cultivating, but many happened to be supporting a young Republican, Frank McNamara, who was running against O'Neill that year.

"I went to Tip and said, 'Lookit. I think we can break this group and not have all oil going against us.' But then all these right-wingers ran this guy against him, supporting him big time. Jesus. I had been out there all over the country trying to put this thing together," Coelho recalled. O'Neill summoned Coelho to his office, and let him have it. "I want those sonsofbitches [hurt]," the Speaker shouted.

O'Neill crushed McNamara but was forced to spend time and money on the race after the Republicans assembled a $700,000 war chest. At one point in the campaign, after alerting local television stations, the young Republican tried to ambush O'Neill in a parking lot to accuse him of ducking debates. The Speaker dazzled him.

"I am delighted to see you," said O'Neill. "I've never seen a McNamara with an 'R' behind his name before."

"Do you think we can debate now, Mr. O'Neill?" McNamara asked, as television crews recorded the scene.

"Listen, it's very interesting," O'Neill said, turning and grasping McNamara's arm. "You've spent three-quarters of a million dollars and our polls show you have a three percent recognition factor. Now, if you think I'm going to help you, the answer is: 'No.'"

In the Democratic caucus, Jim Shannon griped aloud that Ways and Means was supposed to be "a tax-writing committee, not a fund-raising committee," but Coelho persevered and won the independent oilmen their tax break. "Tony and Tip saved the House for the Democrats for another ten years," said Gingrich, who would engineer the Republican takeover in 1994. "Tony had the ideas, but didn't have the power. O'Neill had the power, and saw in Tony the ideas. It was an effective alliance. But it was an armed alliance because neither one trusted or liked the other."

After his success in the 1982 elections, Coelho demanded that the DCCC chairman be added to the party leadership in the House, and threatened to walk away from the job if he did not get his way. He would steam when O'Neill canceled trips, or signed fund-raising appeals for other liberal organizations. During the long years as an aide to Sisk, Coelho had picked up the habit of whispering in members' ears on the floor. "That would drive O'Neill nuts," said O'Donnell. O'Neill had never liked whisperers — nor had Leo Diehl, who handled the DCCC for O'Neill before Coelho took over, and now lost influence to the upstart.

"Leo and I never got along. And I understand it. He realized that once I took over he would no longer control the committee. That was his power and I took it away. People had come to him to get their allocation from the DCCC. But it stopped when I became head of the campaign, and Leo resented it," said Coelho. "Leo always suspected that people were trying to connive against Tip. And after I took over, Tip never understood the need to build up the party structure. Headquarters. Media center. Direct mail and so forth. He thought that what you should do is collect money and distribute money. And that is where he and I had big fights. It was necessary to go out and raise the money to build the structure I was building, and he felt that by doing that I was trying to build an edifice to myself."

Indeed, Coelho never forgot that O'Neill had, at the eleventh hour, declined to formally nominate him for the DCCC job in 1981. "He had sent a signal to everybody else that the leadership was all for me," he said, "but by withdrawing the night before, he didn't have his fingerprints on it," and O'Neill thus kept peace with Coelho's opponents.

"It was very Machiavellian. You could make the argument very strongly that it was a constructive way to do it: get what you want but don't burn bridges," said Coelho. "Or you could say it was destructive: that he decided to pull out at the end in a negative way . . . which really upset me.

"He would give you a commitment verbally but when the time came to sign off he wasn't there. Which was very irritating," Coelho recalled.

Throughout the 1980s, there were serious plots to challenge O'Neill. Gingrich and the boll weevils had conspired in the days after the 1980 election. If the Democrats had not done so well in 1982, O'Neill would assuredly have been challenged by Charlie Stenholm or — the man the Speaker's staff feared — Jim Jones. In early 1983, Gillis Long had approached Coelho and asked him to be on a slate with Long and Tim Wirth to challenge O'Neill, Wright and Tom Foley. O'Neill had confronted Long before the Democratic leadership: "Are you running against me?" Startled, Long said no.

Long's fatal heart ailment, and the fact that Jones just barely kept hold of his own seat in Congress in 1984, removed them as threats. But as the polls showed Mondale falling 30 points behind that autumn, leading members of the class of New Democrats began to conspire. Coelho, Dick Gephardt, Leon Panetta, Martin Russo of Illinois, Thomas Downey of New York, David McCurdy of Oklahoma, Steny Hoyer of Maryland, Mike Synar of Oklahoma, Richard Durbin of Illinois, Martin Frost of Texas, Tim Wirth and a few others gathered on Wednesday nights, at first to ponder ways to make the House Democrats more effective. They concluded, along the way, that changing the leadership might help. The plotters ultimately decided that Gephardt and Coelho should head a slate that would challenge the O'Neill-Wright-Foley team. The group met at first in the Beneficial Finance offices on North Capitol Street, until Coelho offered them his basement as a war room.

"They were talking of how after the 1984 elections — which were going to be a disaster — we should have a change," Coelho recalled. "I always took the view that if we had gotten killed in 1984 the atmosphere would have been set to make a change. There was discontent. It was a real threat. People were very upset with his leadership. They were frightened."

It did not take long for word to reach O'Neill. The Speaker's source was William Gray of Pennsylvania. "Gray left one of the meetings and went to Murtha. He said this wasn't about Gephardt becoming caucus chair, this was a real cabal and Tip better be concerned. Murtha went to O'Neill. That is what blew the whole thing open," said Kirk O'Donnell.

Said Murtha: "We had a coup attempt. 'You find out who the hell is involved,' Tip told me. It was about twenty guys."

When the Democrats fared better than many had feared on Election Day, much of the passion for dumping O'Neill — who had already announced that this was his last term — subsided. The Speaker had let his friends — Diehl, Murtha and members of the Massachusetts delegation — stomp out the fire.

"A bunch of us made it very clear, that there were a lot of us, a lot of young members who were going to be there for a while, who would never forget any treachery," Brian Donnelly recalled. "One time in the cloakroom I told them, 'Okay, shoot him in the back. But there are eleven of us here from Massachusetts and we're all going to be here twenty years and we will fucking never forget!' "

O'Neill's allies would approach the plotters and "pick them off one at a time," said Donnelly. "You would go up to a likely suspect and say, 'Hey, I hear you are a mutineer.' And they would say, 'Oh, no, Brian. I just went to one meeting. I don't know why they had me. I didn't know what the agenda was.' And we would sigh and say, 'Well, you better go tell Tip,' and off they'd run."

O'Neill personally dealt with Coelho. "The word had got out that there was a meeting at my home, of a rump group to take over the leadership," Coelho recalled. "So Tip called me in and I said, 'Lookit, there was really an effort but we lost less than expected and so none of this is real.' But he didn't want to hear any of that. What he heard was yeah, there were meetings, and yeah, there were these things going on, and yes, there is an effort to get rid of you. I was always surprised they were not appreciative of the fact that we had lost so few seats. They were more upset at the fact I had attended these meetings."

O'Neill was a lame duck, and the plotters had youth and the future and Mondale's catastrophic loss on their side. Though their plans for a coup d'état faded, they elected Gephardt caucus chairman and made the whip's job an elected position, which Coelho captured in 1986. Gephardt also insisted on the creation of a Speaker's cabinet, comprised of younger members, to set the direction of the party in the House.

O'Neill had to make the concessions, as he was fighting a war on two fronts at the time. Texans Ralph Hall and Charlie Stenholm were coming at the Speaker from the right, and declining to rule out the possibility they would join the Republicans and elect a Republican Speaker. O'Neill was receiving reports on this second uprising from Silvio Conte, who was motivated by his friendship with O'Neill and his dislike of Gingrich. "It would have been a Republican Speaker. They were going to vote along with the Republicans," said Diehl.

"Two sides came after Tip in 1984," said Chris Matthews. "One was the southern side: the Confederates behind Stenholm. When they began, they had 75 votes, up from the usual 29. Tip said, 'I don't want any press.' And he and Leo were brilliant. They got their list together and started fence-mending. Beverly Byron from Maryland. [Edward] Jenkins from Georgia. It was right out of *The Godfather.* A great tactical thing: penetrating their lines. Undermining. Just Leo and Tip. At the end, the southern commanders were back at 29 votes." In a meeting with Stenholm and Representative Charles Roemer of Louisiana, the Speaker persuaded the boll weevils to drop their challenge.

"We had all had to run having Mondale wrapped around our necks," Stenholm recalled. "It wasn't too pleasant. So at that time the frustrations . . . were pretty great. We had been run over for several years and we didn't like it, so we started looking at what we were going to do to change it."

But O'Neill just had too many friends. "When we first started, we went with the idea that we were going to win, but it didn't take us long to figure out that was not achievable," said Stenholm. "I found out that even some of my friends would not support it." O'Neill was chosen, by acclamation, to serve as Speaker for the fifth time on December 3. In two races for majority leader and five for Speaker, he had never had a challenger in the Democratic caucus. He thanked his colleagues, asked for unity and sought revenge.

Jim Jones and Leon Panetta, who had made political names for themselves in their six years on the Budget Committee, each hoped to be elected chairman of the panel — but needed to change a party rule that restricted any committee member to three consecutive terms. If the attempt to change the rules failed, Bill Gray would be the clear frontrunner for the chairmanship. Jones had been sparring with the Speaker for years, and Panetta had participated in the Gephardt-Coelho putsch. Gray, on the other hand, had warned O'Neill of the coup. When the vote on the rules was taken on December 4, O'Neill worked the floor for Gray, and stood by his side as the votes were cast. The three-term rule was upheld by a 124 to 115 vote; Jones and Panetta were forced to step aside. "When Tip voted against doing it, I knew I didn't have a chance. It was . . . the decisive act," Panetta recalled.

In January, Gray was elected Budget Committee chairman. Disclosing the plot had been "a masterful move by Gray," O'Donnell remembered, with an appreciative smile.[13]

CHAPTER 27

Endgames

AND THEN, in the final two years of his five decades in elected office, Tip O'Neill enjoyed one of the most spectacular last terms any lame duck ever had. His luck returned, his foe had tired, his army was united and some long-nurtured legislative shoots began to bloom. O'Neill's forays into foreign policy paid off, his party came roaring back to recapture the Senate, he basked in the approval of his fellow Americans, bestowed final blessings on Massachusetts, sold his memoirs and became a wealthy man.

To be sure, the new term did not begin with such promise. As the Democrats chose their committee chairmen in January 1985, a group of younger Democrats led by Tony Coelho and Les Aspin had challenged the leadership of Armed Services Committee chairman Melvin Price of Illinois, now a tottering seventy-nine-year-old figure. Jack Murtha and Dan Rostenkowski went to O'Neill and urged him to impose a face-saving compromise on Price. No, the Speaker said, they would defend the chairman's request to serve one more term. As the hour of the vote approached, the younger members of the Speaker's staff urged him to use restraint. He had, after all, just survived two coup attempts.

But the Speaker gave it all he had, summoning Coelho to his office to tell him, "We are going to beat your ass."

"I walked out of that room at ten in the morning and the vote was at three that afternoon," Coelho recalled. "And it seemed that minute-by-minute Les would call me and say, 'We just lost so-and-so. We just lost so-and-so. We just lost so-and-so. We won by two votes, and we had been ahead by thirty. It was Tip, Rosty and Murtha in the Speaker's office and they kept calling and switching votes. If the vote was the next day they would have beaten us."

The Speaker had no better luck when he tried to take revenge on Coelho. The Californian was chairing a meeting of the DCCC when O'Neill arrived, unannounced, to voice his concerns that "we have a system here where one man gets to decide where all the money is spent. I think money was spent in 1984 in places where it shouldn't be spent. There are no checks and balances." He urged the other members to strip Coelho of his decision-making authority. It was a rebuke and a challenge to Coelho, but Rostenkowski came to the chairman's defense. "I deeply resent that," the Chicagoan told O'Neill. The DCCC members already had an oversight committee that met and "approved every goddamn cent." John Dingell, who was also at the meeting, rose and seconded Rostenkowski's remarks. "Tip walked out of the room. He just walked out," Coelho recalled.[1]

But if O'Neill had troubles, Reagan was finding things far more difficult at the White House. The President had a mandate but, given the disappointing Republican performance in the 1984 congressional races, so did the House Democrats. And in a distinct change from 1981, the President was now facing a Democratic House whose core was a group of young, fresh-faced centrists who knew how to run, and win, in the age of Reagan. They didn't fear the President, and voted together with impressive unity. Many of the South's Democrats, who had discovered the rewards of a motivated black constituency, were now more inclined to side with the Gephardts and Panettas than with the President. The federal deficit projections for the next three years, meanwhile, were all in the $230 billion range, threatening the economic recovery. And Reagan had begun his second term by breaking up the White House staff that served him so well. Chief-of-staff Jim Baker swapped jobs with Treasury secretary Donald Regan, and Ed Meese left to become Attorney General. O'Neill had nowhere near as much respect for Regan (whom he viewed as a turncoat to the working-class Cambridge roots they shared) as he had for Baker, and tried to warn the President. It proved to be a disastrous change.

In short order that spring, Reagan was forced to settle for half loaves on the MX missile and Contra aid. He made an ill-advised commitment to visit a military cemetery in Bitburg, West Germany, which contained the graves of SS storm troopers. But it was the annual budget debate that really revealed how far Reagan had slipped. Bill Gray's Budget Committee brought a budget resolution to the floor that was passed by a 258 to 170 vote, with only 15 Democratic defections. Reagan endorsed the Republican Senate's alternative, which attacked the deficit by freezing Social Security cost-of-living adjustments, limiting the increase in defense spending to the rate of inflation and making other politically painful cutbacks. Senator Peter Wilson of California, recovering from an emergency appendectomy, was brought into the Senate in a wheelchair to cast the vote that made it 49 to 49, allowing Vice President George Bush to vote and break the tie. But now it was the GOP's turn at disarray: House Republicans, remembering how O'Neill had used the issue in 1982, were petrified at the idea of a Social Security COLA freeze, and lobbied the White House to reject the Senate plan.

Reagan met with the bipartisan leaders of both houses on July 9, under an oak tree on the South Lawn. The leaders doffed their coats and ordered drinks and O'Neill sat beside the President — a tactical advantage for the Speaker, in that his exchanges with Reagan were masked from the others, from time to time, by jets taking off and landing at nearby National Airport.

The Speaker said Congress should put Reagan's defense buildup on a pay-as-you-go basis, rather than financing it via deficits. He tried to persuade the President to endorse a surtax and, as in 1983, suggested that raising income taxes on Social Security recipients was a fair way to apply a means test to the program. When Reagan rejected the ideas, new taxes were taken off the table. "Do you think I am ever going to have a tax bill? Do you think I'm going to let Mondale say, 'Look, I told you so.' Never!" Reagan said.

The discussion moved on to Social Security, where the Senate had voted to save $22 billion over three years by eliminating the 1986 COLA. O'Neill stated his opposition, and Reagan caved in. Majority leader Bob Dole later insisted that Reagan said the COLAs would be safe only if the Democrats came up with compensating cuts elsewhere in the budget. But O'Neill, taking advantage of the uncertainty caused by the jet traffic, struck quickly and told the waiting press that the President had taken an unqualified position to take Social Security "off the table." It was a virtual replay of the pineapple and cactus summit, except this time Reagan had sawed off a limb on which the Senate Republicans were sitting. Dole scrambled to find compensating revenue by proposing an oil import fee. But a few weeks later, the White House announced Reagan's opposition to the oil tax as well. Dole "was absolutely stunned," O'Neill said. "His chin hit his chest."

"Reagan is angry at Dole for being angry at him, and House Speaker Thomas "Tip" O'Neill Jr. is chortling at the bizarre breakdown in Republican unity at a crucial juncture in the President's second term," the *Los Angeles Times* reported. Any hope for a grand compromise that would close the yawning deficits faded for another year. The Republican senators had been abandoned, with politically fatal repercussions. "People feel they flew a kamikaze mission and ended up in flames and got nothing for it," said Senator Warren Rudman of New Hampshire. In the closing weeks of the 1986 mid-term elections, the Democratic candidates used their television advertising to remind the elderly how Republican senators had voted to freeze their COLAs in 1985. The tactic worked and the Democrats recaptured the Senate.[2]

THOUGH THEY COULD not settle on how to curb the federal budget deficits, most Republicans and Democrats in Congress at least felt the need to do something about them. In late 1985, Rudman joined with O'Neill's old nemesis Phil Gramm — now a Texas senator — and Democratic Senator Ernest Hollings of South Carolina and devised a mechanism to force Congress to restrain itself. Their bill set up deficit reduction targets and a mandatory budget-cutting mechanism that would take effect if the goals were not met. Even Ted Kennedy voted for it. But the Senate postponed the effective date until after the 1986 elections. It was an Augustinian loophole ("Give me chastity and continence, but not yet") that the House Democrats resolved to close. "The purpose of this legislation is to give twenty-two senators credit for being rough and tough budget-cutters without getting their hands dirty," the Speaker fumed. And so, after first placing many social welfare programs off-limits, the House voted to make Gramm-Rudman effective for 1986. The Senate leadership, its bluff called, had to go along and, to meet the Gramm-Rudman goals, proposed modest tax hikes and defense cutbacks. That was the formula that O'Neill had been angling for all year, and the Democrats happily agreed. It was, said the *Times,* "one of the most deft legislative tricks of the year," and *Newsweek* called it "O'Neill's finest hour."

O'Neill's Democrats were united again when work on the budget began the following spring. His final budget battle did not go by without one last confrontation between the Speaker and the President. On January 28, 1986, Reagan spoke up at a briefing and complained about able-bodied welfare recipients. "Don't give me that crap," an angry O'Neill responded. "The guy in Youngstown, Ohio, who's been laid off at the steel mill and has to make his mortgage payments — don't tell me he doesn't want to work. Those stories may work on your rich friends, but they don't work on the rest of us. I'm sick and tired of your attitude, Mr. President. I thought you would have grown in the five years you've been in office, but you're still repeating those same simplistic explanations." Reagan replied in kind, and the two went at it until Senator Alan Simpson of Wyoming intervened. O'Neill backpedaled, insisting he had great respect for the Presidents with whom he served. "With the exception of this incumbent," Reagan barked.

Simpson later wrote to the President: "It really unraveled my underwear to hear that guff going on yesterday. . . . You don't have to be assailed like that right there in the Nation's House — maybe down at 'Charlie's Bar,' but not there." The Democrats departed and Reagan was still discussing the matter with his aides when, at 11:45 that morning, communications director Pat Buchanan walked into the Oval Office and said, "Sir, the shuttle blew up."

"The future doesn't belong to the fainthearted. It belongs to the brave," Reagan told the nation that afternoon. "The crew of the space shuttle *Challenger* honored us by the manner in which they lived their lives. We will never forget them nor the last time we saw them this morning as they prepared for their journey and waved goodbye and 'slipped the surly bonds of earth to touch the face of God.'" The President's televised address was "masterly" and brought tears to O'Neill's eyes. In the course of one day, the Speaker decided, he had seen Reagan "at his worst" and "at his best."[3]

Reagan and O'Neill were aligned in the final great legislative battle of the Speaker's reign: tax reform. The already arcane federal tax code had been made even more complex by the adornments of the

1981 tax cut, TEFRA and other stopgap tax legislation. Both parties saw a political benefit to simplifying the system. The New Democrats, led by Dick Gephardt and Senator Bill Bradley of New Jersey, saw tax reform as a way for the party to address inequity without being seen as tax-and-spenders. Treasury secretary Jim Baker looked upon it as a popular and achievable goal for the President's second term. And Ways and Means chairman Rostenkowski was still looking for a crowning accomplishment after the humiliation he'd suffered during 1981 and 1982. Having endorsed Wright as a successor, O'Neill felt he owed Rosty. At the very worst, the Speaker and his lieutenant reasoned, they could dump "a dead cat" on the Senate's doorstep and use the GOP's failure to pass tax reform as an issue in the 1986 campaign. Indeed, both parties would remain motivated, and persevere through moments of crisis, for fear of being blamed as the ones who killed reform. "I remember O'Neill would say, 'It's dead. I'm outa here,' because he had everybody in the goddamn world whispering in his ear because they don't want to vote for the goddamn thing," said Rostenkowski. "And I would go to Ari Weiss and say, 'You know, it's the Democrats who are going to kill tax reform. Can we afford it?' And Ari would go in there and talk with him and O'Neill would come back and say, 'All right, let's see what you're going to do here.'" The bipartisan alliance proved crucial, since the guts of any meaningful tax reform measure — lower, fairer rates for individual taxpayers — had to be financed by the closing of loopholes that benefited corporate America.

Because of the White House staff shakeup, the effort got off to a slow start. House Republicans muttered about the President's willingness to deal with O'Neill and Rostenkowski on the issue, and suspected that the whole scheme was anti-business. Reagan's legislation lowered the top bracket of the federal income tax to 35 percent (it had been 70 percent when he took office and 50 percent after the 1981 bill); eliminated the investment tax credit and other corporate tax breaks and removed millions of the working poor from the obligation of paying taxes at all.

Rostenkowski had elicited a promise from both Reagan and O'Neill: they would let him wheel and deal without second-guessing. He used that freedom, and some, to produce a bill that nudged the top bracket back up to 38 percent, raised the corporate and capital gains tax, and included a tough and necessary minimum tax on wealthy individuals and corporations. It was easy for O'Neill to drum up

Democratic votes for such a package, but the House Republicans, furious that they had been left out of the Baker-Rostenkowski loop, staged an uprising. When the rule for the bill came up on December 11, the Republican members deserted their President en masse and it was defeated by a 223 to 202 vote.

Rostenkowski, crestfallen, went to O'Neill.

"Jesus, I put too much time on this thing to have it die like this," said the chairman. "What are we going to do?"

"We're gonna put the challenge on the President," said O'Neill. "We're gonna make the President go out and get the votes."

The Republican "robots" had revolted, O'Neill told the press. "December 11 will be remembered as the day Ronald Reagan became a lame duck on the floor of the House," the Speaker said, unless the President got his Republicans back in line and came up with 50 GOP votes. The House Republicans had enjoyed their moment, railing against Baker and Rostenkowski. But now they faced the prospect of serving for three years, and running for reelection, under a champion they themselves had crippled. The President arrived on Capitol Hill to meet with and rally his unruly troops. The Reagan magic worked again.

"He called me that night that he had the 50 votes, and I was down at the Phoenix Park Hotel eating supper, and I didn't return the call," said O'Neill, happily recalling how he had made Reagan sweat. "Three times he called, and they tell me at the White House he was in a dither." The rule passed easily, with 70 Republican votes, and even O'Neill was stunned when no Republican called for a recorded vote on the bill itself. It passed without debate on a voice vote.

"What the hell is going on?" Rostenkowski asked an aide.

"I think we just passed the tax bill," the aide replied.

Senate Finance Committee chairman Robert Packwood of Oregon matched Rostenkowski's heroics in the Senate, and the final legislation was passed by Congress in the fall of 1986. The top rate was fixed at 28 percent for middle-class America, and at 33 percent for the wealthiest Americans, and hundreds of loopholes were shut. Politics being politics, there was a postscript. To grease the bill's path through Congress, a $10 billion package of "transition rules" was assembled to buy off various special interests and influential politicians. Though tax reform was supposed to eliminate loopholes, O'Neill and other members of Congress carved a few new ones. A Cambridge developer (who wanted a tax break on bonds to build a parking garage), the Gillette Company (which asked for tax breaks for its investments in overseas banks and a new corporate airplane), Boston's low-income housing projects (whose investors needed tax shelters), New England Patriots owner Bill Sullivan, Harvard University and O'Neill's old friend George Steinbrenner (worried about the continued deductibility of Yankees baseball tickets) were among those who asked O'Neill to ask Rosty for a "transition" rule.

One rule pushed by the Speaker typified the behind-the-scenes action. The John Hancock Mutual Life Insurance Company, whose Washington lobbyist was O'Neill's old pal Paul McGowan, stood to lose $30 million on bonds it had purchased under the old, lower capital gains tax. It was a fair claim, but too costly to apply to the entire industry, and so available only to firms whose congressmen had clout. After hearing from the Massachusetts Mutual Life Insurance Company, O'Neill told his aides to deal with its concerns as well, and both Massachusetts firms were included on the eventual list of fifteen insurance companies protected by the Ways and Means Committee. "There were some very good companies left off the list," said Representative Pete Stark (of the other 1,800 American insurance firms), "because they didn't have the right friends."[4]

DURING HIS LAST two years as Speaker, O'Neill registered some success in foreign policy as well. Diplomacy was a field that required study of the nuanced positions that nations struck when conducting business with each other. Never a "detail guy," the Speaker had a history of splashing in diplomatic hot water. The Portugal-Angola affair was one good example; Koreagate another. In the midst of the Middle East peace process during the Carter years, O'Neill offended Israeli sensibilities and had to send a note of apology to the White House. And when the Speaker took a congressional delegation to China in 1983, and got an earful from an agitated Vice Chairman Peng Zhen, O'Neill made news with his self-described "astonishment" at the tension that still existed between the mainland Chinese and their cousins on Taiwan. "We don't follow foreign affairs in our country like they do in perhaps Europe or out here in the Orient," he said lamely at a Beijing press conference. The Speaker had mangled Chinese names and ceremonies, showed up late for a meeting with Premier Zhao Ziyang and professed such ignorance of Sino-American relations that his hosts suspected he was being disingenuous. "I am not familiar with the details of U.S. foreign policy, particularly that towards China," O'Neill confessed to Chinese leader Deng Xiaoping.

The visit to China was doubtlessly on O'Neill's mind when, in April 1985, he and Bob Michel led a bipartisan U.S. delegation to Moscow to meet with the new Soviet leader, Mikhail S. Gorbachev, who had taken command in March. This time the Speaker came prepared: the delegation had gotten detailed briefings from the Reagan administration and its own experts, and the members had divvied up the topics of interest — trade, arms control and so on — among themselves to study and prepare. Reagan had decided that the time had come to test the impact of the U.S. arms buildup on the Soviet Union, and to see if he could pressure the Soviets to make concessions at the bargaining table that would culminate in a dramatic arms control agreement. That was a course that O'Neill could support. In an unpublicized meeting before the Speaker left for Moscow, Reagan asked him to try and impress the new Russian leader with the depth of American unity, and to vouch for the President's sincere desire for meaningful negotiations. In this matter, the Speaker could be a particularly credible messenger: O'Neill had warned the former Soviet regime in 1984 that Reagan was "a demagogue" and a "dangerous man."

The Soviets greeted the O'Neill delegation's arrival with the news that Gorbachev accepted Reagan's invitation for a summit meeting. The Americans met first with Foreign Minister Andrey Gromyko, who told O'Neill that the prospects for a successful summit were dimmed by the U.S. insistence on deploying a space-based defense system. "Whatever cross you christen it with, even if it is a golden cross with diamonds, SDI will still be part of a dangerous offensive plan," Gromyko said. As Reagan's leading domestic critic, O'Neill urged Gromyko to look past the Star Wars plan and have faith in the President's desire for improved relations. The other members of the delegation chipped in with detailed suggestions for Soviet-American cooperation.

Apparently impressed by the Americans' preparedness, Gorbachev spent almost four hours with O'Neill, Michel, Rostenkowski and Silvio Conte — twice the usual allotted time — the next day. At the top of his notepad, O'Neill had printed the phonetic pronunciation — "Gor-Ba-Chof" — of the Soviet leader's name. After chatting about their mutual friend U.S. agri-businessman Dwayne Andreas, O'Neill noted that Gorbachev had appeared to arrive on the scene from nowhere. "There are lots of places to hide in the Soviet Union," Gorbachev replied. He reminded O'Neill of a savvy trial lawyer — "articulate, energetic and tough."

The Speaker was pleased with Gorbachev's opening statement, in which the Soviet leader voiced a desire for "long-term stability" in U.S.-Soviet relations.

"Politics is the art of perception. What do you perceive to be the terms?" O'Neill asked.

Until quite recently, Gorbachev said, it was a "time of concern . . . very dangerous . . . an ice age." Perhaps now there was room for change. But the Soviet leader hit the table in anger when O'Neill handed him a letter of complaints about Soviet human rights violations, bristled at Reagan's description of the USSR as an "evil empire," and repeated Gromyko's complaint that strategic arms talks in Geneva would go nowhere as long as Reagan clung to Star Wars.

"Our delegation is sitting around in Geneva eating their way through gold rubles and not making much progress," Gorbachev said. "As long as you consider Star Wars we will have to build our nuclear capacity to make sure we can break through." Such an offensive capability would cost the USSR "20 times less" than the West would spend on SDI, he warned. O'Neill promised to serve as a conduit to both Reagan and Congress, and delivered a personal letter from the President to Gorbachev, reaffirming America's desire for productive negotiations. In his memoirs, Gorbachev expressed his disappointment that the O'Neill delegation had not been more bold or imaginative. But the Speaker had seen it as his duty to prod Reagan and Gorbachev to negotiate with each other — not to tantalize the Soviet leader with the prospect of a divided American government. It was a modest goal, but one he had met.

A little over a year later, in the fall of 1986, O'Neill played a behind-the-scenes role in another superpower summit: the historic meeting between Reagan and Gorbachev in Reykjavik, Iceland. It was the eve of the mid-term elections, and dovish House liberals, after years of frustration, were poised to pass amendments that would set U.S. policy on issues like nuclear disarmament, nuclear testing, chemical weapons and strategic defense. Reagan had asked O'Neill to block the amendments, so that he would have a free hand to negotiate with Gorbachev. The Speaker had given his word to support the liberals, but called a meeting to discuss the President's request. As O'Neill looked on, Les

Aspin warned his colleagues that Reagan, should the summit fail, would have a ready scapegoat if they passed their amendments. "It's up to you," O'Neill said to Ron Dellums and Ed Markey, the leaders of the liberal group. The Speaker had said he would back them either way, but they knew what he was asking. "Dellums stood up and said that it had been a long, hard struggle to get the House on record on these weapons systems. It was disheartening, heartbreaking, to give up after reaching a point where we were so close to put an end to this madness, but that it was necessary that we not be seen as tying the President's hands," Markey recalled. "Tears started coming out of Ron's eyes. So Tip got up and came from behind his desk and he walked over to Dellums and said, 'You're a good man, Ron Dellums.' And Ron said, 'You're a good man, Tip O'Neill.' And they hugged in the middle of the room." Markey elicited a promise from Jim Wright to restage the votes in the next Congress. Once again, O'Neill had provided Reagan with the maximum freedom with which to negotiate with Gorbachev. The two leaders failed to reach an agreement on SDI at Reykjavik, but their talk of abolishing all nuclear arms was a conceptual leap that transformed the cold war.[5]

O'Neill's kinship with the Irish played an important role in the passage of another landmark of his final term — the immigration reform bill of 1986. The purpose of the Simpson-Mazzoli bill, as it was known, was to end the formidable national problem of illegal immigration by granting citizenship to the millions of illegal aliens who had established roots in the United States, and then to close the door behind them. The bill's provisions provoked opposition, at various times, from fiscal conservatives, civil libertarians, organized labor, business organizations and Hispanic Americans who feared it would cause employers to discriminate against them. It died at the end of the session in 1982, and in 1983 as well. The *Times* blistered O'Neill in an editorial as "someone who, for political gain, traffics in consummate unfairness." Senator Alan Simpson, a cosponsor, made the trek across the Capitol rotunda to the House side, where he met with the Speaker, assuaged his fears, and won O'Neill's word that the bill would be brought up in 1984.

"It is just a gut-hard, tough son-of-a-bitch that is going to haunt us all until we grapple with it," Simpson wrote O'Neill in May. "I know you have taken a hell of a battering on this immigration legislation but I sincerely and greatly admire the way you have held tough on your commitment to me." O'Neill sent the bill to the floor in late June, where it passed by a 216 to 211 margin.

Simpson appealed to O'Neill again when the bill went to conference, asking the Speaker to appoint fair-minded House conferees who would at least give the legislation a fighting chance, and expressed his thanks for O'Neill's honorable behavior. "If I am going to get punched full of holes, I'd rather have it happen right out there in the middle of the high plains and the buffalo grass—just like Custer—rather than having someone sneak into my bedroll at night and give me a lethal injection of highly distilled horse crap," Simpson wrote. The bill died again at the end of the session, but O'Neill had given his word. When Simpson brought the legislation back to the House in the Ninety-ninth Congress, the Speaker helped the Wyoming senator overcome a number of obstacles, and it passed in October 1986. It was then that Brian Donnelly got O'Neill to intervene on behalf of Irish immigrants.

When the Great Society Congress passed its historic immigration bill in 1965, it revised the old nationality quotas that were biased toward immigrants from European countries. The 1965 legislation opened America's borders to millions of Hispanics, Asians and Africans and transformed the country's complexion. Ireland, however, was one of those nations that had prospered under the old system, and was hurt by the new one. Throughout the hard economic times of the 1970s, Irish young people arrived in Boston, New York and other cities by the thousands on tourist visas, and stayed on illegally to work, many at the mercy of unscrupulous employers. Lots of legal and illegal Irish immigrants lived in Donnelly's district, and he went to work in Congress on their behalf. As the Simpson-Mazzoli bill moved toward the floor, Donnelly pushed an amendment to boost the number of Irish work visas. The legislation was so tenuously balanced, however, that the Rules Committee turned him down. He gathered with a dozen or so other Irish American legislators in the House dining room and, knowing how close the vote might be, they conspired to vote against the conference committee report.

"When they called for the vote we all went in and hit red," Donnelly recalled. "The Republicans and southern Democrats were voting no, but we were people the leadership had just assumed would be solid. You could see the staff looking up at the screen and running up to the Speaker's rostrum, frantic at the sight of all those Irish voting no."

Ignoring Republican shouts for "regular order," O'Neill held the vote open and summoned Donnelly to the rostrum.

"Jesus, Brian, what are you doing?" O'Neill asked.

"Tip, I didn't want to, but I got ten thousand illegal Irish kids living in Boston," Donnelly replied.

"Ten thousand? Jesus Christ," O'Neill said. "How do we work this out?"

"All you have to do is put an amendment in the rule."

"Arrrgh. Why didn't you guys let me know?"

"It just came up. We didn't have time," said Donnelly. "It's a good deal. A good thing. I promise."

"All right," said O'Neill. "But stay up here for another couple of minutes. I want people to think I'm giving you a good scolding."

O'Neill called the House conferees and members of the Rules Committee to his office. With "a small amendment," he said, he could bring the rebels around. "He became a coconspirator," said Donnelly. The "Donnelly visas" eventually helped 25,000 Irish immigrants. "Some small amendment," the congressman said, laughing. "O'Neill never got any credit for that, but he did it."[6]

IT WAS A NEAR thing, but O'Neill also managed to secure a quite splendid multibillion-dollar plum for Massachusetts before leaving office — the Central Artery/Third Harbor Tunnel project to relieve congestion in downtown Boston. He would not live to see it finished, but the artery project promised to transform Boston by burying a downtown eyesore, pump billions of dollars into its economy and improve the quality of life for thousands of metropolitan residents. It came to be called "Tip's Tunnel."

The original Central Artery had been built by the highway bond measures that O'Neill had pushed through the legislature as Speaker of the Massachusetts House. Constructed in the 1950s, the elevated superhighway ran from the Charles River south through Boston, cutting off the amenities of the North End and the waterfront from the rest of downtown. To minimize costs, all of which were then borne by the state, the highway planners left out merge and breakdown lanes. To allow access from Boston's many twisting streets, there were too many on and off ramps. Moreover, the Artery conveyed more vehicles — 25,000 to 30,000 per lane — than any other urban highway in the country. The dependable result, during rush hour, was an ugly elevated traffic jam through which short-tempered motorists crawled in stop-and-go misery. The two harbor tunnels, which led from the Artery to East Boston and Logan Airport, were equally gridlocked.

O'Neill, faithfully representing his constituents, had moved from being a highway booster in the 1940s and 1950s to a highway foe in the 1960s. He had joined with neighborhood groups and anti-highway activists and played a major role in helping to save Cambridge from being divided by the proposed Inner Belt. He supported the efforts of East Boston's citizenry to block construction of a third harbor tunnel entrance in their community. In Washington, he served the anti-highway cause by helping to free road-building funds for use in mass transit.

When Michael Dukakis was elected governor in 1974, he brought Fred Salvucci into the state government as secretary of transportation. Salvucci had seen his own grandmother's home taken by highway planners, and was no mindless fan of interstate expressways. But he combined a sixties sensibility about growth, and the rights of local communities, with an MIT engineering degree, a grand vision and a sure political touch. He quietly nursed a scheme to move the Artery underground, in league with construction of a third harbor tunnel. "Wouldn't it be cheaper to raise the city than to depress the Artery?" asked Barney Frank. But Salvucci's plan would prove to be a clever way to persuade pro-growth advocates, who wanted a tunnel, to join together with the no-growth forces, who liked the idea of burying the unsightly Artery and freeing its right-of-way for parks and other public open space.

Salvucci's plan went nowhere for years, but state officials were wise enough to keep mention of it in their various requests for transportation funds. O'Neill was a critical help in 1975, when the Federal Highway Administration wanted to drop the project. At one crucial meeting with federal officials, Massachusetts transportation counsel Robert Curry began to tug on his ear. It was a signal to an O'Neill aide in the room that the time was ripe for the then majority leader to interrupt the proceedings with a phone call. That phone call helped win a $311 million federal commitment. For the next six years, O'Neill's watchful pals on the House Public Works Committee kept the plan alive.

When Ed King beat Dukakis in 1978, Salvucci's dream was put on hold. Then Dukakis beat the governor in their 1982 rematch. Salvucci was back, and in early 1983 he persuaded Dukakis to shoot the moon.

Now it was up to O'Neill to get the money — then estimated at $2 billion — from Congress.

"Salvucci, Machiavellian as he was, came up with the master plan, and the biggest problem was convincing O'Neill on the tunnel, which he had spent his career opposing. And the magic stroke was reconfiguring the tunnel so there were no more [property] takings," said Brian Donnelly. "So Fred comes in with a couple of staff. He's got the plan. And Tip is a little cold to Fred. He's got this big cigar and the ashes keep flipping on the plans as he says, 'What about so-and-so?' He keeps throwing out names. 'Are the people in Eastie for this?' And I'm convinced the whole thing, literally, is going to go up in flames. But Salvucci is right there with him, saying 'Yeah. Yeah. They're for it.'"

O'Neill signed on after Salvucci gave the Speaker his personal guarantee that there would be no neighborhood opposition in East Boston. But even with O'Neill's help, finding the money was no easy task. The state's strategy was straightforward: to persuade the government that the Artery/tunnel project should be classified under the Interstate Highway program as new construction, which would make Massachusetts eligible for unlimited U.S. funding on a 90:10 ratio of federal to state money. It was a federal commitment that dated back to the Eisenhower administration, but this was the Reagan era, and though the President had carried the state twice, it still bore a reputation as a haven for unrepentant liberalism. "Massachusetts had screwed around for so many years in such an anti-transportation mode with all their social maneuvering," said highway administrator Ray Barnhart. "Coming from Texas, my first inclination was to let the bastards freeze in the dark."

"Ray was a right-wing Republican who had been with Ronald Reagan forever. He thought Tip O'Neill and Ted Kennedy were like Lenin and Marx. He called them the communists from Massachusetts. A real drum-beating yahoo. He was out to croak us," Salvucci recalled.

O'Neill persevered. While Reagan was President, the Speaker routinely ran across conservative activists in positions of authority at federal agencies who were itching to halt any project connected with his name. "All I would do is pick up the telephone and call Mike Deaver or Jim Baker or Ed Meese. All three of them were talented politicians. They didn't agree with me philosophically but they agreed they had to deal with me and I had to deal with them," O'Neill recalled. "I would say, 'We have authorized this, we have appropriated this, and some flunky over there is trying to stop it because I am Tip O'Neill.' They would say, 'Tip, it will be through.' It was something I couldn't get in the Carter administration."

O'Neill was also close pals with the Public Works chairman, James Howard, a schoolteacher who had been elected in a Republican district only because of Lyndon Johnson's coattails in 1964. As a House leader and DCCC chair, O'Neill had helped deliver the campaign funds and legislative plums that let Howard secure the seat, and the two men became golf and travel buddies as well. "Howard idolized Tip. Whatever Tip wants, Howard is for," said Donnelly, who was on the Public Works panel at the time. Indeed, the Massachusetts delegation was well cast at this moment: Eddie Boland and Silvio Conte were on Appropriations, Joe Moakley on Rules and Brian Donnelly in the process of moving to Ways and Means from Public Works. "We were a tremendously strong delegation at that time. Everybody was in key spots and we were very powerful," O'Neill recalled. "If you have power bases, the power bases operate." It was a good thing. The chief threat that Massachusetts faced was the fierce competition for transportation money among the various states and regions. "There are no vegetarians in Congress when it comes to pork," said Fred Salvucci.

Though under intense pressure from the highway administration and the other states, O'Neill blocked all omnibus transportation bills until the Public Works Committee agreed to authorize the Artery. The Republican Senate refused to bow, however, and the Artery proponents decided that what they needed was a Republican leader for their coalition. They found one in Roger Moore, a senior partner at Ropes and Gray, longtime Massport counsel and a conservative activist with ties to Reagan and Barnhart. Transportation secretary Elizabeth Dole was invited to Boston for a fund-raiser for her husband Bob's presidential campaign, and was deliberately booked by Dole's local supporters to arrive during a Friday rush hour, when she got a firsthand taste of the need for the project. The state also hired the Bechtel Corporation (for whom both George Shultz and Cap Weinberger had served as corporate executives) as construction manager. "When Salvucci hired Bechtel, I blew my stack," said Donnelly. "This wasn't rocket science — anybody could dig a tunnel. Why not give the job to some guys from Dorchester? But that took care of the Republican opposition. That and Moore."

The 1986 transportation bill, which included the Artery and more than $88 billion worth of porky projects, cleared the House. But House and Senate negotiators failed to agree on other provisions, including an effort by Western senators to hike the maximum speed limit from 55 to 65 miles per hour on rural highways. Once again, the legislation died at the end of a session. "Howard used the Speaker as the locomotive to pull this huge pork train across the landscape," said Salvucci, "and it kept getting stuck because it was so goddamn big."

O'Neill retired, but left behind his anointed successor, Speaker Jim Wright, and a Democratic Senate. Congress finally passed the transportation bill after Frank — with an eye on building the largest coalition for a possible veto fight — got a contingent of urban Eastern Democrats to support the 65-mile-per-hour speed limit for their Western colleagues. Sure enough, Reagan vetoed the bill, and the Westerners were crucial in the subsequent votes to override the President's veto. So too were the efforts of O'Neill's old friend Charlie Rose, whose North Carolina delegation had its tobacco subsidies to protect, and persuaded their state's senator, Terry Sanford, to switch his vote at a critical moment. It took until April 2, 1987 — twelve years after O'Neill began to shepherd the project and three months after he had left office — but Tip's Tunnel had its money. The project's cost was then estimated at $3.1 billion, and would soar to $12 billion by the end of the century. Tip came to worry that the Artery would be known as Tip's Folly. But "let me tell you something about Washington," O'Neill said. "The squeaky wheel gets the grease in Washington, there is no question about it. Maybe it's not the way to run a government but that's the way the government runs."[7]

There was one more chapter in the six-year scrap between Reagan and O'Neill. In February 1985, the President launched a final offensive to persuade Congress to provide funding for the Nicaraguan Contra armies, whom Reagan hailed as "freedom fighters." Since the passage of the Boland amendment the previous fall, Ollie North had been keeping the Contras alive by collecting millions of dollars in secret contributions from cooperative foreign nations. At the same time, the Reagan administration was confronting another foreign policy threat — the taking, by Iranian-sponsored terrorists, of American hostages in Lebanon. CIA director William Casey persuaded Reagan and other administration officials to send TOW antitank missiles to Iran. North was put in charge of that operation as well, and both of his activities were kept secret from Congress.

In March 1986, O'Neill made an impassioned speech to close the debate, then broke tradition to cast his vote early in the balloting, and a $100 million military aid package for the Contras was defeated in the House. "You can appreciate how hard I'm working against the President's program," the Speaker wrote an old friend. "I believe his policies are absolutely immoral. It appears he won't be happy until American troops are in Central America fighting for what he believes is the ultimate testing ground between the Soviets and our government."

Yet Democrats were under intense public pressure from the President and his supporters to act against what Reagan called "a Soviet military beachhead." The Speaker was the lame duck and finally, on June 25, 1986, he could hold the line no longer. By a 221 to 209 vote, the House okayed a $100 million package for the Contras that included $70 million in military aid. Les Aspin was among those who switched their votes. It looked like Reagan had won. He celebrated on "Liberty Weekend," another red-white-and-blue July 4 spectacular, commemorating the hundredth birthday of the Statue of Liberty. In fact, it was Reagan who had lost. Frustrated by the restraints of the Boland amendments, North had been diverting profits from the arms sales to Iran to pay for the Contra war. On November 3, a Lebanese magazine broke the news about the U.S. arms trade with Iran. Reagan denied that he had been trading arms for hostages, but asked Ed Meese to conduct an inquiry. On November 22, a Saturday, Meese's investigators discovered a memo in North's office that revealed the diversion of funds to the Contras. It was, North said, the "secret within the secret." On Tuesday, November 25, Jim Wright and Bob Byrd were hastily summoned to the White House to hear the details of what came to be known as the "Iran-Contra" affair. O'Neill, who was meeting about his memoirs with a publisher in Boston, got the news by telephone. "You'll never guess what just happened," he told editor Peter Osnos and ghostwriter William Novak after hanging up the phone.

Earlier that morning, Don Regan had asked North's boss, national security adviser John Poindexter, what had gone so terribly, terribly wrong.

"I knew Ollie was up to something, but I didn't know what, and I just didn't look into it," said Poindexter, looking up from his breakfast and dabbing his mouth clean with a napkin.

"Why not? What the hell? You're a vice admiral. What's going on?" Regan said.

"Well, that damned Tip O'Neill," Poindexter said. "The way he was jerking the Contras around, I was just so disgusted. I didn't want to know what Ollie was doing." Regan later concluded that North "despaired of Tip O'Neill ever bringing up legislation for Contra aid, so he was willing to try anything."[8]

CHAPTER 28

Farewell

IT WAS TIME to say good-bye. After fifty years, Tip O'Neill was leaving public service. Head up. Shoulders back. He did not especially want to go, but recognized that the moment had arrived. His sense of timing, as always, was splendid. He went out on top, and was rewarded with the longest, most affectionate send-off given any Speaker or President of his time. There had been hints of what was to come: while addressing the Tufts University graduating class of 1985, he had been interrupted by the cheering crowd of students chanting: "Tip! Tip! Tip!" A Harris poll, taken in July of 1986, showed the Speaker had a 63 percent favorability rating. *The Almanac of American Politics, 1986* gave the O'Neill years a spectacular review — reaching all the way back to Sam Rayburn's New Deal and World War II leadership for comparison.

O'Neill was "the most effective and accomplished Speaker the nation has had for 40 years," the *Almanac* said. "He does not command automatic majorities, and he sometimes makes mistakes. But well into his 70s he continues to be an active, hard-working, and, to an extent that remains unappreciated even in his fifth term as Speaker, both a shrewd legislator and political strategist.

"During the Carter years, he made the mistake of deferring to others, and while he got the Carter energy program through the House, he found out that the White House had no clear priorities," the *Almanac* said. "In the 1980s, as the Democrats' leading national politician, he did not make that mistake again. He pounced on Reagan administration plans to cut Social Security and gave Democratic House candidates a winning issue in the 1982 elections.

"Without O'Neill's deft strategy, the Republican dreams of capturing control of the House . . . might have come true by 1984," the authors concluded. "The technical and financial advantages which Republican candidates enjoy have been overcome by, among other things, the shrewdness of a white-haired septuagenarian Irish pol."

The round of farewell tributes began in February, when 1,200 Massachusetts Democrats gathered at the Park Plaza Hotel for drinks and filet mignon in O'Neill's honor. State Senate president William Bulger called out, "Up, up — the Speaker!" and joined treasurer Robert Crane in a chorus of "Happy Days Are Here Again" and "If You're Irish, Come into the Parlor." O'Neill was poised and relaxed, and still challenging Reaganism when he told the adoring audience, "Government is not part of the problem, it is part of the solution." The Boston dinner was just a warm-up for the St. Patrick's Day blast that followed. More than 2,000 people, including Presidents Reagan and Ford and Irish prime minister Garret FitzGerald, jammed the main ballroom at the Washington Hilton to raise $2 million for a Tip O'Neill scholarship fund at Boston College. FitzGerald conveyed Irish citizenship to Tip and Millie, who joined a select half-dozen individuals granted that honor. Bob Hope served as the evening's entertainer, and Ted Kennedy told the crowd, "I want to welcome you to the latest in the 1986 weekly series of Tip O'Neill retirement parties."

"For BC, it may have been the greatest single night in the school's history, the time when the school was feted by the power elite, and the BC contingent exulted in its new status," wrote the *Globe*'s David Nyhan. "A Harvardian counted the house and mused that, for a one-night stand, 'Harvard's never had a night like this.' A graying BC man exulted: 'Nor could it.' A BC man theorized later: 'You probably couldn't get elected Speaker of the House if you had a Harvard degree. The skills that it takes to get the one are not the skills you needed to get the other.'"

Reagan almost stole the show. "I've always known that Tip was behind me," the President said, "even if it was only at the State of the

Union address. As I made each proposal, I could hear Tip whispering to George Bush, 'Forget it. No way. Fat chance.'" Then Reagan grew sentimental. "Mr. Speaker, I'm grateful you have permitted me in the past, and I hope in the future, that singular honor — the honor of calling you my friend," he said.

O'Neill, during his turn at the microphone, debuted what he would use, in interviews and speeches over the next year, as a farewell creed. "In the country of my youth, there was no middle class as we know it today — only the very few rich at the top and the millions and millions of poor at the bottom, with a huge and terrible difference in between," he said. "I never forget how far we've come in fifty years." The growth of the American middle class, he said, was his greatest accomplishment.

O'Neill departed from his prepared remarks to say a few words about Millie. "So many of you have talked about my Millie tonight. Well, Millie and I went around together in high school and we've been married forty-five years. She has been mother and father to our family while I have been down here in Washington, while I've been in politics," he said. "It's great to come home and know that when the times are up and the times are tough, there is a loving and caring individual who has so much concern for your life. Mother, if it's possible to love you more, I love you more, but I want to thank you for forty-five years of happiness."

On a swing through the Midwest in May, O'Neill accepted the Harry S. Truman Public Service Award at the presidential library in Independence, Missouri, and attended events in his honor in Kansas City and Chicago. Later that month the Boston Chamber of Commerce did its part, and then it was back to the Washington Hilton for 1,700 Democrats and the DCCC dinner. As the band played "When Irish Eyes are Smiling," he ended his remarks by waving and shouting, "This is it, everybody! I love you!" In September, he was invited to speak at Harvard's 350th anniversary celebration, and got a standing ovation from the students and dignitaries. "Not bad for a young fellow who grew up in the shadow of Harvard . . . who remembered the Yard very well, because he cut the lawns here," O'Neill said. He would get his honorary degree (finally) from Harvard in 1987, and even then would say, "I don't feel as though I've been totally accepted." He still liked to give its graduates the needle, calling it "the Stanford of the East."

In the summer of 1986, O'Neill and Millie sold the house on Russell Street, at or near the listed price of $425,000; they would split their time between Bethesda and Harwichport. When in Washington, Millie warned him, she wanted him out of the house during the day, so he arranged to get an office at Kip's law firm, in a renovated townhouse on Nineteenth Street, near Dupont Circle. As O'Neill entered his final months in office, the press began to appraise his career. "When Republicans took the White House and the Senate in 1980, Mr. O'Neill was suddenly the nation's ranking Democrat, chief defender against the new crowd's assault on 'big government.' Partisan Reaganites were delighted to have him as a stereotypical foil — the bulky old Irish pol, who rumbled on cue against their polished and popular President," said the *New York Times.* "He still rumbles, but the Republicans are no longer delighted.

"O'Neill has been more than speaker; in the Reagan years, he has been the Democrats' national spokesman, doggedly pressing his fractured party's concerns for the underdog," the *Times* said.

"Ten years ago, when Tip O'Neill was about to become Speaker of the House, little was expected from him. The House, conventional wisdom had it, was a collection of committee chairmen's baronies, the backwater of American government, stymied by division and incapable of action," said the *Washington Post*. "Tip O'Neill and the House he has led have proved that conventional wisdom wrong."

More eloquent praise came in a private letter from David Rogers of the *Wall Street Journal,* a former *Globe* reporter who had served in Vietnam as a medic, though a conscientious objector to the war. He had come home from the battlefield with "anger and immense sadness," he told O'Neill. "I bring this up only because you have sometimes expressed mixed feelings about your own early opposition to the war. While firm in your position, you have been sensitive to the hurt your stand might have caused among families whose sons were in the fighting. I understand those emotions, but as one of those sons, I want you to know too that you have done more to heal me toward my government than anyone I have seen since in public life.

"It's not because you were against the war . . . it is what you have been beyond Vietnam, as Speaker and as a person," said Rogers. "You have meant far more than either of us fully knows, and for that I thank you as well."

Colleagues from both parties surprised O'Neill with a closed-door party on the House floor on October 1, after luring him to the chamber under the pretext that they needed a ruling from the chair. "I'd rather fight with someone who really believes in what they say, than with some lukewarm pragmatist who believes what the headlines tell him to believe," GOP leader Bob Michel told him. A third-floor room in the Capitol, and a congressional office building, were named after the departing Speaker, and his portrait was hung in the Speaker's lobby. He wept and spoke of his long-lost mother during his last Speaker's press conference on October 17, then presided over his final session. It had finally hit him — he told his colleagues after the standing ovation ended — when even Republicans came in to have farewell photos taken with him. "I leave with just love and affection for this great body," O'Neill said. "I'll always be a man of the House of Representatives."

"Old pal, we love you, we'll miss you," said Silvio Conte.

O'Neill got to throw out the first ball at Fenway Park when the World Series returned to Boston that fall, and died one of the thousand deaths of Red Sox fans when the New York Mets made a remarkable comeback, with the help of an error by Sox first baseman Bill Buckner. "I still wake up and see the ball go through Buckner's legs," he said months later. O'Neill's last ceremonial duty was to light the Capitol Christmas tree in December, a task at which he was assisted by his three granddaughters. On his final day on the job, in January, the Speaker realized that he was without a car and driver. He phoned an auto dealer, leased an automobile and had it delivered to the Capitol so he could get home.

"Tip was really a miraculous human being," said Democratic pollster Peter Hart, "because there he was being cuffed about the ears on various things, and as he had to listen to these young pollsters and hotshot media people, he had a great ability to understand what we were trying to do, and at the same time could be unmerciful with us for not understanding the importance of the Democratic Party and the tradition which we might be willing to trample on in order to achieve a short-term gain. He never lost sight of where the North Star was. He knew what his party was all about, what it had to be and ought to be, and was able to position the party for 1982 on the issues of fairness and Social Security and at the same time not lose the party's soul.

"He was a remarkable leader in a time that couldn't have been worse for the Democratic Party."

The Republicans were not sad to see him go. Among the younger Reaganauts, he was a villainous figure. "He was a good working-class Irishman, but he operated from complete moral arrogance," speechwriter Peggy Noonan recalled. "He ascribed unthinkingly to the old leftist view that he cared for the little guy, and we did not. And because of that he suffered from a terrible ideological deafness: he could not hear Reagan. And because he could not hear him, he couldn't give him his due. He gave him only backhanded acknowledgement as a charmer, or a performer. It was all backhanded bullshit."

"O'Neill was a very passionate local politician representing the Irish Catholic Boston system that Curley had made famous, and in many ways he never evolved much beyond that," said Gingrich. "He was a pretty effective legislative leader with an occasional instinct for national activity but one who always started from what he knew and learned in the saloons and streets of Boston."[1]

Back in North Cambridge, more than a dozen Democratic contenders had spent the last year jockeying for O'Neill's seat. (Tommy's wife, Jacqueline, had been among those "mentioned" as possible candidates.) Leading the list was Joseph P. Kennedy II, a son of Robert F. Kennedy. After some clumsy political foreplay, Kirk O'Donnell and Ted Kennedy got the candidate down to the Cape to meet with the Speaker. Young Joe had his father's toughness, good political instincts and a commitment to the downtrodden, all of which appealed to both Millie and Tip, who didn't relish seeing his seat go to a "save the whales" liberal. The Speaker agreed to film a 30-second commercial endorsing Kennedy. The ad blanketed Boston on the weekend before the primary. Kennedy's campaign was delighted with the outcome. "I think we had gotten so used to Tip that we had underestimated the regard people had for him," said adviser John Marttila. Kennedy won the seat, keeping its distinctive lineage — Curley, JFK, O'Neill, Kennedy — alive for another decade.

The Democrats picked up 8 seats in the Senate and 5 in the House in the November 1986 election. Jim Wright was nominated by the caucus to be the new Speaker. O'Neill used his last weeks in office to settle a few scores. The Speaker had already hosted one reception for Governor Michael Dukakis when, in December, Gary Hart — the supposed frontrunner for the 1988 Democratic nomination — dropped by for a meeting. Hart opened the session by citing the Mrs. O'Brien story and asking for the Speaker's support, but O'Neill boasted later that he cut him no slack.

"You're not my cup of tea," O'Neill told Hart. "You've been around here for fourteen years: you and I have never had a conversation. You're a loner. Furthermore, you're this new type of liberal. I'm the old work and wages, take care of the poor and the hungry. I don't like your kind of politics.

"I won't say anything mean about you, but in our party, front-runners have a tendency to stumble. You should know. You participated in the destruction of a front-runner. I was a Muskie man. You helped to destroy Muskie. You helped to destroy the party," O'Neill said.[2]

Next up was Les Aspin, who "broke his word to a lot of people" on the MX and Contra issues, the Speaker said. O'Neill and Murtha went to work, and when Aspin's name came before the Democratic caucus on January 7, his colleagues voted to dump him as chairman of the Armed Services Committee. It was only with difficulty that a frantic Aspin was able to turn that vote around, and defeat his challengers in a caucus showdown after O'Neill had departed.[3]

MONEY, FOR ONCE, was not a problem. Irony of ironies: Reagan had made him rich. "You know, in a real perverse way the Republicans created their own worst enemy," Matthews said. "They gave him an identity and he used it, and became the great champion of the little guy." The months of exchanging televised volleys with the President had brought O'Neill's grandfatherly visage into millions of living rooms. Conventioneers clamored to hear him speak. New York advertising agencies wanted to use his image to sell their clients' products. The publishing industry bid for his memoirs, and talk shows begged for his time.

The first windfall arrived when O'Neill signed a contract with Random House in June of 1985. A dozen publishing houses had joined the two-day telephone auction, driving the price up to just over a million dollars. "Don't tell me America isn't a great country," O'Neill said. William Novak, the Newton-based writer who had been the ghostwriter for Chrysler chairman Lee Iacocca's bestselling memoirs, had joined Kip O'Neill in persuading the Speaker to become an author. Novak had also contracted to write *Mayflower Madam,* about a call-girl service run by a former debutante, and was worried that O'Neill would disapprove. Instead, O'Neill would greet him by saying, "Well, how's the hooker?"

Novak interviewed three dozen of O'Neill's family members, friends and former colleagues and got him to talk for hours into a tape recorder that summer on the Cape. Novak combed O'Neill's well-kept scrapbooks, his fragmented diaries, Breslin's *How the Good Guys Finally Won,* and *Tip,* a 1979 book by Paul Clancy and Shirley Elder, for material. After a shaky start, the ghostwriter did a fine job, capturing O'Neill's voice and cataloging anecdotes. Yet the old pol's professional reticence, and Irish distaste for introspection, left huge holes in his story. O'Neill's way of dealing with foes like Phil Burton and Tony Coelho was to leave them out entirely.

Man of the House received a rave write-up on the cover of the Sunday book section of the *New York Times Book Review.* Amazingly, the reviewer was O'Neill's old antagonist, columnist William Safire. He found the former Speaker a "spellbinding Irish charmer" whose "disarming frankness" and "practical political reasoning" and "provocative quips" kept the book "zipping right along."

"For its evocation of the early Boston days alone, *Man of the House* deserves to be a hit," Safire concluded. "Up, up — the Speaker!" With the help of Safire's review (and an equally favorable piece by John Kenneth Galbraith in the *Globe*) the book shot up the bestseller list, going through eight printings and more than 300,000 copies in its first eight weeks of sales. "It's a good book," Safire blithely explained when he ran into O'Neill at a book-signing session, and was asked by the astonished author ("You've got to be kidding. You were always such a sonofabitch. How come you gave it a good review?") about the *Times* review.

Not everyone was impressed. "Sadly, if not surprisingly, *Man of the House* fails to capture the true tang of this American original, not to mention the full reach of his astonishing half-century in public life," wrote J. Anthony Lukas in the *Washington Post.* O'Neill always said that Breslin's book about Watergate was "based on fact." Much the same could be said about *Man of the House.* Some of the anecdotes — like the George Kara story — were verifiable. Others came under attack. Columnists Evans and Novak denied his assertion that they offered to trade him good coverage for leaks. Dave Powers failed to support O'Neill's claim that Powers and Kenny O'Donnell believed there was a second gunman involved in the JFK assassination. "Tip is a great storyteller, as are many politicians," Novak diplomatically told the press. "They tell these stories over and over again. The rough edges get planed off and the story gets a little more dramatic and they get further and further from reality."

One anecdote served as a prime example. In 1975, the young Joe Klein, then working for an alternative paper in Cambridge, spent time with O'Neill for a profile.

"A Cambridge banker and his son come into the office," Klein wrote.

> The banker asks O'Neill to pose for pictures with the boy, which he does graciously. Then, "You have an elderly woman teller in your North Cambridge branch. She's been there for 34 years, an old friend of mine." O'Neill mentions the woman's name. "She tells me she's getting fired."
>
> "The banker shuffles and stumbles a bit. "Yes, well . . . uh, we're being forced to lay off some people to keep our profits stable."
>
> "Well gee," O'Neill says, still very calm and folksy, "it'd be a real shame to let her go."
>
> "Yes . . . uh, I'll speak to the president of the bank about that."
>
> "That's probably a good idea," O'Neill replies. "Because this woman could probably start at Alewife Brook Parkway and walk all the way to Porter Square and lose you 800 accounts."

In 1977, two years after Klein's article appeared, O'Neill told a reporter from the *Chicago Tribune* who asked about the incident that it was "a true story." O'Neill had a name for the elderly woman teller: Mary McHugh. And it wasn't just Mary who would walk across Cambridge, blackening the banker's good name, it was Mary and Tip, arm in arm.

But in 1981, O'Neill needed a story to illustrate the discrimination that Irish Americans faced during his younger years. Now, as the Speaker told the tale to a writer from the *Post,* the story morphed into the version that eventually wound up in *Man of the House.* The 1970s had become the 1940s, and it was not Mary McHugh, but young Billy Askin who had quit a job to take work at the bank, only to find it wouldn't employ him once the managers discovered he was Catholic. "You've got three days to straighten this out," O'Neill said he told the bank president. "If it isn't, then on Monday, $34,000 of our St. Peter and Paul Society money is coming out. And I'll walk this entire district to tell people what a bigoted bastard you are."

The readers didn't mind. And the success of *Man of the House* was fueled by O'Neill's debut as "the latest darling of America's advertising industry . . . [and] full-blown national icon," as Lukas put it. After leaving office, O'Neill had signed with the William Morris Agency and enrolled in the Screen Actors Guild. For American Express, photographer Annie Leibovitz caught O'Neill in a beach chair, with rolled-up pants and a silly striped hat, a pack of cards in his mitts and his cigar shoved into the sand.[4] For Hush Puppies (in which the torsos of five celebrities were posed over another's legs and shoes), O'Neill smiled from above actress Lauren Hutton's slender legs and red high-heeled shoes. After a long, excruciating day of filming at the Faneuil Hall Marketplace, O'Neill appeared in a TV ad for Miller Lite beer. With the help of a pneumatic lift, he rose magically out of a suitcase for Quality International, a budget motel chain; he sparred with seatmate Al Haig on behalf of the Trump Shuttle, and waved a chicken leg for Commodore computers.

The early commercials paid O'Neill from $10,000 to $50,000 each, and his fee rose to $100,000 as advertisers jockeyed for his services. Millie got some nice jewelry, and the O'Neills bought a condo at the Sea View Hotel in Bal Harbour, where Bob Dole, Howard Baker, Bob Strauss and Dwayne Andreas (whose firm ran the place) were neighbors. It was easy money, which helped compensate for the pain of retirement, for O'Neill did not take to the stay-at-home life. His retirement had been a mistake, he told his friend Speed Carroll. He was lonely and near tears in a Cleveland hotel room as he watched Reagan give the 1987 State of the Union address. Visitors noted how C-SPAN's coverage of the House was always on the office television. He was restless; he missed the fame and action, bitter that Jim Wright didn't call for advice and that only a few old pals — like Dan Rostenkowski — took him to lunch. "Chris, it goes away," he told Matthews. He roamed the country, cashing in while he could. The Harry Walker Agency booked him as a guest speaker and, in his first six months of retirement alone, O'Neill was paid from $15,000 to $25,000 an appearance to deliver fifty speeches to various clubs, colleges and business groups. He went home to Harwichport for the summer, then departed on his national book tour.

As the list of commercials grew, old friends, like Mary McGrory, deplored the "tackiness" of O'Neill's new career. He cut her off. Gene McCarthy said that "it was hard to imagine that Rayburn, had he lived beyond his speakership, would have appeared in television advertisements for luggage, or beer."

"These ads I'm in come after 50 years of public service," O'Neill told *Adweek* magazine. "I'm entitled to a new career. I'm happy and my clients are happy." To his defense came an unlikely ally — Republican media guru Roger Ailes — who wrote in *Advertising Age* that O'Neill should not worry about the "stuffy people" he had offended.

"He worked for wages far below what he could have earned in private life, often sacrificing his family and himself for his constituents," Ailes wrote. "This is America. . . . Tip O'Neill is now in his seventies. He may want to leave some money to his children and grandchildren so they never have to work as hard as he did. . . . He's making commercials because it's fun, and if he wants to jump out of a suitcase, it's nobody's damn business."

Even Millie thought some of the advertising antics were unseemly. "Honey, you weren't upset when you put the last check in the bank," he told her.

O'Neill's royalties from his memoirs, advertisements and speeches were supplemented by $69,000 that he had accumulated in a campaign treasury over the years, which the law allowed him to convert to private use. He received a $185,000 annual office allowance and an $80,000 annual pension payment from the U.S. government — all of which were grist for critics. What he kept private were his considerable donations to charities: often he would endorse the entire proceeds from a speech to a Catholic religious order, a charitable foundation, scholarship fund or college. Of the $69,000 in his campaign fund, $25,000 went to charity. In the spring, O'Neill would send out $3,000 in "Easter offerings" to the hard-working clergy. Homeless shelters and boys clubs thanked him for his generosity. The Family Pantry food bank in Harwich relied heavily on O'Neill and his circle of friends and associates. With Diehl, he hosted an annual charity golf tournament at Eastward Ho.[5]

In October 1987, O'Neill traveled to Hyde Park, New York, to receive a Franklin D. Roosevelt Four Freedoms Medal. "I was a New Dealer then and I'm a New Dealer now," he said. Three weeks later, on the first weekend of November, O'Neill attended the Boston College versus Notre Dame football game in South Bend, Indiana. BC managed to lose a lead and the game, but what increasingly bothered O'Neill was the diarrhea and abdominal discomfort he experienced.

He was flown home to Washington on a private jet and late at night suffered "terrible, terrible pains." Alarmed, Millie phoned Kip, who took them to the emergency room at nearby Sibley Memorial Hospital. O'Neill was given medication and painkillers and told to return the following day. He did so, and a specialist discovered a tumor in his colon.

After consulting with cancer experts from the National Institutes of Health and Johns Hopkins University, O'Neill scheduled an operation at Brigham and Women's Hospital in Boston on November 18. "I'll never forget the night before I was operated on. The nurse came in to see me and she said, 'I'm here to measure you.' And I didn't know if she was there to measure me for a coffin, or what. Then the doctor said it is ten to one we are going to get it and we will be able to reconnect you, but I knew then there was a possibility I was going to have to wear a [colostomy] bag," O'Neill recalled.

By then, despite his sons' initial efforts to mislead the press, hospital officials had announced the details of O'Neill's condition to the Boston media. "So I go to bed and wake up in the morning and turn on the TV and there is the news and a doctor explaining to the press and he shows my whole stomach and the cutting and how we are going to try to connect and I am watching the whole thing fifteen minutes before they come to take me downstairs," O'Neill remembered. "I'm telling you, the old prayer beads were really going." The seven-hour operation was a success, as the doctors removed a golf ball–sized tumor and the surrounding rectum. But "I've got good news and bad news," his doctor told him. "The good news is I got the cancer. The bad news is I couldn't connect you. You will have to wear a colostomy bag."

Said O'Neill: "I leaned back and I prayed to die."

Millie was a rock. He got phone calls from President Reagan and Vice President George Bush, spoke to a choked-up Gerry Ford and received 30,000 get-well cards and letters and phone calls from around the country — many from colostomy patients, like football great Otto Graham and Marvin Bush, the vice president's son. They predicted, accurately, that the intense pain O'Neill experienced for the next month would one day disappear, and that he would resume a near-normal lifestyle. While he was in the hospital, another team of surgeons removed O'Neill's enlarged prostate, which had been giving him trouble for more than a decade. He spent his seventy-fifth birthday in the hospital, and left December 10, looking wan but flashing a "V" sign with his fingers to the waiting news photographers.

Recuperating in Harwichport, O'Neill suffered from depression, humiliation and pain. His colon had been drawn through the abdominal wall and sutured to the skin, just below his navel. Because his sphincter muscles had been removed, he could no longer control the timing of his bowel movements. Waste was collected in a plastic bag that, periodically, he would have to change. O'Neill had difficulty with the colostomy rig and was haunted by the memory of an old card-playing buddy who — dependent on the ostomy technology of the 1950s — had lost friends because he had smelled so bad. Yet, over time, O'Neill coped. He returned to Washington in late January and reentered public life. He had to cancel one speaking engagement after discovering that the seal on his ostomy apparatus had broken, and to curtail the passion with which he swung a golf club, but resumed his speaking schedule, the ads and TV commercials — and campaigned for Michael Dukakis in 1988. ("He was really a pretty able guy, but he didn't have the stomach for the fight after he got the nomination," was O'Neill's analysis of the Dukakis defeat.)

Tip O'Neill was now an American archetype. He did a cameo for the motion picture *Dave.* Cartoonist Jeff MacNelly put an O'Neill-like character in the comic strip "Shoe." Joe Klein would use him as the model for congressional boss "Donny O'Brien" (with an Ari Weiss–like aide named "Dov Mandelbaum") in the novel *Primary Colors.*

Bush was a generous victor and pressed O'Neill to be his ambassador to Ireland. It was a tempting proposition, but O'Neill's bout with cancer had taken too great a toll and Millie's respiratory problems — she suffered from asthma and would eventually be diagnosed with emphysema — had grown worse. He would be serving a Republican administration, for a pro-British State Deparment, far from home and his eight grandchildren. "I'm in the autumn of my life," he told the *Times.* "Millie and I are too old to go over there." He watched from home in wonder as the Hungarians and Poles defied an exhausted Soviet Union and then, on November 9, 1989, as the German people tore down the Berlin Wall.

In retrospect, O'Neill made a wise decision when turning down Bush's offer. In January 1990, O'Neill found that he was having difficulty buttoning his collars. "You must have gained weight," Millie suggested. "Mom, I've lost weight," her husband replied. He completed a scheduled speech at Tulane University, then entered Brigham and Women's again in early March for another biopsy. The doctors discovered a series of cancerous lumps under his collarbone and sternum. The diagnosis was lymphoma; the surgeons removed some of the nodules and put O'Neill on a course of chemotherapy and quarterly checkups.

"What about cigars?" O'Neill asked his doctor.

"You inhale?" the physician asked.

"No."

"What the hell. You're seventy-seven. Don't let me take the last pleasure away from you," the doctor said.

"I'm fortunate," O'Neill told the *Herald*'s Andy Miga, referring to the chemotherapy. "I've never lost my hair, never had any side effects, and yet it's done the job. You get tired, but you get tired anyway." Yet Jerry Colbert remembered a time when O'Neill was so sickened by his chemotherapy treatments that he couldn't manage to drive a car — yet kept a commitment to entertain 300 people at a charity fund-raiser. "Hell, it's for the homeless, I can make it," O'Neill said.

O'Neill refused to surrender to cancer. He traveled to Cooperstown to see Carl Yastrzemski's induction to the Baseball Hall of Fame. He watched in dismay as Jim Wright and Tony Coelho were forced to resign from the House — casualties of a storm about ethics brought on by Newt Gingrich. (When Representative Chester Atkins, a Massachusetts Democrat and member of the House Ethics Committee, voted against Wright, the Texan called O'Neill to complain. "I would have told you not to put him on the ethics panel," O'Neill told him, "but you never asked me.") He endorsed John Silber's run for governor in 1990 (Silber had helped out O'Neill's son Michael's insurance agency when the young man was trying to make one last go of it) and offered words of consolation and encouragement to Barney Frank when the congressman was trapped in a sex scandal. There were Red Sox games with his grandsons, golf at Eastward Ho, trips to Ireland (where a flatbed truck carried his golf cart from course to course and the children pressed their faces up against the windows of cafés to see him) and gin rummy by the poolside cabana at the Sea View. "Millie says I'm spending far more time with my grandchildren than I ever did with my kids," he told an interviewer. In January 1991, O'Neill watched the Super Bowl with Silvio Conte, who was suffering from a virulent prostate cancer. Conte died two weeks later. In the spring, in part from a feeling of obligation to Sil, O'Neill went public about the disease, testifying before a Senate committee on behalf of more federal spending for anticancer research. "I am a cancer victim who, because of government funding, has found the means to lengthen my life," O'Neill said.

Though the initial reports of its success in combat were wildly overstated by the Pentagon, the Patriot missile proved to be an effective psychological weapon during the Persian Gulf War in 1991, and O'Neill showed pride in his pork barrel baby. "Jim Dinneen went in to see Tip with this professor-type person. They both work at Raytheon. He says, 'Tip, this is Dr. so-and-so and he's developed a great missile but we are having trouble getting the Army to accept it.' So they sit down and tell Tip the story," Joe Moakley recalled. "Well, Tip is as knowledgeable about missiles as I am. We are both still trying to figure out how a crystal radio works. So they're talking about azimuths and hit ratios and Tip is saying, 'Yeah . . . yeah . . . yeah.' Then Dinneen says, 'Tip, it will put six thousand people to work in the commonwealth.' And Tip says, 'Six thousand people!' and starts paying attention."

"Did I do it for the defense of America or did I do it for the economy of my country?" O'Neill would say with a twinkle. "Well, nevertheless it worked out beautifully."[6]

THE SOVIET UNION collapsed upon itself during the summer and fall of 1991; the Red flag was hauled down from the Kremlin spires on Christmas Day. In November, O'Neill was at the White House to receive the Presidential Medal of Freedom: the nation's highest civilian honor. Among the other recipients was Ted Williams, who broke his personal practice and wore a tie for the occasion. President Bush called O'Neill "a legendary figure in American politics, blessed with the common touch like few others." After the reception, O'Neill walked out to the North Portico where he stood, a giant in a gray suit with a red-white-and-blue ribbon around his neck, looking out upon Pennsylvania Avenue, lost in thought.

A year later, the clan gathered at the Phoenix Park Hotel for O'Neill's eightieth birthday. Ted Kennedy and his new wife, Vicki, were there, and Mary McGrory — now forgiven — and Joe Kennedy and Cokie Roberts. "How ahr ya, dahlin'?" O'Neill would roar to the ladies and, "God love him, he's a beautiful guy," he would say about the men. They told stories and sang and ate corned beef and cabbage. The new Democratic President-elect sent a videotaped greeting.

"I hope that I'll always be the kind of President that you were as Speaker: a person who remembers the folks who sent him to Washington. I've always been impressed by the way you went home to your district and the way you knew the people who cut your hair and sold you your newspaper and made your life in Congress possible," said Bill Clinton. "I want you to know that those are the people who sent me to the White House. And I'll never forget them or the example you set."

O'Neill was pleased. "He quoted my philosophy: the President! I want the Congress to support him and I want him to change this country around," O'Neill said. "I thought he was dead in New Hampshire, and the way he had stick-to-it-iveness, never quit for a minute, he's going to do one hell of a job as President." When Clinton faced a tough fight in Congress in 1993 to win passage of the North American Free Trade Agreement, O'Neill was among those the White House called for help. Though it upset Evelyn Dubrow and other old friends from organized labor, O'Neill telephoned a dozen of his old pals on the Hill, happy that the Democratic President had finally called on him for a favor.

O'Neill had always thought Supreme Court justice William Brennan a great liberal jurist, and had long wanted to meet him. Brennan felt the same way about O'Neill. Marty Tolchin brought them together for lunch at the Cosmos Club after NAFTA had passed the Congress. Brennan's wife, Mary, was startled by the tales O'Neill told of wheeling and dealing — of the trades for VA hospitals and highway projects and other favors granted to secure passage of the trade agreement. Jimmy Carter had never "spoken that language," the Speaker said, but "Clinton sure did and it really paid off."

"Tip," said Mary Brennan, "that's a hell of a way to run a government."

"Mary dahlin', that's the only way to run a government," he replied.

O'Neill's health continued to deteriorate. Jim Shannon caught up with him for a ball game at Fenway Park. "It's a great life," O'Neill told him from the smoky, cluttered backseat of a stretch limousine, "if only I had my health."

Mary McGrory saw him at a reception in Washington. He was leaning on a cane, and told her, "I'm fallin' apart, dahlin' — arthritis, diabetes." He was forced to give up golf, and fretfully started pricing wheelchairs. He gave his last speech to the Nashville City Club on December 1, 1993. He scrawled "Henry Ford" and "Kennedy" at the top of speechwriter Kirk O'Donnell's text to remind himself what anecdotes to use, and had nice things to say about Al Gore and NAFTA and praised Clinton for fighting for national health insurance: "It is long overdue."

"He told me that right before he was to be introduced, he got a dizzy spell, and he didn't know whether he was going to be able to do anything. He had had only a little piece of meat and a half a glass of wine. But they introduced him, and he stood up there and he talked for an hour and a half. Which was typical of Tip O'Neill — kind of forget the physical," said Gary Hymel. "The next day he came back to Washington, went to the doctor and his blood sugar level was about six times what it should have been. It was the diabetes kicking in."

With Hymel, O'Neill had spent more than a year patching together a primer on his art: *All Politics Is Local — And Other Rules of the Game.* (Said Hymel: "He would call me on a Monday and say, 'Gary, I thought of three more stories during the sermon yesterday.'") Though stiffened by the arthritis, he sat for more than two hours at the Harvard Coop on December 15 — a few days past his eighty-first birthday — to sign copies for his sister, Mary, old friends like Lenny Lamkin and other well-wishers. He planned to spend Christmas at the Cape, and then to embark on a two-week, four-state tour to promote the new book in January.

But when the New Year dawned, O'Neill was feeling poorly. A friend who had lunch with him thought he looked and felt awful. He snapped at his grandson. The cancer, and other diseases, were putting great stress on his heart. O'Neill told Mary that the doctors wanted him back at Brigham and Women's for five days of tests.

"What's wrong with you?" she asked.

"I'm deteriorating," he said.

"Tom, we're all deteriorating."

"Yeah, but I'm deteriorating fast."

On Wednesday, January 5, O'Neill checked into the hospital. After work, Tommy came by to see him. O'Neill was sitting up in bed, eating coffee ice cream with Heath Bar chunks on top, watching a BC basketball game on the television, and spitting out the bigger chunks of sticky candy. They chatted about the game, and about BC's winning football season, which included a victory over Notre Dame.

"That Foley kid," O'Neill said, referring to the BC quarterback. "Foley's really a North Cambridge kid, you know?"

Tommy gave him a dubious look.

"You know who his grandmother is? Foley's grandmother? Verna.

From Verna's Doughnut Shop," O'Neill said. He reminisced about that Massachusetts Avenue landmark. "Tommy, do you remember how good those honey-dipped doughnuts were? God, those honey-dipped doughnuts."

The doctors were due to stop by that evening, but now a wave of fatigue enveloped him. His left side and arm felt numb.

"I can't stay awake," he told Tommy.

"You've got to," the son said.

"I'm trying, but I can't," said O'Neill.

"Okay, go to sleep," Tommy said, and put his arm around his father. The heart attack was sudden, and final.

"THE HEAVENS THEMSELVES blaze forth the death of princes," wrote William Shakespeare, and a fierce storm indeed hit Boston on the night that Tip O'Neill died. The third in eight days, it cloaked the city in two feet of snow. In the days of the snow buttons, it would have been a godsend. Word of the great man's death was passed through a series of late-night telephone calls — between friends or from news reporters. At the *Globe,* Mike Barnicle honored the journalistic craft with a graceful tribute, written under an unforgiving deadline. "The heart that called it quits was there for all those causes not quite fashionable in today's downsizing world and all those citizens whose voices are never heard because they contribute nothing to democracy other than their toil, effort, pride and patriotism," Barnicle wrote. "He was a simple man of simple tastes who sought only to use his office to lighten the load of the neediest." The two Martys — Nolan and Tolchin — wrote the obituaries for their papers. At the *Herald,* a shouting match erupted between the news side and the cost-conscious production staff after the editor on duty had taken the rare privilege of saying, "Stop the presses."

Somehow, through the snow, Millie made it up from the Cape. Tommy's home and office hosted great, roiling, working wakes as stories were swapped, drinks taken and the thousand details of the funeral decided. Ted Kennedy stopped by and the Reagans called. The other O'Neill children arrived from Washington. Television crews roamed the streets of North Cambridge, interviewing barber Frank Minnelli and cobbler John Gimigliano, whose shops had been stations on the "ethnic walks" O'Neill took to keep in touch with his constituents.

Though the skies began to clear on Saturday, the temperature was locked below freezing and the flags, at half-mast, snapped and popped in the wind. Still, the people came. Making their way through the cold and drifts, 15,000 of them crossed the Common, climbed Beacon Hill, to Bulfinch's State House. They came to mourn, to walk by O'Neill's body in the Hall of Flags, where the last public figure to lie in state had been James Michael Curley. Peter Lyons, who had served as an advance man for O'Neill in his retirement, slipped some cigars — and a few of those small shampoo bottles that the Speaker had always told him to take from their hotel rooms ("We can use them sometime") — into the casket. Millions watched the televised funeral Mass, held at St. John the Evangelist in North Cambridge on a frigid Monday morning. A cardinal and six priests performed the ritual. More than 200 dignitaries, led by Jimmy Carter, Jerry Ford and Al Gore, packed the pews. There were 38 honorary pallbearers, including congressmen, journalists and Carl Yastrzemski.

"Those of us who have lived through the decades since the 1930s, of dramatic change in the moral dilemmas that modernity brings, in the crisis of wars and threats of war . . . realize that Speaker O'Neill's legendary sense of loyalty, either to old friends or to God, was no dull or wooden conformity," said the Reverend J. Donald Monan, S.J., the president of Boston College. "It has been a creative fidelity to values pledged in his youth that he kept relevant to a world of constant change by dint of effort and imagination and at the cost of personal sacrifice."

There were many other fine and noble words. But it was Tommy who delivered a classic eulogy, mixing humor and pathos in a way that no one who heard him speak would not remember. "Oh, how he loved us. How he loved you, Kippy, and Michael, and you, Susan, God did he love you, and you, Rosemary, and you, Chib, and you, Jackie, and you, Joanne, and all of you grandchildren, you were Pop-Pop's very own honey-dipped doughnuts," Tommy said. "But the man's core, the pulse of his huge heart, the cushna Machree, as the Irish would say, was Mommy, his high school sweetheart, his lifelong love, the great source of his braveness. All the world knows how he loved you; most importantly, you do, too."

Then, fittingly, Tommy closed with a creaky, sentimental bit of doggerel — the yellow journalist's poem about friendship that Curley had given O'Neill to memorize a half century earlier, for those public occasions when he found himself at a loss for words.

Around the corner I have a friend, in this great city that has no end.
Yet days go by and weeks rush on, and before I know it, a year is gone.
And I never see my old friend's face, for life is a swift and terrible race.
He knows I like him just as well, as in the days when I rang his bell.
And he rang mine. We were younger then, and now we are busy, tired men.
Tired with playing a foolish game, tired with trying to make a name.
Tomorrow, I say, I will call on Jim, just to show that I am thinking of him.
But tomorrow comes and tomorrow goes, and the distance between us grows and grows.
Around the corner yet miles away: "Here is a telegram, sir; Jim died today."
And that's what we get and deserve in the end, around the corner, a vanished friend.

The O'Neills long owned a plot in the Catholic cemetery on Rindge Avenue, right down from Barry's Corner, near the railroad crossing where Mummy Kate and her brood had settled so long ago. He used to joke with Millie about it when they would drive by. She didn't like it; there were few trees and no shade. So one day, in his retirement years, O'Neill had told Leo Diehl about a new plot, down there on the Cape, where the O'Neills would take their final rest. And that is where, on that cold January day in 1994, the cortege made its way and Tip O'Neill was buried. It is a large plot at Mount Pleasant Cemetery in Harwich, for there is extra space. As Tip had told Leo: he wanted an old pal by his side.[7]

Notes

Abbreviations Used in the Notes

CHC—Cambridge Historical Commission
ONBC—Thomas P. O'Neill Jr. papers, Boston College
JCL—Jimmy Carter Library
NNA—Nixon Project, National Archives
LBJL—Lyndon B. Johnson Library
JFKL—John F. Kennedy Library
NA—National Archives
LOC—Library of Congress
RRL—Ronald Reagan Library

Prologue

1. Knowing that Cleveland fathered an illegitimate child, O'Neill would suggest to his pals in Congress that the desk may have been "the seat of the occasion." Gary Hymel interview.
2. Or to improve upon the truth. In fact, the chandelier was a replica. *New York Times*, Jan. 31, 1983.
3. Leo Diehl, Eleanor Kelley, Rosemary O'Neill, Christopher O'Neill, Hymel interviews; *Boston Globe*, Jan. 4, 5, 1977, Jan. 6, 1994; *Boston Herald*, Jan. 4, 5, 1977. A coalition government in the pre–Civil War era included a Speaker who called himself a Democrat for a time.
4. Brian Donnelly, Mary McGrory, Frank Staniszewski, Christopher Matthews, Ari Weiss, Jimmy Breslin interviews; Dick Bolling, Tip O'Neill interviews with

Hedrick Smith, Smith papers, Library of Congress; Bolling interview with Paul Clancy and Shirley Elder; *Boston Globe,* Jan. 20, 1981; O'Neill commencement speech, Thomas P. O'Neill Jr. papers, Boston College; *Associated Press,* Sept. 24, Oct. 15, 1984; O'Neill appointment book, 1973, O'Neill family files.

5. Kirk O'Donnell, Leon Panetta, Dan Flynn, Joe Moakley, Susan O'Neill, Barney Frank, Peter Hart, Neil MacNeil, Francine Gannon, Ray Smock, Stan Brand, John Kenneth Galbraith, Marty Nolan, Weiss, Kelley, Hymel interviews; Frank Moore to Jimmy Carter, Jan. 25, 1980, Jimmy Carter Library; *Washington Post,* Mar. 31, 1986; *Boston Globe,* Dec. 10, 1980.
6. Frank Moore interview; MacNeil interview; *Washington Post,* Dec. 7, 1976, Jan. 5, 1977; *Boston Globe,* Jan. 4, 5, 1977; *Boston Herald,* Jan. 4, 5, 1977; *Cambridge Chronicle,* Jan. 1977.
7. Michael Lillis, David Rogers, George Kundanis, Ben Bradlee, Susan O'Neill, Christopher O'Neill, Lester Hyman, Marty Tolchin, Howard Baker, John Murtha, Tony Coelho, Richard Gephardt, Dan Rostenkowski, Eddie Boland, Sidney Yates, Matthews, MacNeil, Diehl, Gannon, Breslin, Kelley, O'Donnell, Hymel interviews; unpublished memoir, Lester Hyman; George Reedy, *From the Ward to the White House* (Charles Scribner's Sons, New York, 1991); *Boston Herald,* Mar. 25, 1979; *Yankee* magazine, July 1978; Kennedy speech, Senate floor, Feb. 10, 1984, contained in *Thomas P. O'Neill Jr., Memorial Addresses and Tributes,* U.S. House of Representatives, 1995; Henry Ford story, multiple citations; PBS, "Mr. Speaker," 1978; Nixon to Kissinger, White House tapes, Nixon Project, National Archives.
8. *Boston Globe,* Jan. 4, 5, 1977; *Washington Post,* Jan. 5, 1977; *Congressional Record,* Jan. 5, 1977.
9. Patrick Caddell memo, JCL; *Boston Globe,* "The Electronic Election," Nov. 13, 1988; Michael Barone, *Our Country* (Free Press, New York, 1990); William Manchester, *The Glory and the Dream* (Little Brown, Boston, 1973); James T. Patterson, *Grand Expectations* (Oxford University Press, New York, 1996); David M. Kennedy, *Freedom from Fear* (Oxford University Press, New York, 1999); Robert J. Samuelson, *The Good Life and Its Discontents* (Times Books, New York, 1995); Paul Johnson, *Modern Times* (Harper & Row, New York, 1983); Theodore White, *America in Search of Itself* (Harper & Row, New York, 1982); Thomas and Mary Edsall, *Chain Reaction* (Norton, New York, 1991); Stanley Greenberg, *Middle Class Dreams* (Times Books, New York, 1995); Arthur M. Schlesinger Jr., *The Age of Roosevelt* (Houghton Mifflin, Boston, 1957); *Economic Report of the President,* Feb. 1995 (U.S. Government Printing Office, Washington, D.C., 1995); *US News & World Report,* Nov. 17, 1980.
10. Edward M. Kennedy, Peggy Noonan, Coelho, Matthews, Hart, Boland, Gephardt, Donnelly interviews; Bolling, Richard Wirthlin interviews, Hedrick Smith papers, LOC; O'Neill interview, WGBH-TV, "Goodbye Mr. Speaker," videotape, ONBC; David Stockman, *The Triumph of Politics* (Avon, New York, 1987); *Boston Globe,* Jan. 4, 5, 1977.

Chapter 1
From Dublin Street to Barry's Corner

1. It is not known whether the O'Connells made landfall in Canada, and then moved south over the years, or arrived directly in Portland. We do know they came well

before the famine, as in July of 1840, from Portland, Daniel placed an ad in the *Boston Pilot,* the Irish-Catholic newspaper, seeking word of a son who had left to work with the railroad in Georgia. Daniel Hayes and John McAleer interviews; *The Search for Missing Friends: Irish Immigrant Advertisements in the Boston Pilot* (New England Historic Genealogical Society, Boston, 1989).

2. *Mallow Field Club Journal,* #6 (Mallow Archaeological & Historical Society, Mallow, 1988).
3. *Northwest Cambridge & Survey Index* (Cambridge Historical Commission, Cambridge, 1977).
4. McAleer and Hayes interviews; Sarah Boyer, *In Our Own Words* (City of Cambridge, Red Sun Press, Boston, 1997); McAleer, a professor at Boston College, married into the O'Connell-Hayes family and compiled extensive oral histories, from which the tale of Mummy Kate is drawn.
5. *Mallow Field Club Journal,* #6.
6. *Mallow Field Club Journal,* #15 (Mallow Archaeological & Historical Society, Mallow, 1997). *The Famine Years in Mallow,* as reported in the *Cork Examiner,* Mallow Archaeological & Historical Society Web site.
7. McAleer interview; O'Neill genealogy file, CHC; O'Neill genealogy file, private family papers.
8. U.S. Census, 1880 and 1900, O'Neill file, CHC; *Northwest Cambridge & Survey Index,* CHC.
9. *Northwest Cambridge & Survey Index,* CHC; Jack Beatty, *The Rascal King* (Addison-Wesley, Reading, Mass., 1992).
10. Oscar Handlin, *Boston's Immigrants* (Atheneum, New York, 1974).
11. Cecil Woodham-Smith, *The Great Hunger* (Old Town Books, New York, 1962).
12. Boyer, *In Our Own Words*; Hayes interview.
13. The O'Neills were sometimes listed as Neil or O'Neil, with the "O" and extra *l* appearing and disappearing in various documents over the years. U.S. Census records and Cambridge directories; O'Neill file, CHC.
14. O'Neill file, CHC; Massachusetts Registry of Vital Records and Statistics, Patrick, Julia and Thomas P. O'Neill death certificates.
15. *Northwest Cambridge & Survey Index,* CHC; S. B. Sutton, *Cambridge Reconsidered* (MIT Press, Cambridge, 1976).
16. Mary O'Neill Mulcahy interview; Rose Tolan O'Neill death certificate; Thomas and Rose O'Neill marriage certificate; O'Neill file, CHC; O'Neill genealogy file, private family papers.
17. Mulcahy interview; O'Neill file, CHC.
18. Thomas P. O'Neill III; Jeremiah Sullivan, Mulcahy interviews; Mildred O'Neill interview with Paul Clancy and Shirley Elder; Thomas P. O'Neill Jr. interviews: Neil MacNeil, Clancy and Elder.
19. Untitled newspaper clipping, O'Neill scrapbook, ONBC.
20. Mulcahy interview.
21. O'Neill III, Mulcahy interviews.
22. *Boston Magazine,* Dec. 1991.
23. Mulcahy interview; *Boston Globe,* Nov. 1, 1998.
24. Thomas P. O'Neill Jr. to S. Dillon Ripley, Nov. 21, 1986, ONBC.
25. Rosemary O'Neill, Mulcahy interviews; O'Neill interview, Clancy and Elder; Thomas P. O'Neill Jr., *Man of the House* (Random House, New York, 1987).

26. Mulcahy interview; *Yankee* magazine, July 1978; *Town Crier,* Wilmington, Mass., Aug. 12, 1981.
27. O'Neill interview, Clancy and Elder; *Cambridge Chronicle,* April 7, 1994; O'Neill, *Man of the House.*
28. O'Neill to Maurice Fleishman, Mar. 3, 1978, ONBC.
29. Leo Diehl and Mulcahy interviews; O'Neill interview, Clancy and Elder; O'Neill, *Man of the House.*
30. Boyer, *In Our Own Words.*
31. Centennial Album, St. John the Evangelist Church; Boyer, p. 127.
32. Centennial Album, St. John the Evangelist Church.
33. James Sullivan, Robert Griffin interviews; Francis Fitzgerald, O'Neill interviews, Clancy and Elder; Boyer, *In Our Own Words;* O'Neill to Harold Clancy, Mar. 6, 1970, ONBC.
34. Leonard Lamkin, Sullivan, Hayes, Mulcahy, Diehl interviews; William McCaffrey, Fitzgerald interviews, Clancy and Elder; Paul Clancy and Shirley Elder, *Tip* (Macmillan, New York, 1980); Yankee, June 1994; Boyer; *Boston Herald,* June 10, 1979.
35. Sullivan interview; *New York Times,* Jan. 15, 1995.
36. Sullivan, Diehl, Lamkin interviews; Fitzgerald, Tom Mullen interviews, Clancy and Elder; *Boston Globe,* June 25, 1976.
37. *Boston Globe,* June 15, 1976.
38. *People* magazine, July 1980.
39. Arthur Schlesinger Jr., *The Age of Roosevelt* (Houghton Mifflin, Boston, 1957).

Chapter 2
People Like to Be Asked

1. *Yankee,* July 1978.
2. Thomas P. O'Neill III interview.
3. Mary O'Neill Mulcahy interview.
4. O'Neill interview, Hedrick Smith, Smith papers, Library of Congress.
5. Christopher O'Neill interview.
6. Kirk O'Donnell, O'Neill III interviews; Mildred Miller interview, Clancy and Elder. See Sue Erikson Bloland, *Atlantic Monthly,* "Fame: The Power and Cost of a Fantasy," Nov. 1999. It is interesting to note how many of O'Neill's great contemporaries also lost a parent as a child, including James Michael Curley, Paul Dever, Martin Lomasney, John "Honey Fitz" Fitzgerald, Michael Neville, David Walsh, Al Smith and John McCormack.
7. Chris Matthews, O'Neill III, Rosemary O'Neill interviews.
8. David Rogers, Matthews interviews.
9. O'Neill, Francis Fitzgerald interviews, Clancy and Elder.
10. "Massachusetts Is Democratic," briefing paper, Democratic National Committee files, JFKL; Michael E. Hennessy, *Four Decades of Massachusetts Politics* (Norwood Press, Norwood, Mass., 1935); J. Joseph Huthmacher, *Massachusetts People and Politics, 1919–1933* (Belknap Press, Cambridge, 1959); Beatty, *The Rascal King;* William V. Shannon, *The American Irish* (Macmillan, New York, 1963); Thomas O'Connor, *The Boston Irish* (Northeastern University Press, Boston, 1995); *Boston Magazine,* Jan. 1985.

11. Beatty, *The Rascal King.*
12. Beatty, *The Rascal King;* O'Connor, *The Boston Irish;* Alan Lupo, *Liberty's Chosen Home* (Beacon Press, Boston, 1977).
13. Nathan Glazer and Daniel P. Moynihan, *Beyond the Melting Pot* (MIT Press, Cambridge, 1963); Steven P. Erie, *Rainbow's End* (University of California Press, Berkeley, 1988); Neil Peirce and Jerry Hagstrom, *The Book of America* (Norton, New York, 1983).
14. *Cambridge Chronicle,* Nov. 1, 1884; O'Connor, *The Boston Irish;* Lupo, *Liberty's Chosen Home;* Beatty, *The Rascal King;* Shannon, *The American Irish.*
15. ONBC; O'Neill, *Man of the House;* O'Neill interview, Clancy and Elder.
16. Matthews, Jeremiah Sullivan interviews; O'Neill interview, Clancy and Elder; O'Neill, *Man of the House.*
17. Mulcahy interview; O'Neill, *Man of the House.*
18. Boyer, *In Our Own Words.*
19. O'Neill, *Man of the House.*
20. *Boston Post;* Doris Kearns Goodwin, *The Fitzgeralds and the Kennedys* (St. Martin's Press, New York, 1987); Beatty, *The Rascal King;* Lupo, *Liberty's Chosen Home.*
21. O'Neill interview, Clancy and Elder; Beatty, *The Rascal King.*
22. *Boston Post,* May 9, 1928, Nov. 6, 1929, Jan. 19, 1932.
23. *Cambridge Chronicle,* Oct. 3, 10, Nov. 8, 1935; *Boston Post,* Oct. 17, 1935.
24. *Boston Post,* Oct. 20, Nov. 1, 1937, *Boston Herald,* Nov. 3, 1937, Nov. 8, 1939; *Boston Traveler,* Nov. 3, 1937.
25. James Dineen, Mulcahy interviews; O'Neill interviews, Clancy and Elder, Neil MacNeil files.
26. Mark Dalton, Bob Griffin, Lamkin interviews; *The Heights,* 1932–36; *Sub Turri.*
27. Lamkin, Diehl, James Sullivan interviews; O'Neill and McCaffrey interviews, Clancy and Elder.
28. Diehl, James Sullivan interviews; Mildred O'Neill interview, Clancy and Elder; *North Cambridge News,* O'Neill commemorative issue, summer, 1994; "Thomas P. O'Neill Jr., A Family Portrait," videotape, ONBC; Boyer, *In Our Own Words.*
29. *Boston Globe,* Dec. 12, 1948; O'Neill, *Man of the House; Cambridge Chronicle,* Oct. 19, 1935; *Cambridge Tribune,* Oct. 18, 1935; Lamkin interview; O'Neill interviews, Neil MacNeil files; *Larry King Live,* Sept. 25, 1987.
30. *Boston Globe,* Oct. 18, 1935; *Cambridge Tribune,* Oct. 18, 1935.
31. Multiple sources, see O'Neill, *Man of the House,* and O'Neill and Gary Hymel, *All Politics Is Local and Other Rules of the Game* (Times Books, New York, 1994); "All politics is local" was a saying of the times, and may be attributed to Finley Peter Dunne.
32. *The Heights,* Oct. 18, 1935; Clancy and Elder, *Tip; Cambridge Chronicle,* Aug. 13, 1936.
33. *Cambridge Chronicle,* Aug. 27, 1936.
34. Diehl interview. It was Coakley who, on Curley's behalf, had driven Honey Fitz from the 1914 mayoral race by threatening to expose Fitzgerald's dalliance with the luscious Elizabeth "Toodles" Ryan, a twenty-three-year-old cigarette girl.
35. Diehl, Mulcahy interviews; Thomas P. O'Neill Jr. interview, Neil MacNeil; O'Neill, *Man of the House.*
36. Lamkin interview; Mildred O'Neill interview, Clancy and Elder; *Cambridge Chronicle,* Sept. 3, 17, 1936; *Cambridge Tribune,* Sept. 18, 1936.

37. *Cambridge Chronicle,* Oct. 22, 29, Nov. 5, 1936; *Cambridge Tribune,* Oct. 23, Nov. 6, 1936.

Chapter 3
Loyalties

1. Cornelius Dalton, *Leading the Way: A History of the Massachusetts General Court* (Office of the Massachusetts Secretary of State, Boston, 1984); Charles H. Trout, *Boston, the Great Depression, and the New Deal* (Oxford University Press, New York, 1977).
2. O'Neill began the year as a Smith supporter, and remembered booing and heckling the traitorous Curley for endorsing Roosevelt.
3. John McCormack oral history, JFKL; Beatty, *The Rascal King;* Trout, *Boston, the Great Depression, and the New Deal.*
4. Edward Boland and Diehl interviews; O'Neill interviews, Clancy and Elder; James Shannon, senior thesis, Johns Hopkins University; Boyer, *In Our Own Words.*
5. Trout, *Boston, the Great Depression, and the New Deal.*
6. James Sullivan interview; John F. Stack Jr., *International Conflict in an American City: Boston's Irish, Italians, and Jews, 1935–1944* (Greenwood Press, Westport, Conn., 1979); Trout, *Boston, the Great Depression, and the New Deal;* O'Connor, *The Boston Irish.*
7. *Cambridge Tribune,* Sept. 11, 1936; *Cambridge Chronicle,* Sept. 10, 1936; *Boston Globe,* Mar. 2, 11, 1937; *Boston Post,* Mar. 2, 3, 12, 1937.
8. By way of comparison, the "Reagan Revolution" of 1981 sought to cut federal spending back to 20 percent of GNP. O'Neill, *Man of the House;* O'Neill interviews, Clancy and Elder; O'Neill oral history, JFKL; Schlesinger, *The Age of Roosevelt;* David M. Kennedy, *Freedom from Fear* (Oxford University Press, New York, 1999); William Manchester, *The Glory and the Dream* (Little, Brown, Boston, 1974).
9. Jerome Grossman and Lamkin interviews; O'Neill interviews, Clancy and Elder, and multiple sources; Doris Kearns Goodwin, *No Ordinary Time* (Simon & Schuster, New York, 1994); Schlesinger, *The Age of Roosevelt;* Kennedy, *Freedom from Fear.*
10. Despite Hurley's veto, there was a half-hearted attempt to revive repeal in 1938, but O'Neill and other supporters declined to spill more blood for a hopeless cause. *Boston Globe,* Mar. 16, 17, 18, 19, 24, 31, Apr. 1, 1937; *Boston Post,* Mar. 17, 25, Apr. 9, 1937; *Cambridge Tribune,* Feb. 18, 25, 1938; Shannon thesis; O'Neill oral history, JFKL; O'Neill interview, Clancy and Elder; O'Neill, *Man of the House.*
11. Jeremiah Sullivan, Diehl, Lamkin interviews; O'Neill, *Man of the House;* Joseph Healey interview, Clancy and Elder; O'Neill interview, WGBH, "Goodbye Mr. Speaker," ONBC. *Cambridge Tribune,* Feb. 9, 1940; *Cambridge Chronicle,* Jan. 13, Apr. 7, July 7, 28, Aug. 4, Sept. 8, 15, 22, Nov. 10, 1938, July 25, Sept. 19, Oct. 17, 1940; *Congressional Record,* Dec. 18, 1979. O'Neill survived one other crisis to win reelection. On an icy midnight in November 1937, the Natick police responded to reports of a wreck on the turnpike. An automobile had rammed a bus, spinning the heavy vehicle 180 degrees. The car was empty, but the troopers found a state parking permit in the window for Rep. Thomas P. O'Neill Jr. The police report sent the city's newspapers into a competitive fury, and it was not until the next day, when a Cambridge hospital phoned the police to inform them that the representative's brother, William, had been admitted with a lacerated forehead at 5 A.M., that the authorities dropped their investigation of Tip O'Neill, and concluded that it was Bill who hit the bus.

12. Cold weather and the day's 55 to 12 upset loss to Holy Cross caused Boston College to cancel its planned victory party at the Cocoanut Grove one Saturday night in November of 1942. A fire killed 492 people there that night — and many a BC fan counted his blessings. Diehl, Lamkin, James Sullivan interviews; O'Neill, McCaffrey interviews, Clancy and Elder; O'Neill interview, Neil MacNeil files; O'Neill, *Man of the House.*
13. Diehl, Lamkin, Mulcahy interviews; *Washington Post,* Mar. 13, 1977, Mildred O'Neill interviews, Clancy and Elder, O'Neill papers, videotape collection, Boston College.
14. Rosemary O'Neill, Terry Segal, Diehl, Boland, Mulcahy interviews; Mildred O'Neill interview, Clancy and Elder; O'Neill interview, MacNeil files; *Boston Post,* June 12, 1938.
15. Diehl, Lamkin interviews; O'Neill classification records, U.S. Selective Service System; O'Neill to Dr. John F. McHugh, Oct. 26, 1979, ONBC; O'Neill interview, *Larry King Live,* Sept. 25, 1987; O'Neill interview, MacNeil files; Kennedy, *Freedom from Fear;* Goodwin, *No Ordinary Time;* Manchester, *The Glory and the Dream;* Stephen Ambrose, *Citizen Soldiers* (Simon & Schuster, New York, 1997).
16. *Cambridge Chronicle,* Aug. 25, 1938, Nov. 7, 1940; *Boston Post,* Oct. 20, Nov. 9, 1938, May 6, 1943; *Boston Advertiser,* April 11, 1942; *Boston Globe,* April 11, 1942.
17. Walter Sullivan, Diehl interviews, O'Neill interview, Clancy and Elder; Glenn Koocher videotape, "Talking with Tip O'Neill," June 30, 1993; *Boston Globe,* Oct. 15, 1941; *Boston Post,* Feb. 6, 1945; *Cambridge Chronicle,* Sept. 20, Nov. 22, 1945, Jan. 10, 24, Feb. 21, Apr. 4, May 23, 1946, Apr. 10, May 29, July 10, 17, Aug. 14, 28, Dec. 4, 1947, Apr. 29, 1948; *Cambridge Recorder,* Jan. 3, 1948; *Boston Herald,* May 27, 1947.

Chapter 4
Crusades

1. Garrison Nelson, Diehl interviews; O'Neill interview, Clancy and Elder; untitled newspaper clipping, O'Neill scrapbook, ONBC; Grant newsletter, ONBC.
2. William Sutton, David Powers, Diehl interviews; Kenneth O'Donnell and David Powers, *Johnny We Hardly Knew Ye* (Little, Brown, Boston, 1972); Nigel Hamilton, *JFK: Reckless Youth* (Random House, New York, 1992); Beatty, *The Rascal King;* Joseph De Guglielmo, Patsy Mulkern, Joseph Healey oral histories, JFKL; Ralph Martin and Ed Plaut, *Front Runner, Dark Horse* (Doubleday, Garden City, N.Y. 1960); O'Neill oral history, ONBC; *Cambridge Chronicle,* Apr. 4, 25, June 13, 20, 1946.
3. Mark Dalton, Sutton, Powers, Diehl interviews; De Guglielmo, Mulkern, Healey, Dalton oral histories, JFKL; O'Neill oral history, ONBC; Burton Hersh, *The Education of Edward Kennedy* (William Morrow, New York, 1972); O'Donnell and Powers, *Johnny We Hardly Knew Ye;* Hamilton, *JFK: Reckless Youth;* Goodwin, *The Fitzgeralds and the Kennedys.*
4. Sutton, Dalton interviews; *Boston Post,* July 8, 1947, Jan. 4, 29, June 18, 1948; *Boston Herald,* Nov. 29, 1947; *Boston Traveler,* Dec. 31, 1946; *Cambridge Chronicle,* Jan. 9, 1947; O'Connor, *The Boston Irish;* Beatty, *The Rascal King;* Goodwin, *The Fitzgeralds and the Kennedys;* O'Neill interviews, Clancy and Elder; O'Neill oral histories, Boston College; O'Neill, *Man of the House.*
5. John Harris, Diehl interviews; John McCormack, Maurice Donahue oral histories, JFKL; Paul Dever to John McCormack, McCormack to Dever and other Massachusetts Democrats, McCormack papers, Boston University; *Boston Globe,*

Feb. 1, 4, 5, 7, 8, 13, 18, 19, 21, 27, 28, Mar. 1, 3, 4, 10, 12, 18, 26, Apr. 2, 21, 27, 1948; *Christian Science Monitor,* Apr. 28, 1948; *Boston Post,* Mar. 23, 1948; O'Neill interview, Clancy and Elder; O'Neill, *Man of the House.*

6. Donahue oral history, JFKL.
7. *Boston Globe,* June 19, 1948, Feb. 3, 1949; O'Neill interview, Clancy and Elder; O'Neill, *Man of the House.*
8. In his memoirs, O'Neill described the measure as an abortion bill, perhaps to make his opposition palatable in a more liberal era. But there was no doubting his position at the time: he listed his stand against birth control in the list of accomplishments on his campaign literature that year. *Boston Globe,* Apr. 1, 6, 7, 21, May 4, 13, Sept. 24, 1948; *Boston Herald,* Mar. 28, June 21, 1948; O'Neill, *Man of the House.*
9. *Boston Globe,* Sept. 26, Oct. 1, 3, 13, 17, 18, 19, 24, 26, 27, 28, 29, 31, Nov. 1, 2, 3, 4, 1948; *Boston Herald,* Nov. 4, 1948; O'Neill, *Man of the House;* "Massachusetts Is Democratic," briefing paper, Democratic National Committee files, JFKL.
10. The Kingston Trio later immortalized this fare increase, and the fate of poor Charlie who was trapped on the subway by it, in the song "M.T.A."
11. Jeremiah Sullivan, Diehl, Lamkin interviews; *Christian Science Monitor,* Nov. 4, 1948, Feb. 3, 1949; *Boston Traveler,* Nov. 4, 1948; *Boston Globe,* Nov. 9, 16, 24, 25, 30, Dec. 9, 1948, Jan. 4, 5, 1949; *Boston Post,* Dec. 10, 1948; O'Neill interviews, Clancy and Elder; Koocher videotape; PBS, Aug. 2, 1983; Pamela Condon, ONBC; Healey interview, Clancy and Elder; O'Neill, *Man of the House.*

Chapter 5
The Baby New Deal

1. Susan O'Neill interview; *Boston Globe,* Dec. 14, 1948, Jan. 4, 5, 6, 1949; *Christian Science Monitor,* Jan. 7, 1949; *Roxbury Citizen,* Jan. 14, 1949.
2. O'Neill interview, David Luberoff; O'Neill interview, Sheridan McCabe, audiotape, ONBC; Richard Grant newsletter, ONBC; *Boston Globe,* Feb. 2, 20, Mar. 2, 16, 23, 24, Apr. 12, 14, 29.
3. Boland interview; O'Neill interview, McCabe; *Boston Globe,* Nov. 5, 28, Dec. 1, 1948, Jan. 6, Feb. 18, May 18, Aug. 15, 1949; *Boston Post,* Feb. 6, 1937, Feb. 27, 1938.
4. O'Neill interview, McCabe.
5. *Springfield Union,* May 21, June 11, 1949; *Boston Globe,* May 8, June 26, 28, 29, July, 3, 7, 11, 12, 13, 15, 17, 19, Aug. 2, 18, 19, 26, 27, 28, 29, 30, 31, Sept. 1, 1949; *Worcester Telegram,* June 1, July 17, 1949; *Lowell Sun,* July 28, 1949; *Boston Herald,* Aug. 4, Sept. 8, 1949; O'Neill, *Man of the House.*
6. Rosemary O'Neill, Jeremiah Sullivan, Diehl interviews; O'Neill interview, Clancy and Elder; *Boston Globe,* May 11, June 24, 1949; *Boston American,* May 11, 1949; *Boston Post,* June 24, 1949.
7. Beatty, *The Rascal King; Beverly Times,* Jan. 31, 1950; O'Neill interview, *Larry King Live,* Jan. 20, 1992.
8. *Boston Traveler,* Jan. 4, 10, Apr. 23, May 7, June 15, Aug. 19, 20, Oct. 15, Nov. 29, Dec. 5, 31, 1950; *Boston Globe,* Jan. 4, 10, Apr. 23, May 7, June 15, Aug. 19, 20, Oct. 15, Nov. 29, Dec. 5, 31, 1950; *Boston Post,* May 15, 18, Aug. 2, Oct. 19, Nov. 8, 1950; *Christian Science Monitor,* Dec. 28, 1949, July 31, Aug. 2, 17, 1950.
9. Edward M. Kennedy, Sutton, Powers interviews; *Cambridge Chronicle,* Nov. 1949; McCaffrey, Healey interviews with Clancy and Elder; O'Neill, *Man of the House;* Healey, oral history, JFKL.

10. In one oral history for the John F. Kennedy library, O'Neill placed the meeting in 1952. In other interviews, and in his memoirs, O'Neill said the dinner took place in 1951.
11. Healey interview, Clancy and Elder; O'Neill oral history, ONBC; *Boston Globe,* Nov. 29, 1950, Jan. 18, Apr. 2, 7, 17, June 24, 1951; *Boston Traveler,* Aug. 19, Dec. 3, Dec. 15, 1950, Apr. 13, 1951; O'Neill, *Man of the House.*
12. *Boston Post,* June 27, July 11, 27, 30, Aug. 10, 1951; *Boston Herald,* Aug. 9, 1951; *Berkshire Eagle,* Aug. 10, 1951.
13. *Boston Post,* Mar. 11, 1952; *Boston Globe,* Aug. 5, 1951, Jan. 1, July 5, 6, 20, Aug. 20, 21, 1952; *Providence Sunday Journal,* Jan. 19, 1986; *Boston Traveler,* July 6, Nov. 4, 18, 20, 1951; *Christian Science Monitor,* Aug. 4, 15, Sept. 20, Oct. 22, 29, Nov. 19, Dec. 26, 1951, May 21, July 1, Aug. 27, 1952; *Boston Record,* Oct. 8, 1951; *Cambridge Courier,* Nov. 22, 1951; *Boston Herald,* Dec. 2, 1951.

Chapter 6
LoPresti

1. Carolina was later rewarded with a job on O'Neill's staff.
2. Diehl interview; *Cambridge Chronicle,* May 22, 1952; *Providence Sunday Journal,* Jan. 19, 1986; *Boston Herald,* July 16, 1980.
3. Mario Umana, Tony Marmo, Michael LoPresti interviews; *New England Quarterly,* "Race Conflicts in the North End of Boston," Dec. 1939.
4. Hymel, Diehl, Mulcahy interviews.
5. "Blanche had an annual fund-raising ball for an Italian orphans' home in Jamaica Plain," Fred Salvucci recalled. "And in the 1980s — it must have been her last ball — Tip was there. And he didn't do the five-minute, hello-howarya out-the-door. He is there for five hours, and he gets up and says, 'Tonight I fly to Europe to meet with Gorbachev and to stop in Rome and meet with the Pope. But I wouldn't be going — I wouldn't be Speaker of the House — if it were not for Blanche Ruffo.'" Diehl, O'Neill III, Salvucci interviews; O'Neill, *Man of the House.*
6. Bob Griffin, Diehl interviews.
7. Brian O'Neill, Walter Sullivan, Rosemary O'Neill, Susan O'Neill, O'Neill III, Diehl interviews; O'Neill, *Man of the House;* O'Neill interview, Clancy and Elder. The Bartolos were to play a crucial role in the Boston mayoralty election of 1959 when an election-eve bookmaking raid on a tavern they owned helped doom the campaign of the man they supported, state senator John Powers.
8. Diehl, Walter Sullivan interviews; O'Neill interview, Clancy and Elder; *Boston Post,* Sept. 1, 1951, Dec. 2, 1951; *Associated Labor Record,* Aug. 1952; Beatty, *The Rascal King.*
9. "Notwithstanding any other provisions of law any person who has served as a member of the General Court, who after attaining age sixty-five and after completing not less than twenty-five years of service in any governmental unit or units and as a member of the General Court, terminated his services under any of the circumstances set forth in subdivisions (1) and (2) of section ten, may at any time within three years after the date of his termination of service apply for and be admitted, as of the date of the termination of his service, into membership in the retirement system," said the bill, which was entitled "An Act Making Certain Changes in the Retirement Law."

10. Diehl, Walter Sullivan interviews; *Springfield Union,* Sept. 2, 1952; *Boston Globe,* Aug. 30, 31, Sept. 1, 2, 3, 4, 5, 6, 7, 8, 9, 10, 11, 12, 13, 14, 15, 16, 1952; *Boston American,* Sept. 5, 1952; *Boston Post,* Aug. 30, 31, Sept. 1, 2, 3, 4, 5, 6, 7, 9, 16, 1952; *Boston Herald,* Sept. 1, 4, 5, 7, 8, 10, 12, 17, 1952.
11. Diehl, O'Neill III interviews; *Boston Herald,* Sept. 15, 1952; *Boston Post,* Sept. 10, 1952; *Boston Globe,* Sept. 13, 16, 1952.
12. Diehl, Lamkin, Walter Sullivan interviews.
13. Diehl, Lamkin, Harris, LoPresti, Umana, Walter Sullivan interviews; *East Boston Leader,* Oct. 10, 1952; *Boston Post,* Sept. 17, 1952; *Boston Globe,* Sept. 17, 1952; *Boston American,* Sept. 17, 1952; *Cambridge Chronicle,* Sept. 18, 1952.
14. Diehl, LoPresti, Umana, Marmo, O'Neill III interviews; Skyline Enterprises, Airport Cocktail Lounge, Inc., records and leases, Massachusetts Port Authority.

Chapter 7
Men's Men

1. Diehl, Lamkin interviews; O'Neill oral histories, ONBC, JFKL; *Boston Globe,* Nov. 5, 1952, Mar. 8, 1953; *Boston Post,* Nov. 20, 1952.
2. Thomas P. O'Neill death certificate, Massachusetts Registry of Vital Records and Statistics; O'Neill, *Man of the House; Cambridge Chronicle,* Aug. 20, 1953.
3. O'Neill to George E. Murphy, Mar. 8, 1954, shipyard and local project files, ONBC; *Boston Globe,* Dec. 3, 1952; July 14, 1953; *Boston Post,* Feb. 22, 1954; *Cambridge Courier,* May 12, 1955; Healey, O'Neill, oral histories, JFKL; D. B. Hardeman and Donald C. Bacon, *Rayburn* (Madison Books, Lanham, Md., 1987); O'Neill interview, WWOR-TV, 1954, ONBC; *Congressional Record,* Mar. 5, 1953; June 2, July 1, 1954.
4. O'Neill, *Man of the House;* Jeremy Isaacs and Taylor Downing, *Cold War* (Little, Brown, New York, 1998); Healey oral history, JFKL; *Boston American,* June 17, 1957; *Boston Post,* Jan. 31, 1954; *Boston Herald,* Apr. 8, 1947; *Congressional Record,* July 15, July 29, Aug. 16, 1954; ONBC.
5. John Harris, J. Joseph Moakley, Diehl interviews; *Washington Post,* Mar. 2, 1954; O'Neill, *Man of the House;* Joseph Martin, *My First Fifty Years in Politics* (Greenwood Press, Westport, Conn., 1975); Yucca Flats briefing paper, Richard Bolling papers, University of Missouri; *Congressional Record,* Aug. 5, 1982.
6. Rosemary, Susan, Christopher, O'Neill III interviews; Mildred O'Neill interview, WBZ-TV, 1986; O'Neill to Dorothy O'Neill, Mar. 23, 1954, ONBC.
7. Diehl, Lamkin, Umana, LoPresti interviews; LoPresti campaign newspaper, ONBC; O'Neill, *Man of the House; Boston Post,* Oct. 15, 1956. The Curley story sounds too good to be true, but Lenny Lamkin remembers O'Neill telling him about it at the time.
8. Richard Donahue, Powers, Sutton, Dalton, Diehl, Kennedy interviews; Edward McCormack, John McCormack, Foster Furcolo, Torbert Macdonald, Francis X. Morrissey, O'Neill oral histories, JFKL; O'Neill oral history; O'Neill to Lester Hyman, Feb. 16, 1968, ONBC; O'Neill, *Man of the House;* O'Donnell and Powers, *Johnny We Hardly Knew Ye;* Burton Hersh, *The Education of Edward Kennedy* (William Morrow, New York, 1972); *Boston Herald,* May 7, 9, 20, 1956; *Boston Post,* May 8, 10, 20, 1956.

9. Donahue, Powers, Sutton interviews; O'Neill oral history, ONBC; O'Neill oral history, JFKL; O'Neill interview, Clancy and Elder; *Boston Post,* Oct. 12, Dec. 5, 1954, Aug. 15, Nov. 15, 1958; clippings, *Salem Evening News, Daily Evening Item, Lawrence Evening Tribune;* O'Neill to Kenneth Harding, DNCC, Oct. 20, 1958; ONBC.
10. *Washington Post,* June 12, 1986.
11. Boland, Diehl, Dinneen interviews; O'Neill interview, Clancy and Elder; *Boston Post,* Feb. 28, Sept. 5, 1956, Aug. 3, 1957, Aug. 7, 1957; *Boston Globe,* June 15, 1957, Feb. 20, 1977, Jan. 9, 1994; *Boston Traveler,* Aug. 2, 1961; *Cape Cod Standard-Times,* May 16, 1961; *Associated Press,* May 12, 1958; *Los Angeles Times,* Aug. 19, 1985; National Historic Sites Commission file, John McCormack papers, Boston University; *Congressional Record,* Feb. 27, 1956, Aug. 17, 1959; *Boston* magazine, Dec. 1973.
12. Correspondence, Davis Taylor, Thomas Winship to the author; Bob Healy interview; Louis M. Lyons, *Newspaper Story: One Hundred Years of The Boston Globe* (Belknap Press, Cambridge, 1971).
13. Healy interview; *Boston Globe,* Apr. 26, 27, 1957, June 6, July 31, 1958; Manchester, *The Glory and the Dream;* Louis Jaffe, "The Scandal in TV Licensing," *Harper's,* Sept. 1957; Drew Pearson column, Dec. 1956.
14. Healy, Ted Sorensen interviews; Thomas Winship, oral history, JFKL; memo to files, January 20, 1959, Ted Sorensen, John F. Kennedy, Senate papers, JFKL; Lyons, *Newspaper Story;* J. Anthony Lukas, *Common Ground* (Alfred Knopf, New York, 1985); *Boston Globe,* Feb. 19, 1959.
15. Dazzi had helped Tobin beat Curley for mayor in 1937, and played a behind-the-scenes role with O'Neill and Davis Taylor in Governor Bradford's appointment of John Hynes as interim mayor in 1947.
16. Francis X. McLaughlin, Healy interviews; O'Neill statement, House Judiciary Committee, 1956, ONBC; *Congressional Record,* Feb. 24, 1956; *Boston Globe,* Feb. 24, 1956; Andrew Dazzi, oral history, JFKL; O'Neill to John J. Graham, May 15, Aug. 7, 1957, ONBC; Drew Pearson to John McCormack, Jan. 23, 1957, McCormack papers, Boston University; *Congressional Quarterly Almanac,* 1957, 1958; Bernard Schwartz, *The Professor and the Commissions* (Alfred Knopf, New York, 1959).
17. Schwartz came to suspect that the whole reason for the oversight probe was to blackmail the Republicans into supporting a natural gas bill that Harris and Rayburn wanted for their oil patch constituents.
18. McLaughlin, Healy interviews; Schwartz, *The Professor and the Commissions;* Lyons, *Newspaper Story.*
19. Schwartz, *The Professor and the Commissions; Congressional Quarterly Almanac,* 1957, 1958.
20. Jack Anderson, Healy, McLaughlin interviews; Schwartz, *The Professor and the Commissions; Congressional Quarterly Almanac,* 1957, 1958; *Congressional Quarterly,* Jan. 31, Feb. 7, 14, 21, 1958; *Boston Globe,* Feb. 13, 1958.
21. McLaughlin and Healy interviews. They differ in their recollections of the toll ticket search. Healy is sure he accompanied the committee investigator to the phone company. McLaughlin says he would not, and did not, take a reporter with him.
22. McConnaughey, while FCC chairman, also negotiated a six-figure agreement to join the law firm that represented an applicant for a Pittsburgh TV license. The sta-

tion got its license. Healy, McLaughlin interviews; *Boston Globe,* Apr. 26, 1957, May 26, June 5, 6, 7, 9, 11, 13, 15, 18, Dec. 14, 31, 1958, Jan. 1, Jan. 27, Feb. 17, 18, 19, Sept. 24, 1959; hearings, Committee on Interstate and Foreign Commerce, U.S. House of Representatives, Apr. 3, June 5, 6, 9, 10, 11, 16, 26, 27, 30, July 2, 3, 7, 1958.

23. Benjamin Bradlee, Anderson, Healy, McLaughlin interviews; *Congressional Quarterly Almanac,* 1958; Bradlee, *A Good Life* (Simon & Schuster, New York, 1995); Joseph Kennedy, statement, June 27, 1958, Senate papers, JFKL.

Chapter 8
Judge Smith

1. Boland interview; O'Neill, *Man of the House.*
2. Hardeman and Bacon, *Rayburn;* Carl Albert, *Little Giant* (University of Oklahoma Press, Norman, 1990); Richard Bolling, *House Out of Order* (E. P. Dutton, New York, 1965); O'Neill oral history, JFKL; Bolling interview, June 26, 1980, Bolling papers, University of Missouri.
3. Neil MacNeil, *Forge of Democracy* (Van Rees Press, New York, 1963); Ronald M. Peters, *The American Speakership* (Johns Hopkins University Press, Baltimore, 1990); Bruce Dierenfield, *Keeper of the Rules: Congressman Howard W. Smith* (University of Virginia Press, Charlottesville, 1987); Bolling, *House Out of Order; Congressional Quarterly,* May 14, 1973.
4. John McCormack, interview with Alan Lupo; Spark Matsunaga and Ping Chen, *Rulemakers of the House* (University of Illinois Press, Chicago, 1976); Ronald M. Peters, The Speaker (CQ Press, Washington, D.C., 1995); O'Neill to Emmanuel Celler, Jan. 25, 1956, and memo from staff, July 21, 1958, ONBC; *National Journal,* Feb. 26, 1977.
5. Lupo, *Liberty's Chosen Home; Boston Herald,* July 1949; *Cambridge Chronicle,* June 7, Nov. 1, 1945; *Congressional Quarterly,* Mar. 16, May 4, 1956.
6. "We could never have passed . . . the act if it hadn't been for the fact that Rayburn was educating me as we went along into some of the tricks that would be pulled to try to defeat me," said Bolling.
7. Committee on Rules, hearings, May 2, 7, 8, 9, 13, 14, 15, 16, 17, June 20, 21, 27, 1957, National Archives; background memo, chronologies and summary of legislative developments, 1957 Civil Rights Act, Bolling papers, University of Missouri; Denton L. Watson, *Lion in the Lobby* (William Morrow, New York, 1990); Bolling, *House Out of Order; Congressional Quarterly Almanac,* 1957; telegram, O'Neill to Rowena Taylor, et al., June 27, 1956, ONBC; *New York Times,* June 22, 1956; Smith papers, University of Virginia.
8. As a measure of the political constancy shown by McCormack and O'Neill, it is instructive to note that Saltonstall and Kennedy each voted for one of these diluting measures.
9. *New York Times,* Aug. 21, 1957; the remark is variously attributed to Rep. Leo Allen, a Republican from Illinois, as well.
10. Clarence Mitchell oral history, JFKL; Watson, *Lion in the Lobby;* Bolling papers, 1957 Civil Rights Act, University of Missouri; *Boston Globe,* July 24, 1956, Mar. 22, Aug. 30, 1957; Dierenfield, *Keeper of the Rules;* Rules Committee hearings, National Archives; *New York Times,* Aug. 20, 26, 1957; Drew Pearson column, June 21, 1956; Smith papers, University of Virginia.

11. In 1959, Smith again tried to bottle up a civil rights bill in committee, and again he capitulated when it was clear that his foes had the votes to force his hand. The liberals used a "discharge petition," which required the signatures of a majority of the members of the House, to free the bill from committee. Though O'Neill, for reasons of committee clout and solidarity, generally declined to sign discharge petitions, he relented in this case. *Congressional Quarterly Almanac,* 1959; *Boston Globe,* Dec. 14, 17, 1958, Mar. 6, 1959; *Boston Traveler,* Jan. 7, 1959; hearings, Special Committee to Investigate Campaign Expenditures, Dec. 15, 16, 17, 1958, National Archives.
12. Hearings, Committee on Rules, Mar. 31, Apr. 19, 1955, Apr. 24, May 2, 1958; O'Neill to Leo O'Brien, Apr. 15, 1969, ONBC; O'Neill to Arthur Schlesinger Jr., May 27, 1958, ONBC.
13. Confidential letter, Rep. Frank Thompson and others to House liberal colleagues, Dec. 2, 1958, ONBC; Donahue interview; MacNeil, *Forge of Democracy;* Bolling, *House Out of Order;* Dierenfield, *Keeper of the Rules;* Hardeman and Bacon, *Rayburn; Time* magazine, Feb. 10, 1961; Lawrence O'Brien, Bolling, oral histories, JFKL; *Congressional Quarterly,* Jan. 2, 9, 1959; *New York Times,* Jan. 29, 1961; Mary McGrory column, *Boston Globe,* Feb. 1, 1961; *CBS Reports,* "The Keeper of the Rules," Jan. 19, 1961; Bolling interview, Bolling papers, University of Missouri; Rayburn correspondence, Feb. 1961, Rayburn papers, Rayburn Library; Hale Boggs correspondence, Boggs papers, Tulane University; *Congressional Record,* Jan. 31, 1961; James Robinson, *The House Rules Committee* (Bobbs-Merrill, Indianapolis, 1963); Smith correspondence, Smith papers, University of Virginia.

Chapter 9
My Beloved Jack

1. The author can remember how, during his childhood, "Kennedy quarters" would show up in small change at the store. With a splash of scarlet nail polish, Catholic-haters gave the image of George Washington a cardinal's hat and robes, as a warning that the Pope would take over the government.
2. Donahue, Powers, Sutton, Dalton interviews; O'Neill oral history, ONBC; Adam Clymer, *Edward M. Kennedy: A Biography* (William Morrow, New York, 1999).
3. Years later, when writing to thank him for donating his papers to her husband's presidential library, Jackie Kennedy would begin her note: "Dear Tim . . . "
4. Dalton, Sutton, Griffin, Edward M. Kennedy interviews; *Boston Herald,* Sept. 29, 1957; O'Neill oral histories, ONBC, JFKL, LBJL; Thomas Broderick, Mulkern oral history, JFKL; O'Neill, *Man of the House.*
5. *Boston Herald,* Sept. 27, 1958; O'Neill-for-governor brochure, author's files; *Christian Science Monitor,* Apr. 28, Oct. 26, 1959; *Boston Globe,* Mar. 20, Apr. 7, Oct. 27, 1959, Feb. 8, 11, Mar. 1, Apr. 3, 1960; Jan. 9, 1960; O'Neill interview, Clancy and Elder.
6. Diehl interview; Mildred O'Neill, Healey interviews, Clancy and Elder; *North Cambridge News,* special tribute edition, summer 1994; Theodore White, *The Making of the President 1960* (Atheneum, New York, 1961); Robert F. Kennedy, *Robert Kennedy: In His Own Words* (Bantam Books, New York, 1988).
7. One of the lucrative practices exposed by Richardson's probe was the way that state legislators employed in the insurance business profited as brokers of the perfor-

mance bonds that Callahan's turnpike authority required of its contractors. As an insurance agent, O'Neill may have participated in the practice, but his name was never linked to scandal, Richardson said. O'Neill once said he was given an insider's opportunity to score by buying land along the right-of-way for Route 6 on Cape Cod, but turned down the offer.

8. Elliot Richardson, Diehl interview; Murray Levin, *Kennedy Campaigning* (Boston: Beacon Press, 1966); Mildred O'Neill interview, Clancy and Elder.
9. Boggs and McCormack also served as conduits between Rayburn and Kennedy, and their version of events mirrored O'Neill's account. O'Neill oral histories, ONBC, LBJL, JFKL; Peter Cloherty oral history, JFKL; Hale Boggs oral histories, Boggs papers, Tulane University; *Worcester Telegram,* July 10, 1960; *Boston Globe,* July 15, Dec. 1, 1963.
10. The *Globe*'s Bob Healy was along on the trip, and later recalled how Kennedy had called him to the stateroom on the campaign airplane, where the bed was covered with more than $100,000 in cash. Even the candidate was impressed. "Did you ever see anything like that?" he asked Healy.
11. Healy, Segal interviews; O'Neill oral history, ONBC; O'Neill oral histories, JFKL, LBJL; O'Neill, *Man of the House;* confidential memorandum to Senator Kennedy from August A. Busch Jr. and confidential memorandum to Kennedy brothers and Kenneth O'Donnell from Lawrence O'Brien, 1960 campaign files, JFKL.
12. Edward M. Kennedy, James Shannon, Powers, Donahue, Boland interviews; *Boston Globe,* Jan. 23, 1961, Oct. 23, 1967; *Congressional Record,* Feb. 10, 1994; *Boston Herald,* July 26, 1973; O'Neill oral history, ONBC; O'Donnell and Powers, *Johnny We Hardly Knew Ye;* O'Neill, *Man of the House.*
13. Arthur Schlesinger Jr., Ted Sorensen, Rosemary O'Neill, Powers, Donahue, Diehl, Boland interviews; Bolling interview, Clancy and Elder; Dear Colleague letter, Richard Bolling, Sept. 20, 1960; Bolling papers, University of Missouri.
14. O'Neill to Rev. Kenneth Hughes, July 24, 1961, ONBC; O'Neill to constituents, 1956, 1957, 1958, 1959, 1960, school construction and education files, ONBC; *New York Times,* Mar. 2, June 16, 1961; *Boston Globe,* July 17, 1957, Mar. 8, 12, 1961; Irving Bernstein, *Promises Kept* (Oxford University Press, New York, 1991); Hugh Douglas Price, "Race, Religion and the Rules Committee," in Alan Westin, *The Uses of Power* (Harcourt, Brace & World, New York, 1962); Frank Munger and Richard F. Fenno, *National Politics and Federal Aid to Education* (University of Syracuse Press, Syracuse, 1962); *Congressional Quarterly Almanac,* 1961; Smith papers, University of Virginia.
15. Sorensen to Kennedy, Mar. 7, Apr. 12, 1961, Sorensen papers, JFKL; memorandum re Federal Aid Meeting, Feb. 28, 1961, National Catholic Welfare Conference papers, Catholic University; memorandum, May 18, 1961, NCWC papers, Catholic University; Robert Bendiner, *Obstacle Course on Capitol Hill* (McGraw Hill, New York, 1964); oral history, Jim Bolling, JFKL.
16. Donahue, Sorensen, Schlesinger interviews; Bernstein, *Promises Kept;* Munger and Fenno, *National Politics and Federal Aid to Education;* Bendiner, *Obstacle Course on Capitol Hill;* O'Neill to Cardinal Cushing, June 2, 9, 1959; Cushing to O'Neill, May 28, June 17, 1959, O'Neill to Mary Mulcahy, Mar. 14, 1960, O'Neill to Walter Hughes, May 10, 1962, school construction and education files, ONBC; confidential memorandum, June 16, 1961, memorandum, Oct. 23, 1961, letter, Aug. 28, 1961, NCWC papers, Catholic University.

17. Aside from Edward Kennedy's proficiency as a legislator, O'Neill liked him as a host. At Jack Kennedy's parties and receptions, the festivities ended early, and "he would have a waiter pass a tray of drinks around and if you grabbed one when it went by, you got your drink." Teddy's parties, however, would go on past midnight with plenty of refreshments, singing and fellowship, O'Neill said. Diehl, Boland, Schlesinger, Edward M. Kennedy, Sorensen, Donahue interviews; O'Neill oral history, ONBC; Lawrence O'Brien to Bill Wilson, May 4, 1962, O'Brien, list of congressional calls, White House papers, JFKL; *Washington Post,* Apr. 5, 1963.
18. "Tip always felt he had to do these things for the Kennedys. They came close to telling him what to do. He resented it; he hated it," said Hyman. Hyman himself ran for Massachusetts attorney general in 1965, and his accounts of the culture clash between Jewish candidate and Irish pols are telling and funny. At one point he called upon Bridget Fitzpatrick, the septuagenarian Irish boss of certain wards in Worcester, and a suspected anti-Semite. "I went up to her door and knocked. It opened a crack and peering out was an old hag who looked very much like the witch in Snow White. 'What d'ya want?' she croaked at me," Hyman recalled. He introduced himself and was admitted to a small vestibule dominated by a card table packed with crucifixes, Virgin Marys, Baby Jesuses and other religious statuary. Hyman's foot caught the leg of the table, and all the statues toppled to the floor. "You dirty Jew," Bridgie said, "you broke my fuckin' madonnas!"
19. Interview and unpublished manuscript, Lester Hyman; Healy, Donahue, Grossman interviews; Martin T. Camacho to O'Neill, 1962 and 1963, O'Neill to Sen. J. W. Fulbright, July 23, 1963, Fulbright to O'Neill, July 12, 1963, Portugal file, ONBC; hearings, Senate Foreign Relations Committee, "Activities of Agents of Foreign Principals in U.S.," May 23, 1963; *Boston Record American,* July 24, 1963; *Boston Globe,* Oct. 1, Nov. 11, Dec. 16, 1962, Mar. 23, July 24, 1963; *Congressional Record,* Oct. 17, 1961, Oct. 15, 1962, July 11, 1963; O'Neill oral history, ONBC; O'Neill oral history, JFKL; O'Neill interview with Adam Clymer; *Christian Science Monitor,* Nov. 20, 1962.
20. Rosemary O'Neill, Susan O'Neill, Edward M. Kennedy, Segal, MacNeil interviews; O'Neill oral histories, ONBC, JFKL; O'Neill, *Man of the House.*
21. Kenneth O'Donnell, oral history, LBJL; tapes and notes of telephone recordings, Dec. 7, 9, 12, 1963, Apr. 28, Apr. 29, May 4, 11, 13, 14, June 9, 1964, LBJL; Evans and Novak column, June 7, 1964; *Boston Globe,* Mar. 24, May 3, 10, 1964; O'Neill oral history, LBJL; House Rules Committee minutes, 1964, National Archives; memorandum, Jack Valenti to Larry O'Brien, Ken O'Donnell and Bill Moyers, Apr. 15, 1964, LBJL; memo, Chuck Daly to Larry O'Brien, May 20, 1964, LBJL; Kenneth BeLieu, assistant secretary of the navy to O'Neill, Sept. 23, 2964; memorandum, Chuck Daly to David McGiffert, legislative assistant, Department of Defense, Aug. 21, 1964; Favors Requested, Favors Granted, Rep. Thomas P. O'Neill Jr., White House files, LBJL; telegram, O'Neill to Larry O'Brien, Aug 19, 1964, LBJL; O'Neill to Lyndon Johnson, Oct. 13, 1966.
22. Deputy Assist. Sect. of State John P. White to Barefoot Sanders, 1967, LBJL.
23. Kennedy had lost the white vote to Nixon but carried 68 percent of the Negro vote after making a well-publicized intercession on behalf of the imprisoned Martin Luther King during the 1960 presidential campaign.
24. Catherine MacKinnon, Rosemary and Susan O'Neill interviews; Watson, *Lion in the Lobby;* Charles and Barbara Whalen, *The Longest Debate* (Seven Locks Press,

Cabin John, Maryland, 1985); minutes, hearings of the House Rules Committee, 1965, 1966, National Archives; *Congressional Record,* Aug. 28, 1963, Mar. 9, July 8, 1965, Aug. 2, 1983; correspondence, O'Neill to Mitchell and other civil rights leaders, civil rights files, ONBC; *Boston Traveler,* Jan. 5, 1964; McCormack interview, McCormack papers, Boston University; Drew Pearson column, July 7, 1964; Mitchell oral history, JFKL; Irving Bernstein, *Guns or Butter* (Oxford University Press, New York, 1996); Bernstein, *Promises Kept;* Robert Dallek, *Flawed Giant* (Oxford University Press, New York, 1998).

25. O'Neill to Rep. John Dent, June 10, 1965, O'Neill to Rep. J. Edward Roush, Aug. 10, 1966, O'Neill to Rep. James G. O'Hara, Sept. 28, 1966; oral history, Barefoot Sanders, LBJL; Dallek, *Flawed Giant;* Bernstein, *Guns or Butter; Congressional Record,* Aug. 25, 1965; Dierenfield, *Keeper of the Rules; New York Times,* July 2, 1989.

Chapter 10
Vietnam, Kooks and Commies

1. Rosaline Herstein, letter to the editor, *New York Times.* Jan. 23, 1994.
2. ONBC.
3. *Boston Traveler,* Aug. 12, 1954.
4. O'Neill to Philip L. Marcus, Sept. 23, 1963, ONBC; Michael Beschloss, *The Crisis Years* (Burlingame Books, New York, 1991).
5. Beschloss, *Taking Charge: The Johnson White House Tapes, 1963-1964* (Simon & Schuster, New York, 1997).
6. Robert S. McNamara, *In Retrospect* (Times Books, New York, 1995).
7. "Hell, those dumb stupid sailors were just shooting at flying fish," Lyndon Johnson told George Ball. Ball memoir quoted in Dallek, *Flawed Giant.*
8. O'Neill, *Man of the House*; O'Neill oral histories, LBJL, JFKL; O'Neill interviews with Clancy and Elder, William Gibbons.
9. William Gibbons, *The U.S. Government and the Vietnam War: Part III* (Washington D.C., U.S. Government Printing Office, 1988); *The U.S. Government and the Vietnam War: Part IV* (Washington, D.C., U.S. Government Printing Office, 1994).
10. Doris Kearns, *Lyndon Johnson and The American Dream* (Signet, New York, 1976).
11. O'Neill to MassPAX activists, Apr. 7, 1967, ONBC.
12. O'Neill to Mrs. Robert Campbell, Feb. 24, 1965; O'Neill to Robert Soboff, Apr. 21, 1965; O'Neill to Mr. and Mrs. J. S. Uleman, Apr. 8, 1965, ONBC.
13. Gibbons, Part III.
14. Gibbons, Part III.
15. *Boston Record-American,* Apr. 30, 1965.
16. *Boston Globe,* June 15, 1965.
17. O'Neill to Chester Hartman, June 16, 1965, ONBC.
18. O'Neill to Jerome Grossman, Jan. 13, 1966, ONBC.
19. Jerome Grossman interview.
20. Judith Kurland interview.
21. Gibbons, Part III. O'Neill to Leonard A. Paolillo, July 21, 1965, ONBC.
22. *Boston Herald,* Jan. 8, 1966.
23. Massachusetts ADA chairman Albert S. Coolidge to O'Neill, Jan. 18, 1966, ONBC; O'Neill to Rosemary O'Neill, Jan. 11, 1966.
24. Elmer Brown, executive secretary of Friends Meeting at Cambridge to O'Neill, Jan. 14, 1966, ONBC.

25. O'Neill to Lawrence J. Straw, Jan. 8, 1966, W. F. Westcott to O'Neill, Jan. 31, 1966, ONBC.
26. O'Neill to Rosemary O'Neill, Jan. 11, 1966; Leslie Gelb and Richard Betts, "The Irony of Vietnam," quoted in Paul Johnson, *A History of the American People* (HarperCollins, New York, 1997).
27. O'Neill to Rosemary O'Neill, Mar. 1966; Gibbons, Part IV.
28. *Boston Globe,* Mar. 6, 1966. "Coalition governments with Communists never work. We know that from experience," O'Neill said. O'Neill to Rosemary O'Neill, Mar. 1966.
29. Legislative files, ONBC.
30. *Boston Herald,* June 7, 1966.
31. Terry Segal interview; *Boston Herald, Boston Globe, Associated Press,* June 16, 1966; O'Neill to Rosemary O'Neill, June 3, 26, 1966; Reports on Congressmen to the President, undated, Charles Roche files, LBJL.
32. O'Neill newsletter, "Report from Washington," June 1966.
33. Charles N. Ascheim II to O'Neill and reply, Aug. 11, 1966, ONBC. O'Neill replied with equal sarcasm. "The weather in Washington is simply beautiful. . . . Nothing is more refreshing than a long mid-week walk through Rock Creek Park on a summer afternoon. . . . If one is bored with serenity, he can even come into the city where, I am told, important political events transpire with consistent frequency."
34. O'Neill to Alice Fehlhaber, Mrs. John Gray and Leonard Kirsch, Apr. 7, 1967, ONBC.
35. At Boston College, only the schools of nursing and education enrolled women, who were not allowed to live in off-campus apartments, or marry.
36. Interviews with Susan O'Neill, Thomas P. O'Neill III, Pat McCarthy; O'Neill interview with William Gibbons; oral histories, LBJL, JFKL; O'Neill, *Man of the House;* O'Neill to Rosemary O'Neill, Feb. 1966; *The Heights,* Boston College newspaper, Feb. through Oct. 1966.
37. Raymond T. McNally to O'Neill, Aug. 5, 1966, and reply, Aug. 10, 1966, ONBC.
38. Interview, Filippa Pizzi; *Boston Sunday Herald,* July 31, 1966; O'Neill, *Man of the House; Boston Magazine,* Dec. 1973. Bretta was convicted for taking kickbacks from developers in 1984. Cammarata had many friends in the press and O'Neill was harshly criticized for trying to muscle the promoter off the ballot in 1964 and 1966. Years later, after publishing his memoirs, O'Neill was again brought to task for piling on poor Sam. Only then did it come out that Cammarata had moved to Houston, gotten involved with organized crime and been convicted as a drug kingpin. He died in prison in 1983.
39. Terry Segal and Judith Kurland interviews.
40. Neil MacNeil interview; MacNeil file to editors.
41. O'Neill to Rosemary O'Neill, May–Sept. 1966; *Boston Globe,* June 22, 1966.
42. Helen Horowitz to O'Neill, July 1967, ONBC.
43. Jerome Grossman interview.
44. Grossman, *Relentless Liberal* (Vantage, New York, 1996).
45. Jerry R. Cole, "Campaign Analysis," ONBC.
46. O'Neill to Morris Friedkin, June 1, 1966; U.S. State Department to O'Neill, Oct. 1966; O'Neill papers, Subject Files, Vietnam, Boston College; O'Neill to Rosemary O'Neill, Jan. 1967.
47. Joseph McLaughlin interview; Gibbons, Part IV.
48. LBJ to W. Marvin Watson, May 2, 1967, LBJL.

49. ONBC.
50. Between 1965 and 1973 the U.S. dropped more than 8 million tons of bombs on Indochina, more than four times what the U.S. dropped during all of World War II. Todd Gitlin, *The Sixties: Years of Hope, Days of Rage* (Bantam, New York, 1987).
51. Gibbons, Part IV; James T. Patterson, *Grand Expectations* (Oxford University Press, New York, 1996).
52. McNamara, *In Retrospect;* Jerome Grossman, *Relentless Liberal*; Patterson, *Grand Expectations.*
53. Gitlin, *The Sixties.*
54. ONBC.
55. O'Neill interviews with Gibbons; Clancy and Elder.
56. CIA analyst Sam Adams and like-minded members of the intelligence community concluded at this time that the number of Communist soldiers in Vietnam was more than 500,000 — about twice as many as the official Pentagon "order of battle" said there were. The bitter dispute outlasted the war, and led to a celebrated lawsuit by Westmoreland against CBS News, which had reported on the dispute.
57. John Walker interview.
58. Interview with Walker; O'Neill interview with Gibbons; Clancy and Elder.
59. Walker later asked William Colby if then-director Richard Helms had known about the meetings, or if the CIA had kept records of its approach to O'Neill. "What meeting?" Colby replied. Thirty years later, Walker said he still did not know if the group of intelligence analysts were acting with or without the knowledge of their superiors.
60. Gibbons interview with O'Neill.
61. O'Neill, *Man of the House.* O'Neill's sons were spared from service in Vietnam by student deferments and, in Tommy's case, service in the reserves.
62. The statistics on Vietnam service were compiled by former Secretary of the Navy James H. Webb, cited in Alexander Haig's memoir *Inner Circles* (Warner Books, New York, 1992).
63. Alan Lupo, "Tip-toeing Toward Impeachment with Tip O'Neill," *Boston Magazine*, Dec. 1973.
64. O'Neill to Marvin Watson, Apr. 27, 1967, ONBC.
65. Joseph McLaughlin interview.
66. O'Neill to John P. White, deputy assistant secretary for congressional relations, U.S. State Department, June 21, 1967, ONBC.
67. Letter to the editor, *Cambridge Chronicle,* by Mrs. Frederick Wiseman, Mrs. Calvin Mooers, Dr. Sanford Gifford and Tom Cole, ONBC.
68. While in Malta, O'Neill received a wire from Rep. Mendel Rivers, the chairman of the House Armed Services Committee, asking him to make an "on-the-spot" inquiry into the flap surrounding the USS *Liberty,* which had been attacked during the Six Day War by Israeli warplanes, and was now in port with elements of the U.S. sixth fleet in Malta. O'Neill came to the conclusion that the *Liberty* was indeed flying the U.S. flag, and therefore unjustly attacked by the Israelis. Rosemary O'Neill interview.
69. O'Neill interview with Gibbons. With hindsight, Johnson's critics insist that the U.S. should have employed its full military might against North Vietnam, and invaded. (Johnson, *A History of the American People.*) To LBJ, O'Neill and others, however, the threat of full-scale war with China was very real — the U.S. had

fought the Chinese under such circumstances just a dozen years before, in Korea. Like Harry Truman, Johnson feared that a limited war could escalate into a general conflagration; unlike Truman, he didn't have nuclear hegemony. The Chinese had detonated a nuclear device in 1964. O'Neill was particularly worried about the perils of escalation.

70. Mrs. Christine DiGrezio to O'Neill, July 16, 1967, ONBC.
71. O'Neill to Lyndon Johnson, July 18, 1967, ONBC.
72. O'Neill to Lyndon Johnson, July 25, 1967, ONBC.
73. Barefoot Sanders to O'Neill, Aug. 9, 1967, ONBC.
74. O'Neill to Christine DiGrezio, July 27, 1967, ONBC.
75. McLaughlin interview.
76. O'Neill newsletter, "Report from Washington," Sept. 1967.
77. McLaughlin interview; Gibbons interview with O'Neill.
78. O'Neill to Rosemary O'Neill, Aug. or Sept. 1967.
79. Mildred O'Neill, "Thomas P. O'Neill Jr. A Family Portrait." Private O'Neill family videotape, ONBC.
80. *Boston Record-American,* Sept. 8, 1967; *Boston Globe,* Sept. 13, 1967.
81. "For one night only, the regular game at the University Club had been moved to the Metropolitan Club (a segregated facility that O'Neill claimed never to have frequented before) . . . so we could avoid Ben Jensen, a member from Iowa who had been losing more money than he could afford," O'Neill recalled.
82. Thomas P. O'Neill III, Kurland, Gibbons, MacNeil, Barefoot Sanders, Ed Boland interviews; O'Neill interviews with Gibbons; Clancy and Elder; MacNeil to editors, 1974; O'Neill, *Man of the House;* oral histories at LBJ and JFK libraries. There is no White House record of Johnson's phone calls, or of O'Neill's visit to the Oval Office. MacNeil and Tommy O'Neill have hazy memories that O'Neill was instead called aside by LBJ in a gathering with other congressmen at the White House; one such "stag dinner" took place, with O'Neill in attendance, on October 24, 1967. Boland remembers the presidential phone call, however, and Kurland remembers a morning her boss was summoned to the White House over Vietnam. Gibbons, author of the definitive history of Congress and Vietnam, and a Johnson aide at the time, said that gaps in the records of Johnson's activities are common, especially regarding the kind of spontaneous events that O'Neill describes.
83. Claude J. Desautels to Lawrence O'Brien, Sept. 27, 1967, LBJL; Lawrence O'Brien to Lyndon Johnson, Sept. 29, 1967, LBJL.
84. Desautels to O'Brien, Sept. 27, 1967.
85. W. Thomas Johnson, Notes of the President's Meeting with Cambridge Educators, Sept. 26, 1967.
86. W. Thomas Johnson, Notes of the President's Meeting with Secretary Rusk, Secretary McNamara, Mr. Rostow, CIA Director Helms, and George Christian, Oct. 3, 1967.
87. Gibbons, Part IV.
88. Martin Sweig interview.
89. W. J. Dolan Jr. to O'Neill, Nov. 14, 1967, ONBC.
90. Gary Hymel interview.
91. Gibbons interview with O'Neill; Clancy and Elder interview with O'Neill; O'Neill, *Man of the House;* oral histories at LBJ and JFK libraries.
92. ONBC.

93. W. M. Byrd to O'Neill, Oct. 1, 1967; ONBC.
94. Grossman, *Relentless Liberal.*
95. Victor A. Campisi to O'Neill, Oct. 2, 1967; ONBC.
96. Leo Corrigan to O'Neill, Sept. 15, 1967; ONBC.
97. O'Neill interview with Gibbons.
98. McNally to O'Neill, Sept. 25, 1967; ONBC.
99. O'Neill to Mrs. George E. Vaillant, Feb. 19, 1968; ONBC. At a whip meeting in 1971, O'Neill got into a shouting match with Rep. Clem Zablocki over why he opposed the war. Zablocki had accused him of political expediency.
100. Grossman, *Relentless Liberal.*
101. 48,195 voted for military victory; 31,641 for immediate withdrawal, and 23,618 for a Nixon-like plan of phased withdrawals, *Boston Globe,* Dec. 4, 1970.
102. ONBC.

Chapter 11
A War That Can Only Be Ended

1. William Gibbons, *The U.S. Government and the Vietnam War* (Washington, D.C., U.S. Government Printing Office, 1994).
2. Harry McPherson, *A Political Education* (Little, Brown, Boston, 1972).
3. Gibbons, Part IV.
4. W. Thomas Johnson, Notes of the President's Meeting with Secretary Rusk, Secretary McNamara, Mr. Rostow, CIA Director Helms, and George Christian, Oct. 3, 1967, LBJL.
5. William Gibbons interview.
6. *Washington Post,* Sept. 19, 1967.
7. *Chicago Tribune,* Sept. 18, 1967.
8. O'Neill, *Man of the House.*
9. O'Neill interview with Clancy and Elder.
10. Judith Kurland interview.
11. Neil MacNeil interview.
12. Segal, Francine Gannon, Joseph McLaughlin interviews.
13. Kurland interview.
14. Segal, Kurland interviews; *Congressional Record,* July 20, Aug. 17, 1966; *Washington Post,* Aug. 6, 18, 1966; *Boston Globe,* Aug. 5, 24, 1966.
15. Kurland interview.
16. Even in times of political crisis, O'Neill maintained his perspective. On October 2, O'Neill told the House that "we in this body lead a busy life, caught up with the problems of our country and the world. We do not often take time out to contemplate the truly beautiful and wonderful things in life. . . . Lest any of the Members of this body were in some isolated area of Antarctica during the past weekend and have not heard the news, let me inform you that the Boston Red Sox won the American League pennant. . . . No one less than a poet could describe the beauty of Sunday's game. The score was 5 to 3 and for once in our busy lives there was true beauty and happiness."
17. McLaughlin interview.
18. Peters, *The American Speakership.*
19. Neil MacNeil, file to editors.
20. Kurland interview.

21. Kurland, "Moral Arguments Against the War in Vietnam," Jan. 17, 1968, ONBC.
22. O'Neill interview with Gibbons; ONBC.
23. *Congressional Record,* Mar. 4, 1968.
24. Jim Wright, *Balance of Power* (Turner Publishing, Atlanta, 1996).
25. Susan O'Neill interview.
26. *Brookline Chronicle Citizen,* Mar. 1968.
27. O'Neill to Rosemary O'Neill, July 25, 1966.
28. Watson, *Lion in the Lobby.*
29. Jack Newfield, *Robert Kennedy: A Memoir* (Bantam, New York, 1970).
30. *Congressional Record,* Jan. 29, 1970; Kurland interview.
31. Watson, *Lion in the Lobby.*
32. *Congressional Record,* Apr. 10, 1968.
33. Charles D. Roche to O'Neill, Apr. 12, 1968, LBJL.
34. O'Neill, *Man of the House.*
35. Healy interview; O'Neill to Rosemary O'Neill, spring 1968.
36. O'Neill to Rosemary O'Neill, summer 1968.
37. *Congressional Record,* June 26, 1968; O'Neill to Rosemary O'Neill, summer 1968.
38. Goodwin, *Remembering America.*
39. Kurland interview.
40. Michael V. DiSalle to O'Neill, O'Neill to DiSalle, ONBC.
41. O'Neill interview with Adam Clymer; O'Neill to Rosemary O'Neill, summer 1968.
42. Healy interview.
43. O'Brien oral history, JFKL.
44. Some journalists insisted that Daley said, "Fuck you, you Jew sonofabitch, you lousy motherfucker, go home." Rostenkowski, insisting that Daley was a daily communicant who never used epithets harsher than "mashed potatoes," said that Daley called Ribicoff "a faker."
45. Kurland interview.
46. *Boston Globe,* Aug. 26, 1968.
47. Larry L. King, "The Road to Power in Congress," in, Morris K. Udall, *Education of a Congressman* (Bobbs-Merrill, Indianapolis, 1972). Udall kept a detailed file on his coup attempt, and how it failed, with a series of memoranda, notes to himself, "postmortem thoughts on the Speaker contest" and "some thoughts on how to win while losing." They are available in his papers at the University of Arizona.
48. MacNeil, file to editors.
49. Gitlin, *The Sixties.*
50. Kennedy was grateful to O'Neill and the other members of the Massachusetts delegation who signed a telegram of support for the senator in the days after the fatal accident. "You've always been a good friend to me, and to my family — and your understanding and friendship will never be forgotten," Kennedy wrote. ONBC.
51. Hersh, *The Education of Edward Kennedy.*
52. O'Neill, graduation address, Matignon High School, June 1, 1969, ONBC.
53. Kurland interview.
54. David Cohen interview.
55. Stephen E. Ambrose, *Nixon: The Triumph of a Politician, 1962-1972* (Simon and Schuster, New York, 1989); Henry Kissinger, *White House Years* (Little, Brown, Boston, 1979).

56. Kissinger, *White House Years.*
57. Cohen interview.
58. *Congressional Record,* Sept. 30, 1969.
59. Grossman, *Relentless Liberal.*
60. *Congressional Record,* Oct. 15, 1969.
61. Richard Nixon, *RN: The Memoirs of Richard Nixon* (Warner Books, New York, 1978); Kissinger, *White House Years;* Ambrose, *Nixon.*
62. Ambrose, *Nixon.*
63. O'Neill to Dennis Milford, Nov. 4, 1969, Wright to O'Neill, Nov. 17, 1969, ONBC.
64. *Congressional Record,* Dec. 2, 1969.
65. Speeches file, ONBC.
66. Nixon, *RN;* Ambrose, *Nixon;* Kissinger, *White House Years;* J. V. Brennan to Rose Mary Woods, NNA.
67. Kissinger, *White House Years.*
68. Ambrose, *Nixon;* Nixon to Robert Haldeman, NNA.
69. Gitlin, *The Sixties.*
70. Kurland to O'Neill, May 6, 1970.
71. *Congressional Record,* May 6, 1970.
72. Richard Conlon interview, Clancy and Elder; Kurland, Cohen interviews.
73. *Congressional Record,* July 27, 1970.
74. Cohen interview.
75. *Newsweek,* Aug. 10, 1970; *Time,* Aug. 10, 1970. Time profiled the O'Neill household, which "teems with five concerned children, aged 18 to 26, plus a constant dozen or so of their friends, all forever debating political issues. . . . A few days ago, the O'Neills had a long discussion about hair: the congressman duly assigned an aide to do some research. 'We discovered that since the time of Christ, the male species has worn long hair and beards about 90 percent of the time. The Western world turned to short hair and clean-shaven faces only after the Prussian victory over France. All the great heroes of America have worn long hair. It's nothing for Americans to get alarmed about.'" Cohen, Kurland interviews.
76. Democratic Study Group, "Special Report, The First Year of Record Teller Voting," Jan. 27, 1972.
77. Mary McGrory, *Washington Star,* Mar. 19, 1971.

Chapter 12
The Leadership Ladder

1. King, "The Road to Power in Congress."
2. Ibid.
3. Carl Albert oral history, University of Oklahoma.
4. Albert, *Little Giant.*
5. Hale Boggs oral history, JFKL.
6. Robert Peabody, *Leadership in Congress* (Little, Brown, Boston, 1976).
7. Hale Boggs file, Federal Bureau of Investigation, Washington, D.C.
8. Patrick J. Buchanan to President Richard Nixon, Oct. 10, 1969, NNA.
9. Jack Anderson, *Parade* magazine, Nov. 9, 1969.
10. MacNeil file to editors.
11. MacNeil file to editors; *Boston Globe,* Jan. 31, 1971.

12. *Congressional Quarterly,* Jan. 6, 1970.
13. Martin Sweig and John L. Monahan interviews; "It was typical of O'Neill . . . he didn't give a damn if he got burned. He loved Martin and was glad to do it," said Monahan.
14. McCormack interview, Clancy and Elder.
15. Bryce Harlow to Nixon, Feb. 12, 1970, NNA; *Congressional Quarterly Almanac,* 1970.
16. King, "The Road to Power in Congress."
17. Albert oral history, University of Oklahoma, "When under stress and pressure [Boggs] has seemed to buckle. This was particularly true in the summer of 1969, when his bizarre and erratic behavior was the talk of the cloakrooms," Mo Udall wrote in a private memo. "The case against Boggs," Udall papers, University of Arizona. As in the 1969 race against McCormack, Udall kept a file of memoranda and notes to himself.
18. King, "The Road to Power in Congress"; transcript of Boggs press conference, Udall papers, University of Arizona.
19. Lindy Boggs, John Brademas interviews; "Hale was drinking and he was popping pills," said Brademas.
20. Dan Rostenkowski interview; *Harpers,* Oct. 1970.
21. Rostenkowski interview.
22. Peabody, *Leadership in Congress;* King, "The Road to Power in Congress"; Albert, *Little Giant;* Rostenkowski, Hymel interviews.
23. Peabody, *Leadership in Congress;* King, "The Road to Power in Congress"; Albert, *Little Giant;* Rostenkowski, Hymel interviews; Udall papers, University of Arizona.
24. MacNeil file to editors; Rostenkowski interview; *New York Times,* Nov. 22, 1970.
25. Bolling interview, Clancy and Elder.
26. Barbara Sinclair, *Majority Leadership in the U.S. House* (Johns Hopkins University Press, Baltimore, 1983).
27. O'Neill, *Man of the House.*
28. MacNeil file to editors; O'Neill interview, Clancy and Elder; Kurland interview.
29. Segal interview.
30. Kurland interview.
31. O'Neill, *Man of the House;* Healy interview; O'Neill interview, Clancy and Elder; *Washington Post,* Dec. 14, 1970; *Boston Globe,* Dec. 4, 1970.
32. Hugh Carey, Coelho interviews; Udall papers, University of Arizona.
33. MacNeil interview.
34. Peabody, *Leadership in Congress;* King, "The Road to Power in Congress"; Hymel interview; O'Neill interview, Clancy and Elder.
35. Hale Boggs to O'Neill, ONBC; Peabody, *Leadership in Congress;* King, "The Road to Power in Congress"; *Congressional Quarterly,* Jan. 11, 1971.
36. King, "The Road to Power in Congress"; Udall papers, University of Arizona.
37. Mo Udall to O'Neill, Jan. 14, 1971, Hale Boggs to O'Neill, Jan. 14, 1971, ONBC; Udall papers, University of Arizona; *Washington Post,* Dec. 14, 25, 1970, Jan. 19, 1971; *New York Times,* Jan. 18, 1971.
38. Peabody, *Leadership in Congress.*
39. King, "The Road to Power in Congress"; Udall papers, University of Arizona; Peabody, *Leadership in Congress.*
40. Albert, *Little Giant.*

41. "Daley was not prowar. Daley was a dove. He had four sons," Rostenkowski recalled. "Every time we would go to the Oval Office he would say, 'Lyndon, get out of that goddamn Vietnam. Please, Mr. President, you don't know. You got problems. Don't be screwing around in Vietnam.' But then he would walk out to the driveway of the White House and the news people would say 'What did you talk about?' 'Domestic issues.' 'You talk about Vietnam?' 'No.' 'Where are you on the war?' 'I'm with the President. Wherever the President is, I'm with him.'" Rostenkowski interview.
42. Albert, *Little Giant.*
43. Peabody, *Leadership in Congress;* Rostenkowski, Jim Wright interviews; Albert, *Little Giant.*
44. Wright, Rostenkowski interviews.
45. Randall B. Ripley, "The Party Whip Organizations in the U.S. House of Representatives," *American Political Science Review,* Sept. 1964.
46. Peabody, *Leadership in Congress;* O'Neill interview, Clancy and Elder.
47. Gary Hymel interview; Albert oral history, University of Oklahoma; Peabody, *Leadership in Congress.*
48. O'Neill, *Man of the House;* Peabody, *Leadership in Congress;* Hymel, Rosemary O'Neill interviews.
49. King, "The Road to Power in Congress"; Hymel, Hugh Carey interviews. It should also be noted that Delaney was a Rules Committee colleague of O'Neill's, at a time when loyalties were forged on committees.
50. Hymel interview; Albert oral history, University of Oklahoma; *Congressional Quarterly,* Jan. 22, 1971.
51. James Shannon interview.
52. Edward Boland and Coelho interviews; Drinan, Bolling interviews, Clancy and Elder.

Chapter 13
The Majority Leader

1. O'Neill, *Man of the House;* Hyman interview, unpublished memoir; *Congressional Quarterly Almanac,* 1967.
2. Speech files, ONBC.
3. Diehl interview.
4. McLaughlin, Kurland, Healy, Thomas Oliphant, Marty Nolan, Jim Dinneen interviews.
5. Diehl interview.
6. O'Brien oral history, JFKL.
7. Lawrence Dodd, untitled paper, Hale Boggs papers, Tulane University.
8. Dodd paper, Boggs papers, Tulane University.
9. Kurland memo, ONBC; Irv Sprague and Kurland interviews; Dodd paper, Hale Boggs papers, Tulane University.
10. Dodd paper, Hale Boggs papers, Tulane University; Kurland interview, ONBC.
11. Rostenkowski interview; Albert oral history, University of Oklahoma; MacNeil file to editors.
12. John Barriere, memo to Albert, Carl Albert papers, University of Oklahoma.
13. Dodd paper, Hale Boggs papers, Tulane University.

14. MacGowan's party lost its luster when Diehl, who was worried that the lobbyist was trading on O'Neill's friendship, joined with the young women on the congressman's staff (who never liked the idea that women were excluded from the stag affairs) to host a rival bash. Diehl, Christine Sullivan Daly interview.
15. Ambrose, *Nixon.*
16. Kissinger, *White House Years;* Ambrose, *Nixon.*
17. White House tape recording, NNA.
18. Kissinger, *White House Years.*
19. *Congressional Record,* Feb. 9, 1971; Kurland to O'Neill, Feb. 9, 1971, ONBC.
20. At home, O'Neill was more secure than ever. He traded Brookline in the 1971 redistricting for the dependably Democratic but more stable suburban towns of Arlington, Belmont and Watertown.
21. Cohen interview.
22. Cohen interview; ONBC; *New York Times,* Mar. 30, 1971.
23. Cohen interview.
24. William Timmons to President Richard Nixon, Apr. 1, 1971; NNA.
25. Kissinger, *White House Years.*
26. Stanley Kutler, *Abuse of Power* (Free Press, New York, 1997); Diehl, Kurland interviews.
27. *Congressional Record,* June 17, 1971.
28. Peters, *The American Speakership.*
29. Jack Anderson, Mar. 10, 1972, *Boston Globe.*
30. *New York Times,* June 7, 1971.
31. Gerald Ford, interview with Trevor Armbrister, Gerald Ford Library.
32. Boggs file, Federal Bureau of Investigation. In the week before his April 5 speech, Boggs had repeatedly lost control, the FBI agents told Hoover. Boggs had challenged a colleague to a fight at a reception at the Mayflower Hotel. On April 3, at a fund-raising dinner for Rep. Bob Sikes in Panama City, Fla., the majority leader "became completely and thoroughly intoxicated," the FBI files showed.
33. *Congressional Quarterly,* Apr. 9, 23, 30, 1971; H. R. Haldeman, *The Haldeman Diaries* (G. P. Putnam's Sons, New York, 1994).
34. Kurland interview.
35. Nixon, *RN.*
36. Gary Hart, *Right From the Start* (Quadrangle, New York, 1973).
37. *Washington Post,* July 11, 1972.
38. Grossman, *Relentless Liberal.*
39. Richard Conlon interview, Clancy and Elder.
40. Phillip Burton to DSG colleagues, Apr. 19, 1972, ONBC.
41. Linda J. Melconian interview; Linda J. Melconian, "A Case Study in the Legislative Process," George Washington University thesis.
42. Conlon to Burton, Apr. 24, 1972; Carl Albert papers, University of Oklahoma.
43. Barriere to Albert, June 14, 1972, Carl Albert papers, University of Oklahoma.
44. Robert Drinan, *New York Times,* Aug. 1972.
45. Richard Cook and William Timmons to Nixon, Oct. 12, 1972, NNA.
46. MacNeil file to editors; Mike Reed interview.
47. Drinan, *New York Times,* Aug. 1972.
48. Lindy Boggs interview.
49. Jim Wright interview. Wright, *Balance of Power.*

50. Hymel interview; Albert, *Little Giant;* O'Neill, *Man of the House.*
51. Richard Cook and William Timmons to President Richard Nixon, Mar. 17, 1972, NNA.
52. *Anchorage Daily News,* Oct. 17, 1972.
53. Lindy Boggs interview; Lindy Boggs, *Washington Through a Purple Veil* (Harcourt Brace, New York, 1994).
54. Hymel interview.
55. Lindy Boggs, *Washington Through a Purple Veil.*
56. Hymel interview.
57. Hale Boggs papers, Tulane University; National Transportation Safety Board, release, Feb. 2, 1973; Secretary of Defense Melvin Laird to W. Pat Jennings, clerk of the House, Jan. 2, 1973; Albert papers, University of Oklahoma; WLAE-TV documentary, "Hale Boggs: The Man, The Mission, The Mystery."
58. Peabody, *Leadership in Congress;* Flying in icy weather "is like playing with the devil — fun, but don't play unless you can cheat," Jonz wrote in an article entitled "Ice: Without Fear." "If you are sneaky, smart and careful you can fly 350 days a year and disregard 99 percent of the BS you hear about icing."
59. Hymel interview.
60. NTSB release, Boggs papers, Tulane University; *Congressional Quarterly,* Oct. 21, 1972.
61. *Congressional Record,* Oct. 17, 1972.
62. O'Neill, *Man of the House.*
63. MacNeil, file to editors.
64. Hymel interview; *Congressional Quarterly,* Dec. 23, 1972.
65. Lindy Boggs interview; Boggs, *Washington Through a Purple Veil.*
66. Christopher O'Neill interview.
67. Diehl interview.
68. Peabody, *Leadership in Congress;* Clancy and Elder, *Tip,* 1980.
69. MacNeil interview; Diehl interview.
70. Rosemary O'Neill interview.
71. Ronald Peters, *The Speaker* (CQ Inc., Washington, D.C., 1995).
72. MacNeil interview; *Kansas City Star,* Aug. 6, 1970. Upon arriving in Washington, Kirwan was told that he could room, as a matter of courtesy to congressmen, at the University Club, where he said his prayers on his knees each night at the side of the bed. He faced an immediate problem at the membership meetings, however, where his fellow boarders traditionally introduced themselves by adding their occupation, alma mater and year of graduation ("lawyer, Harvard, '20" or "physician, Princeton, '31"). When it came his turn, Kirwin called out "Member of Congress, Heidelberg 8." *Congressional Record,* Apr. 21, 1964.
73. Thomas "Lud" Ashley interview.
74. MacNeil file to editors.
75. ONBC.
76. ONBC. Some of the changes were long overdue. A few months after O'Neill took over, the DCCC bragged, "We have gone into the era of color photography."
77. O'Neill, *Man of the House.* The press discovered the account when O'Neill filed a year-end report of his Massachusetts campaign fund, and disclosed the existence of the D.C. committee. The *Globe* published a story on the fund on Jan. 13, 1971, but did not mention Taylor's involvement.

78. Coelho interview.
79. DCCC report, ONBC.
80. ONBC.
81. Coelho interview.
82. ONBC; O'Neill interview with James Cannon.
83. The Democrats were helped by a critical blunder at the White House. Determined to roll up a historic margin, Nixon shared less than 2 percent of his $60 million campaign chest with Republican congressional candidates, thus ending Ford's hopes of being Speaker. In the end, the decision came back to haunt Nixon. "There is no question in my mind that if Nixon and John Mitchell and the other campaign powers had made a major effort we could have gotten a majority in 1972 . . . with just a little extra effort by him campaigning and by them spending money," said Ford in an interview for this book. "And in that case impeachment would "never have come to the forefront."
84. ONBC.
85. Peabody, *Leadership in Congress.*
86. Ibid.
87. Sam Gibbons, letters to colleagues, ONBC; *Congressional Quarterly,* Dec. 23, 1972.
88. Ralph Nader Congress Project, "Citizens Look at Congress," Oct. 22, 1972.
89. Peabody, *Leadership in Congress.*
90. ONBC.
91. Charlie Rose interview.
92. J. Joseph Moakley interview.
93. Hymel, Diehl interviews; *Congressional Quarterly,* Dec. 23, 1972; Peabody, *Leadership in Congress;* Jimmy Breslin, *How the Good Guys Finally Won* (Viking, New York, 1975).
94. Cook and Timmons to Nixon, Nov. 17, 1972, NNA.
95. Myra MacPherson, *Washington Post,* Dec. 31, 1972.
96. Ibid.
97. Nina Totenberg, *National Observer,* Jan. 13, 1973.
98. Peabody, *Leadership in Congress.*
99. Harold Donahue remarks, ONBC.
100. Brand interview; Peabody, *Leadership in Congress.*
101. *Boston Globe,* Jan. 3, 1973.
102. O'Neill diary, 1973.

Chapter 14
Watergate

1. Leonard Garment interview; Kissinger, *White House Years, Years of Upheaval* (Little, Brown, Boston, 1982); Nixon, *RN;* Jim Wright diary.
2. Garment interview; Bryce Harlow oral history, Gerald Ford library; Albert, *Little Giant.*
3. Matt Storin, Brand interviews; O'Neill oral history, JFKL; O'Neill interview with James Cannon; O'Neill Watergate interview, ONBC; O'Neill diary.
4. Charles Colson interview; Nixon White House enemy lists, NNA.
5. James Cannon interview, ONBC; James Patterson, *Grand Expectations* (Oxford University Press, New York, 1996).

6. Kissinger, *White House Years.*
7. O'Neill diary; *Boston Globe,* Jan. 28, 1973.
8. Symington to O'Neill and reply, Jan. 23, 1973, ONBC.
9. Albert oral history, Carl Albert papers, University of Oklahoma; O'Neill daily diary and schedule, 1973; O'Neill diary; O'Neill to Rep. James Symington, ONBC.
10. Diehl interview; O'Neill interview with Clancy and Elder; O'Neill FBI files, obtained through the Freedom of Information Act by the author.
11. O'Neill diary; Kurland, Ray Smock interviews; *Chicago Tribune,* Feb. 4, 1973; Saints and Sinners song sheet, ONBC.
12. Elliot Richardson, Michael Harrington, Eleanor Kelley, Billie Larsen, Rosemary O'Neill, Susan O'Neill, Christopher O'Neill, Thomas P. O'Neill III, Diehl interviews; Bolling, O'Neill III interviews, Clancy and Elder; *Washington Post,* Aug. 4, 1980; *Real Paper,* Mar. 13, 1974.
13. Garment interview; Colson to Haldeman, June 25, 1971; NNA; Bernard Firestone and Alexej Ugrinsky, eds., *Watergate and Afterward: The Legacy of Richard M. Nixon* (Greenwood Publishing, Westport, Conn., 1992).
14. Stanley Kutler, *The Wars of Watergate* (Alfred Knopf, New York, 1990); J. Anthony Lukas, *Nightmare: The Underside of the Nixon Years* (Viking Press, New York, 1976); Kutler, *Abuse of Power.*
15. O'Neill oral history, JFKL; Nixon, *RN.*
16. For years Albert nursed a grievance that Ervin, nearing retirement and thinking how the publicity of a Watergate investigation would boost his speaking fees, had "capitalized on it as a vehicle for making money." Albert oral history, University of Oklahoma; Brand interview; Kutler, *The Wars of Watergate;* Lukas, *Nightmare; Washington Monthly,* Apr. 1973.
17. *Watergate: Chronology of a Crisis* (Congressional Quarterly Inc., Washington, D.C., 1975); O'Neill Watergate interview, ONBC.
18. Jimmy Breslin, Cannon interview; *Watergate,* CQ Inc.; Jimmy Breslin, *How the Good Guys Finally Won* (Viking, New York, 1975); O'Neill to Steinbrenner, June 15, 1970, Steinbrenner to O'Neill, July 3, 1969, ONBC; O'Neill Watergate interview, ONBC; O'Neill oral history, John F. Kennedy library; O'Neill interview with Cannon.
19. Ari Weiss, David Cohen, Neil MacNeil, Jerry Zeifman, Stan Brand, Mike Reed interviews; O'Neill, oral history, JFKL; O'Neill interview with Cannon; O'Neill to Dr. and Mrs. David Sutton, Mar. 17, 1981, ONBC; *Watergate,* CQ Inc.
20. Robert Drinan, Gerald Ford interviews; Drinan to O'Neill, July 31, 1973, ONBC; O'Neill, *Man of the House;* O'Neill Watergate interview, ONBC; O'Neill interview with Cannon.

Chapter 15
Massacre

1. O'Neill diary; Timmons to Nixon, May 10, 1973, NNA; O'Neill, *Man of the House.*
2. White House memos, NNA; *Watergate,* CQ.
3. Thomas W. Benham, Opinion Research Corp., to Alexander Haig, White House papers, NNA; Moakley interview; *Congressional Record,* May 3, 1973; O'Neill diary; *Washington Post,* Sept. 5, 1973; *Time,* Sept. 24, 1973.

4. "When such attacks assume the character of impeachable offenses, and become, in some degree, official, by being placed among the public records, an officer thus assailed, however base the instrument used, if conscious of innocence, can look for refuge only to the Hall of the immediate Representative of the People," Calhoun wrote. The House agreed to investigate, and Calhoun was exonerated.
5. Richard Cohen and Jules Witcover, *A Heartbeat Away* (Viking, New York, 1974); *Wall Street Journal,* Aug. 7, 1973; Spiro Agnew, *Go Quietly . . . or Else* (William Morrow, New York, 1980); Ford, Zeifman, Hymel interviews; Albert oral history, University of Oklahoma.
6. *NBC News,* Sept. 25, 1973; Mike Reed, Zeifman, Hymel interviews; Agnew, *Go Quietly . . . or Else; Washington Post,* Sept. 26, 1973.
7. Zeifman, Hymel, Reed interviews; O'Neill, *Man of the House;* O'Neill and Peter Rodino interviews with Cannon; Albert oral history, University of Oklahoma.
8. Clancy and Elder, *Tip;* Albert oral history, University of Oklahoma; *Congressional Record,* Sept. 26, 1973; Zeifman interview; Rodino interview with Cannon.
9. Kissinger, *Years of Upheaval;* Nixon, *RN;* memorandum to the President from the chairmen of Exxon, Mobil, Texaco, Standard Oil, Oct. 12, 1973, NNA: "Any actions of the US government at this time in terms of increased military aid to Israel will have a critical and adverse effect on our relations with the moderate Arab producing companies . . . the whole position of the United States in the Middle East is on the way to being seriously impaired."; Ray Price to Nixon, Oct. 11, 1973, NNA: Albert oral history, University of Oklahoma; James Cannon, *Time and Chance* (HarperCollins, New York, 1994), O'Neill interview with Cannon.
10. In an interview with the author, Ford said that he "never" picked up the slightest sign that O'Neill tried to delay his confirmation as vice president: "None whatsoever."
11. Ford, MacNeil interviews; Cannon, *Time and Chance;* Albert oral history, University of Oklahoma; Rodino, O'Neill interviews with Cannon; Edward Mezvinsky, *A Term to Remember* (Coward, McCann & Geoghegan, New York, 1977); Breslin, *How the Good Guys Finally Won.*
12. Cox had worked in John Kennedy's presidential campaign, doing opposition research on Nixon in 1960, and in Robert Kennedy's Justice Department; Ted Kennedy attended Cox's May 24 swearing in.
13. Nixon, *RN; Watergate,* CQ Inc.; Lukas, *Nightmare;* Nixon to Haig, July 7, 1973, NNA; O'Neill staff report, "The Saturday Night Massacre and the Impetus to Impeachment," ONBC.
14. Diehl, Zeifman, Hymel interviews; O'Neill staff report, ONBC; Kutler, *The Wars of Watergate;* Fred Emery, *Watergate* (Times Books, New York, 1994); James Doyle, *Not Above the Law* (William Morrow, New York, 1977); Lukas, *Nightmare;* Nixon, *RN.*
15. *Time's* Neil MacNeil stopped by to see Albert on Wednesday. "Carl laid it on the line to me. The damndest thing I ever heard," MacNeil said. "He told me that he was next in line to be President and if Nixon was forced to resign, he would insist that Congress confirm Ford and then he would resign as President immediately. And if Congress refused to confirm Ford as vice president, he would name another prominent Republican as vice president, ask Congress to confirm *him,* and then resign."
16. Diehl, Zeifman, Hymel, Rosemary O'Neill, Francis O'Brien, Al Hunt interviews; O'Neill diary, quoted in MacNeil file to editors; O'Neill, *Man of the House;* O'Neill

and Rodino interviews, Cannon; Alan Lupo, "Tip-toeing Toward Impeachment with Tip O'Neill," *Boston Magazine,* Dec. 1973; *Watergate,* CQ Inc.; Albert oral history, University of Oklahoma; Jerry Zeifman, *Without Honor* (Thunder's Mouth Press, New York, 1995); Breslin, *How the Good Guys Finally Won; Washington Post,* Oct. 24, 1973.

17. *Congressional Record,* Oct. 23, 1973; O'Neill and Albert statements, ONBC.

Chapter 16
Impeachment

1. O'Neill diary; Kissinger, *Years of Upheaval; Congressional Record,* Oct. 25, Nov. 15, 1973; Lukas, *Nightmare;* Kutler, *The Wars of Watergate;* Timmons to Nixon, Nov. 13, 1973, NNA; *Washington Post,* Oct. 26, 1973.
2. Four days later, Housing secretary James Lynn heard O'Neill repeat the jibe at a birthday party thrown by Tongsun Park, a young Korean businessman. "Somebody said, kiddingly, 'Tip, that'll be the last time you ever vote for a Republican in high position.' And Tip said something, softly, under his voice, but loud enough to be heard in the immediate vicinity: 'Don't you count on it.'" Cannon, *Time and Chance;* John Brademas, MacNeil, Brand, Weiss interviews; *Boston Magazine,* Dec. 1973; MacNeil file to editors; Elizabeth Drew, *Washington Journal* (Random House, New York, 1975); James Lynn, oral history, Gerald Ford Library.
3. Kenneth Clawson, talking points to colleagues, Nov. 16, 1973, NNA; MacNeil file to editors; *Buffalo Evening News,* Nov. 2, 1973, Jan. 10, 1994; Nixon interview, *Today* show, videotapes, O'Neill papers, ONBC; Bryce Harlow to Haig, Dec. 17, 1973, NNA; memorandum from staff, Oct. 26, 1973; O'NBC; *Boston Herald,* Nov. 10, 1973; *New York Times,* Nov. 16, 1973; *Congressional Record,* Nov. 7, 1973.
4. J. Kenneth Galbraith to O'Neill, Nov. 1, 1973, O'Neill to Galbraith, Nov. 12, 1973, ONBC; Charles Fountain, *Another Man's Poison* (Globe Pequot Press, Boston, 1984).
5. O'Brien, Reed, Brand, Weiss, Healy, Hymel, MacNeil, Zeifman interviews; O'Neill Watergate interview, ONBC; O'Neill oral history, JFKL; Albert oral history, memorandum to Mike Reed, Carl Albert papers, University of Oklahoma.
6. *Time,* Feb. 4, 1974; MacNeil file to editors; Charles Sandman to George Bush, Nov. 9, 1973, NNA.
7. William Timmons to Haig, Nov. 28, 1973, NNA; Bryce Harlow to Peter Flanigan, Jan. 7, 1974, NNA; *New York Times,* Jan. 22, 1974; *Washington Post,* Jan. 22, 1974; Timmons to Haig, Mar. 8, 1974, NNA; Nixon, *RN;* Nixon on *60 Minutes,* 1984.
8. Garment, Zeifman, O'Brien interviews; *Watergate,* CQ Inc.; Lukas, *Nightmare;* Buchanan to Haig, May 10, 1974, NNA.
9. Breslin, Hymel, Weiss, Charles Daly, Rosemary O'Neill interviews; O'Neill Watergate interview, ONBC; Breslin, *How the Good Guys Finally Won.*
10. Breslin, Weiss, Brand, Hymel, Zeifman, Cannon interviews; *Boston Globe,* May 9, 1974; Breslin, *How the Good Guys Finally Won;* Ari Weiss and staff memoranda to O'Neill, Watergate files, ONBC; Breslin is too dismissive of O'Neill's intellect, as some of the staff memoranda show trenchant underlining and margin notes in his handwriting.
11. "The person that kept me informed was Jerry Zeifman," O'Neill remembered later. "Brilliant man. Of course, he was a little upset that Peter didn't go with him

instead of Doar. But he kept informing me and so did Jack Brooks. And I would get on Peter. Peter used to get furious." O'Brien interview.

12. O'Neill, *Man of the House;* Breslin, *How the Good Guys Finally Won.* The "get off my back" exchange is placed by various witnesses in either the late fall of 1973 or the early summer of 1974. It may have happened more than once. Breslin firmly dates it on Monday, June 25, 1974, but the 25th was a Tuesday.
13. O'Brien interview; Rodino, O'Neill interviews with Cannon; Breslin, *How the Good Guys Finally Won.*
14. Nixon, *RN;* O'Neill oral history, JFKL; Breslin, *How the Good Guys Finally Won.*
15. Zeifman, O'Brien, Hymel interviews; Rodino interview with Cannon; *Watergate,* CQ Inc.; Kutler, *The Wars of Watergate;* Lukas, *Nightmare;* Nixon, *RN;* Khachigian to Haig, July 18, 1974, NNA; Buchanan to Haig, May 23, 1974, NNA.
16. Kutler, *Abuse of Power; Watergate,* CQ Inc.; O'Neill, *Man of the House;* O'Neill interview with Cannon; Breslin, *How the Good Guys Finally Won; Boston Globe,* July 31, Aug. 9, 1974.
17. Garment, Ford interviews; Breslin, *How the Good Guys Finally Won;* O'Neill interview with Cannon; Timmons memorandum, NNA; Nixon, *RN.*
18. Ford, Cannon interviews; O'Neill, *Man of the House;* Breslin, *How the Good Guys Finally Won;* Cannon, *Time and Chance.*
19. Nixon, *RN;* Lukas, *Nightmare;* Cannon, *Time and Chance; Boston Globe,* Aug. 9, 1974; *Newsday,* Apr. 21, 1994.
20. Breslin had moments of doubt. When his book was ready to go to the publisher, he took Hymel out for a drink and asked, "Tell me one more time, just what exactly did O'Neill do?"
21. The book contains a wonderful description of the duet sung by O'Neill and Diehl as they left for the Cape after Nixon's resignation, walking down the Capitol's long hallways "silent and deserted and softly lit for the evening," singing "Ace in the Hole." *Newsweek,* May 5, 1975.
22. Kelley, Hymel, Diehl, Breslin interviews; *Washington Star,* May 5, 1975; *Boston Globe,* May 22, 1975.

Chapter 17
Reform

1. Ford interview; O'Neill interview with Cannon; O'Neill, *Man of the House.*
2. Ford interview; O'Neill statement, ONBC; Cannon, *Time and Chance.*
3. Wright interview; O'Neill interview, Clancy and Elder; *Orlando Sentinel,* Sept. 12, 1993; O'Neill interview, ONBC.
4. Linda Kamm, Christopher O'Neill, Roger Davidson interviews; Albert, *Little Giant;* Tom Foley interview with John Jacobs; John Jacobs, *A Rage for Justice* (University of California, Berkeley, 1995); Norman Ornstein, "Causes and Consequences of Congressional Change: Subcommittee Reforms in the House of Representatives, 1970–73," in *Congress in Change* (Praeger, New York, 1975); *Congressional Quarterly,* Oct. 8, 1969; Rules Committee transcript, Feb. 3, 1965, National Archives; O'Neill to Peter Eckstein, Jan. 20, 1967, ONBC; Walter Oleszek, "The House Democratic Caucus: Its History and Function," 1971, Legislative Reference Service.
5. David Nyhan, Billie Larsen, Brand, Diehl, Hymel, Drinan interviews; O'Neill, Udall, Bolling, Abner Mikva interviews with Jacobs; Jacobs, *A Rage for Justice;*

Judith Robinson, *You're in Your Mother's Arms* (M. J. Robinson, San Francisco, 1994); Hale Boggs's papers show that Boggs, O'Neill and Burton were in Los Angeles for a Democratic Party fund-raiser on Oct. 6, 1972, Boggs papers, Tulane University.

6. Jacobs, *A Rage for Justice;* Robinson, *In Your Mother's Arms;* O'Neill interview with Robinson; *Washington Post,* Jan. 28, 1973.
7. Albert used his new power to face down the South and put three mainstream Democrats on the Rules Committee. "The days of the Rules Committee as an independent power center appear to be over," *Washington Post* reported.
8. Fred Wertheimer, Reed, Cohen, Rose interviews; O'Neill diary; ADA Legislative Newsletter, Feb. 1, 1973; *Congressional Quarterly,* June 2, 1973; "Democratic Caucus Reforms," Bolling papers, University of Missouri; Richard Conlon, undated memo to Walter Oleszek, Oleszek papers; Walter Oleszek, "Role of House Democratic Caucus in Strengthening Subcommittees," Congressional Research Service, 1978; Democratic Study Group, "Reform in the House of Representatives," Nov. 30, 1976.
9. O'Neill's contribution to the new budget process was made in 1975, when it was tested for the first time and he persuaded hostile liberals to drop their opposition to the more austere budget that resulted from the act's first implementation. Timmons and Cook to Nixon, Feb. 23, 1973, NNA; Timmons to Nixon, April 1973, NNA.
10. "O'Neill long had viewed Bolling as his principal political rival for the speakership," note Roger Davidson and Walter Oleszek, two political scientists who served on Bolling's staff, in their book on the episode, *Congress Against Itself* (Indiana University Press, Bloomington, 1977).
11. William Cable, Cohen, Kamm, Davidson, Palumbo interviews; Bolling's papers contain his whip count from the DSG election, and extensive files on the Bolling committee plans; "Effect of the Bolling Committee Recommendations on Democratic Congressmen," Ari Weiss analysis, 1974, ONBC; Albert oral history, University of Oklahoma; Charles Sheldon to Bolling, Dec. 2, 1974, Bolling papers, University of Missouri; memorandum, "Meeting Called by Chairman Mills to discuss the Bolling Select Committee Resolution," Mar. 27, 1974, Bolling papers, University of Missouri.
12. Burton aide Mark Gersh said his boss would never have run against O'Neill for Speaker, but planned all along to run for majority leader.
13. Christopher O'Neill, Cohen, Wertheimer, Coelho, Kamm interviews; Albert oral history, University of Oklahoma; Wright oral history, Wright papers, Texas Christian University; O'Neill interview with Jacobs; Jacobs, *A Rage for Justice;* Ari Weiss to O'Neill, "Campaign Reform," 1974, ONBC; *National Journal,* Dec. 14, 1974; *New York Times,* Dec. 6, 1974; *Wall Street Journal,* Nov. 29, 1974; *Boston Globe,* June 14, 18, Oct. 2, 1974.
14. Christopher O'Neill interview; *Newsweek,* Dec. 16, 1974; *Washington Post,* Nov. 30, Dec. 4, 11, 1974; *Congressional Quarterly,* Dec. 7, 1974; *New York Times,* Dec. 3, 4, 1974.
15. There were plots within plots that day. O'Neill told reporters that he had seen Burton's ballot, and that even Burton had voted against Hays, presumably to clip the chairman's wings, incur his debt and establish himself as the dominant player in the duo.
16. Schroeder, Cohen interviews; Democratic caucus transcripts, Carl Albert papers, University of Oklahoma; Doug Frost interview with Jacobs; Albert oral history,

University of Oklahoma; Jacobs, *A Rage for Justice; Washington Post,* Jan. 17, 19, 20, 1975; Common Cause, "Report on House Committee Chairmen," Jan. 13, 1975; *Congressional Quarterly,* Jan. 18, 25, 1975; "Chronology of 94th Congress Organization," Bolling papers, University of Missouri; *National Journal,* Jan. 25, 1975; Ralph Nader letter to members of Congress, Jan. 20, 1975, Oleszek files; *Washington Star,* Jan. 17, 1975; Mary McGrory columns, Jan. 17, 20, 1975; *Los Angeles Times,* Jan. 20, 1975.

17. *Washington Post,* May 2, 1975; Bernard Firestone and Alexej Ugrinsky, *Gerald R. Ford and the Politics of Post-Watergate America* (Greenwood Press, Westport, Conn., 1992); Weiss to O'Neill, Apr. 1975, ONBC; notes, leadership meeting, Apr. 14, 1975, Carl Albert papers, University of Oklahoma.
18. Irv Sprague, Diehl and Kelley interviews; transcript, Democratic caucus, June 18, 1975, ONBC; Albert, *Little Giant;* Samuel B. Hoff, "Presidential Success in the Veto Process," Firestone and Ugrinsky, *Gerald R. Ford and the Politics of Post-Watergate America; Boston Globe,* June 19, 1975; Irv Sprague to House leadership, confidential "Memo for the Record," June 12, 1975, ONBC; *New York Times,* June 22, 1975; William Brodhead, "Memo to Members of the Democratic Steering and Policy Committee," June 18, 1975, Carl Albert papers, University of Oklahoma; *Washington Star,* June 2, 1975; *Congressional Quarterly,* June 28, 1975; O'Neill staff memorandum "Re Freshman Class Meeting," ONBC; *Washington Post,* June 22, 29, 1975; Albert oral history, University of Oklahoma; *Newsweek,* June 30, 1975.
19. McCarthy interview; *Boston Globe,* Feb. 25, July 27, Sept. 13, Oct. 18, 1975, Apr. 11, 1976; *Washington Star,* Mar. 4, 30, 1975; *Wall Street Journal,* Feb. 26, 1975; *Washington Post,* Feb. 26, 28, 1975; Evans and Novak, Mar. 13, 1975; *Democratic Review,* Feb. 1975; *New York Times,* Mar. 2, July 2, Oct. 12, 1975; Joseph Kraft column, Aug. 5, 1975; memo, Burt Hoffman to John Brademas, Dec. 12, 1975.
20. "I'm careful about what I do in this town now. I never touch anything under 40 and only that which is unavailable," O'Neill told reporters.
21. Margot Dinneen Wilson, Diehl, MacNeil, Cohen interviews; *New York Times,* June 3, 7, 9, 24, 1976; O'Neill, June 3, 1976, press conference transcript, ONBC; *Congressional Quarterly,* June 5, 12, 19, 1976; *Boston Globe,* June 8, 1976; *Newsweek,* June 14, 1976; *Roll Call,* June 17, 1976.
22. MacNeal, Palumbo, Diehl, Brand, Rostenkowski, Wright, Rose interviews; Jacobs, *A Rage for Justice;* Robinson, *You're in Your Mother's Arms;* O'Neill interviews with Jacobs and Robinson; Bolling majority leader files, Bolling papers, University of Missouri; *Congressional Quarterly News Service,* Oct. 7, Dec. 8, 1976; *New York Times,* Dec. 6, 1976; Wright oral history, Texas Christian University.
23. "Sources say O'Neill would prefer anyone to the aggressive Burton, whom O'Neill feels he might have to fight for control of the Democrats," the *Washington Post* reported on November 22.
24. Bill Cable, Charlie Wilson, Wright, Diehl, Rostenkowski, Palumbo, Ashley, Christopher O'Neill interviews; Jacobs, *A Rage for Justice;* Robinson, *You're in Your Mother's Arms;* O'Neill interviews with Jacobs and Robinson; Wright interview with Robert Peabody, Wright papers, Texas Christian University; Wright oral history, Texas Christian University; "Meet the Press," Dec. 5, 1976, transcript; *Congressional Quarterly News Service,* Dec. 8, 1976; *Congressional Quarterly,* Oct. 9, Dec. 11, 1976; *Boston Globe,* Dec. 7, 1976; *New York Times,* Dec. 7, 1976; *Washington Post,* Dec. 7, 8, 1976; *Time,* Dec. 20, 1976; Bruce Oppenheimer and Robert Peabody,

"The House Majority Leadership Contest, 1976," paper for delivery at the 1977 meeting of the American Political Science Association.

Chapter 18
Mr. Speaker

1. When the Senate and such support agencies as the new Congressional Budget Office, the Library of Congress, the General Accounting Office and the Office of Technology Assessment were added to the calculation, the total number of congressional employees topped 31,000.
2. Up from $77 million when O'Neill arrived in 1953.
3. John F. Bibby, Thomas Mann, Norman Ornstein, *Vital Statistics on Congress, 1980* (American Enterprise Institute, Washington, D.C., 1981); *How Congress Works,* CQ Inc., 1984; *Congressional Quarterly,* Jan. 23, 1982; *The Atlantic,* Mar. 1977, Dec. 1984; *Washington Post,* Aug. 28, 1977; Hedrick Smith, *The Power Game* (Random House, New York, 1988); *Chicago Tribune,* May 2, 1986; Roger Davidson and Walter Oleszek, *Congress and Its Members,* CQ Press, Washington, D.C., 1990); William Riordon, *Plunkitt of Tammany Hall* (E. P. Dutton, New York, 1963).
4. "Summary of Major Powers of the Speaker," ONBC; Richard Conlon, *Harvard Political Review,* winter, 1976; *The Atlantic,* Mar. 1977.
5. Linda Melconian, Moakley, Rose, Matthews interviews; Lee Iacocca interview, *Larry King Live,* Dec. 11, 1992; Chrysler bailout briefing papers, ONBC.
6. John McCain, Cohen, Matthews, Dinneen, Ashley interviews; John Ashbrook to O'Neill, ONBC; Melconian thesis, George Washington University; *Hartford Courant,* Jan. 8, 1994; Chris Matthews, *Hardball* (Summit Books, New York, 1988); John Anderson to O'Neill, June 8, 1977, ONBC; *Washington Post,* Oct. 20, 1977; *Providence Sunday Journal,* Jan. 19, 1986.
7. George Kundanis, Jim Healey, Wilson, Rose, Shannon, Donnelly interviews; Rose interview with Clancy and Elder; O'Neill to Rep. Frank Brasco, Feb. 17, 1971, ONBC; O'Neill, *All Politics Is Local; Washingtonian* magazine, Feb.1996.
8. Francine Gannon, Burt Hoffman, Pam Jackson, Billy Sutton, Brand, Cannon, Rose, Brademas, Sprague interviews; Barbara Sutton remarks, O'Neill staff reunion; Bolling interview with Clancy and Elder; foreign trip file, ONBC.
9. In some versions of the tale, it is the very stereo that was identified as a payoff in the investigation of Johnson aide Bobby Baker.
10. Alex Treadway, Jack Lew, Brand, Donnelly, Reed, Ashley, Weiss interviews; John Barry, *The Ambition and the Power* (Penguin, New York, 1989).
11. Lew, Kundanis, Wright, Kamm, Larsen, Rose, Weiss interviews; computerized loyalty records, ONBC; memorandum, Jan. 13, 1977, Bolling papers, University of Missouri; Bolling to Leo Diehl, Feb. 17, 1977, Bolling papers, University of Missouri; Jacobs, *A Rage for Justice;* Wright diary.
12. Barney Frank, J. Kenneth Galbraith, Glenn Koocher, Susan O'Neill, Cable, Coelho, Hymel, Rostenkowski, MacNeil, Weiss, Lew, Breslin interviews; Paul Pilzer, *Other People's Money* (Simon and Schuster, New York, 1989); Michael Waldman, *Who Robbed America?* (Random House, New York, 1990).
13. Coelho, Ford, Cannon interviews; Terry O'Donnell and Max Friedersdorf oral histories, Gerald Ford presidential library; Richard Ottinger to O'Neill, Mar. 18, 1979, and O'Neill to Ottinger, Mar. 26, 1979, ONBC.

Chapter 19
Jimmy

1. Patrick Caddell, "Initial Working Paper on Political Strategy," Dec. 10, 1976, JCL; Jules Witcover, *Marathon* (Viking, New York, 1977); *Rolling Stone,* June 31, 1976; *Arundel Observer,* July 1976; Hamilton Jordan oral history, JCL; Gary Hart, *Right from the Start* (Quadrangle, New York, 1973); *The Atlantic,* Mar. 1989.
2. "There was a fear [in the O'Neill camp] Mo would come back as a national figure and challenge Tip for Speaker. I urged Mo and asked him to do it," said Udall aide Terry Bracy. "He could do it to John McCormack, but not to Tip O'Neill." Jimmy Carter, Terry Bracy interviews.
3. Hamilton Jordan, Carter interviews; Carter interview with WBZ-TV, ONBC; Jordan oral history, JCL; Peter Bourne, *Jimmy Carter* (Scribner, New York, 1997).
4. Jordan interview; Bourne, *Jimmy Carter;* Jordan oral history, JCL; O'Neill, *Man of the House; Boston Globe,* Jan. 2, 1977; *Boston Herald,* July 16, 1979.
5. Anne Wexler, Jordan interviews; Landon Butler, Tom Donilon, Anne Wexler, Frank Moore, Jordan oral histories, JCL; Jimmy Carter, *Keeping the Faith* (Bantam, New York, 1982).
6. Weiss memo, ONBC; O'Neill notes of meeting with Carter, ONBC; White House leadership meeting notes, ONBC; Jim Wright oral history, Wright files, Texas Christian University; Hymel, Diehl, Brademas interviews; O'Neill, *Man of the House;* Wright, *Balance of Power.*
7. Carter wasn't happy about the Richardson and Dobelle affair, and neither was Jordan. After getting chewed out by O'Neill, Jordan warned the cabinet in a memo that "we cannot stand many more situations where the cabinet officer . . . and the President decided to do something and fail to tell anyone here about it. Tip O'Neil [sic] read about it in the paper." Hamilton Jordan to Jack Watson, Jan. 30, 1977, JCL; Frank Moore to Hal Gulliver, Feb. 13, 1980, JCL; Jody Powell, Carter, Jordan, Matthews, Moore, Diehl, Kelley interviews; *Boston Globe,* Jan. 19, 27, 28, 30, 1977; *New York Times,* Jan. 28, 1977; Smith, *The Power Game.*
8. Frank Moore to Jimmy Carter, Nov. 5, 1976, JCL; *Washington Post,* Nov. 5, 1976; Moore interview; Moore oral history, JCL.
9. Rick Merrill to Frank Moore, Jan. 26, 1977, JCL; Frank Moore to Jimmy Carter, Oct. 7, 1977, JCL; Merrill to Moore, Mar. 10, 1977; *Boston Magazine,* Mar. 1983; Moore to Carter, Dec. 23, 1977, JCL; Abner Mikva to Moore, Jan. 4, 1978, JCL.
10. Wexler interview; White House leadership meeting notes, Jan. 25, Feb. 8, 1977, ONBC; steering and policy committee notes, Feb. 2, 1977, ONBC.
11. Moore, Hymel interviews; Wright, *Balance of Power;* Carter and Richard Moe, oral histories, JCL; *New York Times,* July 24, 1977.
12. White House leadership meeting notes, Feb. 8, 1977; Charles Jones, *The Trusteeship President* (Louisiana State University Press, 1988); Weiss to O'Neill, undated memo, ONBC; Bourne, *Jimmy Carter;* Kirk O'Donnell, Jordan interviews.
13. Jones, *The Trusteeship President;* Steven Gillon, *The Democrats' Dilemma* (Columbia University Press, New York, 1992); Moore, Cable oral histories, JCL; White House leadership meeting notes, Apr. 5, 1977, ONBC; Dan Tate to Jimmy Carter, Apr. 18, 1977, JCL; Frank Moore to Jimmy Carter, Apr. 18, 1977, JCL.
14. White House leadership meeting notes, Apr. 19, May 2, 3, 1977, ONBC.
15. Carter interview; *Boston Globe,* June 2, 5, 1977; *Washington Post,* June 3, 1977; *New York Times,* May 24, June 3, 1977; Moore to Carter, June 1, 1977, JCL; Carter to O'Neill, May 22, 1977, JCL; *Boston Herald,* May 9, 1977; Moore to Carter, Mar. 23,

1977, JCL; O'Neill to Carter, Mar. 25, 1977, JCL; Carter to O'Neill, Feb. 20, 1977, JCL; memoranda, Spencer Smith to Irv Sprague, Apr. and May, 1977, ONBC.

16. Moore interview; Jordan to O'Neill, June 20, 1977, JCL; *New York Times,* June 15, 1977; *Washington Post,* June 15, 1977; Carter, *Keeping the Faith.*

Chapter 20
The Politics of Inclusion

1. Daniel Yergin, *The Prize* (Touchstone, New York, 1991); Burton Kaufman, *The Presidency of James Earl Carter* (University Press of Kansas, 1993); "Origins of the Current Energy Crisis," Ari Weiss to O'Neill, 1974, ONBC; Democratic caucus transcript, Apr. 1975, Carl Albert papers, University of Oklahoma; Stuart Eizenstat, oral history, JCL.
2. His aides urged Carl Albert to set up a select committee on energy in 1974, but Albert buckled when confronted by the violent opposition of liberals, environmentalists and the committees affected by the change. He did use his power to appoint an ad hoc committee on offshore oil and gas, which served as a useful forerunner for O'Neill's plan.
3. "Proposal for an Ad Hoc Committee on Energy Policy," Weiss to O'Neill, 1977, ONBC; "Attitude of Outside Groups," and follow-up memoranda, Spencer Smith to John E. Barriere, Jan. 1977, ONBC; *Boston Globe,* Apr. 20, 1977; *Wall Street Journal,* Aug. 5, 1977.
4. Sprague, Moore, Cable interviews; Jordan oral history, JCL; *Newsweek,* June 27, 1977; "Notes for Rules luncheon," July 14, 1977, ONBC; O'Neill, *Man of the House; Wall Street Journal,* Aug. 5, 1977; *New York* magazine, May 16, 1977.
5. *Wall Street Journal,* Aug. 5, 1977; *National Journal,* July 30, 1977; "Notes for Rules luncheon," July 14, 1977, ONBC; *Washington Star,* July 29, Aug. 5, 1977; Democratic steering and policy committee minutes, July 26, 1977, ONBC; *New York Times,* Aug. 1, 1977; *Congressional Record,* Aug. 3, 1977; *Newsweek,* Aug. 15, 1977.
6. *National Journal,* June 18, July 30, 1977, Sept. 2, 1978. "We're happy to try to open the door for them, having been in the town for so many years and knowing so many people. We do know where the bodies are," O'Neill said.
7. "Anatomy of a Victory," Irv Sprague to files, Mar. 1978, ONBC; "Task Forces," Sprague to O'Neill, Nov. 9, 1978, ONBC; James Garand and Kathleen Clayton, "Socialization to Partisanship in the US House: The Speaker's Task Force," *Legislative Studies Quarterly,* Aug. 1986; Barbara Sinclair, "The Speaker's Task Force in the Post-Reform House of Representatives," *American Political Science Review,* June 1981; Wright diary.
8. To further help his cause, O'Neill asked Carter not to veto a measure that would exempt a number of congressmen who lived in Maryland (like the Speaker) from the state income tax. Bob Ginsburg to Stu Eizenstat and Frank Moore, Apr. 26, 1977, JCL; Moore to Eizenstat, Apr. 21, 1977, JCL.
9. MacNeil, Hymel interviews; steering and policy committee minutes, Feb. 3, 22, 1977, ONBC; *Washington Post,* Dec. 6, 1976, Mar. 3, 8, Apr. 3, June 19, 27, 30, Aug. 7, 1977; *Boston Globe,* Jan. 9, 14, Mar. 20, 1977; *US News and World Report,* June 6, 1977; *Wall Street Journal,* June 15, 1977; *New York Times,* Jan. 4, June 30, 1977; *Washington Star,* Feb. 18, Mar. 3, June 29, 1977; *Boston Herald,* Dec. 25, 1977; *Time,* Mar. 14, 1977, Clancy and Elder, *Tip.*

Chapter 21
Trouble

1. Brand interview; *Newsweek,* O'Neill files.
2. Brand, Christopher O'Neill interviews; *Newsweek,* O'Neill files; though it would not be unusual for a grateful institution like Boston College to offer scholarships to the children of a prominent alumnus, O'Neill's sons and daughters say their parents paid for their education.
3. Eliot Spalding, Richardson, Donahue, MacNeil interviews; Richardson to the author, 1999.
4. Charles Breslin, president, Life of America Insurance Corp. to O'Neill, July 20, 1976; O'Neill to Phil Landrum, Aug. 6, 1976; Landrum to O'Neill, Aug. 26, 1976; ONBC.
5. Gannon, MacNeil, Diehl interviews; *Boston Herald,* Aug. 17, 1987; *Congressional Insight,* CQ Inc., Mar. 2, 1984; Associated Press, Aug. 19, 1987; *New York Times,* Dec. 3, 1976.
6. Tolchin, Hymel interviews; *New York Times,* June 22, 23, 1976; *Washington Post,* Oct. 9, 1976.
7. O'Neill interview, Sheridan McCabe, ONBC; federal prison requests, U.S. Department of Justice, Executive Secretariat, obtained by author's Freedom of Information Act request; Barefoot Sanders to Lyndon Johnson, Apr. 1968, LBJL.
8. Healy, Tolchin, Kelley, Murtha, MacNeil, Hymel interviews.
9. "Investigation of Korean-American Relations," Committee on International Relations, 1978; Robert Boettcher, *Gifts of Deceit* (Holt, Rinehart and Winston, New York, 1980); *Washington Post,* Oct. 16, 1977.
10. Reed, Boland interviews; Korea files, ONBC; Kirk O'Donnell, Koreagate files, O'Neill family; *Congressional Record,* Oct. 14, 1969; Korea files, Carl Albert papers, University of Oklahoma; *Washington Post,* July 6, 1976, Apr. 27, 1980; *Congressional Quarterly,* July 17, 1976; Albert oral history, University of Oklahoma; *CBS News Special,* "Anatomy of a Scandal," Apr. 3, 1978.
11. Ford, Brademas, Rostenkowski interviews; O'Neill interview with the Washington Bureau of *New York Times,* May 23, 1977; *Washington Star,* Apr. 4, 1974; *Washington Post,* Dec. 17, 1974; *Washington Monthly,* Apr. 1987; "Contacts of Congressman (later Speaker) Thomas P. O'Neill Jr. with Tongsun Park," House Committee on Standards of Official Conduct, July 13, 1978.
12. Boettcher, *Gifts of Deceit;* "Korean Influence Investigation," House Committee on Standards of Official Conduct, 1977–78; O'Neill daily diaries, O'Neill family files; *Washington Star,* Apr. 20, 1975.
13. *Boston Globe,* Nov. 7, 1976, Nov. 13, 1977; confidential telegram, Philip Habib to State Department, Apr. 1974, Carl Albert papers, University of Oklahoma; Boettcher, *Gifts of Deceit;* O'Donnell Koreagate files, O'Neill family; Mike Reed to Carl Albert, July 24, 1973; "Discussions with Korean and American Parliamentary Delegations," Carl Albert papers, University of Oklahoma.
14. *Washington Post,* July 20, 27, 1977, Feb. 17, 22, 1978; O'Donnell Koreagate files, O'Neill family; O'Neill daily press briefings, July 20, 21, 1977, press files, ONBC; *Congressional Record,* Sept. 7, 1977; *Washington Star,* July 25, 1973, Aug. 30, 1977; correspondence and transcripts, Burt Hoffman and Charles Ferris to ABC News, and reply by Roone Arledge and ABC lawyers, July, Aug. 1977; O'Donnell Korea-

gate file, O'Neill family and Hoffman files; *New York Times,* July 20, 1977; see Safire columns in *New York Times,* Aug. 11, Oct. 13, 1977, Apr. 6, June 22, July 20, 27, 1978; *Newsweek,* Aug. 1, 1977; Von Hoffman column, undated, O'Donnell files, O'Neill family.

15. *People* magazine, Mar. 6, 1978; NBC *Weekend,* Mar. 4, 1978; "Translation of Korean Language Report Seized from Tongsun Park's House Entitled The United States Congressional Delegation's Visit to Korea," House Committee on Standards of Official Conduct, Apr., 1978; statement by Speaker Thomas P. O'Neill, Apr. 4, 1978, O'Donnell Koreagate files, O'Neill family; *Washington Post,* Apr. 4, 5, 1978; *New York Times,* Apr. 4, 5, 1978; *Newsweek,* Apr. 17, 1978; Jim Wright diary.
16. Boettcher, *Gifts of Deceit; Boston Globe,* Apr. 4, 5, July 14, 1978; *Boston Herald,* Apr. 4, 5, 27, July 14, 1978; letter, acting deputy attorney general Benjamin Civiletti to Rep. Bruce Caputo, Apr. 19, 1978, O'Donnell Koreagate files, O'Neill family; "Contacts of Congressman (later Speaker) Thomas P. O'Neill Jr. with Tongsun Park," House Committee on Standards of Official Conduct; Jaworski interview, *US News & World Report,* Aug. 14, 1978; *New York Times,* July 14, 1978; O'Donnell analysis of hearings and final report, O'Donnell Koreagate files, O'Neill family; Jaworski to O'Neill, O'Donnell Koreagate files, O'Neill family; transcript, meeting between O'Neill and Ambassador Kim Yong Shik, Apr. 10, 1978, O'Donnell Koreagate files, O'Neill family.
17. *Washington Post,* June 21, 1978; memoranda and correspondence, O'Donnell and Hymel, O'Donnell Koreagate file, O'Neill family. The "Doonesbury" strips were from June 15 and 16, 1978. After tipping off the Speaker, the *Los Angeles Times* then reported O'Neill's efforts to halt publication of the strips. O'Donnell and Hymel fumed, and forever believed that the *Times* had set them up.
18. *New York Times,* Apr. 8, 1978. FBI and U.S. Department of Justice files, obtained by the author through the U.S. Freedom of Information Act, show that in December 1970, the Glenside Corporation had applied to the U.S. Department of Housing and Urban Development for federal help in buying and improving 60 units of low and moderate income housing on Centre Street in Jamaica Plain. The Glenside group asked for a $1.3 million rehabilitation loan guarantee, a low interest rate, rent supplements and other federal housing benefits.

    As work on the application proceeded in HUD's Boston office, Glenside completed its purchase of the apartment complex. In August 1971, O'Neill — now the House whip — was on a list of directors submitted by Glenside to HUD officials. The HUD managers in Washington took note: writing "new" and "Congress" next to his name. HUD made a "firm commitment" to guarantee the loan in March of 1972. A week before the closing in July, the Glenside Corporation spun off the apartments by selling them to two members of the Glenside board of directors, who received the HUD guarantee. In October 1972, O'Neill and his fellow investors then sold their remaining interest in the Glenside Corporation and its property, on the condition that one of the purchasers win a federal Small Business Administration lease guarantee on the hospital, which was subsequently approved.

    O'Neill earned over $110,000 in the deal: $50,000 in cash and $60,380 in ten annual payments of $6,038. He invested the money in Cape Cod real estate. In October he bought a lot in Chatham, near the Eastward Ho Country Club, for $22,000 in cash. In March 1973 — now majority leader — he closed on the house in Harwichport, paying $42,500 in cash and taking out a $35,000 mortgage.

19. The Bristol Nursing Home had been operated by Bristol County as a tuberculosis hospital and long-term care facility for more than fifty years before Boston lawyer (later judge) Walter J. Hurley, former Massachusetts Turnpike Authority lobbyist and patronage chief John Shea, State House aide Cornelius Owens and two doctors purchased it from the county for $93,600 in 1968. The original partners, who needed funds to make improvements to the nursing home, opened talks with O'Neill and other investors, some of which were held at the Robin Hood Motor Lodge outside Boston. O'Neill and his aide James Rowan joined Maurice Shear and businessman Richard Gens and signed a conditional partnership agreement with the original investors. O'Neill invested from $2,600 to $5,000, he said later. He also put his name on the bank loan when the partners borrowed money for renovations.

    The Massachusetts Health Department at first declined to give the Bristol facility a "grandfathered" license. But the Bristol partners were adept at exercising their clout with the state's Irish American political establishment. Attorney General Robert Quinn issued an unpublished opinion in 1969 that overruled the Health Department. State Senate president Kevin Harrington weighed in on behalf of the Bristol partners as well: pressuring the Health Department in 1970 and 1972. On Beacon Hill the word went out: this nursing home was well connected. "There was a good deal of interest by individual legislators in having the applicants issued a certificate of need," wrote DPH official Peter Hiam in a departmental letter. The state Health Department officials continued to complain about the political heat they felt on behalf of the nursing home. "Apparently several state legislators have a proprietary interest in the home," Dr. Ann Pettigrew suggested in a memo to her superiors in May 1972. "There was considerable pressure to obtain favorable consideration."

    O'Neill was listed on the application form, as a guarantor of a $150,000 loan, when the Bristol group applied for an SBA loan guarantee on Oct. 21, 1972. The guarantee was approved within a month. In July 1973, the nursing home asked the SBA to release the then majority leader O'Neill from his position as a guarantor of the loan, since he had sold his interest. O'Neill said later he had, at best, broken even, and had lent his name and money to the deal only to help out his pal Shea.
20. Brand and O'Donnell interviews.
21. *New York Times,* Dec. 5, 1976, Oct. 27, 1977; William Barnstead, Hymel interviews; *Boston Herald,* Sept. 5, 1976; Barnstead interview, Clancy and Elder; *Boston Globe,* Oct. 23, 28, 1977, Oct. 16, 1978; Barnstead packet.
22. *Boston Herald,* Oct. 29, 30, Nov. 2, 7, 27, 1977; Fred Phillips, Christine Black, Barnstead interviews; Clancy and Elder, *Tip.* In a series of stories, the *Globe* backed up much of the *Herald's* reporting — pointing out that O'Neill had been in on the Glenside deal while all but the last important HUD decision had been made, and quoting Barnstead as saying, "What's happening here is that O'Neill is being used as a magnet. He lends his name to the deal and just before it goes through, he gets out." But affection for O'Neill, and the traditional journalistic scorn for a rival's success, led many in the *Globe* newsroom to dismiss the *Herald's* reporting.
23. Rawls also revealed that O'Neill was a partner with Shear (who was described as a man "twice convicted of financial crimes") in "a high-risk securities investment venture named Broadway Capital Fund." Of the twenty original partners, the *Times* said, "four have been convicted of banking or real estate fraud in other enterprises." It was a classic charge of guilt by association, which the *Times* justified by

noting how O'Neill had tried to disguise his net worth and his dealings with Shear from the press.

24. Shear was convicted in 1971 for meddling in the bank's affairs after being suspended by the Federal Deposit Insurance Corporation.
25. *New York Times,* Apr. 9, 1978; Wendell Rawls interview.
26. Moore to Carter, Apr. 10, 1978, JCL; *New York Times,* Apr. 11, 1978; transcript, O'Neill daily press briefing, Apr. 10, 1978, ONBC.
27. Diehl, Hymel, Sutton, Boland, Breslin, Kelley, Gannon, MacNeil, O'Neill III, Susan O'Neill interviews; Winship to O'Neill and O'Neill to Winship, March, and Apr. 1977, ONBC; *Boston Globe,* May 13, 1977; O'Neill foreign travel records, ONBC; Thomas P. O'Neill III interview with Clancy and Elder.
28. Wright, Donahue, Sweig, O'Neill III interviews; O'Neill interview with Gibbons; O'Neill interview with Clancy and Elder.
29. According to a Drew Pearson column of October 1959, O'Neill bought 3,000 shares, at $1.50 a share, in an oil and gas company from former BC and Notre Dame coach Frank Leahy. The stock plunged to 50 cents a share, and the SEC ordered the firm to halt sales. O'Neill daily press briefing, Apr. 10, 1978, ONBC; MacNeil, Brand and Dineen interviews.
30. O'Neill daily press briefing, Apr. 10, 1978; O'Neill interview with Clancy and Elder; O'Donnell, Matthews interviews; *New York Times,* Apr. 28, 1978; O'Donnell to Diehl, Feb. 13, 1980, ONBC; *Washington Star,* Apr. 28, 1978; *Washington Post,* Apr. 28, 1978.
31. The SBA investigation concluded that there were two "unusual" features in the Bristol loan, but no hint of wrongdoing. "Subsequent events indicate that the company has enjoyed considerable success and profits and the loan has been reduced to somewhere in the vicinity of $25,000," one investigator wrote. "Repayment ability seems to have been there and events apparently have proven the initial judgments." SBA inspector general's report, July 10, 1973, Frank Phillips files.
32. It was not the Bristol group, but the Commonwealth Bank, that had actually applied for the SBA guarantee, O'Neill's lawyers told him, and so "no direct contractual relation existed." Even if a contractual relationship had existed, there was a second loophole to protect him. Though the federal conflict-of-interest law banned congressmen from profiting via government contracts, Congress had specifically exempted the Reconstruction Finance Corporation from its provisions. When the RFC expired in 1957, its duties and immunities were transferred to the SBA — including the exemption. William Ragan to O'Neill, Oct. 23, 1978, ONBC; *Boston Herald,* Oct. 22, 1978; "Confidential Memo on House Speaker O'Neill Investigation," *Boston Herald* internal record, Aug. 2, 1978.
33. "Contacts of Congressman (later Speaker) Thomas P. O'Neill Jr. with Tongsun Park," House Committee on Standards of Official Conduct, July 13, 1978; McLaughlin interview; Montgomery County police records, McLaughlin files. McLaughlin had approached Park in the hope of establishing a joint venture to sell Irish seafood in Asia, but his plans fell through before any money passed hands. To attract investors, McLaughlin said, he asked Tommy O'Neill to serve on the board. Neither O'Neill had invested in the firm.
34. Montgomery County police records, McLaughlin files; McLaughlin interview; McLaughlin to Edward Bennett Williams, McLaughlin files.
35. On at least three occasions in the next 20 months, the source donned the body wire or concealed a listening device in her purse and got O'Neill's friends to talk.

Though the redactions in the FBI file make it difficult to determine if the woman successfully taped all her targets, it is clear that O'Neill was on the list. O'Neill files, FBI, obtained by the author through the Freedom of Information Act.

36. The O'Neill investigation remained an FBI secret, and was not made public until 1999, when the bureau released selected files in response to a Freedom of Information Act request by the author. Richard Ben Veniste, Carter, Jordan interviews; Robert W. Greene, *The Sting Man* (E. P. Dutton, New York, 1981); Jack Anderson column, May 6, 15, 1980; O'Neill, *Man of the House;* UPI, Dec. 14, 1982; *Newsweek,* Feb. 18, 1980.
37. James Baker, Phil Heymann interviews.
38. Sheridan McCabe, Wertheimer interviews; O'Neill interview with McCabe, ONBC; Bolling interview with Clancy and Elder; Hamilton poll, Oct. 1978; O'Donnell Koreagate files, O'Neill family.

Chapter 22
An Uncertain Trumpet

1. Moore to Carter, Aug. 1, 1977, JCL.
2. White House leadership meeting notes, Sept. 27, 1977, ONBC; Bill Cable to Carter, Sept. 8, 1977, JCL; Moore and Eizenstat to Carter, Sept. 13, 1977, JCL; Moore and Tate to Carter, Aug. 23, Oct. 7, 1977, JCL; Ashley to O'Neill, Sept. 22, 1977, ONBC; Tate to Moore, Sept. 24, 1977, JCL; *New York Times,* Sept. 28, 1977.
3. *Washington Post,* Sept. 15, 1977.
4. Moore to Carter, Apr. 7, 1978, JCL; *Newsweek,* Aug. 29, 1977.
5. Ashley interview.
6. Ed Markey, Ashley, Weiss interviews; Eizenstat oral history, JCL; Tate and Thomson to Carter, Oct. 3, 1977, JCL; Tate to Carter, Oct. 18, 1977, JCL; Schultze to Carter, Oct. 19, 1977, JCL; Schlesinger, Eizenstat and McIntyre to Carter, Nov. 1, 1977, JCL; Moore to Carter, Dec. 2, 1977, JCL; Hitz memorandum, Dec. 1, 1977, JCL; Moore and Free to Carter, Mar. 15, 1978, JCL; Schlesinger and Moore to Carter, early 1978, JCL; Eizenstat and Moore to Carter, Mar. 27, 1978; Schlesinger to Carter, Aug. 15, 1978, JCL; Democratic steering and policy committee agenda, Sept. 26, 1978, ONBC; *New York Times,* Oct. 12, 1980; O'Neill to Anita Summer, Nov. 30, 1978, ONBC; Michael Malbin, "Rhetoric and Leadership: A Look Backward at the Carter National Energy Plan," in Anthony King, *Both Ends of the Avenue* (American Enterprise Institute, Washington, D.C., 1983); Jones, *The Trusteeship Presidency;* Kaufman, *The Presidency of James Earl Carter.*
7. Moore interview; O'Neill diary notes, Mar. 7, 1979, ONBC; Jim Wright diary; Carter to O'Neill, Oct. 20, 1977, Feb. 28, 1978, ONBC; Moore to Carter, Oct. 20, 1977, JCL; *Technology Review,* Massachusetts Institute of Technology, Apr. 1988; *Newsweek,* Mar. 19, 26, 1979; *Washington Post,* Oct. 21, 1977, Feb. 9, 1978; *Washington Star,* Oct. 21, 1977.
8. Garret FitzGerald, Sean Donlan, John Hume, Michael Lillis, O'Donnell interviews; *Irish Times,* Jan. 25, 1993, Jan. 8, 1994; *Foreign Affairs,* spring 1986; "Joint St. Patrick's Day Appeal for Peace in Northern Ireland," Mar. 17, 1977, Kirk O'Donnell files, ONBC; "Statement by President Carter on Northern Ireland," ONBC; Carroll to O'Neill, Oct. 27, 1977, O'Neill to Carroll, Nov. 3, 1977; *Washington Post,* Sept. 4, 1977; memorandum, Ferris to O'Neill, "Meeting with Secretary Vance on Northern Ireland," June 8, 1977, ONBC; O'Neill and colleagues to Nixon, June

24, 1969, Harlow reply to O'Neill, July 7, 1969, ONBC; *Congressional Record,* Apr. 10, 1957, June 25, 1969; O'Neill speeches on Ireland, 1953–54, ONBC.

9. O'Donnell, Sullivan interview; *Washington Post,* Sept. 23, 1977, Jan. 31, 1978, Sept. 18, 1979; *New York Times,* Sept. 24, 1977; Note to Carter, June 22, 1978, JCL; "Thoughts Re Policy Committee's Future," ONBC.
10. Griffin, Jordan, Carter, Cable, Moore interviews; Carter to Solomon, July 24, 1978, JCL; Moore to O'Neill, Aug. 3, 1978, ONBC; Moore to Carter, Aug. 7, 1978, JCL; *New York Times,* Feb. 18, 1977, July 29, Aug. 3, 4, 1978; *Washington Post,* Feb. 12, 16, 1977, June 7, 24, July 27, 28, 29, Aug. 4, 5, 9, 11, 12, 1978, Jan. 21, Feb. 2, Apr. 1, 1979; *Washington Star,* Aug. 1, 4, 1978; *Washington Monthly,* Sept. 1980.
11. The Speaker liked to tease Yastrzemski, who had uncharacteristically failed to deliver in a playoff game with the Yankees in 1978, by telling him how the new Polish Pope had summoned him aside on the trip to Rome, as if to consider a matter of great import, and asked, "What the hell happened to Yastrzemski in the ninth inning with two on and two out?"
12. Jody Powell, Cable, Carter, Moore, Wright, Jordan interviews; McIntyre to Carter, Apr. 5, 1978, JCL; Moore to Carter, June 5, 1978, JCL; Wright to Carter, June 14, 1978, JCL; Carter to Wright, June 14, 1978, JCL; Moore to Carter, Aug. 15, 1978, JCL; Wright to Carter, Sept. 26, 1978, JCL; Moore to Mondale, Oct. 2, 1978, JCL; Moore and Cable to Carter, Oct. 3, 1978, JCL; Carter to O'Neill, Oct. 5, 1978, JCL; Moore to Carter, Oct. 5, 1978, JCL; Moore and Cable to Carter, Oct. 6, 1978, JCL; *Newsweek,* Aug. 28, Oct. 16, 1978; *Washington Post,* June 15, 16, Sept. 28, Oct. 5, 6, 7, 1978.
13. Rosemary and Susan O'Neill interviews; O'Neill religion interview, ONBC; O'Neill to Alan Zabel, June 22, 1972, ONBC; O'Neill to Joseph Hart, Feb. 9, 1973, ONBC; O'Neill to Rev. Paul Murphy, Mar. 30, 1973, ONBC; Murphy to O'Neill, Apr. 3, 1973, ONBC; Rev. Michael Bowab to O'Neill, Apr. 16, 1973, ONBC; "Tally on Abortion Mail," June 8, 1973, ONBC; O'Neill to Carroll, June 11, 1973, ONBC; O'Neill to Loretta Capistran, ONBC; Massachusetts Citizens for Life to O'Neill, Oct. 12, 1976, ONBC; Jim Wright diary.
14. Carl Albert papers, University of Oklahoma.
15. "Busing — The Real Issue," O'Neill staff research paper, *Congressional Record,* Aug. 17, 1972; *Boston Globe,* Mar. 5, 6, 7, 8, 13, 17, Apr. 10, 1975, Aug. 23, 24, 28, Sept. 7, 1976; *Cambridge Chronicle,* Mar. 20, 1975; *Washington Post,* Sept. 3, 1975; Lukas, *Common Ground;* Lupo, *Liberty's Chosen Home;* Ronald Formisano, *Boston Against Busing* (University of North Carolina Press, Chapel Hill, 1991); *Boston Herald,* June 10, July 6, 1976; hearing, Committee on Rules, Feb. 17, 1970, National Archives.
16. Between 1973 and 1982, the average growth in the gross national product was a miserable 1.6 percent, with actual declines in GNP and/or double-digit inflation in most of those nine years.
17. Thomas Byrne Edsall with Mary D. Edsall, *Chain Reaction* (Norton, New York, 1991); Theodore H. White, *America in Search of Itself* (Harper & Row, New York, 1982); Daniel Patrick Moynihan, *Came the Revolution* (Harcourt Brace Jovanovich, New York, 1988); Haynes Johnson, *In the Absence of Power* (Viking, New York, 1980); Joseph Califano Jr., *Governing America* (Simon & Schuster, New York, 1981); Patterson, *Grand Expectations;* Barone, *Our Country;* Carter oral history, JCL.
18. Mondale considered resigning, or taking himself off the ticket for 1980. Weiss to O'Neill, Dec. 1978, ONBC; Moore to Carter, Dec. 7, 1978, JCL; Carter to

O'Neill, Dec. 9, 1978, JCL; Carter talking points, undated, JCL; *Washington Post,* Dec. 9, 1978; Weiss to O'Neill, Feb. 13, 1979, ONBC; Jim Wright diary; *Washington Post,* Jan. 15, 21, 1979; *New York Times,* Jan. 23, 1979.

19. Steven Gillon, *The Democrats' Dilemma* (Columbia University Press, New York, 1992); Jones, *The Trusteeship Presidency;* Kaufman, *The Presidency of James Earl Carter;* Daniel Yergin, *The Prize* (Touchstone, New York, 1991); Bourne, *Jimmy Carter;* White House congressional leadership meeting notes, May 1, 8, 1979; Jimmy Carter, *Keeping Faith: Memoirs of a President* (University of Arkansas Press, New York, 1995); Jim Wright diary; Jordan to O'Neill, summer, 1979, ONBC; *Washington Post,* Sept. 28, 1979; *Washington Star,* Sept. 23, 1979; Eizenstat to Carter, Feb. 15, 1978, JCL; Moore to Carter, Nov. 1, 1978, JCL; Carter to O'Neill, Mar. 20, 1979, JCL.
20. O'Neill phoned the Vatican, asking the Holy See to appeal to Khomeini to protect Iran's small Jewish population from reprisals.
21. Kennedy, Carter, Murtha interviews; Carter oral history, JCL; Jack Germond and Jules Witcover, *Blue Smoke and Mirrors* (Viking, New York, 1981); O'Neill interview with Clancy and Elder; *National Journal,* June 2, 1979; *Washington Post,* Sept. 11, 17, 18, Oct. 19, 1979; *Washington Star,* Sept. 21, 1979; O'Neill daily press briefings, Sept. 1979, ONBC; O'Neill interview with Clymer.
22. Leon Panetta, Joe Moakley, Moore interviews; Barbara Sinclair, *Majority Leadership in the U.S. House* (Johns Hopkins University Press, Baltimore, 1983); Jim Wright diary; Jack Lew to O'Neill, Feb. 28, 1980, ONBC; *Congressional Quarterly,* Sept. 13, 1980; O'Neill to colleagues, Aug. 25, 1980, ONBC; Associated Press, Aug. 27, 1980; *National Journal,* Jan. 19, Mar. 22, Apr. 12, June 14, Oct. 4, 1980; *Newsweek,* Mar. 24, June 23, 1980; *Washington Post,* Mar. 6, Aug. 27, 1980; Weiss to O'Neill, undated memoranda, spring and summer, 1980, ONBC.
23. O'Donnell interview; Lew to O'Neill, July 17, 1980, ONBC; O'Donnell to O'Neill, July 23, 1980, ONBC; *Washington Post,* Aug. 14, 1980; *New York Times,* Aug. 13, 16, 1980; *Newsweek,* Aug. 25, 1980; *Boston Globe,* Aug. 14, 1980. John Anderson's entrance into the race as an independent candidate led the Speaker to ask his staff to research an intriguing possibility. What could happen if none of the three candidates captured a majority of the votes in the Electoral College? "If Anderson can win one or two big states and President Carter and Ronald Reagan split the rest, the election could very well end up in the House," read the resultant memo. If both House and Senate remained deadlocked, "Mr. O'Neill could become acting President of the United States," the memo noted.
24. Jordan, Moore interviews; O'Neill, *Man of the House;* 1980 campaign polls and analyses, ONBC; Germond and Witcover, *Blue Smoke and Mirrors.*

Chapter 23
Reeling on the Ropes

1. O'Donnell interview; Hoffman to O'Neill, Nov. 10, 1980, ONBC; *New York Times,* Nov. 15, 1980; *Washington Post,* Nov. 6, 1980; O'Donnell interview, Hedrick Smith papers, LOC.
2. Diehl, Hoffman, O'Donnell, Brademas interviews; O'Donnell interview, Hedrick Smith papers, LOC; Speaker's press conferences, June 11, Sept. 9, 1980, ONBC; *Newsweek,* Nov. 24, 1980.
3. Hoffman to O'Neill, Nov. 10, 1980, ONBC.

4. "The real key to power in Congress is power over the deadlines. When there are no deadlines you can let the matters drift and the votes drift away," said GOP leadership aide William Pitts. To ensure that O'Neill stuck to his timetable, Pitts and Stockman threatened to employ an obscure provision of the Budget Act, which would have allowed them to call individual cuts in the 1981 budget up for votes on a daily basis, thus tying the House in knots. William Pitts, Charles Stenholm, O'Donnell interviews; *Washington Post,* Nov. 17, 1980; Associated Press, Nov. 19, 1980; *Newsweek,* Nov. 24, 1980.
5. Speaker's press conference, Nov. 18, 1980, ONBC; White House leadership meeting notes, Dec. 2, 1980, ONBC; *New York Times,* Dec. 17, 1980; Associated Press, Jan. 7, 1981.
6. Michael Deaver, Gary Hart, O'Donnell, Wright interviews; *Boston Globe,* Jan. 20, Aug. 14, 1981; Stockman, *The Triumph of Politics; New York Times,* Feb. 12, 1981; Reuters, Feb. 5, 1981; *Newsweek,* Feb. 2, 1981; *Time,* Feb. 2, 1981.
7. Deaver, James Baker, Ken Duberstein interviews; Duberstein oral history, RRL; Max Friedersdorf to Reagan, Mar. 3, 11, 1981, RRL; O'Neill interview, *MacNeil-Lehrer Report,* July 27, 1981; Stockman, *The Triumph of Politics; National Journal,* Mar. 7, 1981; memorandum, Steve Smith to Ari Weiss, 1981, ONBC; "Final Report of the Initial Action Project," Jan. 29, 1981, RRL; Laurence Barrett, *Gambling with History* (Doubleday, Garden City, N.Y., 1983).
8. Duberstein interview; Duberstein oral history, RRL; O'Neill talking points and notes for Mar. 4, 1981, leadership meeting, ONBC; Jim Wright diary; Stockman, *The Triumph of Politics; New York Times,* Feb. 18, Mar. 11, 1981; *Washington Post,* Feb. 19, 1981.
9. Wright was with him. "George Bush is very calm. He shows no sign whatsoever of nervous distress, nor of indecision," Wright later told his diary.
10. Hymel, Matthews interviews; Jim Wright diary; Lou Cannon, *President Reagan* (Touchstone, New York, 1991); Herbert Abrams, *The President Has Been Shot* (W. W. Norton, New York, 1992); Richard Darman, *Who's In Control?* (Simon & Schuster, New York, 1996); O'Neill, *Man of the House;* O'Neill untitled videotape interview, ONBC; *Washington Post,* Apr. 1, 1981; *Congressional Quarterly,* Apr. 4, 1981.
11. The President told Duberstein later that when he discovered it was 3 A.M. in New Zealand, he was tempted to say, "This is Jimmy Carter," and hang up.
12. Pitts, O'Donnell interview; Jim Wright diary; Reagan congressional call sheets, RRL; Duberstein oral history; O'Donnell, Atwater interviews, Hedrick Smith papers, LOC; O'Neill press conference transcript, Apr. 27, 1981, ONBC; Stockman, *The Triumph of Politics; Washington Post,* Apr. 28, 1981; *New York Times,* Apr. 28, 30, 1981; *Boston Globe,* Apr. 30, 1981; *Congressional Quarterly,* May 9, 1981.
13. O'Donnell, Hymel, Matthews, Moakley interviews; *Washington Star,* Apr. 30, 1981; *Boston Globe,* May 1, 3, 17, 1981; Congressman Les Aspin newsletter, O'Donnell files, ONBC; O'Neill press conference transcript, Apr. 28, May 7, 1981, ONBC; O'Neill caucus remarks, ONBC; *Washington Post,* May 31, 1981; *New York Times,* May 1, 1981; videotape of O'Neill during floor debate, ONBC; meeting of Legislative Strategy Group, agendas, May 12, 1981, RRL; Associated Press, May 13, 14, 1981; *Time,* May 18, 1981; *Congressional Record,* May 7, 1981.
14. WETA-TV, "The Lawmakers," May 14, 1981; "This man Reagan, whatever else he may be, is a consummate politician," Wright told his diary. "He skillfully flimflammed Tip and me, to say nothing of Dan Rostenkowski, into believing

him sincere about wanting to compromise his tax bill. The public charade was artful. By the time we met with him, however, he already had satisfied himself he could get a better deal from the conservatives . . . and the whole meeting was an ultimatum."

15. The beer mugs illustrate the level of detail in the White House lobbying operation. As the congressmen got up to leave, Baker announced that the mugs would be collected, boxed and forwarded to their offices because, as Duberstein later recalled, "if they got off the helicopter carrying beer mugs they would never be able to vote for us. We knew there would be a lot of press at the Reflecting Pool when we got back and the image to America would be these congressmen . . . went up there for a party, a barbecue . . . [and] drank a lot of beer." Duberstein oral history, RRL.
16. Pitts, Brand, Weiss, Matthews, Wright, Baker, Deaver, O'Donnell, Wilson interviews; O'Neill interview, C-SPAN, Sept. 18, 1986; O'Neill oral history, JFKL; Stockman, *The Triumph of Politics;* Darman, *Who's In Control?;* Hedrick Smith, *The Power Game* (Random House, New York, 1988); Barrett, *Gambling With History;* Duberstein oral history, RRL; Darman to Reagan, June 18, 24, 1981, RRL; Jim Wright diary; Reagan congressional call sheets, June–Aug. 1981, RRL; *New York Times,* July 5, Aug. 9, 16, 1981; Friedersdorf to Reagan, May 15, 1981, RRL; Darman to Reagan, June 1, 1981, RRL; Duberstein to Baker, June 5, 1981, RRL; "Gramm-Latta II Briefing," minutes, June 12, 1981, RRL; Duberstein to Friedersdorf, July 22, 1981, RRL; "In the Oval Office after the Tax Cut Vote," notes and conversation, undated, RRL; Spencer Smith to O'Neill, May 1981, ONBC; steering and policy committee minutes, May 20, 1981, ONBC; Lew to O'Neill, July 8, 1981, ONBC; O'Donnell to O'Neill, June 16, 1981, ONBC; *Congressional Quarterly,* July 4, 18, Aug. 1, 8, 1981.

Chapter 24
An Old Dog Can Learn New Tricks

1. Rick Stearns, who was later appointed to the federal bench, was the other leading contender for the job.
2. Dick Gephardt, O'Donnell, Weiss, Matthews, Coelho, Hymel interviews; O'Neill, Bolling interviews with Hedrick Smith, Smith papers, LOC; "Media Plan," Apr. 4, 1981, ONBC; Al From to O'Donnell, Apr. 6, 1981, ONBC; *Washington Post,* Apr. 8, 1981; *Washington Star,* Apr. 12, 1981; *Newsday,* Apr. 8, 1981.
3. Jerry Colbert, Matthews, Diehl, Deaver, Coelho, Kelley, O'Donnell interviews; Roper Center Poll, May 12, 1981; *Newsweek,* May 11, 1981; "A Television Plan for Tip O'Neill," Colbert to O'Neill, spring, 1981, ONBC; Speaker's press conference transcript, Feb. 28, 1985, ONBC; Gingrich interview with Hedrick Smith, Smith papers, LOC.
4. James Shannon, O'Donnell, Baker interviews; *Boston Globe,* May 22, 1981; Stockman, *The Triumph of Politics;* "Final Report on the Initial Actions Project," Jan. 29, 1981, RRL; "Strategic Planning Memorandum #1," July 16, 1981, RRL; O'Neill press conference transcript, May 13, 1981, ONBC; Jim Wright diary; *New York Times,* May 15, 1981; Associated Press, May 13, 21, 1981.
5. Matthews interview; *Washington Post,* June 18, 1981; ABC-TV, "Issues & Answers," June 7, 1981; Nancy Reagan, letter to author; *Washington Post,* June 17, 1981; *Boston Herald,* June 17, 1981; *New York Times,* June 2, 17, 1981.

6. Jack Lew, Deaver, Matthews, O'Donnell interviews; O'Donnell and Bolling interviews, Hedrick Smith papers, LOC; *Boston Herald,* June 25, 1981; UPI, June 23, July 7, 1981; Associated Press, July 7, 8, 1981; *New York Times,* July 9, 1981; *Newsweek,* July 6, 1981; Jim Wright diary; *Congressional Record,* July 29, 1981; videotape, O'Neill July 29 floor speech, ONBC; O'Neill speech cards, ONBC; UPI, July 21, 1981.
7. Baker, Deaver interviews; *Washington Post,* Aug. 7, 1981; Robert Michel to colleagues, May 29, 1981, RRL; Darman to Reagan, June 1, 1981, RRL; *Boston Herald,* July 24, 1981; Stockman, *The Triumph of Politics;* Darman, *Who's in Control?; Newsweek,* July 20, 1981; *New York Times,* July 21, 1981.
8. Newt Gingrich, O'Donnell, Ashley interviews; O'Donnell "Memorandum: Political Agenda for House Democrats," Aug. 4, 1981, ONBC; Richard Wirthlin to Richard Richards, July 29, 31, 1981, RRL; Pepper to O'Neill, July 14, 1981, ONBC.
9. Shannon interview; Stockman, *The Triumph of Politics;* "The State of the Social Security Trust Fund" and "The Financial Status of the Social Security System," Weiss files, ONBC; *New York Times,* Sept. 18, 21, 26, 1981; *Washington Post,* Sept. 18, Oct. 16, 1981.
10. Stockman, *The Triumph of Politics; Congressional Record,* Oct. 21, 1981; *New York Times,* Sept. 20, 1981; Associated Press, Sept. 16, 1981; *Washington Post,* Sept. 11, 1981; *Atlantic Monthly,* Dec. 1981; Weiss files, ONBC; *National Journal,* Oct. 31, 1991; UPI, Oct.21, 1981; Cannon, *President Reagan.*
11. Dotty Lynch, Peter Hart, O'Donnell, Matthews, Coelho interviews; Coelho to O'Neill, Sept. 21, 1981, ONBC; Hart focus group report, Oct. 1981, ONBC; "Leadership — Campaign Meeting" minutes, Oct. 19, 22, 26, 29, Nov. 2, 5, 30, Dec. 3, 7, 1981, Jan. 6, 12, Feb. 8, 11, 16, 22, 25, Mar. 25, 29, Apr. 5, 19, 22, May 3, 10, 1982, ONBC; Dotty Lynch to O'Donnell, Oct. 28, 1981; strategic memoranda, Oct. 22, Nov. 4, 1981, Mar. 1982, ONBC; Patrick Caddell, "A Democratic Strategy," Feb. 20, 1982, ONBC; "Fairness Issues: An Executive Briefing Book," White House Office of Policy Information, June 1, 1982, RRL.
12. Howard Baker, Jim Baker, O'Donnell, Matthews, Weiss interviews; draft budget speech, Apr. 27, 1981, RRL; Fred Barnes, *Policy Review,* spring, 1983, with cover letter, David Gergen to Jim Baker, Mar. 15, 1983, RRL; Smith, *The Power Game;* Stockman, *The Triumph of Politics;* Barrett, *Gambling with History; Newsweek,* May 10, 1982; *Time,* May 10, 1982; *Washington Post,* Feb. 9, Mar. 30, Apr. 22, 29, 30, May 2, 1982; *New York Times,* Feb. 9, Mar. 20, Apr. 21, 29, 30, 1982; *Boston Globe,* Feb. 9, 1982; Associated Press, Feb. 8, 1982. There are several variations of Reagan's "pineapple" remark.
13. *Newsweek,* Aug. 16, 30, 1982; *Washington Post,* June 11, 24, Aug. 20, 24, 1982; Associated Press, July 29, 1982; *New York Times,* Aug. 19, 20, 1982; UPI, June 8, 1982.
14. Christopher O'Neill, Coelho, Matthews, O'Donnell, Ashley interviews; O'Donnell to O'Neill, talking points and itinerary of October 1981 trip to Texas, ONBC; "The Speaker's Club," promotional literature, ONBC; talking points for DCCC meeting, Jan. 19, 1981, ONBC; Coelho to O'Neill, Mar. 19, 1981, ONBC; Coelho to O'Neill, May 27, 1982, ONBC; *New York Times,* Mar. 1, 1981, Mar. 24, 1983; *Washington Post,* Aug. 26, 1982; *Newsweek,* Apr. 12, 1982; *Atlantic Monthly,* Oct. 1986; Brooks Jackson, *Honest Graft* (Farragut Publishing, Washington, D.C., 1990).
15. Massachusetts and New Jersey each lost a seat and New York lost five. Pennsylvania, Ohio and Illinois each lost two seats and the rest of the Midwest four. California

picked up two seats, the rest of the West seven, Florida four, Tennessee one and Texas three.

16. In 1984, Republicans got 49.3 percent of the popular vote in California congressional races, and Democrats 48.4 percent, yet 60 percent of the delegation was Democratic. "Dear Colleague" letter, June 20, 1985, Richard Cheney, ONBC.
17. Mark Gersh, Matthews interview; William Greider, *Secrets of the Temple* (Simon & Schuster, New York, 1987); Albert Hunt and Alan Ehrenhalt in Thomas Mann and Norman Ornstein, *The American Elections of 1982* (American Enterprise Institute, Washington, D.C., 1983); Rollins transcript, Mar. 5, 1990, Federal News Service; Jacobs, *A Rage for Justice;* Dan Smith to Martin Anderson, Jan. 21, 1982, RRL; Don Devine to Richard S. Beal, Dec. 7, 1981, RRL; Associated Press, July 27, Sept. 16, 1982; UPI, Oct. 12, 29, 1982; *New York Times,* Sept. 10, 17, Oct. 2, 1982; *Washington Post,* Aug. 7, Sept. 10, Oct. 2, 1982.
18. Diehl interview; *Boston Globe,* Dec. 20, 1990, Apr. 16, 18, 1993; DCCC list of fundraising events, ONBC; *Newsday,* Dec. 19, 1990; "Repeal O'Neill" literature and LeBoutillier newsletters, ONBC.
19. Though the average mid-term loss for a party in power over the preceding fifty years was 31 seats, the average in the first mid-term elections of a new presidency were much lower. FDR had actually picked up nine House seats and ten Senate seats in the realigning election of 1934: neither Eisenhower (lost 18 in 1954) nor Kennedy (lost 4 in 1962) nor Nixon (lost 12 in 1970) nor Carter (lost 15 in 1978) had fared as poorly as Reagan. Matthews, O'Donnell, Baker interviews; *New York Times,* Oct. 30, 1982; Hunt, *The American Elections of 1982.*
20. O'Donnell interview; Mary McGrory column, Nov. 5, 1982; *Newsweek,* Nov. 15, 1982.
21. Hunt, *The American Elections of 1982; Washington Post,* Oct. 10, Nov. 7, 1982; WGBH-TV, "Goodbye Mr. Speaker," ONBC.
22. "He fought hard. He believed deeply. He felt passionately. He argued vehemently. He worked persistently. And in the end he just burned himself out before his time," Burton's old foe Jim Wright told his diary. "He never did live to be an angry old man because he consumed himself in this fierce determination to right wrongs."
23. Despite all the tax hikes O'Neill forced upon Reagan (who would raise taxes in five of the seven years after 1981), it would take two huge deficit-cutting packages — pushed by Presidents Bush and Clinton — and a roaring economy that had made the transition to the post–cold war information age before the budget got back to black in Clinton's second term. The national debt by then stood at five trillion dollars. Al From, O'Donnell interviews; "New Aspects of the Enforcement of Party Discipline in the U.S. House of Representatives," Ross K. Baker, 1984; UPI, Jan. 26, 1983; *Time,* Sept. 26, 1983; Richard Beal to Ed Meese, Oct. 16, 1981, RRL; *New York Times,* June 7, 10, 24, 30, Nov. 24, Dec. 4, 1982; Jim Wright diary; *Washington Post,* Mar. 24, 26, 30, 1983.
24. Lew, Duberstein, Baker, Rostenkowski, O'Donnell interviews; *New York Times,* Nov. 7, 1982, Jan. 13, 18, 20, Mar. 10, 11, 1983; Duberstein oral history, RRL; *Washington Post,* Jan. 12, 1983; Associated Press, Apr. 20, 1983.
25. O'Donnell, Baker, Gingrich interviews; Darman, *Who's in Control?;* Stockman, *The Triumph of Politics;* Cannon, *President Reagan;* Edsall, *Chain Reaction; Washington Post,* Aug. 26, 1983; Barnes, *Policy Review; Boston Globe,* Jan. 24, 1996.

Chapter 25
Maryknolls and Marines

1. The deficit spending and tax cuts of the Reagan-Bush years also acted as a palliative — like a loan from the bank — as the Federal Reserve crushed inflation and the U.S. economy made the painful transformation to the computer age. Deaver interview; Jim Wright diary; Adriana Bosch, *Reagan* (TV Books, New York, 1998); Kirsten Lundberg, "CIA and the Fall of the Soviet Empire," Kennedy School of Government, case program, 1994; Benjamin Fisher, ed., *At Cold War's End,* U.S. Central Intelligence Agency, 1999.
2. Elliott Abrams, Armen Der Marderosian, Charlie Wilson, Moakley, Deaver, Baker, O'Donnell, Matthews interviews; *New York Times,* Nov. 23, 1982, May 14, 1983.
3. *Congressional Record,* Apr. 23, 1968, June 5, 1980; *Guardian,* Jan. 8, 1994; Jim Wright diary; Speaker's press conference transcript, Feb. 23, 1982, ONBC; O'Neill interview, PBS, Aug. 2, 1983; O'Donnell to O'Neill, "Haig Meeting — El Salvador," Mar. 2, 1981; Jim Wright, *Worth It All* (Brassey's, Washington, D.C., 1993); *New York Times,* Sept. 12, 1984; *Washington Post,* June 5, 1985; O'Neill commencement address, Stonehill College, May 20, 1984, ONBC.
4. In early 1982, as Reagan pressed Congress to authorize more aid for El Salvador, O'Neill dispatched O'Donnell and Jack Murtha to El Salvador to give him a "first-hand report." They found a military stalemate. "American aid is absolutely necessary to prevent a guerilla victory," Murtha reported. "Some military aid is definitely coming [to the Marxist forces] from Nicaragua." Murtha, O'Donnell interviews; Murtha, O'Donnell reports, ONBC; O'Donnell notes, El Salvador, Feb. 16, 1981, ONBC; Robert White briefing transcript, Feb. 26, 1981, ONBC; O'Donnell to O'Neill, Mar. 2, 1981, ONBC; UPI, Mar. 24, 1982; Associated Press, Mar. 24, 1982.
5. O'Donnell, Boland interviews; Theodore Draper, *A Very Thin Line* (Hill & Wang, New York, 1991); Bob Woodward, *Veil* (Simon & Schuster, New York, 1987).
6. Baker, Duberstein, O'Donnell interviews; Duberstein oral history, RRL; *Washington Post,* Sept. 21, Oct. 25, 26, 1983; *Congressional Record,* Sept. 28, 1983; Reagan to O'Neill, Sept. 27, 1983, ONBC; Speaker's press conference transcript, Sept. 24, 1983; Jim Wright diary; O'Neill, *Man of the House.*
7. To quell the ensuing flap, O'Neill had to send a letter of apology to Nancy Reagan. Baker, O'Donnell interviews; transcript of Democratic caucus, Oct. 26, 1983, ONBC; O'Neill press conference transcript, Oct. 28, 1983; *New York Times,* Oct. 29, Nov. 1, 1983.
8. Murtha, O'Donnell interview; Smith, *The Power Game;* O'Neill interview with Hedrick Smith, Smith papers, Library of Congress; *New York Times,* Dec. 30, 1983; *Washington Post,* Feb. 9, Apr. 5, 6, 1984.
9. Speaker's press conference transcript, May 24, 1984; *Congressional Quarterly,* June 2, 1984; Smith, *The Power Game.*
10. Matthews, O'Donnell, Deaver interviews; O'Neill and O'Donnell interviews with Hedrick Smith, Smith papers, Library of Congress; O'Neill file, RRL; Reagan to Jerry Granat, May 31, 1984, RRL; letter, Ann Gorsuch to O'Neill, ONBC; Ronald Reagan, *An American Life* (Simon & Schuster, New York, 1990); Reagan to Sinatra and Sinatra to Reagan, 1987, released to author under the Freedom of Information Act, RRL.
11. In 1980, the election of a new Irish government tilted the Republic toward the nationalist position, and put Sean Donlon's job and strategy in jeopardy. An upset

O'Neill and Kennedy got on the phone to Dublin and personally persuaded the new Irish prime minister, Charles Haughey, to retain Donlon. Donlon, Lillis interviews.

12. William Clark, Paul Quinn, Hume, Donlon, FitzGerald, Lillis, O'Donnell, Murtha interviews; O'Neill letter to Irish POW Committee, June 9, 1981, ONBC; James Sharkey to O'Donnell, "Private and Confidential: Meeting to Review 'Friends of Ireland' Initiative," Nov. 30, 1982, ONBC; "Secret and Personal" draft regarding the creation of U.S. aid fund for Ireland, Aug. 31, 1985, ONBC; O'Donnell notes on Anglo-Irish agreement, ONBC. In 1985 the Speaker returned to Ireland for a sentimental journey, during which he was honored with the "Freedom of the City of Cork" — the city's highest honor — and paid a visit to nearby Mallow, the O'Neill family's ancestral home.

Chapter 26
Newt

1. Newt Gingrich, Bob Walker interviews; Ronald M. Peters, "The Republican Speakership," 1996; *Time,* Dec. 25, 1995; John Barry, *The Ambition and the Power* (Penguin, New York, 1990); *Vanity Fair,* Sept. 1995.
2. Al Gore, Brian Lamb, Walker, Rose, Gingrich, Matthews, Hymel, Colbert interviews; Hardeman and Bacon, *Rayburn;* Colbert to O'Neill, "Broadcast Coverage of House Floor Proceedings," Feb. 17, 1976, ONBC; news release, Coalition for Professional Broadcast Coverage of the House Floor, ONBC; "Memo for Record," Mar. 1, 1976, Richard Bolling papers, University of Missouri; Brademas to O'Neill, Mar. 4, 1976, ONBC; "Legislative Reorganization Act of 1970," Bolling papers, University of Missouri ("O'Neill came up with the compromise which saved broadcasting," Bolling wrote); "C-SPAN and Congress," symposium, Woodrow Wilson Center, Mar. 19, 1999; *Boston Herald,* Mar. 20, 1979.
3. "They do *what*?" he roared, after a staffer explained the mechanics of how men were having sex with men in Capitol Hill men's rooms. Christine Sullivan Daly, Matthews interviews.
4. Gingrich to GOP colleagues, Feb. 8, 1983, ONBC; Tom O'Donnell to O'Neill, June 22, 1988, ONBC; Gingrich to Weyrich, Dec. 18, 1980, ONBC; William F. Connelly, *Congress' Permanent Minority?* (Rowman & Littlefield, Lanham, Md., 1994); Dan Renberg, *A House of Ill Repute* (Princeton University Press, Princeton, 1987).
5. Geraldine Ferraro, Ray Smock, Charles Johnson, Rose, Gingrich, Moakley, Walker, Pitts, Diehl interviews; *Congressional Record,* May 8, 10, 14, 15, 1984; "Words Taken Down," Bob Michel, Oct. 8, 1993; Jim Wright diary.
6. It was not the first time that O'Neill had lost control and let a Republican provocateur get the better of him. He had been forced to apologize to Rep. Bruce Caputo during the Koreagate scandal in 1978. In 1974, as majority leader, O'Neill's words were taken down and he was silenced by Carl Albert for accusing Rep. Robert Bauman of "a cheap, sneaky, sly way to operate." As Speaker, in 1980, O'Neill had again fenced with Bauman and, for fear of being silenced, agreed to withdraw the charge that a Republican opponent had been "duped."
7. Gingrich, Walker, Rostenkowski interviews; O'Neill, *Man of the House;* videotape clips, O'Neill papers, ONBC; Connelly, *Congress' Permanent Minority?;* Renberg, *A*

House of Ill Repute; investigative report on Gingrich, Phil Noble Associates, July 6, 1984, ONBC; *Atlantic Monthly,* Dec. 1985; *Newsweek,* May 28, 1984; *Washington Post,* Apr. 23, 26, 29, May 1, 1985.

8. The famous description of King's success came from Angelo Berlandi, a campaign worker.
9. John Sasso, Michael Dukakis, Rosemary O'Neill, Susan O'Neill, Thomas P. O'Neill III, Kip O'Neill, Diehl, Kelley, Healy, Gannon interviews; O'Neill interview with John K. White, ONBC; Richard Gaines and Michael Segal, *Dukakis and the Reform Impulse* (Quinlan Press, Boston, 1987); *Boston Globe,* May 4, 5, 1980, Nov. 22, 1981; *New York Times,* Dec. 1972; *Congressional Record,* June 29, 1977; *Boston Herald,* Feb. 28, 1973.
10. The Speaker had originally supported Ted Kennedy. O'Neill interview with Clymer.
11. Gary Hart, Peter Hart, Pat Schroeder, Stanley Greenberg, David Rogers, O'Donnell, From, Matthews, Healy, Tolchin interviews; O'Neill, *Man of the House; New York Times,* Mar. 1, 1984; *Boston Globe,* Mar. 1, 1984; *Washington Post,* Feb. 2, 1984; memo, Hamilton to O'Neill, Mar. 23, 1984, ONBC; *Time,* July 16, 1984.
12. Geraldine Ferraro, Gary Hart, Peter Hart, Susan O'Neill, Daly, Schroeder, Matthews, O'Donnell interviews; *Washington Post,* June 8, July 20, Aug. 9, Sept. 6, Oct. 10, 1984 ; Geraldine Ferraro, *Ferraro: My Story* (Bantam, New York, 1985); Ferraro to O'Neill, July 30, 1980, May 5, 1982, Mar. 29, 1984, ONBC; *Boston Globe,* May 4, 1984; *Time,* July 23, Sept. 17, 1984; *Newsweek,* Aug. 27, Nov./Dec. 1984; Associated Press, Oct. 13, 1984; *New York Times,* Aug. 22, 1984; Peter Goodman and Tony Fuller, *The Quest for the Presidency, 1984* (Bantam Books, New York, 1985).
13. Peter Hart, Charles Stenholm, Leon Panetta, Richard Gephardt, Ashley, Matthews, Gingrich, Coelho, Murtha, Diehl, O'Donnell, Donnelly interviews; DCCC records, ONBC; Jackson, *Honest Graft;* videotape collections, ONBC.

Chapter 27
Endgames

1. Missy Tessier, Coelho, Matthews, Murtha interviews; Matthews diary; *Washington Post,* Jan. 5, 1985; *New York Times,* Mar. 5, 1985.
2. O'Neill interview with Hedrick Smith, Smith papers, Library of Congress; Cannon, *President Reagan;* Smith, *The Power Game; New York Times,* July 10, 1985; *Washington Post,* July 12, 1985.
3. Simpson interview; Simpson to Reagan, Jan. 29, 1986, RRL; O'Neill interview with Hedrick Smith, Smith papers, Library of Congress; Smith, *The Power Game;* O'Neill, *Man of the House; New York Times,* Oct. 28, Nov. 2, 1985; *Newsweek,* Nov. 11, 1985; Jim Wright diary; *Washington Post,* Jan. 29, 1986.
4. Rostenkowski, Pitts interviews; O'Neill interview with Hedrick Smith, Smith papers, Library of Congress; *Washington Post,* June 27, 1982, May 28, Dec. 7, 12, 1985; *New York Times,* Sept. 22, Dec. 12, 18, 1985, Sept. 25, 26, Oct. 23, 1986; Associated Press, Dec. 19, 1985; *Time,* Dec. 30, 1985; Jeffrey Birnbaum and Alan Murray, *Showdown at Gucci Gulch* (Random House, New York, 1987); Derek Bok to O'Neill, July 7, 1986, ONBC; O'Neill to Steinbrenner, July 10, 1985, ONBC; Raeburn Hathaway to O'Neill, Sept. 9, 1986, ONBC; John McElwee to O'Neill, Aug. 4, 1986, ONBC; Joseph Mullaney to Jack Lew, Aug. 27, 1986, ONBC; Edward Glazer

to Jack Lew, Aug. 20, 1986; Edward Sibble to O'Neill, July 22, 1986, ONBC; Eric Elfman to Jack Lew, Aug. 22, 1986, ONBC; States News Service, Oct. 3, 1986.

5. Rosemary O'Neill, Markey, O'Donnell interviews; O'Neill notes on Gorbachev meeting, ONBC; *Newsweek,* Apr. 11, 1983; *US News & World Report,* Apr. 11, Dec. 12, 1983; telegrams, U.S. Embassy in Beijing to U.S. State Department, Mar. 1983, ONBC; memoranda of conversations, Codel O'Neill and Chinese leaders, Mar. 1983, ONBC; Associated Press, Apr. 8, 9, 10, 19, Nov. 12, 13, 1985; *New York Times,* Apr. 9, 11, Sept. 12, 1985; *Washington Post,* Apr. 11, 18 1985; "Soviet Union: General Findings and Conclusions," report of Apr. 1985 trip to Soviet Union, ONBC; "Summary of Meetings in the Soviet Union," April 1985, ONBC; U.S. State Department telegram, Codel O'Neill, Apr. 1985, ONBC; Anatoly Dobrynin, *In Confidence* (Times Books, New York, 1995).
6. Simpson, Donnelly interviews; Simpson to O'Neill, May 3, Aug. 1, 1984, ONBC; *New York Times,* Oct. 9, Nov. 30, 1983, June 21, 1984, Oct. 21, 1986; *Newsweek,* Oct. 17, 1983; *Time,* Oct. 17, 1983.
7. Fred Salvucci, David Luberoff, Donnelly, Rose interviews; O'Neill interview with Luberoff; Luberoff and Alan Altshuler, "Mega-Project: A Political History of Boston's Multibillion Dollar Artery/Tunnel Project," John F. Kennedy School of Government, Harvard University; Kenneth R. Geiser, "Political Processes of Urban Freeway Controversies," Massachusetts Institute of Technology; Michael D. Nolan, "Big Buyoff: Participation in the Planning of Boston's Third Harbor Tunnel/Depressed Central Artery Project," honors thesis, Harvard University; *Boston Globe,* May 13, 1976; Associated Press, Feb. 26, 1984, Apr. 2, 1987; *National Journal,* Mar. 3, 1984; *Business Week,* Mar. 5, 1984; UPI, Oct. 12, 1984, Apr. 6, 1987; *Washington Post,* Oct. 12, 1984; *New York Times,* Feb. 21, 1985, Mar. 30, July 13, 1987.
8. O'Neill to Thomas J. White, Mar. 14, 1986, ONBC; "Third Country Assistance," talking points on Boland amendments, RRL; Draper, *A Very Thin Line;* Woodward, *Veil;* Jane Mayer and Doyle McManus, *Landslide* (Houghton Mifflin, Boston, 1988); Novak to O'Neill, undated, ONBC; *Washington Post,* Apr. 19, May 5, 7, June 6, 13, 1985, Mar. 9, 20, 21, Apr. 15, 17, June 24, 26, 1986, Feb. 9, 1989; *Time,* Apr. 29, 1985; *New York Times,* Jan. 22, 23, Feb. 21, 26, Mar. 5, 12, 19, 20, 21, 23, 25, 26, 1986, July 31, 1987; Associated Press, July 20, 1987.

Chapter 28
Farewell

1. Peter Hart, Peggy Noonan, David Rogers, Gingrich, O'Donnell interviews; Rogers letter, ONBC; *Boston Herald,* May 20, 1985, May 22, July 8, Oct. 18, 1986; Michael Barone and Grant Ujifusa, *The Almanac of American Politics, 1986* (National Journal, Washington, D.C., 1985); farewell dinners videotapes, ONBC; *Boston Globe,* Feb. 25, 1986; Public Papers of the Presidents, Mar. 17, 1986; *Washington Post,* Mar. 18, June 5, Oct. 19, 1986; "Farewell, Tip," Boston College alumni magazine, spring, 1986; UPI, May 9, July 25, Aug. 5, 1986; *Chicago Tribune,* May 13, 1986; *New York Times,* Sept. 6, Oct. 18, 23, 1986; Associated Press, Oct. 1, 18, Dec. 10, 1986.
2. Hart disputes O'Neill's version of this meeting.
3. Gary Hart, O'Donnell interview; *Larry King Live* videotapes, ONBC; Gerald Sullivan and Michael Kenney, *Race for the Eighth* (Harper & Row, New York, 1988); Joe Kennedy to O'Neill, Jan. 1987, ONBC; *Boston Herald,* Sept. 11, 1986; correspon-

dence, O'Neill to Ortega; Ortega to O'Neill; O'Neill to Law, January and February 1987.

4. "If the old fart had been a beachbum for the past 40 years, as shown in the ad, this country would be a lot better off," a friend of Jerry Ford's wrote the former President, in a letter he forwarded to O'Neill, ONBC.
5. Joe Klein, Thomas P. O'Neill III, Christopher O'Neill; O'Donnell, Matthews, Hymel; *Boston Globe,* Apr. 28, 1991, Sept. 6, 1987, Dec. 11, 1989; Associated Press, Oct. 14, 1987; *Adweek,* Nov. 11, 1989; *New York Times,* June 14, 1985, Sept. 6, 1987, Nov. 6, 1989; *Man of the House* drafts, ONBC; *Boston Herald,* Oct. 20, 1989; O'Neill speaking and advertisement contracts and charitable donation records, O'Neill family files; *Washington Post,* May 31, 1981, June 16, 1985, Sept. 6, 1987, Sept. 20, 1989; *Wall Street Journal,* June 29, 1987; *Chicago Tribune,* May 8, 1977, Apr. 18, 1993, June 30, 1994; *Real Paper,* Mar. 13, 1974; *Advertising Age,* Jan. 8, 1990; Matthews interview, *Charlie Rose,* Jan. 6, 1994.
6. Christopher O'Neill, Jim Cannon, Joe Moakley interviews; O'Neill interview, Rolf Benirschke, *Ostomy Quarterly;* O'Neill interview, Andrew Miga; O'Neill interview, Steve Kurkjian; O'Neill interview, *Larry King Live,* May 7, 1991; *Boston Globe,* Dec. 7, 1988, Apr. 26, 1991; Barney Frank to O'Neill, Dec. 18, 1990, ONBC; *New York Times,* Oct. 17, Dec. 4, 1987, Dec. 8, 1988; *Boston Herald,* Nov. 11, 1987; July 24, 1989, May 31, Oct. 10, 1990; Associated Press, Nov. 13, 14, 15, 16, 17, 18, 19, Dec. 1, 4, 11, 1987.
7. Rosemary O'Neill, O'Neill III, Mulcahy, Diehl, Tolchin, Shannon, Hymel, McGrory, Lamkin, Moakley; O'Neill interview with the author; *Boston Globe,* Nov. 19, 1991, Dec. 10, 1992, Jan. 6, 7, 8, 9, 10, 11, Apr. 12, 1994; *Boston Herald,* Mar. 30, 1994; *New York Times,* Jan. 6, 1994; *The Hill,* Apr. 14, 1999; O'Neill Nashville City Club speech, O'Neill family files; *North Cambridge News,* Special Tribute Edition, summer 1994.

O'Neill donated his papers to Boston College, which agreed to exhibit the Speaker's desk and chair in a campus library. But after O'Neill's death, when the Reverend Donald Monan stepped down as BC's president, the college needed space for his retirement office and shut down the exhibit. The Grover Cleveland desk and other furniture were crated and put in storage, bruising the feelings of O'Neill's family and friends.

BC officials were then dismayed to discover that Joe Moakley, the ranking Democrat on the Rules Committee, was blocking further appropriations for the college. "They were dismantling Tip's office, and I couldn't believe it because of the millions and millions of dollars he had gotten for that school," Moakley recalled. "A year later there is a bill going through Congress, greased, for $6 million for BC. All of a sudden the light hit me: they are not entitled to it. Not after the way they treated the Speaker. It was the most disloyal act I can think of, against a guy who put his heart, his soul, everything for Boston College. So I did my thing."

A lobbyist for the college called on Moakley and was rebuffed. A BC representative met with Moakley and asked him to relent. Influential BC alumni telephoned. The college prevailed upon the Speaker's family to ask him to desist. Moakley refused. "The thing of it is," Moakley said, "he was my friend."

BC built a new exhibit, containing the desk and office furnishings, even better than the old one. It opened in the Thomas P. O'Neill Jr. Library in 1999. At the dedication ceremonies, Joe Moakley was the featured speaker.

Bibliography

Abrams, Herbert. *The President Has Been Shot.* New York: W. W. Norton, 1992.
Adams, Sam. *War of Numbers.* South Royalton, Vermont: Steerforth Press, 1994.
Adams, Sherman. *Firsthand Report.* New York: Harper and Bros., 1961.
Agnew, Spiro T. *Go Quietly . . . or Else.* New York: William Morrow & Co., 1980.
Albert, Carl, with Goble, Danny. *Little Giant.* Norman: University of Oklahoma Press, 1990.
Ambrose, Stephen E. *Nixon,* vol. 2: *The Triumph of a Politician 1962–1972.* New York: Simon & Schuster, 1977.
———. *Nixon,* vol. 3: *Ruin and Recovery 1973–1990.* New York: Simon & Schuster, 1991.
———. *Citizen Soldiers.* New York: Simon & Schuster, 1997.
Bailey, Stephen K. *Congress in the Seventies.* New York: St. Martin's Press, 1970.
Balz, Dan, and Brownstein, Ronald. *Storming the Gates.* Boston: Little, Brown, 1996.
Barone, Michael. *Our Country.* New York: Free Press, 1990.
Barone, Michael, and Ujifusa, Grant. *The Almanac of American Politics.* Washington, D.C.: National Journal, various editions.
Barrett, Lawrence. *Gambling with History.* Garden City: Doubleday, 1983.
Barry, John M. *The Ambition and the Power.* New York: Penguin, 1989.
Bartley, Robert. *The Seven Fat Years.* New York: Free Press, 1992.
Beatty, Jack. *The Rascal King.* Reading, Mass.: Addison-Wesley, 1992.
Bendiner, Robert. *Obstacle Course on Capitol Hill.* New York: McGraw Hill, 1964.
Bernstein, Irving. *Promises Kept.* New York: Oxford University Press, 1991.
———. *Guns or Butter.* New York: Oxford University Press, 1996.

Beschloss, Michael. *The Crisis Years.* New York: Burlingame Books, 1991.
———. *Taking Charge, The Johnson White House Tapes, 1963–1964.* New York: Simon & Schuster, 1997.
Bibby, John F., Mann, Thomas, and Ornstein, Norman. *Vital Statistics on Congress, 1980.* Washington, D.C.: American Enterprise Institute, 1980.
Bibby, John F., and Davidson, Roger H. *On Capitol Hill.* Hinsdale, Illinois: Dryden Press, 1972.
Birnbaum, Jeffrey, and Murray, Alan. *Showdown at Gucci Gulch.* New York: Random House, 1987.
Blumenthal, Sidney, and Edsall, Thomas. *The Reagan Legacy.* New York: Pantheon, 1988.
Boettcher, Robert. *Gifts of Deceit.* New York: Holt, Rinehart and Winston, 1980.
Boggs, Lindy. *Washington Through a Purple Veil.* New York: Harcourt Brace, 1994.
Bolling, Richard. *Power in the House.* New York: E. P. Dutton, 1968.
———. *House Out of Order.* New York: E. P. Dutton, 1965.
Bosch, Adriana. *Reagan: An American Story.* New York: TV Books, 1998.
Bourne, Peter. *Jimmy Carter.* New York: Scribner, 1997.
Boyer, Sarah. *In Our Own Words.* Boston: City of Cambridge, Red Sun Press, 1977.
Bradlee, Benjamin. *A Good Life.* New York: Simon & Schuster, 1995.
Branch, Taylor. *Parting the Waters.* New York: Simon & Schuster, 1988.
Breslin, Jimmy. *How the Good Guys Finally Won.* New York: Viking, 1975.
Califano, Joseph. *Governing America.* New York: Simon & Schuster, 1981.
Cambridge Historical Commission. *Northwest Cambridge & Survey Index.* Cambridge: 1977.
Cannon, James. *Time and Chance.* New York: HarperCollins, 1994.
Cannon, Lou. *President Reagan.* New York: Touchstone, 1991.
Carter, Dan. *The Politics of Rage.* New York: Simon & Schuster, 1995.
Caro, Robert A. *The Years of Lyndon Johnson: The Path to Power.* New York: Alfred A. Knopf, 1982.
———. *The Years of Lyndon Johnson: Means of Ascent.* New York: Alfred A. Knopf, 1990.
Carter, Jimmy. *Keeping Faith: Memoirs of a President.* Arkansas: University of Arkansas Press, 1995.
Cheney, Richard, and Cheney, Lynne. *Kings of the Hill.* New York: Continuum, 1983.
Chester, Lewis, Hodgson, Godfrey, and Page, Bruce. *An American Melodrama.* New York: Viking, 1969.
Clancy, Paul, and Elder, Shirley. *Tip.* New York: Macmillan, 1980.
Clymer, Adam. *Edward M. Kennedy: A Biography.* New York: William Morrow, 1999.
Cohen, Richard, and Witcover, Jules. *A Heartbeat Away.* New York: Viking, 1974.
Cohen, Richard E. *Rostenkowski.* Chicago: Ivan R. Dee, 1999.
Congressional Quarterly, Inc. *Politics in America.* Washington, D.C.: various editions.
———. *Watergate: Chronology of a Crisis.* Washington, D.C., 1975.
———. *Congressional Quarterly Almanac.* Washington, D.C., 1953–1986.
———. *Congress and the Nation.* Washington, D.C., various editions.
———. *Guide to the Congress of the United States.* Washington, D.C., various editions.
Connelly, William F. *Congress' Permanent Minority?* Lanham, Md.: Rowman & Littlefield, 1994.
Coogan, Tim Pat. *The Troubles.* Boulder, Colo.: Roberts Rinehart Publishers, 1996.
Dallek, Robert. *Lone Star Rising.* New York: Oxford University Press, 1991.
———. *Flawed Giant.* New York: Oxford University Press, 1998.

Dalton, Cornelius. *Leading the Way: A History of the Massachusetts General Court*. Boston: Office of the Massachusetts Secretary of State, 1984.

Darman, Richard. *Who's in Control?* New York: Simon & Schuster, 1996.

Davidson, Roger H., *The Postreform Congress.* New York: St. Martin's Press, 1992.

———. *Masters of the House.* Boulder, Colo.: Westview Press, 1998.

Davidson, Roger H., and Oleszek, Walter J. *Congress Against Itself.* Bloomington: Indiana University Press, 1977.

———. *Congress and Its Members.* Washington, D.C.: CQ Press, 1990.

Day, Kathleen. *S & L Hell.* New York: W. W. Norton, 1993.

Dean, John. *Blind Ambition.* New York: Simon & Schuster, 1976.

Deaver, Michael. *Behind the Scenes.* New York: William Morrow, 1987.

Dierenfield, Bruce. *Keeper of the Rules: Congressman Howard W. Smith*. Charlottesville: University of Virginia Press, 1987.

Dionne, E. J. *Why Americans Hate Politics.* New York: Simon & Schuster, 1991.

Dobrynin, Anatoly. *In Confidence.* New York: Times Books, 1995.

Dodd, Lawrence C., and Oppenheimer, Bruce I. *Congress Reconsidered*. Washington, D.C.: CQ Press, 1985.

Doyle, James. *Not Above the Law.* New York: William Morrow, 1977.

Draper, Theodore. *A Very Thin Line.* New York: Hill & Wang, 1991.

Drew, Elizabeth. *Washington Journal.* New York: Random House, 1975.

Dumbrell, John. *The Carter Presidency.* Manchester, England: Manchester University Press, 1995.

Edsall, Thomas and Edsall, Mary. *Chain Reaction*. New York: Norton, 1991.

Emery, Fred. *Watergate.* New York: Times Books, 1994.

Erie, Steven P. *Rainbow's End*. Berkeley: University of California Press, 1988.

Evans, Rowland, and Novak, Robert. *Lyndon B. Johnson: The Exercise of Power.* New York: New American Library, 1966.

Ferraro, Geraldine. *Ferraro: My Story.* New York: Bantam, 1985.

Fields, Howard. *High Crimes and Misdemeanors.* New York: W. W. Norton, 1978.

Firestone, Bernard, and Ugrinsky, Alexej. *Gerald R. Ford and the Politics of Post-Watergate America*. Westport, Conn.: Greenwood Press, 1992.

———. *Watergate and Afterward: The Legacy of Richard M. Nixon*. Westport, Conn.: Greenwood Press, 1992.

Fisher, Benjamin, ed. *At Cold War's End*. U.S. Central Intelligence Agency, 1999.

Foley, Thomas, and Biggs, Jeffrey. *Honor in the House.* Pullman, Wash.: Washington State University Press, 1999.

Ford, Gerald. *A Time to Heal*. Norwalk, Conn.: Easton Press, 1987.

Formisano, Ronald P. *Boston Against Busing.* Chapel Hill, N.C.: University of North Carolina Press, 1991.

Fountain, Charles. *Another Man's Poison*. Boston: Globe Pequot Press, 1984.

Froman, Lewis A. *The Congressional Process.* Boston: Little, Brown, 1967.

Gaines, Richard, and Segal, Michael. *Dukakis and the Reform Impulse.* Boston: Quinlan Press, 1987.

Garment, Leonard. *Crazy Rhythm*. New York: Times Books, 1997.

Germond, Jack, and Witcover, Jules. *Blue Smoke and Mirrors.* New York: Viking, 1981.

Gibbons, William. *The U.S. Government and the Vietnam War.* Washington, D.C.: U.S. Government Printing Office.

Gillon, Steven. *The Democrats' Dilemma*. New York: Columbia University Press, 1992.

Gitlin, Todd. *The Sixties: Years of Hope, Days of Rage.* New York: Bantam Books, 1987.
Glazer, Nathan, and Moynihan, Daniel Patrick. *Beyond the Melting Pot.* Cambridge: MIT Press, 1963.
Goodman, Peter, and Fuller, Tony. *The Quest for the Presidency, 1984.* New York: Bantam Books, 1985.
Goodwin, Doris Kearns. *The Fitzgeralds and the Kennedys.* New York: St. Martin's Press, 1987.
———. *No Ordinary Time.* New York: Simon & Schuster, 1994.
———. *Lyndon Johnson and the American Dream.* New York: Signet, 1967.
Goodwin, Richard. *Remembering America.* New York: Little, Brown, 1988.
Greenberg, Stanley. *Middle Class Dreams.* New York: Times Books, 1995.
Greene, John Robert. *The Presidency of Gerald Ford.* Lawrence, Kansas: University Press of Kansas, 1995.
Greene, Robert. *The Sting Man.* New York: E. P. Dutton, 1981.
Greider, William. *Secrets of the Temple.* New York: Simon & Schuster, 1987.
Grossman, Jerome. *Relentless Liberal.* New York: Vantage, 1996.
Haig, Alexander. *Inner Circles.* New York: Warner Books, 1992.
Haldeman, H. R. *The Haldeman Diaries.* New York: G.P. Putnam's Sons, 1994.
Hale, Dennis. *The United States Congress.* New Brunswick: Transaction Books, 1982.
Hamilton, Nigel. *JFK: Reckless Youth.* New York: Random House, 1992.
Handlin, Oscar. *The Uprooted.* New York: Grosset & Dunlap, 1951.
———. *Boston's Immigrants.* New York: Atheneum, 1974.
Hardeman, D. B., & Bacon, Donald. *Rayburn.* Lanham, Md.: Madison Books, 1987.
Hart, Gary. *Right from the Start.* New York: Quadrangle, 1973.
Hartmann, Robert. *Palace Politics.* New York: McGraw-Hill, 1980.
Hennessey, Michael. *Four Decades of Massachusetts Politics.* Norwood, Mass.: Norwood Press, 1935.
Hersh, Burton. *The Education of Edward Kennedy.* New York: William Morrow, 1972.
Hersh, Seymour. *The Price of Power.* New York: Summit Books, 1983.
Hougan, Jim. *Secret Agenda.* New York: Random House, 1984.
Huthmaker, J. Joseph. *Massachusetts People and Politics, 1919–1933.* Cambridge, Mass.: Belknap Press, 1959.
Hyman, Lester. Unpublished memoirs.
Jackson, Brooks. *Honest Graft.* Washington, D.C.: Farragut Publishing, 1990.
Jacobs, John. *A Rage for Justice.* Berkeley: University of California Press, 1990.
Johnson, Haynes. *In the Absence of Power.* New York: Viking, 1980.
Johnson, Paul. *Modern Times.* New York: Harper & Row, 1983.
———. *A History of the American People.* New York: HarperCollins, 1997.
Jones, Charles O. *The Trusteeship Presidency.* Baton Rouge: Louisiana State University Press, 1988.
———. *The Reagan Legacy.* Chatham, N.J.: Chatham House Publishers, 1988.
Jones, Howard M., and Jones, Bessie Z. *The Many Voices of Boston.* Boston: Little, Brown, 1975.
Jordan, Hamilton. *Crisis.* New York: G. P. Putnam's Sons, 1982.
Karnow, Stanley. *Vietnam.* New York: Penguin, 1991.
Kaufman, Burton I. *The Presidency of James Earl Carter Jr.* Lawrence: University Press of Kansas, 1993.
Kennedy, David. *Freedom from Fear.* New York: Oxford University Press, 1999.

Kennedy, Robert. *Robert Kennedy: In His Own Words.* New York: Bantam Books, 1988.
Kenney, Charles, and Turner, Robert. *Dukakis: An American Odyssey.* Boston: Houghton Mifflin, 1988.
King, Anthony. *Both Ends of the Avenue.* Washington, D.C.: American Enterprise Institute, 1983.
King, Larry L. *Of Outlaws, Con Men, Whores, Politicians and Other Artists.* New York: Viking, 1980.
Kissinger, Henry. *White House Years.* Boston: Little, Brown, 1979.
———. *Years of Upheaval.* Boston: Little, Brown, 1982.
Kutler, Stanley. *The Wars of Watergate.* New York: Alfred A. Knopf, 1990.
———. *Abuse of Power.* New York: Free Press, 1997.
Leamer, Larry. *Playing for Keeps in Washington.* New York: Dial Press, 1977.
Levin, Murray. *Kennedy Campaigning.* Boston: Beacon Press, 1966.
Levin, Murray, and Blackwood, George. *The Compleat Politician.* Indianapolis: Bobbs-Merrill, 1962.
Loverd, Richard A. *Leadership for the Public Service.* Upper Saddle River, N.J.: Prentice Hall, 1997.
Lukas, J. Anthony. *Nightmare: The Underside of the Nixon Years.* New York: Viking Press, 1976.
———. *Common Ground.* New York: Alfred A. Knopf, 1985.
Lupo, Alan. *Liberty's Chosen Home.* Boston: Beacon Press, 1977.
Lyons, Louis. *Newspaper Story: One Hundred Years of the Boston Globe.* Cambridge, Mass.: Belknap Press, 1971.
MacNeil, Neil. *Forge of Democracy: The House of Representatives.* New York: Van Rees Press, 1963.
MacPherson, Myra. *The Power Lovers.* New York: G. P. Putnam's Sons, 1975.
Mailer, Norman. *Some Honorable Men: Political Conventions 1960–1972.* Boston: Little, Brown, 1976.
Mallow Archaeological & Historical Society. *Mallow Field Club Journal.* Mallow: 1988.
Manchester, William. *The Glory and the Dream.* Boston: Little, Brown, 1973.
Mann, Thomas E., and Ornstein, Norman J. *The New Congress.* Washington, D.C.: American Enterprise Institute, 1981.
———. *The American Elections of 1982.* Washington, D.C.: American Enterprise Institute, 1983.
Martin, Joseph W. *My First Fifty Years in Politics.* Westport, Conn.: Greenwood Press, 1975.
Martin, Ralph, and Plaut, Edward. *Front Runner, Dark Horse.* Garden City, N.Y.: Doubleday, 1960.
Matthews, Christopher. *Hardball.* New York: Summit Books, 1988.
Matsunaga, Spark, and Chen, Ping. *Rulemakers of the House.* Chicago: University of Illinois Press, 1976.
Matusow, Allen J. *The Unraveling of America.* New York: Harper and Row, 1984.
Mayer, Jane, and McManus, Doyle. *Landslide.* Boston: Houghton Mifflin, 1988.
McCaffrey, Lawrence J. *Textures of Irish America.* Syracuse: Syracuse University Press, 1992.
McCubbins, Mathew D., and Sullivan, Terry. *Congress: Structure & Policy.* Cambridge: Cambridge University Press, 1987.
McCullough, David. *Truman.* New York: Simon & Schuster, 1992.

McNamara, Robert. *In Retrospect*. New York: Times Books, 1995.
McPherson, Harry. *A Political Education*. Boston: Little, Brown, 1972.
Meese, Edwin. *With Reagan*. Washington, D.C.: Regnery Gateway, 1992.
Mezvinksy, Edward. *A Term to Remember.* New York: Coward, McCann & Geoghegan, 1977.
Miller, Clem. *Member of the House.* New York: Charles Scribner's Sons, 1962.
Miller, Kerby, and Wagner, Paul. *Out of Ireland*. Washington, D.C.: Elliott & Clark Publishing, 1994.
Mollenhoff, Clark. *The President Who Failed*. New York: Macmillan, 1980.
Morris, Charles R. *American Catholic.* New York: Times Books, 1997.
Morris, Edmund. *Dutch: A Memoir of Ronald Reagan*. New York: Random House, 1999.
Moynihan, Daniel Patrick. *Came the Revolution*. New York: Harcourt Brace Jovanovich, 1988.
Munger, Frank, and Fenno, Richard F. *National Politics and Federal Aid to Education*. Syracuse: University of Syracuse Press, 1962.
New England Genealogical Society. *The Search for Missing Friends, Irish Immigrant Advertisements in the Boston Pilot*. Boston: 1989.
New York Times. The Pentagon Papers. New York: Bantam, 1971.
Newfield, Jack. *Robert Kennedy: A Memoir.* New York: Bantam, 1970.
Nixon, Richard. *RN: The Memoirs of Richard Nixon*. New York: Grosset & Dunlap, 1978.
Noonan, Peggy. *What I Saw at the Revolution*. New York: Random House, 1990.
O'Brien, Lawrence. *No Final Victories.* Garden City, N.Y.: Doubleday, 1974.
O'Connor, Edwin. *The Last Hurrah*. Boston: Atlantic Monthly Press, 1956.
O'Connor, Thomas. *The Boston Irish*. Boston Northeastern University Press, 1995.
O'Donnell, Kenneth, and Powers, David. *Johnny We Hardly Knew Ye.* Boston: Little, Brown, 1972.
Oleszek, Walter J. *Congressional Procedures and the Policy Process.* Washington, D.C.: CQ Press, 1984.
O'Neill, Thomas P. Jr., with Gary Hymel. *All Politics Is Local.* New York: Times Books, 1994.
O'Neill, Thomas P. Jr., with William Novak. *Man of the House.* New York: Random House, 1987.
Ornstein, Norman. *Congress in Change.* New York: Praeger, 1975.
Oudes, Bruce. *From: The President*. New York: Harper & Row, 1989.
Palazzolo, Daniel J. *The Speaker and the Budget: Leadership in the Post-Reform House of Representatives.* Pittsburgh: University of Pittsburgh Press, 1992.
Patterson, James. *Grand Expectations.* New York: Oxford University Press, 1996.
Parmet, Herbert S. *JFK*. New York: Dial Press, 1983.
Peabody, Robert L. *Leadership in Congress.* Boston: Little, Brown, 1976.
———. *Cases in American Politics.* New York: Praeger, 1976.
Peabody, Robert L., and Polsby, Nelson W. *New Perspectives on the House of Representatives.* Baltimore: Johns Hopkins University Press, various editions.
Peirce, Neil, and Hagstrom, Jerry. *The Book of America*. New York: Norton, 1983.
Pertshuk, Michael. *Giant Killers.* New York: W. W. Norton, 1986.
Peters, Ronald M. *The Speaker.* Washington, D.C.: CQ Inc., 1995.
———. *The American Speakership: The Office in Historical Perspective.* Baltimore: Johns Hopkins University Press, 1990.
Phillips, Kevin P. *The Emerging Republican Majority.* New Rochelle: Arlington House, 1969.

Pilzer, Paul. *Other People's Money*. New York: Simon & Schuster, 1989.
Polsby, Nelson W. *Congress and the Presidency*. Englewood Cliffs, N.J.: Prentice-Hall, 1986.
———. *Consequences of Party Reform*. Oxford: Oxford University Press, 1983.
Powers, Thomas. *The Man Who Kept the Secrets: Richard Helms and the CIA*. New York: Alfred A. Knopf, 1979.
Prochnau, William. *Once Upon a Distant War*. New York: Times Books, 1995.
Ranney, Austin. *The American Elections of 1980*. Washington, D.C.: American Enterprise Institute, 1981.
Reagan, Ronald. *An American Life*. New York: Simon & Schuster, 1990.
Reedy, George. *From the Ward to the White House*. New York: Charles Scribner's Sons, 1991.
Reeves, Richard. *President Kennedy*. New York: Simon & Schuster, 1993.
Regan, Donald. *For the Record*. New York: Harcourt Brace Jovanovich, 1988.
Renberg, Dan. *A House of Ill Repute*. Princeton: Princeton University Press, 1987.
Reid, T. R. *Congressional Odyssey*. New York: W. H. Freeman, 1980.
Riordan, William. *Plunkitt of Tammany Hall*. New York: E. P. Dutton, 1963.
Robinson, James. *The House Rules Committee*. Indianapolis: Bobbs-Merrill, 1963.
Robinson, Judith. *You're in Your Mother's Arms*. San Francisco: M. J. Robinson, 1994.
Rothenberg, Randall. *The Neoliberals*. New York: Simon & Schuster, 1984.
Rudman, Warren. *Combat: Twelve Years in the U.S. Senate*. New York: Random House, 1996.
Ryan, Dennis P. *Beyond the Ballot Box*. Amherst: University of Massachusetts Press, 1983.
Safire, William. *Before the Fall*. New York: Doubleday, 1975.
Samuelson, Robert. *The Good Life and Its Discontents*. New York: Times Books, 1995.
Scammon, Richard, and Wattenberg, Ben. *The Real Majority*. New York: Coward-McCann, 1970.
Schlesinger, Arthur M. Jr. *The Age of Roosevelt*. Boston: Houghton Mifflin, 1957.
———. *A Thousand Days*. Boston: Houghton Mifflin, 1965.
Schram, Martin. *The Great American Video Game*. New York: William Morrow, 1987.
Schwartz, Bernard. *The Professor and the Commissions*. Westport, Conn.: Greenwood Press, 1978.
Shannon, William. *The American Irish*. New York: Macmillan, 1963.
Siff, Ted, and Weil, Alan. *Ruling Congress*. New York: Penguin Books, 1975.
Sinclair, Barbara. *Majority Leadershp in the U.S. House*. Baltimore: Johns Hopkins University Press, 1983.
———. *Congressional Realignment*. Austin: University of Texas Press, 1982.
Smith, Hedrick. *The Power Game*. New York: Random House, 1988.
Smith, Steven S. *Call to Order*. Washington, D.C.: Brookings Institution, 1989.
Smith, Steven S., and Deering, Christopher. *Committees in Congress*. Washington, D.C.: CQ Press, 1984.
Sorensen, Theodore. *Kennedy*. New York: Harper & Row, 1965.
Stack, John F. *International Conflict in an American City: Boston's Irish, Italians, and Jews, 1935–1944*. Westport, Conn.: Greenwood Press, 1979.
Stockman, David. *The Triumph of Politics*. New York: Harper & Row, 1986.
Sullivan, Gerald, and Kenney, Michael. *The Race for the Eighth*. New York: Harper & Row, 1987.
Sundquist, James L. *The Decline and Resurgence of Congress*. Washington, D.C.: Brookings Institution, 1981.
Sutton, S. B. *Cambridge Reconsidered*. Cambridge: MIT Press, 1976.

Thernstrom, Stephan. *The Other Bostonians.* Cambridge: Harvard University Press, 1973.

Thomson, Suzi Park. *Suzi: The Korean Connection.* Westport, Conn.: Condor Publishing, 1978.

Trout, Charles H. *Boston, the Great Depression, and the New Deal.* New York: Oxford University Press, 1977.

Udall, Morris K. *Education of a Congressman: The Newsletters of Morris K. Udall.* Indianapolis: Bobbs-Merrill, 1972.

U.S. House of Representatives. *Memorial Addresses and Tributes in Honor of Thomas P. "Tip" O'Neill, Jr.* Washington, D.C.: U.S. Government Printing Office, 1995.

Waldman, Michael. *Who Robbed America?* New York: Random House, 1990.

Warner, Sam B. *Streetcar Suburbs: The Process of Growth in Boston, 1870–1900.* New York: Atheneum, 1973.

Watson, Denton. *Lion in the Lobby.* New York: William Morrow, 1990.

Weaver, Warren. *Both Your Houses.* New York: Praeger Publishers, 1972.

Westin, Alan. *The Uses of Power.* New York: Harcourt, Brace & World, 1962.

Whalen, Charles, and Whalen, Barbara. *The Longest Debate.* Cabin John, Md.: Seven Locks Press, 1985.

White, Theodore. *The Making of the President 1960.* New York: Atheneum, 1961.

———. *The Making of the President 1964.* New York: Atheneum, 1965.

———. *The Making of the President 1968.* New York: Atheneum, 1968.

———. *The Making of the President 1972.* New York: Atheneum, 1973.

———. *America in Search of Itself.* New York: Harper & Row, 1982.

White, William S. *Home Place: The Story of the U.S. House of Representatives.* Boston: Houghton Mifflin, 1965.

Wills, Gary. *Reagan's America.* New York: Doubleday, 1987.

Winik, Jay. *On the Brink.* New York: Simon & Schuster, 1996.

Witcover, Jules. *Marathon.* New York: Viking, 1977.

Woodham-Smith, Cecil. *The Great Hunger.* New York: Old Town Books, 1962.

Woodward, Bob. *Veil.* New York: Simon & Schuster, 1987.

Woodward, Bob, and Bernstein, Carl. *All the President's Men.* New York: Simon & Schuster, 1974.

Wright, Jim. *Balance of Power.* Atlanta: Turner Publishing, 1996.

Yergin, Daniel. *The Prize.* New York: Touchstone, 1991.

Zeifman, Jerry. *Without Honor.* New York: Thunder's Mouth Press, 1995.

Sources and Acknowledgments

MANY GOOD HEARTS helped make this book. It is dedicated to my wife, Catharina, with love. My daughter, Caitlin, was my hardy research assistant and driving companion on our cross-country journeys. My dad, John, and son, John, are my best pals. My sister, Marjorie, and good friends Peter Gosselin, Robin Toner and Steve Kurkjian offered keen advice, welcome meals and spare bedrooms in New York and Boston.

At the *Boston Globe,* my home of more than a dozen years, Bill and Ben Taylor, Matt Storin, Bob Healy, Tom Oliphant, David Shribman, Cindy Taylor and my colleagues in the newspaper's Washington bureau lead a list of great journalists who offered their patient, unflagging support. Two superb professionals, my agent, David Black, and editor, William Phillips, gave me lessons in craftsmanship. A Dirksen Congressional Center grant helped me assemble the resources to complete this book.

Though I covered Tip on several occasions as a reporter, I started working on this biography a year after he died and could not interview him or many of his deceased pals and colleagues for this book. I was able to recapture many of those lost voices, however, owing to the special generosity of Paul Clancy, Shirley Elder, Hedrick Smith, Neil MacNeil, Gary Hymel, James Cannon, Walter

Oleszek, Adam Clymer, Judith Robinson and the late John Jacobs, who opened parts or all of their files, interview tapes and transcripts to me. Chris Matthews and Jim Wright shared their diaries and also deserve special thanks.

The lion's share of my research was conducted at Boston College, which houses the papers of Tip O'Neill, Ed Boland and Bob Drinan, and where Robert O'Neill, Leah Weisse, Ron Patkus and John Atteberry top the list of those who helped me out. The staffs of the National Archives, the Library of Congress and the Ronald Reagan, Jimmy Carter, Gerald Ford, Richard Nixon, Lyndon Johnson, John F. Kennedy, Harry Truman, Franklin Roosevelt and Sam Rayburn libraries were unfailingly professional, as were the librarians and curators of the Jim Wright papers at Texas Christian University, the papers of Mo Udall at the University of Arizona, the John McCormack papers at Boston University, the Howard Smith papers at the University of Virginia, the Hale Boggs papers at Tulane University, the Edmund Muskie papers at Bates College and the papers of Richard Bolling at the University of Missouri in Kansas City.

This is not an "authorized" biography. Members of the O'Neill clan welcomed this book with varying degrees of enthusiasm. Some talked to me for hours; others declined to be interviewed. Some opened their personal files; others politely turned down my requests. But without the family's at least tacit approval, and in some cases active intervention, I doubt that so many of the late Speaker's friends and colleagues would have agreed to share their memories with me, and for that I am quite grateful. The twin pillars of my research were the O'Neill papers and the interviews I conducted with the members of his family, his friends, his aides and former colleagues. Some of these folks spent days with me, many others gave me a few hours and even those who answered a few questions over the telephone were key to my understanding:

Elliott Abrams, George Allen, Jack Anderson, Scott Armstrong, Skip Ascheim, Lud Ashley, Howard Baker, Jim Baker, William Barnstead, Richard Ben-Veniste, Peter Benson, Chris Black, Lindy Boggs, Ed Boland, David Bonior, Adriana Bosch, Terry Bracy, John Brademas, Ben Bradlee, Stan Brand, Jimmy Breslin, Lynne Brown, Michael Bucciero, Pat Buchanan, William Bundy, James MacGregor Burns, Bill Cable, Jim Cannon, Hugh Carey, Jimmy Carter, Paul Clancy, William Clark, Adam Clymer, Tony Coelho, David Cohen, Jerry Colbert, Chuck Colson, John Culver, Mark Dalton, Charles Daly, Christine Sullivan Daly, Roger Davidson, Michael Deaver, Geri Denterlein, Armen Der Marderosian, Tandy Dickerson, Leo Diehl, Christine DiGrezio, Jim Dinneen, Dick Donahue, Sean Donlon, Brian Donnelly, Jim Doyle, Bob Drinan, Ken Duberstein, Michael Dukakis, Don Edwards, John Ehrlichman, Shirley Elder,

Mary Fahey, Geraldine Ferraro, Garret FitzGerald, Gerald Ford, Barney Frank, Jonny Frank, Al From, John Kenneth Galbraith, Francine Gannon, Leonard Garment, Richard Gephardt, Mark Gersh, William Gibbons, Newt Gingrich, Al Gore, Joe Grandmaison, Stan Greenberg, Bob Greene, Bob Griffin, Jerome Grossman, Kevin Harrington, Michael Harrington, John Harris, Gary Hart, Peter Hart, Dan Hayes, Jim Healey, Bob Healy, Richard Helms, Phil Heymann, Burt Hoffman, John Hume, Al Hunt, Mark Hunt, Lester Hyman, Gary Hymel, Harold Ickes, Brooks Jackson, Pam Jackson, John Jacobs, Joel Jankowsky, Charles Johnson, Hamilton Jordan, Linda Kamm, Ron Kaufman, Eleanor Kelley, Ted Kennedy, John Kerry, Paul Kirk, Joe Klein, Glenn Koocher, Molly Kreimer, George Kundanis, Judith Kurland, Stanley Kutler, Brian Lamb, Lenny Lamkin, Billie Larsen, Jack Lew, Michael Lillis, Nick Littlefield, Michael LoPresti, David Luberoff, Kirsten Lundberg, Marshall Lynam, Dotty Lynch, Catherine MacKinnon, Ray MacNally, Neil MacNeil, Jeff MacNelly, Frank Mankiewicz, Ed Markey, Tony Marmo, Chris Matthews, John McAlear, Ruth Delaney McAlear, Sheridan McCabe, John McCain, Pat McCarthy, Mike McCurry, Jim McDermott, Ray McGovern, James McIntyre, Tom McCoy, Mary McGrory, Frank McLaughlin, Joseph McLaughlin, Linda Melconian, Rick Merrill, Bob Michel, Joe Moakley, John Monahan, Frank Moore, Mary Mulcahy, Jack Murtha, Garrison Nelson, Bob Neuman, Marty Nolan, Peggy Noonan, David Nyhan, Francis O'Brien, Ray O'Brien, Kirk O'Donnell, Lawrence O'Donnell, Walt Oleszek, Tom Oliphant, Rosemary O'Neill, Tommy O'Neill, Susan O'Neill, Christopher O'Neill, Jackie O'Neill, Ben Palumbo, Leon Panetta, Tongsun Park, Jim Peterson, Frank Phillips, Bill Pitts, Fillippa Pizzi, Jody Powell, Dave Powers, Paul Quinn, Wendell Rawls, Nancy Reagan, Mike Reed, Bill Richardson, Elliot Richardson, Gary Roberts, David Rogers, Charlie Rose, Dan Rostenkowski, Jim Rowan, Warren Rudman, Fred Salvucci, Barefoot Sanders, Paul Sarbanes, Lou Sarris, John Sasso, Arthur Schlesinger, Patricia Schroeder, Terry Segal, Jim Shannon, Mark Shields, David Shribman, Alan Simpson, Ray Smock, Ted Sorensen, Eliot Spalding, Irv Sprague, Frank Staniszewski, Charles Stenholm, Matt Storin, James Sullivan, Jeremiah Sullivan, Walter Sullivan, Bill Sutton, John Sweeney, Martin Sweig, Davis Taylor, Missy Tessier, Martin Tolchin, Alex Treadway, Paul Tsongas, Mario Umana, Jack Valenti, Bob Walker, John Walker, Denton Watson, Ari Weiss, Steve Wermeil, Fred Wertheimer, Anne Wexler, Charlie Wilson, Margot Dinneen Wilson, Tom Winship, Jim Wright, Sidney Yates, Jerry Zeifman.

Another group of folks passed on tips and anecdotes, replied to my letters or phone calls, helped with research or publication and supplied the odd meal, memo or word of encouragement:

The Anspach clan, Craig Baker, Mike Barnicle, Jack Beatty, Peter Blute, Susan Brophy, William Bulger, Sheila Burke, Ken Burns, Mrs. Victor Campisi, Carl Cannon, Jim Carroll, Tom Coakley, Michael Colbert, Mrs. Leo Corrigan, John Cronin, Robert Dallek, Richard Darman, Brian and Ellen Donadio, Helen Donovan, Paul Donovan, Len Downie, H. G. Dulaney, Jeff Duncan, Jack Dunn, John Ellement, Dan Flynn, Jim Gallagher, Jeff Gerth, Michael Gillette, Doris Kearns Goodwin, Richard Goodwin, Ryan Harbage, Sy Hersh, Jerry Howard, Steve Jacobs, Jill James, Lady Bird Johnson, Tom Johnson, Caledonia Kearns, Nancy Keebler, Kitty Kelley, Larry L. King, Adam Kurkjian, George Lardner, John LeBoutillier, Trent Lott, Al Lupo, Jim Manley, Bruce Martin, Miguel Martinez, Rudy Maxa, Ann McDaniel, Ed McDonough, Red McGrail, Harry Middleton, Andy Miga, Melody Miller, Dan Moldea, Brian Mooney, Edmund Morris, Bill Novak, Mort Olshon, Adrian O'Neill, Brian O'Neill, Gerard O'Neill, William O'Neill, Peter Osnos, Bob Packwood, Carey Parker, Robert Pear, Nancy Porter, Sister Ellen Powers, Michael Putzel, Tom Quinn, Marie Reilly, Cokie Roberts, Walter Robinson, Peter Rodino, David Rosenbaum, Tim Russert, Lloyd Salvetti, Bob and Ellen Sessa, Cate Sewell, Geoff Shandler, James Smith, George Stephanopoulos, Charles Sullivan, Barbara Sutton, Bill Turque, Larry Tye, Barclay Walsh, Joseph White, Carter Wilkie, Curtis Wilkie, Bob Woodward.

The works of Michael Barone, Grant Ujifusa, Richard E. Cohen, Robert Peabody, Barbara Sinclair, Ronald Peters and Alan Ehrenhalt and the CQ staff were invaluable references. With the exception of a few segments of dialogue that were captured on the White House taping systems during the Johnson and Nixon years, the conversations quoted in this book are the recreations of one or more participants or observers. I have identified the source in every case and, where there are differing renditions over the years, tried to use the most timely and reliable account: favoring a version Tip gave to an oral historian from a presidential library, for example, over those he presented to newspaper reporters or in after-dinner speaking engagements.

Index